Solaris 10:
The Complete Reference

About the Author

Paul A. Watters, Ph.D, is a Senior Lecturer in the Department of Computing at Macquarie University. He has worked as a Solaris and e-commerce consultant for many corporate and nongovernmental entities in Australia, designing systems and software on the Solaris platform. His current consulting work, through the Centre for Policing, Intelligence, and Counter Terrorism at Macquarie University, is in the area of cyberterrorism and prevention of attacks on critical system and network infrastructure. His current research projects involve biometric authentication for accessing enterprise systems, and statistical and structural approaches to filtering pornography on the Internet. He has previously written *Solaris 9: The Complete Reference* and *Solaris 9 Administration: A Beginner's Guide*, as well as contributed to *Web Services Security*, all published by McGraw Hill/Osborne.

Solaris 10:
The Complete Reference

Dr. Paul A. Watters

McGraw-Hill/Osborne

New York   Chicago   San Francisco
Lisbon   London   Madrid   Mexico City
Milan   New Delhi   San Juan
Seoul   Singapore   Sydney   Toronto

The *McGraw-Hill* Companies

McGraw-Hill/Osborne
2100 Powell Street, 10th Floor
Emeryville, California 94608
U.S.A.

To arrange bulk purchase discounts for sales promotions, premiums, or fund-raisers, please contact **McGraw-Hill/Osborne** at the above address. For information on translations or book distributors outside the U.S.A., please see the International Contact Information page immediately following the index of this book.

Solaris 10: The Complete Reference

1234567890 DOC DOC 0198765

ISBN 0-07-222998-5

Acquisitions Editor Jane Brownlow	**Proofreader** Paul Medoff
Project Editor Emily Rader	**Indexer** Valerie Robbins
Acquisitions Coordinator Jessica Wilson	**Composition** Apollo Publishing Services
Technical Editor Nalneesh Gaur	**Illustrator** Sue Albert
Copy Editor William McManus	**Series Design** Peter F. Hancik, Lyssa Wald

This book was composed with Corel VENTURA™ Publisher.

This book is dedicated to my niece Jasmine.

Contents at a Glance

Contents

Part II   System Essentials

Acknowledgments

I would like to acknowledge the professionalism and support of the team at McGraw-Hill/Osborne. Jane Brownlow has worked tirelessly to ensure that this title arrived on the market to coincide with the release of Solaris 10. Jessica Wilson and Emily Rader provided valuable insight and feedback on each chapter, while Bill McManus graciously corrected every typo and error in the manuscript. The technical editor, Nalneesh Gaur, was tough but fair, as always. Thanks Nalneesh!

To everyone at my agency, Studio B, thanks for your past and continued support. To Neil Salkind, my agent, thanks for your wisdom and pragmatic advice.

Finally, thanks to my family, especially my wife Maya, for always being there, through good times and bad.

Introduction

This book is intended as an easy-to-access reference point for Solaris 10, the latest version of the enterprise network operating system developed by Sun Microsystems. Solaris 10 is now free for all users, making it just as accessible as competing, "free" UNIX-style systems, such as Linux, and pay-per-seat systems such as Microsoft Windows.

Each chapter provides a concise overview of the technologies that comprise Solaris 10, a review of the typical operations used for installation and configuration, worked examples, and a command reference. While it is not possible to provide information on every command—the online reference material at **http://docs.sun.com/** is excellent, after all—this book provides you with easily accessible examples, where the reason why you might use certain commands is clearly explained. This is usually what is missing from man pages and other system documentation, which are designed to be concise.

This reference is divided into six parts that cover all of the tactical activities associated with Solaris 10 system administration. The sections are roughly ordered by complexity and timeline—for example, you need to install a system and application software before implementing security plans and setting up logical volumes, usually in preparation for deployment of enterprise applications into a networked environment.

Part I, "Installation," covers system installation and the selection of hardware for various workload mixes. Chapter 1 introduces the scope of the now-free version of Solaris 10 for the SPARC and Intel hardware platforms in the context of competing UNIX and UNIX-like systems. A major benefit of using Solaris over Linux, for example, is getting access to hardware that scales up to over 100 CPUs in a single box. Chapter 2 reviews hardware decision choices. Chapter 3 provides walkthroughs of the main system installation methods—Web Start Wizard, JumpStart, and suninstall—as well as preinstallation planning issues. Chapter 4 covers system booting and working with the PROM boot monitor on SPARC-based systems, which is much more sophisticated than its PC counterparts.

Part II, "System Essentials," covers the installation of end-user and third-party software packages, writing scripts, and managing processes. Chapter 5 reviews how to install new software using the package tools, and how to update software installations by using Live Upgrade and patching. Because editing text files is a basic skill for system administrators, Chapter 6 covers how to use the vi text editor and also how to use various text-processing utilities, such as cat, head, tail, sed, and awk. Much of the interaction system administrators have with Solaris is through a command-line shell, rather than a GUI, so Chapter 7 reviews how to work with shells and write scripts to perform repetitive tasks. Chapter 8 investigates how processes and threads are managed to enable multitasking.

Part III, "Security," covers system security configuration, including authorization and authentication. Chapter 9 covers basic security concepts that underlie Solaris technologies, such as integrity and authenticity. Chapter 10 explains two broad types of authorization enabled in Solaris—user- and group-based access control—with which most users will be familiar, and Chapter 11 explains the newer and far more sophisticated role-based access control. Chapter 12 discusses managing users and groups, including the new Sun Management Console, which is much easier to use than the command line! Chapter 13 reviews distributed authentication, provided by the MIT Kerberos system, along with configuration of the Pluggable Authentication Module (PAM), which allows different authentication systems to be used across all applications.

Part IV, "Managing Devices," provides an in-depth review of how to install, configure, and tune the performance of hardware devices. Chapter 14 covers generic device configuration procedures, while Chapter 15 covers file system installation. Chapter 16 discusses logical volume management and associated RAID levels, and Chapter 17 reviews the backup and restoration of file systems, including snapshots. Chapter 18 discusses printing devices and the printing commands, including a review of print classes, services, and queue management. Chapter 19 covers special file systems, such as the process file system (PROCFS) and virtual memory configuration; and the section finishes with Chapter 20, which presents configuration for system logging and usage accounting, along with kernel tuning hints.

Part V, "Networking," covers basic and advanced configuration for IPv4 and IPv6 stacks, including IPSec, and firewall configuration for routers. Chapter 21 introduces core networking concepts, including OSI layers, the TCP/IP stack, and Ethernet, while Chapter 22 investigates how IP addresses can be allocated dynamically using DHCP and how consistent network time can be managed through NTP. Chapter 23 covers how to prevent network intrusion by using firewalls and discusses appropriate router configuration, and Chapter 24 covers connecting to the Internet using a modem. Finally, Chapter 25 reviews advanced network security technologies such as IPSec and the Internet Key Exchange.

Part VI, "Services, Directories, and Applications," covers distributed system support through naming and directory services, as well as development and deployment of enterprise systems and J2EE applications. Chapter 26 describes the Network File System (NFS), which is the distributed file-sharing technology developed specifically for Solaris. Chapters 28, 29, and 30 present three different naming services—the Domain Name Service (DNS), which maps IP addresses to user-friendly names on the Internet; the Network Information Service (NIS/NIS+), a Solaris innovation; and the industry standard Lightweight Directory Access Protocol (LDAP), which is likely to supersede NIS/NIS+ for all directory services in the very near future. Chapter 31 describes Samba, a heterogeneous file-sharing environment in which Solaris systems work within a Microsoft

Windows environment. Samba provides similar file-sharing capabilities to NFS, as well as domain control. Chapter 32 covers application development issues in the Solaris environment, focusing on system calls and how they can be accessed from C programs. On the enterprise front, Chapter 33 presents the Sun Java System Application Server, which provides J2EE services (Enterprise JavaBean deployment, JDBC database connectivity, and so on) from within the Solaris environment without requiring a third-party system.

Solaris 10 introduces many refinements to existing technology, and affected entries in this book have been updated accordingly. Newer technologies, such as the Sun Management Console and Pluggable Authentication, are covered in their own right.

As the requirements of Sarbanes-Oxley filter down to the CIO's office, the ability to ensure proper access controls to data will become critical—and Solaris 10 provides the best set of tools for this task because of its built-in support for user-, group-, and role-based approaches. Security receives a strong emphasis in this book because we, system administrators, will be called on to account for the implementation of our authorization and access control policies if they are inadequate.

Solaris's integrated support for J2EE web applications and XML web services means that there is consistent checking of authorization from end to end. In this edition, I've expanded the discussion of security and included material on integrating J2EE into the Solaris 10 environment.

I hope you find this book useful. Please don't hesitate to contact me at **paul@ cassowary.net** if you have any questions, comments, or corrections.

Installation

PART

I

Introduction to Solaris 10

Operating systems are the building blocks of computer systems, and provide the interface between user applications and computer hardware. Solaris 10 is a multiuser, multitasking, multithreading operating environment, developed and sold by Sun Microsystems (**http://www.sun.com/**). Solaris is one implementation of the UNIX operating system that draws on both the System V (AT&T) and Berkeley (BSD) traditions. It has risen from little more than a research project to become the dominant UNIX operating system in the international marketplace today. Solaris 10 is the latest in a long line of operating environment releases based around the SunOS operating system, which is currently in version 5.10. Solaris is commonly found in large corporations and educational institutions that require concurrent, multiuser access on individual hosts and between hosts connected via the Internet. However, it is also rapidly being adopted by small businesses and individual developers, through Sun's promotion of the "Free Solaris" program (**http://wwws.sun.com/software/solaris/binaries/**). In this book, many of the references to the commands and procedures of Solaris 10 apply equally to earlier versions of Solaris 9, 8, 7, and 2.*x*.

Many desktop computer users have never heard of the word "Sun" in the context of computing, nor are they usually familiar with the term "Solaris" as an operating environment. However, almost every time that an Internet user sends an e-mail message or opens a file from a networked server running Sun's Network File System (NFS) product, Solaris is transparently supporting many of today's existing Internet applications. In the enterprise computing industry, Sun is synonymous with highly available and reliable high-performance hardware, while Solaris 10 is often the operating environment of choice to support database servers, message queues, XML Web services, and Java 2 Enterprise Edition (J2EE) application servers. Sun's hardware solutions are based around the UltraSPARC integrated circuit technologies, which currently support more than 100 processors in a single StarFire 15K server system. Sun systems are typically used to run financial databases, large-scale scientific computing environments, such as genetic sequencing, and complex graphics rendering required by movie studios in post-production.

In recent times, two of Sun's innovations have moved the spotlight from the server room to the desktop. First, Sun's development of the Java programming language, which promises "write once, read anywhere" application execution across any platform that supports the Java Virtual Machine (JVM), has revolutionized the development of networked applications. Java "applets" now appear on many Web pages, being small, encapsulated applications that execute on the client side. J2EE application servers and their associated distributed component models (Enterprise Java Beans) power the back end of many *n*-tier applications, such as CRM, ERP, and HR systems.

Second, Sun is promoting a "free" version of Solaris 10 for the SPARC and Intel hardware platforms (**http://wwws.sun.com/software/solaris/binaries/**). Sun has also made Solaris 10 more accessible for desktop users, offering the OpenOffice productivity suite for a relatively small cost. OpenOffice is a product that is competitive to Microsoft Office—it contains word processing, spreadsheet, presentation, and database components that are fully integrated. In addition, OpenOffice runs on many different platforms, and in eight languages, meaning that a user on an UltraSPARC system can share documents seamlessly with users on Linux and Microsoft Windows. The combination of a solid operating system with a best-of-breed productivity suite has given Solaris new exposure in the desktop market.

This book is a "complete reference" for the Solaris 10 operating environment, and for the SunOS 5.10 operating system, meaning that I will try to cover, in detail, the operational aspects of Solaris and SunOS. If you simply need to look up a command's options, you can usually make use of Sun's own online "manual pages," which you can access by typing **man** *command*, where *command* is the command for which you require help. You can also retrieve the text of man pages and user manuals online by using the search facility at **http://docs.sun.com/**. This reference will be most useful when you need to implement a specific solution, and you need practical, tried-and-tested solutions. Although Solaris 10 comes with a set of tools for process management, for example, there may be others that improve productivity. Thus, while ps and psig are supplied with Solaris 10, lsof is not. In outlining a solution to a problem, we generally introduce Sun-supplied software first, and then discuss the installation and configuration of third-party alternatives. You can also use this book as a reference for previous versions of Solaris, since much of the command syntax remains unchanged across operating system releases. Command syntax is typically identical across different platforms as well (SPARC and Intel), except where hardware differences come into play, such as disk configuration and layout.

If you've been keeping track of recent press releases, you may be wondering why Solaris has a version number of 10, while SunOS has a revision level of 5.10. Since the release of Solaris 7 (SunOS 5.7), Sun has opted to number its releases sequentially with a single version number, based on the old minor revision number, coinciding with the introduction of 64-bit CPU architectures. This means that the release sequence for Solaris has been 2.5.1, 2.6, 7, 8, 9, and now 10. Sun provides "jumbo patches" for previous operating system releases, which should always be installed when released, to ensure that bugs (particularly security bugs) are resolved as soon as possible. Some changes between releases may appear cosmetic; for example, Larry Wall's Perl interpreter has been included since the Solaris 8 distribution, meaning that a new generation of system administrators will no longer have the pleasure of carrying out their first post-installation task. However, other quite important developments in the area of networking (such as IPv6) and administration (Sun Management Console tools) may not directly affect users, but are particularly important for enterprise administration.

In this chapter, we cover the background to the Solaris 10 operating environment, which really begins with the invention and widespread adoption of the UNIX operating system. In addition, we also cover the means by which Solaris 10 can run cross-platform applications—Sun's development of Java can be seen as a strong commitment to cross-platform interoperability. In addition, Solaris 10 uses Samba to allow a Solaris server to act as a Windows NT or 2000 domain controller. Thus, if you want the reliability of SPARC hardware coupled with the widespread adoption of Microsoft Windows as a desktop operating system, Solaris 10 running Samba is an ideal solution.

Finally, we review some of the many sites on the Internet that provide useful information, software packages, and further reading on many of the topics that we cover in this book.

What Is UNIX?

UNIX is not easily defined, since it is an "ideal" operating system that has been instantiated by different vendors over the years, in some quite nonstandard ways. It is also the subject of litigation, as vendors fight over the underlying intellectual property in the system. However, there are a number of features of UNIX and UNIX-like systems (such as Linux) that can be readily described. UNIX systems have a core kernel, which is responsible for managing core system operations, such as logical devices for input/output (such as */dev/pty*, for pseudo-terminals), and allocating resources to carry out user-specified and system-requisite tasks. In addition, UNIX systems have a hierarchical file system that allows both relative and absolute file path naming, and is extremely flexible. UNIX file systems can be mounted locally, or remotely from a central file server. All operations on a UNIX system are carried out by processes, which may spawn child processes or other lightweight processes to perform discrete tasks. Processes can be uniquely identified by their process ID (PID).

Originally designed as a text-processing system, UNIX systems share many tools that manipulate and filter text in various ways. In addition, small, discrete utilities can be easily combined to form complete applications in rather sophisticated ways. These applications are executed from a user shell, which defines the user interface to the kernel. Although GUI environments can be constructed around the shell, they are not mandatory.

UNIX is multiprocess, multiuser, and multithreaded. This means that more than one user can execute a shell and applications concurrently, and that each user can execute applications concurrently from within a single shell. Each of these applications can then create and remove lightweight processes as required.

Because UNIX was created by active developers, rather than operating system gurus, there was always a strong focus on creating an operating system that suited programmers' needs. A *Bell System Technical Journal* article ("The Unix shell," by S.R. Bourne, 1978) lists the key guiding principles of UNIX development:

- *Create small, self-contained programs that perform a single task.* When a new task needs to be solved, either create a new program that performs it, or combine tools from the toolset that already exists, to arrive at a solution. This is a similar orientation to the current trend toward encapsulation and independent component building (such as Enterprise Java Beans), where complicated systems are built from smaller, interacting but logically independent modules.

- *Programs should accept data from standard input and write to standard input*; thus, programs can be "chained" to process each other's output sequentially. Avoid interactive input in favor of command-line options that specify a program's actions to be performed. Presentation should be separated from what a program is trying to achieve. These ideas are consistent with the concept of piping, which is still fundamental to the operation of user shells. For example, the output of the ls command to list all files in a directory can be "piped" using the | symbol to a program such as grep to perform pattern matching. The number of pipes on a single command-line instruction is not limited.

- *Creating a new operating system or program should be undertaken on a scale of weeks not years: the creative spirit that leads to cohesive design and implementation should be exploited.* If software doesn't work, don't be afraid to build something better. This process of iterative revisions of programs has resurfaced in recent years with the rise of object-oriented development.

- *Make best use of all the tools available, rather than asking for more help.* The motivation behind UNIX is to construct an operating system that supports the kinds of toolsets required for successful development.

This is not intended to be an exhaustive list of the characteristics that define UNIX; however, these features are central to understanding the importance that UNIX developers often ascribe to the operating system. It is designed to be a programmer-friendly system.

The History of UNIX

UNIX was originally developed at Bell Laboratories as a private research project by a small group of people, starting in the late 1960s. This group had experience with research efforts on a number of different operating systems in the previous decade, and its goals with the UNIX project were to design an operating system to satisfy the objectives of transparency, simplicity, and modifiability, with the use of a new third-generation programming language. At the time of conception, typical vendor-specific operating systems were extremely large, and all written in assembly language, making them difficult to maintain. Although the first attempts to write the

UNIX kernel were based on assembly language, later versions were written in a high-level language called C, which was developed during the same era. Even today, most modern operating system kernels, such as the Linux kernel, are written in C. After the kernel was developed using the first C compiler, a complete operating environment was developed, including the many utilities associated with UNIX today (e.g., the visual editor, `vi`). In this section, we examine the timeline leading to the development of UNIX, and the origins of the two main "flavors" of UNIX: AT&T (System V) and BSD.

Origins of UNIX

In 1969, Ken Thompson from AT&T's Bell Telephone Labs wrote the first version of the UNIX operating system, on a DEC PDP-7. Disillusioned with the inefficiency of the Multics (Multiplexed Information and Computing Service) project, Thompson decided to create a programmer-friendly operating system that limited the functions contained within the kernel and allowed greater flexibility in the design and implementation of applications. The PDP-7 was a modest system on which to build a new operating system—it had only an assembler and a loader, and it would allow only a single user login at any one time. It didn't even have a hard disk—the developers were forced to partition physical memory into an operating system segment and a RAM disk segment. Thus, the first UNIX file system was emulated entirely in RAM!

After successfully crafting a single-user version of UNIX on the PDP-7, Thompson and his colleague Dennis Ritchie ported the system to a much larger DEC PDP-11/20 system in 1970. This project was funded with the requirement of building a text-processing system for patents, the descendents of which still exist in text filters such as `troff`. The need to create application programs ultimately led to the development of the first C compiler by Ritchie, which was based on the B language. C was written with portability in mind—thus, platform-specific libraries could be addressed using the same function call from source code that would also compile on another hardware platform. Although the PDP-11 was better than the PDP-7, it was still very modest compared to today's scientific calculators—it had 24KB of addressable memory, with 12KB reserved for the operating system. By 1972, the number of worldwide UNIX installations had grown to ten.

The next major milestone in the development of UNIX was the rewriting of the kernel in C, by Ritchie and Thompson, in 1973. This explains why C and UNIX are strongly related—even today, most UNIX applications are written in C, even though other programming languages have long been made available. Following the development of the C kernel, the owners of UNIX (being AT&T) began licensing the source code to educational institutions within the United States and abroad. However, these licenses were often restrictive, and the releases were not widely advertised. No support was offered, and no mechanism was available for officially fixing bugs. However, because users had access to the source code, the ingenuity in hacking code—whose legacy exists today in community projects like Linux—gathered steam, particularly in the University of California at Berkeley (UCB). The issue of licensing and AT&T's control over UNIX would determine the future fragmentation of the operating system in years to come.

In 1975, the first distribution of UNIX software was made by the Berkeley group, and was known as the BSD. Berkeley was Ken Thompson's alma mater, and he teamed up with two graduate students (Bill Joy and Chuck Haley) who were later to become leading figures in the UNIX world. They worked on a UNIX Pascal compiler that was released as part of BSD, and Bill Joy also wrote the first version of `vi`, the visual editor, which continues to be popular even today.

In 1978, the seventh edition of the operating system was released, and it supported many different hardware architectures, including the IBM 360, Interdata 8/32, and Interdata 7/32. The version 7 kernel was a mere 40KB in size, and included the following system calls: `_exit, access, acct, alarm, brk, chdir, chmod, chown, chroot, close, creat, dup, dup2, exec*, exit, fork, fstat, ftime, getegid, geteuid, getgid, getpid, getuid, gtty, indir, ioctl, kill, link, lock, lseek, mknod, mount, mpxcall, nice, open, pause, phys, pipe, pkoff, pkon, profil, ptrace, read, sbrk, setgid, setuid, signal, stat, stime, stty, sync, tell, time, times, umask, umount, unlink, utime, wait, write`. Indeed, the full manual for version 7 is now available online at **http://plan9.bell-labs.com/7thEdMan/index.html**.

With the worldwide popularity of UNIX version 7, AT&T began to realize that UNIX might be a valuable commercial product, and attempted to restrict the teaching of UNIX from source code in university courses, thereby protecting valuable intellectual property. In addition, AT&T began to charge license fees for access to the UNIX source for the first time. This prompted the UCB group to create its own variant of UNIX—the BSD distribution now contained a full operating system in addition to the traditional applications that originally formed the distribution. As a result, version 7 forms the basis for all the UNIX versions currently available. This version of UNIX also contained a full Brian Kernighan and Ritchie C compiler, and the Bourne shell. The branching of UNIX into AT&T and BSD "flavors" continues even today, although many commercial systems—such as SunOS, which is derived from BSD—have now adopted many System V features, as discussed in the upcoming section, "Features of System V Release 4." Mac OS X is the latest UNIX system to be based around a BSD kernel.

The most influential BSD versions of UNIX were 4.2, released in 1983, and 4.3, released in 1987. The DARPA-sponsored development of the Internet was largely undertaken on BSD UNIX, and most of the early commercial vendors of UNIX used BSD UNIX rather than pay license fees to AT&T. Indeed, many hardware platforms even today, right up to Cray supercomputers, can still run BSD out of the box. Other responses to the commercialization of UNIX included Andrew Tanenbaum's independent solution, which was to write a new UNIX-like operating system from scratch that would be compatible with UNIX, but without even one line of AT&T code. Tanenbaum called it Minix, and Minix is still taught in operating systems courses today. Minix was also to play a crucial role in Linus Torvalds' experiments with his UNIX-like operating system, known today as Linux.

Bill Joy left Berkeley prior to the release of 4.2BSD, and modified the 4.1c system to form SunOS. In the meantime, AT&T continued with its commercial development of the UNIX platform. In 1983, AT&T released the first System V Release 1 (SVR1), which had worked its way up to Release 3 by 1987. This is the release that several of the older generation of mainframe hardware vendors, such as HP and IBM, based their HP-UX and AIX systems upon, respectively. At this time, Sun and AT&T also began planning a future merging of the BSD and System V distributions. In 1990, AT&T released System V Release 4, which formed the basis for the SunOS 5.*x* release in 1992—this differed substantially from the previous SunOS 4.*x* systems, which were entirely based on BSD. Other vendors, such as IBM and DEC, eschewed this new spirit of cooperation and formed the Open Software Foundation (OSF).

In recent years, a number of threats have emerged to the market dominance of UNIX systems: Microsoft's enterprise computing products and frameworks, such as Windows 2003, 2000, and NT servers, and the .NET Framework. Together, these are designed to deliver price-competitive alternatives to UNIX on inexpensive Intel hardware. In the same way that UNIX outgunned the dominant mainframe vendors with a faster, leaner operating system, Microsoft's strategy has also been based on arguments concerning total cost of ownership (TCO), and a worldwide support scheme for an enormous installed base of desktop Microsoft Windows clients. With the development of XML Web services, providing platform-independent transports, data descriptions, and message-based Remote Procedure Call (RPC), there has been a strong push to move toward common standards for system integration. Thus, integrating .NET components with J2EE EJBs can now be performed with a few mouse clicks.

The greatest threat to UNIX is the increasing popularity of Linux, for which different vendors sell distributions based on a "free" kernel. Initially, these companies provided distributions for free, in the spirit of the "free software" movement, and only charged for support and services. Nowadays, the reverse is true: Linux vendors charge for distributions, while the Solaris distribution is free (see **http://wwws.sun.com/ software/solaris/binaries/** for details)!

UNIX will still have an important role to play in the future; however, as desktop computing systems rapidly become connected to the Internet, they will require the kinds of services typically available under Solaris 10. As part of their territorial defense of the UNIX environment, many former adversaries in the enterprise computing market, such as IBM, HP, and Sun, have agreed to work toward a Common Open Software Environment (COSE), which is designed to capitalize on the common features of UNIX provided by these vendors. By distributing common operating system elements such as the common desktop environment (CDE), based on X11, these vendors will be looking to streamline their competing application APIs, and to support emerging enterprise data-processing standards, such as the Object Management Group's CORBA object management service, and XML Web services.

Features of BSD

Solaris was originally derived from the BSD distribution from the University of California. Thus, commands in SunOS 4.*x* were very similar to those found in other BSD distributions, although these changed significantly in SunOS 5.*x* when System V Release 4 was adopted. For example, many veteran system administrators would still find themselves typing **ps aux** to display a process list, which is BSD style, rather than the newer **ps -eaf**, which is correct for SVR4. Before AT&T commercialized UNIX, the BSD distribution required elements of the AT&T system to form a fully operational system. By the early 1990s, the UCB groups had removed all dependencies on the AT&T system. This led to the development of many of the existing BSD systems available today, including FreeBSD and NetBSD.

The innovations pioneered at UCB included the development of a virtual memory system for UNIX, a fast file system (which supported long filenames and symbolic links), and the basic elements of a TCP/IP networking system (including authentication with Kerberos). The TCP/IP package included support for services such as Telnet and FTP, and the Sendmail mail transport agent, which used the Simple Mail Transfer Protocol (SMTP). In addition, alternate shells to the default Bourne shell—such as the C shell, which uses C-like constructs to process commands within an interpreted framework—were also first seen in the BSD distribution, as were extensions to process management, such as job control. Standard terminal-management libraries, such as termcap and curses, also originated with BSD. Products from other vendors were also introduced into BSD, including NFS clients and servers from Sun Microsystems. Later releases also included support for symmetric multiprocessing (SMP), thread management, and shared libraries.

It is often said that the BSD group gave rise to the community-oriented free software movement, which underlies many successful software projects being conducted around the world today. However, BSD is not the only attempt to develop a "free" version UNIX. In 1984, Richard Stallman started developing the GNU (GNU's Not UNIX) system, which was intended to be a completely free replacement for UNIX. The GNU C and C++ compilers were some of the first to fully support industry standards (ANSI), and the GNU Bourne Again Shell (BASH) has many more features than the original Bourne shell. You can find more information about the GNU project at **http://www.gnu.org/**. In addition, several versions of BSD are still freely distributed and available, such as FreeBSD.

Features of System V Release 4

Solaris 10 integrates many features from the AT&T System V releases, including support for interprocess communication, which were missing in the BSD distributions. As discussed earlier, many legal battles were fought over the UNIX name and source. System V was developed by the UNIX System Laboratories (USL), which was still majority-owned by AT&T in the early 1980s. However, Novell bought USL in early 1993. Eventually, USL sold UNIX to Novell, which ultimately sold it to X/Open. In 1991, the OSF-1 specification was released, and although DEC is the only major manufacturer to fully implement the standard, there is much useful cross-fertilization between System V and other operating systems. Since Sun joined OSF in 1994, there has been new hope of standardizing UNIX services and APIs across platforms.

The major contributions of System V to the UNIX platform are as follows:

- Enhancement of the Bourne shell, including shell functions
- The STREAMS and TLI networking libraries
- Remote file sharing (RFS)
- Improved memory paging
- The Application Binary Interface (ABI)

The major differences between SVR4 and BSD UNIX can be summarized as follows:

Feature	System V	BSD
Boot scripts	/etc/init.d	/etc/rc.d
Default shell	Bourne shell	C shell
File system mount database	/etc/mnttab	/etc/mtab
Kernel name	/unix	/vmunix
Printing system	lp	lpr
String functions	memcopy	bcopy
Terminal initialization	/etc/inittab	/etc/ttys
Terminal control	termio	termios

The Solaris Advantage

Sun Microsystems was formed by former graduate students from Stanford and Berkeley, who used Stanford hardware and Berkeley software to develop the workstation market in the enterprise. Sun aimed to compete directly with the mainframe vendors by offering CPU speed and a mature operating system on the desktop, which was unprecedented. For a given price, greater performance could be obtained from the Sun workstations than was ever possible using mainframes. From one perspective, this success destroyed the traditional client/server market, which used very dumb terminals to communicate with very clever but horrendously expensive mainframe systems. The vendors of some proprietary systems, such as HP and DEC, saw their market share rapidly decline in the enterprise market because Sun delivered more "bang per buck" in performance. By 1986, UNIX was the dominant force at the expense of operating systems like VAX/VMS, although VMS would later come back to haunt UNIX installations in the form of Windows NT. When users could have a workstation with graphics instead of a dumb terminal, there were few arguments about adopting Sun.

However, Sun's innovation enabled departments and workgroups to take control of their own computing environments and to develop productively with the C programming language. Sun took BSD and transformed it into a commercial product, adding some useful innovations, such as NFS, along the way. This was similar in some ways to the approach of Linux companies that create distributions of useful software packages and bundle them with the Linux kernel. However, one significant difference between Sun and Red Hat Linux is that Sun has always been a company with a hardware focus—its systems were designed with the SPARC chipset, and more recently the UltraSPARC chipset, in mind. This has enabled Sun to create very fast workstations and servers with typically lower CPU speeds than Intel, but faster and more efficient bus performance. Sun invests heavily in hardware design and implementation for an expected commercial reward, all the more so now that Sun gives away the Solaris 10 operating system.

The major innovations of SunOS 4.*x* can be summarized as follows:

- Implementation of the network file system (NFS version 2.0, running over UDP)
- The OpenWindows 2.0 graphical user environment, based on X11
- The OpenBoot monitor
- The DeskSet utilities
- Multiprocessing support

The major innovations of SunOS 5.*x* can be summarized as follows:

- Support for SMP of more than 100 processors in a single server
- The OpenWindows graphical user environment and OpenLook
- Integration with MIT X11R5, Motif, PostScript, and the CDE
- Support for Gnome 2.0 as an alternative desktop, enhancing Linux integration
- The Network Information Service (NIS/NIS+)
- Kerberos integration for authentication
- Support for static and dynamic linking
- Full-moon clustering and N1 grid containers, ensuring high availability
- The ability to serve Windows 2003, 2000, and NT clients as a domain controller
- Tooltalk
- Java
- POSIX-compliant development environment, including single threads, multithreading, shared memory, and semaphores
- Real-time kernel processing
- X/OPEN-compliant command environment
- Compliance with UNIX 95 and UNIX 98 standards
- Support for very large (>2GB) files

- Microsoft Windows emulation on the desktop with Windows Application Binary Interface (WABI)
- Advanced volume management (`vold`)
- Standardized package administration and deployment tools
- Standardized patch management and integration
- Software-based power management
- Access control lists for resource authorization
- Support for centralized management of user home directories using the automounter
- Improvements to NFS (version 4), running over TCP
- Support for advanced networking, such as IPv6, ATM, frame relay, and Gigabit Ethernet
- JumpStart customization of local site installation and deployment
- 64-bit kernel architecture with Solaris 7 and later
- Simplified backup and restore procedures
- Simplified site administration with the AdminSuite toolkit and now the Solaris Management Console

Hardware Support (SPARC and *x*86)

The original CPU for Sun systems was the SPARC chip, with processor speeds of around 40–60 MHz. However, current systems use the UltraSPARC chipset, with processor speeds in the GHz range. The bus architectures of Sun systems are typically much faster than their PC counterparts, more than making up for their sometimes slower chip speeds.

With the introduction of Solaris 2.1 came support for the Intel platform, supporting ISA, EISA, MCA, and PCI bus types. Version 2.1 performed adequately on high-end 486 systems. Given the significant variation in types and manufacturers of PC hardware, not all devices are currently supported under Solaris 10, although newer innovations, such as the Universal Serial Bus (USB), are supported. Solaris 10 for Intel runs very fast on modern Pentium-IV systems, meaning that Intel devotees now have a wider choice of operating system, if they don't want to buy Sun hardware. There was also a single port of Solaris to the PowerPC platform (with version 2.5.1); however, this failed to impress MacOS users, and was deprecated in Solaris 2.6.

Solaris for Intel users will require the Hardware Compatibility List (HCL) to determine whether their particular system or their peripheral devices are supported. You can find this list at **http://access1.sun.com/drivers/hcl/hcl.html**. The HCL lists all tested systems, components, and peripherals that are known to work with Solaris for Intel. Chances are, if your hardware is not listed, it won't be supported. However, many Intel-based standards have been adopted by Sun, including the PCI bus, which is now integrated in the desktop Ultra workstations.

Cross-Platform Interoperability

The main focus of interoperability of different operating systems lies with the Java programming language, developed by Sun. Starting life as the "Oak" project, Java promises a "write once, run anywhere" platform, which means that an application compiled on Windows NT, for example, can be copied to Solaris 10 and executed without modification and without recompilation. Even in the 1970s, when C was being implemented far and wide across different hardware platforms, it was often possible to transfer source and recompile it without modification, but binary compatibility was never achieved. The secret to Java's success is the two-stage compile and interpretation process, which differs from many other development environments. Java source is compiled on the source platform to an intermediary bytecode format, which can then be transferred to any other platform and interpreted by a JVM. Many software vendors, including SunSoft and Microsoft, have declared support for the Java platform, even though some vendors have failed to meet the specifications laid out by Sun. Until a standard is developed for Java, Sun will retain control over its direction, which is a risk for non-Solaris sites especially. However, organizations with Solaris 10 installations should have few qualms about integrating Java technology within their existing environments. With the release of free development tools, such as Borland's JBuilder Foundation (**http://www.borland.com/**), development in Java is becoming easier for C and experienced UNIX developers. Java is the best attempt yet at complete binary compatibility between operating systems and architectures. More recently, XML Web services have emerged as an important set of technologies for system integration, and these are generally supported by Java.

Recent Solaris Innovations

Recent Solaris releases have contained many enhancements and new features compared to earlier versions, on both the client and server side, and specifically for administrators. For example, security has been overhauled with the inclusion of Kerberos version 5, and IPSec for both IPv4 and IPv6. This security makes it easy to create virtual private networks (VPNs) through improved tunneling and encryption technologies. In the next section, we review some of the recent Solaris innovations.

Server Tools

Many Solaris tools are targeted at implementing nonfunctional requirements, such as scalability, availability, security, integrity, and manageability. For example, Sun's multiprocessing systems are highly available because of their hot-swapping capabilities, meaning that components can be replaced while the system is running—no need for a reboot! The systems are also highly scalable, because the CPU capacity of many systems can be combined using Sun's Cluster product, which offers high system availability through management of hardware redundancy.

Clustering

Increased performance is often gained by the use of hardware redundancy, which can be achieved on a file system–by–file system basis, by using a software solution, such as volume management, or a hardware-based solution, such as a Redundant Array of Independent Disks (RAID) appliance. This allows partitions to be actively mirrored, so that in the event of a hardware failure, you can rapidly resume service and restore missing data.

This approach is fine for single-server systems that do not require close to 100 percent uptime. However, for mission-critical applications, where the integrity of the whole server is at stake, it makes sense to invest in clustering technology. Quite simply, clusters are what the name suggests: groups of similar servers (or "nodes") that have similar function, and that share responsibility for providing system and application services. Clustering is commonly found in the financial world, where downtime is measured in hundreds of thousands of dollars, and not in minutes. Large organizations need to undertake a cost-benefit analysis to determine whether clustering is an effective technology for their needs. However, Sun has made the transition to clustering easier by integrating the Cluster product with Solaris 10, featuring a clustered virtual file system and cluster-wide load balancing.

Grids, Zones, and Resource Management

Clustering is generally restricted to a set of co-located servers with similar capabilities. The real innovation in Solaris 10 is the introduction of N1 grid containers, providing a framework for logically partitioning a single system. Advanced resource management features ensure that applications can be run in separate zones, with logical isolation ensuring true encapsulation. Applications can be allocated CPU capacity on demand, reducing overall waste.

The Resource Manager extends a number of existing tools that provide for monitoring and allocation of system resources to various tasks and services. This is particularly useful in high-end systems, where a large pool of resources can be allocated to specific processes. Although the existing `nice` command allows priorities to be set on specific processes, and `top` displays the resources used by each process, the Resource Manager is an integrated toolkit, featuring a scheduler, accounting, and billing. Again, although accounting tools are supplied as part of the standard Solaris toolkit, they have never been integrated with useful real-time monitoring tools. The Resource Manager also features a command-line interface and optional GUI for configuring and monitoring resource allocation and usage.

Volume Management

Although software RAID support has been previously provided in Solaris through Solstice Disk Suite (SDS), this product has now been superseded by Volume Manager (VM). VM supports RAID levels 0, 1, and 5, and allows a wide range of mirroring and striping facilities. Cross-grade and migration tools are also available to assist SDS users who are currently using metadevices as their primary virtual file systems for boot and nonboot disks and their associated slices.

Live Upgrade

Live Upgrade allows a Solaris system to continue running while components of its operating system are upgraded. This is particularly useful in production environments, where system downtime costs money and customers, particularly on shared platforms, like the StarFire 15K. A separate boot environment is constructed during run time, after which the system is rebooted with the new configuration, thereby minimizing downtime.

System Management

Solaris Management Tools 2.1 is the only supported GUI management environment for Solaris 10—admintool, AdminSuite 2.3 and 3.0, and Solaris Management Tools 1.0 and 2.1 have all been deprecated. For console-based system administration, new command sets are integrated into the Solaris Management Console command set. This makes system management tasks easier because there is now a single GUI or console interface. The Solaris Management Console Tools Suite includes the following tools:

- Computers and Networks Tool
- Diskless Client Support
- Disks Tool
- Enhanced Disk Tool (Solaris Volume Manager)
- Job Scheduler
- Log Viewer
- Mail Alias Support
- Mounts and Shares Tool
- Name Service Support
- Patch Tool
- Performance Tool
- Projects Tool
- RBAC Support
- RBAC Tool
- Serial Port Tool
- Software Package Tool
- System Information Tool
- User and Group Tool

Security Innovations

Security is a major concern for Solaris administrators. The Internet is rapidly expanding, with the new IPv6 protocol set to completely supercede IPv4 sometime in the next few years. This will make many more addresses available for Internet hosts than are currently available. It also means that the number of crackers, thieves, and rogue users will also increase exponentially. Solaris 10 prepares your network for this "virtual onslaught" by embracing IPv6, not only for its autoconfiguration and network numbering features, but also because of the built-in security measures that form part of the protocol. In particular, authentication is a key issue, after many highly publicized IP-spoofing breaches reported in the popular press over the past few years. A second layer of authentication for internal networks and intranets is provided in Solaris 10 by the provision of Kerberos version 5 clients and daemons.

Kerberos Version 5

Kerberos is the primary means of network authentication employed by many organizations to centralize authentication services. As a protocol, it is designed to provide strong authentication for client/server applications by using secret-key cryptography. Recall that Kerberos is designed to provide authentication to hosts inside and outside a firewall, as long as the appropriate realms have been created. The protocol requires a certificate granting and validation system based around "tickets," which are distributed between clients and the server. A connection request from a client to a server takes a convoluted but secure route from a centralized authentication server, before being forwarded to the target server. This ticket authorizes the client to request a specific service from a specific host, generally for a specific time period. A common analogy is a parking ticket machine that grants the drivers of motor vehicles permission to park in a specific street for one or two hours only.

Kerberos version 5 contains many enhancements, including ticket renewal, removing some of the overhead involved in repetitive network requests. In addition, there is a pluggable authentication module, featuring support for RPC. The new version of Kerberos also provides both server- and user-level authentication, featuring a role-based access-control feature that assigns access rights and permissions more stringently, ensuring system integrity. In addition to advances on the software front, Solaris 10 also provides integrated support for Kerberos and smart card technology using the Open Card Framework (OCF) 1.1. More information concerning Kerberos is available from MIT at **http://web.mit.edu/network/kerberos-form.html**.

IPv6 and IPSec

IPv6, described in RFC 2471, is the replacement IP protocol for IPv4, which is currently deployed worldwide. The Internet relies on IP for negotiating many transport-related transactions on the Internet, including routing and the Domain Name Service. This means that host information is often stored locally (and inefficiently) at each network node. It is clearly important to establish a protocol that is more general in function, but more centralized for administration, and that can deal with the expanding requirements of the Internet.

One of the growing areas of the Internet is obviously the number of hosts that need to be addressed; many subnets are already exhausted, and the situation is likely to get worse. In addition, every IP address needs to be manually allocated to each individual machine on the Internet, which makes the usage of addresses within a subnet sparse and less than optimal. Clearly, there is a need for a degree of centralization when organizing IP addresses that can be handled through local administration, and through protocols like Dynamic Host Configuration Protocol (DHCP). However, one of the key improvements of IPv6 over IPv4 is its autoconfiguration capabilities, which make it easier to configure entire subnets and to renumber existing hosts. In addition, security is now included at the IP level, making host-to-host authentication more efficient and reliable, even allowing for data encryption.

One way security is achieved is by authentication header extensions: this allows a target host to determine whether a packet actually originates from a source host. This prevents common attacks, such as IP spoofing and denial of service (DoS), and reduces reliance on a third-party firewall by locking in security at the packet level. Tools are also included with Solaris 10 to assist with IPv4 to IPv6 migration.

VPN technology is also provided with Solaris 10, using IPSec. IPSec is compatible with both IPv4 and IPv6, making it easier to connect hosts using both new and existing networking protocols. IPSec consists of a combination of IP tunneling and encryption technologies to create sessions across the Internet that are as secure as possible. IP tunneling makes it difficult for unauthorized users (such as intruders) to access data being transmitted between two hosts on different sites. This is supported by encryption technologies, and an improved method for exchanging keys, using the Internet key exchange (IKE) method. IKE facilitates inter-protocol negotiation and selection during host-to-host transactions, ensuring data integrity. Implementing encryption at the IP layer will make it even more difficult for rogue users to "pretend" to be a target host, intercepting data with authorization.

What's New in Solaris 10

Each new release of Solaris brings about changes at the client, server, and system levels. These changes affect users, administrators, and developers in different ways. The following features have been released for the first time with Solaris 10:

- N1 containers, allowing systems to be logically partitioned into zones with specific functions. Containers can be "booted" within a few seconds, ensuring high availability.

- Resource management changes, ensuring that specific limits can be set on resource usage by applications, preventing "runaway" applications from bringing a system to its knees.

- Integrated firewall technology, not requiring a separate install.

- Support for smart card authentication.

- Kernel instrumentation through dynamic tracing, allowing system fine-tuning and problem identification.

- Binary compatibility between different Solaris versions and Linux, and source compatibility between different Solaris platforms.

- Failure prediction of hardware components, ensuring that they can be replaced before impacting on system performance.

Sources for Additional Information

In this chapter, we have so far examined the history of UNIX, and what distinguishes UNIX systems from other operating systems. We have also traced the integration of both "flavors" of UNIX into the current Solaris 10 release. With the ever-rising popularity of Solaris 10, there are many Web sites, mailing lists, and documentation sets that new and experienced users will find useful when trying to capitalize on an investment in Sun equipment or the latest Solaris 10 operating environment. In this section, we present some pointers to the main Internet sites on which you can find reliable information about Solaris 10.

Sun Documentation/Sun Sites

Unlike some operating systems, Solaris 10 comes with a complete set of online reference manuals and user guides on the Documentation CD-ROM, which is distributed with all Solaris 10 releases (Intel and SPARC). The manuals, which are in PDF format and cover a wide range of system administration topics, include the following:

- *System Administration Guide: Basic Administration*

- *System Administration Guide: Advanced Administration*

- *System Administration Guide: Devices and File Systems*

- *System Administration Guide: IP Services*

- *System Administration Guide: Naming and Directory Services (DNS, NIS, and LDAP)*

- *System Administration Guide: Naming and Directory Services (NIS+)*

- *System Administration Guide: Network Services*

- *System Administration Guide: Security Services*

The best thing about the manuals is that they are available for download and interactive searching through **http://docs.sun.com/**. This means that if you are working in the field and need to consult a guide, you don't need to carry around a CD-ROM or a printed manual. Just connect through the Internet and read the guide in HTML, or download and retrieve a PDF format chapter or two.

The two main Sun sites for Solaris 10 are at **http://www.sun.com/solaris** (for SPARC users) and **http://www.sun.com/intel** (for Intel users). Both of these pages contain internal and external links that are useful in finding out more information about Solaris 10 and any current offerings. The Sun Developer Connection (**http://developers.sun.com/**) is a useful resource that users can join to obtain special pricing and to download many software components for free.

Web Sites

Many third-party Web sites are also available that deal exclusively with Sun and Solaris 10. For example, if you are looking for a Solaris 10 FAQ, or pointer to Sun information, try the Sun Help site (**http://www.sunhelp.org/**). If it's free, precompiled software that you're after, check the Sun Freeware site (**http://www.sunfreeware.com/**) or one of the many mirrors. Here you can find the GNU C compiler in a precompiled package. For Solaris for Intel users, there is also an archive of precompiled binaries available at **ftp://x86.cs.duke.edu/pub/solaris-x86/bins/**.

In case you are interested in seeing what the pioneers of UNIX are doing these days, check out the home pages of these famous UNIX developers:

- **Brian Kernighan**   http://cm.bell-labs.com/cm/cs/who/bwk/index.html
- **Dennis Ritchie**   http://cm.bell-labs.com/cm/cs/who/dmr/index.html
- **Ken Thompson**   http://cm.bell-labs.com/who/ken/

USENET

USENET is a great resource for asking questions, finding answers, and contributing your skills and expertise to help others in need. This is not necessarily a selfless act—there will always be a Solaris 10 question that you can't answer, and if you've helped others before, they will remember you. The **comp.unix.solaris** forum is the best USENET group for Solaris 10 information and discussion. The best source of practical Solaris 10 information is contained in the Solaris FAQ, maintained by the legendary Casper Dik. You can always find the latest version at **http://www.wins.uva.nl/pub/solaris/solaris2/**. For Solaris for Intel users, there is the less formal **alt.solaris.x86** forum, where you won't be flamed for asking questions about dual-booting with Microsoft Windows, or mentioning non-SPARC hardware. For Solaris Intel, the best FAQ is at **http://sun.pmbc.com/faq/**. For both SPARC and Intel platforms, there is a **comp.sys.sun.admin** group that deals with system administration issues, which also has a FAQ available at **ftp://thor.ece.uc.edu/pub/sun-faq/FAQs**.

Mailing Lists

Mailing lists are a good way of meeting colleagues and engaging in discussions in a threaded format. The Sun Manager's List is the most famous Sun list, and contains questions, answers, and, most importantly, summaries of previous queries. All Solaris-related topics are covered. Details are available at **ftp://ftp.cs.toronto.edu/pub/jdd/sun-managers/faq**. In addition, there is a Solaris for x86 mailing list archived at **http://www.egroups.com/group/solarisonintel/**, which has some great tips, tricks, and advice for those who are new to Solaris 10, or who are having difficulties with specific hardware configurations.

Summary

Solaris 10 is an exciting, innovative operating environment. It can provide more functionality than existing desktop operating systems; however, there is an increased administrative overhead that you must consider. In this book, we hope to convey sound management practices and divulge practical techniques for solving many Solaris-related problems, and to implement the best-of-breed methods for all enterprise-level installations. By the end of this book, you should feel confident in managing all aspects of Solaris 10 system administration, and feel confident in transferring those skills to the management of related operating systems, such as Linux.

How to Find Out More

The main site for all Sun technologies in **http://www.sun.com/**. For further information on Java technologies, users should browse Sun's Java site at **http://java.sun.com/**.

System Concepts and Choosing Hardware

U nderstanding what makes Solaris different from other operating systems is critical to appreciating why it is the environment of choice for high-availability client/server environments. In this chapter we review the terms used to describe Solaris systems and major components, as well as networking terminology associated with Solaris networks. Understanding these terms will ensure that you understand some of the concepts discussed in later chapters. Much Solaris terminology is particular to the context of Solaris systems, and some generic terms may have one meaning in Solaris but another meaning for other operating systems. For example, while the term *host* may be used generically to identify any system attached to a network, it may be used more specifically in Solaris, when referring to *multihomed hosts.*

One of the main reasons for using Solaris is its SPARC-based hardware. While Solaris has supported Intel-based systems for supported for some time, many characteristics of SPARC-based systems make them appealing. For example, all new SPARC-based CPUs are capable of 64-bit processing, which has been available for several years on Solaris. This mature support is reflected in the current Sun Fire 15K configurations that allow more than 100 CPUs to be combined into a single physical system that features completely redundant hardware devices, including power supplies and buses. This configuration enables high availability and hot swapping of failed components while the system is still running.

At the lower end of the market, 64-bit UltraSPARC workstations are now price comparable to many PC systems that offer only 32-bit CPU performance. While these systems generally have faster CPUs, they simply don't have the processing capacity of 64-bit CPUs. In addition, the UltraSPARC series features both Small Computer System Interface (SCSI) and PCI local buses, which allow a wide variety of third-party hardware devices to be attached to the workstations. (The PCI local bus is now the dominant bus technology in the PC market.)

You might be wondering what SPARC hardware can do, where it came from, and why you should (or shouldn't) use it. Some administrators may be concerned about the use of proprietary hardware, given the "vendor lock-in" they may have experienced in the past. However, Solaris complies with many open standards, and the SPARC platform is supported by multiple hardware vendors. Alternatively, if you have an existing investment in Intel-based systems, it may be more sensible to migrate those to Solaris instead of using one or more of the alternatives.

This chapter reviews some of the main hardware components used in building both SPARC- and Intel-based systems, and it reviews some of the common workstation and server systems currently available for Solaris 10. If you need to find out more about specific servers and workstations, Sun offers PDF and HTML versions of hardware manuals for all supported systems at **http://docs.sun.com/**.

Key Concepts

This chapter reviews the role of the kernel, shells, and file systems. The distinction between a multiuser system and a multitasking system is also examined, and the role of clients and servers is explored. You will also learn how to define hosts, hostnames, networks, and IP addresses, and explore the range of SPARC and Intel hardware supported by Solaris.

UNIX and the Kernel

Operating systems are the building blocks of computer systems, and they provide the interface between user applications and computer hardware. Solaris is a multiuser, multitasking operating system developed and sold by Sun Microsystems (**http://www.sun.com/**), and it is one implementation of the UNIX operating system that draws on both the System V (AT&T) and Berkeley (BSD) systems. Solaris has evolved from little more than a research project to become the dominant UNIX operating system in the international marketplace.

Solaris 10 is the latest in a long line of operating environment releases that are based around the SunOS operating system, which is currently in version 5.10. Solaris 10 is considered a minor release, in the sense that it maintains complete binary compatibility with the previous release (Solaris 9). However, there are many new innovations—such as system minimization, extensible password encryption, and the thread-safe base security model—that make upgrading worthwhile.

Solaris is commonly found in large corporations and educational institutions that require concurrent, multiuser access on individual hosts and between hosts connected via the Internet.

In the enterprise computing industry, Sun is synonymous with highly available, highly reliable performance hardware, while Solaris is often the operating environment of choice to support database servers and application servers. Sun's hardware solutions are based around the SPARC and UltraSPARC integrated circuit technologies, which can currently support more than 100 processors in a single server system. These high-end systems, such as the Sun Fire 15K, can be logically partitioned into a number of dedicated multiprocessor "domains," allowing each domain to act as an independent system. This partitioning assists with the design and implementation of fail-over and replication strategies designed to ensure high availability.

UNIX is hard to define because different vendors have historically introduced different features to arrive at the entities that most users would think of as UNIX. However, it is easy enough to list the fundamental characteristics that are common to all UNIX and UNIX-like systems:

- They have a *kernel,* written in the C programming language, which mainly manages input/output processing rather than being a complete operating system. The kernel has ultimate responsibility for allocating system resources to complete various tasks.

- They have a hierarchical file system, which begins with a root directory and from which the branches of all other directories (and file systems) are mounted.

- System hardware devices are represented logically on the file system as special files (such as */dev/pty*, for pseudoterminals).

- They are process based, with all services and user shells being represented by a single identifying number (the process ID, or PID).

- They share a set of command-line utilities that can be used for text and numeric processing of various kinds, such as `troff`, `col`, `cat`, `head`, `tbl`, and so on.

- User processes can be spawned from a shell, such as the Bourne shell, which interactively executes application programs.

- Multiple processes can be executed concurrently by a single user and sent into the background by using the *&* operator.

- Multiple users can execute commands concurrently by logging in from pseudoterminals.

Note that a graphical user interface (GUI) is not necessarily a defining feature of UNIX, unlike other desktop operating systems, which place much stock in "look and feel." The common desktop environment (CDE) remains the default desktop for Solaris 10, but the Linux-developed GNOME desktop is also available for each user (**http://www.gnome.org/**). GNOME is currently the leading desktop of Linux users. Full integration of GNOME into Solaris 10 will lead to greater interoperability between Solaris and Linux systems, particularly in terms of GUI application development. It will also make porting GUI applications between Solaris and Intel easier, because Linux back-end applications have been able to be executed on Solaris Intel for some time by using `lxrun`.

For operating systems that are not layered, changing the window manager or even the look and feel involves rewriting significant portions of back-end code. In the Solaris environment, where the interface and display technologies are appropriately abstracted from the underlying kernel, moving from CDE to GNOME involves simply changing the command to initialize the X11 display manager; the kernel remains unmodified. The layering of the various components of a UNIX system is shown in Figure 2-1.

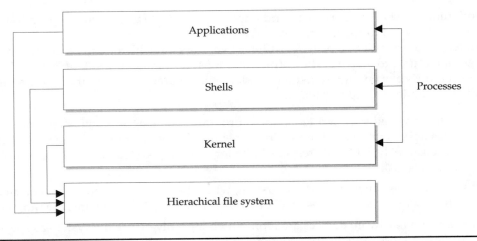

FIGURE 2-1 Components of a UNIX system

Broadly speaking, a UNIX system is layered according to applications that are invoked through user shells, which are managed by a kernel—which in turn uses file systems to create a persistent storage mechanism. Since the kernel provides the interface between shells and the file system (and by extension, between applications and the file system), it is considered the central part of UNIX technology.

Solaris kernels can trace their origins to both the System V and BSD variants of UNIX, while Microsoft Windows NT was based on the Virtual Memory System (VMS) kernel originally developed for the high-end VAX systems. Most kernels during the 1960s were written using assembly language or machine (binary) code, so the development of a high-level language for writing kernels (the C language) was one of the founding ideas of UNIX. This level of abstraction from hardware meant that kernels could be ported to other hardware platforms without having to be completely rewritten. The tradition of writing kernels in C continues today, with the Linux kernel (for example) being written in C. Obviously, a kernel alone is not a complete operating environment, so many additional applications (such as the visual editor, vi) were later added to what UNIX users would recognize as the suite of standard UNIX tools.

All UNIX systems have a kernel, which is the central logical processor that provides an interface between the system hardware, the system services, and the user shells that directly enable applications. For example, support for network interfaces is provided in the form of a kernel module and a device file that logically represents the physical device. Services are defined in the services database, and network daemons provide the final layer for supporting applications that use the network to transmit data. Since UNIX kernels are typically written in the C programming language, many systems-level applications and daemons are also written in C.

Of course, UNIX systems share some common characteristics with other operating systems, including the use of a hierarchical file system in which special files called *directories* are used to arrange related files logically. But UNIX has some distinctive features as well: explicit permissions to read, execute, and modify files on the UNIX file system can be granted to specific users or groups of users, making it easy to share work and collaborate with other users on the system.

The Shell

A key Solaris concept is the functional separation between the user interface and the operating system. This distinction means that a user can access a Solaris system by using either a terminal-based character user interface (CUI) or a high-resolution GUI without modifying the underlying operating system.

With so much attention paid to GUIs, why are CUI environments still important to Solaris? Are they just a historical hangover that Windows has managed to overcome? Are they simply the tools of choice for long-haired network administrators who have never used a mouse? In fact, mastering the Solaris command line is one of the most effective tools available under any UNIX environment, and the good news is that it's not that difficult to learn. Using the command line (or *shell*) has several advantages over GUI environments.

The shell is essential for programming repetitive tasks that can be performed only laboriously through a GUI. For example, searching a file system for all document files that have changed each day and making a copy of all these files (with the extension .doc) to a backup directory (with the extension .bak) takes time.

The shell can be used to search for, modify, edit, and replace Solaris configuration files, which are typically storied in text format. This is much like the approach taken with Windows .ini configuration files, which were text-based. However, after Windows 95, Windows versions store configuration information in the Registry in a binary format, making it impossible to edit manually. Most Solaris configuration files, including the startup scripts, are text based, and there is a move in many applications to standardize around XML.

The shell has a number of built-in commands that typically mirror those provided in the C programming language. This means that it is possible to write small programs as shell statements that are executed as sequential steps, without having to use a compiler (just like MS-DOS batch files are interpreted without requiring a compiler).

The shell can be used to launch applications that use a CUI, which is especially useful for logging onto a remote system and enabling access to the commands an administrator can use on the console, a valuable point in this era of global information systems. While Windows applications like Symantec's pcAnywhere can be used for remote access to the Windows Desktop, they don't easily support multiuser access (or multiuser access where one user requires a CUI and another a GUI).

The shell can be used to execute commands for which no equivalent GUI application exists. Although many operations could conceivably be performed using a GUI, it is usually easier to write a shell script than to create a completely new GUI application.

Many applications in Solaris, Linux, and Windows are now available through a GUI. If you feel more comfortable using GUIs, there is little reason to stop using them as long as you can find the tools to perform all of the tasks you need to undertake regularly, such as monitoring resource usage, setting process alarms and diagnostics, and/or facilitating remote access. However, if you want to make the most of Solaris and competently administer the system, you will need to become familiar with the shell and command-line utilities.

In keeping with the philosophy that different administrators have different needs and styles, Solaris makes several different shells available:

- **Bourne shell (sh)**   The original UNIX shell used to write all system scripts by convention
- **Korn shell (ksh)**   Provides enhanced input/output features, including the `print` and `read` commands
- **C shell (csh)**   Offers a command syntax similar to the C programming language
- **Bourne Again shell (bash)**   An open source, much improved version of the Bourne shell
- **Z shell (zsh)**   A freely available Bourne-like shell with a focus on sophisticated scripting features

The File System

UNIX also features a hierarchical file system that makes it easy for you to separate related files logically into directories, which are themselves special files. While MS-DOS and similar operating systems feature a hierarchical file system with simple file access permissions (such as read only), UNIX has a complete user-based file access permission system. Like process management, each file on the system is "owned" by a specific user, and by default only that user can perform operations on that file. *Privileged* users can perform all operations on all files on the file system. Interestingly, a special file permission allows *unprivileged* users to execute certain commands and applications with *superuser* privileges (such as `setuid`).

The following file system types are supported by the kernel:

- **cachefs**   The CacheFS cached file system
- **hsfs**   The High Sierra file system
- **nfs**   The Network File System (NFS)
- **pcfs**   The MS-DOS file system
- **tmpfs**   A file system that uses memory
- **ufs**   The standard UNIX File System (UFS)

The default local file system type is contained in the */etc/default/fs* file, while the default remote file system type is contained in the */etc/default/fstypes* file.

Multiuser, Multitasking, and Zoning

Modern enterprise operating systems like Solaris are able to support multiple users, executing multiple applications concurrently. Users can spawn multiple shells, which in turn can execute multiple applications. In addition, Solaris supports lightweight processes such as threads, which allow the traditional concept of multitasking to be generalized to execute multiple threads within a single process.

Solaris also supports symmetric multiprocessing, meaning that the physical execution of processes, threads, and user applications may occur on one of many different supported processors. In addition, the computing resources of multiple servers can be requested on demand through the N1 grid computing initiative, allowing a virtualization of the multiprocess, multiuser, multiprocessor scheme. Here, "zones" are configured as virtual instances that operate within the resource management framework, and form the basic containers for working with N1. More details on zoning can be found at **http://www.blastwave.org/docs/Solaris-10-b51/DMC-0002/dmc-0002.html**.

All of these functions are targeted at ensuring high availability and scalability of computationally intensive applications.

Client/Server Networks

While PC operating systems were designed in response to the waning of client/server systems, Solaris and other UNIX systems are firmly designed as client/server systems. While a PC is designed to run many high-powered applications using the local CPU, a client/server network is designed around the concept of multiple *thin* clients that access data and execute applications on a *fat* centralized server, or on a number of servers that are dedicated to one particular purpose. For example, a typical Solaris network might consist of hundreds of Sun Ray thin client systems, which are supported on the front line by several E450 departmental servers, as well as a set of rack-mounted 420R systems that run database, Web server, and development systems.

The client/server topology is also reflected in the structure of UNIX services: client applications running on client systems are designed to connect through to server applications running on server systems. Sun was instrumental in initiating key distributed computing technologies, such as the Remote Procedure Call (RPC) technology used in the NFS protocol. In addition, the Remote Method Invocation (RMI) technology developed as part of the Java networking and distributed computing APIs allows objects to be passed around the network as seamlessly as RPC.

Processes

Processes lie at the heart of all modern multiuser operating systems. By dividing system tasks into small, discrete elements that are each uniquely identified by a PID, Solaris is able to manage all the applications that may be concurrently executed by many different users. In addition, individual users may execute more than one application at any time. Each Solaris process is associated with a user ID (UID) and a group ID (GID), just like a standard file. This means that only users may send signals to their own processes (except for the superuser, who may send signals to any process on the system). Signals are typically used to restart or terminate processes. The multiuser, multitasking process model in Solaris ensures that system resources can be shared equally among all competing processes or allocated preferentially to the most important applications. For example, a firewall application would probably take precedence over all other system processes. Individual users and the superuser may allocate a priority level to active processes in real time.

Solaris provides a number of command-line tools that can be used to manage processes. In addition, APIs are provided for C programmers to allow them to operate directly on processes—spawning, managing, and killing as necessary. Solaris also provides lightweight processes (LWPs) that don't require as much overhead to operate as "normal" processes.

Naming Services

Every computer connected to the Internet must have an IP address, which identifies it uniquely within the network. For example, *192.18.97.241* is the IP address of the Web server at Sun. IP addresses are difficult for humans to remember, and they don't adequately describe the network on which a host resides. Thus, by examining the Fully Qualified Domain Name (FQDN) of *192.18.97.241—www.sun.com—*it's immediately obvious that the host, *www*, lies within the *sun.com* domain. The mapping between human-friendly domain names and machine-friendly IP addresses is performed by a distributed naming service known as the Domain Name Service (DNS). DNS is the standard protocol used by UNIX systems (and other operating systems) for mapping IP addresses to hostnames, and vice versa.

Although Solaris provides complete support for DNS, it uses its own domain management and naming system, known as the Network Information Service (NIS). NIS is not only responsible for host naming and management, but it is a comprehensive resource management solution that can be used to structure and administer groups of local and remote users.

NIS uses a series of maps to create namespace structures. Sometimes administrators ask why this extra effort is required to manage hosts and naming, because DNS already provides this function for Internet hosts by converting computer-friendly IP addresses to human-friendly "names." However, NIS does not just provide naming services; a NIS server also acts as a central repository of all information about users, hosts, Ethernet addresses, mail aliases, and supported RPC services within a network. This information is physically stored in a set of maps that are intended to replace the network configuration files usually stored in a server's /etc directory, ensuring that configuration data within the local area network (LAN) is always synchronized. Many large organizations use NIS alongside DNS to manage both their Internet and LAN spaces effectively. Linux also supports NIS.

In the past, Sun introduced an enhanced version of NIS known as NIS+. Instead of a simple mapping system, it uses a complex series of tables to store configuration information and hierarchical naming data for all networks within an organization. Individual namespaces may contain up to 10,000 hosts, with individual NIS+ servers working together to support a completely distributed service. NIS+ also includes greater capabilities in the area of authentication, security (using DES encryption), and resource access control.

Recently, Solaris has begun a transition to Lightweight Directory Access Protocol (LDAP) directory services as an alternative source of authoritative information for naming, identification, and authentication. LDAP is based on the original Directory Access Protocol (DAP), which provided X.500-type services for centralized directory lookups. Like NIS and NIS+, LDAP performs lookups, given a token, and returns a result. However, the query is much more generalized than what can be returned from NIS or NIS+: text, sounds, and graphics can all be associated with an entry in the directory.

While LDAP does not provide any kind of programmatic query language, like SQL, to query the directory, it does provide a standard interface to search the hierarchical namespace (`ldapsearch`). Since it works directly over TCP/IP and can support directory services for clients on different operating systems, LDAP is often viewed as the future central naming and directory service for Solaris.

Java 2 Enterprise Edition (J2EE)

Java is a relatively new programming language that is often used to create platform-independent GUIs that a user can interact with in complex and sophisticated ways. However, Java *applets*—the bits of code that are transmitted over the Internet and executed on the user's machine—are only one side of the whole Java story. This section focuses on the *server* side of Java.

Simple Java applications that execute on the server are called *servlets,* and they have their own standard API specification that has now been widely implemented in Web server extension products known as servlet *runners* (such as Apache's Tomcat server). Servlets are useful in developing Web-enabled, Solaris-based enterprise applications.

Increasingly, applications in the enterprise are being implemented using Web interfaces, partly in response to the persistent heterogeneity of computing platforms within organizations that span cities, states, and even nations. Accepting platform diversity does not mean losing control of standards, however. Sun Microsystems has pioneered a platform-independent programming language in which applications run on top of a logical Java Virtual Machine (JVM) that presents a consistent API for developers. Most major hardware platforms and operating systems now have virtual machines implemented, including (obviously) Solaris. In fact, the Solaris JVM produced by Sun has been highly optimized in its production release series. JVMs have also been integrated into popular Web browsers, so that Java programs can be downloaded from a server and executed within these browsers. (HTML has an `<applet>` tag that facilitates this process.) Applets have increased the complexity of Web-based user interfaces from simple arrays of buttons and forms to dynamic interaction with the user in a way that is similar to a normal desktop application.

The Java 2 Enterprise Edition (J2EE) is an extension of Java that aims to provide a complete enterprise architecture for delivering applications over the Web. J2EE is designed around a basic four-tier model—including client, presentation, business logic, and data tiers—that is sufficient to build new applications in a way that separates display logic from back-end data processing functions. In addition, J2EE features a component model that supports both stateless and stateful operations, transactional access to relational databases, and components that participate in asynchronous messaging. J2EE allows platform-independent enterprise applications to be executed through a standard Web interface, changing the way that users, developers, and software interact. The "write once, run anywhere" philosophy means that servers with totally different operating systems and hardware can be replaced with newer systems, without concern for application stability and porting.

How does server-side Java compare to Web-based client/server techniques such as the combination of a Common Gateway Interface (CGI) and a non-object-oriented language such as C? Although a compiled language like C is faster on a byte-per-byte basis than an interpreted language like Java, performance increases for Java can be gained by the combination of optimizing just-in-time (JIT) compilers for specific platforms and reducing the process and memory overhead associated with the CGI. For example, if you wrote a search application in Perl that is accessed by 1,000 Web users per hour, that would mean an extra 1,000 invocations of Perl that the server has to deal with, unless you used a specialized module. Of course, if you are running on a Sun Fire 15K, this would probably result in a negligible system strain. For other systems, invoking a Java servlet that occupies only a single process after being loaded into memory, and which *persists* across sessions, is both memory and process efficient. Servlets are therefore more appropriate for applications that are constantly being executed by multiple users, because they take advantage of Java's multithreading and synchronization capabilities.

On the flip side, CGI programs are often better suited to single-user, infrequently used, and numerically intensive applications that might be invoked only once per hour. In addition, CGI programs written in C are logically isolated from each other in the server's memory space: if Java servlets are executed using a single instance of a service manager (for example, Live Software's JRun), an unhandled exception arising from malformed or unexpected input could potentially impact all servlets running through the manager, especially if the JVM crashes.

SPARC Hardware

Sun has developed a wide range of hardware systems over the past few years, much of which are still supported by Solaris 10. These systems are based on the Scalable Processor Architecture (SPARC), which is managed by a SPARC member organization (**http://www.sparc.org/**). In addition to Sun Microsystems, Fujitsu (**http://www.fujitsu.com/**) and T.Sqware (**http://www.tsqware.com/**) also build SPARC-compliant CPU systems. System vendors that sell systems based on SPARC CPUs include Amdahl Corporation (**http://www.amdahl.com/**), Tatung (**http://www.tatung.com/**), Tadpole (**http://www.tadpole.com/**), and Toshiba (**http://www.toshiba.com/**). Vendors of system boards and peripherals for SPARC CPU–based systems include Hitachi (**http://www.hitachi.com/**), Seagate (**http://www.seagate.com/**), and Kingston Technology (**http://www.kingston.com/**).

Although media critics and competitors often paint SPARC systems from Sun as stand-alone, vendor-specific traps for the unwary, the reality is that a large number of hardware vendors also support the SPARC platform. It should also be noted that software vendors, such as Red Hat, also support SPARC versions of Linux, which proves that Solaris is not the only operating system that powers the SPARC platform. The SPARC standards can be downloaded free of charge from **http://www.sparc.org/standards.html**.

Often, administrators of Linux and Microsoft Windows systems who are used to "PC" hardware are incredulous to discover that some supported systems (such as the SPARCclassic) have CPUs that run below 100 MHz. This must seem a slow CPU speed in the age of Intel CPUs and their clones reaching the 1 GHz mark. However, CPU speed is only one component that contributes to the overall performance of a system—SPARC systems are renowned for their high-speed buses and very fast I/O performance. In addition, many SPARC systems were designed for continuous operation—it is not unheard of for systems to have several year of uptime, compared to several days for some operating systems. The many impressive features of the Solaris operating systems were developed with the SPARC hardware platform as a target, and these systems naturally have the best performance.

However, Sun has not ignored hardware developments and emerging standards—in recent years, Sun has created the UltraSPARC series of workstations and servers that features a PCI local bus, USB, and compatibility with Super Video Graphics Array (SVGA) multisync monitors commonly sold with PC systems. Of course, SPARC systems have always supported the SCSI standard, and all SCSI devices will work with Solaris. At the same time, Sun has proceeded with innovations, such as the Sun Fire 15K system, which can operate as a single system with massively parallel computational abilities, or it can be logically partitioned to act as 18 different systems. It has 106 UltraSPARC III Cu 1.2 GHz CPUs, and each domain can address more than half a terabyte of memory (576GB). Imagine being able to control an entire Application Service Provider (ASP) with no apparent "shared hosting" to the client, which is actually being serviced by a single physical system. Although the up-front cost of a Sun Fire 15K exceeds that required for 106 systems running Linux or Microsoft Windows, only one administrator is required to manage a Sun Fire 15K, while 106 different systems might require more than one administrator. More details on the Sun Fire platform can be found at **http://www.sun.com/servers/highend/sunfire15k/specs.xml**.

Supported Platforms

SPARC systems have an application architecture and a kernel architecture: most modern Sun systems have an application architecture of type 4, while the latest UltraSPARC systems have a kernel architecture of type *u*. Thus, UltraSPARC systems are known as *Sun4u* systems, and are the minimum requirement to run Solaris 10. One of the great advantages of SPARC is that systems with the same application architecture can run the same binaries; thus, the binary of an application compiled on an Ultra 5 should work on a Sun Fire 15K. This protects your investment in existing software, and acts as a protection against future changes in technology. However, the kernel architecture has changed significantly over the years, so that systems with different kernel architectures cannot boot the same kernel.

Table 2-1 shows a list of system types and platforms that are support for Solaris 10.

Desktop	Workgroup	Midrange	High End	Netra
Sun Blade 100 and 1000	Sun Fire V880	Sun Fire 6800 and 4810	Sun Fire 15K	Netra 20
Ultra 2	Sun Fire V480	Sun Fire 3800	Enterprise 10000	Netra T1
Ultra 5	Sun Fire V240	Sun Fire V1280		Netra ct800
Ultra 10	Sun Fire V210	Enterprise 6500		Netra ct400
Ultra 30	Sun Fire V120	Enterprise 6000		Netra t1400
Ultra 60	Sun Fire V100	Enterprise 5500		Netra t1425
Ultra 80	Enterprise 450	Enterprise 5000		Netra t1120 and t1125
Ultra 450	Enterprise 250 and 150	Enterprise 3500 and 4500		Netra t1100 and t1105

TABLE 2-1   Supported Systems for Solaris 10

You will need at least a Sun4u architecture system to run Solaris 10, and its CPU must run at 200 MHz or above. Sun4m and Sun4c systems are still supported by Solaris 9 and Linux. A minimum of 96MB of RAM is required to install Solaris 10—the Web Start Wizard will not let you proceed unless it can detect this amount of physical RAM, so be sure to check that your system meets the basic requirements before attempting to install Solaris 10. All SPARC kernels are now 64-bit only.

Full compatibility details are available at **http://wwws.sun.com/software/solaris/ solaris-express/supported_platforms.html**.

Intel Hardware

If Solaris was originally designed to run on SPARC hardware, and if SPARC hardware is where Sun makes its money, why would Sun support an Intel version? For starters, many more Intel systems exist in the world than SPARC systems. Sun also has a historical relationship with Intel, which supported SunOS 4.*x* for several 80386 and 80486 systems. At this point, however, Sun introduced the SPARC range of CPUs, which was the forerunner of the current UltraSPARC series. Intel-based systems are also suitable for workstation environments, and were (until the recent release of the Sun Blade 100) much cheaper than SPARC systems. Since Sun is primarily in the server hardware business, it made sense to develop a reliable operating system for Intel workstations that was supported by its high-end servers.

For many potential Solaris users, SPARC systems are still prohibitively expensive, even though these users want the features of the UNIX operating system. Often, organizations need to make best use of their existing investment in PC hardware. However, some PC operating systems may not currently meet their needs. While PCs have become the de facto standard for desktop computers, investments in PC-based solutions have sometimes met with dissatisfaction from users because some PC operating systems lack stability—particularly regarding application-specific issues, although operating systems have also caused concern. Some of the problems included the perceived lack of reliability of operating systems that were prone to crash during important business operations. Although Intel CPUs featured modes that should logically isolate such failures to the operation that causes them (such as protected mode), this requires operating system support that was never fully perfected by some vendors. In other words, PC hardware is up to the task, but operating systems have not always taken full advantage of the PC's abilities.

Perhaps more frustratingly, errors in existing PC operating systems could not be corrected by talented developers, because most PC operating systems are proprietary—in some instances, operating system vendors actually charged users to report operating system bugs, only refunding the charge if the bug was verified. In addition, frustration was often caused by so-called "standard" hardware, which often had incompatibilities with application and server software. For example, at the time when 80286 CPU systems were being touted as "IBM compatible," most were using an ISA bus, while IBM was actually using the Micro Channel Architecture (MCA) as the bus on its PS/2 systems. However, PC hardware has converged on a number of standards, such as the PCI bus, which has vastly improved the performance figures for data throughput on PCs.

There are some key benefits to using Solaris for Intel over SPARC hardware. For a start, "plug and play" devices are supported, meaning that explicit device configuration is often not required. In addition, you can get access to modern bus architectures like PCI, without having to purchase an UltraSPARC system. This point relates to overall system cost: If SPARC systems are going to use PCI for the foreseeable future, why use SPARC when PCI is supported by Intel systems at a smaller cost? In addition, Solaris for Intel supports multiple CPUs, each of which is much cheaper in cost than the equivalent SPARC CPU.

There are, however, some limitations to using Solaris for Intel. These limitations may be specific to Solaris, but some relate to the architecture itself. For example, while some versions of Microsoft Windows support up to four Enhanced Integrated Drive Electronics (EIDE) controllers, Solaris will "see" only the first two. Granted, IDE disks and controllers are generally less favorable than SCSI-3 drives, but they do exist and they are cheap. In addition, support for the Universal Serial Bus (USB) is still experimental, making it harder to add new devices that don't use the serial port for connection. Many new modems also won't work on anything but Windows (so-called "Winmodems") because they rely on Windows to control the modem hardware rather than having a built-in controller.

Because Sun makes no direct revenues from Solaris Intel, the bottom line is that, with the growing popularity of Linux for the Intel platform, continued development of the Solaris Intel edition may receive less attention than the SPARC edition. This doesn't mean that you shouldn't continue to use Solaris Intel, though, because it is a mature and stable product. In terms of contemplating future server purchases, however, it might be wiser to go with SPARC.

The Hardware Compatibility List (HCL), which is available at **http://www.sun.com/bigadmin/hcl/**, is the definitive guide to all hardware devices supported by the Solaris Intel platform. If a device does not appear in the HCL, it is unlikely that it will be supported under Solaris Intel—with some exceptions: motherboards, for example, often follow fairly loose standards, with clone boards often working correctly under Solaris even if they don't appear in the HCL. The most common compatibility issue occurs with video cards—many are not supported at all or, if they are, their full feature set is unsupported. For example, some video cards have hardware support for receiving TV signals. While their graphical rendering ability will be supported, the TV functions will generally not work with Solaris.

Fortunately, if your video card is not supported, it is possible to replace the X server provided by Solaris with the XFree-86 X server (**http://www.xfree.org/**). This server is functionally equivalent to any other server that supports the X11R6 standard, meaning that the CDE and all other Solaris GUI applications will run if you have installed XFree. The main advantage of using XFree-86 is that it supports a much larger array of hardware devices than the Solaris X server.

Devices Supported Under Solaris Intel

This section reviews some of the families of devices supported under Solaris Intel and provides examples of products that are likely to be supported. Most common motherboards are supported, including those developed by Acer, ASUS, EPoX, and Intel. Some examples are the Acer M9N MP, the ASUS A7V, and the EPoX EP-MVP3G. In addition, motherboard support has been established for many prebuilt systems, including the Acer AcerAcros T7000 MT, Bull Information Systems Express5800-HX4500, and Compaq Deskpro EN 6400. Many symmetric multiprocessing (SMP)-capable motherboards are also supported. No special configuration is required to support SMP devices—they are plug and play—and some popular models include the Dell PowerEdge 6300, the Fujitsu TeamSERVER-T890I, and the Gateway 8400.

Video cards from many different manufacturers are supported, including those operating from ISA, PCI, or AGP buses. Five display resolutions are supported:

- 800 × 600 pixels
- 1024 × 768 pixels
- 1152 × 900 pixels
- 1280 × 1024 pixels
- 1600 × 1200 pixels

Both 8- and 24-bit color are supported in all of these modes, depending on the chipset and onboard memory. Many cards are supported, including the ATI 3D RAGE, the Boca Voyager 64, and the Chips & Technology 65540. All multisync monitors are supported. However, the kdmconfig application used for setting up the display does not show 14-inch monitors in its selection list: in most cases, you will be able to use the 15-inch setting, as long as the frequency specified is supported by your monitor. Fixed-sync monitors should work as long as their frequency is supported by the video card at the resolution you require. Serial, bus, and PS/2 mouse devices are supported under Solaris. In addition, many third-party pointing devices are supported, including the MicroSpeed MicroTRAC trackball, the LogiTech MouseMan cordless, and the Kraft Systems MicroTrack.

In terms of SCSI host adapters, both standard and UltraSCSI support is included for the most popular host adapters, including the Adaptec AHA-2940/2940W, the AMD

Pcscsi, and the Compaq 32-bit Fast-Wide SCSI-2. Many Iomega Jaz/Zip devices are supported under Solaris, including the SCSI 2250S Zip (250MB) and the V2008I Jaz (2GB) drives, and the ATAPI and IDE Z100A Zip drives (100MB).

Many different types of network adapters are supported, including 10 Mbps and 100 Mbps data transfer rates. Supported adapters include the 3Com EtherLink III PCI Bus Master, the Adaptec ANA-6901, and the AMD PCnet-PCI.

For laptops, common PCMCIA devices are generally supported, such as modems and network adapters, including the ATI Technologies 14400 ETC-EXPRESS, the Compaq SpeedPaq 192, and the Hayes 5361US.

Solaris 10 also has full support for USB technology, allowing communication with peripheral devices at very high speeds.

Examples

In the following section, you will examine the basic components of a Solaris system, and two sample systems that demonstrate the difference between a workstation and a server.

System Components

A typical Solaris SPARC workstation consists of the following components:

- Base unit (aka "pizza box"), which contains the motherboard, SCSI controller, and SBUS cards
- Frame buffer or graphics card
- SCSI or IDE units connected by SCSI or IDE cables to the SCSI or IDE controller in the pizza box
- CD-ROM drive, internal or external (SCSI or IDE)
- DVD-ROM drive, internal on newer systems
- Speaker box and microphone, external
- Two serial ports (A and B)
- A parallel port
- A tape drive, internal or external (DAT/DDS/QIC and so on)
- Mouse (mechanical or infrared) and keyboard (type 4 or type 5)

As noted, most desktop workstations come in a "pizza box" chassis, although earlier Internetwork Packet Exchange (IPX) and similar systems had a "lunch box" chassis. Both of these designs were more compact than their PC counterparts. Servers generally come in two versions: stand-alone or rack-mountable. The version numbers on servers also differ with their chassis type. The 220R, for example, is the rack-mounted version of the stand-alone E-250, while the 420R is the rack-mounted version of the stand-alone 420. The 220R and E-250 have two CPUs each, while the 420R and E-450 have four CPUs each.

Example Systems

Let's examine two SPARC systems in detail; a workstation (UltraSPARC 5) and a server (UltraSPARC E-450). The UltraSPARC 5 system is a popular, low-end desktop model. Although it has been replaced in this category by the new, lower-cost Sun Blade 100 (available for around $1,000), it remains a popular workstation for business and home use. It supports UltraSPARC-IIi CPUs with speeds ranging from 270 to 400 MHz. Internally, it features 16KB instruction and data caches, while it supports from 256KB to 2MB of external cache memory. In terms of memory and disk capacity, the system supports up to 512MB of physical RAM, a CD-ROM drive, a 1.44MB floppy disk drive, and two hard drives, making it possible to enable volume management. The system has three peripheral ports—two serial and one parallel—and it has a built-in Ethernet adapter and supports 10 Mbps and 100 Mbps transmission rates. The system also features a PCMCIA bay, which allows a wide variety of PC-type hardware to be connected.

While the UltraSPARC 5 is comparable in performance to desktop PCs, the E-450 is a workgroup-level server that features SMP, larger numbers of disks, fast buses, hot swapping, and more cache RAM per CPU. The E-450 supports up to four UltraSPARC-IIi CPUs, operating at 250–480 MHz. Internally, it features 16KB instruction and data caches per CPU, and up to 4MB of external cache per CPU—for a four-CPU system, that's a total of 16MB of external cache. The system also features two Ultra Port Architecture (UPA) buses operating at 100 MHz, supporting up to two CPUs on each bus. With respect to mass storage and memory, the system accepts up to 16 dual inline memory modules (DIMMs), giving up to 4GB of physical RAM. Some 20 slots for hard disks provide a large pool of hot-swappable volumes on a fast SCSI-3 bus. A CD-ROM and floppy disk drive are also supplied, and a DDS-3 internal Digital Audio Tape (DAT) drive for backups. In addition, hot-swappable power supplies can be installed into the chassis, enabling two different power sources to be utilized.

Procedures

In the following sections, you will learn how to examine system and network configuration, in order to prepare you for system and upgrade installation tasks.

System Configuration

Solaris provides a simple way to view all the hardware devices on your system. This information can be used to configure your system. For example, by identifying the disk devices on your system, you can correctly select targets for formatting.

The `prtconf` command is used for displaying system information:

```
prtconf
System Configuration:  Sun Microsystems  sun4u
Memory size: 128 Megabytes
```

This section shows the hardware architecture (Sun4u, which means that this is a Sun-4 system with an UltraSPARC CPU) and that it has 128MB of RAM.

The following section identifies the terminal emulator, keyboard, and UFS. These devices are necessary to boot a Solaris system.

```
System Peripherals (Software Nodes):
SUNW,Ultra-5_10
    packages (driver not attached)
        terminal-emulator (driver not attached)
    disk-label (driver not attached)
        SUNW,builtin-drivers (driver not attached)
        sun-keyboard (driver not attached)
        ufs-file-system (driver not attached)
```

The next section shows the OpenBoot PROM (programmable read-only memory), physical memory, and virtual memory monitor devices:

```
    chosen (driver not attached)
    openprom (driver not attached)
        client-services (driver not attached)
    options, instance #0
    aliases (driver not attached)
    memory (driver not attached)
    virtual-memory (driver not attached)
```

The final section displays devices attached to the first PCI local bus. This includes an Integrated Device Electronics (IDE) hard disk, IDE hard drive, and network interface.

```
pci, instance #0
        pci, instance #0
            ebus, instance #0
                auxio (driver not attached)
                power, instance #0
                SUNW,pll (driver not attached)
                se, instance #0
                su, instance #0
                su, instance #1
                ecpp (driver not attached)
                fdthree, instance #0
                eeprom (driver not attached)
                flashprom (driver not attached)
                SUNW,CS4231 (driver not attached)
            network, instance #0
            SUNW,m64B (driver not attached)
            ide, instance #0
                disk (driver not attached)
                cdrom (driver not attached)
                dad, instance #0
                sd, instance #30
```

NOTE   *Obviously, the specific devices installed on each system vary, and so will the configuration displayed when using* `prtconf`.

Basic Networking Terminology

A Solaris network consists of a number of different hosts that are interconnected using a switch or a hub. Solaris networks connect to one another via routers, which can be dedicated hardware systems, or Solaris systems, which have more than one network interface. Each host on a Solaris network is identified by a unique hostname; these hostnames often reflect the function of the host in question. For example, a set of four FTP servers may have the hostnames *ftp1, ftp2, ftp3,* and *ftp4.*

Every host and network that is connected to the Internet uses the Internet Protocol (IP) to support higher-level protocols such as Transmission Control Protocol (TCP) and User Datagram Protocol (UDP). Every interface of every host on the Internet has a unique IP address that is based on the network IP address block assigned to the local network. Networks are addressable by using an appropriate netmask that corresponds to a class A (255.0.0.0), class B (255.255.0.0), or class C (255.255.255.0) network.

Solaris supports multiple Ethernet interfaces that can be installed on a single machine. These are usually designated as */etc/hostname.hmen*, where *n* is the interface number and *hme* is the interface type. Interface files contain a single unqualified domain name, with the primary network interface being designated with an interface number of zero. Thus, the primary interface of a machine called *ftp* would be defined by the file */etc/hostname.hme0*, which might contain the unqualified domain name *ftp*. A secondary network interface, connected to a different subnet, might be defined in the file */etc/hostname.hme1*. In this case, the file might contain the unqualified domain name *mail*.

Enabling multiple interfaces is commonly used in organizations that have a provision for a failure of the primary network interface or to enable load balancing of server requests across multiple subnets (for example, for an intranet Web server processing HTTP requests). A system with a second network interface can act either as a router or as a multihomed host. Hostnames and IP addresses are locally administered through a naming service, which is usually DNS for companies connected to the Internet, and the Network Information Service (NIS/NIS+) for companies with large internal networks that require administrative functions beyond what DNS provides, including centralized authentication. Large organizations may also use a directory service such as LDAP for naming.

It is also worth mentioning at this point that it is possible for you to assign different IP addresses to the same network interface; this configuration can be useful for hosting "virtual" interfaces that require their own IP address, rather than relying on application-level support for multihoming (for example, when using the Apache Web server). You simply create a new */etc/hostname.hmeX:Y* file for each IP address required, where X represents the physical device interface and Y represents the virtual interface number.

The subnet mask used by each of these interfaces must also be defined in */etc/netmasks*. This is particularly important if the interfaces lie on different subnets, or if they serve different network classes. In addition, it might also be appropriate to assign an FQDN to each of the interfaces, although this will depend on the purpose to which each interface is assigned.

Summary

In this chapter, we have examined some of the key concepts that underlie the Solaris 10 Operating Environment and the SunOS 5.10 Operating System. From the kernel to the shell to different file system types, Solaris 10 provides a number of sophisticated methods for managing systems and deploying applications in the enterprise. We have also examined the basic hardware support for systems that run the Solaris 10 Operating Environment and the SunOS 5.10 Operating System. From SPARC-based systems, specifically designed for Solaris with a mature 64-bit architecture, to the ubiquitous Intel-based systems that can now run Solaris Intel, the range of servers and workstations is enormous. Given Sun's efforts in presenting a unified desktop and office suite, many more systems will run Solaris in the future.

## CHAPTER 3

Solaris 10 Installation

Solaris 10 provides more installation methods than any previous version. These include the Web Start Wizard, JumpStart, `suninstall`, and Live Upgrade. The Web Start Wizard is the easiest method for installing Solaris 10: it uses a GUI-based front end that presents a series of configuration choices. For those who prefer a command-line installation, the `suninstall` program is available. This is particularly useful for installing servers that are attached to a simple terminal on the console port, using the `tip` command, rather than a high-resolution monitor. Large organizations are more likely to create a JumpStart configuration to install a standard operating environment (SOE) on all Solaris 10 systems. Using JumpStart ensures that all systems have an identical installation base, which makes it easy for you to manage patches and maintain production systems. Live Upgrade is a new innovation that minimizes the downtime of production servers: a new boot environment is constructed while the server is still operating under its existing operating environment release. Once the second boot environment has been installed, the system is quickly rebooted into the new operating environment, and the previous version is uninstalled in the background.

In most cases, installing from a high-speed CD-ROM with a modern system will take around 30 minutes. However, JumpStart, Live Upgrade, and all network-based installations will be slower on a per-machine basis, since network bandwidth limits the data that can be transmitted from the install server to the install client.

Preinstallation Planning

The basic process of installing Solaris remains the same, regardless of the installation method selected. A number of planning tasks must be performed prior to installation:

1. Choose the appropriate installation method: the Web Start Wizard, JumpStart, `suninstall`, or Live Upgrade.

2. Decide whether you want to upgrade an existing installation or perform a clean install of the operating system. If your system is currently running Solaris 7, 8, or 9, you can perform an upgrade. If your system is running Solaris 2.6 or earlier,

or if it is not running Solaris at all, you need to perform a clean installation. An upgrade preserves many of the system settings from the previous installation and generally takes less time to complete than a completely new installation. If you are performing an upgrade, you should first back up the current system by using `ufsdump` or a similar method so that it can be restored in the event of an upgrade failure.

3. Analyze your existing hardware devices to determine whether Solaris 10 will run on your system without an upgrade. For example, Solaris 9 on SPARC would run with only 96MB of RAM; however, at least 128MB of RAM is required to run Solaris 10. To perform an upgrade installation, you would need to add RAM to an existing Solaris 9 system with only 96MB of RAM.

4. Determine whether your storage devices have sufficient capacity to install Solaris 10 and all required third-party applications. A complete Solaris 10 installation requires around 3GB of disk space. In addition, an amount of swap space equivalent to twice your physical memory should be factored into the sum, along with third-party and user disk space requirements.

5. Choose an appropriate installation medium. Possibilities include a JumpStart, CD-ROM, DVD-ROM, or net-based installation from a remotely mounted CD-ROM or DVD-ROM drive. For enterprises, it's often convenient to set up a single network server with a Network File System (NFS)-exported DVD-ROM or CD-ROM drive that is publicly available for mounting. In addition, enterprises might also choose a customized JumpStart installation, which also requires network access to a centralized boot server. Smaller organizations will almost certainly use a CD-ROM or DVD-ROM drive attached to the local system for installation.

6. Gather all of the necessary system configuration information. This includes the system hostname, IP address, subnet mask, name service type, name server IP address, default router IP address, time zone, locale, and proxy server IP address. These values, and when they are required, will be discussed in the "Configuration" section.

By undertaking a comprehensive preinstallation review, you can ensure a successful installation. In addition to making a decision about the installation type and gathering basic system data, you need to understand the network context in which the system will operate. You can define the network context by answering several key questions:

- Will the system be networked? If so, you will need an IP address, subnet mask, and default router (unless the system itself is intended to be a router).

- Will the system use the Dynamic Host Configuration Protocol (DHCP)? If so, you will not need to supply an IP address, as a lease over an IP address will automatically be granted to you at boot time. However, you will need the IP address of the DHCP server to enable DHCP.

- Will the system use IPv6, the newest version of the Internet Protocol?

- Will the system form part of a Kerberos v5 realm to allow centralized authentication? If so, you will need the name of the realm, the administration server's IP address, and the address of the primary Key Distribution Center (KDC).

- Will the system use the Domain Name Service (DNS)? If so, you will need the IP address of a primary and secondary DNS server that is authoritative for the local domain.

- Will the system use Network Information Service (NIS) or NIS+? If so, you will need to supply the IP address of the local NIS or NIS+ server.

- Will the system use the Lightweight Directory Access Protocol (LDAP) for centralized authentication and authorization? If so, you will need to supply the profile server's IP address.

- Will the system use a proxy server to access the Internet? If so, you will need to provide the IP address of the proxy server.

You will need to answer these questions before you can completely configure the system during installation.

Disk Space Planning

You can determine how much disk space you require to install Solaris 10 only by examining the purpose of the server. For a SPARC system, with 512MB of RAM, a complete installation will require around 3GB of space for software, 1024MB for swap, and more space for user data and applications. You need to set aside extra disk space for special features such as internationalization, and you need to estimate the size of print and mail spooling directories that are located in */var*. Although the default size of */var* is usually small in the installation program, mail and print servers will require that you increase this amount by allowing for a reasonable allocation of spooling space per user. Since a full */var* file system caused by a large print job can affect other tasks such as mail, it's important that you overestimate rather than underestimate the size of */var*.

In terms of applications, an Oracle database server, for example, will require at least 1–2GB of disk space for software packages, mount points, and table data. For a development system with multiple users, you should compute a projection based on the maximum quota for each user. For example, if each of 50 users is allowed 100MB of disk space, at least 5GB of disk space must be available for the users' exclusive use—as a rule, if users have quotas imposed on them, they should always be guaranteed access to that space. If data on a server is mission critical, you should consider installing some volume management software.

In terms of specific layouts, the typical file system layout for a SPARC system follows a set of customary disk slice allocations. Slice 0 holds the root partition, while slice 1 is allocated to swap space. For systems with changing virtual memory requirements, using a swap file on the file system might be better than allocating an entire slice for swap. Slice 2 often refers to the entire disk, while */export* on slice 3 traditionally holds older versions of the operating system that are used by client systems with lower performance (for example, older systems that use the trivial FTP daemon `tftpd` to download their operating system upon boot). These systems may also use slice 4 as exported swap space. */export* may also be used for file sharing using NFS. Slice 5 holds the */opt* file system, which is the default location under Solaris 10 for local packages installed using the `pkgadd` command. Under earlier versions of Solaris, the */usr/local* file system held local packages, and this convention is still used by many sites. The system package file system */usr* is usually located on slice 6, while */export/home* usually contains user home directories on slice 7. Again, earlier systems located user home directories under */home*, but since */home* is used by the `automounter` program in Solaris 10, some contention can be expected.

The typical file system layout for an Intel-based system also follows a set of customary disk slice allocations. Slice 0 again holds the root partition, while slice 1 is allocated to swap space. Slice 2 continues to refer to the entire disk, while */export* on slice 3 again holds older versions of the operating system that are used by client systems, and slice 4 contains exported swap space for these clients. The local package file system */opt* is still located on slice 5, and the system package file system */usr* is again located on slice 6. Slice 7 contains the user home directories on */export/home*. However, the two extra slices serve different purposes: boot information for Solaris is located on slice 8 and is known as the *boot slice,* while slice 9 provides space for alternative disk blocks and is known as the *alternative slice.*

Device Names

One of the most challenging aspects of understanding Solaris hardware is to learn the device names and references used by Solaris to manage devices. Solaris uses a specific set of naming conventions to associate physical devices with instance names on the operating system. In addition, devices can also be referred to by their device name, which is associated with a device file created in the */dev* directory after configuration. For example, a hard disk may have the physical device name */pci@1f,0/pci@1,1/ide@3/dad@0,0*, which is associated with the device file */dev/dsk/c0t0d0*. The benefit of the more complex Solaris device names and physical device references is that it is easy to interpret the characteristics of each device by looking at its name. For the preceding physical device name example, you can see that the Integrated Device Electronics (IDE) hard drive is located on a PCI local bus at target 0. When you view the amount of free disk space on the system, for example, it is easy to identify slices on the same disk by looking at the device name:

```
# df -k
Filesystem              kbytes     used    avail capacity  Mounted on
/proc                        0        0        0     0%    /proc
/dev/dsk/c0t0d0s0      1982988   615991  1307508    33%    /
fd                           0        0        0     0%    /dev/fd
/dev/dsk/c0t0d0s3      1487119   357511  1070124    26%    /usr
swap                    182040      416   181624     1%    /tmp
```

Here you can see that */dev/dsk/c0t0d0s0* and */dev/dsk/c0t0d0s3* are slice 0 and slice 3 of the disk.

If you're ever unsure of which physical disk is associated with a specific disk device name, you can use the format command to find out:

```
# format
Searching for disks...done
AVAILABLE DISK SELECTIONS:
0. c1t3d0 <SUN2.1G cyl 2733 alt 2 hd 19 sec 80>
          /pci@1f,0/pci@1/scsi@1/sd@3,0
```

Here you can see that physical device */pci@1f,0/pci@1/scsi@1/sd@3,0* is matched with the disk device */dev/dsk/c1t3d0*. In addition, a list of mappings between physical devices and instance names is always kept in the */etc/path_to_inst* file.

SPARC Preinstallation

One of the main hardware differences between SPARC systems that run Solaris and PC systems that run Linux or Microsoft Windows is that SPARC systems have an Open Boot PROM monitor program that can be used to modify firmware settings prior to booting. It is based on the Forth programming language and can be used to run Forth programs that perform the following functions:

- Boot the system using the boot command
- Perform diagnostics on hardware devices using the diag command
- Test network connectivity using the watch-net command

Prior to installing or upgrading Solaris on a SPARC system, you should perform a few basic checks of the system to obtain the data necessary for installation (such as the device name of the boot disk) and to verify that all system components are functional. The three most commonly performed tasks are to check network connectivity, check the disks that have been detected on the SCSI bus, and review how much memory is installed.

If you are booting over a network or if your system needs to access a DNS, NIS/NIS+, Kerberos, or LDAP server, and you want support for these services to be installed, your network connection needs to be operational. To ensure that packets are being sent to and received from your system, you can use the watch-net command:

```
ok watch-net
Internal Loopback test - succeeded
External Loopback test - succeeded
Looking for Ethernet packets.
'.' is a good packet. 'X' is a bad packet.
Type any key to stop
......X.........XXXX........XX............
```

If the output reports that a large number of packets are bad, you should check for hardware errors on your network cable and/or use a packet analyzer to determine whether a structural fault exists on the local area network (LAN).

To check whether all the disk devices attached to the system have been correctly detected, you can use the `probe-scsi` command to print a list of available devices:

```
ok probe-scsi
Target 1
Unit 0 Disk SUN0104 Copyright (C) 2004 Sun Microsystems All rights reserved
```

You can see the default boot disk at target 1 unit 0.

To check that sufficient memory is available on the local system for the installation of Solaris 10, you can use the `banner` command:

```
ok banner
Sun Ultra 5/10, Keyboard present
OpenBoot 3.25, 256 MB memory (50 ns) installed, Serial #12345353
Ethernet address 5:2:12:c:ee:5a HostID 456543
```

In this case, 256MB of RAM is available, which is sufficient for installation.

Intel Preinstallation

To install Solaris Intel, first switch on the system and insert the Solaris 10 Installation CD-ROM into the drive. If a high-resolution graphics monitor is attached to the system, the GUI-based Configuration Assistant will start. Alternatively, if you are using a low-resolution terminal to connect, the Configuration Assistant will be text based.

After the BIOS messages have been displayed, the following message is displayed:

```
SunOS Secondary Boot
Solaris Intel Platform Edition Booting System
Running Configuration Assistant...
```

The Configuration Assistant is responsible for performing a number of preinstallation tasks and must be executed prior to starting the Web Start Wizard or any other installation program. At the opening screen, simply press F2 to proceed with the installation, unless you are performing an upgrade.

The first task performed by the Configuration Assistant is to determine the bus types supported by your system and to collect data about the devices installed in your system. During this process, the following message is displayed on your screen:

```
Determining bus types and gathering hardware configuration data ...
```

After all the devices have been discovered by scanning, a list of identified devices is printed on the screen:

```
The following devices have been identified on this system. To identify
devices not on this list or to modify device characteristics, chose Device
Task. Platform types may be included in this list.

        ISA: Floppy disk controller
        ISA: IDE controller
        ISA: IDE controller
        ISA: Motherboard
        ISA: PS/2 Mouse
        ISA: PnP bios: 16550-compatible serial controller
        ISA: PnP bios: 8514-compatible display controller
        ISA: PnP bios: Audio device
        ISA: System keyboard (US-English)
```

If you are satisfied that the devices required for installation have been correctly detected (video card and RAM size, for example), press F2 again to proceed with booting. Alternatively, you may perform several other tasks on this screen, including the following:

- View and edit devices
- Set the keyboard type
- Save the current configuration
- Delete a saved configuration
- Set the default console device

If your system does not already have a UNIX File System (UFS) installed, or if it is a completely new system, you need to use *fdisk* to create new partitions at this point so that your system may be installed. However, if you have an existing Linux installation that you want to dual boot with Solaris, you must ensure that the Linux swap partition is not confused with a Solaris UFS device, because they have the same type within *fdisk*. You should be able to distinguish Linux swap partitions by their maximum size (127MB). The following page will be displayed during bootup and prior to the execution of *fdisk*:

```
<<< Current Boot Parameters >>>
Boot path: /pci@1,0/pci-ide@6,1/ide@2/sd@1,0:a
Boot args: kernel/unix
<<< Starting Installation >>>
SunOS Release 5.10 Version Generic 32-bit
Copyright 1983-2001 Sun Microsystems, Inc. All rights reserved.
Configuring /dev and /devices
```

```
Using RPC Bootparams for network configuration information.
Solaris Web Start installer
English has been selected as the language in which to perform the install.
Starting the Web Start Solaris installer
Solaris installer is searching the system's hard disks for a
location to place the Solaris installer software.
No suitable Solaris fdisk partition was found.
Solaris Installer needs to create a Solaris fdisk partition
on your root disk, c0d0, that is at least 395 MB.
WARNING: All information on the disk will be lost.
May the Solaris Installer create a Solaris fdisk [y,n,?]
```

You should heed the warning that all data will be lost if you choose to overwrite an existing partition with *fdisk*.

Disk Partitions

If you consent to using *fdisk*, you will see a screen similar to the following:

```
Total disk size is 2048 cylinders
Cylinder size is 4032 (512 byte) blocks
Cylinders
Partition  Status  Type  Start  End   Length  %
=========  ======  ====  =====  ====  ======  ===
1                  UNIX  0      1023  1024    50
2                  DOS   1024   2047  1024    50
SELECT ONE OF THE FOLLOWING:
1. Create a partition
2. Specify the active partition
3. Delete a partition
4. Exit (update disk configuration and exit)
5. Cancel (exit without updating disk configuration)
Enter Selection:
```

In this example, you can see that two existing partitions occupy 1,204 cylinders each. Partition 1 is a UNIX partition (perhaps from SCO UNIX, from the Santa Cruz Operation), while partition 2 is an MS-DOS partition. If you want to use the entire disk for Solaris, you need to select option 3 on this menu, twice, to delete each existing partition in turn. Alternatively, if you wished to retain the UNIX partition but delete the MS-DOS partition, you would select option 3 only once, and then select partition 2 for deletion.

After you have freed up space (if necessary), you will be required to select option 1 to create a partition. You will then be required to select option A from the following menu to create a Solaris partition:

```
Select the partition type to create:
1=SOLARIS 2=UNIX 3=PCIXOS 4=Other
5=DOS12 6=DOS16 7=DOSEXT 8=DOSBIG
A=x86 Boot B=Diagnostic 0=Exit?
```

NOTE *It is not possible to run Solaris from a non-UFS partition; however, it is possible to mount non-Solaris file systems after the system has been installed.*

Next, you need to specify the size of the partition, in either the number of cylinders or the percentage of the disk to be used. In this example, you enter either 100 percent or 2,048 cylinders:

```
Specify the percentage of disk to use for this partition
(or type "c" to specify the size in cylinders).
```

Next, you need to indicate whether the target partition is going to be activated. This means that the system will attempt to boot the default operating system loader from this partition. If you are going to use the Solaris boot manager, you may activate this partition. However, if you are using Boot Magic or LILO to manage existing Microsoft Windows or Linux partitions, and you wish to continue using either of these systems, you should answer no.

After you have created the partition, the *fdisk* menu will be updated and displayed as follows:

```
2 Active x86 Boot 8 16 9 1
Total disk size is 2048 cylinders
Cylinder size is 4032 (512 byte) blocks
Cylinders
Partition  Status  Type       Start  End  Length  %
=========  ======  =========  =====  ====  ======  ===
2          Active  x86 Boot   0      2047  2048    100
SELECT ONE OF THE FOLLOWING:
1. Create a partition
2. Specify the active partition
3. Delete a partition
4. Exit (update disk configuration and exit)
5. Cancel (exit without updating disk configuration)
Enter Selection:
```

At this point, you should select option 4. You will then be prompted with the following message:

```
No suitable Solaris fdisk partition was found.
Solaris Installer needs to create a Solaris fdisk partition
on your root disk, c0d0, that is at least 395MB.
WARNING: All information on the disk will be lost.
May the Solaris Installer create a Solaris fdisk [y,n,?]
```

Since you've just created the appropriate partition using *fdisk*, you should type **n** here. You will then see this message:

```
To restart the installation, run /sbin/cd0_install.
```

After restarting the installer, you will see the formatting display shown in the next section.

Disk Formatting and Virtual Memory

If your system already has a UFS partition, or if you have just created one, you will see a screen containing text similar to the following:

```
<<< Current Boot Parameters >>>
Boot path: /pci@1,0/pci-ide@6,1/ide@2/sd@1,0:a
Boot args: kernel/unix
<<< Starting Installation >>>
SunOS Release 5.10 Version Generic 32-bit
Copyright 1983-2001 Sun Microsystems, Inc. All rights reserved.
Configuring /dev and /devices
Using RPC Bootparams for network configuration information.
Solaris Web Start installer
English has been selected as the language in which to perform the install.
Starting the Web Start Solaris installer
Solaris installer is searching the system's hard disks for a
location to place the Solaris installer software.
The default root disk is /dev/dsk/c0d0.
The Solaris installer needs to format
/dev/dsk/c0d0 to install Solaris.
WARNING: ALL INFORMATION ON THE DISK WILL BE ERASED!
Do you want to format /dev/dsk/c0d0? [y,n,?,q]
```

At this point, you simply type **y** and the disk will be formatted so that you can create new partitions. You will then be prompted to enter the size of the swap partition:

```
NOTE: The swap size cannot be changed during filesystem layout.
Enter a swap partition size between 384MB and 1865MB, default = 512MB [?]
```

You are then asked to confirm that the swap slice can be installed at the beginning of the partition:

```
The Installer prefers that the swap slice is at the beginning of the
disk. This will allow the most flexible filesystem partitioning later
in the installation.
Can the swap slice start at the beginning of the disk [y,n,?,q]
```

After you create the swap partition, the other slices can be created on the target disk, because the installation program requires a UFS to install correctly. However, the system must first be rebooted to perform the disk layout:

```
The Solaris installer will use disk slice, /dev/dsk/c0d0s1.
After files are copied, the system will automatically reboot, and
installation will continue.
Please Wait...
Copying mini-root to local disk....done.
Copying platform specific files....done.
Preparing to reboot and continue installation.
Need to reboot to continue the installation
Please remove the boot media (floppy or cdrom) and press Enter
Note: If the boot media is cdrom, you must wait for the system
to reset in order to eject.
```

After you press the ENTER key, you will see the standard Solaris shutdown messages, including this one:

```
Syncing file systems... 49 done
rebooting...
```

The Boot Manager

After you eject the installation CD-ROM from your drive, the standard Solaris boot manager menu should appear:

```
SunOS - Intel Platform Edition Primary Boot Subsystem
Current Disk Partition Information
Part#    Status   Type      Start  Length
========================================
1        Active   X86 BOOT  0      2048
Please select the partition you wish to boot:
```

After you enter **1** and press the ENTER key, the following message appears:

```
SunOS Secondary Boot
Solaris Intel Platform Edition Booting System
Running Configuration Assistant...
Autobooting from boot path: /pci@1,0/pci-ide@6,1/ide@2/sd@1,0:a
If the system hardware has changed, or to boot from a different
device, interrupt the autoboot process by pressing ESC.
```

A few seconds later, the boot interpreter that is responsible for initializing the system is started:

```
Initializing system
Please wait...
<<< Current Boot Parameters >>>
Boot path: /pci@0,0/pci-ide@7,1/ata@1/cmdk@0,0:b
```

```
Boot args:
Type b [file-name] [boot-flags] <ENTER> to boot with options
or i <ENTER> to enter boot interpreter
or <ENTER> to boot with defaults
<<< timeout in 5 seconds >>>
Select (b)oot or (i)nterpreter:
SunOS Release 5.10 Version Generic 32-bit
Copyright 1983-2004 Sun Microsystems, Inc. All rights reserved.
Configuring /dev and /devices
Using RPC Bootparams for network configuration information.
```

Next, you need to use kdmconfig to set up your graphics card and monitor so that the Web Start Wizard can correctly display its windows. To start kdmconfig, press F2. Then, you are taken to the kdmconfig introduction screen. After pressing F2 again, you will be asked to perform the kdmconfig view/edit system operation. In the configuration window, you can make changes to the settings detected on your system. If your system is listed on the Hardware Compatibility List (HCL), you shouldn't have any problems with hardware detection.

Web Start Wizard Installation

To use the Web Start Wizard installer using a local DVD-ROM or CD-ROM drive, you need to bring the system to run-level 0 so that commands can be entered into the PROM boot monitor. The following command can be used from a root shell to bring the system to run-level 0:

```
# sync; init 0
```

When the system has reached init level 0, the following prompt will be displayed:

```
ok
```

Next, place the Solaris 10 Installation CD-ROM or DVD-ROM into the local drive, and type the following command:

```
ok boot cdrom
```

NOTE *This command is the same whether a DVD or CD-ROM is used as the source. If you are using a Solaris Intel system, you cannot upgrade from Solaris versions 2.6 or from versions 7 through 9 to 10 by using the Web Start Wizard from the CD-ROM: you must use a DVD-ROM or JumpStart, or you must perform an Internet-based installation. In addition, your BIOS and hard disk controller for the boot device must support Logical Block Addressing (LBA) to work with Solaris 10.*

Soon after the system has started booting, you see output similar to the following:

```
Boot device: /sbus/espdma@e,8400000/esp@e,8800000/sd@6,0:f File and args:
SunOS Release 5.10 Version Generic 32-bit
Copyright 1983-2004 Sun Microsystems, Inc. All rights reserved.
Configuring /dev and /devices
Using RPC Bootparams for network configuration information.
Solaris Web Start installer
English has been selected as the language in which to perform the install.
Starting the Web Start Solaris installer
Solaris installer is searching the system's hard disks for a
location to place the Solaris installer software.
Your system appears to be upgradeable.
Do you want to do a Initial Install or Upgrade?
1) Initial Install
2) Upgrade
Please Enter 1 or 2 >
```

If this message appears in the boot messages, you may elect to perform an upgrade of the existing Solaris installation. However, most administrators would back up their existing software, perform a fresh install, and then restore their data and applications after the system is operational. In this example, the option to perform an Initial Install is chosen, which will overwrite the existing operating system.

Type **1**, and then press ENTER. You will see a message like this:

```
The default root disk is /dev/dsk/c0t0d0.
The Solaris installer needs to format
/dev/dsk/c0t0d0 to install Solaris.
WARNING: ALL INFORMATION ON THE DISK WILL BE ERASED!
Do you want to format /dev/dsk/c0t0d0? [y,n,?,q]
```

Formatting the hard drive overwrites all existing data on the drive—you must ensure that if you have previously installed an operating system on the target drive (*c0t0d0*), you have backed up all data that you will need in the future. This includes both user directories and application installations.

After you answer by typing **Y**, the following screen appears:

```
NOTE: The swap size cannot be changed during filesystem layout.
Enter a swap slice size between 384MB and 2027MB, default = 512MB [?]
```

Press the ENTER key to accept the default of 512MB, if your system has 256MB of physical RAM, as this example system has. However, as a general rule, you should allocate twice the amount of physical RAM as swap space; otherwise, system performance will be impaired. The swap partition should be placed at the beginning of the drive, as the following message indicates, so that other slices are not dependent on its physical location:

```
The Installer prefers that the swap slice is at the beginning of the
disk. This will allow the most flexible filesystem partitioning later
in the installation.
Can the swap slice start at the beginning of the disk [y,n,?,q]
```

After you type **Y** to answer this question, you will be asked to confirm the formatting settings:

```
You have selected the following to be used by the Solaris installer:
Disk Slice : /dev/dsk/c0t0d0
Size : 1024 MB
Start Cyl. : 0
WARNING: ALL INFORMATION ON THE DISK WILL BE ERASED!
Is this OK [y,n,?,q]
```

If you answer by typing **Y**, the disk will be formatted and a mini-root file system will be copied to the disk. Then the system will reboot, and the Web Start Wizard installation process can begin:

```
The Solaris installer will use disk slice, /dev/dsk/c0t0d0s1.
After files are copied, the system will automatically reboot, and
installation will continue.
Please Wait...
Copying mini-root to local disk....done.
Copying platform specific files....done.
Preparing to reboot and continue installation.
Rebooting to continue the installation.
Syncing file systems... 41 done
rebooting...
Resetting ...
Sun Ultra 5/10, Keyboard present
OpenBoot 3.25, 256 MB memory (50 ns) installed, Serial #12345353
Ethernet address 5:2:12:c:ee:5a HostID 456543
Rebooting with command: boot /sbus@1f,0/espdma@e,8400000/
esp@e,8800000/sd@0,0:b
Boot device: /sbus@1f,0/espdma@e,8400000/esp@e,8800000/
sd@0,0:b File and args:
SunOS Release 5.10 Version Generic 32-bit
Copyright 1983-2004 Sun Microsystems, Inc. All rights reserved.
Configuring /dev and /devices
Using RPC Bootparams for network configuration information.
```

Configuration

The Web Start Wizard asks a number of configuration questions that are used to determine which files are copied to the target drive and how the new system's key parameters will be set. Many of these questions involve network and software configuration, because these are the two foundations of the Solaris installation. The following sections review each of the configuration options and provide examples of appropriate settings.

Network Support

The Network Support screen gives you the option to select either a networked or nonnetworked system. Some examples of nonnetworked systems include standalone workstations and offline archives. If you don't want or need to install network support, however, you still need a unique hostname to identify the localhost.

DHCP Server

Network users must first identify how their system is identified using the IP. One possibility is that the system will use DHCP, which is useful when IP addresses are becoming scarce on a class C network. DHCP allows individual systems to be allocated only for the period during which they are "up." Thus, if a client machine is operated only between 9 A.M. and 5 P.M. every day, for example, it is only "leased" an IP address for that period of time. When an IP address is not leased to a specific host, it can be reused by another host. Solaris DHCP servers can service Solaris clients as well as Microsoft Windows and Linux clients.

Hostname

A hostname is used to uniquely identify a host on the local network; when combined with a domain name, the hostname allows a host to be uniquely identified on the Internet. Solaris administrators often devise related sets of hostnames that form part of a single domain. Alternatively, a descriptive name can be used to describe systems with a single purpose, such as *mail* for mail servers.

IP Address

If your network does not provide DHCP, you need to enter the IP address assigned to this system by the network administrator. It is important to ensure that the IP address is not currently being used by another host, because packets may be misrouted if identical IP addresses exist. Like a hostname, the IP address needs to be unique to the local system.

Netmask

You need to enter the netmask for the system: *255.0.0.0* (class A), *255.255.0.0* (class B), or *255.255.255.0* (class C). If you're not sure what the correct netmask is, ask your network administrator.

IPv6 Support

You need to indicate whether IPv6 needs to be supported by this system. The decision of whether or not to use DHCP will depend on whether your network is part of MBone, the IPv6-enabled version of the Internet. As proposed in RFC 2471, IPv6 will replace IPv4 in the years to come, as version 6 provides for many more IP addresses than IPv4. Once IPv6 is adopted worldwide, less reliance on DHCP will be necessary.

However, IPv6 also incorporates a number of innovations above and beyond the addition of more IP addresses for the Internet. Enhanced security provided by authenticating header information, for example, will reduce the risk of IP spoofing and denial of service (DoS) attacks. Since IPv6 support does not interfere with existing IPv4 support, most administrators will want to support version 6.

Kerberos Server

Kerberos is a network authentication protocol that is designed to provide centralized authentication for client/server applications by using secret-key cryptography, which is based around ticketing. Once a ticket has expired, the trust relationship between two hosts is broken. To use Kerberos, you need to identify the name of the local KDC.

Name Services

A name service allows your system to find other hosts on the Internet or on the LAN. Solaris supports several different naming servers, including NIS/NIS+, DNS, and file-based name resolution. Solaris supports the concurrent operation of various naming services, so it's possible to select NIS/NIS+ and set up DNS manually later. However, because most hosts are now connected to the Internet, it may be more appropriate for you to install DNS first and then install NIS/NIS+.

DNS Server

DNS maps IP addresses to hostnames. If you select DNS, you will be asked to enter a domain name for the local system. This should be the FQDN, or Fully Qualified Domain Name (for example, *cassowary.net*). You need to either search the local subnet for a DNS server or enter the IP address of the primary DNS server for your domain. You may also enter up to two secondary DNS servers that have records of your domain, which can be a useful backup if your primary DNS server goes down. It is also possible that, when searching for hosts with a hostname rather than an FQDN, you would want to search multiple local domains. For example, the host *www.buychapters.com* belongs to the *buychapters.com* domain. However, your users may wish to locate other hosts within the broader *cassowary.net* domain by using the simple hostname, in which case you can add the *cassowary.net* domain to a list of domains to be searched for hosts.

NIS/NIS+ Server

NIS/NIS+ is used to manage large domains by creating maps or tables of hosts, services, and resources that are shared between hosts. NIS/NIS+ centrally manages the naming and logical organization of these entities. If you choose NIS or NIS+ as a naming service, you need to enter the IP address of the local NIS or NIS+.

LDAP Server

LDAP provides a "white pages" service that supersedes existing X.500 systems and runs directly over TCP/IP. The LDAP server is used to manage directory information for entire organizations, using a centralized repository. If you want to use an LDAP server, you need to provide both the name of your profile and the IP address of the LDAP server. If the machine that you're installing will be the LDAP server, you shouldn't set up the system as an LDAP client. Note that it might be wiser to configure LDAP after system installation, or at the very least, if you should ensure that the system can connect to the LDAP server. A client system will not come up until the LDAP server is up, and the client system can hang for a long time if the LDAP server is not available.

Router

To access the LAN and the Internet, you need to supply the IP address of the default router for the system. A router is a multihomed host that is responsible for passing packets between subnets.

Time Zone and Locale

The next section requires that you enter your time zone as specified by geographic region—the number of hours beyond or before Greenwich Mean Time (GMT) or by time-zone file. Using the geographic region is the easiest method, although if you already know the GMT offset or the name of the time-zone file, you may enter that instead. Next, you are required to enter the current time and date, with a four-digit year, a month, day, hour, and minute. In addition, you need to specify support for a specific geographic region in terms of locales, if required.

Power Management

Do you want your system to switch off automatically after 30 minutes of inactivity? If your answer is yes (e.g., because you have a workstation that does not run services), then you should enable power management, as it can save costly power bills. However, if you're administering a server, you'll definitely want to turn power management *off*. A case in point: once your server shuts down in the middle of the night, and consequently your clients cannot access data, you'll understand why disabling power management is so important.

Proxy Server

A proxy server acts as a buffer between hosts on a local network and the rest of the Internet. A proxy server passes connections between local hosts and any other host on the Internet. It sometimes acts in conjunction with a firewall to block access to internal systems, thereby protecting sensitive data. One of the most popular proxy servers is squid, which also acts as a caching server. To enable access to the Internet through a proxy server, you need to enter the hostname of the proxy server, and the port on which the proxy operates.

64-Bit Support

Solaris 10 provides support for 64-bit kernels for the SPARC platform. By default, only a 32-bit kernel will be installed. For superior performance, a 64-bit kernel is preferred, because it can natively compute much larger numbers than can the 32-bit kernel. In the 64-bit environment, 32-bit applications run in compatibility mode. However, only some UltraSPARC systems support the 64-bit kernel.

Disk Selection and Layout

If you are performing an upgrade or installing a new system, you need to decide whether you want to preserve any preexisting data on your target drives. For example, you may have five SCSI disks attached, only one of which contains slices used for a previous version of Solaris. Obviously, you will want to preserve the data on the four nonboot disks. However, partitions on the boot disk will be overwritten during installation, so it's important that you back up and/or relocate files that need to be preserved. Fortunately, if you choose to perform an upgrade rather than a fresh installation, many system configuration files will be preserved.

The Web Start Wizard will also ask whether you want to "auto-layout" the boot disk slices or configure them manually. You should be aware that the settings supplied by the installation program are conservative, and trying to recover a system that has a full root file system can be time consuming, especially given the low cost of disk space. It's usually necessary to increase the size of the / and /var partitions by at least 50 percent over what the installer recommends. If you have two identical disks installed, and you have more space than you need, you can always set up volume management to ensure high availability through root partition mirroring; thus, if your primary boot disk fails, the system can continue to work uninterrupted until the hardware issue is resolved.

Finally, some client systems use NFS to mount disks remotely on central servers. While this can be a useful way of accessing a centralized home directory from a number of remote clients (by using the automounter), database partitions should never be mounted remotely. If you need to access remote partitions via NFS, you can nominate these partitions during the installation program.

Root Password

An important stage of the installation process involves selecting the root password for the superuser. The root user has the same powers as the root user on Linux or the Administrator account on Windows NT. If an intruder gains root access, he or she is free to roam the system, deleting or stealing data, removing or adding user accounts, or installing Trojan horses that can transparently modify the way your system operates.

One way to protect against an authorized user gaining root access is to use a difficult-to-guess root password, which makes it difficult for a cracker to use a password-cracking program to guess your password successfully. The optimal password is a completely random string of alphanumeric and punctuation characters. Some password-generating applications can be used to generate passwords that are easy to remember but that contain almost random combinations of characters.

You should never write down the root password, and you should change it often, unless it is locked in the company safe. The root password should not be known by anyone who doesn't need to know it. If users require levels of access that are typically privileged (such as mounting CD-ROMs), using the `sudo` utility to limit the access of each user to specific applications for execution as the superuser is better than giving out the root password to everyone who asks for it.

The root password must be entered twice—just in case you make a typographical error, as the characters that you type are masked on the screen.

Software Selection

After you have entered all the configuration settings, the following message appears:

```
Please wait while the system is configured with your settings...
```

The installation Kiosk then appears on the screen. In the Kiosk, you select the type of installation that you want to perform. To begin the software selection process, you need to eject the Web Start CD-ROM and insert the Software (1) CD-ROM. Next, you have the option of installing all Solaris software using the default options or customizing your selection before copying the files from the CD-ROM. Obviously, if you have a lot of disk space and a fast system, you may prefer to install the entire distribution and then, after installation, delete the packages that you no longer require. This is definitely the fastest method. Alternatively, you can elect to perform a custom installation.

You are then presented with a list of all the available software groups. You can select or deselect individual package groups, or package clusters, depending on your requirements. For example, you may decide to install the Netscape Navigator software, but not install the NIS/NIS+ server for Solaris.

After choosing the packages that you want to install, you are required to enter your locale based on geographic region (the U.S. entry is selected by default). You may also elect to install third-party software during the Solaris installation process—this is particularly useful if you have a standard operating environment that consists of using the Oracle database server in conjunction with the Solaris operating environment, for example. You would need to insert the product CD-ROM at this point so that it could be identified.

After selecting your software, you need to lay out the disks, which involves defining disk slices that will store the different kinds of data on your system. The fastest configuration option involves selecting the boot disk and allowing the installer to lay out the partitions automatically according to your software selections. For example, you may want to expand the size of the */var* partition to allow for large print jobs to be spooled or Web server logs to be recorded.

Finally, you will be asked to confirm your software selections and proceed with installation. All the packages will then be installed to your system. A progress bar indicates which packages have been installed at any particular point, and how many remain to be installed. After you have installed the software, you must reboot the system. After restarting, your system should boot directly into Solaris unless you have a dual-booting system—in which case you will need to select the Solaris boot partition from the Solaris boot manager.

Upon reboot, a status message is printed on the console, looking something like this:

```
ok boot
Resetting ...
Sun Ultra 5/10, Keyboard present
OpenBoot 3.25, 256 MB memory (50 ns) installed, Serial #12345353
Ethernet address 5:2:12:c:ee:5a HostID 456543
Boot device: /iommu/sbus/espdma@f,400000/esp@f,800000/sd@1,0
File and args:
SunOS Release 5.10 Version generic [UNIX(R) System V Release 4.0]
Copyright (c) 1983-2001, Sun Microsystems, Inc.
configuring network interfaces: le0.
Hostname: server
The system is coming up. Please wait.
add net default: gateway 204.58.62.33
NIS domainname is paulwatters.net
starting rpc services: rpcbind keyserv ypbind done.
Setting netmask of le0 to 255.255.255.0
Setting default interface for multicast: add net 224.0.0.0: gateway client
syslog service starting.
Print services started.
volume management starting.
The system is ready.
client console login:
```

By default, the common desktop environment (CDE) login screen is displayed.

Network Installation

Although the discussion up to this point has looked in detail at CD-ROM and DVD-ROM installation from a local drive, it's actually possible to set up a single install server from which installation clients read all of their data, using a variation of the JumpStart install program. This approach is useful when a number of clients will be installing from the same disk and/or if installation is concurrent. Thus, it's possible for a number of users to install Solaris from a single server, which can be very useful when a new release of Solaris is made. For example, the Solaris 10 beta was distributed in a form suitable for network installation, allowing multiple developers to get their systems running as quickly as possible. For existing install servers, this reduces administration overhead, since different versions of Solaris (Solaris 8 and 9, for example) can be distributed from the same server.

The install server reads copies of the installation CD-ROMs and DVD-ROMs and creates a distributable image that can then be downloaded by remote clients. In addition, you can create images for both SPARC and Intel versions that can be distributed from a single system; thus, a high-end SPARC install server could distribute images to many Intel clients. The install server uses DHCP to allocate IP addresses dynamically to all install clients. Alternatively, a name server can be installed and used to allocate permanent IP addresses to install clients.

To create SPARC disk images on the install server, you use the `setup_install_server` command. For a SPARC DVD-ROM or CD-ROM, this command is located in */cdrom/cdrom0/s0/Solaris_10/Tools*. For an Intel DVD-ROM or CD-ROM, this command is located in */cdrom/cdrom0/Solaris_10/Tools*. The only parameter that needs to be supplied to the command is the path where the disk images should be installed. You should ensure that the path can be exported to clients and that the partition selected has sufficient disk space to store the images.

The same command is used to create Intel disk images, but the path is different: for a SPARC DVD-ROM or CD-ROM, the command is located in */cdrom/cdrom0/Solaris_10/Tools*, whereas for an Intel DVD-ROM or CD-ROM, the command is located in */cdrom/cdrom0/s2/Solaris_10/Tools*.

To set up individual clients, execute the `add_install_client` command on the install server—once for each client. You need to specify the name of the client to be installed, as well as its architecture. For a Sun4m system named *pink*, for example, you would use the following command:

```
# /export/install/boot/Solaris_10/Tools/add_install_client pink sun4m
```

You also need an entry in the */etc/ethers* file and */etc/hosts* file for *pink*. On the client side, instead of typing **boot cdrom** at the OK prompt, you would need to enter the following command:

```
ok boot net
```

suninstall Installation

To boot with the `suninstall` program, you don't use the Solaris 10 Installation CD-ROM; rather, you use the Solaris 10 Software 1 CD-ROM, which is bootable. `suninstall` has the advantage of not requiring high-resolution graphics to complete installation, so you can use a low-resolution monitor or terminal. It requires a minimal amount of RAM and allows you flexibility in configuring your system prior to installation (including internationalization). The order of questions and procedures followed are generally the same as those used in the Web Start Wizard. However, `suninstall` does not allow you to install third-party software as part of the installation process.

Using the `suninstall` method is more reliable than the Web Start Wizard when installing Solaris Intel, because `suninstall` relies less on graphic cards and displays, which may not be compatible with the Solaris X11 server.

JumpStart

JumpStart is an installation technology that allows a group of systems to be installed concurrently, using a standard file system layout and software package selection. For sites with hundreds of systems that are maintained by a small staff, JumpStart is the ideal tool for upgrading or reinstalling systems.

For example, when a staff member leaves the organization, her workstation can be simply reinstalled using JumpStart. By enforcing an SOE, there is no need to configure individually every system that needs to be installed, greatly reducing the administrative burden on system administrators.

When using JumpStart on a large number of clients, installation can be expedited by using a *sysidcfg* file, which defines a number of standard parameters for installation. The *sysidcfg* file can contain configuration entries for the following properties:

Current date and time	DHCP server IP address	Local domain name
Graphics card	Local hostname	Local IP address
IPv6 support	Locale	Security policy
Monitor type	DNS server	NIS/NIS+ server
LDAP server	Netmask	Network interface
Pointing device	Power management	Root password
Security policy	Terminal type	Time zone

The following is a sample *sysidcfg* file:

```
system_locale=en_US
timezone=US/Eastern
timeserver=192.168.34.3
network_interface=le0 {netmask=255.255.255.0 protocol_ipv6=yes}
security_policy=NONE
terminal=dtterm
name_service=NONE
root_password=5fg48;r3f
name_service=NIS {domain_name=cassowary.net name_server=
nis(192.168.44.53)}
```

Here, you can see that the system locale has been set to standard U.S. English, the time zone to the U.S. East Coast, the timeserver to *192.168.34.3*, and the network interface running *IPv6 to /dev/le0*. While the default terminal and root password are also set, the name service and security policy have not been set because these might change from system to system. In addition, the name service selected is NIS, with the NIS server set to *nis.cassowary.net (192.168.44.53)*.

JumpStart has three roles, which are filled by different systems on the network:

- An install server, which provides all the data and services required to install the system
- A boot server, where the RARP daemon is used to boot client systems that have not been installed
- An install client, which is the target system for installation

Boot Servers

A boot server provides a copy of the operating system to be installed on a target host. Once the target host has been booted using the network and install options, a kernel is downloaded to the target host from an install server, and booted locally. Once the system has been loaded, the operating system is then downloaded from the boot server. The rules for downloading and installing specific files are located in the *rules.ok* file. Individual systems can have their own entries in the *rules* file, or generic rules can be inserted. After loading the system from the boot server, the install client executes a post-installation script, and then is ready for use.

Installing Servers

The install server uses RARP to listen for requests to install the system from target hosts. Once such a request is received, a mini-root system is downloaded from the install server to the target host.

To set up an install server, you need to enter the following commands:

```
# mkdir -p /export/install /export/config
# cp -r /cdrom/Sol_10_sparc/s0/Solaris_2.10/Misc/jumpstart_sample/ * /export/config
# /cdrom/Sol_10_sparc/s0/Solaris_2.10/Tools
     ./setup_install_server /export/install
```

This assumes that */export/install* has sufficient space to store the installation files, and that the JumpStart configuration data, such as the *rules* file, will be stored in */export/config*. Here is a sample *host_class* file, which is referred to in *rules*, that specifies the UFS disk layout for all boot clients:

```
install_type initial_install
system_type standalone
partitioning explicit
filesys c1t2d0s0 512 /
filesys c1t2d0s3 2048 /usr
filesys c1t2d0s4 256 /var
filesys c0t3d1s0 1024 swap
filesys c0t3d1s1 free /export
cluster SUNWCall
```

Here, you can see that the standard layout allocated 512MB to /, 2048MB to /usr, 256MB to /var, 1024MB to swap, and all free space to /export. In addition, the cluster SUNWCall is to be installed.

Once the *rules* file has been customized, its contents must be verified by using the check command. Once the check command parses the *rules* file and validates its contents, a *rules.ok* file is created.

Boot Clients

To set up a boot client, you must shut down the target system to init level 0, by using the init 0 command or equivalent. Next, you need to boot the system by using the following command from the "ok" prompt:

```
boot net - install
```

At this point, a broadcast is made on the local subnet to locate an install server. Once an install server is located, a mini-root system is downloaded to the target system. Once the kernel is loaded from the mini-root system, the operating system in then downloaded from the boot server:

```
Resetting ...

Sun Ultra 5/10, Keyboard present
OpenBoot 3.25, 256 MB memory (50 ns) installed, Serial #12345353
Ethernet address 5:2:12:c:ee:5a HostID 456543
Initializing Memory |
Boot device: /iommu/sbus/ledma@f,400010/le@f,c00000 File and args: -
hostname: paul.cassowary.net
domainname: cassowary.net
root server: installserv
root directory: /Solaris_2.10/export/exec/kvm/sparc.sun
Copyright (c) 1983-2004, Sun Microsystems, Inc.
The system is coming up. Please wait.
```

Once the system has started, you'll see individual clusters being installed:

```
Selecting cluster: SUNWCXall

Total software size: 324.55 MB

Preparing system to install Solaris. Please wait.

Setting up disk c1t2d0:

Creating Solaris disk label (VTOC)
```

```
Creating and checking UFS file systems:

- Creating / (c1t2d0)
- Creating /var (c1t2d0)
- Creating /scratch (c1t2d0)
- Creating /opt (c1t2d0)
- Creating /usr (c1t2d0)
- Creating /staff (c1t2d0)
Beginning Solaris package installation...
SUNWcsu.....done. 321.23 MB remaining.
SUNWcsr.....done. 277.34 MB remaining.
SUNWcsd.....done. 312.23 MB remaining.
```

sysidcfg

When installing JumpStart on a large number of clients, you can expedite installation by using a *sysidcfg* file, which defines a number of standard parameters for installation. The *sysidcfg* file can contain configuration entries for the properties shown in Table 3-1.

The following is a sample *sysidcfg* file:

```
system_locale=en_US
timezone=US/Eastern
timeserver=localhost
network_interface=le0 {netmask=255.255.255.0 protocol_ipv6=yes}
security_policy=NONE
terminal=dtterm
name_service=NONE
root_password=f7438:;H2ef
```

Property	*sysidcfg* Parameter
Date and time	*timeserver*
DHCP	*dhcp*
DNS domains to search	*search*
DNS, LDAP, or NIS/NIS+ name server	*name_server*
DNS, LDAP, or NIS/NIS+ name service	*name_service*
Domain name	*domain_name*
Graphics card	*display*
Hostname	*hostname*
IP address	*ip_address*
IPv6	*protocol_ipv6*
Kerberos administration server	*admin_server*
Kerberos KDC	*kdc*

TABLE 3-1   Configurable *sysidcfg* Properties

Property	*sysidcfg* Parameter
Kerberos realm	*default_realm*
Keyboard language	*keyboard*
LDAP profile	*profile*
Monitor type	*monitor*
Netmask	*netmask*
Network interface	*network_interface*
Pointing device	*pointer*
Root password	*root_password*
Security policy	*security_policy*
Terminal type	*terminal*
Time zone	*timezone*

TABLE 3-2   Configurable *sysidcfg* Properties *(continued)*

Summary

This chapter has shown you how to perform preinstallation planning and how to estimate the amount of disk space required for installation. In addition, you have walked through how to perform a Web Start Wizard installation, and how to configure a Solaris system for first-time operation. These techniques must be employed whenever a Solaris system is installed.

Initialization, OpenBoot PROM, and Run Levels

One of the main hardware differences between SPARC systems that run Solaris and PC systems that run Linux or Microsoft Windows is that SPARC systems have an OpenBoot PROM monitor program, which can be used to modify firmware settings prior to booting. In this chapter, we examine how to use the OpenBoot PROM monitor to manage SPARC system firmware.

Solaris 10 uses a flexible boot process that is based on the System V Release 4.0 specification for UNIX systems. The System V approach makes it easier to create and customize startup and shutdown procedures that are consistent across sites and systems. The aim of this chapter is to introduce you to the basic terminology and initialization elements that play an important role in bringing a Solaris system to single- and multiuser *run levels* or `init states`. Each run level is a mutually exclusive mode of operation. Transitions between run levels are managed by the init process. After reading this chapter, you should feel confident in tailoring the startup and shutdown of your own system.

Key Concepts

The following concepts are required knowledge for starting up and shutting down a system.

OpenBoot

The OpenBoot PROM monitor is based on the Forth programming language and can be used to run Forth programs that perform the following functions:

- Boot the system, by using the `boot` command
- Perform diagnostics on hardware devices by using the `diag` command
- Test network connectivity by using the `watch-net` command

The OpenBoot PROM monitor has two prompts from which you can issue commands: the ok prompt and the > prompt. In order to switch from the > prompt to the ok prompt, you simply need to type **n**:

```
> n
ok
```

Commands are typically issued from the ok prompt. These commands include boot, which boots a system either from the default system boot device or from an optional device specified at the prompt. Thus, if a system is at run-level 0 and needs to be booted, the boot command with no options specified will boot the system:

```
ok boot
Sun Ultra 5/10 UPA/PCI (UltraSPARC Iii 360 MHz), Keyboard Present
OpenBoot Rev. 3.25, 512 MB memory installed, Serial #13018400.
Ethernet address 5:2:12:c:ee:5a Host ID: 456543
Rebooting with command:
Boot device: /iommu@f,e0000000/sbus@f,e0001000/espdma@f,400000/esp@f,8...
SunOS Release 5.10 Version s10_48 64-bit
Copyright (c) 1983-2003 by Sun Microsystems, Inc. All rights reserved
configuring IPv4 interfaces: hme0.
Hostname: winston
The system is coming up. Please wait.
checking ufs filesystems
/dev/rdsk/c0t0d0s1: is clean.
NIS domainname is Cassowary.Net.
starting rpc services: rpcbind keyserv ypbind done.
Setting netmask of hme0 to 255.255.255.0
Setting default IPv4 interface for multicast: add net 224.0/
4: gateway winston
syslog service starting.
Print services started.
volume management starting.
The system is ready.
winston console login:
```

If you have modified your hardware configuration since the last boot and want the new devices to be recognized, you should always reboot using this command:

```
ok boot -r
```

This is equivalent to performing a reconfiguration boot using either of the following command sequences in a shell as the superuser:

```
# touch /reconfigure; sync; init 6
```

or

```
# reboot -- -r
```

So far, we've looked at automatic booting. However, sometimes, performing a manual boot is desirable, using the command `boot -a`, where you can specify parameters at each stage of the booting process. These parameters include the following:

- The path to the kernel that you wish to boot
- The path to the kernel's modules directory
- The path to the system file
- The type of the root file system
- The name of the root device

For example, if you wished to use a different kernel, such as an experimental kernel, you would enter the following parameters during a manual boot:

```
Rebooting with command: boot -a
Boot device: /pci@1f,0/pci@1,2/ide@1/disk@0,1:a File and args: -a
Enter filename [kernel/sparcv9/unix]: kernel/experimental/unix
Enter default directory for modules [/platform/SUNW,Sparc-20/kernel
/platform/sun4m/kernel /kernel /usr/kernel]:
Name of system file [etc/system]:
SunOS Release 5.10 Version Generic 64-bit
Copyright (c) 1983-2003 by Sun Microsystems, Inc.
root filesystem type [ufs]:
Enter physical name of root device
[/pci@1f,0/pci@1,2/ide@1/disk@0,1:a]:
```

To accept the default parameters, simply press ENTER when prompted. Thus, to change only the path to the experimental kernel, you would enter **kernel/experimental/unix** at the Enter Filename prompt.

/sbin/init

Upon booting from OpenBoot, Solaris has several different modes of operation, which are known as *run levels* or *init states,* so called because the init command is often used to change run levels, although init-wrapper scripts (such as shutdown) are also used. These init states, which can be single- or multiuser, often serve different administrative purposes and are mutually exclusive (i.e., a system can only ever be in one init state).

Typically, a Solaris system that is designed to "stay up" indefinitely cycles through a predefined series of steps in order to start all the software daemons necessary for the provision of basic system services, primary user services, and optional application services. These services are often provided only during the time that a Solaris system operates in a multiuser run state, with services being initialized by run control (rc) shell scripts. Usually, one run control script is created to start each system, user, or application service. Fortunately, many of these scripts are created automatically for administrators during the Solaris installation process. However, if you intend to install third-party software (such as a database server), you may need to create your own run control scripts in the */etc/init.d* directory to start up these services automatically at boot time. This process is fully described in the "Writing Control Scripts" section, later in the chapter.

If the system needs to be powered off for any reason (e.g., a scheduled power outage) or switched into a special maintenance mode to perform diagnostic tests, there is also a cycle of iterating through a predefined series of run control scripts to kill services and preserve user data. It is essential that you preserve this sequence of events so that data integrity is maintained. For example, operating a database server typically involves communication between a server-side, data-writing process and a daemon listener process, which accepts new requests for storing information. If the daemon process is not stopped prior to the data-writing process, it could accept data from network clients and store it in a cache, while the database has already been closed. This could lead to the database being shut down in an inconsistent state, potentially resulting in data corruption and/or record loss. It is essential that you apply your knowledge of shell scripting to rigorously manage system shutdowns and startups using run control scripts.

In terms of system startup, Solaris has some similarities to Microsoft Windows and Linux. Although Solaris doesn't have an *autoexec.bat* or *config.sys* file, it does have a number of script files that are executed in a specific order to start services, just like Linux. These scripts are typically created in the */etc/init.d* directory as Bourne shell scripts and are then symbolically linked into the "run level" directories. Just as Microsoft Windows has Safe Modes, Solaris supports a number of different modes of operation, from restricted, single-user modes to full, multiuser run levels. The complete set of run levels, with their respective run control script directories, is displayed in Table 4-1.

Run Level	Description	User Status	Run Control Script Directory
0	Hardware maintenance mode	Console access	*/etc/rc0.d*
1	Administrative state; only root file system is available	Single user	*/etc/rc1.d*
2	First multiuser state; NFS resources unavailable	Multiuser	*/etc/rc2.d*
3	NFS resources available	Multiuser	*/etc/rc3.d*
4	User-defined state	Not specified	N/A
5	Power down firmware state	Console access	*/etc/rc5.d*
6	Operating system halted for reboot	Single user	*/etc/rc6.d*
S	Administrative tasks and repair of corrupted file systems	Console access	*/etc/rcS.d*

TABLE 4-1   Solaris Run Levels and Their Functions

Run Level	Run Control Script
0	/etc/rc0
1	/etc/rc1
2	/etc/rc2
3	/etc/rc3
4	N/A
5	/etc/rc5
6	/etc/rc6
S	/etc/rcS

TABLE 4-2   Solaris Run-Level Scripts

Each run level is associated with a run-level script, as shown in Table 4-2. The run-level script is responsible for the orderly execution of all run-level scripts within a specific run-level directory. The script name matches the run level and directory name.

When a Solaris system starts, the `init` process is spawned, which is responsible for managing processes and the transitions between run levels. You can actually switch manually between run levels by using the `init` command; to halt the operating system and reboot (run-level 6), you can simply type the following command:

```
# init 6
```

Note that a `reboot` command exists as an alias to `init 6`.

Firmware

In many respects, Solaris startup and shutdown is similar to many other systems. However, recognizing and appreciating the distinguishing features of the Solaris operating system from other operating systems is important. One of the outstanding facilities for SPARC hardware is the firmware monitoring system (OpenBoot PROM), which is responsible for key prebooting tasks:

- Starting the Solaris operating system by typing **ok boot** at the OpenBoot prompt, which boots the Solaris kernel
- Setting system configuration parameters, such as the boot device, which could be one of the hard disks (specified by a full device pathname), another host on the network, or a CD-ROM
- Watching network traffic by issuing the command **ok watch-net** at the OpenBoot prompt
- Performing simple diagnostic tests on system devices (e.g., testing the termination status of a SCSI bus, or the Power-On Self-Test [POST] tests)

Rather than just being a simple operating system loader, OpenBoot also permits programs written in the stack-based Forth programming language to be written, loaded, and run before booting commences. You can also set variables post-boot during single- and multiuser `init` states by using the `eeprom` command as superuser. For example, you can use `eeprom` to change the amount of RAM self-tested at boot to 64MB:

```
# eeprom selftest-#megs=64
```

On Solaris *x*86 systems, the firmware does not directly support this kind of `eeprom` functionality; every PC manufacturer has a different "BIOS" system, making it difficult. Instead, storage is simulated by variables set in the */boot/solaris/bootenv.rc* file.

A second distinguishing feature of the Solaris operating system is the aim of maximized uptime, through efficient kernel design and the user application model. In some non-Solaris server environments, the system must be rebooted every time a new application is installed, or a kernel rebuild might be required to change a configuration. Fortunately, rebooting is rarely required for Solaris systems, because applications are logically isolated from system configuration options, and you can set many system-level configuration options in a superuser shell. For example, you can set many TCP/IP stack options dynamically using the following command:

```
# ndd /dev/tcp
```

With most hardware configurations, you don't even need to reboot to install new hardware—for example, if a drive fails that is part of a RAID array, it can usually be hot-swapped without interrupting the operation of any applications or rebooting. If the original drive is mirrored, then the replacement drive will be resynchronized. These are the kinds of benefits that will be a welcome relief to new Solaris administrators.

Control Scripts and Directories

Every Solaris `init` state (such as `init` state 6) has its own run-level script directory (e.g., */etc/rc6.d*). This contains a set of symbolic links (like shortcuts in Microsoft Windows) that are associated with the service startup files in the */etc/init.d* directory. Each linked script starts with the letter *S* ("start") or the letter *K* ("kill"), and is used to either start or kill processes. When a system is booted, processes are started. When a system is shut down, processes are killed. The start and kill links are typically made to the same script file, which interprets two parameters: *start* and *stop*. The scripts are executed in numerical order, so a script like */etc/rc3.d/S20dhcp* is executed before */etc/rc3.d/S21sshd*.

Boot Sequence

Booting the kernel is a straightforward process, once the operating system has been successfully installed. You can identify the Solaris kernel by the pathname */platform/* PLATFORM_NAME/*kernel/unix*, where *PLATFORM_NAME* is the name of the current architecture. For example, sun4u systems boot with the kernel */platform/sun4u/kernel/*. Kernels can also be booted from a CD-ROM drive or through a network connection (by using the `boot cdrom` or `boot net` command, respectively, from the OpenBoot PROM monitor).

When a SPARC system is powered on, the system executes a series of basic hardware tests before attempting to boot the kernel. These Power-On Self-Tests (POSTs) ensure that your system hardware is operating correctly. If the POST tests fail, you will not be able to boot the system.

Once the POST tests are complete, the system attempts to boot the default kernel using the path specified in the firmware; or if you wish to boot a different kernel, you can press STOP-A, enter **boot kernel/name**, and boot the kernel specified by *kernel/name*. For example, to boot a kernel called `newunix`, you would use the command `boot kernel/newunix`, especially if `kernel/newunix` is an experimental kernel.

Systems boot either from a UFS file system (whether on the local hard disk or on a local CD-ROM drive) or across the network. Two applications facilitate these different boot types: `ufsboot` is responsible for booting kernels from disk devices, and `inetboot` is responsible for booting kernels using a network device (such as another Solaris server). Although servers typically boot themselves using `ufsboot`, diskless clients must use `inetboot`.

The `ufsboot` application reads the bootblock on the active partition of the boot device, and `inetboot` performs a broadcast on the local subnet, searching for a trivial FTP (TFTP) server. Once located, the kernel is downloaded using NFS and booted.

Procedures

The following procedures can be used to interact with the OpenBoot PROM monitor.

Viewing Release Information

To view the OpenBoot release information for your firmware and the system configuration, use this command:

```
ok banner
Sun Ultra 5/10 UPA/PCI (UltraSPARC Iii 360 MHz), Keyboard Present
OpenBoot Rev. 3.25, 512 MB memory installed, Serial #13018400.
Ethernet address 5:2:12:c:ee:5a Host ID: 456543
```

Here, you can see that the system is an UltraSPARC 5, with a keyboard present, and that the OpenBoot release level is 3.25. 512MB of RAM is installed on the system, which has a host ID of 456543. Finally, the Ethernet address of the primary Ethernet device is 5:2:12:c:ee:5a.

Changing the Default Boot Device

To boot from the default boot device (usually the primary hard drive), you would type this:

```
ok boot
```

However, you can also boot using the CD-ROM by using this command:

```
ok boot cdrom
```

You may boot the system from a host on the network by using this command:

```
ok boot net
```

Or, if you have a boot floppy, you may use the following command:

```
ok boot floppy
```

Because many early Solaris distributions were made on magnetic tape, you can also boot using a tape drive with the following command:

```
ok boot tape
```

Instead of specifying a different boot device each time you want to reboot, you can set an environment variable within the OpenBoot PROM monitor, so that a specific device is booted by default. For example, to set the default boot device to be the primary hard disk, you would use the following command:

```
ok setenv boot-device disk
boot-device = disk
```

To verify that the boot device has been set correctly to disk, you can use the following command:

```
ok printenv boot-device
boot-device disk disk
```

To reset the system to use the new settings, you simply use the reset command:

```
ok reset
```

To set the default boot device to be the primary network device, you would use the following command:

```
ok setenv boot-device net
boot-device = net
```

The preceding configuration is commonly used for diskless clients, such as Sun Rays, which use the Reverse Address Resolution Protocol (RARP) and NFS to boot across the network. To verify that the boot device has been set correctly to the primary network device, you can use the following command:

```
ok printenv boot-device
boot-device net disk
```

To set the default boot device to be the primary CD-ROM device, you would use the following command:

```
ok setenv boot-device cdrom
boot-device = cdrom
```

This is often useful when installing or upgrading the operating system. To verify that the boot device has been set correctly to cdrom, you can use the following command:

```
ok printenv boot-device
boot-device cdrom disk
```

To set the default boot device to be the primary floppy drive, you would use the following command:

```
ok setenv boot-device floppy
boot-device = floppy
```

To verify that the boot device has been set correctly to floppy, you can use the following command:

```
ok printenv boot-device
boot-device floppy disk
```

To set the default boot device to be the primary tape drive, you would use the following command:

```
ok setenv boot-device tape
boot-device = tape
```

To verify that the boot device has been set correctly to tape, you can use the following command:

```
ok printenv boot-device
boot-device tape disk
```

Testing System Hardware

The `test` command is used to test specific hardware devices, such as the loopback network device. You could test this device by using this command:

```
ok test net
Internal Loopback test - (OK)
External Loopback test - (OK)
```

This indicates that the loopback device is operating correctly.

You can also use the `watch-clock` command to test the clock device:

```
ok watch-clock
Watching the 'seconds' register of the real time clock chip.
 It should be ticking once a second.
 Type any key to stop.
1
2
3
```

If the system is meant to boot across the network, but a boot attempt does not succeed, you can test network connectivity by using the `watch-net` program. This determines whether the system's primary network interface is able to read packets from the network it is connected to. The output from the `watch-net` program looks like this:

```
Internal Loopback test - succeeded
External Loopback test - succeeded
Looking for Ethernet packets.
'.' is a good packet. 'X' is a bad packet.
Type any key to stop
......X.........XXXX......…..XX...........
```

In this case, a number of packets are marked as bad, even though the system has been connected successfully to the network. This can occur because of network congestion.

In addition to the `watch-net` command, the OpenBoot PROM monitor can perform a number of other diagnostic tests. For example, you can detect all the SCSI devices attached to the system by using the `probe-scsi` command. The output of `probe-scsi` looks like this:

```
ok probe-scsi
Target 1
Unit 0 Disk SUN0104 Copyright (C) 1995 Sun Microsystems All rights reserved
Target 1
Unit 0 Disk SUN0207 Copyright (C) 1995 Sun Microsystems All rights reserved
```

Here, you can see that two SCSI disks have been detected. If any other disks or SCSI devices were attached to the chain, they have not been detected, indicating a misconfiguration or hardware error.

Because most modern SPARC systems also ship with a PCI bus, you can display the appropriate PCI devices by using the `probe-pci` and `probe-pci-slot` commands.

Creating and Removing Device Aliases

The OpenBoot PROM monitor is able to store certain environment variables in nonvolatile RAM (NVRAM) so that they can be used from boot to boot by using the `nvalias` command. For example, to set the network device to use RARP for booting, you would use the following command:

```
ok nvalias net /pci@1f,4000/network@1,1:rarp
```

This output indicates that booting using the network device, as shown in the following example, would use the */pci@1f,4000/network@1,1* device to boot the system across the network:

```
ok boot net
```

However, if you wanted to use the Dynamic Host Configuration Protocol (DHCP) to retrieve the host's IP address when booting, instead of using RARP, you would use the following command:

```
ok boot net:dhcp
```

To remove the alias from NVRAM, you simply use the `nvunalias` command:

```
ok nvunalias net
```

This would restore the default value of *net*.

Startup

You should be aware of three kinds of boots. In addition to a normal reboot, which is initiated by the command # `shutdown` from a superuser shell, you should be familiar with these two kinds of boots:

- **Reconfiguration boot**   Involves reconstructing device information in the */dev* and */devices* directories. A reconfiguration boot is commonly undertaken in older SPARC systems when new hard disks are added to the system, although this may not be necessary with newer systems, which have hot-swapping facilities. You can initiate this kind of boot by typing **# boot –r** at the OpenBoot PROM monitor prompt, or by issuing the command # touch /reconfigure prior to issuing a shutdown command from a superuser shell.

- **Recovery boot** Involves saving and analyzing crash dump files if a system does not respond to commands issued on the console. A recovery boot is a rare event on a Solaris system—although hardware failures, kernel module crashes, and incorrect kernel parameters can sometimes result in a hung system. A stack trace is usually provided if a system crash occurs, which can provide vital clues to tracking the source of any system problems using the kernel debugger (kadb).

Although Solaris has eight init states, only five are commonly encountered by administrators during normal operations. Run-level S is a single-user init state that is used for administrative tasks and the repair of corrupted file systems, using the following command:

/usr/sbin/fsck

In run-level 2, the init state changes to multiuser mode for the first time, with the exception of NFS-exported network resources. In run-level 3, all users can log in and all system and NFS network resources are available. Run-level 6 halts the operating system and initiates a reboot. Finally, in run-level 0, the operating system is shut down, ensuring that it is safe to power down. In older SPARC systems, you need to bring the system down to run-level 0 to install new hardware, such as disk drives, peripheral devices, and memory modules. However, newer systems are able to continue to operate in multiuser init states while disks are hot swapped into special drive bays. This means that these machines may not have a need to enter run-level 6. Further, uptimes of many months are not uncommon.

The Solaris software environment provides a detailed series of run control (rc) scripts to control run-level changes. In this section, we examine each of the control scripts in turn. Each run level has an associated rc script located in the */sbin* directory, which is also symbolically linked into the */etc* directory: *rc0*, *rc1*, *rc2*, *rc3*, *rc5*, *rc6*, and *rcS*.

/sbin/rc0 is responsible for the following:

- Executing all scripts in */etc/rc0.d*, if the directory exists
- Terminating all system services and active processes, initially using */usr/sbin/killall* and then */usr/sbin/killall 9* for any stubborn processes
- Syncing all mounted file systems, using */sbin/sync*
- Unmounting all mounted file systems, using */sbin/umountall*

/sbin/rc5 and */sbin/rc6* are just symbolic links to */sbin/rc0* and do not need to be maintained separately.

/sbin/rc1 is responsible for executing all scripts in the */etc/rc1.d* directory, if it exists. This terminates all system services and active processes, initially using */usr/sbin/killall*,

and */usr/sbin/killall 9* for any stubborn processes. The differences between */etc/rc0* and */etc/rc1* are that the latter brings up the system into single-user mode after shutting down all processes in multiuser mode, and does not unmount any file systems.

In run-level 2 state, */sbin/rc2* executes all scripts in the */etc/rc2.d* directory, bringing the system into its first multiuser state. Thus, all local file systems listed in */etc/vfstab* are mounted, disk quotas and file system logging are switched on if configured, temporary editor files are saved, the */tmp* directory is cleared, system accounting is enabled, and many network services are initialized.

In run-level 3 state, */sbin/rc3* executes all scripts in the */etc/rc3.d* directory, bringing the system into its final multiuser state. These services are mainly concerned with shared network resources, such as NFS, but Solstice Enterprise Agents, and other SNMP-based systems, may also be started here.

/sbin/rcS executes all scripts in the */sbin/rcS.d* directory, to bring the system up to the single-user run level. A minimal network configuration is established if a network can be found, otherwise an interface error is reported. Essential system file systems (such as */*, */usr*, and */proc*) are mounted if they are available, and the system name is set.

To the superuser on the console, the transition between run levels is virtually invisible: most daemons, whether starting in a single- or multiuser `init` state, display a status message when starting up, which is echoed to the console.

Obviously, when booting into single-user mode, fewer messages appear on the console, because multiuser `init` state processes are not started. The single-user run-level messages appear as something like this:

```
ok boot -s
SunOS Release 5.10 Version [UNIX(R) System V Release 4.0]
Copyright (c) 1983-2003, Sun Microsystems, Inc.
configuring network interfaces: hme0.
Hostname: sakura
INIT: SINGLE USER MODE
Type Ctrl-d to proceed with normal startup,
(or give root password for system maintenance):
```

At this point, you enter the password for the superuser account (it will not be echoed to the display). Assuming that you enter the correct password, the display then proceeds with another banner and a Bourne shell prompt:

```
Sun Microsystems Inc. SunOS 5.10 November 2003
#
```

After maintenance is complete, simply exit the shell by using CTRL-D, after which the system proceeds with a normal multiuser boot.

The */sbin/init* daemon is responsible for process control initialization and is a key component of the booting process. Although */sbin/init* is not significant in many day-to-day operations after booting, its configuration for special purposes can be confusing for first-time users. In this section, we examine the initialization of init using the */etc/inittab* file, and explain in detail what each entry means. The primary function of init is to spawn processes, usually daemon processes, from configuration information specified in the file */etc/inittab* in ASCII format. Process spawning always takes place in a specific software context, which is determined by the current run level.

After booting the kernel from the OpenBoot PROM monitor, init reads the system environment variables stored in */etc/default/init* (e.g., the time zone variable *TZ*) and sets them for the current run level. init then reads the */etc/inittab* file, setting the init level specified in that file by the *initdefault* entry. In most multiuser systems, this entry corresponds to run-level 3 and the entry looks like this:

```
is:3:initdefault:
```

If the file */etc/inittab* does not exist during booting, the superuser will be asked to manually enter the desired run level for the system. If this event ever occurs unexpectedly for a multiuser system, it is a good strategy to enter single-user mode (by typing **s**) to perform maintenance on the */etc/inittab* file. Another potential problem is if */etc/inittab* does contain an empty *rstate* value in the *initdefault* entry: the system will go to firmware and continuously reboot! If this occurs, exit from the operating system into the OpenBoot PROM monitor by holding down the STOP key and pressing A. You can now boot directly into single-user mode and add an appropriate *rstate* entry to the */etc/inittab* file. Safeguards are built into init; however, if the system discovers that any entry in */etc/inittab* is respawning rapidly (i.e., more than five times per minute), init assumes that a typographical error has been made in the entry, and a warning message is printed on the system console. init will then not respawn the affected entry until at least five minutes has elapsed since the problem was identified.

After entering a multiuser run level for the first time since booting from the OpenBoot PROM monitor, init reads any appropriate *boot* and *bootwait* entries in */etc/inittab*. This provides for basic initialization of the operating system, such as mounting file systems, which is generally performed before users may be allowed to operate on the system.

In order to spawn processes specified in */etc/inittab*, init reads each entry and determines the process requirements for the commands to be executed. For example, for entries that must be respawned in the future, a child process is created using fork(). After reading all entries and spawning all processes, init simply waits until it receives a signal to change the system's init state (this explains why init is always visible in the process list). */etc/inittab* is always reread at this point to ensure that any modifications to its specified behavior are used. In addition, init can be initialized at any time by passing a special parameter to force rereading of */etc/inittab*:

```
# init q
```

When init receives a valid request to change run levels, it sends a warning signal to all affected processes and then waits five seconds, after which it sends to any processes that do not behave well a kill signal to forcibly terminate them. Affected processes are those that will be invalid under the target init state (e.g., when going from multiuser to single-user mode, daemons started in multiuser mode will be invalid). Because five seconds may not be sufficient to shut down an entire database server and close all open files, it is best to ensure that such activities precede any change of state that affects the main applications running on your system (e.g., by executing the appropriate command in /etc/init.d with the *stop* parameter).

/sbin/init can be executed only by a superuser, because changes in the system's init state executed by a normal user could have serious consequences (e.g., using init to power down a live server). Thus, it is always wise to ensure that file permissions are correctly set on the /sbin/init binary. The "Command Reference" section later in the chapter contains further details about the format of the /etc/inittab file.

Shutdown

A Solaris system is designed to stay up continuously, with as few disruptions to service through rebooting as possible. This design is facilitated by a number of key high-availability and redundancy features in Solaris, including the following:

- **Dual power supplies**   A secondary supply can continue to power the system if the primary power supply fails.

- **Mirroring of disk data**   The system can generally continue to operate even in the face of multiple disk failure.

- **Hot-swappable disks**   You can remove a faulty disk and replace it while the system is still online. You can format and use the new disk immediately, especially when you use DiskSuite.

- **The use of domains on StarFire and E10000 systems**   You can perform maintenance on one "virtual" host while a second domain acts in its place.

However, there are two situations in which a Solaris system must be halted by the superuser:

- Performing a reconfiguration boot
- Powering down the system

Note that you can use the drvconfig command to recognize most new hardware devices, further reducing the need for rebooting. A number of different commands are available to shut down and halt a system, and which one to use depends on the specific situation at hand. For example, some commands cycle through a series of shutdown scripts that ensure that key applications and services, such as databases, are cleanly shut down. Others commands are designed to ensure that a system is powered down as rapidly as possible. For example, if a storm strikes out the main power system and you're left with only a few minutes of battery backup, it might be wise to perform a rapid powerdown, to protect equipment from further damage. The next several sections investigate the following commands: init, shutdown, reboot, poweroff, and halt. These commands can only be run as the root user.

Shutting Down the System

The shutdown command is used to change a system's state, performing a similar function to init, as described earlier. However, shutdown has several advantages over init:

- You can specify a grace period, so that the system can be shut down at some future time rather than immediately.
- A confirmation message requires the superuser to confirm the shutdown before it proceeds. If an automated shutdown is to be executed at some future time, you can avoid the confirmation message by using the –y option.
- Only init states 0, 1, 5, 6, and S can be reached using shutdown.

For example, to shut down the system to run-level 5, so that you can move the system, you would use the following command, giving 60 seconds' notice:

```
# shutdown -i 5 -g 60 "System will be powered off for
maintenance. LOGOUT NOW."
```

This prints the following messages at 60 and 30 seconds, respectively:

```
Shutdown started.    Tue Feb    12  12:00:00 EST   2004
Broadcast Message from root (pts/1) on cassowary Tue Feb    12
    12:00:00 EST   2004...
            The system will be shut down in 1 minute
System will be powered off for maintenance. LOGOUT NOW.
Shutdown started.    Tue Feb    12  12:00:30 EST   2004
Broadcast Message from root (pts/1) on cassowary Tue Feb    12
    12:00:30 EST   2004...
            The system will be shut down in 30 seconds
System will be powered off for maintenance. LOGOUT NOW.
```

Once the countdown has been completed, the following message appears:

```
Do you want to continue? (y or n):
```

If you type **Y**, the shutdown proceeds. If you type **N**, the shutdown is cancelled and the system remains at the current run level.

Rebooting

The reboot command is used to reboot the system, from the current run level to the default run level, and not to change to any other run level. The reboot command has several options. You can use the *–l* flag to prevent the recording of the system halt in the system log, which it normally attempts before halting the CPU. The *–n* option prevents the refreshing of the superblock, which is performed by default, to prevent damage to mounted file systems. The most extreme option is *–q*, which does not attempt any kind of fancy actions before shutting down the system and rebooting.

In addition, `reboot` accepts the standard parameters passed to the `boot` command, if they are preceded by two dashes and are placed after the `reboot` parameters (described in the preceding paragraph) on the command line.

For example, to perform a configuration reboot, without recording an entry in the system log, you could use the following command:

```
# reboot -l -- -r
```

Reconfiguration Boot

Performing a reconfiguration boot involves updating the hardware configuration for the system. If you add new hardware to the system, other than a disk, you must bring the system down to the hardware maintenance state (level 0) before you can insert the new device. In addition, you must notify the system of a reconfiguration reboot either by booting from the OpenBoot PROM monitor with the command `boot -r` or by creating an empty file called */reconfigure* before changing to run-level 0. You can achieve this by using the command `touch /reconfigure`. Be sure to remove the `/reconfigure` file after the system has been reconfigured (if necessary).

Powering Down

The `poweroff` command is used to rapidly shut down the system and switch off power (like switching to run-level 5), without cycling through any intermediate run levels and executing the kill scripts specified for those run levels. This ensures that you can achieve a very fast shutdown when emergency situations dictate that the system cannot remain live, even with the risk of data loss. For example, if a system is under a denial of service attack, and the decision is made to pull the plug on the service, the `poweroff` command shuts it down much faster than `init` or `shutdown`. The CPU is halted as quickly as possible, no matter what the run level.

The `poweroff` command has several options. You can use the *–l* flag to prevent the recording of the system halt in the system log, which it normally attempts before halting the CPU. The *–n* option prevents the refreshing of the superblock, which is performed by default, to prevent damage to mounted file systems. The most extreme option is *–q*, which does not attempt any kind of fancy actions before shutting down.

Halting the System

You can use the `halt` command to rapidly shut down the system, to the OpenBoot PROM monitor, without cycling through any intermediate run levels and executing the kill scripts specified for those run levels. Like the `poweroff` command, this ensures a rapid shutdown. Also, the `halt` command has the same options as `poweroff`.

Examples

The following examples demonstrate how to use the OpenBoot PROM monitor effectively, and provide some real-world cases for starting up and shutting down a Solaris system.

Single-User Mode

If a system fails to start correctly in multiuser mode, it's likely that one of the scripts being run in */etc/rc2.d* is the cause. To prevent the system from going multiuser, you can boot directly into single-user mode from the ok prompt:

```
INIT: SINGLE USER MODE
Type Ctrl-d to proceed with normal startup,
(or give root password for system maintenance):
```

At this point, you can enter the root password, and the user will be given a root shell. However, not all file systems will be mounted, although you can then check individual scripts for misbehaving applications.

Recovering the System

If the system will not boot into single-user mode, the solution is more complicated, because you cannot use the default boot device. For example, if an invalid entry has been made in the */etc/passwd* file for the root user, the system will not boot into single- or multiuser mode. To recover the installed system, you need to boot the host from the installation CD-ROM into single-user mode. At this point, you can mount the default root file system on a separate mount point, edit the */etc/passwd* file, and reboot the system with the default boot device. This sequence of steps is shown here, assuming that */etc* is located on */dev/dsk/c0t0d0s1*:

```
ok boot cdrom
...
INIT: SINGLE USER MODE
Type Ctrl-d to proceed with normal startup,
(or give root password for system maintenance):
# mkdir /temp
# mount /dev/dsk/c0t0d0s1 /temp
# vi /temp/etc/passwd
# sync; init 6
```

If a system is hung and you cannot enter commands into a shell on the console, you can use the key combination STOP-A to halt the system and access the OpenBoot PROM monitor. If you halt and reboot the system in this way, all data that has not been written to disk will be lost, unless you use the go command to resume the system's normal operation. Another method of accessing a system if the console is locked is to telnet to the system as an unprivileged user, use the su command to obtain superuser status, and kill whatever process is hanging the system. You can then resume normal operation.

Writing Control Scripts

For a multiuser system, the most important control scripts reside in the */etc/rc2.d* and */etc/rc3.d* directories, which are responsible for enabling multiuser services and NFS network resource sharing, respectively. A basic script for starting up a Web server looks like this:

```
#!/bin/sh
# Sample webserver startup script
# Should be placed in /etc/rc2.d/S99webserver
case "$1" in
    'start')
            echo "Starting webserver...\c"
            if [ -f /usr/local/sbin/webserver ]; then
                    /usr/local/sbin/webserver start
            fi
            echo ""
            ;;
    'stop')
            echo "Stopping webserver...\c"
            if [ -f /usr/local/sbin/webserver ]; then
                    /usr/local/sbin/webserver stop
            fi
            echo ""
    ;;
    *)
            echo "Usage: /etc/rc2.d/S99webserver { start | stop }"
            ;;
    esac
```

This file should be created by root (with the group sys) and placed in the file */etc/rc2.d/S99webserver*, and should have executable permissions:

```
# chmod 0744 /etc/rc2.d/S99webserver
# chgrp sys /etc/rc2.d/S99webserver
```

This location of the file is a matter of preference. Many admins treat the Web server similar to an NFS server. In this regard the system run-level 3 represents a "share" state.

Note that because a Web server is a shared service, you could also start it from a script in */etc/rc3.d*. When called with the argument start (represented in the script by *$1*), the script prints a status message that the Web server daemon is starting, and proceeds to execute the command if the Web server binary exists. The script can also act as a kill script, because it has a provision to be called with a stop argument. Of course, a more complete script would provide more elaborate status information if the Web server binary did not exist, and may further process any output from the Web server by using a pipe (e.g., mailing error messages to the superuser).

One of the advantages of the flexible boot system is that you can execute these scripts to start and stop specific daemons without changing the `init` state. For example, if you were going to update a web site and needed to switch off the Web server for a few minutes, the command

```
# /etc/rc2.d/S99webserver stop
```

would halt the Web server process, but would not force the system back into a single-user state. You could restart the Web server after all content was uploaded by typing the following command:

```
# /etc/rc2.d/S99webserver start
```

In order to conform to System V standards, it is actually more appropriate to create all the run control scripts in the */etc/init.d* directory and create symbolic links back to the appropriate *rc2.d* and *rc3.d* directories. This means that all scripts executed by `init` through different run levels are centrally located and can be easily maintained. With the Web server example, you could create a file in */etc/init.d* with a descriptive filename:

```
# vi /etc/init.d/webserver
```

After adding the appropriate contents, you could save the file and create the appropriate symbolic link by using the symbolic link command `ln`:

```
# ln -s /etc/init.d/webserver /etc/rc2.d/S99webserver
```

Using this convention, kill and startup scripts for each service can literally coexist in the same script, with the capability to process a `start` argument for startup scripts, and a `stop` argument for kill scripts. In this example, you would also need to create a symbolic link to */etc/init.d/webserver* for *K99webserver*.

Writing Kill Scripts

Under System V, kill scripts follow the same convention as startup scripts, in that a `stop` argument is passed to the script to indicate that a kill rather than a startup is required, in which a `start` argument would be passed. A common approach to killing off processes is to find them by name in the process list. The following script kills the asynchronous PPP daemon, which is the link manager for the asynchronous data link protocol. This daemon is started by using `aspppd`—thus, the script generates a process list, which is piped through a `grep` to identify any entries containing `aspppd`, and the process number is extracted using `awk`. This value is assigned to a variable (*$procid*), which is then used by the `kill` command to terminate the appropriate process. Alternatively, you could use `pgrep` or `pkill`.

```
procid=`ps -e | grep aspppd | awk '{print $1}'`
if test -n "$procid"
then
      kill $procid
fi
```

Alternatively, you could use `sed` to match the process name:

```
procid=`/usr/bin/ps -e |
   /usr/bin/grep aspppd |
   /usr/bin/sed -e 's/^   *//' -e 's/ .*//'`
```

When multiple processes are to be terminated using a single script (for example, when the NFS server terminates), you can write a shell function, `killprocid()`, which takes an argument and searches for it in the process list, terminating the named process if its exists:

```
killprocid() {
procid=`/usr/bin/ps -e |
          /usr/bin/grep -w $1 |
          /usr/bin/sed -e 's/^   *//' -e 's/ .*//'`
      [ "$procid" != "" ] && kill $procid
}
```

You can then terminate individual processes by using the same function:

```
killproc nfsd
killproc mountd
killproc rpc.boot
killproc in.rarpd
killproc rpld
```

There are two problems with these approaches to process termination. First, there is an ambiguity problem in that different daemons and applications can be identified by the same name. For example, a system may be running the Apache Web server, which is identified by the process name `httpd`, as well as a Web server from another vendor (such as iPlanet) that is also identified by `httpd`. If you write a script to kill the Apache Web server, but the first process identified actually belongs to the iPlanet Web server, the iPlanet Web server process would be terminated. One solution to this problem is to ensure that all applications are launched with a unique name, or from a wrapper script with a unique name. The second problem is that for a system with even a moderately heavy process load (e.g., 500 active processes), executing the `ps` command to kill each process is going to generate a large CPU overhead, leading to excessively slow shutdown times. An alternative solution to this problem would be to use a kill script.

Control Script Examples

If you're curious about what kind of scripts are started or killed in Solaris during startup and shutdown, Table 4-3 lists some sample startup scripts in */etc/rc2.d*, and Table 4-4 lists some example kill scripts found in */etc/rc0.d*. You need to realize that these scripts change from system to system. In addition, if you modify these standard scripts, it's important to realize that subsequent patch installs could wipe out the changes—so, it's worthwhile to verify each script after a patch has been installed.

If you want to stop a script from being loaded at startup, you can simply preface the filename with NO. If you simply add a .bak extension or similar, then the script will still load because the script name still starts with S*nn*, where *nn* is an integer representing the order in which each script should be loaded. The lower-numbered scripts are executed before the higher-numbered scripts.

Script	Description
S05RMTMPFILES	Removes temporary files in the */tmp* directory.
S20sysetup	Establishes system setup requirements and checks */var/crash* to determine whether the system is recovering from a crash.
S21perf	Enables system accounting using */usr/lib/sa/sadc* and */var/adm/sa/sa*.
S30sysid.net	Executes */usr/sbin/sysidnet*, */usr/sbin/sysidconfig*, and */sbin/ifconfig*, which are responsible for configuring network services.
S69inet	Initiates the second phase of TCP/IP configuration, following on from the basic services established during single-user mode (*rcS*). Setting up IP routing (if */etc/defaultrouter* exists), performing TCP/IP parameter tuning (using *ndd*), and setting the NIS domain name (if required) are all performed here.
S70uucp	Initializes the UNIX-to-UNIX Copy (UUCP) program by removing locks and other unnecessary files.
S71sysid.sys	Executes */usr/sbin/sysidsys* and */usr/sbin/sysidroot*.
S72autoinstall	Executes JumpStart installation if appropriate.
S72inetsvc	Performs final network configuration using */usr/sbin/ifconfig* after NIS/NIS+ have been initialized. Also initializes the Internet Domain Name System (DNS) if appropriate.
S80PRESERVE	Preserves editing files by executing */usr/lib/expreserve*.
S92volmgt	Starts volume management for removable media using */usr/sbin/vold*.

TABLE 4-3   Typical Multiuser Startup Scripts Under Solaris 10

Script	Description
K00ANNOUNCE	Announces that "System services are now being stopped."
K10dtlogin	Initializes tasks for the CDE (common desktop environment), including killing the `dtlogin` process.
K20lp	Stops printing services using */usr/lib/lpshut*.
K22acct	Terminates process accounting using */usr/lib/acct/shutacct*.
K42audit	Kills the auditing daemon (*/usr/sbin/audit*).
K47asppp	Stops the asynchronous PPP daemon (*/usr/sbin/aspppd*).
K50utmpd	Kills the `utmp` daemon (*/usr/lib/utmpd*).
K55syslog	Terminates the system logging service (*/usr/sbin/syslogd*).
K57sendmail	Halts the `sendmail` mail service (*/usr/lib/sendmail*).
K66nfs.server	Kills all processes required for the NFS server (*/usr/lib/nfs/nfsd*).
K69autofs	Stops the automounter (*/usr/sbin/automount*).
K70cron	Terminates the `cron` daemon (*/usr/bin/cron*).
K75nfs.client	Disables client NFS.
K76nscd	Kills the name service cache daemon (*/usr/sbin/nscd*).
K85rpc	Disables remote procedure call (*rpc*) services (*/usr/sbin/rpcbind*).

TABLE 4-4   Typical Single-User Kill Scripts Under Solaris 10

Shutting Down the System

In order to manually change run levels, the desired `init` state is used as an argument to */sbin/init*. For example, to bring the system down to a single-user mode for maintenance, you could use the following command:

```
#  init s
INIT: New run level: S
The system is coming down for administration. Please wait.
Print services stopped.
syslogd: going down on signal 15
Killing user processes: done.
INIT: SINGLE USER MODE
Type Ctrl-d to proceed with normal startup,
(or give root password for system maintenance):
Entering System Maintenance Mode ...
#
```

The system is most easily shut down by using the new */usr/sbin/shutdown* command (not the old BSD-style */usr/ucb/shutdown* command discussed later). This command is issued with the form

```
# shutdown -i run-level -g grace-period -y
```

where *run-level* is an `init` state that is different from the default `init` state S (i.e., one of the run levels 0, 1, 2, 5, or 6). However, most administrators typically are interested in using `shutdown` with respect to the reboot or powerdown run levels. The *grace-period* is the number of seconds before the shutdown process is initiated. On single-user machines, the superuser can easily determine who is logged in and what processes need to be terminated gracefully. However, on a multiuser machine, it is more useful to warn users in advance of a powerdown or reboot. If the change of `init` state is to proceed without user intervention, including the *–y* flag at the end of the `shutdown` command is useful; otherwise, the message

```
Do you want to continue? (y or n):
```

is displayed and you must type **Y** for the shutdown to proceed. The default *grace-period* on Solaris is 60 seconds, so if the administrators wanted to reboot with two minutes' warning given to all users, without user intervention, the command would be as follows:

```
# shutdown -i 5 -g 120 -y
```

The system then periodically displays a message that warns all users of the imminent `init` state change:

```
Shutdown started. Tue Feb 12 10:22:00 EST 2004
Broadcast Message from root (console) on server Tue Feb 12 10:22:00...
The system server will be shut down in 2 minutes
```

The system then reboots without user intervention, and does not enter the OpenBoot PROM monitor. If you need to issue commands using the monitor (i.e., an `init` state of 0 is desired), you can use the following command:

```
# shutdown -i0 -g180 -y
Shutdown started. Tue Feb 12 11:15:00 EST 2004
Broadcast Message from root (console) on server Tue Feb 12 11:15:00...
The system will be shut down in 3 minutes
.
.
.
INIT: New run level: 0
The system is coming down. Please wait.
.
.
.
The system is down.
syncing file systems... [1] [2] [3] done
Program terminated
Type help for more information
ok
```

There are many ways to warn users in advance of a shutdown. One way is to edit the "message of the day" file (*/etc/motd*) to contain a warning that the server will be down and/or rebooted for a specific time. This message will be displayed every time a user successfully logs in with an interactive shell. The following message gives the date and time of the shutdown, expected duration, and a contact address for enquiries:

```
System server will be shutdown at 5 p.m. 2/12/2004.
Expected downtime: 1 hour.
E-mail root@system for further details.
```

At least 24 hours' notice is usually required for users on a large system, because long jobs need to be rescheduled. In practice, many administrators shut down or reboot only outside of business hours to minimize inconvenience; however, power failure and hardware problems can necessitate unexpected downtime.

This method works well in advance, but because many users are continuously logged in from remote terminals, they won't always read the new message of the day. Another approach is to use the "write all" command (`wall`), which sends a message to all terminals of all logged-in users. You can send this command manually at hourly intervals prior to shutdown, or you could establish a `cron` job to perform this task automatically. An example command would be this:

```
# wall
System server will be shutdown at 5 p.m. 2/12/2004.
Expected downtime: 1 hour.
E-mail root@system for further details.
^d
```

After sending the `wall` message, you can perform a final check of logged-in users prior to shutdown by using the `who` command:

```
# who
root        console     Feb 12 10:15
pwatters    pts/0       Feb 12 10:15        (client)
```

You can send a message to the user *pwatters* on *pts/0* directly to notify him of the imminent shutdown:

```
# write pwatters
Dear pwatters,
Please logout immediately as the system server is going down.
If you do not logout now, your unsaved work may be lost.
Yours Sincerely,
System Administrator (root@system)
CTRL+d
```

Depending on the status of the user, you may also want to request a talk session, by using the following command:

```
# talk pwatters
```

If all these strategies fail to convince the user *pwatters* to log out, you have no choice but to proceed with the shutdown.

Command Reference

The following commands can be used within the OpenBoot PROM monitor to manage the SPARC firmware and the commands that are commonly used to manage `init` states.

STOP Commands

The STOP commands are executed on the SPARC platform by holding down the special STOP key, located on the left side of the keyboard, and any one of several other keys, each of which specifies the operation to be performed. The following functions are available:

STOP	Enters the POST environment
STOP-A	Enters the OpenBoot PROM monitor environment
STOP-D	Performs diagnostic tests
STOP-F	Enters a program in the Forth language
STOP-N	Initializes the NVRAM settings to their factory defaults

Boot Commands

You can use the `boot` command with any one of the following options:

net	Boots from a network interface
cdrom	Boots from a local CD-ROM drive
disk	Boots from a local hard disk
tape	Boots from a local tape drive

In addition, you can specify the name of the kernel to boot by including its relative path after the device specifier. You can also pass the *–a* option on the command line to force the operator to enter the path to the kernel on the boot device.

Using eeprom

Solaris provides an easy way to modify the values of variables stored in the PROM, through the `eeprom` command. The `eeprom` command can be used by the root user when the system is running in either single- or multiuser mode. The following variables can be set, shown here with their default values:

```
# /usr/sbin/eeprom
tpe-link-test?=true
scsi-initiator-id=7
keyboard-click?=false
keymap: data not available.
ttyb-rts-dtr-off=false
ttyb-ignore-cd=true
ttya-rts-dtr-off=false
ttya-ignore-cd=true
ttyb-mode=9600,8,n,1,-
ttya-mode=9600,8,n,1,-
pcia-probe-list=1,2,3,4
pcib-probe-list=1,2,3
mfg-mode=off
diag-level=max
#power-cycles=50
system-board-serial#: data not available.
system-board-date: data not available.
fcode-debug?=false
output-device=screen
input-device=keyboard
load-base=16384
boot-command=boot
auto-boot?=true
watchdog-reboot?=false
diag-file: data not available.
diag-device=net
boot-file: data not available.
boot-device=disk net
local-mac-address?=false
ansi-terminal?=true
screen-#columns=80
screen-#rows=34
silent-mode?=false
use-nvramrc?=false
nvramrc: data not available.
security-mode=none
security-password: data not available.
security-#badlogins=0
oem-logo: data not available.
oem-logo?=false
oem-banner: data not available.
oem-banner?=false
hardware-revision: data not available.
last-hardware-update: data not available.
diag-switch?=false
```

You can also change the values of the boot device and boot command from within Solaris by using the eeprom command, rather than having to reboot, jump into the OpenBoot PROM monitor, and set the values directly.

/sbin/init

In addition to being the process spawner, `init` can be used to switch run levels at any time. The following are some examples of what you can do with `init`:

Task	Command
Perform hardware maintenance	# init 0
Enter the administrative state	# init 1
Enter the first multiuser state	# init 2
Enter the second multiuser state	# init 3
Enter a user-defined state	# init 4
Power down the system	# init 5
Halt the operating system	# init 6
Enter the administrative state, with all the file systems available	# init S

Before using `init` in this way, preceding its execution with a call to `sync` is often advisable. The `sync` command renews the disk superblock, which ensures that all outstanding data operations are flushed and that the file system is stable before shutting down.

/etc/inittab

After the kernel is loaded into memory, the */sbin/init* process is initialized and the system is bought up to the default `init` state, which is determined by the *initdefault* value contained in */etc/inittab*, which controls the behavior of the `init` process. Each entry has the form

```
identifier:runlevel:action:command
```

where *identifier* is a unique two-character identifier, *runlevel* specifies the run level to be entered, *action* specifies the process characteristics of the command to be executed, and *command* is the name of the program to be run. The program can be an application or a script file. The run level must be one of S, A, B, C, 1, 2, 3, 4, 5, or 6. If the process is to be executed by all run levels, no run level should be specified.

The following is a standard *inittab* file:

```
ap::sysinit:/sbin/autopush -f /etc/iu.ap
ap::sysinit:/sbin/soconfig -f /etc/sock2path
fs::sysinit:/sbin/rcS sysinit            >/dev/msglog 2<>/dev/msglog \
   </dev/console
is:3:initdefault:
p3:s1234:powerfail:/usr/sbin/shutdown -y -i5 -g0 >/dev/msglog 2<>/dev/msglog
sS:s:wait:/sbin/rcS                      >/dev/msglog 2<>/dev/msglog \
   </dev/console
```

```
s0:0:wait:/sbin/rc0                          >/dev/msglog 2<>/dev/msglog \
   </dev/console
s1:1:respawn:/sbin/rc1                       >/dev/msglog 2<>/dev/msglog \
   </dev/console
s2:23:wait:/sbin/rc2                         >/dev/msglog 2<>/dev/msglog \
   </dev/console
s3:3:wait:/sbin/rc3                          >/dev/msglog 2<>/dev/msglog \
   </dev/console
s5:5:wait:/sbin/rc5                          >/dev/msglog 2<>/dev/msglog \
   </dev/console
s6:6:wait:/sbin/rc6                          >/dev/msglog 2<>/dev/msglog \
   </dev/console
fw:0:wait:/sbin/uadmin 2 0                    >/dev/msglog 2<>/dev/msglog \
   </dev/console

of:5:wait:/sbin/uadmin 2 6                    >/dev/msglog 2<>/dev/msglog \
   </dev/console
rb:6:wait:/sbin/uadmin 2 1                    >/dev/msglog 2<>/dev/msglog \
   </dev/console
sc:234:respawn:/usr/lib/saf/sac -t 300
co:234:respawn:/usr/lib/saf/ttymon -g -h -p "`uname -n` console login: "\
   -T sun -d /dev/console -l console -m ldterm,ttcompat
```

This *etc/inittab* file contains only entries for the actions sysinit, respawn, initdefault, wait, and powerfail. These are the common actions found on most systems. However, Solaris provides a wide variety of actions that may be useful in special situations (e.g., when powerwait is more appropriate than powerfail). Potential actions are identified by any one of the following:

- **initdefault**   This is a mandatory entry found on all systems and is used to configure the default run level for the system. This is specified by the highest init state specified in the *rstate* field. If this field is empty, init interprets the *rstate* as the highest possible run level (run-level 6), which forces a continuous reboot of the system. In addition, if the entry is missing, you must supply one manually on the console for booting to proceed.

- **sysinit**   This entry is provided as a safeguard for asking which run level is required at boot time if the *initdefault* entry is missing. Only devices required to ask the question are affected.

- **boot**   This entry is parsed only at boot time and is mainly used for initialization following a full reboot of the system after powerdown.

- **off**   This entry ensures that a process is terminated upon entering a particular run level. A warning signal is sent, followed by a kill signal, again with a five-second interval.

- **once**   This entry is similar to boot but is more flexible, because the named process runs only once and is not respawned.

- **ondemand**   This entry is similar to the respawn action.

- **powerfail**   This entry runs the process associated with the entry when a power fail signal is received.

- **powerwait**   This entry is similar to `powerfail`, except that `init` waits until the process terminates before further processing entries in */etc/inittab*. This is especially useful for enforcing sequential shutdown of services that are prioritized.

- **bootwait**   This entry is parsed only on the first occasion that the transition from a single- to multiuser run levels occurs after a system boot.

- **wait**   This entry starts a process and waits for its completion upon entering the specified run level; however, the entry is ignored if */etc/inittab* is reread during the same run level.

- **respawn**   This entry ensures that if a process that should be running is not, it is respawned.

The */etc/inittab* file follows conventions for text layout used by the Bourne shell: A long entry can be continued on the following line by using a backslash (\), and comments can be inserted into the process field only by using a hash character (#). There is a limitation of 512 characters for each entry imposed on */etc/inittab*; however, there is no limit on the number of entries that may be inserted.

Summary

The OpenBoot PROM monitor is one of the outstanding features of the SPARC architecture. It allows a wide range of system parameters to be configured using a high-level programming language that is independent of the installed operating system. OpenBoot includes a variety of diagnostic and testing applications. In this chapter, you have also learned the basic elements of booting and initializing a Solaris system. These procedures are used across the entire range of SPARC hardware and, in most cases, across Solaris x86 systems. While the process of booting and initializing a Solaris system may seem complicated, it allows for a greater amount of flexibility when building systems for high availability.

System Essentials

Installing Software, Live Upgrade, and Patching

All Solaris software installed as part of the operating environment is included in an archive known as a *package*. Solaris packages provide an easy way to bring together application binaries, configuration files, and documentation for distribution to other systems. In addition to the Solaris packaging system, Solaris also supports standard UNIX archiving and compression tools, such as `tar` (tape archive) and `compress`. This chapter examines how you can manage packages using the standard Solaris packaging tools and the command-line interface (CLI). Operations that are reviewed in this chapter include installing packages, displaying information about packages, and removing packages primarily using the CLI tools.

One of the most important aspects of system maintenance involves identifying, downloading, and installing patches that have been released for a specific revision level. Patches are binary code modifications that generally fix bugs but may also introduce new, urgently required features into existing applications and system services. This chapter looks at the process of patch installation and backing out of patches that have already been applied.

Key Concepts

Packages are text files that contain archives of binary applications, configuration files, documentation, and even source code. All files in the Solaris operating environment are supplied as part of a package, making it easy for you to group files associated with different applications. If files are installed without packaging, it can become difficult over the years for administrators to remember which files were installed with particular applications. Packaging makes it easy to recognize application dependencies, because all files required by a specific application can be included within the archive.

Getting Information about Packages

Administrators can use the `pkgchk` command to examine the package properties of a file that has already been installed:

```
# pkgchk -l -p /usr/bin/mkdir
Pathname: /usr/bin/mkdir
Type: regular file
Expected mode: 0555
Expected owner: bin
Expected group: bin
Expected file size (bytes): 9876
Expected sum(1) of contents: 38188
Expected last modification: Oct 06 05:47:55 PM 1998
Referenced by the following packages:
        SUNWcsu
Current status: installed
```

Another advantage of using packages is that they make use of the standard installation interface provided to install Solaris packages. This means that all Solaris applications are installed using one of two standard installation applications (`pkgadd` or the `admintool`), rather than each application having its own installation program. This reduces coding time and makes it easier for administrators to install software, because they need to learn only a single interface with standard options, such as overwriting existing files. Using packages reduces the administrative overhead in software management on Solaris 10.

In this chapter, we examine how to install new packages, display information about downloaded packages, and remove packages that have been previously installed on the system, by using the command-line package tools.

Live Upgrade

All the installation methods reviewed so far require that an existing system be brought to run-level 0 to start the installation process. In addition, you can expect any system that is being upgraded to be in single-user mode for a matter of hours while distribution files are copied and third-party software is reinstalled. This kind of downtime may be unacceptable for a production server. While many departmental servers no doubt have a backup server that can take their place during upgrading and installation testing, many high-end servers, such as the Sun Fire 15K, are logically divided into domains that run on a single system. A second standby system may not be available to replace a high-end server, just for the purpose of an upgrade. Note that while it's possible to configure each domain individually, many sites would prefer to keep all servers at the same release level.

For such sites, Solaris 10 offers a Live Upgrade facility that allows a separate boot environment to be created, with the distribution of the new operating system files installed to an alternative location. Once the installation of the new boot environment has been completed, the system needs to be rebooted only once to allow it to run the new operating environment. If the new boot environment fails for some reason, the old boot environment can be reinstated as the default and the system can be rebooted to its previous state. This allows operations to resume as quickly as possible in the event of a failure.

One of the nice features of Live Upgrade is that the file system layout and configuration can be different from your existing installation. This allows you to fine-tune your existing settings before you upgrade. For example, if print and mail jobs have continually caused the */var* partition to overfill on a regular basis, you can increase the size of the */var* partition in the new boot environment. You can make changes to the */, /usr, /var,* and */opt* partitions. Other file systems continue to be shared between the existing and new boot environments, unless otherwise specified.

To create a new boot environment, you must identify and format a separate partition before the procedure can begin. This partition must have sufficient disk space to install the new boot environment. The current contents of */, /usr,* and */opt* are then copied to the new partition prior to upgrade. Alternatively, if you have a second disk installed on the system, you can copy the existing files to the appropriate slices on the new disk. Once these files are in place, the new boot environment is ready to be upgraded. All these processes can occur without interfering with the current boot environment.

Upgrading typically involves overwriting the files stored on the new boot environment in */, /usr,* and */opt*. After this has been completed, you can activate the new boot environment and boot the system into the new environment.

Live Upgrade operates through a terminal-based menu that allows the following operations to be performed:

Operation	Description
Activate	Activates a newly installed boot environment
Cancel	Cancels a file-transfer operation
Compare	Checks for differences between the new and current boot environments
Copy	Begins a file-transfer operation
Create	Initializes a new boot environment
Current	Prints the name of the current boot environment
Delete	Uninstalls a boot environment
List	Displays the file systems in a boot environment
Rename	Modifies the name of a new or existing boot environment
Status	Prints the condition of any boot environment
Upgrade	Begins the upgrade process on the new boot environment
Help	Prints the Help menu
Exit	Quits the program

Patches

Patches are binary code modifications that affect the way Sun-supplied software operates. Sun may release a patch to fix previously identified bugs or to remove a security exploit in a piece of software for which a simple workaround is inadequate to prevent intrusion or disruption of normal system activity. For example, until recently, many of the older Solaris daemons suffered from buffer-overflow vulnerabilities, which allowed a rogue client to deliberately overwrite the fixed boundaries on an array to crash the system. Many of the system daemons, such as Web servers, may be crashed by overwriting memory with arbitrary values outside the declared size of an array. Without appropriate bounds checking, passing a GET request of 1025 bytes to a Web server when the array size is 1024 would clearly result in unpredictable behavior, because the C language does not prevent a program from doing this. Since Solaris daemons are typically written in C, a number of them have been fixed in recent years to prevent this problem (but you may be surprised at just how often new weaknesses are exposed). Sendmail, IMAP, and POP daemons for Solaris have all experienced buffer-overflow vulnerabilities in the past that have required urgent installation of security patches.

For security-related patches (e.g., CVE 1999-0977), the CVE number matches descriptions of each security issue from the Common Vulnerabilities and Exposures database (**http://cve.mitre.org/**). Each identified vulnerability contains a hyperlink back to the CVE database, so that information displayed about every issue is updated directly from the source. New patches and bug fixes are also listed.

Keep in mind that although security-related patches are important, other significant upgrades and patches are also released. These patches might involve upgrading the kernel, or fixing identified bugs in system libraries or applications. It's important to apply patches as they are released by Sun, to ensure that your system avoids known problems. Sun also releases so-called "recommended" patch clusters, each of which is a large set of patches that should be applied to all systems. A script is provided to install patches automatically. The patch clusters are usually updated every month, so it pays to check the SunSolve site regularly (for Solaris 10, the recommended file is *10_recommended.zip*). Sun also releases a patch order file, which can be edited to selectively install patches.

Procedures

This section examines how to work with packages and patches in the Solaris environment, including how to view package information, install and uninstall a Solaris package using the CLI, create new packages, create and compress archives, and find patches.

Viewing Package Information with pkginfo

At any time, you can examine which packages have been installed on a system by using the pkginfo command:

```
bash-2.05# pkginfo
system          IPLTadcon               Administration Server Console
system          IPLTadman               Administration Server Documentation
system          IPLTadmin               Administration Server
system          IPLTcons                Console Client Base
system          IPLTdscon               Directory Server Console
```

```
system      IPLTdsman                Directory Server Documentation
system      IPLTdsr                  Directory Server (root)
system      IPLTdsu                  Directory Server (usr)
system      IPLTjss                  Network Security Services for Java
system      IPLTnls                  Nationalization Languages and Localization Support
system      IPLTnspr                 Portable Runtime Interface
system      IPLTnss                  Network Security Services
system      IPLTpldap                PerLDAP
application SUNWlur                  Live Upgrade (root)
application SUNWluu                  Live Upgrade (usr)
```

As you can see, this system has quite a few packages installed in both the system and application categories, including `lxrun`, the application that allows Linux binaries to be executed on Solaris Intel, and the Gimp, a graphics manipulation program. There are no restrictions on the kinds of files and applications that can be installed with packages.

Installing a Solaris Package Using the CLI

The best way to learn about adding packages is to use an example. In this section, you'll download a package from **http://www.sunfreeware.com** called gpw-6.94-sol10-sparc-local.gz, an application developed by Tom Van Vleck that generates random passwords. Let's look more closely at the package name to determine what software this package contains:

- The .gz extension indicates that the package file has been compressed using `gzip` after it was created. Other possible extensions include .Z, which indicates compression with the `compress` program, and .z, which indicates compression with the `pack` program.

- The local string indicates that the package contents will be installed under the directory */usr/local*. Other typical installation targets include the */opt* directory, where optional packages from the Solaris distribution are installed.

- The sparc string states that the package is intended for use on Solaris SPARC and not Solaris Intel.

- The 6.94 string indicates the current software revision level.

- The gpw string states the application's name.

To use the package file, you first need to decompress it using the `gzip` command:

```
bash-2.05# gzip -d gpw-6.94-sol10-sparc-local
```

You can then examine the contents of the file by using the `head` command:

```
bash-2.05# head gpw-6.94-sol10-sparc-local
# PaCkAgE DaTaStReAm
TVVgpw 1 150
```

```
# end of header
NAME=gwp
ARCH=sparc
VERSION=6.94
CATEGORY=application
VENDOR=Tom Van Vleck
EMAIL=steve@smc.vnet.net
```

This kind of header exists for all Solaris packages and makes it easy to understand what platform a package is designed for, who the vendor was, and who to contact for more information.

Now that the package is decompressed and ready, you can begin the installation process by using the pkgadd command. To install the gpw-6.94-sol10-sparc-local package, use the following command:

```
# pkgadd -d gpw-6.94-sol10-sparc-local
```

You'll see the following output:

```
The following packages are available:
  1  TVVgpw       gwp
                  (sparc) 6.94

Select package(s) you wish to process (or 'all' to process
all packages). (default: all) [?,??,q]:   all
```

Press ENTER at this point to proceed with the installation:

```
Processing package instance <TVVgpw> from </tmp/gpw-6.94-sol10-sparc-local>

gwp
(sparc) 6.94
Tom Van Vleck
Using </usr/local> as the package base directory.
## Processing package information.
## Processing system information.
   2 package pathnames are already properly installed.
## Verifying disk space requirements.
## Checking for conflicts with packages already installed.
## Checking for setuid/setgid programs.

Installing gwp as <TVVgpw>

## Installing part 1 of 1.
/usr/local/bin/gpw
/usr/local/doc/gpw/README.gpw
[ verifying class <none> ]

Installation of <TVVgpw> was successful.
```

After processing package and system information and checking that the required amount of disk space is available, the `pkgadd` command copies only two files from the archive to the local file system: */usr/local/bin/gpw* and */usr/local/doc/gpw/README.gpw*.

Uninstalling a Solaris Package Using the CLI

After a package has been installed on the system, you can easily remove it by using the `pkgrm` command. For example, if you wanted to remove the `gpw` program after it was installed in the */usr/local* directory, you would use

```
# pkgrm TVVgpw
```

and respond to the following information:

```
The following package is currently installed:
   TVVgpw          gwp
                   (sparc) 6.94

Do you want to remove this package? y

## Removing installed package instance <TVVgpw>
## Verifying package dependencies.
## Processing package information.
## Removing pathnames in class <none>
/usr/local/doc/gpw/README.gpw
/usr/local/doc/gpw
/usr/local/doc <shared pathname not removed>
/usr/local/bin/gpw
/usr/local/bin <shared pathname not removed>
## Updating system information.

Removal of <TVVgpw> was successful.
```

The `pkgrm` command also operates in an interactive mode, in which multiple packages can be removed using the same interface:

```
# pkgrm

The following packages are available:
  1  GNUlstdc       libstdc++
                    (i86pc) 2.8.1.1
  2  GNUmake        make
                    (i86pc) 3.77
  3  NCRos86r       NCR Platform Support, OS Functionality (Root)
                    (i386) 1.1.0,REV=1998.08.07.12.41
  4  SFWaalib       ASCII Art Library
                    (i386) 1.2,REV=1999.11.25.13.32
```

```
 5   SFWaconf        GNU autoconf
                     (i386) 2.13,REV=1999.11.25.13.32
 6   SFWamake        GNU automake
                     (i386) 1.4,REV=1999.11.25.13.32
 7   SFWbison        GNU bison
                     (i386) 1.28,REV=1999.11.25.13.32
 8   SFWemacs        GNU Emacs
                     (i386) 20.4,REV=1999.11.25.13.32
 9   SFWflex         GNU flex
                     (i386) 2.5.4,REV=1999.11.25.13.32
10   SFWfvwm         fvwm virtual window manager
                     (i386) 2.2.2,REV=1999.11.25.13.32

... 288 more menu choices to follow;
<RETURN> for more choices, <CTRL-D> to stop display:
```

At this point, you can enter the number of the package that you wish to remove.

Creating New Packages

Creating a package is easy if you follow a few simple steps. In this example, you compile and build the Apache Web server from source, which is then customized for your local environment. Instead of rebuilding Apache on every Web server from source, if you compile it once and then distribute it as a package to all the local systems, you can save valuable time and CPU cycles.

The first step is to download the Apache source and build it according to the instructions supplied with the source package. After compiling the application into the source directory (e.g., */usr/local/apache*), make local customizations as appropriate. Next, you need to create the two files that are used to create the package: the *prototype* file, which contains a list of all the files to be stored in the archive, and their file permissions, and the *pkginfo* file, which contains all the descriptive information regarding the package, including the creator, architecture, and base directory.

To create the *pkginfo* file, you use the find command to create a list of all the files below the base directory of the package installation. In the case of Apache, the base directory is */usr/local/apache*, if that is where the source was compiled:

```
# cd /usr/local/apache
# find . -print | pkgproto > prototype
```

This command produces the prototype file in */usr/local/apache*. It contains entries like this:

```
d none bin 0755 nobody nobody
f none bin/httpd 0755 nobody nobody
f none bin/ab 0755 nobody nobody
```

```
f none bin/htpasswd 0755 nobody nobody
f none bin/htdigest 0755 nobody nobody
f none bin/apachectl 0755 nobody nobody
f none bin/dbmmanage 0755 nobody nobody
f none bin/logresolve 0755 nobody nobody
f none bin/rotatelogs 0755 nobody nobody
f none bin/apxs 0755 nobody nobody
d none libexec 0755 nobody nobody
d none man 0755 nobody nobody
d none man/man1 0755 nobody nobody|
f none man/man1/htpasswd.1 0644 nobody nobody
f none man/man1/htdigest.1 0644 nobody nobody
f none man/man1/dbmmanage.1 0644 nobody nobody
d none man/man8 0755 nobody nobody
f none man/man8/httpd.8 0644 nobody nobody
f none man/man8/ab.8 0644 nobody nobody
f none man/man8/apachectl.8 0644 nobody nobody
```

Each entry is either an f (file) or a d (directory), with the octal permissions code, user and group ownership also being displayed. After you verify that all the files that you wish to package are listed in the *pkginfo* file, you need to manually add an entry for the *pkginfo* file itself into the *pkginfo* file:

```
i pkginfo=./pkginfo
```

The *pkginfo* file contains a description of your archive. Adding this entry ensures that the *pkginfo* file is added to the archive. Next, you need to actually create the *pkginfo* file in the base directory of the package (i.e., */usr/local/apache* for this example). The file needs to contain several customized entries like the following:

```
PKG="EDapache"
NAME="Apache"
ARCH="sparc"
VERSION="1.3.12"
CATEGORY="application"
VENDOR="Cassowary Computing Pty Ltd"
EMAIL="paul@cassowary.net"
PSTAMP="Paul Watters"
BASEDIR="/usr/local/apache"
CLASSES="none"
```

Although these tags are self-explanatory, Table 5-1 contains a description of each of the options available for the *pkginfo* file.

Command Tag	Description
PKG	The name of the package
NAME	The name of the application contained in the package
ARCH	The target system architecture (SPARC or Intel)
VERSION	The package version number
CATEGORY	A package contains either an "application" or a "system" application
VENDOR	The supplier of the software
EMAIL	The e-mail address of the vendor
PSTAMP	The package builder's name
BASEDIR	The base directory where package files will be installed

TABLE 5-1   Command Options for *pkginfo* Files

Once the *pkginfo* file has been created, you're ready to begin building the package. After changing into the package base directory, execute the following command:

```
# pkgmk -o -r /usr/local/apache
## Building pkgmap from package prototype file.
## Processing pkginfo file.
## Attempting to volumize 362 entries in pkgmap.
part  1 -- 6631 blocks, 363 entries
## Packaging one part.
/var/spool/pkg/EDapache/pkgmap
/var/spool/pkg/EDapache/pkginfo
/var/spool/pkg/EDapache/reloc/.bash_history
/var/spool/pkg/EDapache/reloc/.profile
/var/spool/pkg/EDapache/reloc/bin/ab
/var/spool/pkg/EDapache/reloc/bin/apachectl
/var/spool/pkg/EDapache/reloc/bin/apxs
/var/spool/pkg/EDapache/reloc/bin/dbmmanage
/var/spool/pkg/EDapache/reloc/bin/htdigest
/var/spool/pkg/EDapache/reloc/bin/htpasswd
```

A directory called *EDapache* will have been created in */var/spool/pkg*, containing a copy of the source files, which are now ready to be packaged in the archive, by using the pkgtrans command:

```
# cd /var/spool/pkg
# pkgtrans -s /var/spool/pkg /tmp/EDapache-1.3.12.tar

The following packages are available:
  1  EDapache      Apache
                      (sparc) 1.3.12
```

```
Select package(s) you wish to process (or 'all' to process
all packages). (default: all) [?,??,q]:
```

You need to select the EDapache package to be built, by pressing the ENTER key:

```
Transferring <EDapache> package instance
```

The package (EDapache-1.3.12) has now been successfully created in the */tmp* directory:

```
-rw-r--r--   1 root      other      3163648 Oct 18 10:09 EDapache-1.3.12
```

To reduce the size of the package file, use the `gzip` command to compress its contents:

```
# gzip EDapache-1.3.12
# ls -l EDapache-1.3.12.gz
-rw-r--r--   1 root      other       816536 Oct 18 10:09 EDapache-1.3.12.gz
```

The compressed package file may now be distributed to other users, and installed using the `pkgadd` command.

Archiving and Compression

Using packages gives you the greatest level of control over how an archive is distributed and installed. However, creating the *pkginfo* and *prototype* files can be a time-consuming process for creating packages that are simply designed for a tape backup or for temporary use. In this case, it may be appropriate to create a tape archive (*tar file*) rather than a package. Another advantage of using a tar file is that it can be distributed to colleagues who are using operating systems other than Solaris (such as Microsoft Windows and Linux), and unpacked with ease.

Creating Archives

Creating a tar file is easy. For example, to create a tape archive containing the Apache distribution that you packaged in the previous section, you would use the following command:

```
# tar cvf /tmp/apache.tar *
a bin/ 0K
a bin/httpd 494K
a bin/ab 28K
a bin/htpasswd 39K
a bin/htdigest 16K
a bin/apachectl 7K
a bin/dbmmanage 7K
a bin/logresolve 10K
a bin/rotatelogs 7K
a bin/apxs 20K
```

```
a cgi-bin/ 0K
a cgi-bin/hello.c 1K
a cgi-bin/printenv 1K
a cgi-bin/test-cgi 1K
a cgi-bin/hello 7K
a cgi-bin/hello.cgi 7K
a cgi-bin/hello.sh 1K
a cgi-bin/prt 1K
a conf/ 0K
```

The cvf part of the `tar` command can be read as "*c*reate file using *v*erbose mode and copy to a *file*." Originally, the `tar` command was designed to copy an archive to a tape device, thus, an extra modifier is required to specify that the archive should be copied to a file instead. Table 5-2 summarizes the main modifiers used with the `tar` command.

The `tar` command takes either function letters or functions modifiers. The main function letters used with tar, to specify operations, are given with examples in the following three sections.

Replacing Files

The function letter r is used to replace files in an existing archive. The named files are written at the end of the tar file, as shown in this example:

```
# tar rvf /tmp/apache.tar *
a bin/ 0K
a bin/httpd 494K
a bin/ab 28K
a bin/htpasswd 39K
a bin/htdigest 16K
a bin/apachectl 7K
a bin/dbmmanage 7K
a bin/logresolve 10K
a bin/rotatelogs 7K
a bin/apxs 20K
a cgi-bin/ 0K
a cgi-bin/hello.c 1K
a cgi-bin/printenv 1K
a cgi-bin/test-cgi 1K
a cgi-bin/hello 7K
a cgi-bin/hello.cgi 7K
a cgi-bin/hello.sh 1K
a cgi-bin/prt 1K
```

Modifier	Name	Description
b	Blocking factor	Specifies the number of tape blocks to be used during each read and write operation.
e	Error	Specifies that tar should exit if an error is detected.
f	File	Output is written to a file rather than to a tape drive.
h	Symbolic links	Archives files accessed through symbolic links.
i	Ignore	Checksum errors are ignored during archive creation.
k	Kilobytes	Specifies the size of the archive in kilobytes. If an archive is larger than this size, it will be split across multiple archives.
o	Ownership	Modifies the user and group ownership of all archive files to the current owner.
v	Verbose	Displays information about all files extracted or added to the archive.

TABLE 5-2 Tape Archive Function Modifiers

Displaying Contents

The function letter t is used to extract the table of contents of an archive, which lists all the files that have been archived within a specific file, as shown in this example:

```
# tar tvf /tmp/apache.tar *
drwxr-xr-x 1003/10        0 Mar 30 13:45 2004 bin/
-rwxr-xr-x 1003/10   505536 Mar 30 13:45 2004 bin/httpd
-rwxr-xr-x 1003/10    27896 Mar 30 13:45 2004 bin/ab
-rwxr-xr-x 1003/10    38916 Mar 30 13:45 2004 bin/htpasswd
-rwxr-xr-x 1003/10    16332 Mar 30 13:45 2004 bin/htdigest
-rwxr-xr-x 1003/10     7065 Mar 30 13:45 2004 bin/apachectl
-rwxr-xr-x 1003/10     6456 Mar 30 13:45 2004 bin/dbmmanage
-rwxr-xr-x 1003/10     9448 Mar 30 13:45 2004 bin/logresolve
-rwxr-xr-x 1003/10     6696 Mar 30 13:45 2004 bin/rotatelogs
-rwxr-xr-x 1003/10    20449 Mar 30 13:45 2004 bin/apxs
drwxr-xr-x 1003/10        0 Oct  5 14:36 2004 cgi-bin/
-rwxr-xr-x 1003/10      279 Oct  5 15:04 2004 cgi-bin/hello.c
-rwxr-xr-x 1003/10      274 Mar 30 13:45 2004 cgi-bin/printenv
-rwxr-xr-x 1003/10      757 Mar 30 13:45 2004 cgi-bin/test-cgi
-rwxr-xr-x 1003/10     7032 Oct  5 15:04 2004 cgi-bin/hello
-rwxr-xr-x 1003/10     6888 Oct  5 14:31 2004 cgi-bin/hello.cgi
-rwxr-xr-x 1003/10      179 Oct  5 15:09 2004 cgi-bin/hello.sh
-rwxr-xr-x 1003/10      274 Oct  5 14:34 2004 cgi-bin/prt
```

PART II

Extracting Files

The function letter x is used to extract files from an archive, as shown in this example:

```
# tar xvf apache.tar
x bin, 0 bytes, 0 tape blocks
x bin/httpd, 505536 bytes, 988 tape blocks
x bin/ab, 27896 bytes, 55 tape blocks
x bin/htpasswd, 38916 bytes, 77 tape blocks
x bin/htdigest, 16332 bytes, 32 tape blocks
x bin/apachectl, 7065 bytes, 14 tape blocks
x bin/dbmmanage, 6456 bytes, 13 tape blocks
x bin/logresolve, 9448 bytes, 19 tape blocks
x bin/rotatelogs, 6696 bytes, 14 tape blocks
x bin/apxs, 20449 bytes, 40 tape blocks
x cgi-bin, 0 bytes, 0 tape blocks
x cgi-bin/hello.c, 279 bytes, 1 tape blocks
x cgi-bin/printenv, 274 bytes, 1 tape blocks
x cgi-bin/test-cgi, 757 bytes, 2 tape blocks
x cgi-bin/hello, 7032 bytes, 14 tape blocks
x cgi-bin/hello.cgi, 6888 bytes, 14 tape blocks
x cgi-bin/hello.sh, 179 bytes, 1 tape blocks
x cgi-bin/prt, 274 bytes, 1 tape blocks
```

Compressing Files

Archives and other files can occupy a large amount of disk space if they contain data that is redundant. For example, text files often have large segments of empty space, and images with segments of the same color are clearly redundant. Solaris provides tools to exploit this redundancy by allowing files to be stored in a compressed format. When tape archives are created as shown in the preceding section, it's wise to maximize the availability of disk space to other applications by compressing archives before they are moved to offline storage, such as backup tapes.

Two compression commands are typically used under Solaris: the compress command, which creates compressed files with a .Z extension, and the GNU gzip command, which creates compressed files with a .gz extension. Since compress and gzip use different compression algorithms to pack data, the size of a file compressed by gzip may differ from the size of the same file compressed by compress. In general, gzip can achieve a higher compression ratio than compress.

To compress an archive called *backup.tar*, you would use the following command:

```
$ compress backup.tar
```

Once the compressed file *backup.tar.Z* has been created, the original file *backup.tar* will be deleted. Alternatively, you could use the following gzip command to compress *backup.tar*:

```
$ gzip backup.tar
```

Again, once the `gzip`-compressed file *backup.tar.gz* has been created, the original file *backup.tar* will be deleted. To perform repeat packing on the file, to achieve maximum compression, the following command can be used:

```
$ gzip -9 backup.tar
```

Keep in mind that repeat packing is a CPU-intensive and lengthy process. To restore a file that has been compressed by using the `compress` program, the `uncompress` command is used:

```
$ uncompress backup.tar.Z
```

Once the file *backup.tar* has been restored, the *backup.tar.Z* file will be automatically removed. Alternatively, to restore a file compressed using `gzip`, use the following command:

```
$ gzip -d backup.tar.gz
```

Once again, after the file *backup.tar* has been restored, the *backup.tar.gz* file will be removed automatically.

Finding Patches

To find out information about current patches, sysadmins are directed to the **http:// sunsolve.sun.com/** site. Here, details about current patches for each operating system release can be found. There are two basic types of patches available from SunSolve: single patches and jumbo patches. Single patches have a single patch number associated with them, and are generally aimed at resolving a single outstanding issue; they usually insert, delete, or update data in a small number of files. Single patches are also targeted at resolving specific security issues. Each patch is associated with an internal bug number from Sun's bug database. For example, patch number 108435-01 aims to fix BugId 4318566, involving a shared-library issue with the 64-bit C++ compiler.

In contrast, a jumbo patch consists of many single patches that have been bundled together, on the basis of operating system release levels, to ensure that the most common issues for a particular platform are resolved by the installation of the jumbo patch. It's standard practice to install the current jumbo patch for Solaris 10 once it's been installed from scratch, or if the system has been upgraded from Solaris 9, for example.

Some of the latest patches released for Solaris 10 include the following:

- 110322-01: Patch for /usr/lib/netsvc/yp/ypbind
- 110853-01: Patch for Sun-Fire-880

- 110856-01: Patch for /etc/inet/services
- 110888-01 : Patch for figgs
- 110894-01: Patch for country name
- 110927-01: Patch for SUNW_PKGLIST
- 111078-01: Patch Solaris Resource Manager
- 111295-01: Patch for /usr/bin/sparcv7/pstack and /usr/bin/sparcv9/pstack
- 111297-01: Patch for /usr/lib/libsendfile.so.1
- 111337-01: Patch for /usr/sbin/ocfserv
- 111400-01: Patch for KCMS configure tool
- 111402-01: Patch for crontab
- 111431-01: Patch for /usr/lib/libldap.so.4
- 111439-01: Patch for /kernel/fs/tmpfs
- 111473-01: Patch for PCI Host Adapter
- 111562-01: Patch for /usr/lib/librt.so.1
- 111564-01 Patch for SunPCi 2.2.1
- 111570-01: Patch for uucp
- 111588-01: Patch for /kernel/drv/wc
- 111606-01: Patch for /usr/sbin/in.ftpd
- 111624-01: Patch for /usr/sbin/inetd
- 111648-01 Patch for env3test, cpupmtest, ifbtest, and rsctest
- 111656-01: Patch for socal and sf drivers
- 111762-01 Patch for Expert3D and SunVTS

One of the most useful guides to the currently available patches for Solaris 10 is the SunSolve Patch Report (**ftp://sunsolve.sun.com/pub/patches/Solaris10.PatchReport**). This report provides a quick reference to all newly released patches for the platform, as well as updates on previous patches that have now been modified. A list of suggested patches for the platform is also contained in the Patch Report, while recommended security patches are listed separately. Finally, a list of obsolete patches is provided. Some of the currently listed security patches available include the following:

- 108528-09: Patch for kernel update
- 108869-06: Patch for snmpdx/mibiisa/libssasnmp/snmplib
- 108875-09: Patch for c2audit
- 108968-05: Patch for vol/vold/rmmount
- 108975-04: Patch for /usr/bin/rmformat and /usr/sbin/format

- 108985-03: Patch for /usr/sbin/in.rshd
- 108991-13: Patch for /usr/lib/libc.so.1
- 109091-04: Patch for /usr/lib/fs/ufs/ufsrestore
- 109134-19: Patch for WBEM
- 109234-04: Patch for Apache and NCA
- 109279-13: Patch for /kernel/drv/ip
- 109320-03: Patch for LP
- 109322-07: Patch for libnsl
- 109326-05: Patch for libresolv.so.2 and in.named
- 109354-09: Patch for dtsession
- 109783-01: Patch for /usr/lib/nfs/nfsd
- 109805-03: Patch for pam_krb5.so.1
- 109887-08: Patch for smartcard
- 109888-05: Patch for platform drivers
- 109892-03: Patch for /kernel/drv/ecpp driver
- 109894-01: Patch for /kernel/drv/sparcv9/bpp driver
- 109896-04: Patch for USB driver
- 109951-01: Patch for jserver buffer overflow

Example

In the following example, you'll examine how to use the Solstice Launcher GUI to manage packages. The flexible package format is independent of the interface used to install specific packages. In previous Solaris versions, admintool would have been used to perform these operations, but this tool has now been deprecated.

Reviewing Patch Installation

To determine which patches are currently installed on your system, you need to use the showrev command as follows:

```
# showrev -p
Patch: 107430-01 Obsoletes:    Requires:    Incompatibles:    Packages: SUNWwsr
Patch: 108029-01 Obsoletes:    Requires:    Incompatibles:    Packages: SUNWwsr
Patch: 107437-03 Obsoletes:    Requires:    Incompatibles:    Packages: SUNWtiu8
Patch: 107316-01 Obsoletes:    Requires:    Incompatibles:    Packages: SUNWploc
Patch: 107453-01 Obsoletes:    Requires:    Incompatibles:    Packages: SUNWkvm,
SUNWcar
Patch: 106541-06 Obsoletes: 106976-01, 107029-01, 107030-01, 107334-01
Requires:  Incompatibles:  Packages: SUNWkvm, SUNWcsu, SUNWcsr, SUNWcsl,
```

```
SUNWcar, SUNWesu, SUNWarc, SUNWatfsr, SUNWcpr, SUNWdpl, SUNWhea, SUNWtoo,
SUNWpcmci, SUNWtnfc, SUNWvolr
Patch: 106541-10 Obsoletes: 106832-03, 106976-01, 107029-01, 107030-01,
107334-01, 107031-01, 107117-05, 107899-01 Requires: 107544-02
Incompatibles:  Packages:
SUNWkvm, SUNWcsu, SUNWcsr, SUNWcsl, SUNWcar, SUNWesu, SUNWarc, SUNWatfsr,
SUNWscpu, SUNWcpr, SUNWdpl, SUNWhea, SUNWipc, SUNWtoo, SUNWpcmci, SUNWpcmcu,
SUNWtnfc, SUNWvolr
Patch: 106541-15 Obsoletes: 106832-03, 106976-01, 107029-01, 107030-01,
107334-01, 107031-01, 107117-05, 107899-01, 108752-01, 107147-08, 109104-04
Requires: 107544-02 Incompatibles:  Packages: SUNWkvm, SUNWcsu, SUNWcsr,
SUNWcsl, SUNWcar, SUNWesu, SUNWarc, SUNWatfsr, SUNWscpu, SUNWcpr, SUNWdpl,
SUNWhea, SUNWipc, SUNWtoo, SUNWnisu, SUNWpcmci, SUNWpcmcu, SUNWtnfc, SUNWvolu,
SUNWvolr
```

From the preceding example, you can see that showrev reports several different properties of each patch installed:

- The patch number
- Whether the patch obsoletes a previously released patch (or patches) and, if so, which version numbers
- Whether there are any prerequisite patches (and their version numbers) on which the current patch depends
- Whether the patch is incompatible with any other patches
- What standard Solaris packages are affected by installation of the patch

As an example, consider the last several lines of the preceding output regarding patch 106541-15. As you can see, this patch obsoletes a large number of other patches, including 106832-03, 106976-01, 107029-01, 107030-01, 107334-01, 107031-01, 107117-05, 107899-01, 108752-01, 107147-08, and 109104-04. In addition, it depends on patch 107544-02, and is compatible with all other known patches. Finally, it affects a large number of different packages, including SUNWkvm, SUNWcsu, SUNWcsr, SUNWcsl, SUNWcar, SUNWesu, SUNWarc, SUNWatfsr, SUNWscpu, SUNWcpr, SUNWdpl, SUNWhea, SUNWipc, SUNWtoo, SUNWnisu, SUNWpcmci, SUNWpcmcu, SUNWtnfc, SUNWvolu, and SUNWvolr.

Command Reference

The following commands are commonly used to install packages and files on Solaris.

Package Commands

Table 5-3 summarizes the various commands used to create, install, and remove packages.

Command	Description
pkgproto	Creates a prototype file that specifies the files contained in a package
pkgmk	Creates a package directory
pkgadd	Installs a package from a package file
pkgtrans	Converts a package directory into a file
pkgrm	Uninstalls a package
pkgchk	Verifies that a package is valid
pkginfo	Prints the contents of a package

TABLE 5-3   Solaris Packaging Commands

install

The `install` command is not part of the standard package tools, but is often used in scripts to copy files from a source to a destination directory, as part of an installation process. It does not require superuser privileges to execute, and will not overwrite files unless the effective user has permission. However, if the superuser is executing the command, then files can be written with a specific username, group membership, and octal permissions code. This allows a superuser to install multiple files with different permissions, and ownership different to root.

The three ownership and permission options are specified by:

- *–m*   Octal permissions code
- *–u*   File owner
- *–g*   Group membership

There are four options that indicate which operations are to be performed:

- *–c*   Copies a source file to a target directory
- *–f*   Overwrites the target file with a source file if the former exists
- *–n*   Copies a source file to a target directory if and only if it does not exist in any of a specified set of directories
- *–d*   Creates a directory

To install the file */tmp/setup_server.sh* to the directory */opt/scripts*, as the user bin and group sysadmin, you would use the following command:

```
# install -c /opt/scripts -m 0755 -u bin -g sysadmin /tmp/setup_scripts
```

patchadd

To install single patches, use the patchadd command:

```
# patchadd /patches/106541-15
```

where */patches* is the directory in which your patches are downloaded, and 106541-15 is the patch filename (it should be the same as the patch number).

To add multiple patches from the same directory, use the following command:

```
# patchadd /patches/106541-15 106541-10 107453-01
```

where 106541-15, 106541-10, and 107453-01 are the patches to be installed. Once the patches have been successfully installed, you can verify them by using the showrev command, as shown here for 106541-15:

```
# showrev -p | grep 106541-15
```

patchadd has a large number of options that you can use for nonstandard patch installations. For example, if you need to patch a net install image, you need to specify the path to the image. Alternatively, if you don't want to have the option to back out of a patch, then you can flag this. As a strategy, this is not recommended, because you won't be able to revert your system to a prepatched state. The following are the options for patchadd:

- *–B* Specifies a directory for storing backout information other than the default
- *–C* Specifies the path to the net install image that is to be patched, if required
- *–d* Disallows backing out of patch installations
- *–M* Specifies an alternative directory where patches are located
- *–p* Prints a list of all installed patches
- *–u* Does not validate file installations
- *–R* Specifies an alternative root directory for client installations
- *–S* Patches a client from a server, where clients share the server's operating system directories

Let's look at how some of these options can be used in practice. In order to patch a client system called mars, with its root directory mapped to */export/mars*, you could use the following command:

```
# patchadd -d -R /export/mars /var/spool/patch/106541-15
```

Note that this command would disallow backing out of the patch installation. To add the patch to a net install image, located in */export/Solaris_2.10/Tools/boot*, you would use the following command:

```
# patchadd -C /export/Solaris_2.10/Tools/boot /var/spool/patch/106541-15
```

Since patches overwrite system files, you may experience some potential pitfalls when applying patches. The most common problem is running out of disk space on the /*var* partition. If this occurs during patch installation, you see the following error message:

```
Insufficient space in /var/sadm/pkg/106541-15/save to save old files
```

In this situation, there are several possible courses of action, listed in order of desirability:

- Increase the available space on */var* by removing unnecessary files, even temporarily, until the patch can be applied.
- Specify an alternative backout directory that is located on a different file system.
- Create a symbolic link from */var/sadm/pkg/106541-15/save* to a directory on another file system, such as */usr/local/var/sadm/pkg/106541-15/save*.
- Switch off backing out of the patch installation.

Any error messages for the patch installation generally are logged in */tmp/ log.106541-15*, which may indicate other reasons for installation failure. For example, if a patch is applied twice to a system, then the following entry will appear in the log:

```
This appears to be an attempt to install the same architecture
and version of a package which is already installed. This
installation will attempt to overwrite this package.
```

patchrm

Patches can be easily removed using the `patchrm` command. For example, to remove the patch 106541-15, the following command would be used:

```
# patchrm 106541-15
```

If the patch was previously installed, it would now be removed.

However, if the patch was not previously installed, the following error message would be displayed:

```
Checking installed packages and patches...
Patch 106541-15 has not been applied to this system.
patchrm is terminating.
```

Like `patchadd`, `patchrm` has a number of options that may be passed on the command line:

- *–B*   Specifies a directory for storing backout information for the patch removal, other than the default
- *–C*   Specifies the path to the net install image from which a patch is to be removed, if required
- *–f*   Forces a package to be removed
- *–R*   Specifies an alternative root directory for patch removal from client installations
- *–S*   Removes a patch from a client system, executed from the server

For example, to remove patch 106541-15 from the client system jupiter, the following command could be used:

```
# patchrm -C /export/Solaris_2.10/Tools/boot 106541-15
```

Summary

In this chapter, you have examined how to install software in the Solaris environment using GUI and CUI tools. In previous Solaris versions, `admintool` would have been used in this context, but future versions of Solaris will not ship with `admintool`, so it's a good practice to stop using it.

Text Processing and Editing

In this chapter, we focus on basic and advanced text processing in Solaris. An editor is used primarily to create new text files or edit existing text files. Few UNIX users would have escaped learning about the visual editor (vi) when first learning how to use a Solaris shell. In this chapter, the aim is to review some of the more esoteric vi usages, and to review commonly used command-mode and ex-mode commands. We also present examples of how to use text-processing utilities like PERL, sed, and awk.

Key Concepts

The following concepts are required knowledge for working with text processing.

Visual Editor

vi is a text-processing tool that carries out the following tasks on Solaris and other UNIX systems:

- Creates new text files
- Modifies existing files
- Searches for a text string in a file
- Replaces one string with another in a file
- Moves or copies a string within a file
- Removes a string from a file

To run vi from the command line and create a new file, you use the following command:

```
$ vi
```

To run vi from the command line and edit an existing file, use the following command:

```
$ vi file.txt
```

where *file.txt* is the filename of the file to be edited. The result of editing a file (such as /etc/passwd.txt) is shown in Figure 6-1.

When editing an existing file, `vi` copies the bytes from disk into a memory buffer, which is then operated on according to user commands. Text can be inserted during edit mode, while commands are executed during command mode. Changes are not written to disk until the appropriate `save` command is executed. During edit mode, special keys such as the arrow keys do not operate as commands to move the cursor around the screen; instead, the actual code is inserted into the file. These keys can be used only when the editor is in command mode. During edit mode, you can switch to command mode by pressing the ESCAPE key. When in command mode, you can switch to edit mode by pressing the I key.

The following commands can be executed in command mode:

- **/**   Performs a forward search for a text string.
- **?**   Performs a backward search for a text string.
- **:**   Runs an ex editor command on the current line.
- **!**   Executes a shell within `vi`.
- **ZZ**   Saves a file and exits.
- **h**   Moves the cursor left.
- **j**   Moves the cursor down.
- **k**   Moves the cursor up.

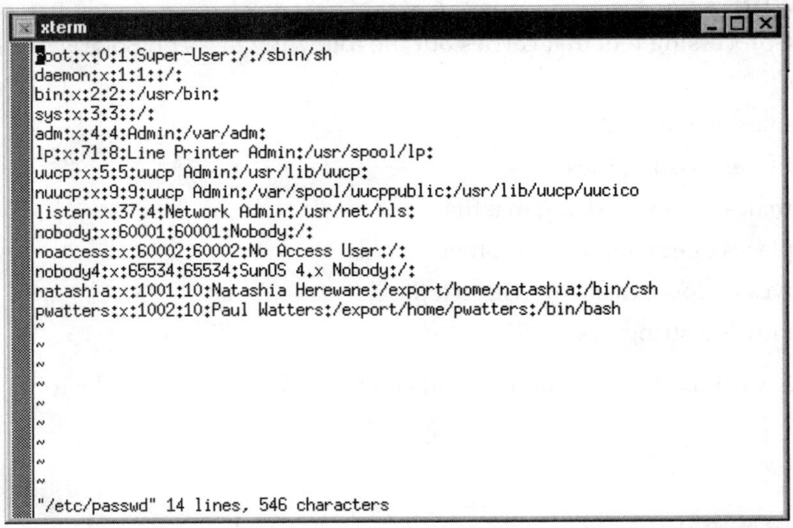

```
xterm                                                          _ □ X
root:x:0:1:Super-User:/:/sbin/sh
daemon:x:1:1::/:
bin:x:2:2::/usr/bin:
sys:x:3:3::/:
adm:x:4:4:Admin:/var/adm:
lp:x:71:8:Line Printer Admin:/usr/spool/lp:
uucp:x:5:5:uucp Admin:/usr/lib/uucp:
nuucp:x:9:9:uucp Admin:/var/spool/uucppublic:/usr/lib/uucp/uucico
listen:x:37:4:Network Admin:/usr/net/nls:
nobody:x:60001:60001:Nobody:/:
noaccess:x:60002:60002:No Access User:/:
nobody4:x:65534:65534:SunOS 4.x Nobody:/:
natashia:x:1001:10:Natashia Herewane:/export/home/natashia:/bin/csh
pwatters:x:1002:10:Paul Watters:/export/home/pwatters:/bin/bash
~
~
~
~
~
~
~
~
"/etc/passwd" 14 lines, 546 characters
```

FIGURE 6-1   Editing the */etc/passwd* file

- **l**   Moves the cursor right.
- **nG**   Moves the cursor to line *n*.
- **w**   Moves to next the word.
- **b**   Moves back one word.
- **dw**   Deletes words.
- **ndw**   Deletes *n* words.
- **d^**   Deletes all words to the beginning of the line.
- **dd**   Deletes the current line.
- **dG**   Deletes all lines to the end of the file.
- **D**   Deletes all words to the end of the line.
- **x**   Deletes the current character.
- **nx**   Deletes the *n* characters to the right.
- **nY**   Yanks *n* lines into the buffer.
- **p**   Pastes to the right of the cursor.
- **P**   Pastes to the left of the cursor.

A separate set of commands, called the ex commands, can be run by using the colon in conjunction with one of these commands:

- **:n**   Moves the cursor to line *n*.
- **:$**   Moves the cursor to the end of the file.
- **: s/a/b/g**   Replaces all occurrences of string *a* with string *b* on the current line.
- **:%s/a/b/g**   Replaces all occurrences of string *a* with string *b* in the entire file.
- **:wq**   Saves the modified file and quits.
- **:q!**   Quits without saving any changes.
- **:set**   Sets a number of different options.

Let's examine the result of using the ex command `:%s/a/b/g`. Figure 6-2 shows the */etc/passwd* file with an ex command that searches for all occurrences of "export" and replaces them with "staff".

Figure 6-3 shows the result output, with the string `/export/home`, for example, now changed to `/staff/home`.

.exrc File

`vi` can be customized on a per-user basis by creating an .exrc file in each user's home directory, which they can then modify with their own settings. You can map commands to function keys on the keyboard, and set various modes to be the default.

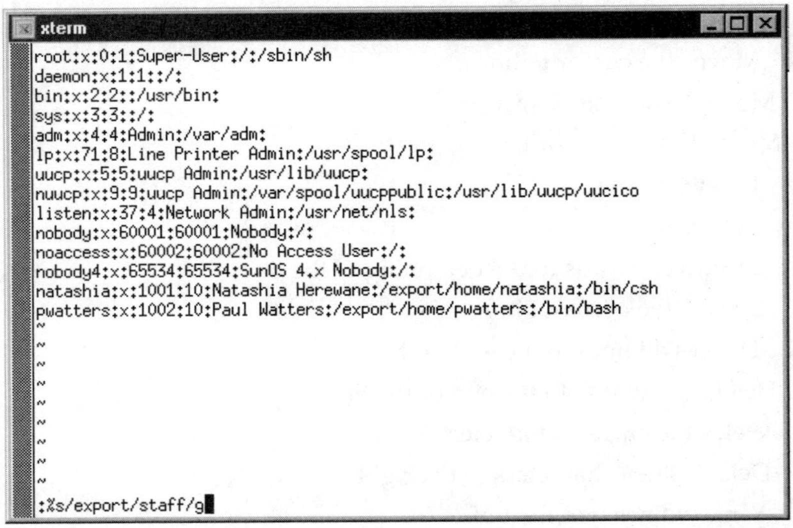

```
┌──────────────────────────────────────────────────────────────┐
│ ⊠  xterm                                            _ □ ✕     │
├──────────────────────────────────────────────────────────────┤
│ root:x:0:1:Super-User:/:/sbin/sh                             │
│ daemon:x:1:1::/:                                             │
│ bin:x:2:2::/usr/bin:                                         │
│ sys:x:3:3::/:                                                │
│ adm:x:4:4:Admin:/var/adm:                                    │
│ lp:x:71:8:Line Printer Admin:/usr/spool/lp:                  │
│ uucp:x:5:5:uucp Admin:/usr/lib/uucp:                         │
│ nuucp:x:9:9:uucp Admin:/var/spool/uucppublic:/usr/lib/uucp/uucico │
│ listen:x:37:4:Network Admin:/usr/net/nls:                    │
│ nobody:x:60001:60001:Nobody:/:                               │
│ noaccess:x:60002:60002:No Access User:/:                     │
│ nobody4:x:65534:65534:SunOS 4.x Nobody:/:                    │
│ natashia:x:1001:10:Natashia Herewane:/export/home/natashia:/bin/csh │
│ pwatters:x:1002:10:Paul Watters:/export/home/pwatters:/bin/bash │
│ ~                                                            │
│ ~                                                            │
│ ~                                                            │
│ ~                                                            │
│ ~                                                            │
│ ~                                                            │
│ ~                                                            │
│ ~                                                            │
│ :%s/export/staff/g▮                                          │
└──────────────────────────────────────────────────────────────┘
```

FIGURE 6-2   Using an ex command

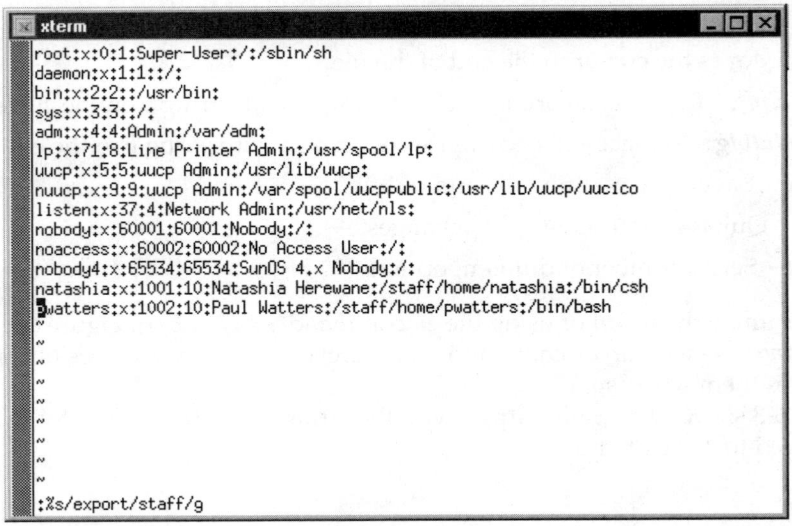

```
┌──────────────────────────────────────────────────────────────┐
│ ⊠  xterm                                            _ □ ✕     │
├──────────────────────────────────────────────────────────────┤
│ root:x:0:1:Super-User:/:/sbin/sh                             │
│ daemon:x:1:1::/:                                             │
│ bin:x:2:2::/usr/bin:                                         │
│ sys:x:3:3::/:                                                │
│ adm:x:4:4:Admin:/var/adm:                                    │
│ lp:x:71:8:Line Printer Admin:/usr/spool/lp:                  │
│ uucp:x:5:5:uucp Admin:/usr/lib/uucp:                         │
│ nuucp:x:9:9:uucp Admin:/var/spool/uucppublic:/usr/lib/uucp/uucico │
│ listen:x:37:4:Network Admin:/usr/net/nls:                    │
│ nobody:x:60001:60001:Nobody:/:                               │
│ noaccess:x:60002:60002:No Access User:/:                     │
│ nobody4:x:65534:65534:SunOS 4.x Nobody:/:                    │
│ natashia:x:1001:10:Natashia Herewane:/staff/home/natashia:/bin/csh │
│ ▮watters:x:1002:10:Paul Watters:/staff/home/pwatters:/bin/bash │
│ ~                                                            │
│ ~                                                            │
│ ~                                                            │
│ ~                                                            │
│ ~                                                            │
│ ~                                                            │
│ ~                                                            │
│ ~                                                            │
│ :%s/export/staff/g                                          │
└──────────────────────────────────────────────────────────────┘
```

FIGURE 6-3   Performing text substitutions

In the following example .exrc, we set showmode and autoindent to be the default modes when opening all text files, and map the F1 and F2 keys to set line numbering and then turn it off, respectively:

```
set showmode
set autoindent
map #1: set number
map #2: set nonumber
```

Any valid ex command can be included in the .exrc file.

Text-Processing Utilities

Solaris has many user commands available to perform tasks ranging from text processing, to file manipulation, to terminal management. In this section, we look at some standard UNIX utilities that are the core of using a shell in Solaris. However, readers are urged to obtain an up-to-date list of the utilities supplied with Solaris by typing this command:

```
$ man intro
```

The `cat` command displays the contents of a file to standard output, without any kind of pagination or screen control. It is most useful for viewing small files, or for passing the contents of a text file through another filter or utility (e.g., the `grep` command, which searches for strings). To examine the contents of the *groups* database, for example, you would use the following command:

```
$ cat /etc/group
root::0:root
other::1:
bin::2:root,bin,daemon
sys::3:root,bin,sys,adm
adm::4:root,adm,daemon
uucp::5:root,uucp
mail::6:root
tty::7:root,tty,adm
lp::8:root,lp,adm
nuucp::9:root,nuucp
staff::10:
postgres::100:
daemon::12:root,daemon
sysadmin::14:
nobody::60001:
noaccess::60002:
nogroup::65534:
```

The cat command is not very useful for examining specific sections of a file. For example, if you need to examine the first few lines of a web server's log files, using cat would display them, but they would quickly scroll off the screen out of sight. However, you can use the head command to display only the first few lines of a file. This example extracts the lines from the log file of the Borland Application Server:

```
$ head access_log
203.16.206.43 - - [31/Jan/2004:14:32:52 +1000]
  "GET /index.jsp HTTP/1.0" 200 24077
203.16.206.43 - - [31/Jan/2004:14:32:52 +1000]
  "GET /data.jsp HTTP/1.0" 200 13056
203.16.206.43 - - [31/Jan/2004:14:32:52 +1000]
  "GET /names.jsp HTTP/1.0" 200 15666
203.16.206.43 - - [31/Jan/2004:14:32:52 +1000]
  "GET /database.jsp HTTP/1.0" 200 56444
203.16.206.43 - - [31/Jan/2004:14:32:52 +1000]
  "GET /index.jsp HTTP/1.0" 200 24077
203.16.206.43 - - [31/Jan/2004:14:32:52 +1000]
  "GET /index.jsp HTTP/1.0" 200 24077
203.16.206.43 - - [31/Jan/2004:14:32:52 +1000]
  "GET /names.jsp HTTP/1.0" 200 15666
203.16.206.43 - - [31/Jan/2004:14:32:53 +1000]
  "GET /database.jsp HTTP/1.0" 200 56444
203.16.206.43 - - [31/Jan/2004:14:32:53 +1000]
  "GET /index.jsp HTTP/1.0" 200 24077
203.16.206.43 - - [31/Jan/2004:14:32:53 +1000]
  "GET /search.jsp HTTP/1.0" 200 45333
```

Instead, if you just want to examine the last few lines of a file, you could use the cat command to display the entire file, ending with the last few lines, or you could use the tail command to specifically display these lines. If the file is large (e.g., an Inprise Application Server log file of 2MB), displaying the whole file using cat would be a large waste of system resources, whereas tail is very efficient. Here's an example of using tail to display the last several lines of a file:

```
$ tail access_log
203.16.206.43 - - [31/Aug/2004:14:32:52 +1000] "GET /index.jsp HTTP/1.0" 200 24077
203.16.206.43 - - [31/Aug/2004:14:32:52 +1000] "GET /index.jsp HTTP/1.0" 200 24077
203.16.206.43 - - [31/Aug/2004:14:32:52 +1000] "GET /index.jsp HTTP/1.0" 200 24077
203.16.206.43 - - [31/Aug/2004:14:32:52 +1000] "GET /index.jsp HTTP/1.0" 200 24077
203.16.206.43 - - [31/Aug/2004:14:32:52 +1000] "GET /index.jsp HTTP/1.0" 200 24077
203.16.206.43 - - [31/Aug/2004:14:32:52 +1000] "GET /index.jsp HTTP/1.0" 200 24077
203.16.206.43 - - [31/Aug/2004:14:32:52 +1000] "GET /index.jsp HTTP/1.0" 200 24077
203.16.206.43 - - [31/Aug/2004:14:32:53 +1000] "GET /index.jsp HTTP/1.0" 200 24077
203.16.206.43 - - [31/Aug/2004:14:32:53 +1000] "GET /index.jsp HTTP/1.0" 200 24077
203.16.206.43 - - [31/Aug/2004:14:32:53 +1000] "GET /index.jsp HTTP/1.0" 200 24077
```

Now, imagine that you were searching for a particular string within the *access_log* file, such as a 404 error code, which indicates that a page has been requested that does not exist. Webmasters regularly check log files for this error code, to create a list of links that need to be checked. To view this list, you can use the `grep` command to search the file for a specific string (in this case, "404"), and you can use the `more` command to display the results page by page:

```
$ grep 404 access_log | more
203.16.206.56 - - [31/Aug/2004:15:42:54 +1000]
  "GET /servlet/LibraryCatalog?command=mainmenu HTTP/1.1" 200 21404
203.16.206.56 - - [01/Sep/2004:08:32:12 +1000]
  "GET /servlet/LibraryCatalog?command=searchbyname HTTP/1.1" 200 14041
203.16.206.237 - - [01/Sep/2004:09:20:35 +1000]
  "GET /images/LINE.gif HTTP/1.1" 404 1204
203.16.206.236 - - [01/Sep/2004:10:10:35 +1000]
  "GET /images/black.gif HTTP/1.1" 404 1204
203.16.206.236 - - [01/Sep/2004:10:10:40 +1000]
  "GET /images/white.gif HTTP/1.1" 404 1204
203.16.206.236 - - [01/Sep/2004:10:10:47 +1000]
  "GET /images/red.gif HTTP/1.1" 404 1204
203.16.206.236 - - [01/Sep/2004:10:11:09 +1000]
  "GET /images/yellow.gif HTTP/1.1" 404 1204
203.16.206.236 - - [01/Sep/2004:10:11:40 +1000]
  "GET /images/LINE.gif HTTP/1.1" 404 1204
203.16.206.236 - - [01/Sep/2004:10:11:44 +1000]
  "GET /images/LINE.gif HTTP/1.1" 404 1204
203.16.206.236 - - [01/Sep/2004:10:12:03 +1000]
  "GET /images/LINE.gif HTTP/1.1" 404 1204
203.16.206.41 - - [01/Sep/2004:12:04:22 +1000]
  "GET /data/books/576586955.pdf HTTP/1.0" 404 1204
--More--
```

These log files contain a line for each access to the Web server, with entries relating to the source IP address, date and time of access, the HTTP request string sent, the protocol used, and the success/error code. When you see the *--More--* prompt, you can press the SPACEBAR to advance to the next screen, or you can press ENTER to advance by a single line in the results. As you have probably guessed, the pipe operator (|) was used to pass the results of the `grep` command through to the `more` command.

In addition to the pipe, you can use four other operators on the command line to direct or append input streams to standard output, or output streams to standard input. Although that sounds convoluted, directing the output of a command into a new file (or appending it to an existing file) can be very useful when working with files. You can also generate the input to a command from the output of another command. These operations are performed by the following operators:

- > Redirects standard output to a file.
- >> Appends standard output to a file.

- < Redirects file contents to standard input.
- << Appends file contents to standard input.

bash also has logical operators, including the "less than" (*lt*) operator, which uses the test facility to make numerical comparisons between two operands. Other commonly used operators include the following:

a –eq b	a equals b
a –ne b	a does not equal b
a –gt b	a is greater than b
a –ge b	a is greater than or equal to b
a –le b	a is less than or equal to b

Let's look at an example with the cat command, which displays the contents of files, and the echo command, which echoes the contents of a string or an environment variable that has been previously specified. For example, imagine that you want to maintain a database of endangered species in a text file called *animals.txt*. If you want to add the first animal "zebra" to an empty file, you could use this command:

```
$ echo "zebra" > animals.txt
```

You could then check the contents of the file *animals.txt* with this command:

```
$ cat animals.txt
zebra
```

Thus, the insertion was successful. Now, imagine that you want to add a second entry (the animal "emu") to the *animals.txt* file. You could try using this command:

```
$ echo "emu" > animals.txt
```

However, the result may not be what you expected:

```
$ cat animals.txt
emu
```

You get this result because the > operator always overwrites the contents of an existing file, whereas the >> operator always appends to the contents of an existing file. Let's run that command again with the correct operators:

```
$ echo "zebra" > animals.txt
$ echo "emu" >> animals.txt
```

This time, the output is just what we expected:

```
$ cat animals.txt
zebra
emu
```

Once you have a file containing a list of all the animals, you would probably want to sort it alphabetically, which simplifies searching for specific entries. To do this, you can use the sort command:

```
$ sort animals.txt
emu
zebra
```

The sorted entries are then displayed on the screen in alphabetical order. You can also redirect the sorted list into another file (called *sorted_animals.txt*) by using this command:

```
$ sort animals.txt > animals_sorted.txt
```

If you want to check that the sorting process actually worked, you could compare the contents of the *animals.txt* file line by line with the *sorted_animals.txt* file, by using the diff command:

```
$ diff animals.txt sorted_animals.txt
1d0
< zebra
2a2
> zebra
```

This result indicates that the first and second lines of the *animals.txt* and *sorted_animals.txt* files are different, as expected. If the sorting process had failed, the two files would have been identical, and no differences would have been reported by diff.

A related facility is the basename facility, which is designed to remove file extensions from a filename specified as an argument. This is commonly used to convert files with one extension to another extension. For example, imagine that you have a graphics file–conversion program that takes as its first argument the name of a source JPEG file, and takes the name of a target bitmap file. Somehow, you need to convert a filename of the form *filename.jpg* to a file of the form *filename.bmp*. You can do this with the basename command. In order to strip a file extension from an argument, you need to pass the filename and the extension as separate arguments to basename. For example, the command

```
$ basename maya.gif .gif
```

produces this output:

```
maya
```

If you want the .gif extension to be replaced by a .bmp extension, you could use the command

```
$ echo `basename maya.gif`.bmp
```

to produce the following output:

```
maya.bmp
```

Of course, you are not limited to extensions like .gif and .bmp. Also, keep in mind that the `basename` technique is entirely general—and because Solaris does not have mandatory filename extensions, you can use the `basename` technique for other purposes, such as generating a set of strings based on filenames.

Procedures

The following procedures are required for advanced text processing.

sed and awk

So far, we've looked at some fairly simple examples of text processing. However, the power of Solaris-style text processing lies with advanced tools like `sed` and `awk`. `sed` is a command-line editing program that can be used to perform search-and-replace operations on very large files, as well as to perform other kinds of noninteractive editing. `awk`, on the other hand, is a complete text-processing programming language that has a C-like syntax and can be used in conjunction with `sed` to program repetitive text-processing and editing operations on large files. These combined operations include double- and triple-spacing files, printing line numbers, left- and right-justifying text, performing field extraction and field substitution, and filtering on specific strings and pattern specifications. We examine some of these applications shortly.

To start this example, create a set of customer address records stored in a flat-text, tab-delimited database file called *test.dat*:

```
$ cat test.dat
Bloggs   Joe      24 City Rd       Richmond      VA     23227
Lee      Yat Sen  72 King St       Amherst MA    01002
Rowe     Sarah    3454 Capitol St  Los Angeles   CA     90074
Sakura   Akira    1 Madison Ave    New York      NY     10017
```

This is a fairly common type of record, storing a customer's surname, first name, street address, city, state, and ZIP code. For presentation, we can double-space the records in this file by redirecting the contents of the *test.dat* file through sed, with the *G* option:

```
$ sed G < test.dat
Bloggs   Joe      24 City Rd        Richmond          VA       23227

Lee      Yat Sen 72 King St         Amherst MA        01002

Rowe     Sarah    3454 Capitol St Los Angeles         CA       90074

Sakura   Akira    1 Madison Ave     New York          NY       10017
```

The power of sed lies in its ability to be used with pipe operators; thus, an action can literally be performed in conjunction with many other operations. For example, to insert double spacing and then remove it, simply invoke sed twice with the appropriate commands:

```
$ sed G < test.dat | sed 'n;d'
Bloggs   Joe      24 City Rd        Richmond          VA       23227
Lee      Yat Sen 72 King St         Amherst MA        01002
Rowe     Sarah    3454 Capitol St Los Angeles         CA       90074
Sakura   Akira    1 Madison Ave     New York          NY       10017
```

If you are printing reports, you'll probably be using line numbering at some point to uniquely identify records. You can generate line numbers dynamically for display by using sed:

```
$ sed '/./=' test.dat | sed '/./N; s/\n/ /'
1 Bloggs          Joe      24 City Rd      Richmond        VA       23227
2 Lee    Yat Sen 72 King St         Amherst MA     01002
3 Rowe   Sarah    3454 Capitol St Los Angeles    CA    90074
4 Sakura          Akira    1 Madison Ave    New York       NY       10017
```

You could also use *nl*. For large files, counting the number of lines is often useful. Although you can use the wc command for this purpose, you can also use sed in situations where wc is not available in the PATH environment variable:

```
$ cat test.dat | sed -n '$='
4
```

When you're printing databases for display, you might want to have comments and titles left-justified but have all records displayed with two blank spaces before each line. You can achieve this by using sed:

```
$ cat test.dat | sed 's/^/  /'
  Bloggs    Joe      24 City Rd        Richmond      VA        23227
  Lee    Yat Sen 72 King St       Amherst MA       01002
  Rowe   Sarah   3454 Capitol St Los Angeles    CA       90074
  Sakura     Akira    1 Madison Ave    New York         NY        10017
```

Imagine that due to some municipal reorganization, all cities currently located in CT were being reassigned to MA. sed would be the perfect tool to identify all instances of *CT* in the data file and replace them with *MA*:

```
$ cat test.dat | sed 's/MA/CT/g'
Bloggs  Joe      24 City Rd       Richmond        VA        23227
Lee       Yat Sen 72 King St      Amherst CT      01002
Rowe     Sarah   3454 Capitol St Los Angeles     CA        90074
Sakura  Akira    1 Madison Ave    New York        NY        10017
```

If a data file has been entered as a first-in, last-out (FILO) stack, you'll generally be reading records from the file from top to bottom. However, if the data file is to be treated as a last-in, first-out (LIFO) stack, reordering the records from the last to the first would be useful:

```
$ cat test.dat | sed '1!G;h;$!d'
Sakura  Akira    1 Madison Ave    New York        NY        10017
Rowe     Sarah   3454 Capitol St Los Angeles     CA        90074
Lee       Yat Sen 72 King St      Amherst MA      01002
Bloggs  Joe      24 City Rd       Richmond        VA        23227
```

Some data-hiding applications require that data be encoded in some way that is nontrivial for another application to detect a file's contents. One way to foil such programs is to reverse the character strings that comprise each record, which you can achieve by using sed:

```
$ cat test.dat | sed '/\n/!G;s/\(.\)\(.*\n\)/&\2\1/;//D;s/.//'
72232    AV       dnomhciR         dR ytiC 42        eoJ       sggolB
20010    AM       tsrehmA tS gniK 27        neS taY eeL
47009    AC       selegnA soL      tS lotipaC 4543 haraS     ewoR
71001    YN       kroY weN         evA nosidaM 1     arikA     arukaS
```

Some reporting applications might require that the first line of a file be processed before deletion. Although you can use the head command for this purpose, you can also use sed:

```
$ sed q < test.dat
Bloggs  Joe     24 City Rd      Richmond        VA      23227
```

If you want to print a certain number of lines, you can use sed to extract the first *q* lines:

```
$ sed 2q < test.dat
Bloggs  Joe     24 City Rd      Richmond        VA      23227
Lee     Yat Sen 72 King St      Amherst MA      01002
```

The grep command is often used to detect strings within files. However, you can also use sed for this purpose, as shown in the following example, where the string *CA* (representing California) is searched for:

```
$ cat test.dat | sed '/CA/!d'
Rowe    Sarah   3454 Capitol St Los Angeles     CA      90074
```

However, this is a fairly gross and inaccurate method, because *CA* might match a street address like "1 CALGARY Rd", or "23 Green CAPE". Thus, you need to use the field-extraction features of awk. In the following example, use awk to extract and print the fifth column in the data file, representing the state:

```
$ cat test.dat | awk 'BEGIN {FS = "\t"}{print $5}'
VA
MA
CA
NY
```

Note that the tab character (\t) is specified as the field delimiter. Now, if you combine the field-extraction capability of awk with the string-searching facility of sed, you should be able to print out a list of all occurrences of the state *CA*:

```
$ cat test.dat | awk 'BEGIN {FS = "\t"}{print $5}' | sed '/CA/!d'
CA
```

or, you could simply count the number of records that contain *CA* in the state field:

```
$ cat test.dat | awk 'BEGIN {FS = "\t"}{print $5}' | sed '/CA/!d' \
  | sed -n '$='
1
```

When you are producing reports, selectively displaying fields in a different order is useful. For example, although surname is typically used as a primary key, and is generally the first field, most reports would display the first name before the surname, which you can achieve by using awk:

```
$ cat test.dat | awk 'BEGIN {FS = "\t"}{print $2,$1}'
Joe Bloggs
Yat Sen Lee
Sarah Rowe
Akira Sakura
```

You can also split such reordered fields across different lines, and use different format specifiers. For example, the following script prints the first name and surname on one line, and the state on the following line. Such code is the basis of many mail-merge and bulk-printing programs.

```
$ cat test.dat | awk 'BEGIN {FS = "\t"}{print $2,$1,"\n"$5}'
Joe Bloggs
VA
Yat Sen Lee
MA
Sarah Rowe
CA
Akira Sakura
NY
```

Because awk is a complete programming language, it contains many common constructs, like *if/then/else* evaluations of logical states. These states can be used to test business logic cases. For example, in a mailing program, you could check the bounds of valid ZIP codes by determining whether the ZIP code lay within a valid range. For example, the following routine checks to see whether a ZIP code is less than 9999, and rejects it as invalid if it is greater than 9999:

```
$ cat test.dat | awk 'BEGIN {FS = "\t"}{print $2,$1}{if($6<9999) \
   {print "Valid zipcode"} else {print "Invalid zipcode"}}'
Joe Bloggs
Invalid zipcode
Yat Sen Lee
Valid zipcode
Sarah Rowe
Invalid zipcode
Akira Sakura
Invalid zipcode
```

PERL Programming

PERL stands for the Practical Extraction and Reporting Language, and was originally developed by Larry Wall. One of the things that developers really like about PERL is how quickly it is possible to write a full-blown application literally within a few minutes. When teamed up with the Common Gateway Interface (CGI) provided by Web servers such as Apache, PERL provides an easy way to write applications that can be executed on a server when requested by a client. This means that HTML pages can be generated dynamically by a PERL application and streamed to a client. Coupled with PERL's database access libraries (known as the PERL Database Interface, or DBI), PERL can be used to create multitiered applications, which is especially useful for system-management applications.

To create a PERL application, simply follow these five steps:

1. Create a text file by using the `vi` editor or `pico` editor.
2. Give the file executable permissions, by using the `chmod` command.
3. Instruct the shell to execute the PERL interpreter by including a directive in the first line of the script.
4. Write the PERL code.
5. Run the application.

As an example, let's create a PERL program that simply prints a line of text to the screen (for example, the string "Hello World!"). First, create a file called *helloworld.pl* by using the command `touch`:

```
$ touch helloworld.pl
```

Next, set the permissions on the file to be executable:

```
$ chmod +x helloworld.pl
```

Next, edit the file like this:

```
$ vi helloworld.pl
```

and insert a directive to the shell to execute the PERL interpreter contained in the */usr/ bin* directory (it may also be installed in */usr/local/bin*):

```
#!/usr/bin/perl
```

Next, insert the PERL code that actually constitutes the program:

```
print "Hello World\n";
```

Finally, save the file in the current directory and execute it on the command line:

```
$ ./helloworld.pl
Hello World!
```

Like most programming languages, PERL uses variables to store values that can change over time. These are represented as names with the $ symbol preceding them. So, for example, if you develop a program that prints the balance of a checking account, you might create and assign values to variables with names like *$date*, *$transaction*, *$amount*, and *$balance*. You can use variables to store just about any kind of information, including simple messages. A revision of the "Hello World" program code using a variable to store the message you want to print out would look like this:

```
#!/usr/bin/perl
$message="Hello World!";
print $message, "\n";
```

When you run this program, you get exactly the same output as before,

```
$ ./helloworld.pl
Hello World!
```

because the comma symbol here acts to concatenate the string contained in the *$message* variable and the `newline` command contained between the quotes directly after the comma symbol.

Variables in PERL do not necessarily just contain strings; they can also store numeric values, and PERL has a series of operators that you can use to perform arithmetic operations on variables. For example, you may want to perform a simple addition:

```
#!/usr/bin/perl
$val1=10;
$val2=20;
print $val1, " + ", $val2, " = ", $val1+$val2, "\n";
```

This program assigns the value of 10 to the variable *$val1*, and the value of 20 to the variable *$val2*. It then prints the addition expression that is going to be evaluated, and then actually performs the addition of *$val1* and *$val2* by using the + operator. Here's the result, which is unsurprising:

```
$ ./addition.pl
10 + 20 = 30
```

Other operators for PERL include the following:

−	Subtraction operator
*	Multiplication operator
/	Division operator
==	Equivalence operator
!=	Nonequivalence operator

<	Less-than operator, also called *le*
>	Greater-than operator, also called *gt*
<=	Less-than or equal-to operator, also known as *le*
>=	Greater-than or equal-to operator, also known as *ge*

So far, we've only seen the special escape character \n, which comes from C and means "newline character." It's also possible to use other escape characters from C, such as \t, which is the tab escape character. Let's have a look at the results of combining the tab escape character to produce tabulated output, and then examine other arithmetic operators from PERL:

```
#!/usr/bin/perl
$val1=10;
$val2=20;
print $val1, " + ", $val2, " =\t", $val1+$val2, "\n";
print $val1, " - ", $val2, " =\t", $val1-$val2, "\n";
print $val1, " * ", $val2, " =\t", $val1*$val2, "\n";
print $val1, " / ", $val2, " =\t", $val1/$val2, "\n";
```

Once again, the results are as expected, with the result column being separated from the expression by a tab character:

```
$ ./operators.pl
10 + 20 =        30
10 - 20 =       -10
10 * 20 =        200
10 / 20 =        0.5
```

Other escape characters commonly used in PERL include the following:

\a	Terminal bell
\b	Backspace
\f	Form feed
\r	Return
\\	Inserts \ as a character literal
\"	Inserts " as a character literal

In many cases, applications require that some kind of decision be taken on the basis of the current value of a specific variable. One way of making this decision is to use an *if/else* construct, which separates two blocks of code, one that is executed if a statement is true, and one that is executed if a statement is false. For example, imagine that you want to test whether a particular file exists. There are many reasons why you would want to do this. If a password file does not exist, for example, you might want to notify the system administrator, or if a shadowed password file does not exist, you might want to suggest that one be created for improved security. You can perform a file test by creating an expression using the *–e* operator, which tests for existence. Thus, an expression like this,

```
(-e /etc/passwd)
```

when evaluated, returns true if the file *letc/passwd* exists, and returns false if the file does not exist. Other file operators used in PERL include the following:

–B	Tests whether the file contains binary data
–d	Tests whether the file is a directory entry
–T	Tests whether the file contains text data
–w	Tests whether the file is writeable

To test for the existence of both the password file and the shadowed password file, you can create a program like this:

```
#!/usr/bin/perl
$passwdfile="/etc/passwd";
$shadowfile="/etc/shadow";
if (-e $passwdfile)
{
        print "Found standard Solaris password file\n";
}
else
{
        print "No standard Solaris password file found\n";

}
if (-e $shadowfile)
{
        print "Found shadow password file - good security move!\n";
}
else
{
        print "No shadow password file found!\n";
}
```

When executing the file on a Solaris 9 system, you should see output like this:

```
$ ./checkpasswords.pl
Found standard Solaris password file
Found shadow password file - good security move!
```

This kind of check could be added as a `cron` job for the root user, meaning that it could be executed on a regular basis as part of a security check. If any errors were detected, instead of writing a message to standard output, a mail message could be sent to the system administrator. Of course, password files are not the only kinds of files that might be included as part of a security check. Imagine the situation where a Trojan horse or virus has deleted one of the major shells or changed its permissions to render it inoperable. Thus, it is not adequate to just check for the existence of a file. You may also need to check other characteristics, such as being executable (–x), being readable (–r), and having a file size greater than zero (–s). Imagine that you want to check the status of the default Bourne Again Shell (/bin/bash): You can define a valid shell state as existing, being readable, being executable, and having a file size greater than zero, where logical AND is represented by the operator &&. If the shell does not have these attributes, you can generate a warning message. A simple program to achieve this could look like this:

```perl
#!/usr/bin/perl
$shell="/bin/bash";
if (-e $shell && -x $shell && -r $shell && -s $shell)
{
        print "Valid shell found\n";
}
else
{
        print "No valid shell found\n";
}
```

When executed, the program prints the following message:

```
$ ./checkbash.pl
Valid shell found
```

Other logical operators commonly used in PERL include the following:

//	Logical OR
!	Logical NOT
/	Bitwise OR
^	Bitwise XOR

Of course, there is more than one shell to be found on Solaris systems, and users are free to choose any one of them for their default login. You can modify the shell-checking program to verify the attributes of each of these shells by using an array that contains the name of each shell, rather than just creating a single scalar variable (e.g., *$shell* in the previous example). If you create an array called *@shell* that stores the names of all shells on the system, you can just iterate through the list using the `foreach` command, as shown in this program:

```perl
#!/usr/bin/perl
@shells=("/bin/sh", "/bin/csh", "/bin/sh", "/bin/tcsh", "/bin/zsh");
foreach $i (@shells)
{
        if (-e $i && -x $i && -r $i && -s $i)
        {
                print "Valid shell: ".$i."\n";
        }
        else
        {
                print "Invalid shell: ".$i."\n";
        }
}
```

When you execute the program on a Solaris system, you might see output like this:

```
Valid shell: /bin/sh
Valid shell: /bin/csh
Valid shell: /bin/sh
Valid shell: /bin/tcsh
Invalid shell: /bin/zsh
```

Oops—you can see that the first four shells check out okay, but a problem occurs with the */bin/zsh* shell. This means that a system administrator should check whether there is a problem. Again, this could be achieved by creating a `cron` job that runs once per day, and e-mails the administrator if a problem is detected. However, it may be much more useful to actually run this application through a Web browser, which is possible by using CGI. Few modifications are necessary to convert a PERL program to use the CGI: you simply need to print out a content-type header and then continue to print output as usual. For example, the earlier program could be restated in CGI terms as follows:

```perl
#!/usr/bin/perl
print "Content-type: text/html\n\n";
@shells=("/bin/sh", "/bin/csh", "/bin/sh", "/bin/tcsh", "/bin/zsh");
foreach $i (@shells)
{
        if (-e $i && -x $i && -r $i && -s $i)
        {
                print "<b>Valid shell:</b> ".$i."<br>\n";
        }
        else
```

```
        {
            print "<b>Invalid shell:</b> ".$i."<br>\n";
        }
    }
}
```

Command Reference

The following commands are used to process text.

sed

The standard options for `sed` are shown here:

–n	Prevents display of pattern space
–e filename	Executes the script contained in the file *filename*
–V	Displays the version number

awk

The standard POSIX options for `awk` are shown here:

–f filename	Where *filename* is the name of the `awk` file to process
–F field	Where *field* is the field separator
–v x=y	Where *x* a variable, and *y* is a value
–W lint	Turns on lint checking
–W lint-old	Uses old-style lint checking
–W traditional	Enforces traditional usage
–W version	Displays the version number

Summary

In this chapter, we have examined basic text editing and command-line processing, as well as more advanced text-processing utilities like `sed` and `awk`. As predecessors to PERL, `sed` and `awk` were widely used within shell scripts (see next chapter) to perform pattern analysis and matching.

PART II

## CHAPTER 7

Shells, Scripts, and Scheduling

Graphical user interfaces (GUIs) are an increasingly popular metaphor for interacting with computer systems, including the GNOME GUI included with Solaris 10. However, character user interfaces (CUIs) are a core feature of Solaris 10, because they provide a programmatic environment in which commands can be executed. Many operations on Solaris systems are performed in the context of a script, whether starting services at boot time or processing text to produce a report. Indeed, one of the key advantages of UNIX and UNIX-like environments over non-UNIX systems is the capability to combine large numbers of small commands in a CUI, in conjunction with pipes and filters, to create complex command sets that perform repetitive tasks that can be scheduled to run at a specific time.

Key Concepts

The following key concepts are required knowledge for understanding shells, scripts, and the scheduling of operations.

The Shell

All shells have a command prompt—the prompt usually tells the user which shell is currently being used, the user who owns the shell, and the current working directory. For example, the following prompt

```
#
```

usually indicates that the current user has superuser privileges. Shell prompts are completely customizable—the default for the Bourne Again Shell (bash) is just the name of the shell:

```
bash-2.05$
```

When you start a new terminal window from within the CDE, a shell is automatically spawned for you. This will be the same shell that is specified in your */etc/passwd* entry:

```
apache:x:1003:10:apache user:/usr/local/apache:/usr/local/bin/bash
```

In this case, the apache user has `bash` set as the default. To be a valid login shell, */usr/local/bin/bash* must also be included in the shells database (stored in the file */etc/shells*).

If the default shell prompt is not to your liking, you can easily change its format by setting two environment variables—*PS1* and *PS2*. I cover environment variables in the "Setting Environment Variables" section later in the chapter. For now, simply note that the Solaris environment space is similar to that found in Linux and Windows. For example, to set the prompt to display the username and host, you would use the following command in `bash`:

```
PS1='\u@\H> '; export PS1
```

The prompt displayed by the shell would then look like this:

```
oracle@db>
```

Many users like to display their current username, hostname, and current working directory, which can be set using the following command:

```
PS1='\u@\H:\w> '; export PS1
```

When executed, this shell prompt is changed to

```
oracle@db:/usr/local>
```

where *oracle* is the current user, *db* is the hostname, and */usr/local* is the current working directory. A list of different customization options for shell prompts is given in Table 7-1.

At the shell prompt, you enter commands in the order in which you intend for them to be executed. For example, to execute the `admintool` from the command prompt, you would type this command:

```
oracle@db:/usr/sbin> ./admintool
```

The ./ in this example indicates that the `admintool` application resides in the current directory—you could also execute the application using this command:

```
oracle@db:/usr/sbin> /usr/sbin/admintool
```

Setting	Description	Output
\a	ASCII beep character	"beep"
\d	Date string	Wed Sep 6
\h	Short hostname	www
\H	Full hostname	www.paulwatters.com
\s	Shell name	bash
\t	Current time (12-hour format)	10:53:44
\T	Current time (24-hour format)	10:53:55
\@	Current time (A.M./P.M. format)	10:54 A.M.
\u	Username	Root
\v	Shell version	2.05
\W	Shell version with revision	2.05.0
\!	Command history number	223
\$	Privilege indicator	#
\u\$	Username and privilege indicator	root#
\u:\!:\$	Username, command history number, and privilege indicator	root:173:#

TABLE 7-1   Environment Variable Settings for Different Command Prompts Under bash

The admintool window would then appear on the desktop, assuming that you're using a terminal window to execute a shell. Once the shell is executing a command in the "foreground" (like admintool), no other commands can be executed. However, by sending a command process into the "background," you can execute more than one command in the shell. You can send a process into the background immediately by adding an ampersand (&) to the end of the command line:

```
oracle@db:/usr/sbin> ./admintool &
```

Once a command has been executed, you can suspend it by pressing CTRL-Z, and then send it into the background by using the command bg:

```
oracle@db:/usr/sbin> ./admintool
^Z[1] + Stopped (SIGTSTP)          admintool
oracle@db:/usr/sbin> bg
[1] admintool&
oracle@db:/usr/sbin>
```

The application name is displayed along with the job number

You can bring an application back into the foreground by using the following command:

```
oracle@db:/usr/sbin> fg
admintool
```

This brings job number 1 back into the foreground by default. However, if you had multiple jobs suspended, you would need to specify a job number with the `fg` command:

```
oracle@db:/usr/local/bin> ./netscape
^Z[2] + Stopped (SIGTSTP)           netscape
oracle@db:/usr/sbin> bg
[2] netscape&
oracle@db:/usr/sbin> fg
netscape
```

You can obtain a list of all running jobs in the current shell by typing the following command:

```
$ jobs
[2] +  Running                  ./netscape&
[1] -  Running                  admintool&
```

Procedures

The following procedures are required knowledge for understanding the shell and how operations can be scripted and scheduled.

Writing Shell Scripts

Shell scripts are combinations of shell and user commands that are executed in noninteractive mode for a wide variety of purposes. Whether you require a script that converts a set of filename extensions, a script that alerts the system administrator by e-mail that disk space is running low, or a script that performs some other function, you can use shell scripts. The commands that you place inside a shell script should normally execute in the interactive shell mode as well, making it easy to take apart large scripts and debug them line by line in your normal login shell. In this section, we examine only shell scripts that run under `bash`—although many of the scripts will work without modification using other shells, it is always best to check the syntax chart of your own shell before attempting to run the scripts in another shell.

Processing Shell Arguments

A common goal of writing shell scripts is to make them as general as possible so that you can use them with many different kinds of input. Fortunately, shell scripts are able to make use of command-line parameters, which are numerically ordered arguments that are accessible from within a shell script. For example, a shell script to move files from one computer to another computer might require parameters for the source host, the destination host, and the name of the file to be moved. Obviously, you want to be able to pass these arguments to the script, rather than hard-wiring them into the code. This is one advantage of shell scripts (and PERL programs) over compiled languages like C: scripts are easy to modify, and their operation is completely transparent to the user.

Arguments to shell scripts can be identified by a simple scheme—the command executed is referred to with the argument $0, with the first parameter identified as $1, the second parameter identified as $2, and so on, up to a maximum of nine parameters. Thus, a script executed with these parameters

```
$ display_hardware.sh cdrom scsi ide
```

would refer internally to *cdrom* as $1, *scsi* as $2, and *ide* as $3.

Let's see how arguments can be used effectively within a script to process input parameters. The first script simply counts the number of lines in a file (using the wc command), specified by a single command-line argument ($1). To begin with, create an empty script file:

```
$ touch count_lines.sh
```

Next, set the permissions on the file to be executable:

```
$ chmod +x count_lines.sh
```

Next, edit the file

```
$ vi count_lines.sh
```

and add the appropriate code:

```
#!/bin/bash
echo "Number of lines in file " $1
wc -l $1
```

The script takes the first command-line argument, prints the number of lines, and then exits. Run the script with the command

```
$ ./count_lines.sh /etc/group
```

which gives the following output:

```
Number of lines in file /etc/group
43
```

PART II

Although the individual activity of scripts is quite variable, the procedure of creating the script file, setting its permissions, editing its contents, and executing it on the command line remains the same across scripts. Of course, you may want to make the script available only to certain users or groups for execution. You can enable this by using the chmod command and explicitly adding or removing permissions when necessary.

Testing File Properties

One of the assumptions that we made in the previous script was that the file specified by $1 actually exists; if it doesn't exist, we obviously cannot count the number of lines it contains. If the script is running from the command line, we can safely debug it and interpret any error conditions that arise (such as a file not existing or having incorrect permissions). However, if a script is intended to run as a scheduled job (using the cron or at facility), debugging it in real time is impossible. Thus, writing scripts that can handle error conditions gracefully and intelligently is often useful, rather than leaving administrators wondering why a job didn't produce any output when it was scheduled to run.

The number one cause of run-time execution errors is the incorrect setting of file permissions. Although most users remember to set the executable bit on the script file itself, they often neglect to include error checking for the existence of data files that are used by the script. For example, if you want to write a script that checks the syntax of a configuration file (like the Apache configuration file, *httpd.conf*), you need to check that the file actually exists before performing the check—otherwise, the script may not return an error message, and you may erroneously assume that the script file is correctly configured.

Fortunately, bash makes it easy to test for the existence of files by using the (conveniently named) test facility. In addition to testing for file existence, the test facility can determine whether files have read, write, and execute permissions, prior to any read, write, or execute file access being attempted by the script. The following example revises the previous script that counted the number of lines in a file. The script first verifies whether the target file (specified by $1) exists. If a file exists, the command should count the number of lines in the target file as before:

```
#!/bin/bash
if test -a $1 then
echo "Number of lines in file " $1
wc -l $1
else
        echo "The file" $1 "does not exist"
fi
```

Otherwise, an error message will be printed. If the *etc/group* file does not exist, for example, you'd really want to know about it:

```
bash-2.05# ./count_lines.sh /etc/group
The file /etc/group does not exist
```

There may be some situations in which you want to test another file property. For example, the */etc/shadow* password database must be readable only by the superuser. Thus, if you execute a script to check whether the */etc/shadow* file is readable by a nonprivileged user, it should not return a positive result. You can check file readability by using the *–r* option rather than the *–a* option. Here's the revised script:

```
#!/bin/bash
if test -r $1 then
echo "I can read the file " $1
else
        echo "I can't read the file" $1
fi
```

You can also test the following file permissions using the `test` facility:

–b	File is a special block file
–c	File is a special character file
–d	File is a directory
–f	File is a normal file
–h	File is a symbolic link
–p	File is a named pipe
–s	File has nonzero size
–w	File is writeable by the current user
–x	File is executable by the current user

Looping

All programming languages have the capability to repeat blocks of code for a specified number of iterations. This makes performing repetitive actions very easy for a well-written program. The Bourne shell is no exception. It features a *for* loop, which repeats the actions of a code block for a specified number of iterations, as defined by a set of consecutive arguments to the `for` command. It also features a while loop and an until loop. In addition, an iterator is available within the code block to indicate which of the sequence of iterations that will be performed is currently being performed. If that sounds a little complicated, take a look at the following concrete example, which uses a *for* loop to generate a set of filenames. These filenames are then tested using the `test` facility, to determine whether they exist.

```
#!/bin/bash
for i in apple orange lemon kiwi guava
do
        DATAFILE=$i".dat"
        echo "Checking" $DATAFILE
        if test -s $FILENAME
```

```
        then
                echo "$DATAFILE "has zero-length"
        else
                echo $FILENAME "is OK"
        fi
done
```

The *for* loop is repeated five times, with the variable *$i* taking on the values *apple, orange, lemon, kiwi,* and *guava*. Thus, on the first iteration, when *$i=apple*, the shell interprets the *for* loop in the following way:

```
FILENAME="apple.dat"
echo "Checking apple.dat"
if test -s apple.dat
then
echo "apple.dat has zero-length"
else
echo "apple.dat is OK"
fi
```

If you run this script in a directory with files of zero length, you would expect to see the following output:

```
$ ./zero_length_check.sh
Checking apple.dat
apple.dat is zero-length
Checking orange.dat
orange.dat is zero-length
Checking lemon.dat
lemon.dat is zero-length
Checking kiwi.dat
kiwi.dat is zero-length
Checking guava.dat
guava.dat is zero-length
```

However, if you entered data into each of the files, you should see them receive the OK message:

```
$ ./zero_length_check.sh
Checking apple.dat
apple.dat is OK
Checking orange.dat
orange.dat is OK
Checking lemon.dat
lemon.dat is OK
Checking kiwi.dat
kiwi.dat is OK
```

```
Checking guava.dat
guava.dat is OK
```

Using Shell Variables

In the previous example, you assigned different values to a shell variable, which was used to generate filenames for checking. It is common to modify variables within scripts by using export, and to attach error codes to instances where variables are not defined within a script. This is particularly useful if a variable that is available within a user's interactive shell is not available in their noninteractive shell. For example, you can create a script called *show_errors.sh* that returns an error message if the *PATH* variable is not set:

```
#!/bin/bash
echo ${PATH:?PATH_NOT_SET}
```

Of course, because the *PATH* variable is usually set, you should see output similar to the following:

```
$ ./path_set.sh
/sbin:/bin:/usr/games/bin:/usr/sbin:/root/bin:/usr/local/bin:
/usr/local/sbin/:/usr/bin:
/usr/X11R6/bin: /usr/games:/opt/gnome/bin:/opt/kde/bin
```

However, if *PATH* was not set, you would see the following error message:

```
./show_errors.sh: PATH_NOT_SET
```

You can use system-supplied error messages as well, by not specifying the optional error string:

```
$ ./path_set.sh
#!/bin/bash
echo ${PATH:?}
```

Thus, if the *PATH* variable is not set, you would see the following error message:

```
$ ./path_set.sh
./showargs: PATH: parameter null or not set
```

You can also use the numbered shell variables (*$1, $2, $3*, and so on) to capture the space-delimited output of certain commands, and perform actions based on the value of these variables, using the set command. For example, the command

```
$ set `ls`
```

sequentially assigns each of the fields within the returned directory listing to a numbered shell variable. For example, if the directory listing contains the entries

```
apple.dat    guava.dat    kiwi.dat    lemon.dat    orange.dat
```

you could retrieve the values of these filenames by using the echo command:

```
$ echo $1
apple.dat
$ echo $2
guava.dat
$ echo $3
kiwi.dat
$ echo $4
lemon.dat
$ echo $5
orange.dat
```

This approach is very useful if your script needs to perform some action based on only one component of the date. For example, if you want to create a unique filename to assign to a compressed file, you could combine the values of each variable, with a .Z extension, to produce a set of strings like *orange.dat.Z*.

Scheduling Jobs

Many system administration tasks need to be performed on a regular basis. For example, log files for various applications need to be archived nightly, and a new log file needs to be created. Often, a short script is created to perform this, by following these steps:

1. Kill the daemon affected, using the kill command.
2. Compress the logfile, using the gzip or compress command.
3. Use the time command to change the logfile name to include a timestamp, so that it can be distinguish from other logfiles.
4. Move the logfile to an archive directory, using the mv command.
5. Create a new logfile by using the touch command.
6. Restart the daemon by calling the appropriate */etc/init.d* script.

Instead of the administrator having to execute these commands interactively at midnight, they can be scheduled to run daily using the cron scheduling command. Alternatively, if a job needs to be run only once at a particular time, like bringing a new Web site online at 7 A.M. one particular morning, then you can use the at scheduler. In the next section, we look at the advantages and disadvantages of each scheduling method.

The at Command

You can schedule a single system event for execution at a specified time by using the at command. The jobs are specified by files in the */var/spool/cron/atjobs* directory, while configuration is managed by the file */etc/cron.d/at.deny*. The job can either be a single command or refer to a script that contains a set of commands. Imagine that you want to start up sendmail at a particular time. Perhaps some scheduled maintenance of the network infrastructure is scheduled to occur until 8:30 A.M. tomorrow morning, but you really don't feel like logging in early and starting up sendmail (you've switched it off completely during the outage to prevent users from filling the queue). The following adds to the queue a job that is scheduled to run at 8:40 A.M., giving the network guys a ten-minute window:

```
bash-2.05$ at 0840
at> /usr/lib/sendmail -bd
at> <EOT>
commands will be executed using /bin/ksh
job 954715200.a at Mon Apr  3 08:40:00 2004
```

After submitting a job using at, you can check that the job is properly scheduled by checking whether an atjob has been created:

```
bash-2.05$ cd /var/spool/cron/atjobs
bash-2.05$ ls -l
total 8
-r-Sr--r--   1 paul      other       3701 Apr  3 08:35 954715200.a
```

The file exists, which is a good start. Now check that it contains the appropriate commands to run the job:

```
bash-2.05$ cat 954715200.a
: at job
: jobname: stdin
: notify by mail: no
export PWD; PWD='/home/paul'
export _; _='/usr/bin/at'
cd /home/paul
umask 22
ulimit unlimited
/usr/lib/sendmail -bd
```

This looks good. After 8:40 A.M. the next morning, the command should have executed at the appropriate time, and some output should have been generated and sent to you as a mail message. Take a look at what the message contains:

```
From paul Sat Apr  1 08:40:00 2004
Date: Sat Apr  1 2000 08:40:00 +1000 (EST)
From: paul <paul>
To: paul
Subject: Output from "at" job
Your "at" job on tango
"/var/spool/cron/atjobs/954715200.a"
produced the following output:
/bin/ksh[5]: sendmail: 501 Permission denied
```

Oops! The job needs to be submitted as root: normal users don't have permission to start sendmail in the background daemon mode. You would need to submit this job as root to be successful.

The cron Command

An at job executes only once at a particular time. However, cron is much more flexible, because you can schedule system events to execute repetitively, at regular intervals, by using the crontab command. Each user on the system can have a *crontab* file, which allows them to schedule multiple events to occur at multiple times, on multiple dates. The jobs are specified by files in the */var/spool/cron/cronjobs* directory, while configuration is managed by the files */etc/cron.d/cron.allow* and */etc/cron.d/cron.deny*.

To check your own *crontab*, you can use the crontab -l command:

```
bash-2.05$ crontab -l root
10 3 * * 0,4 /etc/cron.d/logchecker
10 3 * * 0   /usr/lib/newsyslog
15 3 * * 0 /usr/lib/fs/nfs/nfsfind
1 2 * * * [ -x /usr/sbin/rtc ] && /usr/sbin/rtc -c > /dev/null 2>&1
30 3 * * * [ -x /usr/lib/gss/gsscred_clean ] && /usr/lib/gss/gsscred_clean
```

This is the standard *crontab* generated by Solaris for root, and it performs tasks like checking if the cron logfile is approaching the system *ulimit* at 3:10 A.M. on Sundays and Thursdays, creating a new system log at 3:10 A.M. only on Sundays, and reconciling time differences at 2:01 A.M. every day of the year.

The six fields in the *crontab* stand for the following:

- Minutes, in the range 0–59
- Hours, in the range 0–23
- Days of the month, in the range 1–31

- Months of the year, in the range 1–12
- Days of the week, in the range 0–6, starting with Sundays
- The command to execute

If you want to add or delete an entry from your *crontab*, you can use the crontab -e command. This starts up your default editor (vi on the command line, textedit in CDE), in which you can make changes interactively. After saving your job, you then need to run crontab by itself to make the changes.

Examples

The following examples demonstrate how to use the shell.

Setting Environment Variables

Environment variables are used to store information in a form that is accessible to commands within the shell and other applications that are spawned from the shell. You can obtain a list of all environment variables that have been set in a shell by using the following command:

```
BASH=/bin/bash
BASH_VERSINFO=([0]="2" [1]="05b" [2]="7" [3]="1" [4]="release"
[5]="sparc-sun-solaris2.10")
BASH_VERSION='2.05b.7(1)-release'
COLUMNS=80
DIRSTACK=()
EUID=1001
GROUPS=()
HISTFILE=/export/home/pwatters/.bash_history
HISTFILESIZE=500
HISTSIZE=500
HOME=/export/home/pwatters
HOSTNAME=sakura
HOSTTYPE=sparc
HZ=100
IFS=$' \t\n'
LC_COLLATE=en_US.ISO8859-1
LC_CTYPE=en_US.ISO8859-1
LC_MESSAGES=C
LC_MONETARY=en_US.ISO8859-1
LC_NUMERIC=en_US.ISO8859-1
LC_TIME=en_US.ISO8859-1
```

Although this seems to be a lot of shell variables, the most significant ones include the following:

BASH	The path to the shell on the file system
COLUMNS	The columns width for the terminal
DISPLAY	The display variable that is used for X11 graphics
HOME	The default home directory for the user
HOSTNAME	The hostname of the current system
LD_LIBRARY_PATH	The path to system and user libraries
LOGNAME	The username of the shell owner
MANPATH	The path to the system manuals
NNTPSERVER	The hostname of the NNTP server
PATH	The path that is searched to find applications where no absolute path is specified on the command line
PPID	The parent process ID
TERM	The terminal type (usually VT100)
UID	The user ID
WINDOWMANAGER	The name of the X11 window manager

The values of all shell variables can be set on the command line by using the `export` command. For example, if you want to set the terminal type to VT220, you use this command:

```
$ TERM=vt220; export TERM
```

Command Reference

The following commands are commonly used to get the most from the shell. Help for each of these commands is usually available through the man facility or the GNU info command.

Source (.)

The source command, represented as a single dot, reads in and executes the lines of a shell script. The format of this command is

```
. file
```

where *file* is a valid filename that contains a Bourne shell script. The first line should contain a directive that points to the absolute location of the shell:

```
#!/bin/sh
```

You also can execute Bourne shell scripts by calling them with a new shell invocation, or by calling them directly if the executable bit is set for the executing user. For example, the following three commands would each execute the script file *myscript.sh*:

```
$ . myscript.sh
$ sh myscript.sh
$ ./myscript.sh
```

However, only the source command (.) preserves any environment variable settings made in the script.

basename

The basename command strips a filename of its extension. The format of this command is

```
basename filename.ext
```

where *filename.ext* is a valid filename like *mydata.dat*. The basename command parses *mydata.dat*, and extracts *mydata*. Because file extensions are not mandatory in Solaris, this command is very useful for processing files copied from Windows or MS-DOS.

cat

The cat command prints out the contents of the file, without any special screen-control features like scrolling backward or forward in a file. The format of this command is as follows:

```
cat filename
```

To display the *groups* database, for example, you could run the following command:

```
$ cat /etc/group
root::0:root
other::1:
bin::2:root,bin,daemon
sys::3:root,bin,sys,adm
adm::4:root,adm,daemon
uucp::5:root,uucp
mail::6:root
tty::7:root,tty,adm
lp::8:root,lp,adm
nuucp::9:root,nuucp
staff::10:
```

cd

The `cd` command changes the current working directory to a new directory location, which you can specify in either absolute or relative terms. The format of this command is as follows:

```
cd directory
```

For example, if the current working directory is */usr/local*, and you type the command

```
cd bin
```

the new working directory would be */usr/local/bin*. However, if you type the command

```
cd /bin
```

the new working directory would be */bin*. For interactive use, relative directory names are often used; however, scripts should always contain absolute directory references. Typing **cd** by itself takes the user to their home directory.

chgrp

The `chgrp` command modifies the default group membership of a file. The format of this command is

```
chgrp group file
```

where *group* is a valid group name, defined in the groups database (*/etc/groups*), and *file* is a valid filename. Because permissions can be assigned to individual users or groups of users, assigning a nondefault group membership can be useful for users who need to exchange data with members of different organizational units (e.g., the Webmaster who swaps configuration files with the database administrator and also exchanges HTML files with Web developers). Only the file owner or the superuser can modify the group membership of a file.

date

The `date` command prints the current system date and time. The format of this command is as follows:

```
date
```

The default output for the command is of this form:

```
Tuesday February  12 13:43:23 EST 2002
```

You can also modify the output format by using a number of parameters corresponding to days, months, hours, minutes, and so on. For example, the command

```
date '+Current Date: %d/%m/%y%nCurrent Time:%H:%M:%S'
```

produces the following output:

```
Current Date: 06/09/00
Current Time:13:45:43
```

grep

The grep command searches a file for a string (specified by *string*) and prints the line wherever a match is found. The format of this command is as follows:

```
grep string file
```

The grep command is very useful for interpreting log files, where you just want to display a line that contains a particular code (e.g., a Web server logfile can be grepped for the string 404, which indicates a page was not found).

head

The head command displays the first page of a file. The format of this command is as follows:

```
head filename
```

The head command is very useful for examining the first few lines of a very long file. For example, to display the first page of the name service switch configuration file (*/etc/nsswitch.conf*), you could use this command:

```
$ head /etc/nsswitch.conf
# /etc/nsswitch.nisplus:
# An example file that could be copied over to /etc/nsswitch.conf; it
# uses NIS+ (NIS Version 3) in conjunction with files.
# "hosts:" and "services:" in this file are used only if the
# /etc/netconfig file has a "-" for nametoaddr_libs of "inet" transports.
# the following two lines obviate the "+" entry in /etc/passwd and /etc/group.
```

less

The less command prints a file on the screen, and it allows you to search backward and forward through the file. The format of this command is as follows:

```
less filename
```

To scroll through the contents of the system log configuration file (*/etc/syslog.conf*), you would use the following command:

```
less /etc/syslog.conf
#ident  "@(#)syslog.conf       1.4     96/10/11 SMI"    /* SunOS 5.0 */
# Copyright (c) 1991-1993, by Sun Microsystems, Inc.
# syslog configuration file.
# This file is processed by m4 so be careful to quote ('') names
# that match m4 reserved words.  Also, within ifdef's, arguments
# containing commas must be quoted.
*.notice                                    @loghost
*.err;kern.notice;auth.notice               /dev/console
*.err;kern.debug;daemon.notice;mail.crit;daemon.info   /var/adm/
messages
*.alert;kern.err;daemon.err                 operator
*.alert                                     root
```

The `less` command has a number of commands that can be issued interactively. For example, to move forward one window, just type **F**, or to move back one window, just type **B**. `less` also supports searching with the `/pattern` command.

ls

The `ls` command prints the names of files contained in the directory *dir* (by default, the contents of the current working directory are displayed). The format of the command is

```
ls directory
```

where *directory* is the name of the directory whose contents you wish to list. For example, to list the contents of the */var/adm* directory, which contains a number of system logs, you could use the following command:

```
$ ls /var/adm
aculog        log            messages.1    passwd      utmp      wtmp
ftpmessages   messages       messages.2    spellhist   utmpx     wtmpx
lastlog       messages.0     messages.3    sulog       vold.log
```

mkdir

The `mkdir` command makes new directory entries. The format of this command is as follows:

```
mkdir directory
```

For example, if the current working directory is */sbin*, and you type the command

```
mkdir oracle
```

the new directory would be */sbin/oracle*. However, if you type the command

```
mkdir /oracle
```

the new directory would be */oracle*. For interactive use, relative directory names are often used; however, scripts should always contain absolute directory references.

more

The more command prints the contents of a file, like the less command, but just permits the scrolling forward through a file. The format of this command is as follows:

```
more filename
```

To scroll through the contents of the disk device configuration file (*/etc/format.dat*), you would use the following command:

```
more /etc/format.dat
#pragma ident    "@(#)format.dat 1.21    98/01/24 SMI"
# Copyright (c) 1991,1998 by Sun Microsystems, Inc.
# All rights reserved.
# Data file for the 'format' program.  This file defines the known
# disks, disk types, and partition maps.
# This is the list of supported disks for the Emulex MD21 controller.
disk_type = "Micropolis 1355" \
        : ctlr = MD21 \
        : ncyl = 1018 : acyl = 2 : pcyl = 1024 : nhead = 8 : nsect = 34 \
        : rpm = 3600 : bpt = 20832
```

The more command has a number of subcommands that can be issued interactively. For example, to move forward one window, just press the SPACEBAR, or to move forward one line, just press ENTER. The more command also supports searching with the /pattern command.

pwd

The pwd command prints the current working directory in absolute terms. The format of the command is as follows:

```
pwd
```

For example, if you change the directory to /etc and issue the pwd command, you would see the following result:

```
$ cd /etc
$ pwd
/etc
```

rmdir

The rmdir command deletes a directory. However, the directory concerned must be empty for the rmdir command to be successful. The format of this command is as follows:

```
rmdir directory
```

For example, if the current working directory is /usr/local, and you want to remove the directory oldstuff, you would use this command:

```
rmdir oldstuff
```

However, you could use the command

```
rmdir /usr/local/oldstuff
```

to remove the directory as well. For interactive use, relative directory names are often used; however, scripts should always contain absolute directory references.

tail

The tail command displays the last page of a file. The format of this command is as follows:

```
tail filename
```

The tail command is very useful for examining the last few lines of a very long file. For example, to display the first page of a Web logfile (/usr/local/apache/logs/access_log), you could use the following command:

```
$ tail /usr/local/apache/logs/access_log
192.168.205.238 - - [12/Feb/2002:09:35:59 +1000]
  "GET /images/picture10.gif HTTP/1.1" 200 53
192.168.205.238 - - [12/Feb/2002:09:35:59 +1000]
  "GET /images/ picture1.gif HTTP/1.1" 200 712
192.168.205.238 - - [12/Feb/2002:09:35:59 +1000]
  "GET /images/ picture5.gif HTTP/1.1" 200 7090
192.168.205.238 - - [12/Feb/2002:09:35:59 +1000]
  "GET /images/ picture66.gif HTTP/1.1" 200 997
```

```
192.168.205.238 - - [12/Feb/2002:09:35:59 +1000]
  "GET /images/ picture49.gif HTTP/1.1" 200 2386
192.168.205.238 - - [12/Feb/2002:09:36:09 +1000]
  "GET /servlet/SimpleServlet HTTP/1.1" 200 10497
```

The `tail` command also has an option that allows you to continuously monitor all new entries made to a file. This is very useful for monitoring a live service such as Apache, where you need to observe any error made in real time. The format for this command is as follows:

```
tail -f filename
```

Summary

In this chapter, we have examined how to manage files and directories, and how to work with the shell. In addition, we have examined the commands used to write shell scripts, and other commonly used shell commands. Since the shell is the administrator's interface to the operating system, it's important that you become familiar with shell commands and procedures.

CHAPTER 8

Process Management

rocesses lie at the heart of modern multiuser operating systems, providing the ability to run multiple applications and services concurrently on top of the kernel. In user terms, process management is a central feature of using a single login shell to start and stop multiple jobs running concurrently, often suspending their execution while waiting for input. Solaris 10 provides many tools for process management. This chapter highlights the new process-management tools and command formats, and discusses the innovative /*proc* file systems and associated tools that allow administrators to deal with "zombie" processes.

Key Concepts

One of the appealing characteristics of Solaris and other UNIX-like systems is that applications can execute (or *spawn*) other applications: after all, user shells are nothing more than applications themselves. A shell can spawn another shell or application, which can spawn another shell or application, and so on. Instances of applications, such as the Sendmail mail transport agent or the Telnet remote access application, can be uniquely identified as individual processes and are associated with a unique process identifier (PID), which is an integer.

You may be wondering why PIDs are not content addressable—that is, why the Sendmail process cannot be identified as simply Sendmail. Such a scheme would be quite sensible if it were impossible to execute multiple, independent instances of the same application (like early versions of the MacOS). However, Solaris allows the same user or different users to concurrently execute the same application independently, which means that an independent identifier is required for each process. This also means that each PID is related to a user identifier (UID) and to that user's group identifier (GID). The UID in this case can be either the *real* UID of the user who executed the process or the *effective* UID if the file executed is *setUID*. Similarly, the GID in this case can be either the *real* GID, which is the GID that identifies the group to which the user who executed the process belongs, or the *effective* GID if the file executed is *setGID*. When an application can be executed as *setUID* and *setGID*, other users can execute that application as the user who owns the file. This means that setting a file as *setGID* for root can be dangerous in some situations, albeit necessary.

An application, such as a shell, can spawn another application by using the system call `system()` in a C program. This is expensive performance-wise, however, because a new shell process is spawned in addition to the target application. An alternative is to use the `fork()` system call, which spawns child processes directly, with applications executed using `exec()`. Each child process is linked back to its parent process: if the parent process exits, the parent process automatically reverts to PID 1, which exits when the system is shut down or rebooted.

In this section, you'll look at ways to determine which processes are currently running on your system and how to examine process lists and tables to determine what system resources are being used by specific processes.

The main command used to list commands is `ps`, which is highly configurable and has many command-line options. These options, and the command format, use System V–style parameters, like `ps -eaf`. However, whereas `ps` takes only a snapshot of the current process list, many administrators find that they need to interactively monitor processes on systems that have a high load so that they can kill processes that are consuming too much memory, or at least assign them a lower execution priority. One popular process-monitoring tool is `top`, which is described later in this chapter in the section "Using the top Program."

Sending Signals

Since all processes are identifiable by a single PID, the PID can be used to manage that process, by means of a *signal*. Signals can be sent to other processes in C programs using the `signal()` function, or they can be sent directly from within the shell. Solaris supports a number of standard signal types that can be used as a means of interprocess communication.

A common use for signals is to manage user applications that are launched from a shell. For example, you can send to an application running in the foreground a "suspend" signal by pressing CTRL-Z at any time. To run this application in the background in the C-shell, for example, you would need to type **bg** at the command prompt. A unique background job number is then assigned to the job. To bring the process back to the foreground, you type **fg** *n*, where *n* is its job number. You can run as many applications as you like in the background.

In the following example, `httpd` is run in the foreground. When you press CTRL-Z, the process is suspended, and when you type **bg**, it is assigned the background process number 1. You can then execute other commands, such as `ls`, while `httpd` runs in the background. When you then type **fg**, the process is brought once again into the foreground.

```
client 1% httpd
^z
Suspended
client 2% bg
[1] httpd&
```

```
client 3% ls
httpd.conf  access.conf  srm.conf
client 4% fg
```

A useful command is the `kill` command, which is used to send signals directly to any process on the system. It is usually called with two parameters—the signal type and the PID. For example, if you have made changes to the configuration file for the Internet super daemon, you must send a signal to the daemon to tell it to reread its configuration file. Note that you don't need to restart the daemon itself: this is one of the advantages of a process-based operating system that facilitates interprocess communication. If `inetd` had the PID 167, typing

```
# kill -1 167
```

would force `inetd` to reread its configuration file and update its internal settings. The *–1* parameter stands for the SIGHUP signal, which means "hang up." However, imagine a situation in which you want to switch off `inetd` temporarily to perform a security check. You can send a `kill` signal to the process by using the *–9* parameter (the SIGKILL signal):

```
# kill -9 167
```

Although SIGHUP and SIGKILL are the most commonly used signals in the shell, several others are used by programmers and are defined in the *signal.h* header file. Another potential consequence of sending a signal to a process is that instead of "hanging up" or "being killed," the process could exit and dump a *core file,* which is a memory image of the process to which the message was sent. This result is useful for debugging, although too many core files will quickly fill up your file system! You can always obtain a list of available signals to the `kill` command by passing the *–l* option:

```
$ kill -l
HUP INT QUIT ILL TRAP ABRT EMT FPE KILL BUS SEGV SYS PIPE
ALRM TERM USR1 USR2 CLD PWR WINCH URG POLL STOP TSTP CONT
TTIN TTOU VTALRM PROF XCPU XFSZ WAITING LWP FREEZE THAW
RTMIN RTMIN+1 RTMIN+2 RTMIN+3 RTMAX-3 RTMAX-2 RTMAX-1
RTMAX
```

Procedures

The following procedures are commonly used to manage processes.

Listing Processes

You can use the `ps` command to list all currently active processes on the local system. By default, `ps` prints the processes belonging to the user who issues the `ps` command:

```
$ ps
PID TTY       TIME CMD
 29081 pts/8    0:00 ksh
```

The columns in the default ps list are the process identifier (PID), the terminal from which the command was executed (TTY), the CPU time consumed by the process (TIME), and the actual command that was executed (CMD), including any command-line options passed to the program.

Alternatively, if you would like more information about the current user's processes, you can add the –f parameter:

```
$ ps -f
    UID     PID    PPID   C STIME    TTY        TIME CMD
    pwatters 29081 29079  0 10:40:30 pts/8      0:00 /bin/ksh
```

Again, the PID, TTY, CPU time, and command are displayed. However, the UID is also displayed, as is the PID of the parent process identifier (PPID), along with the starting time of the process (STIME). In addition, a deprecated column (C) is used to display processor utilization. To obtain the maximum detail possible, you can also use the –l option, which means "long"—and long it certainly is, as shown in this example:

```
$ ps -l
 F S  UID    PID   PPID C PRI NI     ADDR   SZ    WCHAN TTY     TIME CMD
 8 S 6049  29081  29079 0  51 20 e11b4830 372 e11b489c pts/8  0:00 ksh
 8 R 6049  29085  29081 0  51 20 e101b0d0 512          pts/8  0:00 bash
```

Here, you can see the following:

- The flags (F) associated with the processes
- The state (S) of the processes (29081 is sleeping, S, 29085 is running, R)
- The process identifier (29081 and 29085)
- Parent process identifier (29079 and 29081)
- Processor utilization (deprecated)
- Process priority (PRI), which is 51
- Nice value (NI), which is 20
- Memory address (ADDR), which is expressed in hex (e11b4830 and e101b0d0)
- Size (SZ), in kilobytes, which is 372KB and 512KB
- The memory address for sleeping process events (WCHAN), which is e11b489c for PID 29081
- CPU time used (TIME)
- The command executed (CMD)

If you're a system administrator, you're probably not interested in the status of just your own processes; you probably want details about all or some of the processes actively running on the system, and you can do this in many ways. You can generate a process list using the *–A* or the *–e* option, for example, and either of these lists information for all processes currently running on the machine:

```
# ps -A
   PID TTY       TIME CMD
     0 ?         0:00 sched
     1 ?         0:01 init
     2 ?         0:01 pageout
     3 ?         9:49 fsflush
   258 ?         0:00 ttymon
   108 ?         0:00 rpcbind
   255 ?         0:00 sac
    60 ?         0:00 devfseve
    62 ?         0:00 devfsadm
   157 ?         0:03 automount
   110 ?         0:01 keyserv
   112 ?         0:04 nis_cache
   165 ?         0:00 syslogd
```

Again, the default display of PID, TTY, CPU time, and command is generated. The processes listed relate to the scheduler, `init`, the system logging facility, the NIS cache, and several other standard applications and services.

It is good practice for you to become familiar with the main processes on your system and the relative CPU times they usually consume. This can be useful information when troubleshooting or when evaluating security. One of the nice features of the `ps` command is the ability to combine multiple flags to print out a more elaborate process list. For example, you can combine the *–A* option (all processes) with the *–f* option (full details) to produce a process list with full details. Here's the full details for the same process list:

```
# ps -Af
   UID   PID  PPID  C    STIME TTY   TIME CMD
  root     0     0  0   Mar 20 ?    0:00 sched
  root     1     0  0   Mar 20 ?    0:01 /etc/init -
  root     2     0  0   Mar 20 ?    0:01 pageout
  root     3     0  0   Mar 20 ?    9:51 fsflush
  root   258   255  0   Mar 20 ?    0:00 /usr/lib/saf/ttymon
  root   108     1  0   Mar 20 ?    0:00 /usr/sbin/rpcbind
  root   255     1  0   Mar 20 ?    0:00 /usr/lib/saf/sac -t 300
  root    60     1  0   Mar 20 ?    0:00 /usr/lib/devfsadm/devfseventd
  root    62     1  0   Mar 20 ?    0:00 /usr/lib/devfsadm/devfsadmd
  root   157     1  0   Mar 20 ?    0:03 /usr/lib/autofs/automountd
  root   110     1  0   Mar 20 ?    0:01 /usr/sbin/keyserv
```

```
    root    112     1  0   Mar 20 ?     0:05 /usr/sbin/nis_cachemgr
    root    165     1  0   Mar 20 ?     0:00 /usr/sbin/syslogd
```

Another common use for ps is to print process information in a format that is suitable for the scheduler:

```
% ps -c
   PID  CLS PRI TTY        TIME CMD
 29081   TS  48 pts/8      0:00 ksh
 29085   TS  48 pts/8      0:00 bash
```

Doing this can be useful when used in conjunction with the priocntl command, which displays the parameters used for process scheduling. This allows administrators, in particular, to determine the process classes currently available on the system, or to set the class of a specific process to interactive or time-sharing. You can obtain a list of all supported classes by passing the –l parameter to priocntl:

```
# priocntl -l
CONFIGURED CLASSES
==================
SYS (System Class)
TS (Time Sharing)
        Configured TS User Priority Range: -60 through 60
IA (Interactive)
        Configured IA User Priority Range: -60 through 60
FX (Fixed priority)
        Configured FX User Priority Range: 0 through 60
```

You can combine this with a –f full display flag to ps –c to obtain more information:

```
$ ps -cf
     UID    PID  PPID  CLS PRI    STIME TTY        TIME CMD
    paul 29081 29079   TS  48 10:40:30 pts/8      0:00 /bin/ksh
    paul 29085 29081   TS  48 10:40:51 pts/8      0:00 /usr/local/bin/bash
```

If you want to obtain information about processes being executed by a particular group of users, this can be specified on the command line by using the –g option, followed by the GID of the target group. In this example, all processes from users in group 0 will be printed:

```
$ ps -g 0
   PID TTY       TIME CMD
     0 ?         0:00 sched
     1 ?         0:01 init
     2 ?         0:01 pageout
     3 ?         9:51 fsflush
```

Another common configuration option used with ps is *–j*, which displays the session identifier (SID) and the process group identifier (PGID), as shown here:

```
$ ps -j
   PID  PGID   SID TTY       TIME CMD
 29081 29081 29081 pts/8    0:00 ksh
 29085 29085 29081 pts/8    0:00 bash
```

Finally, you can print out the status of lightweight processes (LWP) in your system. These are virtual CPU or execution resources, which are designed to make the best use of available CPU resources based on their priority and scheduling class. Here is an example:

```
$ ps -L
   PID  LWP TTY       LTIME CMD
 29081    1 pts/8    0:00 ksh
 29085    1 pts/8    0:00 bash
```

Using the top Program

If you're an administrator, you probably want to keep an eye on all processes running on a system, particularly if the system is in production use. Buggy programs can consume large amounts of CPU time, preventing operational applications from carrying out their duties efficiently. Monitoring the process list almost constantly is necessary, especially if performance begins to suffer on a system. Although you could keep typing **ps –eaf** every five minutes or so, a much more efficient method is to use the top program to monitor the processes in your system interactively, and to use its "vital statistics," such as CPU activity states, real and virtual memory status, and the load average. In addition, top displays the details of the leading processes that consume the greatest amount of CPU time during each sampling period.

The display of top can be customized to include any number of these leading processes at any one time, but displaying the top 10 or 20 processes is usually sufficient to keep an eye on rogue processes. The latest version of top can always be downloaded from **ftp://ftp.groupsys.com/pub/top**.

top reads the */proc* file system to generate its process statistics. This usually means that top runs as a *setUID* process, unless you remove the read and execute permissions for nonroot users and run it only as root. Paradoxically, doing this may be just as dangerous, because any errors in top may impact the system at large if executed by the root user. Again, *setUID* processes are dangerous, and you should evaluate whether the trade-off between accessibility and security is worthwhile in this case.

One of the main problems with top running on Solaris is that top is very sensitive to changes in architecture and/or operating system version. This is particularly the case if the GNU gcc compiler is used to build top, as it has its own set of include files. These files must exactly match the version of the current operating system, otherwise top will not work properly: the CPU state percentages may be wrong, indicating that processes are consuming all CPU time, when the system is actually idle. The solution is to rebuild gcc so that it generates header files that are appropriate for your current operating system version.

Let's examine a printout from top:

```
last PID: 16630;  load averages:  0.17,  0.08,  0.06     09:33:29
72 processes:  71 sleeping, 1 on cpu
CPU states: 87.6% idle, 4.8% user, 7.5% kernel, 0.1% iowait, 0.0% swap
Memory: 128M real, 3188K free, 72M swap in use, 172M swap free
```

This summary tells us that the system has 72 processes, with only 1 running actively and 71 sleeping. The system was 87.6 percent idle in the previous sampling epoch, and there was little swapping or iowait activity, ensuring fast performance. The load average for the previous 1, 5, and 15 minutes was 0.17, 0.08, and 0.06 respectively—this is not a machine that is taxed by its workload. The last PID to be issued to an application, 16630, is also displayed.

```
  PID USERNAME THR PRI NICE  SIZE   RES STATE   TIME    CPU COMMAND
  259 root       1  59    0   18M 4044K sleep  58:49  1.40% Xsun
16630 pwatters    1  59    0 1956K 1536K cpu     0:00  1.19% top
  345 pwatters 8  33    0 7704K 4372K sleep   0:21  0.83% dtwm
16580 pwatters 1  59    0 5984K 2608K sleep   0:00  0.24% dtterm
 9196 pwatters 1  48    0   17M 1164K sleep   0:28  0.01% netscape
13818 pwatters 1  59    0 5992K  872K sleep   0:01  0.00% dtterm
  338 pwatters 1  48    0 7508K   0K sleep    0:04  0.00% dtsession
  112 pwatters 3  59    0 1808K  732K sleep   0:03  0.00% nis_cachemgr
  157 pwatters 5  58    0 2576K  576K sleep   0:02  0.00% automountd
  422 pwatters 1  48    0 4096K  672K sleep   0:01  0.00% textedit
 2295 pwatters 1  48    0 7168K   0K sleep    0:01  0.00% dtfile
 8350 root      10  51    0 3000K 2028K sleep  0:01  0.00% nscd
 8757 pwatters 1  48   10 5992K 1340K sleep   0:01  0.00% dtterm
 4910 nobody     1   0    0 1916K   0K sleep   0:00  0.00% httpd
  366 pwatters 1  28    0 1500K   0K sleep    0:00  0.00% sdtvolcheck
```

This top listing shows a lot of information about each process running on the system, including the PID, the user who owns the process, the nice value (priority), the size of the application, the amount resident in memory, its current state (active or sleeping), the CPU time consumed, and the command name. For example, the Apache Web server runs as the httpd process (PID=4910), by the user nobody, and is 1916KB in size.

Changing the nice value of a process ensures that it receives more or less priority from the process scheduler. Reducing the nice value ensures that the process priority is decreased, while increasing the nice value increases the process priority. Unfortunately, while ordinary users can decrease their nice value, only the superuser can increase the nice value for a process. In the preceding example for top, the dtterm process is running with a nice value of 10, which is low. If the root user wanted to increase the priority of a new dtterm process by 20, they would issue the following command:

```
# nice --20 dtterm
```

Reducing the nice value can be performed by any user. To reduce the nice value of a new top process, the following command would be used:

```
$ nice -20 top
```

Now, if you execute an application that requires a lot of CPU power, you will be able to monitor the impact on the system as a whole by examining the changes in the processes displayed by top. If you execute the command

```
$ find . -name apache -print
```

the impact on the process distribution is immediately apparent:

```
last PID: 16631;   load averages: 0.10, 0.07, 0.06    09:34:08
73 processes:   71 sleeping, 1 running, 1 on cpu
CPU states:   2.2% idle,   0.6% user, 11.6% kernel, 85.6% iowait, 0.0% swap
Memory: 128M real, 1896K free, 72M swap in use, 172M swap free
```

This summary tells you that the system now has 73 processes, with only 1 running actively, 1 on the CPU, and 71 sleeping. The new process is the find command, which is actively running. The system is now only 2.2 percent idle, a large increase on the previous sampling epoch. There is still no swapping activity, but iowait activity has risen to 85.6 percent, slowing system performance. The load average for the previous 1, 5, and 15 minutes was 0.10, 0.07, and 0.06 respectively—on the average, this machine is still not taxed by its workload and wouldn't be unless the load averages grew to greater than 1. The last PID to be issued to an application, 16631, is also displayed, and in this case it again refers to the find command.

```
  PID USERNAME THR PRI NICE  SIZE   RES STATE   TIME    CPU COMMAND
16631 pwatters 1   54   0   788K  668K run     0:00  1.10% find
  259 root         1   59   0   18M 4288K sleep  58:49  0.74% Xsun
16630 pwatters 1   59   0 1956K 1536K cpu     0:00  0.50% top
 9196 pwatters 1   48   0   17M 3584K sleep   0:28  0.13% netscape
 8456 pwatters 1   59   0 5984K   0K sleep   0:00  0.12% dtpad
  345 pwatters 8   59   0 7708K   0K sleep   0:21  0.11% dtwm
16580 pwatters 1   59   0 5992K 2748K sleep   0:00  0.11% dtterm
13838 pwatters 1   38   0 2056K  652K sleep   0:00  0.06% bash
13818 pwatters 1   59   0 5992K 1884K sleep   0:01  0.06% dtterm
  112 root         3   59   0 1808K  732K sleep   0:03  0.02% nis_cachemgr
  337 pwatters 4   59   0 4004K   0K sleep   0:00  0.01% ttsession
  338 pwatters 1   48   0 7508K   0K sleep   0:04  0.00% dtsession
  157 root         5   58   0 2576K  604K sleep   0:02  0.00% automountd
 2295 pwatters 1   48   0 7168K   0K sleep   0:01  0.00% dtfile
  422 pwatters 1   48   0 4096K   0K sleep   0:01  0.00% textedit
```

find now uses 1.1 percent of CPU power, which is the highest of any active process (i.e., in the "run" state) on the system. It uses 788KB of RAM, less than most other processes; however, most other processes are in the "sleep" state and do not occupy much resident memory.

Using the truss Program

If you've identified a process that appears to be having problems and you suspect an application bug is the cause, the solution involves more than just going back to the source to debug the program or making an educated guess about what's going wrong. In fact, one of the great features of Solaris is the ability to trace system calls for every process running on the system. This means that if a program is hanging, for example, because it can't find its initialization file, the failed system call revealed using truss would display this information. truss prints out each system call, line by line, as it is executed by the system. The syntax is rather like a C program, making it easy for C programmers to interpret the output. The arguments are displayed by retrieving information from the appropriate headers, and any file information is also displayed.

As an example, let's look at the output from the cat command, which we can use to display the contents of */etc/resolv.conf*, which is used by the Domain Name Service (DNS) to identify domains and name servers. Let's look at the operations involved in this running this application:

```
# truss cat /etc/resolv.conf
execve("/usr/bin/cat", 0xEFFFF740, 0xEFFFF74C)   argc = 2
open("/dev/zero", O_RDONLY)                  = 3
mmap(0x00000000, 8192, PROT_READ|PROT_WRITE|PROT_EXEC, MAP_PRIVATE, 3, 0) =
 0xEF7B0000
open("/usr/lib/libc.so.1", O_RDONLY)         = 4
fstat(4, 0xEFFFF2DC)                         = 0
mmap(0x00000000, 8192, PROT_READ|PROT_EXEC, MAP_PRIVATE, 4, 0) = 0xEF7A0000
mmap(0x00000000, 704512, PROT_READ|PROT_EXEC, MAP_PRIVATE, 4, 0) =
 0xEF680000
munmap(0xEF714000, 57344)
            = 0
mmap(0xEF722000, 28368, PROT_READ|PROT_WRITE|PROT_EXEC, MAP_PRIVATE|
MAP_FIXED, 4, 598016) = 0xEF722000
mmap(0xEF72A000, 2528, PROT_READ|PROT_WRITE|PROT_EXEC, MAP_PRIVATE|
MAP_FIXED, 3, 0) = 0xEF72A000
close(4)                                     = 0
open("/usr/lib/libdl.so.1", O_RDONLY)        = 4
fstat(4, 0xEFFFF2DC)                         = 0
mmap(0xEF7A0000, 8192, PROT_READ|PROT_EXEC, MAP_PRIVATE|
MAP_FIXED, 4, 0) = 0xEF7A0000
close(4)                                     = 0
open("/usr/platform/SUNW,Ultra-2/lib/libc_psr.so.1", O_RDONLY) = 4
fstat(4, 0xEFFFF0BC)                         = 0
mmap(0x00000000, 8192, PROT_READ|PROT_EXEC, MAP_PRIVATE, 4, 0) = 0xEF790000
```

```
mmap(0x00000000, 16384, PROT_READ|PROT_EXEC, MAP_PRIVATE, 4, 0) =
  0xEF780000
close(4)                                        = 0
close(3)                                        = 0
munmap(0xEF790000, 8192)                        = 0
fstat64(1, 0xEFFFF648)                          = 0
open64("resolv.conf", O_RDONLY)                 = 3
fstat64(3, 0xEFFFF5B0)                          = 0
llseek(3, 0, SEEK_CUR)                          = 0
mmap64(0x00000000, 98, PROT_READ, MAP_SHARED, 3, 0) = 0xEF790000
read(3, " d", 1)                                = 1
memcntl(0xEF790000, 98, MC_ADVISE, 0x0002, 0, 0) = 0
domain paulwatters.com
nameserver 192.56.67.16
nameserver 192.56.67.32
nameserver 192.56.68.16
write(1, " d o m a i n   p a u l w a t t e r s ."..., 98)      = 98
llseek(3, 98, SEEK_SET)                         = 98
munmap(0xEF790000, 98)                          = 0
llseek(3, 0, SEEK_CUR)                          = 98
close(3)                                        = 0
close(1)                                        = 0
llseek(0, 0, SEEK_CUR)                          = 57655
_exit(0)
```

First, cat is called using execve(), with two arguments (the application name, cat, and the file to be displayed, */etc/resolv.conf*). The arguments to execve() include the name of the application (*/usr/bin/cat*), a pointer to the argument list (0xEFFFF740), and a pointer to the environment (0xEFFFF74C). Next, library files such as */usr/lib/libc.so.1* are read. Memory operations (such as mmap()) are performed continuously. The *resolv.conf* file is opened as read only, after which the contents are literally printed to standard output. Then the file is closed. truss can be used in this way to trace the system calls for any process running on your system.

Examples

The following examples demonstrate some advanced process-management features of Solaris 10.

Using Process File System

Now that you have examined what processes are, you are ready to look at some special features of processes as implemented in Solaris. One of the most innovative characteristics of processes under Solaris is the process file system (PROCFS), which is mounted as the */proc* file system. Images of all currently active processes are stored in the */proc* file system by their PID.

Here's an example: first, a process is identified—in this example, the current Korn shell for the user pwatters:

```
# ps -eaf | grep pwatters
 pwatters 310    291  0   Mar 20 ?          0:04 /usr/openwin/bin/Xsun
 pwatters 11959 11934  0 09:21:42 pts/1    0:00 grep pwatters
 pwatters 11934 11932  1 09:20:50 pts/1    0:00 -ksh
```

Now that you have a target PID (11934), you can change to the */proc/11934* directory and view the image of this process:

```
# cd /proc/11934
 # ls -l
total 3497
-rw-------   1 pwatters     other     1769472 Mar 30 09:20 as
-r--------   1 pwatters     other         152 Mar 30 09:20 auxv
-r--------   1 pwatters     other          32 Mar 30 09:20 cred
--w-------   1 pwatters     other           0 Mar 30 09:20 ctl
lr-x------   1 pwatters     other           0 Mar 30 09:20 cwd ->
dr-x------   2 pwatters     other        1184 Mar 30 09:20 fd
-r--r--r--   1 pwatters     other         120 Mar 30 09:20 lpsinfo
-r--------   1 pwatters     other         912 Mar 30 09:20 lstatus
-r--r--r--   1 pwatters     other         536 Mar 30 09:20 lusage
dr-xr-xr-x   3 pwatters     other          48 Mar 30 09:20 lwp
-r--------   1 pwatters     other        2016 Mar 30 09:20 map
dr-x------   2 pwatters     other         544 Mar 30 09:20 object
-r--------   1 pwatters     other        2552 Mar 30 09:20 pagedata
-r--r--r--   1 pwatters     other         336 Mar 30 09:20 psinfo
-r--------   1 pwatters     other        2016 Mar 30 09:20 rmap
lr-x------   1 pwatters     other           0 Mar 30 09:20 root ->
-r--------   1 pwatters     other        1440 Mar 30 09:20 sigact
-r--------   1 pwatters     other        1232 Mar 30 09:20 status
-r--r--r--   1 pwatters     other         256 Mar 30 09:20 usage
-r--------   1 pwatters     other           0 Mar 30 09:20 watch
-r--------   1 pwatters     other        3192 Mar 30 09:20 xmap
```

Each of the directories with the name associated with the PID contains additional subdirectories, which contain state information, and related control functions. In addition, a watchpoint facility is provided, which is responsible for controlling memory access. A series of proc tools interpret the information contained in the */proc* subdirectories, which display the characteristics of each process.

Using proc Tools

The proc tools are designed to operate on data contained within the */proc* file system. Each utility takes a PID as its argument and performs operations associated with the

PID. For example, the `pflags` command prints the flags and data model details for the PID in question.

For the preceding Korn shell example, you can easily print out this status information:

```
# /usr/proc/bin/pflags 29081
29081:  /bin/ksh
        data model = _ILP32  flags = PR_ORPHAN
  /1:   flags = PR_PCINVAL|PR_ASLEEP [ waitid(0x7,0x0,0x804714c,0x7) ]
```

You can also print the credential information for this process, including the effective and real UID and GID of the process owner, by using the `pcred` command:

```
$ /usr/proc/bin/pcred 29081
29081:  e/r/sUID=100  e/r/sGID=10
```

Here, both the effective and the real UID is 100 (user pwatters), and the effective and real GID is 10 (group staff).

To examine the address space map of the target process, you can use the `pmap` command and all the libraries it requires to execute:

```
# /usr/proc/bin/pmap 29081
29081:  /bin/ksh
08046000      8K read/write/exec     [ stack ]
08048000    160K read/exec           /usr/bin/ksh
08070000      8K read/write/exec     /usr/bin/ksh
08072000     28K read/write/exec     [ heap ]
DFAB4000     16K read/exec           /usr/lib/locale/en_AU/en_AU.so.2
DFAB8000      8K read/write/exec     /usr/lib/locale/en_AU/en_AU.so.2
DFABB000      4K read/write/exec     [ anon ]
DFABD000     12K read/exec           /usr/lib/libmp.so.2
DFAC0000      4K read/write/exec     /usr/lib/libmp.so.2
DFAC4000    552K read/exec           /usr/lib/libc.so.1
DFB4E000     24K read/write/exec     /usr/lib/libc.so.1
DFB54000      8K read/write/exec     [ anon ]
DFB57000    444K read/exec           /usr/lib/libnsl.so.1
DFBC6000     20K read/write/exec     /usr/lib/libnsl.so.1
DFBCB000     32K read/write/exec     [ anon ]
DFBD4000     32K read/exec           /usr/lib/libsocket.so.1
DFBDC000      8K read/write/exec     /usr/lib/libsocket.so.1
DFBDF000      4K read/exec           /usr/lib/libdl.so.1
DFBE1000      4K read/write/exec     [ anon ]
DFBE3000    100K read/exec           /usr/lib/ld.so.1
DFBFC000     12K read/write/exec     /usr/lib/ld.so.1
 total     1488K
```

It's always surprising to see how many libraries are loaded when an application is executed, especially something as complicated as a shell, leading to a total of 1488KB memory used. You can obtain a list of the dynamic libraries linked to each process by using the `pldd` command:

```
# /usr/proc/bin/pldd 29081
29081:   /bin/ksh
/usr/lib/libsocket.so.1
/usr/lib/libnsl.so.1
/usr/lib/libc.so.1
/usr/lib/libdl.so.1
/usr/lib/libmp.so.2
/usr/lib/locale/en_AU/en_AU.so.2
```

As discussed earlier in the section "Sending Signals," signals are the way in which processes communicate with each other, and they can also be used from shells to communicate with spawned processes (usually to suspend or kill them).

By using the `psig` command, it is possible to list the signal actions associated with each process:

```
$ /usr/proc/bin/psig 29081
29081:   /bin/ksh
HUP      caught  RESTART
INT      caught  RESTART
QUIT     ignored
ILL      caught  RESTART
TRAP     caught  RESTART
ABRT     caught  RESTART
EMT      caught  RESTART
FPE      caught  RESTART
KILL     default
BUS      caught  RESTART
SEGV     default
SYS      caught  RESTART
PIPE     caught  RESTART
ALRM     caught  RESTART
TERM     ignored
USR1     caught  RESTART
USR2     caught  RESTART
CLD      default NOCLDSTOP
PWR      default
WINCH    default
URG      default
POLL     default
STOP     default
TSTP     ignored
CONT     default
TTIN     ignored
TTOU     ignored
```

```
VTALRM    default
PROF      default
XCPU      caught    RESTART
XFSZ      ignored
WAITING   default
LWP       default
FREEZE    default
THAW      default
CANCEL    default
LOST      default
RTMIN     default
RTMIN+1   default
RTMIN+2   default
RTMIN+3   default
RTMAX-3   default
RTMAX-2   default
RTMAX-1   default
RTMAX     default
```

It is also possible to print a hexadecimal format stack trace for the lightweight process (LWP) in each process by using the pstack command. This can be useful and can be used in the same way that the truss command was used:

```
$ /usr/proc/bin/pstack 29081
29081:   /bin/ksh
 dfaf5347 waitid    (7, 0, 804714c, 7)
 dfb0d9db _waitPID  (ffffffff, 8047224, 4) + 63
 dfb40617 waitPID   (ffffffff, 8047224, 4) + 1f
 0805b792 job_wait  (719d) + 1ae
 08064be8 sh_exec   (8077270, 14) + af0
 0805e3a1 ???????? ()
 0805decd main      (1, 8047624, 804762c) + 705
  0804fa78 ???????? ()
```

Perhaps the most commonly used proc tool is the pfiles command, which displays all the open files for each process. This is useful for determining operational dependencies between data files and applications:

```
$ /usr/proc/bin/pfiles 29081
29081:   /bin/ksh
  Current rlimit: 64 file descriptors
   0: S_IFCHR mode:0620 dev:102,0 ino:319009 UID:6049 GID:7 rdev:24,8
      O_RDWR|O_LARGEFILE
   1: S_IFCHR mode:0620 dev:102,0 ino:319009 UID:6049 GID:7 rdev:24,8
      O_RDWR|O_LARGEFILE
   2: S_IFCHR mode:0620 dev:102,0 ino:319009 UID:6049 GID:7 rdev:24,8
      O_RDWR|O_LARGEFILE
```

```
63: S_IFREG mode:0600 dev:174,2 ino:990890 UID:6049 GID:1 size:3210
    O_RDWR|O_APPEND|O_LARGEFILE FD_CLOEXEC
```

In addition, it is possible to obtain the current working directory of the target process by using the pwdx command:

```
$ /usr/proc/bin/pwdx 29081
29081:   /home/paul
```

If you need to examine the process tree for all parent and child processes containing the target PID, you can use the ptree command. This is useful for determining dependencies between processes that are not apparent by consulting the process list:

```
$ /usr/proc/bin/ptree 29081
247    /usr/dt/bin/dtlogin -daemon
  28950 /usr/dt/bin/dtlogin -daemon
    28972 /bin/ksh /usr/dt/bin/Xsession
      29012 /usr/dt/bin/sdt_shell -c        unset DT;      DISPLAY=lion:0;
        29015 ksh -c         unset DT;     DISPLAY=lion:0;
              /usr/dt/bin/dt
          29026 /usr/dt/bin/dtsession
            29032 dtwm
              29079 /usr/dt/bin/dtterm
                29081 /bin/ksh
                  29085 /usr/local/bin/bash
                    29230 /usr/proc/bin/ptree 29081
```

Here, ptree has been executed from bash, which was started from the Korn shell (ksh), spawned from the dtterm terminal window, which was spawned from the dtwm window manager, and so on. Although many of these proc tools will seem obscure, they are often very useful when trying to debug process-related application errors, especially in large applications like database management systems.

Using the lsof Command

The lsof command (*lsof* stands for "list open files") lists information about files that active processes running on Solaris currently have open. The lsof command is not included in the Solaris distribution; however, the current version can always be downloaded from **ftp://vic.cc.purdue.edu/pub/tools/unix/lsof**.

What can you use lsof for? The answer largely depends on how many problems you encounter that relate to processes and files. Often, administrators are interested in knowing which processes are currently using a target file or files from a particular directory. This can occur when a file is locked by one application, for example, but is required by another application (again, a situation in which two database instances simultaneously attempt to write to a database system's data files is one example in which this might happen). If you know the path to a file of interest, you can use lsof to determine which processes are using files in that directory.

To examine the processes that are using files in the /tmp file system, use this:

```
$ lsof /tmp
COMMAND     PID USER      FD   TYPE DEVICE SIZE/OFF      NODE NAME
ssion       338 pwatters  txt  VREG    0,1   271596 471638794 /tmp (swap)
(unknown)   345 pwatters  txt  VREG    0,1   271596 471638794 /tmp (swap)
le         2295 pwatters  txt  VREG    0,1   271596 471638794 /tmp (swap)
le         2299 pwatters  txt  VREG    0,1   271596 471638794 /tmp (swap)
```

Obviously, there's a bug in the routines that obtain the command name (the first four characters are missing!), but since the PID is correct, this is enough information to identify the four applications that are currently using files in /tmp. For example, dtsession (PID 338) manages the CDE session for the user pwatters, who is using a temporary text file in the /tmp directory.

Another common problem that lsof is used for, with respect to the /tmp file system, is the identification of processes that continue to write to unlinked files: thus, space is being consumed, but it may appear that no files are growing any larger! This confusing activity can be traced back to a process by using lsof. However, rather than using lsof on the /tmp directory directly, you would need to examine the root directory (/) on which /tmp is mounted. After finding the process that is writing to an open file, you can kill the process. If the size of a file is changing across several different sampling epochs (e.g., by running the command once a minute), you've probably found the culprit:

```
# lsof /
COMMAND     PID  USER   FD   TYPE DEVICE SIZE/OFF   NODE NAME
(unknown)    1   root   txt  VREG  102,0   446144 118299 / (/dev/dsk/c0d0s0)
(unknown)    1   root   txt  VREG  102,0     4372 293504 / (/dev/dsk/c0d0s0)
(unknown)    1   root   txt  VREG  102,0   173272 293503 / (/dev/dsk/c0d0s0)
sadm        62   root   txt  VREG  102,0   954804 101535 / (/dev/dsk/c0d0s0)
sadm        62   root   txt  VREG  102,0   165948 101569 / (/dev/dsk/c0d0s0)
sadm        62   root   txt  VREG  102,0    16132 100766 / (/dev/dsk/c0d0s0)
sadm        62   root   txt  VREG  102,0     8772 100765 / (/dev/dsk/c0d0s0)
sadm        62   root   txt  VREG  102,0   142652 101571 / (/dev/dsk/c0d0s0)
```

One of the restrictions on mounting a file system is that you can't unmount that file system if files are open on it: if files are open on a file system and it is dismounted, any changes made to the files may not be saved, resulting in data loss. Looking at a process list may not always reveal which processes are opening which files, and this can be very frustrating if Solaris refuses to unmount a file system because some files are open. Again, lsof can be used to identify the processes that are opening files on a specific file system.

The first step is to consult the output of the df command to obtain the names of currently mounted file systems:

```
$ df -k
Filesystem           kbytes    used    avail capacity  Mounted on
/proc                     0       0        0      0%   /proc
/dev/dsk/c0d0s0     2510214  929292  1530718     38%   /
fd                        0       0        0      0%   /dev/fd
/dev/dsk/c0d0s3     5347552  183471  5110606      4%   /usr/local
swap                 185524   12120   173404      7%   /tmp
```

If you wanted to unmount the */dev/dsk/c0d0s3* file system but were prevented from doing so because of open files, you could obtain a list of all open files under */usr/local* by using this command:

```
$ lsof /dev/dsk/c0d0s3
COMMAND PID     USER   FD TYPE DEVICE SIZE/OFF   NODE NAME
postgres    423 pwatters txt VREG  102,3   1747168 457895 /usr/local (/dev/dsk/
c0d0s3)
d      4905      root txt VREG  102,3    333692  56455 /usr/local (/dev/dsk/c0d0s3)
d      4906    nobody txt VREG  102,3    333692  56455 /usr/local (/dev/dsk/c0d0s3)
d      4907    nobody txt VREG  102,3    333692  56455 /usr/local (/dev/dsk/c0d0s3)
d      4908    nobody txt VREG  102,3    333692  56455 /usr/local (/dev/dsk/c0d0s3)
d      4909    nobody txt VREG  102,3    333692  56455 /usr/local (/dev/dsk/c0d0s3)
d      4910    nobody txt VREG  102,3    333692  56455 /usr/local (/dev/dsk/c0d0s3)
d      4911    nobody txt VREG  102,3    333692  56455 /usr/local (/dev/dsk/c0d0s3)
d      4912    nobody txt VREG  102,3    333692  56455 /usr/local (/dev/dsk/c0d0s3)
d      4913    nobody txt VREG  102,3    333692  56455 /usr/local (/dev/dsk/c0d0s3)
```

Obviously, all of these processes will need to stop using the open files before the file system can be unmounted. If you're not sure where a particular command is running from, or on which file system its data files are stored, you can also use lsof to check open files by passing the PID on the command line. First, you need to identify a PID by using the ps command:

```
$ ps -eaf | grep apache
  nobody 4911  4905  0   Mar 22 ?        0:00 /usr/local/apache/bin/httpd
  nobody 4910  4905  0   Mar 22 ?        0:00 /usr/local/apache/bin/httpd
  nobody 4912  4905  0   Mar 22 ?        0:00 /usr/local/apache/bin/httpd
  nobody 4905     1  0   Mar 22 ?        0:00 /usr/local/apache/bin/httpd
  nobody 4907  4905  0   Mar 22 ?        0:00 /usr/local/apache/bin/httpd
  nobody 4908  4905  0   Mar 22 ?        0:00 /usr/local/apache/bin/httpd
  nobody 4913  4905  0   Mar 22 ?        0:00 /usr/local/apache/bin/httpd
  nobody 4909  4905  0   Mar 22 ?        0:00 /usr/local/apache/bin/httpd
  nobody 4906  4905  0   Mar 22 ?        0:00 /usr/local/apache/bin/httpd
```

Now examine the process 4905 for Apache to see what files are currently being opened by it:

```
$ lsof -p 4905
COMMAND  PID   USER   FD    TYPE DEVICE   SIZE/OFF       NODE NAME
d        4905 nobody txt   VREG  102,3   333692  56455 /usr/local
(/dev/dsk/c0d0s3)
d        4905 nobody txt   VREG  102,0    17388 100789 / (/dev/dsk/c0d0s0)
d        4905 nobody txt   VREG  102,0   954804 101535 / (/dev/dsk/c0d0s0)
d        4905 nobody txt   VREG  102,0   693900 101573 / (/dev/dsk/c0d0s0)
d        4905 nobody txt   VREG  102,0    52988 100807 / (/dev/dsk/c0d0s0)
d        4905 nobody txt   VREG  102,0     4396 100752 / (/dev/dsk/c0d0s0)
d        4905 nobody txt   VREG  102,0   175736 100804 / (/dev/dsk/c0d0s0)
```

Apache has a number of open files!

Command Reference

The following commands are commonly used to manage processes.

ps

The following table summarizes the main options used with ps.

Option	Description
–a	Lists most frequently requested processes
–A, –e	List all processes
–c	Lists processes in scheduler format
–d	Lists all processes
–f	Prints comprehensive process information
–g	Prints process information on a group basis for a single group
–G	Prints process information on a group basis for a list of groups
–j	Includes SID and PGID in printout
–l	Prints complete process information
–L	Displays LWP details
–p	Lists process details for list of specified processes
–P	Lists the CPU ID to which a process is bound
–s	Lists session leaders
–t	Lists all processes associated with a specific terminal
–u	Lists all processes for a specific user

kill

The following table summarizes the main signals used to communicate with processes using `kill`.

Signal	Code	Action	Description
SIGHUP	1	Exit	Hangup
SIGINT	2	Exit	Interrupt
SIGQUIT	3	Core	Quit
SIGILL	4	Core	Illegal instruction
SIGTRAP	5	Core	Trace
SIGABRT	6	Core	Abort
SIGEMT	7	Core	Emulation trap
SIGFPE	8	Core	Arithmetic exception
SIGKILL	9	Exit	Killed
SIGBUS	10	Core	Bus error
SIGSEGV	11	Core	Segmentation fault
SIGSYS	12	Core	Bad system call
SIGPIPE	13	Exit	Broken pipe
SIGALRM	14	Exit	Alarm clock
SIGTERM	15	Exit	Terminate

pgrep

The `pgrep` command is used to search for a list of processes whose names match a pattern specified on the command line. The command returns a list of corresponding PIDs. This list can then be piped to another command, such as `kill`, to perform some action on the processes or send them a signal.

For example, to kill all processes associated with the name "java," the following command would be used:

```
$ kill -9 `pgrep java`
```

pkill

The `pkill` command can be used to send signals to processes that have the same name. It is a more specific version of `pgrep`, since it can be used only to send signals, and the list of PIDs cannot be piped to another program.

To kill all processes associated with the name "java," the following command would be used:

```
$ pkill -9 java
```

killall

The `killall` command is used to kill all processes running on a system. It is called by `shutdown` when the system is being bought to run-level 0. However, since a signal can be passed to the `killall` command, it is possible for a superuser to send a different signal (other than 9) to all processes. For example, to send a SIGHUP signal to all processes, the following command could be used:

```
# killall 1
```

Summary

In this chapter, we have examined how to manage and monitor processes. Since processes and threads are the entities that actually carry out the execution of applications, it's important that you understand how to send signals to manage their activity.

PART II

PART

III

Security

CHAPTER

System Security

Security is a central concern of system administrators of all network operating systems, because all services may potentially have inherent flaws or weaknesses revealed through undetected bugs that can compromise a system. Solaris is no exception, and new Solaris administrators will find themselves visiting issues that they may have encountered with other operating systems. For example, Linux, Microsoft Windows, and Solaris all run database systems that have daemons that listen for connections arriving through the Internet. These servers may be shipped with default user accounts with well-known passwords that are not inactivated by local administrators after configuration and administration. Consequently, exploits involving such services are often broadcast on Usenet newsgroups, cracking mailing lists, and Web sites. This chapter covers the basic security requirements for Solaris systems, including assurances of integrity, authenticity, privacy, trust, and confidentiality. The focus will be on securing Solaris systems for the enterprise at all levels.

Key Concepts

The following key concepts are important for understanding system security in the context of Solaris.

Security Requirements

Security from the enterprise perspective is essentially an exercise in risk management, whether those risks arise from randomly occurring accidental events or intentionally malevolent events. Examples of accidents include fire, hardware failure, software bugs, and data entry errors, while malevolence manifests itself in fraud, denial of service, theft, and sabotage. To some extent, the end result to the enterprise is lost business, which translates to lost money, regardless of whether a realized risk is accidental or intentional. However, the legal means of recourse can be quite different. In each case, data and applications may be deleted or modified, while physical systems may be damaged or destroyed. For example, Web sites with inadequate access controls on their source files that are displayed as Web pages are often defaced, with their contents modified for fun or profit. Computer systems that are stolen obviously have to be replaced, but the amount of reconfiguration required can be significant, as can the underlying loss of data.

Given that so many "mission critical" systems, such as those in banking and government, are now completely electronic, how would end users cope with the complete loss of their records? Worse still, personal data may be exposed to the world—embarrassing for the subscribers of an "adult" site, very dangerous for participants of a witness protection program.

Managing risk obviously involves a human element that is beyond the scope of this book—social-engineering attacks are widespread, and few technological solutions (except biometrics!) may ameliorate such problems. However, failures attributable to human factors can be greatly reduced with the kinds of automation and logical evaluation provided by computation. For example, an automated identification system that recognizes individuals entering an office suite, classifying them as employees or visitors, would reduce the requirements on local staff to "know" everybody's face in the organization. Because employees may object to the storage of their photographs on a work computer, you may want to consider using a one-way hash—instead of storing a photograph, a one-way hash can be computed from the image data and stored, while the original image is discarded. When an employee enters the building, a hash is computed of that image, and if a match is made against any of the hashes stored in the database, then the employee can be positively identified. In this way, organizational security can be greatly enhanced while not compromising the privacy of individual workers. The relationship between security and privacy need not be orthogonal, since well-designed technology can often provide solutions that ensure both privacy and security.

Security Architecture

Solaris security includes the need to protect individual files, as well as entire systems, from unauthorized access, especially using remote-access tools. However, these individual actions need to be placed within a context that logically covers all aspects of security, typically known as levels. A *level* is an extra barrier that must be breached to obtain access to data.

In terms of physical security, a bank provides an excellent analogy. Breaking into a bank's front counter and teller area is as easy as walking through the door, because these doors are publicly accessible. However, providing this level of access sometimes opens doors deeper inside the building. For example, the private banking area, which may normally be accessed only by staff and identified private banking customers, may allow access using a smart card. If a smart card is stolen from a staff member, it could be used to enter the secure area, because the staff member's credentials would be authenticated. Entering this level would not necessarily provide access to the vault: superuser privileges would be required. However, a thorough physical search of the private banking area might yield the key required for entry, or a brute-force attack on the safe's combination might be used to guess the correct combination. Having accessed the vault, if readily negotiated currency or bullion is contained therein, an intruder could easily steal it. However, if the vault contains checks that need to be countersigned, the intruder may not be able to make use of the contents. The lesson here is simple: banks provide public services that open up pathways straight to the cash. Banks know that any or all of the physical security layers may be breached. That's why the storage of negotiable securities is always minimized, because any system designed by humans can be broken by humans, with enough time and patience. The only sensible strategy is to make sure that external layers are as difficult to breach as possible and to ensure that security experts are immediately notified of breaches.

Similarly, public file areas, such as FTP and Web servers, are publicly accessible areas on computer systems that sometimes provide entry to a different level in the system. An easily guessed or stolen password may provide user-level (but unprivileged) access to the system. A brute-force attack against the local password database might even yield the superuser password. Accessing a local database might contain the target records of interest. However, instead of storing the data plaintext within tables, data may have been written using a stream cipher, making it potentially very difficult to obtain the data. However, because 40-bit ciphers have been broken in the past, obtaining the encrypted data might eventually lead to its dissemination. Again, a key strategy is to ensure that data is secured by as many external layers as possible, and also that the data itself is difficult to negotiate.

Increasing the number of levels of security typically leads to a decrease in system ease-of-use. For example, setting a password for accessing a printer requires users to remember and enter a password when challenged. Whether printer access needs this level of security will depend on organizational requirements. For a printer that prints on plain paper, no password may be needed. However, for a printer that prints on bonded paper with an official company letterhead, a password should be used to protect the printer and, optionally, a copy of the file being sent to the printer may need to be stored securely, for auditing purposes.

For government and military systems, a number of security specifications and policy documents are available that detail the steps necessary to secure Solaris systems in "top secret" installations. The U.S. Department of Defense, for example, publishes the "Orange Book," formally known as the "Department of Defense Trusted Computer System Evaluation Criteria." This publication describes systems that it has evaluated in terms of different protection levels, from weakest to strongest, including the following:

- **Class D** Systems that do not pass any tests and are therefore untrusted. No sensitive data should be stored on Class D systems.

- **Class C1** Systems that require authentication based on a user model.

- **Class C2** Systems that provide auditing and logging on a per-user basis, ensuring that file accesses and related operations can always be traced to the initiating user.

- **Class B1** Systems that require security labeling for all files. Labels range from "top secret" to "unclassified."

- **Class B2** Systems that separate normal system administration duties from security activities, which are performed by a separate security officer. This level requires covert channels for data communications and verified testing of an installation's security procedures.

- **Class B3**   Systems that requires that a standalone request monitor be available to authenticate all requests for file and resource access. In addition, the request monitor must be secured and all of its operations must be logged.

- **Class A1**   Systems that are formally tested and verified installations of a Class B3 system.

All of the strategies that are discussed in this chapter are focused on increasing the number of layers through which a potential cracker (or disgruntled staff member) must pass to obtain the data that they are illegally trying to access. Reducing the threat of remote-access exploits and protecting data are key components of this strategy.

Trusted Solaris

Trusted Solaris implements much stricter controls over UNIX than the standard releases, and it is capable of meeting B1-level security by default. It is designed for organizations that handle military-grade or commercially sensitive data. In addition to the mandatory use of Role-Based Access Control (as reviewed in Chapter 11), Trusted Solaris actually has no superuser at all: no single user is permitted to have control over every aspect of system service. This decentralization of authority is necessary in situations where consensus and/or authorization is required to carry out specific activities. For example, a system administrator installing a new Web server might inadvertently interfere with the operations of an existing service. For a server that's handling sensitive production data, the results could be catastrophic.

Once a system has been installed in production, it's crucial to define a set of roles that specifies what operations need to be performed by a particular individual. For example, the role of managing a firewall is unrelated to the database administration role, so the two roles should be separated rather than run from a single superuser account. In addition, access to files is restricted by special access control lists, which define file contents as being anything from "unclassified" up to "top secret." Access to data that is labeled as more secret requires a higher level of authentication and authorization than does access to unclassified data.

Four roles are defined by default under Trusted Solaris for system management purposes:

- **Security officer**   Manages all aspects of security on the system, such as auditing, logging, and password management

- **System manager**   Performs all system management tasks that are not related to security, except for installing new software

- **Root account**   Used for installing new software

- **Oper account**   Used for performing backups

New roles can be created for other tasks, such as database and Web server administration, where necessary. Some aspects of a Trusted Solaris installation already form part of a standard Solaris installation. For example, Trusted Solaris requires that centralized authentication be performed across an encrypted channel using NIS+. This feature is also available on Solaris, although many sites are now moving to LDAP-based authentication.

Trust

When two or more parties communicate with each other, they must have some level of trust. This trust level will determine the extent to which most of the requirements discussed in this section will be required. For example, if your "trust domain" includes your lawyer's network, then the level of authorization required to access resources inside your network would be lower than the level required if an untrusted entity made a request for access. Similarly, if a principal is authenticated from a trusted domain, then they do not need to be separately authenticated for all subsequent resource requests.

The extent to which parties trust each other underlies the different types of security architectures that can be implemented. If a dedicated ISDN line connects two business partners, then they may well trust their communications to be more secure than if connections were being made across the public Internet. Again, it's a question of assessing and managing risks systematically before implementing a specific architecture.

Part of the excitement concerning the "Trusted Computing Platform" developed by Microsoft and others is that the trust equation is reversed between clients and servers, and becomes more symmetric. Currently, clients trust servers to process and store their data correctly—so, when you transfer $100 from a savings to a checking account using Internet banking, you trust that the bank will perform the operation. Indeed, the bank has sophisticated messaging and reliable delivery systems to ensure that such transactions are never lost. However, when server data is downloaded to a client, the client is pretty much free to do what they want to it, and the server is essentially powerless to control what the client does with this data. For example, imagine that a user pays to download an MP3 file to her computer from a music retailer. Once that physical file is stored on the client's hard drive, it can be easily e-mailed to others or shared using a file-swapping program. Even if each MP3 file was digitally watermarked on a per-client basis, so that illegally shared files could be traced back to the original purchaser, this is still not going to prevent sharing.

So, the notion of making the trust relationship between client and server symmetric simply means that the client trusts the server to honor certain types of data and operations. Thus, even if an MP3 file is downloaded to a client's hard drive, the client operating system must ensure that this cannot be accessed by any application other than an MP3 player. The only question is whether users will permit this kind of trust level, given that malicious server applications could potentially take control of the client's computer. For example, if an illegal MP3 file were detected on the client's system, would the server have the ability, if not the explicit right, to delete it?

Integrity and Accuracy

Integrity refers to whether data is valid or invalid. Invalid data may result from a number of different sources, both human and computer in origin. For example, many (flawed) business processes require multiple entry of the same data multiple times, potentially by multiple users. This can lead to integrity breaches if errors are made. More commonly, though, communication errors can occur when data is transmitted over a network, or when data is being transferred in memory. Most network protocols use *parity* to ensure data integrity—an extra bit is added to every 8 bits of data, which is used with a checksum algorithm to determine whether an error has been detected. Parity mechanisms can detect errors in data but are not capable of fixing errors—typically, a retransmission is required, but this is better than losing data altogether.

Memory corruption can occur when a program reads memory that is allocated to a different application or, more seriously, attempts to overwrite data of another application. Fortunately, most modern memory hardware contains error-correction coding (ECC) that ensures that data errors can be easily identified and fixed before they cause any problems.

Since network protocols and hardware protocols generally handle invalid data caused by system hardware and software, the Application layer is generally where there is great concern over data integrity, especially where that data has been transmitted over a network, because data can potentially be intercepted, modified, and then relayed by a malicious third party (for pleasure or profit). For example, a share-trading application might require traders to authenticate themselves over a Secure Sockets Layer (SSL) connection, but then revert to plaintext mode for processing all buy and sell requests, because SSL is too slow to encrypt all traffic to and from the broker's Web site, particularly when thousands of users are trading concurrently. A malicious third party might take control of a downstream router and write a filter that changes all co-occurrences of "BUY" and "1000" shares to "10000" shares. Such an attack would be difficult to thwart, unless SSL was used for all transmissions.

One way to determine data integrity is to use a one-way hash function, like a message digest. These functions can be computed from a string of arbitrary length and return an almost unique identifier, such as b6d624gaf995c9e7c7da2a816b7deb33. Even a small change in the source string changes the computed function, so the message digests can be used to detect data tampering. There are several algorithms available to compute such hash functions, including MD5 and SHA-1, which all generate a different bit length digest—the longest digests provide a relatively stronger guarantee of collision resistance; that is, when the same digest is computed from the same piece of data. Fortunately, the probability of doing this is very low. The bit lengths of MD5 and SHA-1 are 128 and 160 bits, respectively.

Accurate data has all the properties of data integrity, plus an assurance that what a piece of data claims to be is what it actually is. Thus, a username of nine characters cannot be an accurate login if the maximum length is eight characters. Indeed, the many buffer-overflow attacks of recent years have exploited excess data length as a key mechanism for bringing down applications that don't explicitly check for data accuracy.

Authenticity and Consistency

An issue related to integrity is authenticity—that is, given a piece of data that has demonstrated integrity, how do you know that it is authentic? If multiple copies of data exist, and they all pass integrity checks, how do you know whether they are consistent with each other? If multiple copies of a piece of data exist, and one or more copies are inconsistent, how do you establish which one (or more) copies is authentic? The issues of authenticity and consistency are closely related in distributed systems.

Identification and Authentication

How can you determine whether data is authentic? The most common method is to authenticate the principal who is presenting the data. The most common form of authentication is a username and password combination. The username represents the identity of a specific principal, and is known publicly, while the password is a secret token that (in theory) is known only by the user. In practice, users create passwords that can be easily guessed (e.g., birth date, middle name, vehicle registration) or that are written down somewhere (e.g., on a Post-it Note, a sheet of paper in the top drawer, or a whiteboard). If the password consists of a string of random characters of sufficient length that is equally probable as any other random string to be guessed, and if the password is secret, then the system works well. Defining sufficient length is sometimes difficult—the UNIX standard for passwords is eight case-sensitive alphanumeric characters, while most ATM PINs are four digits. Thus, there are 10^4 (10,000) possible ATM PIN permutations, while there are approximately 94^8 (6,095,689,385,410,816) possible UNIX password permutations.

UNIX authentication typically permits three incorrect logins before a delay of 15 seconds, to prevent brute-force attacks. If an automated sequence of three login attempts took 1 second, without any delays, then a search of all possible passwords would take around 193,293,042 years. Of course, there are potentially ways around this—if the shadow password file can be directly obtained, then the search space can be partitioned and the generation of candidate passwords can be parallelized. Using a good password-guessing program like *Crack* on a fast computer with a shadow password file can usually yield results within a matter of minutes or hours if passwords are weak.

There are more sophisticated mechanisms for authentication that revolve around two different strategies—strong identification and strong authentication. Strong identification typically means using an identifier that cannot be presented by anyone other than the intended user. These identifiers are usually biometric—iris scans, face recognition, and fingerprint recognition are becoming more commonly used as identifiers. Of course, there are concerns that the strength of identification can be easily compromised—an eye could be plucked and presented to the monitor, or its patterns transcribed holographically. In these cases, the scanners are sensitive enough to detect whether the eye is living and will reject scans that do not meet this criteria. Face recognition systems are very reliable with a small number of samples, but often have problems "scaling up" to identify individuals within pools of thousands, millions, or even billions of potential users.

Fingerprint systems have been shown to be weak because an imprint is left on the glass of the device—a mould can be easily taken and used to produce fake prints that fool most devices.

While these teething problems should be overcome with further research, it is always recommended to combine strong identification with strong authentication. The username and password combination can be greatly enhanced by the use of a one-time pad, to implement two-factor authentication. Here, a user is authenticated using the fixed user password—when this is accepted by the system, it computes a second password that is not transmitted and is (say) time dependent. This password is also generated by a device or physical pad that the user carries with them. Once the one-time password is transmitted by the user, and she is authenticated a second time, the password becomes invalid. The password need not be time based—a random or chaotic function could be iterated with a different seed or initial parameter to generate a fixed sequence of passwords for each user. As long as that function remains secret, strong authentication can be assured.

One reason why these strong authentication measures are necessary is that usernames and passwords transmitted in the clear over a network can be intercepted by a malicious third party who is promiscuously reading the contents of packets from a network. Thus, if a sniffer application runs on a router between the client and server, the username and password can be intercepted. If the link cannot be secured by using a Virtual Private Network (VPN) of some description, or even a secure client such as Secure Shell (SSH), then a one-time pad is ideal—all tokens can be intercepted because they are valid for a single session only; the tokens cannot be used to successfully log in a second time, because the generated password is invalidated once the first login has been accepted. Even if the link can be secured, a one-time pad is still useful because the client may not be trusted, and all keystrokes could be logged and saved for future malicious use. For example, keyboard listeners installed on Internet café PCs could record username and password combinations and automatically e-mail them to a cracker. These would be unusable if a one-time pad were used because of the expiry time of the second factor.

Procedures

The following procedures can be used to implement basic Solaris security measures.

Confidentiality

A secret is a piece of information known only to one or more persons—that is, something kept hidden from others or known only to oneself or to a few other people. To ensure secrecy, the data is encoded in a form that can be decoded only by the intended persons. Cryptology is the field of study underlying the development of new methods of encoding secrets (cryptology), and inverse methods to break those techniques (cryptanalysis). Cryptography involves the design of new ciphers and enhancement of existing ciphers, which are algorithms that convert the source data (plaintext) into a secret (ciphertext). The encoding process is known as encryption, and the decoding process is called decryption. A large integer, known as a key, is central to the encryption and decryption process—and, depending on the algorithm, a different key may be used for encryption and decryption. Algorithms that use only a single key for encryption and decryption are called symmetric, while algorithms that use two separate keys are known as asymmetric.

An individual user usually wants to encrypt their own data and ensure secrecy from everyone else, in which case a symmetric algorithm typically suffices. The drawback for sharing data secretly with multiple users is that once the key is known to one unauthorized user, then all users' data is compromised. This is where asymmetric algorithms come into play—the encoding key can be compromised, but the data will still be protected unless the decoding key is known to an attacker, because the decoding key cannot be derived from the encoding key.

Given that much data in defense, commerce, and government spheres must be kept secret, it's little surprise that cryptography is what most lay people associate with security. However, as you've seen from the other requirements of security in this chapter, secrecy is only one part of the overall equation—if data is inauthentic, inaccurate, and lacks integrity, then there's little point in keeping it secret.

This section examines basic aspects of how both symmetric and asymmetric cryptography are used in modern applications to ensure secrecy of data.

Symmetric Key Cryptography

In UNIX, a simple symmetric key encryption system is made available through the `crypt` command. `crypt` takes a passphrase entered on the command line and uses it to encrypt plaintext from standard input. The plaintext is passed through a stream cipher, and `crypt` then sends the ciphertext to standard output.

Consider a simple example. Imagine that a list of secret agents' names is stored in a flat-file database called *agents.txt*. To protect these identities, you need to encrypt the data and store the ciphertext in a file called *agents.crypt*. You also need to select an appropriate passphrase in order to protect the data—in this case, use a random string of *78hg65df*. Thus, to encrypt the file, you would use the following command:

```
% crypt 78hg65df < agents.txt > agents.crypt; rm agents.txt
```

Since the contents of *agents.crypt* would contain binary data, you could view the ciphertext using the following command:

```
% strings agents.crypt
8rgj5kg_-90fg++fg8ijrfssfjghkdfmvv
8dg0gf90ggd,rkf8b8fdk234,k_+_7gfsg
...
```

To decrypt the ciphertext, and recover the plaintext, the `crypt` command can also be used. The passphrase 78hg65df will need to be supplied. If the passphrase is lost, then the data is not recoverable—unless brute-force cracking is attempted.

It looks like `crypt` solves all of your secrecy problems, but actually there are several problems with this simple scenario. The first problem is that when the `crypt` command is executed, the passphrase appears in the clear in the process list, making it visible to any user who is scanning the list on a regular basis for the token "crypt". A cracker might be able to determine the average file size on the system and the average time it takes to encrypt that file size under an average system load. If average encryption time for an average file is ten minutes, then a simple `cron` using the command `ps -eaf | grep crypt` would intercept many of the `crypt` invocations. These could be e-mailed to the attacker when detected, thereby bypassing the secrecy measures implemented.

The second problem with the preceding simple example is that the cipher used by the `crypt` program is much less secure than current standards, making it susceptible to brute-force cracking attacks. Other symmetric key ciphers that could be used include the 56-bit Data Encryption Standard (DES). A modified DES variant known as triple-DES encrypts the plaintext, then further encrypts this first ciphertext, and again encrypts the second ciphertext to yield a third and final ciphertext. Clearly, this is more secure than one pass—but the success of cryptanalytic attacks depends on the size of the keys involved, and also on the nature of the plaintext. Many attacks are based on the fact that in natural language, there are differences in character and word frequency—so the word "the" appears in natural language much more frequently than "hippopotamus." Also, knowing even a small section of the plaintext can assist in cryptanalysis. Imagine if every company invoice was encrypted—the company's name would appear on every invoice and would provide an excellent starting point for examining commonalities between the ciphertext of all invoices.

If data is only available for a short period of time, and just needs to be scrambled, then a compression algorithm may be utilized. These make use of the redundancies previously described to recode the plaintext into a compressed text. By inspection, the compressed text appears to be ciphertext. There is much interest in combining compression and cryptography where data security is required, in applications where bandwidth is limited. For example, studio-quality video streaming should be encrypted between sender and receiver, but should be compressed as much as possible without sacrificing quality to minimize bandwidth use.

Asymmetric Key Cryptography

One major limitation of symmetric key cryptography is that the same key is required to encrypt and decrypt data. This is fine for protecting individual files from unauthorized users, but many data-protection scenarios require multiple users to interact with each other, when trust has never been established. For example, if a manager in New York needs to exchange sales data with a manager in Buffalo, and this data requires encryption, both managers could simply share the key required to decrypt the data. However, this approach has two problems. First, users tend to apply the same password and key to multiple purposes, meaning that one manager might be able to access the other manager's files; second, what if more than two managers were involved? Clearly, passing a password around a user group of 1,000 users is tantamount to having no security at all! A system is required that allows individual users to encrypt data using one key, and for the file to be decrypted using a separate key for each user.

Asymmetric encryption allows separate keys to be used for encrypting and decrypting data. How is this possible? Basically, every user is assigned a private key, which they never release to anyone else, and a public key, which is supplied to other users who need to send the user encrypted data. For example, the New York manager would have a private key stored on a floppy disk, locked in a safe, as would the Buffalo manager. Both would also exchange their public keys via e-mail, or another offline method such as floppy disk, verifying that the keys were genuine by using a key "fingerprints" check over the telephone. To encrypt a file for the Buffalo manager, the New York manager would need to use both his/her own private key and the Buffalo manager's public key. Conversely, the Buffalo manager would need to use her private key and the New York manager's public key to encrypt a file for him. Remember that if you exchange public keys via e-mail, and have no other method of verifying who is on the other end of the line, then you're ripe for a "man in the middle attack," because the person you think you are exchanging data with could be an intermediary. For example, imagine if Joe substitutes his key in place of his manager's, and manages to place his machine between a manager's machine and an external router. Now Joe is able to pretend to be his manager, issuing his own public key with his manager's name for which he actually has the corresponding private key.

The most important feature (or limitation, depending on your requirements) of asymmetric key cryptography is that obtaining the private key used to encrypt data is not sufficient to decrypt that data: only the private key of the individual whose public key was used for signing can be used for this purpose. This can be very important in situations where data may be compromised in a specific location. For example, an embassy in a foreign country under threat of attack may decide to encrypt all data by using the public key of an officer in the State Department in Washington, send it via e-mail, and then delete the on-site originals. Even if the encrypted data and the embassy's private key were obtained by force, they could not be used to decrypt the data.

Of course, asymmetry implies that if you lose your original data accidentally, you must rely on the public key holder's private key to decrypt the data. However, at least one avenue of recourse is available, unlike when using symmetric key cryptography, where a lost key almost certainly means lost data.

Public Key Cryptography

One of the most commonly used *public key* systems that uses asymmetric keys is the Pretty Good Privacy (PGP) application (**http://www.pgp.com/**). PGP is available for a wide variety of operating systems, making it very popular among PC and UNIX users, because data can be exchanged without conversion. PGP works both on the command line, to facilitate secure storage of files, and as a plug-in to e-mail programs, allowing messages to be exchanged securely. This ensures that intermediate mail servers and routers cannot intercept the decrypted contents of transmitted messages, even if they can intercept packets containing the encrypted data.

To use PGP, each user needs to generate their own public/private key pair. This can be performed by using the following command:

```
$ pgp -kg
```

The following prompt will be displayed:

```
Choose the type of your public key:
  1)  DSS/Diffie-Hellman - New algorithm for 5.0 (default)
  2)  RSA
Choose 1 or 2:
```

The public key format that you choose will determine what types of block ciphers can be used to encrypt your data. The DSS/Diffie-Hellman algorithm allows Triple DES, CAST, or IDEA, while RSA keys work only with IDEA, so most users will want to select the DSS/Diffie-Hellman algorithm.

Next, you need to select the key size:

```
Pick your public/private keypair key size:
(Sizes are Diffie-Hellman/DSS; Read the user's guide for more information)
  1)    768/768  bits- Commercial grade, probably not currently breakable
  2)   1024/1024 bits- High commercial grade, secure for many years
  3)   2048/1024 bits- "Military" grade, secure for foreseeable
future(default)
  4)   3072/1024 bits- Archival grade, slow, highest security
Choose 1, 2, 3 or 4, or enter desired number of Diffie-Hellman bits
(768 - 4096):
```

Keep in mind that although a large key provides greater security, it also slows down operations significantly because it is CPU-intensive. Thus, if your needs are commercial rather than military, you should use the 768- or 1024-bit key. Military users should certainly select the largest key size available (currently 4096 bits).

Next, you need to enter a user ID. This should be recognizable by your intended recipients. For example, a programmer called Yayoi Rei from Rei Corporation would have a user ID of Yayoi Rei <yayoi@rei.com>. Even in countries in which the family name is usually written first, the expectation for the key server is that the family name will appear last, followed by an e-mail address:

```
You need a user ID for your public key.  The desired form for this
user ID is your FULL name, followed by your E-mail address enclosed in
<angle brackets>, if you have an E-mail address.  For example:
  Joe Smith <user@domain.com>
Enter a user ID for your public key:
```

If you wish your key to be valid for a specific time period, you can enter its period of validity in days next; or if the key is intended to be permanent, you can enter zero days:

```
Enter the validity period of your key in days from 0 - 999
0 is forever (and the default):
```

You need a password to be associated with the private key for future use, and you will need to enter it twice for verification:

```
You need a pass phrase to protect your private key(s).
Your pass phrase can be any sentence or phrase and may have many
words, spaces, punctuation, or any other printable characters.
Enter pass phrase:
Enter again, for confirmation:
```

Finally, a number of random numbers needs to be generated from the intervals between random key presses on your keyboard. Try to insert some variation in the key press latency to ensure security:

```
We need to generate 595 random bits.  This is done by measuring the
time intervals between your keystrokes.  Please enter some random text
on your keyboard until you hear the beep:
```

Once the keypair has been created, you can list all the keys on your local keyring by using the following command:

```
$ pgp -kl
Type Bits KeyID       Created     Expires      Algorithm        Use
sec+  768 0x71849810 2002-01-07 ----------  DSS              Sign & Encrypt
sub   768 0x78697B9D 2002-01-07 ----------  Diffie-Hellman
uid  Yayoi Rei <yayoi@rei.com>
1 matching key found
```

The keypair is now available for use. To generate a copy of your public key for your correspondents and colleagues to use, you need to extract this from your keyring as follows:

```
$pgp -x Yayoi
-----BEGIN PGP PUBLIC KEY BLOCK-----
mQFCBDw5+oURAwDBKeBtW+0PdDvCC7KO1/gUAF9X//uGRhbPkg6m83QzaA7pr6T+
QAVQE4q74NXFCakX8GzmhzHtA2/Hoe/yfpfHGHMhJRZHZIWQWTS6W+r5wHYRSObm
NNNTeJ4C+3/klbEAoP/Mjlim4eMkfvYwNmifTUvak5zRAv48SrXOHmVI+5Mukx8Z
1T7txut60VeYd34QvidwtUbbL7p2IVVa3fGW/gsuo7whblaW//+5Z/+4wxbaqnu6
WxT5vFObm1sJ7E20OW3SDLxdVjeTlYbzTUfNwbN/KHoUzMsC/2EZ3aDB6mGZuDPL
```

```
0SMT8sOoxlbpPouuBxnF/sbcxgOVKkGZDS5XrhodUbp2RUflwFSMyqjbmoqITnNq
xzpSXEhT0odwjjq3YeHj1icBaiy9xB/j0CBXe3QQKAXk5bXMEbQZWWF5b2kgUmVp
IDx5YXlvaUByZWkuY29tPokASwQQEQIACwUCPDn6hQQLAwECAAoJEHCOVqNxhJgQ
riMAn18a5kKYaepNk8BEksMJOTbRgDQmAKC0JD6wvYfo5zmziGr7TAv+uFWN5LkA
zQQ8OfqHEAMA6zd3dxeMkyKJmust3S3IrKvQzMLlMoRuQdb+N2momBYDF1+slo8k
EMK8F/Vrun+HdhJW+hWivgZRhTMe9fm6OL7PDYESkwuQsMizqAJJ1JF0yhbfTwE5
GjdVPcUMyPyTAAICAwCgdBO1XyiPbwdQtjxq+8CZ7uchASvJXsU28OFqbLzNcAW2
Q641WSs6qr2HNfgf+ikG8S8eVWVKEBgm6md9trr6CK25SYEu4oB3o1f45X4daa/n
iNytKUglPPOJMK/rhJOJAD8DBRg8OfqHcI5Wo3GEmBARAs3mAJ0ZPQjmlYyNsMDY
ZVbR9/q2xQl8gACgkqVCNYR40mPIaxrd5Cw9ZrHqlkQ=
=Gsmt
-----END PGP PUBLIC KEY BLOCK-----
```

To encrypt a file using standard, symmetric encryption, you simply pass the *-c* option on the command line along with the name of the file that you want to encrypt. This provides Solaris users with an alternative to `crypt`, where a more secure encryption algorithm is desired.

```
$ pgp -c secret.doc
You need a passphrase to encrypt the file
Enter pass phrase:
Enter same passphrase again
Enter pass phrase:
Creating output file secret.pgp
```

After entering a password to protect the data in *secret.doc*, the encrypted file *secret.pgp* is created. In order to sign the file for another user, you need to pass the *-e* option, along with the name of the user from your keyring who will have the power to decrypt your data:

```
$ pgp -e Henry secret.doc
   4096 bits, Key ID 76857743, Created 2002-01-07
   "Henry Bolingbroke <henry@bolingbroke.co.uk>"
Creating output file secret.pgp
```

The file can then be transmitted to Henry by uuencoding it, by sending it as an e-mail attachment, or by directly generating the file in ASCII format:

```
$ pgp -ea Henry secret.doc
```

Disabling IP Ports

The first step in network security is to prevent unauthorized entry by disabling access to specific IP ports, as defined by individual entries in the services database. This action prevents specific services from operating, even if the `inetd` attempts to accept a connection for a service because it is still defined in */etc/inetd.conf*. This section examines how to disable specific services from `inetd`, in conjunction with the services database.

It's also important to shut down unnecessary services outside of inetd, such as disabling startup scripts, as discussed in Chapter 4.

The following services are typically enabled in */etc/services* and configured in */etc/inetd.conf*. Most sites will want to disable them and install more secure equivalents. For example, the ftp and telnet services may be replaced by the encrypted secure copy (scp) and secure shell (ssh) programs, respectively. To disable the ftp, telnet, shell, login, exec, comsat, talk, uucp, and finger services, you would comment out their entries in */etc/inetd.conf* by inserting a hash character (#) at the first character position of the line that defines the service. The following configuration enables the ftp, telnet, shell, login, exec, comsat, talk, uucp, and finger services in */etc/inetd.conf*:

```
ftp      stream  tcp  nowait  root    /usr/sbin/in.ftpd      in.ftpd -l
telnet   stream  tcp  nowait  root    /usr/sbin/in.telnetd   in.telnetd
shell    stream  tcp  nowait  root    /usr/sbin/in.rshd      in.rshd
login    stream  tcp  nowait  root    /usr/sbin/in.rlogind   in.rlogind
exec     stream  tcp  nowait  root    /usr/sbin/in.rexecd    in.rexecd
comsat   dgram   udp  wait    root    /usr/sbin/in.comsat    in.comsat
talk     dgram   udp  wait    root    /usr/sbin/in.talkd     in.talkd
uucp     stream  tcp  nowait  root    /usr/sbin/in.uucpd     in.uucpd
finger   stream  tcp  nowait  nobody  /usr/sbin/in.fingerd   in.fingerd
```

The following configuration disables the ftp, telnet, shell, login, exec, comsat, talk, uucp, and finger services in */etc/inetd.conf*:

```
#ftp      stream  tcp  nowait  root    /usr/sbin/in.ftpd      in.ftpd -l
#telnet   stream  tcp  nowait  root    /usr/sbin/in.telnetd   in.telnetd
#shell    stream  tcp  nowait  root    /usr/sbin/in.rshd      in.rshd
#login    stream  tcp  nowait  root    /usr/sbin/in.rlogind   in.rlogind
#exec     stream  tcp  nowait  root    /usr/sbin/in.rexecd    in.rexecd
#comsat   dgram   udp  wait    root    /usr/sbin/in.comsat    in.comsat
#talk     dgram   udp  wait    root    /usr/sbin/in.talkd     in.talkd
#uucp     stream  tcp  nowait  root    /usr/sbin/in.uucpd     in.uucpd
#finger   stream  tcp  nowait  nobody  /usr/sbin/in.fingerd   in.fingerd
```

Similarly, the following configuration enables the ftp, telnet, shell, login, exec, comsat, talk, uucp, and finger services in */etc/services*:

```
ftp                 21/tcp
telnet              23/tcp
shell               514/tcp       cmd
login               513/tcp
exec                512/tcp
biff                512/udp       comsat
talk                517/udp
uucp                540/tcp       uucpd
finger   stream  tcp    nowait    nobody  /usr/sbin/in.fingerd    in.fingerd
```

Similarly, the following configuration disables the `ftp`, `telnet`, `shell`, `login`, `exec`, `comsat`, `talk`, `uucp`, and `finger` services in *etc/services*:

```
#ftp            21/tcp
#telnet         23/tcp
#shell          514/tcp         cmd
#login          513/tcp
#exec           512/tcp
#biff           512/udp         comsat
#talk           517/udp
#uucp           540/tcp         uucpd
#finger  stream tcp      nowait nobody  /usr/sbin/in.fingerd    in.fingerd
```

Don't forget that you need to HUP the `inetd` daemon for these changes to be enabled.

Checking User and Group Identification

The concept of the user is central to Solaris—all processes and files on a Solaris system are "owned" by a particular user and are assigned to a specific user group. No data or activities on the system may exist without first establishing a valid user or group. Managing users and groups as a Solaris administrator can be a challenging activity— you will be responsible for assigning all the privileges granted or denied to a user or group of users, and many of these permissions carry great risk. For example, a user with an inappropriate privilege level may execute inappropriate commands as the superuser, causing damage to your system.

You can determine which user is currently logged in from a terminal session by using the `id` command:

```
$ id
uid=1001(natashia) gid=10(dialup)
```

The output shows that the currently logged-in user is *natashia*, with UID=1001. In addition, the current group of *natashia* is a dialup group with GID=10. It is possible for the user and group credentials to change during a single terminal session. For example, if the `su` facility is used effectively to "become" the superuser, the UID and GID associated with the current terminal session will also change:

```
$ su root
Password:
# id
uid=0(root) gid=1(other)
```

Here, the root user (UID=0) belonging to the group *other* (GID=1) has spawned a new shell with full superuser privileges.

You can obtain a list of all groups that a user belongs to by using the `groups` command. For example, to view all the groups that the root user belongs to, use the following command:

```
# groups root
other root bin sys adm uucp mail tty lp nuucp daemon
```

Protecting the Superuser Account

You've just examined how to use the `su` facility to invoke superuser privileges from an unprivileged account. The user with UID=0 (typically the root user) has unlimited powers to act on a Solaris system. The root user can perform the following potentially dangerous functions:

- Add, delete, or modify all other user accounts
- Read and write all files, and create new ones
- Add or delete devices to the system
- Install new system software
- Read everyone's e-mail
- Snoop network traffic for usernames and passwords of other systems on the LAN
- Modify all system logs to remove all traces of superuser access
- Pretend to be an unprivileged user and access their accounts on other systems where login access is authenticated against a username

These powers combine to make the root account sound rather sinister: however, many of these activities are legitimate and necessary system administration routines that are undertaken daily. For example, network traffic can be snooped to determine where network outages are occurring, and copying user files to backup tapes every night is generally in everyone's best interest. However, if an intruder gains root access, they are free to roam the system, deleting or stealing data, removing or adding user accounts, or installing Trojan horses that can transparently modify the way that your system operates.

One way to protect against an authorized user gaining root access is to use a hard-to-guess root password. This makes it difficult for a cracker to use a password-cracking program to guess your password successfully. The optimal password is a completely random string of alphanumeric and punctuation characters.

In addition, the root password should never be written down unless it is locked in the company safe, nor should it be told to anyone who doesn't need to know it. The root password must usually be entered twice—just in case you should happen to make a typographical error, as the characters that you type are masked on the screen.

The root user should never be able to log in using Telnet: instead, the su facility should be used by individual users to gain root privileges where necessary. This protects the root account, since at least one other password is required to log in, unless the root user has access to the console. In addition, the su command should be owned by a sysadmin group (or similar) so that only those users who need access to the root account should be able to obtain it. Once su has been used to gain root access, the root user can use su to spawn a shell with the effective ID of any other user on the system. This is a security weakness, because the root user could pretend to be another user and perform actions or modify data which is traceable to the effective user, and not root.

A more practical and secure solution in a large Solaris environment is to use solutions such as one-time passwords or a mechanism that employs two-factor authentication such as SecurID. It's also very important to check for obvious flaws in the content of the password and group files, such as empty passwords or group affiliations, which should always be checked and fixed.

Monitoring User Activity

System access can be monitored interactively using a number of measures. For example, syslog entries can be automatically viewed in real time using this command:

```
$ tail -f /var/adm/messages
```

However, most administrators want to view interactively what remote users are doing on a system at any time. This section examines two methods for viewing remote-user activity. The command who displays who is currently logged into the system. The output of who displays the username, connecting line, date of login, idle time, process ID, and a comment. Here's an example output:

```
$ who
root          console        Nov 22 12:39
natashia      pts/0          Nov 19 21:05      (client.site.com)
```

This command can be automated to update the list of active users. An alternative to who is the w command, which displays a more detailed summary of the current activity on the system, including the current process name for each user. The header output from w shows the current time, the uptime of the current system, and the number of users actively logged into the system. The average system load is also displayed as a series of three numbers at the end of the w header, indicating the average number of jobs in the run queue for the previous 1, 5, and 15 minutes. In addition to the output generated by who, the w command displays the current foreground process for each user, which is usually a shell. For example, the following command shows that the root user has an active perl process, while the user *natashia* is running the Cornell shell:

```
7:15pm   up 1 day(s),   5:11,   2 users,   load average: 1.00, 1.00, 1.01
User      tty            login@ idle   JCPU   PCPU   what
```

```
root      console      Thu12pm 3days      6      6    perl
natashia  pts/12         Thu11am  8:45         9         /usr/local/bin/tcsh
```

The w and who commands are useful tools for getting an overview of current usage patterns on any Solaris system. Another useful command is last, which displays historical usage patterns for the current system in a sequential format:

```
$ last
natashia   pts/4       hp           Wed Apr 11 19:00    still logged in
root       console     :0           Tue Apr 10 20:11    still logged in
natashia   pts/2       nec          Tue Apr 10 19:17 - 19:24  (00:06)
natashia   pts/6       austin       Tue Apr 10 15:53 - 15:53  (00:00)
root       console     :0           Tue Apr 10 14:24 - 16:25  (02:01)
reboot     system boot              Tue Apr 10 14:04
natashia   pts/5       hp           Thu Apr  5 21:38 - 21:40  (00:01)
natashia   pts/5       hp           Thu Apr  5 21:22 - 21:37  (00:15)
natashia   pts/5       10.64.18.1   Thu Apr  5 19:30 - 20:00  (00:30)
natashia   pts/5       hp           Thu Apr  5 19:18 - 19:29  (00:11)
root       console     :0           Thu Apr  5 19:17 - 22:05  (4+02:48)
reboot     system boot              Thu Apr  5 19:14
natashia   pts/5       hp           Tue Apr  3 16:14 - 18:26  (02:11)
natashia   pts/5       hp           Tue Apr  3 08:48 - 10:35  (01:47)
root       console     :0           Tue Apr  3 08:45 - 22:01  (13:15)
reboot     system boot              Tue Apr  3 08:43
root       console     :0           Fri Mar 30 18:54 - 19:27  (00:32)
reboot     system boot              Fri Mar 30 18:46
natashia   pts/6       hp           Tue Mar 27 20:46 - 21:51  (01:04)
root       console     :0           Tue Mar 27 19:50 - 21:51  (02:01)
reboot     system boot              Tue Mar 27 19:48
root       console     :0           Mon Mar 26 17:43 - 17:47  (00:04)
```

Securing Remote Access

Remote access is the hallmark of modern multiple-user operating systems such as Solaris and its antecedents, such as VAX/VMS. Solaris users can concurrently log into and interactively execute commands on Solaris server systems from any client that supports Transmission Control Protocol/Internet Protocol (TCP/IP), such as Solaris, Windows, and Macintosh OS.

This section examines several historically popular methods of remote access, such as Telnet. It also outlines the much-publicized security holes and bugs that have led to the innovation of secure remote-access systems, such as SSH. These "safer" systems facilitate the encryption of the contents of user sessions and/or authentication sequences and provide an important level of protection for sensitive data. Although remote access is useful, the administrative overhead in securing a Solaris system can be significant, reflecting the increased functionality that remote-access services provide.

Telnet

Telnet is the standard remote-access tool for logging into a Solaris machine from a client using the original DARPA Telnet protocol. A client can be executed on most operating systems that support TCP/IP. Alternatively, a Java Telnet client is available (**http://srp.stanford.edu/binaries.html**), which is supported on any operating system that has a browser that runs Java natively or as a plug-in. Telnet is a terminal-like program that gives users interactive access to a login shell of their choice (for example, the C-shell, or csh). Most Telnet clients support VT100 or VT220 terminal emulations. The login shell can be used to execute scripts, develop applications, and read e-mail and news—in short, everything a Solaris environment should provide to its users, with the exception of X11 graphics and Open Windows, and, more recently, the common desktop environment (CDE). A common arrangement in many organizations is for a Solaris server to be located in a secure area of a building with Telnet-only access allowed. This arrangement is shown in Figure 9-1.

The sequence of events that occurs during a Telnet session begins with a request for a connection from the client to the server. The server either responds (or times out) with a connection being explicitly accepted or rejected. A rejection may occur because the port that normally accepts Telnet client connections on the server has been blocked by a packet filter or firewall. If the connection is accepted, the client is asked to enter a username followed by a password. If the username and password combination is valid, a shell is spawned, and the user is logged in. This sequence of events is shown in Figure 9-2.

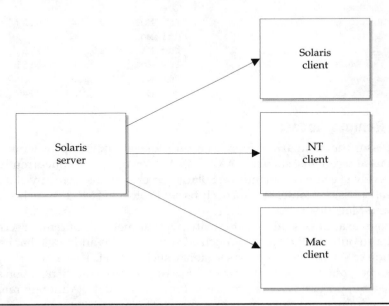

FIGURE 9-1   Typical remote-access topology for client/server technology

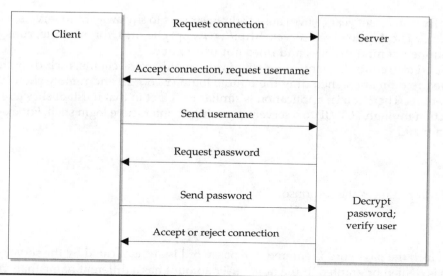

FIGURE 9-2 Identification and authentication of a Telnet session

The standard port for Telnet connections is 23. Thus, a command like this,

```
$ telnet server
```

is expanded to give the effective command:

```
$ telnet server 23
```

This means that Telnet can be used as a tool to access a service on virtually any port. Telnet is controlled by the super Internet daemon (`inetd`), which invokes the *in.telnetd* server. An entry is made in */etc/services* that defines the port number for the Telnet service, which looks like this:

```
telnet    23/tcp
```

The configuration file */etc/inetd.conf* also contains important details of the services provided by `inetd`. The `telnet` daemon's location and properties are identified here:

```
telnet stream tcp nowait root /pkgs/tcpwrapper/bin/tcpd in.telnetd
```

In this case, you can see that *in.telnetd* is protected by the use of TCP *wrappers,* which facilitate the logging of Telnet accesses through the Solaris `syslog` facility. In addition, `inetd` has some significant historical security holes and performance issues that, although mostly fixed in recent years, have caused administrators to shy away from servers invoked by inetd. The Apache Web server (**http://www.apache.org**), for example, runs as a standalone daemon process and does not use inetd.

inetd also controls many other standard remote-access clients, including the so-called r-commands, including the remote login (rlogin) and remote shell (rsh) applications. The rlogin application is similar to Telnet in that it establishes a remote connection through TCP/IP to a server, spawning an interactive login shell. For example, the command

```
$ rlogin server
```

by default produces the response

```
password:
```

after which the password is entered, the password is authenticated by the server, and access is denied or granted. If the target user account has a different name than your current user account, you can try this:

```
$ rlogin server -l user
```

There are two main differences between Telnet and rlogin, however, which are significant. The first is that rlogin attempts to use the username on your current system as the account name to connect to on the remote service, whereas Telnet always prompts for a separate username. This makes remotely logging into machines on a single logical network with rlogin much faster than with Telnet. Second, on a trusted, secure network, it is possible to set up a remote authentication mechanism by which the remote host allows a direct, no-username/no-password login from authorized clients. This automated authentication can be performed on a system-wide level by defining an "equivalent" host for authentication purposes on the server in */etc/hosts.equiv*, or on a user-by-user basis with the file *.rhosts*. If the file */etc/hosts.equiv* contains the client machine name and your username, you will be permitted to automatically execute a remote login. For example, if the */etc/hosts.equiv* file on the server contains this line,

```
client
```

any user from the machine client may log into a corresponding account on the server without entering a username and password. Similarly, if your username and client machine name appear in the *.rhosts* file in the home directory of the user with the same name on the server, you will also be permitted to remotely log in without an identification/ authentication challenge. This means that a user on the remote system may log in with all the privileges of the user on the local system, without being asked to enter a username or password—clearly a dangerous security risk. The sequence of identification and authentication for rlogin is shown in Figure 9-3.

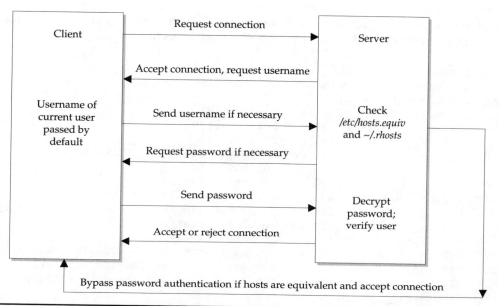

FIGURE 9-3   Identification and authentication sequence for rlogin

Remote-shell (rsh) connects to a specified hostname and executes a command. rsh is equivalent to rlogin when no command arguments are specified. rsh copies its standard input to the remote command, the standard output of the remote command to its standard output, and the standard error of the remote command to its standard error. Interrupt, quit, and terminate signals are propagated to the remote command. In contrast to commands issued interactively through rlogin, rsh normally terminates when the remote command does.

As an example, the following command executes the command df −k on the server, returning information about disk slices and creating the local file *server.df.txt* that contains the output of the command:

```
$ rsh server df -k > server.df.txt
```

Clearly, rsh has the potential to be useful in scripts and automated command processing.

Vulnerabilities

One of the unfortunate drawbacks of the Telnet system is that usernames and, especially, unencrypted passwords are transmitted in cleartext around the network. Thus, if you were using a Telnet client to connect from a cyber café in Paris to a server in New York, your traffic might pass through 20 or 30 routers and computers, all of which can be programmed to "sniff" the contents of network packets. A sample `traceroute` of the path taken by packets from AT&T to Sun's Web page looks like this:

```
$ traceroute www.sun.com
Tracing route to wwwwseast.usec.sun.com [192.9.49.30]
over a maximum of 30 hops:
  1    184 ms    142 ms    138 ms   202.10.4.131
  2    147 ms    144 ms    138 ms   202.10.4.129
  3    150 ms    142 ms    144 ms   202.10.1.73
  4    150 ms    144 ms    141 ms   ia4.optus.net.au [202.139.32.17]
  5    148 ms    143 ms    139 ms   202.139.1.197
  6    490 ms    489 ms    474 ms   sf1.optus.net.au [192.65.89.246]
  7    526 ms    480 ms    485 ms   gn.cwix.net [207.124.109.57]
  8    494 ms    482 ms    485 ms   core7.SanFrancisco.cw.net [204.70.10.9]
  9    483 ms    489 ms    484 ms   core2.SanFrancisco.cw.net
[204.70.9.132]
 10    557 ms    552 ms    561 ms   xcore3.Boston.cw.net [204.70.150.81]
 11    566 ms    572 ms    554 ms   sun.Boston.cw.net [204.70.179.102]
 12    577 ms    574 ms    558 ms   wwwwseast.usec.sun.com [192.9.49.30]
Trace complete.
```

That's a lot of intermediate hosts, any of which could potentially be sniffing passwords and other sensitive data. If the network packet that contains the username and password is sniffed in this way, a rogue user could easily log into the target account using a Telnet client. This risk has led to the development of SSH and similar products that encrypt the exchange of username and password information between client and server, making it difficult for sniffers to extract useful information from network packets. OpenSSH, an open source version of SSH, is now supplied with Solaris.

Although `rlogin` is the fastest kind of remote login possible, it can be easily exploited on systems that are not trusted and secure. Systems that are directly connected to the Internet, or those that form part of a subnet that is not firewalled, should never be considered secure. These kinds of configurations can be dangerous in some circumstances, even if they are convenient for remotely administering many different machines.

The most dangerous use of /etc/hosts.equiv occurs, for example, when the file contains the single line

```
+
```

This allows any users from any host that has equivalent usernames to remotely log in.

The .rhosts file is also considered dangerous in some situations. For example, it is common practice in some organizations to allow the root and privileged users to permit automatic logins by root users from other machines by creating a /.rhosts file. A more insidious problem can occur when users define their own .rhosts files, however, in their own home directories. These files are not directly controlled by the system administrator and may be exploited by malicious remote users. One way to remove this threat is to enforce a policy of disallowing user .rhosts files and activating a nightly cron job to search for and remove any files named *.rhosts* in the user directories. A `cron` entry for a root like this

```
0 2 * * * find /staff -name .rhosts -print -exec rm{} \;
```

should execute this simple `find` and `remove` command every morning at 2 A.M. for all user accounts whose home directories lie within the */staff* partition.

Secure Shell

OpenSSH (or just plain SSH) is a secure client and server solution that facilitates the symmetric and asymmetric encryption of identification and authentication sequences for remote access. It is designed to replace the Telnet and `rlogin` applications on the client side, with clients available for Solaris, Windows, and many other operating systems. On the server side, it improves upon the nonsecure services supported by `inetd`, such as the r-commands. Figure 9-4 shows a typical SSH client session from a Windows client.

SSH uses a generic Transport layer encryption mechanism over TCP/IP, which uses either the popular Blowfish algorithm or the U.S. government–endorsed triple-DES algorithm for the encryption engine. This is used to transmit encrypted packets whose contents can still be sniffed like all traffic on the network by using public key cryptography, implementing the Diffie-Hellman algorithm for key exchange. Thus, the contents of encrypted packets appear to be random without the appropriate "key" to decrypt them.

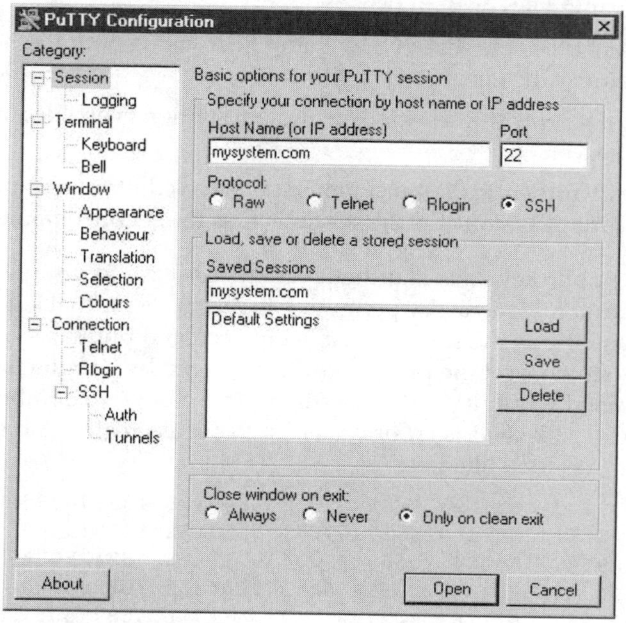

FIGURE 9-4 Typical SSH client session

The use of encryption technology makes it extremely unlikely that the contents of the interactive session will ever be known to anyone except the client and the server. In addition to the encryption of session data, identification and authentication sequences are also encrypted using RSA encryption technology. This means that username and password combinations also cannot be sniffed by a third party. SSH also provides automatic forwarding for graphics applications, based around the X11 windowing system, which is a substantial improvement over the text-only Telnet client.

The sequence of events for establishing an SSH client connection to a server is demonstrated in Figure 9-5, for the standard username/password authentication, and proceeds as follows:

1. The client connects to a server port (usually port 22, but this can be adapted to suit local conditions) and requests a connection.

2. The server replies with its standard public RSA host key (1024 bits), as well as another RSA server key (768 bits) that changes hourly. Since the server key changes hourly, even if the key for the traffic of one session was cracked, historic data would still remain encrypted, limiting the utility of any such attack.

3. The server can be configured to reject connections from hosts that it doesn't know about, but by default, it will accept connections from any client.

4. If the connection is accepted, the client generates a session key composed of a 256-bit random number and chooses an encryption algorithm that the server supports (triple-DES or Blowfish).

5. The client encrypts the session key using RSA, using both the host and server key, and returns the encrypted key to the server.

6. The server decrypts the session key and encryption is enabled between the client and server.

7. If the default authentication mechanism is selected, the client passes the username and password for the server across the secure channel.

SSH supports public key–based authentication: it is easy to disable the username/ password authentication sequence by permitting logins to clients that have an appropriate private RSA key, as long as the server has a list of accepted public keys. However, if a client computer is stolen, and the private key is retrieved by a rogue user, access to the server can be obtained without a valid username and password combination.

On the client side, a *knwnhsts.txt* or *known_hosts* file is created and server keys are recorded there. Entries look like this:

```
server 1024 35 07448318855220650928863459182148090008748760313126
632026365561406995692291726767198155252016701986067549820423736
393736593998729350847306606972263971147429524250769197415119584
295606317662645984226922061878553598043326806246000016982513757266
29275565929877042118101421261757154527967488715061318946854015766
4183
```

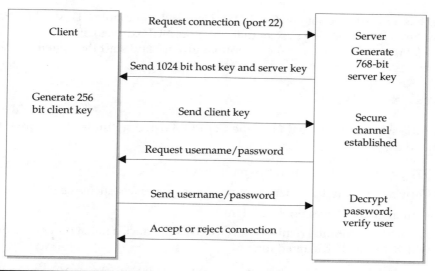

FIGURE 9-5 Authenticating an SSH connection

In addition, a private key for the client is stored in *Identity*, and a public key for the client is stored in *Identity.pub*. Entries in this file are similar to the server key file:

```
1024 37 2590984202231997581736656902901504139087369478896425656 7
21464229667226227437398365816534529060328087939018802894227642 52
42596146365495189984505249238114810023604394738523635422335986 8
11461925396194818530944668193356297977415807086095058777077424 73
73117735318506922304377996946111769127284747352249217710411 51
Paul Watters
```

It is sensible in a commercial context to enforce a policy of SSH-only remote access for interactive logins. This can easily be enforced by enabling the SSH daemon on the server side and removing entries for the Telnet and `rlogin` services in */etc/services* and */etc/inetd.conf*. Now that OpenSSH is supplied with Solaris, there is no excuse for not deploying SSH across all hosts in your local network. Also, there are many items in the */etc/ssh/ssh_config* and */etc/ssh/sshd_config* files that can be configured, such as whether X11 can be forwarded, or whether to support IPv4, IPv6, or both.

Examples

The following examples show how to implement basic security measures for Solaris.

Ensuring Physical Security

It may seem obvious, but if an intruder can physically access your system, then they may be able to take control of your system without the root password, bypassing all the software-based controls that normally limit such activity. How is this possible? If the intruder has access to a bootable CD-ROM drive and a bootable CD-ROM (of Solaris, Linux, or any other operating system that can mount UFS drives), it's a trivial matter to enter the following command at the OpenBoot prompt and start the system without a password:

```
ok boot cdrom
```

Once the system has booted from the CD-ROM drive, a number of options are available to the intruder:

- FTP any file on the system to a remote system.
- Copy any file on the system to a mass storage device (such as a DAT tape).
- Format all the drives on the system.
- Launch a distributed denial of service (DDoS) attack against other networks, which you will be blamed for.

Of course, the possibilities are endless, but the result is the same. You may ask why compromising a system in this way is so easy. One good reason is that if you forget your root password, you can boot from the CD-ROM, mount the boot disk, and manually edit the shadow password file.

This requirement doesn't really excuse poor security, and the OpenBoot monitor provides some options to secure the system. There are three security levels available:

- **None**   Surprisingly, this is the default. No password is required to execute any of the commands in OpenBoot. This is convenient but dangerous, for the reasons outlined earlier.
- **Command**   This level needs a password to be entered for all commands except boot and go. Thus, details of the SCSI bus and network traffic can't be observed by the casual browser, but an intruder could still boot from the CD-ROM.
- **Full**   This level requires a password for every command except go, including the boot command. Thus, even if the system is interrupted and rebooted using the boot command, only the default boot device will be available through go.

To set the security level, use the eeprom command. To set the command level, use the following command:

```
# eeprom security-mode=command
```

Or, to set the command level, use the following command:

```
# eeprom security-mode=full
```

The password for the command and full security levels must be set by using the eeprom command:

```
# eeprom security-password
Changing PROM password:
New password:
Retype new password:
```

Note that if the root password and the full-level password are lost, there is no way to recover the system by software means. You will need to order a new PROM from Sun.

Security Auditing

After installing a new Solaris system and applying the local security policy, you must perform a security audit to ensure that no known vulnerabilities exist in the system, particularly threats posed by remote access. As examined earlier in this chapter, there are a number of strategies, such as switching off ports, that should be adopted prior to releasing a system into production and making it accessible through the Internet.

A security audit should first examine what services are being offered and determine an action plan based on services that should be disabled. In addition, monitoring and logging solutions should be installed for services that are sanctioned, so that it is possible at all times to determine what activity is occurring on any service. For example, a DoS attack may involve hitting a specific port (such as port 80, the Web server port) with a large number of packets, aimed at reducing overall performance of the Web server and the host system. If you don't have logs of all this activity, it will be difficult to determine why your system performance is slow and/or where any potential attacks have originated— that's why TCP wrappers are so important. The final phase of a security audit involves comparing the current list of services running on the system to the security bulletins that are released by the Computer Emergency Response Team (CERT) (**http://www.cert.org/**) and similar computer security groups. After determining the versions of software running on your system, you should determine which packages require patching and/ or upgrading in order to eliminate the risks from known vulnerabilities.

SAINT

Running a security audit and implementing solutions based on the audit can be a time-consuming task. Fortunately, a number of tools are available that can significantly reduce the amount of time required to conduct security audits and cross-check existing applications with known security holes. One of these programs is called SAINT (Security Administrator's Integrated Network Tool), which is freely available from World Wide Digital Security at **http://www.saintcorporation.com/products/saint_engine.html**. SAINT, currently in version 3.0, is based in part on an earlier auditing tool known as SATAN. Both SATAN and SAINT have the ability to scan all of your system services and identify potential and/or known vulnerabilities. These are classified according to their risk: Some items may be classified as critical, requiring immediate attention, whereas other items may come in the form of suggestions rather than requirements. For example, while many local services are vulnerable to a buffer overflow, where the fixed boundaries on an array are deliberately overwritten by a remote client to "crash" the system, other issues, such as the use of r-commands, may be risky but acceptable in suitably protected LANs. Thus, SAINT is not prescriptive in all cases, and suggested actions are always to be performed at the discretion of the local administrator.

Some administrators are concerned that using programs such as SAINT actually contributes to cracking and system break-ins, because they provide a ready-made toolkit that can be used to identify system weaknesses in preparation for a break-in. However, if sites devote the necessary resources to monitoring system usage and identifying potential security threats, the risk posed by SAINT is minimal (particularly if its "suggestions" are acted upon). Indeed, World Wide Digital Security actually offers a Web version of SAINT (called WebSAINT) as the basis for security consulting. For a fee, they will conduct a comprehensive security audit of your network, from the perspective of a remote (rather than a local) user. This can be very useful when attempting to identify potential weaknesses in your front-line systems, such as routers, gateways, and Web servers.

This section examines how to install and configure the SAINT program and how to run an audit on a newly installed Solaris 10 system. This will reveal many of the common issues that arise when Solaris is installed out of the box. Most of these issues are covered by CERT advisories. Sun often releases patches very soon after a CERT vulnerability is discovered on shipped Solaris products. For example, a patch is available for a well-known vulnerability existing in the Berkeley Internet Daemon (BIND) package, which matches IP addresses with Fully Qualified Domain Names (FQDNs) (**http://www.cert.org/ advisories/CA-1999-14.html**). However, some CERT advisories are of a more general nature, because no specific code fix will solve the problem. One example is the identification of a DDoS system known as *Stacheldraht*, which combines the processing power and network resources of a group of systems (which are geographically distributed) and can prevent Web servers from serving pages to clients (**http://www.cert.org/ advisories/CA-2000-01.html**). CERT releases advisories on a regular basis, so it's advisable to keep up-to-date with all current security issues by reading CERT's news.

One of the great strengths of the SAINT system is that it has an extensive catalog of CERT advisories and in-depth explanations of what each CERT advisory means for the local system. Every SAINT vulnerability is associated with a CVE number that matches descriptions of each security issue from the Common Vulnerabilities and Exposures database (**http://cve.mitre.org/**). Each identified vulnerability contains a hyperlink back to the CVE database, so that information displayed about every issue is updated directly from the source. New patches and bug fixes are also listed.

SAINT has the ability to identify security issues for the following services:

- **Domain Name Service (DNS)**   Responsible for mapping the FQDN of Internet hosts to a machine-friendly IP address. In particular, BIND, which is commonly used for DNS resolution, is susceptible to vulnerabilities.

- **File Transfer Program (FTP)**   Allows remote users to retrieve files from the local file system. FTP has historically been associated with serious daemon buffer-overflow problems.

- **Internet Message Access Protocol (IMAP)**   Supports advanced e-mail exchange facilities between mail clients and mail servers. Like FTP, IMAP has buffer-overflow issues, which have previously allowed remote users to execute privileged commands arbitrarily on the mail server.

- **Network File System (NFS) service**   Shares disk partitions to remote client systems. NFS service is often misconfigured to provide world read access to all shared volumes, when this access should be granted only to specific users.

- **Network Information Service (NIS)**   A distributed network service that shares maps of users, groups, and passwords between hosts to minimize administrative overheads. NIS can be compromised if a rogue user can detect the NIS service operating.

- **Sendmail Mail Transport Agent (MTA)**   Once allowed Solaris commands to be embedded within e-mails, which were executed without authentication on the server side.

SAINT works by systematically scanning ports for services that have well-known exploits, and then reporting these exploits back to the user. In addition, it runs a large number of password checks for default passwords on system accounts, or accounts that often have no passwords. SAINT checks all the services and exploits that it knows about, and the database of known exploits grows with each new release. SAINT also tests the susceptibility of your system to DoS attacks, where a large number of large-sized packets are directed to a specific port on your system. This tactic is typically used against Web servers, where some high-profile cases in recent years have highlighted the inherent weakness of networked systems that allow traffic on specific ports without some kind of regulation. Many of the system daemons checked by SAINT have a so-called "buffer overflow" problem, where a system may be crashed because memory is overwritten with arbitrary values outside the declared size of an array. Without appropriate bounds checking, passing a GET request to a Web server of 1025 bytes when the array size is 1024 would clearly result in unpredictable behavior, because the C language does not prevent a program from doing this. Because Solaris daemons are typically written in C, a number of them have been fixed in recent years to prevent this problem from occurring (but you may be surprised at just how often new weaknesses are exposed).

You can download the latest release of SAINT from the SAINT corporation web site. To run SAINT, you need to install the GNU C compiler or use the Sun C compiler. The Perl interpreter and Netscape Web browser supplied with Solaris 10 are also required. After using make to build the SAINT binary, you can start SAINT by typing this command:

```
# ./saint
```

This starts up the Netscape Web browser.

SAINT has several pages, including Data Management, Target Selection, Data Analysis, and Configuration Management. You can visit these pages sequentially to conduct your audit. The Data Management page, shown in Figure 9-6, allows you to create a new

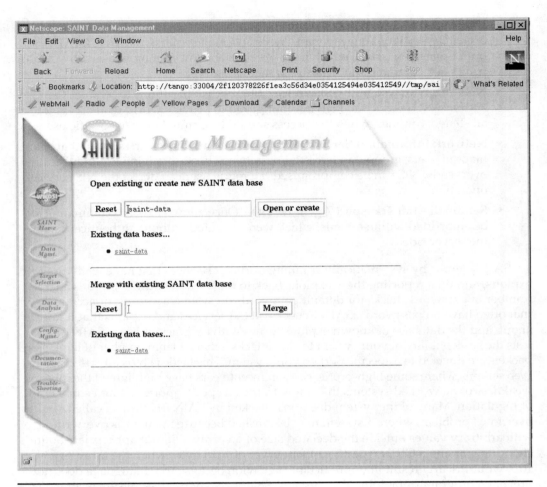

FIGURE 9-6 SAINT Data Management page

SAINT database in which to store the results of your current audit. You can also open an existing SAINT database if you have created one previously, and/or you can merge data from other SAINT scans.

Next, you need to use the Target Selection page to identify the host system that you wish to scan using SAINT, as shown in Figure 9-7. Here, you need to enter the FQDN of the host that you wish to scan. If you have a large number of hosts to scan, it may be more useful to create a file containing a list of hosts. This file could then be used by a system behind the firewall to identify locally visible weaknesses, and used by a system external to the firewall to reveal any threats visible to the outside world. You may also elect to scan all hosts in the LAN, which should be performed only after hours, because it places a heavy load on network bandwidth.

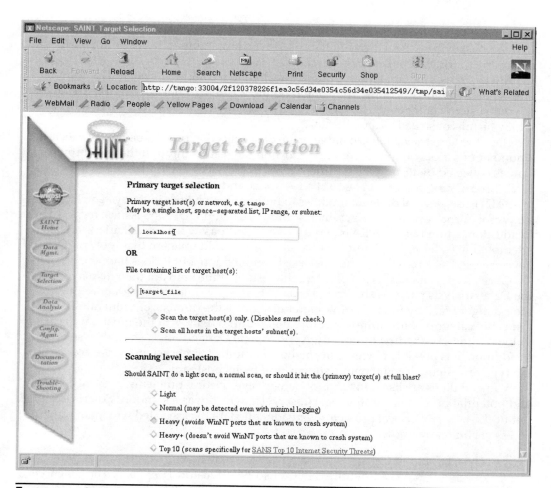

FIGURE 9-7   SAINT Target Selection page

On the Target Selection page, you also need to select a scanning level option, which include the following:

- **Light scanning**   Difficult to detect
- **Normal scanning**   Easy to detect
- **Heavy scanning**   Won't crash Windows NT targets
- **Heavy+ scanning**   May well crash Windows NT targets

There is a final option that just checks the "top ten" security flaws, as identified by the report at **http://www.sans.org/top20/top10.php**. These flaws include BIND weaknesses, vulnerable CGI programs, Remote Procedure Call (RPC) weaknesses, Sendmail buffer overflow, mountd exploits, UNIX NFS exports, user IDs (especially root/administrator with no passwords), IMAP and POP buffer-overflow vulnerabilities, and SNMP community strings set to *public* and *private*.

Always remember that attempting to break in to a computer system is a criminal offense in many jurisdictions: You should obtain written authorization from the owner of your system before embarking on a security-related exercise of this kind; otherwise, it may be misconstrued as a real attack.

Once the target selection is complete, the data collection process begins by executing a number of scripts on the server and reporting the results through the Web browser. Data is collected by testing many different Solaris services, including ping, finger, RPC, login, rsh, sendmail, tooltalk, snmp, and rstatd.

SAINT uses several different modules to probe vulnerabilities in the system, including tcpscan, udpscan, and ddos, which scan for TCP and UDP DoS issues, respectively. In addition, a number of well-known username and password combinations are also attempted in order to break into an account—you would imagine that root/root would never be used as a username and password combination, but it does happen.

Once all the data has been collected, the results of the scan are then displayed on the Data Analysis page, as shown in Figure 9-8. It is possible to list vulnerabilities by their danger level, by the type of vulnerability, or by the number of vulnerabilities in a specific category. Most administrators will want to deal with the most dangerous vulnerabilities, so the first option, By Approximate Danger Level, should be selected. In addition, it is possible to view information about the target system by class of service, the type of system, domain name, subnet, and by its hostname.

Vulnerabilities are listed in terms of danger level: critical problems, areas of concern, and potential problems. For the local host *okami*, which was a standard Solaris install out-of-the-box, two critical problems were identified, both associated with gaining root access via buffer overflow:

- The CDE-based Calendar Manager service may be vulnerable to a buffer-overflow attack, as identified in CVEs 1999-0320 and 1999-0696. The Calendar Manager is used to manage appointments and other date/time–based functions.

- The remote administration daemon (sadmind) may be vulnerable to a buffer-overflow attack, as described in CVE 1999-0977. The remote administration daemon is used to manage system administration activities across a number of different hosts.

There were also two areas of concern identified, with information-gathering vulnerabilities exposed:

- The finger daemon returned personal information about users that could be used to stage an attack. For example, the home directory, full name, and project were displayed (CVE 1999-0612).

- The remote users list daemon was active, providing a list of users on the system to any remote user (CVE 1999-0626). Like the finger daemon, information gathered from the ruserd could be used to stage an attack.

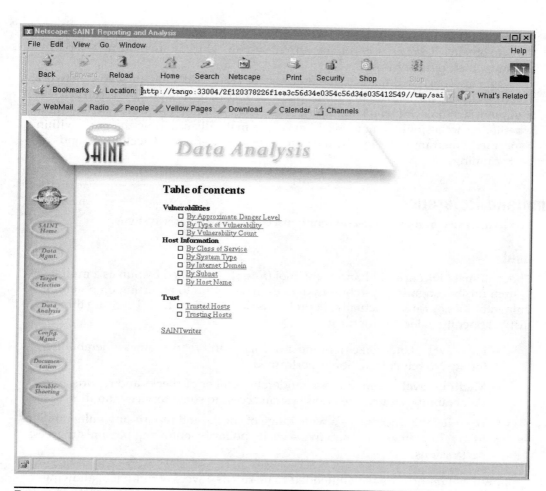

FIGURE 9-8   SAINT Data Analysis page

Two possible vulnerabilities were identified:

- The `chargen` program is vulnerable to UDP flooding used in DoS attacks, such as Fraggle (CVE 1999-0103).
- The `sendmail` server allows mail relaying, which may be used by remote users to forward mail using the server. This makes it easy for companies promoting spam to make it appear as if their mail originated from your server.

Six recommendations were made to limit Internet access, including stopping all the "r" services. These make it easy for a remote user to execute commands on the local system, such as spawning a shell or obtaining information about system load, but have been used in the past to break into systems. In addition, some `sendmail` commands (such as EXPN and VRFY) are allowed by the `sendmail` configuration: this allows remote users to obtain a list of all users on the current system, which is often the first step to obtaining their passwords.

If you are concerned that a rogue user may be using SAINT against your network, you may download and run one of the many SAINT-detecting programs (**http://ciac .llnl.gov/ciac/ToolsUnixNetMon.html**). These tools monitor TCP traffic to determine whether or not a single remote machine is systematically scanning the ports within a specified timeframe. Obviously, such programs are useful for detecting all kinds of port scanning.

Command Reference

The following commands are commonly used to secure Solaris systems.

aset

The Automated Security Enhancement Tool (`aset`) is supplied by Sun as a multilevel system for investigating system weaknesses. In addition to reporting on potential vulnerabilities, `aset` can actually fix problems that are identified. There are three distinct operational levels for `aset`:

- **Low level**   Undertakes a number of checks and reports any vulnerabilities found. No remedial action is performed.

- **Medium level**   Undertakes a moderate number of checks and reports any vulnerabilities found. Restricts system access to some services and files.

- **High level**   Undertakes a wide range of checks and reports any vulnerabilities found. Implements a restrictive security policy by enforcing pessimistic access permissions.

Low-level reports are recommended to be run as a weekly `cron` job, allowing administrators to determine if newly installed applications, services, or patches have compromised system security. In contrast, a medium-level `aset` run should be performed on all newly installed systems that lie behind a firewall. For all systems that are directly connected to the Internet, such as Web and proxy servers, a high-level `aset` run should be performed directly after installation. This ensures that many of the default system permissions that are assigned to system files are reduced to an appropriate scope. It is possible to modify the *asetenv* file to change the actions that are performed when `aset` is executed. The individual tasks performed by `aset` include the following:

tune	Checks all file permissions
cklist	Validates system directories and file permissions
usrgrp	Checks user accounts and groups for integrity
sysconf	Verifies the system files stored in */etc*

env	Parses environment variables stored in configuration files
eeprom	Checks the security level of the OpenBoot PROM monitor
firewall	Determines whether the system is secure enough to operate as a packet filter

TCP Wrappers

Logging access information can reveal whether an organization's networks have an authentication problem. In addition, specific instances of unauthorized access to various resources can be collated and, using statistical methods, can be assessed for regular patterns of abuse. Monitoring of log files can also be used by applications to accept or reject connections, based on historical data contained in centralized logging mechanisms provided under Solaris, such as the `syslogd` system-logging daemon.

One reason why access monitoring is not often discussed is that implementations of the standard UNIX network daemons that are spawned by the Internet super server `inetd` (discussed earlier) do not have a provision to write directly to a `syslog` file. Later Internet service daemons, such as the Apache Web server, run as standalone services not requiring `inetd`, but have enhanced logging facilities that are used to track Web site usage.

Wietse Venema's TCP Wrappers are a popular method of enabling daemons launched from `inetd` to log their accepted and rejected connections, because the wrapper programs that are installed for each service do not require alterations to existing binary software distributions or to existing configuration files. You can download TCP Wrappers in source form from **ftp://ftp.porcupine.org/pub/security/ index.html**.

In their simplest form, TCP wrappers are used for monitoring only, but they could be used to build better applications that can reject connections on the basis of failed connections. For example, a flood of requests to log in using `rsh` from an untrusted host could be terminated after three failed attempts from a single host. TCP wrappers work by compiling a replacement daemon that points to the "real" daemon file, often located in a subdirectory below the daemon wrappers. The wrappers log the date and time of a service request, with a client hostname and whether the request was rejected or accepted. The current version of TCP Wrappers supports the SVR4 (System V Release 4) TLI network programming interface under Solaris, which has equivalent functionality to the Berkeley socket programming interface. In addition, the latest release supports access control and detection of host address or hostname spoofing. The latter is particularly important in the context of authentication services that provide access to services based on IP subnet ranges or specific hostnames in a LAN; if these are spoofed, and access is granted to a rogue client, the entire security infrastructure has failed. It is critical to detect and reject any unauthorized connections at any early stage, and TCP wrappers are an integral part of this mechanism.

When writing access information to `syslog`, the output looks like this:

```
Nov 18 11:00:52 server in.telnetd[1493]: connect from client.site.com
Nov 18 11:25:03 server in.telnetd[1510]: connect from workstation.site.com
```

```
Nov 18 11:25:22 server in.telnetd[1511]: connect from client.site.com
Nov 18 12:16:30 server in.ftpd[1556]: connect from workstation.site.com
```

These entries indicate that between 11:00 A.M. and 1:00 P.M. on November 18, clients connected using Telnet from *client.site.com* and *workstation.site.com*. In addition, there was an FTP connection from *workstation.site.com*. Although this section has examined wrappers only for *in.ftpd* and *in.telnetd*, wrappers can be compiled for most services launched from inetd, including finger, talk, tftp (trivial FTP), and rsh (remote shell).

Summary

In this chapter, you have learned about the basic security services and paradigms that underlie Solaris and its ability to withstand many common attacks while still providing many networked services.

File System Access Control

One of the aspects of Solaris that is most confusing for novice users is the Solaris file access permissions system. The basic approach to setting and interpreting relative file permissions is to use a set of symbolic codes to represent users and permission types. However, even advanced users may find it difficult to understand the octal permission codes that are used to set absolute permissions. When combined with a default permission mask set in the user's shell (the *umask*), octal permission codes are more powerful than symbolic permission codes. In this chapter, we examine how to set and manage basic access controls.

Key Concepts

The following key concepts are required knowledge for understanding access controls.

Symbolic File Permissions

The Solaris file system permits three basic kinds of file access—the ability to read (*r*), to write (*w*), and to execute (*x*) a file or directory. These permissions can be granted exclusively or nonexclusively on individual files, or on a group of files specified by a wildcard (*). These permissions can be set by using the chmod command, in combination with the + operator. Permissions can be easily removed with the chmod command by using the – operator.

For example, to set read permissions (for the current user) on the file */usr/local/lib/libproxy.a*, you would use this command:

```
$ chmod +r /usr/local/lib/libproxy.a
```

or to set read permissions for all users on the file */usr/local/lib/libproxy.a*, you would use this command:

```
$ chmod a+r /usr/local/lib/libproxy.a
```

To remove read permissions on the file */usr/local/lib/libproxy.a* for all users who are not members of the current user's default group, you would use this command:

```
$ chmod o-r /usr/local/lib/libproxy.a
```

This does not remove the group and user read permissions that were set previously. Similarly, you can set execute and write permissions. For example, to set execute permissions on the */usr/local/bin/gcc* files, for each class of user (current user, group, and world), you would use the following commands:

```
$ chmod u+x /usr/local/bin/gcc
```

```
$ chmod g+x /usr/local/bin/gcc
```

```
$ chmod o+x /usr/local/bin/gcc
```

To explicitly remove write permissions on the */usr/local/bin/gcc* files for each class of user (current user, group, and world), you would use these commands:

```
$ chmod u-w /usr/local/bin/gcc
```

```
$ chmod g-w /usr/local/bin/gcc
```

```
$ chmod o-w /usr/local/bin/gcc
```

It makes sense to combine these settings into a single command:

```
$ chmod oug-w /usr/local/bin/gcc
```

The rationale behind using read and write permissions should be clear: permitting read access on a file allows an identified user to access the text of a file by reading it byte by byte; write access permits the user to modify or delete any file on which the write permission is granted, regardless of who originally created the file. Thus, individual users can create files that are readable and writeable by any other user on the system.

The permission to execute a file must be granted on scripts (such as shell scripts or Perl scripts) in order for them to be executed; compiled and linked applications must also have the execute bit set on a specific application. The executable permission must also be granted on the special files that represent directories on the file system, if the directory's contents are to be accessed by a specific class of user.

The different options available for granting file access permissions can sometimes lead to interesting but confusing scenarios. For example, permissions can be set to allow a group to delete a file, but not to execute it. More usefully, a group might be given execute permission on an application, but be unable to write over it. In addition, setting file permissions by using relative permission strings, rather than absolute octal permission codes, means that permissions set by a previous change of permission command (i.e., chmod) are not revoked by any subsequent chmod commands.

However, the permissions themselves are only half the story. Unlike single-user file systems, permissions on Solaris are associated with different file owners (all files and processes on a Solaris system are "owned" by a specific user). In addition, groups of users can be granted read, write, and execute permissions on a file or set of files stored in a directory. Or, file permissions can be granted on a system-wide basis, effectively granting file access without respect to file ownership. Because file systems can be exported using NFS and/or Samba, it's bad practice to grant system-wide read, write, and execute permissions on any file, unless every user needs access to that file. For example, all users need to read the password database (*/etc/passwd*), but only the root user should have read access to the shadow password database (*/etc/shadow*). Blindly exporting all files with world read, write, or execute permissions on a NFS-shared volume is inviting trouble.

The three file system categories of ownership are defined by three permission-setting categories: the user (*u*), who owns the file; group members (*g*), who have access to the file; and all other users (*o*) on the system. The group specified by *g* can be the user's primary group (as defined in */etc/passwd*), or a secondary group to which the file has been assigned (defined in */etc/group*). Remember that there are ultimately few secrets on a Solaris file system: The root user has full access at all times (read, write, and execute) on all files on the file system: even if a user removes all permissions on a file, the rule of root is absolute. If the contents of a file really need to be hidden, encrypting a file's contents using PGP, crypt, or similar is best. A root user can also change the ownership of a file—thus, a user's files do not absolutely belong to a specific user. The chown command can be used only by the superuser for this purpose.

Policies regarding default file permissions need to be set selectively in different environments. For example, in a production Web server system that processes sensitive and personal data, access should be denied by default to all users except those required to conduct online transactions (e.g., the "apache" user for the Apache Web server). On a system that supports team-based development, permissions obviously need to be set that allow the exchange of data between team partners but prevent the access to development files by others. Very few Solaris systems would allow a default world-writeable policy on any file system, except for the temporary swap (*/tmp*) file system.

Enforcing system-wide permissions is possible by using a default umask, which sets the read, write, and execute permissions on all new files created by a specific user. If a user wishes to use a umask other than the default system-wide setting, the user can achieve this by setting it on the command line when required, or in the user's shell startup file (e.g., *.kshrc* for Korn shell).

We start our examination of Solaris file permissions by examining how to create files, set permissions, change ownerships and group memberships, and how to use the ls command to examine existing file permissions. All of these commands can be used by nonprivileged users, except for the chown command.

Procedures

You need to know the following procedures to be able to understand the shell and file permissions.

Octal File Permissions

Some expert users prefer not to separate user and permission information by using the user symbols (*o, u, g*) and the permission symbols (r, w, x). Instead, these users choose to use a numeric code to combine both user and permission information. If you use a lot of common permissions settings, it may be easier for you to remember a single octal code than to work out the permissions string symbolically. The octal code consists of three numbers, which represent owner permissions, group permissions, and other user permissions, respectively (from left to right). Using the equivalence of 4 = r, 2 = w, and 1 = x, any cumulative combination of these provides the octal mode.

For example, to set a file to have read, write, and execute permissions for the file owner, you can use the octal code 700 with the chmod command:

```
$ chmod 700 *
```

You can now check to see if the correct permissions have been granted:

```
$ ls -l
total 4
drwx------   2 root      users        4096 Jun  8 20:10 test
-rwx------   1 root      users           0 Jun  8 20:10 test.txt
```

You can also grant read, write, and execute permissions to members of the group *users* by changing the middle number from 0 to 7:

```
$ chmod 770 *
```

Again, the changes are reflected in the symbolic permissions string displayed by ls:

```
$ ls -l
total 4
drwxrwx---   2 root      users        4096 Jun  8 20:10 test
-rwxrwx---   1 root      users           0 Jun  8 20:10 test.txt
```

If you want to grant read, write, and execute permissions to all users, simply change the third permissions number from 0 to 7:

```
$ chmod 777 *
```

Now, all users on the system have read, write, and execute permissions on all files in the directory:

```
$ ls -l
total 4
drwxrwxrwx    2 root      users        4096 Jun  8 20:10 test
-rwxrwxrwx    1 root      users           0 Jun  8 20:10 test.txt
```

Of course, the codes that can be used to specify permissions are usually not just 0 or 7. For example, the code 5 gives read and execute access, but not write access. So, if you wanted to grant read and execute access to members of the group, but deny write access, you could use the code 750:

```
$ chmod 750 *
```

This produces the following result:

```
$ ls -l
total 4
drwxr-x---    2 root      users        4096 Jun  8 20:10 test
-rwxr-x---    1 root      users           0 Jun  8 20:10 test.txt
```

If you wanted to remove all access permissions from the files in the current directory, you could use the code 000 (you should not normally need to do this):

```
$ chmod 000 *
```

Let's examine the result of the command:

```
$ ls -l
total 4
d---------    2 root      users        4096 Jun  8 20:10 test
----------    1 root      users           0 Jun  8 20:10 test.txt
```

All access permissions have been removed, except for the directory indicator on the special file *test*. Note the main difference between setting files using symbolic codes rather than octal codes: symbolic codes are relative; numeric codes are absolute. This means that unless you explicitly revoke a file permission when setting another using symbolic codes, it will persist. Thus, if a file already has group write access, and you grant group execute access (or remove group execute access), the write access permission is not removed. However, if you specify only group execute access using an octal code, the group write access is automatically removed if it has been previously set (i.e., when using the symbolic codes, the administrator has more granularity in assigning permissions). You may well find that in startup scripts and situations where the permissions are unknown in advance, using octal codes is wiser.

Setting Default Permissions (umask)

You can enforce system-wide permissions by using a default "user mask" (umask), which sets the read, write, and execute permissions on all new files created by a specific user. If a user wants to use a umask other than the default system-wide setting, he or she can achieve this by setting it on the command line when required, or in the user's shell startup file (e.g., *.kshrc* for Korn shell), or in the global system default file, */etc/default/ login*. In addition, the mask that is set for the current user can be displayed by using the umask command by itself.

Like file permissions, the umask is set using octal codes. There are two different strategies for computing umasks. For directories, you must subtract the octal value of the default permission you want to set from octal 777; for files, you often subtract the octal value of the default permission you want to set from octal 666. For example, to set the default permission to 444 (all read only), you would subtract 444 from 666 for files, to derive the umask of 222. For the default permission 600 (user read/write, no other access), you would subtract 600 from 666, leaving a umask of 066 (which often is displayed as 66). The two mask modes are 2 for read and 4 for write.

If you want all users to have full access permissions on all files that you create, except executable permissions, you would set the umask to 000 (666 – 000 = 666):

```
$ umask 000
```

Let's examine the results, after creating a file called *data.txt*, after setting the umask to 000:

```
$ touch data.txt
$ ls -l
total 4
-rw-rw-rw-   1 root      users         0 Jun  8 20:20 data.txt
```

Everyone now has full access permissions. However, you are more likely to set a umask such as 022, which would give new files the permissions 755 (777 – 022 = 755). This would give the file owner read, write, and execute access, but only read permissions for group members and other users:

```
$ umask 022
```

If you now create a new file called *newdata.txt* with the new umask, you should see that the default permissions have changed:

```
$ touch newtest.txt
 $ ls -l
total 4
-rw-r--r--    1 root      root           0 Jun   8 20:21 newdata.txt
-rwxrwxrwx    1 root      users          0 Jun   8 20:20 data.txt
```

If you're more conservative and don't want to grant any access permissions to other users (including group members), you can set the umask to 077, which still gives the file owner full access permissions:

```
bash-2.03$ umask 077
```

Let's see what happens when you create a new file called *lastminute.txt*:

```
bash-2.03$ touch lastminute.txt
bash-2.03$ ls -l
total 4
-rw-r--r--    1 root      root           0 Jun   8 20:21 newdata.txt
-rw-------    1 root      root           0 Jun   8 20:22 lastminute.txt
-rwxrwxrwx    1 root      users          0 Jun   8 20:20 data.txt
```

The new file has full access permissions for the owner, but no access permissions for other users. Resetting the umask does not affect the permissions of other files that have already been created.

setUID and *setGID* Permissions

The file permissions we've covered so far are used by users in their day-to-day file-management strategies. However, administrators can use a different set of file permissions that allows files to be executed as a particular user (*setUID*) and/or as a member of a particular group (*setGID*). These facilities are very powerful, because they allow unprivileged users to gain access to limited superuser privileges in many cases, without requiring superuser authentication. For example, the volume daemon (vold) allows unprivileged users logged into the console to mount and unmount CD-ROMs and floppy disks, an operation that required superuser privileges in previous Solaris releases. Here, the effective user ID is set to 0, meaning that unprivileged users can effectively run processes as root.

The downside to this is obvious: *setGID* and *setUID* permissions open a Pandora's box in terms of security, because normal authentication procedures are bypassed. For example, imagine a device management tool that needed to run as *setUID* 0 in order to read and write device files. If the tool had a standard feature of many UNIX programs, the ability to spawn a shell, the shell spawned would have full root privileges, rather than the privileges of the original user. For this reason, some administrators refuse to allow *setGID* and *setUID* permissions to be set. The find command, for example, can be used to scan all local file systems and show files with *setUID* or *setGID* privileges:

```
# find / -local -type f \( -perm -4000 -o -perm -2000 \) -print
```

You can determine whether a file is *setUID* by root by first checking for files that are owned by root and then checking whether those files have the *s* flag assigned to the user's permissions. For example, if a file-management tool called filetool were *setUID* root, the following directory listing would clearly indicate this property:

```
-r-sr-sr-x 3 root sys 1220334 Jul 18 11:01 /usr/local/bin/filetool
```

The first *s* in the permissions table refers to *setUID* root. In addition, this file is also *setGID* for the *sys* group, which is indicated by the second *s* in the permissions table.
The *setUID* bit can be set by using a command like this

```
# chmod u+s file.txt
```

where *file.txt* is the file that requires *setUID* to be set.
The *setGID* bit can be set by using a command like this

```
# chmod g+s file.txt
```

where *file.txt* is the file that requires *setGID* to be set. Setting chmod o+s has no impact on the file.

Sticky Bit Permissions

A network administrator once explained to me that sticky bits were those bits that slowed down network transmission rates, because they were highly attracted to magnetic qualities of the Ethernet. This is not true! A sticky bit is a special permission that prevents files in common file areas from being deleted by other users. For example, a download area consisting of a large, 10GB partition may be set aside for user downloads, which are not counted against individual user quotas. This means that users could download up to 10GB of data without infringing on their allocated directory space. However, although a shared public file area sounds like a great idea, it would be unwise to allow users to overwrite one another's files. In this case, the sticky bit can be set on the top-level directory of the public file area, allowing only users who created individual files to delete them.
You can set the sticky bit by using a command like this

```
# chmod +t somedir
```

where *somedir* is the directory that requires the sticky bit to be set.

Example

The following example demonstrates how to use the shell.

Access Control Lists

One problem with assigning file access permissions is that users other than one's self fall into two categories: group members or nongroup members. Thus, if you want to make some files available to one group of users but not to another group of users, you need to ask the system administrator to create a group for you. Of course, the main problem with the random group-creation approach is group sprawl—administrators are generally unwilling to create groups at the request of users because of the overhead in administering potentially hundreds of different groups on each system, and since the number of groups that one user can be in is limited.

The best solution to the problem is to structure group membership to reflect organizational divisions and to use access control lists (ACLs) to manage file access. While it may seem like creating more work to have two sets of file access permissions operating, in reality it's the simplest solution for users who don't require superuser permissions.

To grant the user charles read-only access to the file *secret.doc*, which is owned by the user ainsley and has read-write permissions only for ainsley, the following command would be executed by ainsley:

```
$ setfacl -m user:charles:r-- secret.doc
```

Alternatively, to allow charles to have read-write access to the file, the following command can be used:

```
$ setfacl -m user:charles:rw- secret.doc
```

When an ACL has been set, the file listing shows a + symbol at the end of the permissions string:

```
# ls -l /home/charles/secret.doc
-rw-------+   1 charles    admin        105433  Jan 24 12:07
      /home/charles/secret.doc
```

The output of getfacl for a file (*/etc/passwd* in this example) looks like this:

```
$ getfacl /etc/passwd
# file: /etc/passwd
# owner: root
# group: sys
user::rw-
```

```
group::r--                    #effective:r--
mask:r--
other:r--
```

Command Reference

The following command is commonly used to work with access controls.

ls

The `ls` command is the main directory and file permission listing program used in Solaris. When displaying a long listing, it prints file access permissions, user and group ownerships, file size and creation date, and the filename. For example, for the password file */etc/passwd*, the output from `ls` would look like this:

```
$ ls -l /etc/passwd
-r--r--r--    1 root      other          256 Sep  18 00:40 passwd
```

This directory entry can be read from left to right in the following way:

- The password file is not a directory, indicated by the first –. This could also indicate a character or block special device.
- The password file has read-only permissions for the owner `r--` (but not execute or write permissions).
- The password file has read-only permissions for group members `r--`.
- The password file has read-only permissions for other staff `r--`.
- The password file is owned by the root user.
- The password file has other group permissions.
- The password file size is 256 kilobytes.
- The password file was created on September 18, at 00:40 A.M.
- The name of the password file is *passwd*.

The permissions string shown changes depending on the permissions that have been set by the owner. For example, if the password file had execute and write permissions for the root user, then the permissions string would read `-rwxr--r--`, rather than just `-r--r--r--`. Each of the permissions can be set using symbolic or octal permission codes, by using the `chmod` command.

You've seen how a normal file looks under `ls`, but let's compare this with a directory entry, which is a special kind of file that is usually created by the `mkdir` command:

```
# mkdir samples
```

You can check the permissions of the directory entry by using the `ls` command:

```
# ls -l
total 8
drwxrwxr-x   2 root      other        512 Sep  5 13:41 samples
```

The directory entry for the directory *samples* can be read from left to right in the following way:

- The directory entry is a special file denoted by a leading d.
- The directory entry has read, write, and execute permissions for the owner rwx.
- The directory entry has read, write, and execute permissions for group members rwx.
- The directory entry has read and execute permissions for other staff r-x.
- The directory entry is owned by the root user.
- The directory entry has other group permissions.
- The directory entry size is 512 kilobytes.
- The directory entry was created on September 5, at 1:41 P.M.
- The name of the directory is *samples*.

For a directory to be accessible to a particular class of user, the executable bit must be set using the `chmod` command.

Summary

In this chapter, we have examined the basic facilities for user-based access controls provided in Solaris. While these controls are important, they have been enhanced with the inclusion of Role-Based Access Control (RBAC), which is covered in Chapter 11.

Role-Based Access Control

One of the most frustrating aspects of setting a strict security policy is that some actions that require a form of access privilege must occasionally be undertaken by nonprivileged users. Although you don't want normal users to have all of root's privileges, for obvious reasons, there are occasions when normal users could conveniently and securely perform certain actions without jeopardizing system integrity. In other words, a number of specific roles require superuser privileges, which you may need to grant to users who should not have complete root access.

In early Solaris versions, the solution to this problem was to prevent normal users from having any kind of privileged access. Normal users, for example, could not eject a floppy disk or CD-ROM drive without root access! However, this draconian solution just led to the root password being shared around to every user who needed to eject a floppy (not very security-conscious!). Alternatively, applications can be compiled as *setuid* root, allowing an unprivileged user to execute specific commands as the root user, without requiring a password. This approach is fine, as long as the scope of the application is restricted. A given user running any application with the *setuid* bit can cause a buffer overflow to compromise and obtain overall privileged access. For example, any application that allows the effective user to spawn a shell is not suited to be *setuid* root, because an unprivileged user could then spawn a root shell without a password. Relying on a single superuser to protect a system's resources is one of the great strengths and weaknesses of UNIX and UNIX-like systems.

More often than not, operations on a system can be classified as being associated with a specific role. For example, a network administrator who is responsible for backups needs write access really only to tape devices, not to any local file systems, other than for spooling. Thus, a backup "role" can have its scope limited in a way that doesn't overlap with a printer administrator, who needs to be able to manage print jobs and write to spooling areas, while being denied write access to tape drives. Identifying tasks and roles is the first step to ensuring that privileges are granted only to those who need them.

Three approaches are commonly used to provide "role-based" access to Solaris systems: installing Trusted Solaris, installing sudo, or using the Role-Based Access Control (RBAC) features built into Solaris. Using Trusted Solaris requires a new operating system installation, to take advantage of its role-based features, which build on top of

RBAC by introducing security labels, ranging from "top secret" to "unclassified." In contrast, sudo is a small utility that you can download and install, providing a simple role-based access system. However, RBAC provides a system for role-based access that is integrated into the operating system, providing a superior solution to sudo.

Key Concepts

The following key concepts will assist you to understand RBAC.

sudo

sudo allows privileged roles to be assigned to various users by maintaining a database of privileges mapped to usernames. These privileges are identified by sets of different commands listed in the database. In order to access a privileged item, a qualified user simply needs to re-enter their own password (not the root password) after the command name has been entered on the command line. sudo permits a user to format disks, for instance, but have no other root privileges. sudo can be obtained from **http://www.courtesan.com/sudo/**.

One of the most useful features of sudo is its logging. By maintaining a logfile of all operations performed using the sudo facility, system administrators can audit the logfile and trace any actions that may have had unintended consequences. This is something that the normal su facility does not provide. Alternatively, patterns of malicious behavior can also be identified: sudo logs all successful and unsuccessful attempts to perform privileged actions. This can be very important in a security context, because brute-force attacks against weak passwords of unprivileged accounts might now be able to access some superuser functions through sudo. Thus, if the user *nobody* is given access via sudo to format disks, and the password for the user *nobody* is guessed, an intruder would be able to format disks on the system without requiring the root password. In addition, because the effective user ID of a user executing a privileged application through sudo is set to zero (i.e., the superuser), such applications should not allow shells to be spawned.

All of the roles in sudo are independent. Thus, granting one or more roles to one user and one or more roles to another is possible. User roles can be shared, or they may be completely separate. For example, the user *harry* may have the privilege to format disks, and the user *butler* may have the privilege to both format disks and write to tape drives. To access these privileges, *harry* and *butler* do not need to know the root password.

sudo has some limitations, and that's why you need RBAC. For example, it's not possible to stipulate that a user can only execute a single command on a specific file or set of files, and have no other privileges. It might be possible to wrap up some commands and permissions in a shell script, but doing this on a per-user, per-file basis would be time-consuming.

RBAC

Role-Based Access Control (RBAC) was first introduced in Solaris 8 as a means of defining roles for managing a specific task or set of tasks, based on a set of administrator-defined profiles. Although the RBAC implementation supplied with Solaris is a Sun-specific product, it is based on a standard developed by NIST (see **http://csrc.nist.gov/rbac/** for more information). Broadly defined, *access control* extends beyond the notion of administrative access: it can be defined as the ability to create, read, update, and delete data from a system. Standard file system permissions are based on this principle: various users and groups have access permissions to data stored in files based on a permission string that is associated with every file on the file system. However, although file access can be easily demarcated along organizational lines, deciding who should and who should not have administrative access to execute applications can be a more complex issue. What if a secretary needs to have "root access" to a system to add or delete users as they join an organization? Data entry of this kind seems like a reasonable task for a secretary, but it is usually assigned to system administrators, because it requires root access. RBAC allows tasks like these to be separated from other tasks that do require a high level of technical knowledge, such as managing metadevices.

Roles

The first stage of implementing RBAC is to define roles, which are then assigned to individual users. Access rights to various resources can then be associated with a specific role name. As with any organization, change to roles and the users who are associated with roles is inevitable, so the process for reflecting these changes in the list of roles and users needs to be as easy to implement as possible. In addition, individual tasks are not always easy to associate with a single role: indeed, in a large organization, some tasks will be performed by a number of different employees. It's also possible to assign specific authorizations to specific users, bypassing roles, but this defeats the whole "role-based" purpose of RBAC, and is not recommended.

One way of dealing with task overlap is to introduce the notion of hierarchies: profiles and authorizations at the bottom of a conceptual hierarchy are "inherited" by the assignment of a role at a higher level. For example, a role defined as "backup maintainer" involves running `ufsdump`, which in turn requires write access to the tape device. Thus, the backup role inherently requires access to lower-level profiles for which new roles do not need to be separately defined. Another role, such as "device manager," may also require write access to the tape device, through the `tapes` command. Again, no separate role is required to be created for those tasks that form part of the role by inference. However, although Solaris RBAC does support hierarchies of profiles and authorizations, it does not support hierarchies of roles. When a user assumes a role, the effect is all-or-nothing: no inheritance of roles is allowed.

By default, Solaris 10 supports three different system-management roles:

- **Primary Administrator (PA)**   Assigns rights to other users and is responsible for security

- **System Administrator (SA)**   Is responsible for day-to-day administration that is not security-related

- **Operator**   Performs backups and device maintenance

Figure 11-1 shows the hierarchy of rights associated with the different roles. The distinction between PA and SA will depend on the local security policy. For example, whereas the default PA role permits both adding users and changing passwords, the default SA role does not permit password modifications. However, for many sites, denying SAs access to passwords would be impractical. One of the great benefits of RBAC is that the rights granted to different profiles can be easily modified and customized to suit local requirements. Parallels can be drawn with Trusted Solaris and the assignment of tasks with different levels of authority to completely different roles.

Profiles

Associated with the concept of overlapping roles are the notions of authority and operational responsibility. Two individuals may use similar roles to carry out mutually exclusive operations. For example, a clerk in a supermarket may be allowed to enter cash transactions into the cash register, but only a supervisor can void transactions already entered. Conversely, a supervisor cannot enter cash transactions, because the organizational requirements mandate a separation of supervisory and procedural roles, even though both operate on the same set of data and devices. Clearly, these roles and their associated operations must be defined offline before being implemented using the Solaris RBAC facility.

A profile is a specific command or set of commands for which an authorization can be granted. These authorizations are linked together to form a role, which is in turn associated with a single user, or a number of different users, as shown in Figure 11-2. Profiles can list files as well, and can be executed several ways:

- The new `pfexec` command can be used to execute a single command contained in a profile.

- Commands in profiles can be executed through new, restricted versions of the standard shells, such as `pfsh` (profile Bourne shell) and `pfcsh` (profile C shell).

- A new user account for each role can be created, with its own home directory and password. To execute commands contained in a profile, users who have access to the role can just `su` to the new account—they are not allowed to log in directly. Note that if two users `su` to the same role account, they will both be operating on the same files and could potentially overwrite each other's data. The same is true for the normal root account. However, one difference between using `su` to access a role and using `su` to access a normal account is auditing—all of the operations carried out when using `su` to access a role are logged with the user's original UID. Thus, the operations of individual users who access roles can be logged (and audited) distinctively.

NOTE   *You can't directly log in to a role account.*

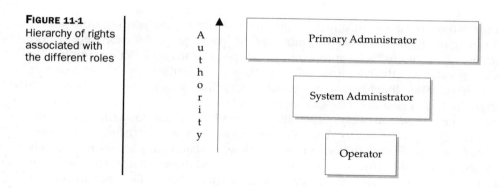

FIGURE 11-1
Hierarchy of rights
associated with
the different roles

Authorizations

Let's look more closely at authorizations before examining how they are assigned to different roles. An *authorization* is a privilege, defined in the file */etc/security/auth_attr*, that is granted to a role to allow that role to perform operations. Some applications allow RBAC authorizations to be checked before allowing an action to be performed, including the device-management commands (e.g., `allocate` and `deallocate`), as well as the batch-processing commands (e.g., `at`, `crontab`).

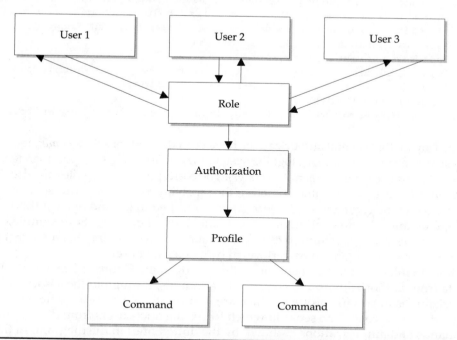

FIGURE 11-2 Profiles and authorizations are associated with roles that are granted to individual users.

Authorizations have a form similar to Internet domain names: reading from left to right, the company name is followed by more specific package and function information. For example, *net.cassowary.** is an authorization that pertains to any function supplied by the vendor *cassowary.net*. By default, all Solaris packages are identified by the prefix *solaris*. Thus, the authorization for changing passwords is identified as *solaris.admin.usermgr.pswd* rather than the longer *com.sun.solaris.admin.usermgr.pswd*.

Many authorizations are fine-grained, allowing read access but not write access, and vice versa. For example, a Primary Administrator may have the *solaris.admin.usermgr.read* and *solaris.admin.usermgr.write* authorizations that allow read and write access, respectively, to user configuration files. However, an SA may be granted the *solaris.admin.usermgr.read* authorization but not the *solaris.admin.usermgr.write* authorization, effectively preventing him or her from changing the contents of user configuration files, even if they have read access to the same files. The following examples show some of the common *solaris.admin* authorizations currently defined:

```
solaris.admin.fsmgr.:::Mounts and Shares::
solaris.admin.fsmgr.read:::View Mounts and Shares::help=AuthFsmgrRead.html
solaris.admin.fsmgr.write:::Mount and Share Files::help=AuthFsmgrWrite.html
solaris.admin.logsvc.:::Log Viewer::
solaris.admin.logsvc.purge:::Remove Log Files::help=AuthLogsvcPurge.html
solaris.admin.logsvc.read:::View Log Files::help=AuthLogsvcRead.html
solaris.admin.logsvc.write:::Manage Log Settings::help=AuthLogsvcWrite.html
solaris.admin.serialmgr.:::Serial Port Manager::
solaris.admin.usermgr.:::User Accounts::
solaris.admin.usermgr.pswd:::Change Password::help=AuthUserMgrPswd.html
solaris.admin.usermgr.read:::View Users and Roles::
   help=AuthUsermgrRead.html
solaris.admin.usermgr.write:::Manage Users::help=AuthUsermgrWrite.html
```

You can see that several authorizations have been defined for *solaris.admin*, including file system management (*fsmgr*), logging system management (*logsvc*), port management (*serialmgr*), and user management (*userxmgr*). The corresponding help files are also listed.

An important aspect of authorizations is the capability to transfer permissions to other users by using the *grant* keyword. Once *grant* is attached to the end of an authorization string, it enables the delegation of authorizations to other users. For example, the *solaris.admin.usermgr.grant* authorization, in conjunction with *solaris.admin.usermgr.pswd*, allows password changing to be performed by a delegated user.

How do roles, profiles, and authorizations fit together? Figure 11-3 shows the flow of data from authorizations and command definitions, through to the association of authorizations to specific profiles, which are in turn utilized by users who have been assigned various roles. The sense in which RBAC abstracts users from directly using commands and authorizations is shown by the dotted lines in the diagram. In this diagram, it is easy to see how central roles are in systems where profiles for different tasks are well defined.

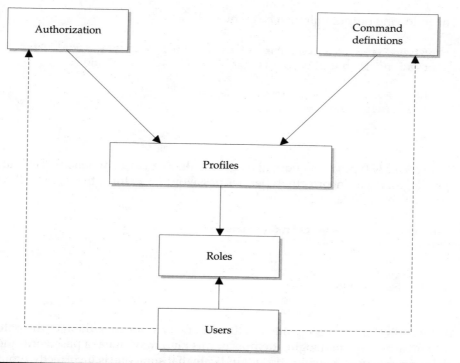

FIGURE 11-3   Integrating roles, profiles, and authorizations

Operations

The following operations are commonly performed when implementing RBAC.

sudo

The `sudo` facility is configured by the file */etc/sudoers*. This file contains a list of all users who have access to the `sudo` facility and defines their privileges. A typical entry in */etc/sudoers* looks like this:

```
jdoe    ALL=(ALL) ALL
```

This entry gives the user *jdoe* access to all applications as the superuser. For the user *jdoe* to run commands as the superuser, she simply needs to prefix the command string with `sudo`. Thus, to execute the `format` command as root, *jdoe* would enter the following command string:

```
$ sudo format
```

The following output will then be displayed:

```
We trust you have received the usual lecture from the local System
Administrator. It usually boils down to these two things:

        #1) Respect the privacy of others.
        #2) Think before you type.

Password:
```

If *jdoe* correctly types in her normal password, the format command will execute with root privileges. If *jdoe* incorrectly types her password up to three times, the following messages appear after each prompt:

```
Take a stress pill and think things over.
Password:
You silly, twisted boy you.
Password:
He has fallen in the water!
Password not entered correctly
```

At this point, an alert is e-mailed to the superuser, informing them of the potential security breach—repeated login attempts of this kind may signal a password-guessing attack by a rogue user. Equally, it could indicate that someone is incorrectly typing their password (perhaps the CAPS LOCK key is on) or that they are entering the root password rather than their own.

In order to list all of the privileges currently allowed for a user, that user simply needs to run sudo with the *–l* option:

```
$ sudo -l
You may run the following commands on this host:
    (ALL) ALL
```

In addition to granting full superuser access, sudo can more usefully delegate authority to specific individuals. For example, you can create command aliases that correspond to the limited set of commands that sudoers can execute:

```
Cmnd_Alias  TCPD=/usr/sbin/tcpd
```

In this case, you are giving users control over the TCP daemon. You can also specify a group of users other than ALL that share the ability to execute different classes of commands:

```
User_Alias  DEVELOPERS=pwatters,tgibbs
User_Alias  ADMINS=maya,natashia
```

Thus, the DEVELOPERS group can be assigned access to specific facilities that are not available to ADMINS. Putting it all together, you can create complex user specifications like this:

```
ADMINS ALL=(ALL) NOPASSWD: ALL
DEVELOPERS    ALL=TCPD
```

This specification allows ADMINS to perform operations without a password, while giving developers privileges to operate on the TCP daemon. Notice that we've included administrators in the user specification, even though these users probably know the root password. This is because sudo leaves an audit trail for every command executed, meaning that you can trace actions to a specific user account. This makes it easy to find out which individual is responsible for system problems. Of course, these administrators can just use the su facility to bypass the sudo facility, if they know the root password. This is the main drawback of using sudo on Solaris—it is not integrated into the operating system, but rather is just an application.

RBAC

Common operations performed in the context of RBAC include setting up profiles and defining roles. The following commands are commonly used:

- **smexec**   Create, read, update, and delete rows in the *exec_attr* database
- **smmultiuser**   Perform batch functions
- **smuser**   Perform operations on user accounts
- **smprofile**   Create, read, update, and delete profiles in the *prof_attr* database
- **smrole**   Create, read, update, and delete role accounts
- **rolemod**   Modify roles
- **roledel**   Delete roles
- **roleadd**   Add roles

The *prof_attr* database contains all of the profile definitions for the system. For example, profiles might be created for the Primary Administrator, System Administrator, Operator, Basic Solaris User, and Printer Manager. A special profile is the All Rights profile, which is associated with all commands that have no security restrictions enforced on their use. This is the default profile, which covers all commands not designated as requiring specific authorization. In contrast, the PA is granted explicit rights over all security-related commands and operations, as defined by the *solaris.** authorization. The PA can then delegate tasks to other users where appropriate if the *solaris.grant* authorization is granted. The scope of the PA can be limited if this role is considered too close in power to the superuser.

The SA, in contrast, has a much more limited role. Specific authorizations are granted to the SA, rather than using wildcards to allow complete access. Typical commands defined in this profile allow auditing and accounting, printer administration, batch processing, device installation and configuration, file system repairs, e-mail administration, name and directory service configuration, process administration, and new software installation and configuration. The Operator profile has very few privileges at all: only printer and backup administration is permitted. Note that the Operator is not allowed to restore data: this privilege is reserved for the SA or PA. As an alternative to the Operator, the Printer Manager profile allows only printer administration tasks to be performed. Typical authorizations that are permitted include *solaris.admin.printer.delete*, *solaris.admin.printer.modify*, and *solaris.admin.printer.read*, encompassing commands like `lpsched`, `lpstat`, and `lpq`.

A slightly different approach is taken for the definition of the Basic Solaris User: this policy is contained within the *policy.conf* file. Typical authorizations permitted for the Basic Solaris User include the following:

solaris.admin.dcmgr.read	*solaris.admin.diskmgr.read*	*solaris.admin.fsmgr.read*
solaris.admin.logsvc.read	*solaris.admin.printer.read*	*solaris.admin.procmgr.user*
solaris.admin.prodreg.read	*solaris.admin.serialmgr.read*	*solaris.admin.usermgr.read*
solaris.compsys.read	*solaris.jobs.user*	*solaris.profmgr.read*

Database Reference

The following reference provides details on the different databases that are used with RBAC.

user_attr

The *user_attr* file is the RBAC user database. This file primarily shows the relationship between the user and profiles that apply to the user. It contains a single entry by default, which defines the security information for every user that has access to RBAC. The following entry gives the root user permission to do everything on the system:

```
root::::type=normal;auths=solaris.*,solaris.grant;profiles=All
```

Clearly, if the power of root were to be reduced, *solaris.** would need to be replaced with something more restricted in scope, such as *solaris.admin.**. For an explanation of the fields not shown, please see the man page.

auth_attr

The *auth_attr* file is the RBAC authorization database. This file primarily depicts the available authorizations. It contains lists of all authorizations defined on the system. Some sample entries are shown here:

```
solaris.admin.fsmgr.:::Mounts and Shares::
solaris.admin.fsmgr.read:::View Mounts and Shares::help=
```

```
AuthFsmgrRead.html
solaris.admin.fsmgr.write:::Mount and Share Files::help=
AuthFsmgrWrite.html
solaris.admin.logsvc.:::Log Viewer::
solaris.admin.logsvc.purge:::Remove Log Files::help=
AuthLogsvcPurge.html
solaris.admin.logsvc.read:::View Log Files::help=AuthLogsvcRead.html
solaris.admin.logsvc.write:::Manage Log Settings::help=
AuthLogsvcWrite.html
solaris.admin.serialmgr.:::Serial Port Manager::
solaris.admin.usermgr.:::User Accounts::
solaris.admin.usermgr.pswd:::Change Password::help=AuthUserMgrPswd.html
solaris.admin.usermgr.read:::View Users and Roles::
help=AuthUsermgrRead.html
solaris.admin.usermgr.write:::Manage Users::help=AuthUsermgrWrite.html
```

prof_attr

The *prof_attr* file is the RBAC profile database. This file displays the relationship between the profiles and the corresponding authorizations. Sample *prof_attr* entries for the Basic Solaris User, User Management, and User Security are shown here:

```
Basic Solaris User:::Automatically assigned rights:
auths=solaris.profmgr.read,solaris.jobs.users,
solaris.admin.usermgr.read,solaris.admin.logsvc.read,
solaris.admin.fsmgr.read,solaris.admin.serialmgr.read,
solaris.admin.diskmgr.read,solaris.admin.procmgr.user,
solaris.compsys.read,solaris.admin.printer.read,
solaris.admin.prodreg.read,solaris.admin.dcmgr.read;
profiles=All;help=RtDefault.html
User Management:::Manage users, groups, home directory:
auths=profmgr.read,solaris.admin.usermgr.write,
solaris.admin.usermgr.read;help=RtUserMngmnt.html
User Security:::Manage passwords, clearances:
auths=solaris.role.*,solaris.profmgr.*,solaris.admin.usermgr.*;
help=RtUserSecurity.html
```

exec_attr

The *exec_attr* file is the RBAC command database. It contains lists of commands associated with a specific profile. For example, a set of entries for the User Manager profile would look like this:

```
User Management:suser:cmd:::/etc/init.d/utmpd:uid=0;gid=sys
User Management:suser:cmd:::/usr/sbin/grpck:euid=0
User Management:suser:cmd:::/usr/sbin/pwck:euid=0
```

Example

Although much of the material in this chapter is conceptual, the following example shows you how to use RBAC practically. For each role that you want to create, you should develop a planning table and then follow the steps required to configure and activate the role on the system. By preplanning roles, scripts can be created to automate the process across a number of different servers. An example of planning table entries is shown here:

Role	Purpose/Description	Users Assigned	Commands Used
User Administration	Add users to the system	*paul, nalneesh*	`useradd, usermod, userdel, pwck,`
Web Management	Allow the Web server to be operated	*paul, jane, jessica*	`httpd, apachectl`

Once you've identified the roles, users, and commands, the following three steps need to be taken:

1. Create each role using the `smrole` command.
2. Create each profile using `smprofile`.
3. Assign each user to the role using `smrole`.
4. Verify the changes in the files.

Command Reference

The following reference provides details on the different commands that are used with RBAC.

smexec

The `smexec` command is used to create, update, and delete rows in the *exec_attr* database. One of three options must be passed to the command upon execution: *add*, which adds an entry; *delete*, which deletes an entry; or *modify*, which updates an entry. In order to use `smexec`, the user must have the *solaris.profmgr.execattr.write* authorization. There are two sets of parameters that can be passed to `smexec` (depending on which option has been selected): authorization parameters and specific parameters for each option.

The authorization parameters are common to each option, and they specify the following characteristics:

–domain	The domain to be administered
–hostname:port	The hostname and port on which operations are to be performed (default port is 898)
–rolepassword	The password for role authentication

–password	The password for the user rather than the role
–rolename	The name of the role
–username	The name of the user

For adding entries using `smexec add`, the following parameters can be passed on the command line:

_–c_	Specifies the full path to the new command name to be added
_–g_	Specifies the effective GID for executing the new command
_–G_	Specifies the actual GID for executing the new command
_–n_	Specifies the profile name with which the command is associated
–t cmd	Specifies that the operation is a command
_–u_	Specifies the effective UID for executing the new command
_–U_	Specifies the actual UID for executing the new command

An example `smexec add` operation looks like this:

```
# smexec add -hostname localhost -password xyz123 -username root -- -n
"Print Manager" -t cmd -c /usr/sbin/lpsched -u 0 -g 0
```

This entry adds the capability to start the printing service to the Printer Manager profile, with the effective UID and GID of 0 (i.e., root).

For removing entries using `smexec delete`, the following parameters can be passed on the command line:

_–c_	Specifies the full path to the command name to be deleted
_–n_	Specifies the profile name with which the command is currently associated
–t cmd	Specifies that the operation is a command

To remove the entry for `lpsched`, you would use the following command:

```
# smexec delete -hostname localhost -password xyz123 -username root -- -n
"Print Manager" -t cmd -c /usr/sbin/lpsched
```

For changing entries using `smexec modify`, the following parameters can be passed on the command line:

_–c_	Specifies the full path to the command name to be modified
_–g_	Specifies the modified effective GID for executing the new command
_–G_	Specifies the modified actual GID for executing the new command

–n	Specifies the modified profile name with which the command is associated
–t cmd	Specifies that the operation is a command
–u	Specifies the modified effective UID for executing the new command
–U	Specifies the modified actual UID for executing the new command

An example `smexec modify` operation looks like this:

```
# smexec modify -hostname localhost -password xyz123 -username root -- -n
"Print Manager" -t cmd -c /usr/some/new/path/lpsched -u 0 -g 0
```

This entry modifies the command to start the printing service for the Printer Manager profile, from the path */usr/sbin/lpsched* to */usr/some/new/path/lpsched*.

smmultiuser

The `smmultiuser` command is used to perform batch functions, such as adding or deleting a large number of users. This is particularly useful when a file already exists that specifies all of the required user data. For instance, a backup system may need a setup that is similar to a current production system. Rather than just copying the file systems directly, all of the operations associated with new account creation can be performed, such as creating home directories. In addition, the file that specifies the user data can be updated to include pathname changes. For example, if the original system's home directories were exported using NFS, they could be mounted under the */export* mount point on the new system, and the data in the user specification file could be updated accordingly before being processed; or if mount points were to change at a later time, user data on the system could be modified by using the `smmultiuser` command as well.

Like `smexec`, `smmultiuser` has three options, one of which must be passed to the command upon execution: *add*, which adds multiple user entries; *delete*, which deletes one or more user entries; or *modify*, which modifies a set of existing entries. In order to use `smmultiuser` to change passwords, the user must have the *solaris.admin.usermgr.pswd* authorization. Two sets of parameters—authorization parameters and operation parameters—can be passed to `smmultiuser`, depending on which option has been selected.

The authorization parameters are common to each option, and they specify the following characteristics:

–domain	The domain to be administered
–hostname:port	The hostname and port on which operations are to be performed (default port is 898)
–password	The password for the user rather than the role
–rolename	The name of the role
–rolepassword	The password for role authentication

–trust	Required when operating in batch mode
–username	The name of the user

For *add, delete,* and *modify* operations using `smmultiuser`, the following parameters can be passed on the command line:

–i	Specifies the input file to be read, which contains data for all entries to be added, modified, or deleted
–L	Specifies the name of the logfile that records whether individual operations in the batch job were a success or failure

In the following example, a set of records is read in from */home/paul/newaccounts.txt* and added to the system:

```
# smmultiuser add -hostname localhost -p xyz123 -username root -- -I
/home/paul/newaccounts.txt
```

smuser

The `smuser` command is used to perform operations on user accounts, whether the data is retrieved from the local user databases or from NIS/NIS+. Although it is similar to `smmultiuser`, it is generally used only to add single users rather than a set of users in batch mode. In addition to adding, deleting, and modifying user records, existing user data can be retrieved and listed. One of four options must be passed to the command upon execution: *add*, which adds an entry; *delete*, which deletes an entry; *list*, which lists all existing entries; or *modify*, which updates an entry. In order to use `smuser add`, `delete`, or `modify`, the user must have the *solaris.profmgr.execattr.write* authorization. However, only the *solaris.admin.usermgr.write* authorization is required to list entries.

There are two sets of parameters that can be passed to `smuser` (depending on which option has been selected): authorization parameters and specific parameters for each option. The authorization parameters are common to each option, and they specify the following characteristics:

–domain	The domain to be administered. This can be the local databases (*file*), NIS (*nis*), NIS+ (*nisplus*), DNS (*dns*), or LDAP (*ldap*). To administer the host *foxtrot.cassowary.net* using LDAP, you would specify the domain as *ldap://foxtrot/cassowary.net*.
–hostname:port	The hostname and port on which operations are to be performed. The default port is 898.
–password	The password for the user rather than the role.
–rolename	The name of the role.
–rolepassword	The password for role authentication.
–username	The name of the user.

For adding entries using `smuser add`, the parameters are similar to those discussed for adding users using `useradd`, as described in Chapter 12. The following parameters can be passed on the command line:

–c	Specifies an account description, such as "Joe Bloggs"
–d	Specifies the user's home directory
–e	Specifies the account expiration date
–f	Specifies a limit on the number of inactive days before an account is expired
–F	Specifies a full name for the account, which must not be used by another account within the domain
–g	Specifies the account GID
–n	Specifies the account name
–P	Specifies the account password
–s	Specifies the default shell
–u	Specifies the account UID

An example `smuser add` command is shown here:

```
# smuser add -H localhost -p xyz123 -u root -- -F "Paul Watters"
 -n walrus -c "Paul A Watters Director" -P jimmy123 -g 10 -u 1025
```

This command adds an account called *walrus* to the system for *Paul Watters*, with the password *jimmy123*. The UID for the account is 1025, and the GID is 10.

For removing entries using `smuser delete`, only the *–n* parameter, specifying the account name, needs to be passed on the command line. The following command would remove the account for *walrus* on the localhost:

```
# smuser delete -H localhost -p xyz123 -u root -- -n walrus
```

The `smuser list` command can display a list of users without any parameters, by using a command like this:

```
# smuser list -H localhost -p xyz123 -u root --
```

For modifying entries using `smuser modify`, the same parameters can be passed on the command line as for `smuser add`, with any new supplied values resulting in the appropriate fields being updated. For example, to modify the default shell for a user to the Korn shell, the following command would be used:

```
# smuser update -H localhost -p xyz123 -u root -- -n walrus -s /bin/ksh
```

smprofile

The `smprofile` command is used to create, list, update, and delete profiles in the *prof_attr* database, using `smprofile add`, `smprofile list`, `smprofile modify`, and `smprofile delete`, respectively. The authorization arguments are similar to those used for `smuser` and `smexec`. For adding entries using `smprofile add`, the following parameters can be passed on the command line:

–a	Adds a single authorization or a set of authorizations
–d	Adds a description for the new profile
–m	Specifies the path to the HTML help file associated with the profile
–n	Specifies a name for the profile

An example `smprofile add` command is shown here:

```
# smprofile add -H localhost -p xyz123 -u root -- -n "Password Manager" \
  -d "Change user passwords" -a solaris.admin.usermgr.pswd \
  -m PasswordManager.html
```

This command adds a profile for the Password Manager who has the authorization *solaris.admin.usermgr.pswd* to change passwords.

For listing entries using `smprofile list`, only the *–n* parameter can be passed on the command line, which optionally specifies the name of the profile to list. An example `smprofile list` command is shown here:

```
# smprofile list -H localhost -p xyz123 -u root --
```

For modifying entries using `smprofile modify`, the same parameters can be passed on the command line as for `smprofile add`. Any parameters specified will result in the corresponding field being updated. An example `smprofile modify` command is shown here:

```
# smprofile modify -H localhost -p xyz123 -u root -- \
  -n "Password Manager" -d "Modify user passwords
```

This example changes the description for the profile Password Manager.

For deleting entries using `smprofile delete`, only the *–n* parameter can be passed on the command line, which specifies the name of the profile to delete. An example `smprofile delete` command is shown here:

```
# smprofile delete -H localhost -p xyz123 -u root -- \
  -n "Password Manager"
```

smrole

The smrole command is used to perform operations on role accounts. It is generally used to add single roles rather than a set of roles in batch mode. In addition to adding, deleting, and modifying role account records, existing role data can be retrieved and listed. One of four options must be passed to the command upon execution: *add*, which adds an entry; *delete*, which deletes an entry; *list*, which lists all existing entries; or *modify*, which updates an entry. In order to use smrole add, delete, or modify, the user must have the *solaris.role.write* authorization. However, only the *solaris.admin.usermgr.read* authorization is required to list entries. There are two sets of parameters that can be passed to smrole (depending on which option has been selected): authorization parameters and specific parameters for each option. The authorization parameters are similar to those used for smuser.

For adding entries using smrole add, the following parameters can be passed on the command line:

–c	Specifies a role account description, such as "System Manager"
–d	Specifies the role account's home directory
–G	Specifies any secondary GIDs for the role account, because the primary GID is always *sysadmin*
–n	Specifies the role name
–P	Specifies the account password
–s	Specifies the default shell
–u	Specifies the account UID

An example smrole add command is shown here:

```
# smrole add -H localhost -p xyz123 -u root -- -F "System Manager" \
  -n bofh -P abc123 -G 10 -u 666
```

This command adds an account called *bofh* to the system for System Manager, with the password *jimmy123*. The UID for the account is 666, and the secondary GID is 10.

For removing entries using smrole delete, only the *–n* parameter, specifying the role account name, needs to be passed on the command line. The following command would remove the account for *bofh* on the localhost:

```
# smrole delete -H localhost -p xyz123 -u root -- -n bofh
```

The smrole list command can display a list of roles without any parameters, by using a command like this:

```
# smrole list -H localhost -p xyz123 -u root --
```

For modifying entries using `smrole modify`, the same parameters can be passed on the command line as for `smrole add`, with any new supplied values resulting in the appropriate fields being updated. For example, to modify the default shell for a role to the Bourne shell, the following command would be used:

```
# smrole update -H localhost -p xyz123 -u root -- -n walrus -s /bin/sh
```

Summary

In this chapter, we have examined some alternative models of access control that are based around roles rather than users. This approach provides a useful abstraction that caters to situations in which individual users are deleted, but the applications that they run or the files that they own must be preserved or kept running.

Users, Groups, and the Sun Management Console

The concept of the user is central to Solaris—all processes and files on a Solaris system are "owned" by a particular user and are assigned to a specific user group. No data or activities on the system may exist without a valid user or group. Managing users and groups as a Solaris administrator can be a challenging activity—you will be responsible for assigning all of the privileges granted or denied to a user or group of users, and many of these permissions carry great risk. For example, a user with an inappropriate privilege level may execute commands as the superuser, causing damage to your system. In this chapter, you will learn how to add users to the system and add and modify groups. In addition, the contents and structure of key user databases, including the password, shadow password, and group files, are examined in detail.

In the past, several attempts have been made to develop an extensible, easy-to-use GUI for managing individual Solaris systems and groups of Solaris systems. Until recently, the `admintool` was the main GUI administration tool supplied with the Solaris distribution. However, since the Solaris 8 Admin Pack release, a new tool has been made available— the Solaris Management Console (SMC). This chapter examines all of the functionality available through the SMC to manage individual servers and groups of servers.

Key Concepts

The following concepts are required knowledge for managing users and groups, and for using the SMC.

Users

All users on a Solaris system have a number of unique identifiers and characteristics that can be used to distinguish individual users from one another and to logically group related users. Most physical users of a Solaris system have a unique login assigned to them, which is identified by a username with a maximum of eight characters. Once a user account is created, it can be used for the following purposes:

- Spawning a shell
- Executing applications interactively
- Scheduling applications to run at specific times and on specific dates
- Accessing database applications and other system services

In addition to user accounts, Solaris also uses a number of predefined system accounts (such as *root*, *daemon*, *bin*, *sys*, *lp*, *adm*, and *uucp*) to perform various kinds of routine maintenance, including the following:

- Allocating system resources to perform specific tasks
- Running a mail server
- Running a Web server
- Managing processes

Users may access a Solaris system by accessing the console, or through a remote terminal, in either graphical or text mode. In each case, a set of authentication credentials is presented to the system, including the username and password. When entered, a user's password is compared to an encrypted string stored in the password database (*/etc/passwd*) or the shadow password database (*/etc/shadow*). Once the string entered by the user has been encrypted, it is matched against the already encrypted entry in the password database. If a match is made, authentication occurs, and the user may spawn a shell.

A Solaris username may have a maximum of eight characters, as may a Solaris password. Because the security of a Solaris system relies heavily on the difficulty of guessing passwords, user policies should be developed to either recommend or enforce the use of passwords containing random or semirandom character strings. The specific characteristics of the password can be defined in the */etc/default/passwd* file.

A number of other user characteristics are associated with each user, in addition to a username and password. These features include the following:

- **User ID (UID)**   A unique integer that begins with the *root* user (UID=0), with other UIDs typically (but not necessarily) being allocated sequentially. Some systems reserve all UIDs below 1023 for system accounts (e.g., the "apache" user for managing the Apache Web server); UIDs 1023 and above are available for ordinary users. The UID of 0 designates the superuser account, which is typically called "root."

- **A flexible mechanism for distinguishing different classes of users, known as groups**   Groups are not just sets of related users. The Solaris file system allows for group-designated read, write, and execute file access for groups, in addition to permissions granted to the individual user and to all users. Every UID is associated with a primary group ID (GID); however, UIDs may also be associated with more than one secondary group.

- **Home directory**   The default file storage location for all files created by a particular user. If the `automounter` is used, then home directories may be exported using NFS on */home*. When a user spawns a login shell, the current working directory is always the home directory.

- **Login shell**   Can be used to issue commands interactively or to write simple programs. A number of different shells are available under Solaris, including the Bourne shell (`sh`), C-shell (`csh`), the Bourne Again Shell (`bash`), and the Cornell shell (`tcsh`). The choice of shell depends largely on personal preference, user experience with C-like programming constructs, and terminal handling.

- **Comment**   Typically, this is the user's full name, such as "Paul Watters." However, system accounts may use names that describe their purpose (e.g., the comment "Web Server" might be associated with the apache user).

Groups

Solaris provides a facility for identifying sets of related users into groups. Each user is associated with a primary GID, which is associated with a name. The group name and GID can be used interchangeably. In addition, users can be associated with one or more secondary groups. This flexibility means that although a user might have a primary group membership based on their employment or organizational status (e.g., "staff" or "managers"), they can actively share data and system privileges with other groups based on their workgroup needs (e.g., "sales" or "engineer").

All information about groups in Solaris is stored in the groups database (*/etc/group*). The following is a typical set of groups:

```
# cat /etc/group
root::0:root
other::1:
bin::2:root,bin,daemon
sys::3:root,bin,sys,adm
adm::4:root,adm,daemon
uucp::5:root,uucp
mail::6:root
tty::7:root,tty,adm
lp::8:root,lp,adm
nuucp::9:root,nuucp
staff::10:paul,maya,brad,natashia
postgres:a.mBzQnr1ei2D.:100:postgres, paul
daemon::12:root,daemon
sysadmin::14:
nobody::60001:
noaccess::60002:
nogroup::65534:
```

You can see that the lower group numbers are associated with all the system functions and accounts, such as the *bin* group, which has the members *root*, *bin*, and *daemon*, and the *sys* group, which has the members *root*, *bin*, *sys*, and *adm*. Higher-numbered groups, such as *staff*, contain several different users, such as *paul*, *maya*, *brad*, and *natashia*. Notice also that *paul* has a secondary group membership in the *postgres* group, giving him database access privileges. A group password can also be set for each group to restrict access, although most groups don't use this facility. In this group database, you can see that the *postgres* group is the only group that has an encrypted password (*a.mBzQnr1ei2D.*).

You can obtain a list of all groups that a user belongs to by using the `groups` command. For example, to view all the groups that the *root* user belongs to, use this command:

```
# groups root
other root bin sys adm uucp mail tty lp nuucp daemon
```

Passwords

All Solaris users have a username and password associated with their account, except where a user account has been explicitly locked (designated *LK*) or a system account has been specified not to have a password at all (NP). Many early exploits of Solaris systems were associated with default passwords used on some system accounts, and the most common method of gaining unauthorized access to a Solaris system remains password cracking and/or guessing. This section examines the password database (*/etc/passwd*) and its more secure counterpart, the shadow database (*/etc/shadow*). It also presents strategies for making passwords safer.

The standard password database is stored in the file */etc/passwd*, and it looks like this:

```
# cat /etc/passwd
root:x:0:1:Super-User:/:/sbin/sh
daemon:x:1:1::/:
bin:x:2:2::/usr/bin:
sys:x:3:3::/:
adm:x:4:4:Admin:/var/adm:
lp:x:71:8:Line Printer Admin:/usr/spool/lp:
uucp:x:5:5:uucp Admin:/usr/lib/uucp:
nuucp:x:9:9:uucp Admin:/var/spool/uucppublic:/usr/lib/uucp/uucico
listen:x:37:4:Network Admin:/usr/net/nls:
nobody:x:60001:60001:Nobody:/:
noaccess:x:60002:60002:No Access User:/:
nobody4:x:65534:65534:SunOS 4.x Nobody:/:
postgres:x:1001:100:Postgres User:/usr/local/postgres:/bin/sh
htdig:x:1002:10:htdig:/opt/www:/usr/local/bin/bash
apache:x:1003:10:apache user:/usr/local/apache:/bin/sh
```

You have already seen some of the fields shown here when adding users to the system:

- The username field, which has a maximum of eight characters.
- The encrypted password field, which in a system using shadow passwords is crossed with an x.

- The user ID field, which contains the numeric and unique UID.
- The primary group ID field, which contains the numeric GID.
- The user comment, which contains a description of the user.
- The path to the user's home directory.
- The user's default shell.

In older versions of Solaris, the encrypted password field would have contained an encrypted password string like *X14oLaiYg7bO2*. However, this presented a security problem, because the login program required all users to have *read* access to the password file:

```
# ls -l /etc/passwd
-rw-r--r--   1 root       sys          605 Jul 24 11:04 /etc/passwd
```

Thus, any user with the lowest form of privilege would be able to access the encrypted password field for the *root* user and attempt to gain root access by guessing the password. A number of programs were specifically developed for this purpose, such as `crack`, which takes a standard Solaris password file and uses a dictionary and some clever lexical rules to guess passwords (note that `crack` is not supplied with the Solaris distribution). Once a rogue user obtains a root password, he or she may perform any operation on a Solaris system, including formatting hard disks, installing Trojan horses, launching attacks on other systems, and so on.

The cryptographic algorithm used by Solaris is not easy to crack. Indeed, a brute-force guess of a password composed of a completely random set of characters would take many CPU years to compute. The task would be made even more difficult (if not impossible) if the root password were changed weekly, again with a random set of characters. However, the reality is that most users enter passwords that are easily guessed from a dictionary or from some knowledge about the user. Because users are constantly required to use PINs and passwords, they generally choose passwords that are easy to remember. However, easily remembered passwords are also the easiest to crack.

Solaris has reduced the chances of a rogue user obtaining the password file in the first place, by implementing a shadow password facility. This creates a file called */etc/ shadow*, which is similar to the password file (*/etc/passwd*), but is readable only by *root* and contains the encrypted password fields for each UID. Thus, if a rogue user cannot obtain the encrypted password entries, using them as the basis for a "crack" attack is very difficult.

UNIX passwords are created by calling the `crypt` function, which requires a salt and the password to create an encrypted string. Because the `crypt` function is one-way (i.e., it is not mathematically reversible), there is no corresponding function called `decrypt`. Thus, the only way to obtain a password from an encrypted string is by passing the salt plus a "guess string" containing what you think the password might be and seeing if the encrypted string generated matches the one stored in the shadow password file. In this case, "guess strings" are often generated by reading a dictionary file containing thousands of possible passwords or by using a list of commonly used passwords (such as "root," "system," "manager," "tiger," and so on).

Introduction to SMC

The Solaris Management Console (SMC) is designed as a replacement for the `admintool`, which was used in versions of Solaris prior to Solaris 9. `admintool` provided a limited and nonextensible set of tools for GUI system management. The motivation for providing GUI tools to seasoned command-line hackers may seem unclear—however, SMC provides methods for managing a large number of servers from a single interface and provides easy methods for extending the functionality of the core interface. This means you can add customized applications to the toolbox, or to the collection of administration applications for a specific system, by using the appropriate commands. SMC may not be of great benefit to administrators who manage a single system—it is an advanced tool that suits sites that deal with large numbers of systems.

SMC allows you to manage system and application packages, along with users and groups. You can manage multiple systems from a single system and user interface based on Java. SMC enables you to reboot or shut down managed systems, set their root passwords, enable Point-to-Point Protocol (PPP) support, and administer naming services like Domain Name Service (DNS). You can review processes in real time, along with system resources, such as virtual and physical memory.

The following administrative tasks can be performed by software contained within SMC toolboxes:

- Assign rights and roles to users
- Configure and format new disks for the system, including laying out partitions and copying configurations from one disk to another in preparation for RAID
- Create a single user account or generate multiple accounts using a consistent specification
- Create new groups or modify existing groups
- Create user policies and apply them
- Execute jobs in real time or schedule them for regular, repeated execution
- Install support for serial ports, modems, and related Physical layer technologies such as PPP
- Monitor processes and search for resumed, deleted, or suspended processes
- Review system logs and search for anomalous or suspicious entries
- Set up mailing lists
- View mounted file systems

These management operations and applications are not provided intrinsically by SMC—however, SMC provides an interface to access them.

Procedures

The following procedures must be performed to add users and groups to the system.

Adding Users

Adding a user to a Solaris system is easy; however, this operation may be performed only by the *root* user. There are two options. The first option is to edit the */etc/passwd* file directly, which includes incrementing the UID, adding the appropriate GID, adding a home directory (and remembering to physically create it on the file system), inserting a comment, and choosing a login name. In addition, you must set a password for the user by using the `passwd` command.

Does this sound difficult? If so, you should consider using the second option: the automated `useradd` command, which does all the hard work for you, as long as you supply the correct information. The `useradd` command has the following format:

```
# useradd -u uid -g gid -d home_directory -s path_to_shell
-c comment login_name
```

Let's add a user to the system and examine the results:

```
# useradd -u 1004 -g 10 -d /opt/www -s /bin/sh -c
"Web User" www
```

Here, you are adding a Web user called *www* with the UID 1004, GID 10, the home directory */opt/www*, and the Bourne shell as their login shell.

At the end of the `useradd` script, an appropriate line should appear in the */etc/passwd* file, as follows:

```
# grep www /etc/passwd
www:x:1004:10:Web User:/opt/www:/bin/sh
```

However, the `useradd` command may fail under the following conditions:

- The UID that you specified has already been taken by another user. UIDs may be recycled, as long as precautions are taken to ensure that a previous owner of the UID no longer owns files on the file system.

- The GID that you specified does not exist. Verify its entry in the groups database (*/etc/group*).

- The comment contains special characters, such as double quotes (""), exclamation marks (!), or slashes (/).

- The shell that you specified does not exist. Check that the shell actually exists in the path specified and that the shell has an entry in the shells database (*/etc/shells*).

Modifying User Attributes

Once you have created a user account, you can change any of its characteristics by directly editing the password database (*/etc/passwd*) or by using the `usermod` command. For example, if you wanted to modify the UID of the *www* account from 1004 to 1005, you would use this command:

```
# usermod -u 1005 www
```

Again, you can verify that the change has been made correctly by examining the entry for *www* in the password database:

```
# grep www /etc/passwd
www:x:1005:10:Web User:/opt/www:/bin/sh
```

Remember that if you change a UID or GID, you must manually update existing directory and file ownerships by using the `chmod`, `chgrp`, and `chown` commands where appropriate.

Once a user account has been created, the next step is to set a password, which you can perform by using the `passwd` command:

```
# passwd user
```

where *user* is the login name for the account whose password you want to change. In all cases, you are required to enter the new password twice—if you happen to make a typing error, the password will not be changed, and you will be warned that the two password strings entered do not match. Here's an example for the user *www*:

```
# passwd www
New password:
Re-enter new password:
passwd(SYSTEM): They don't match; try again.
New password:
Re-enter new password:
passwd (SYSTEM): passwd successfully changed for www
```

After a password has been entered for a user, such as the *www* user, it should appear as an encrypted string in the shadow password database (*/etc/shadow*):

```
# grep www /etc/shadow
www:C4dMH8As4bGTM:::::::
```

Once a user has been granted an initial password, he or she may then enter a new password by using the `passwd` command with no options.

Deleting Users

Now imagine that one of your prized employees has moved on to greener pastures unexpectedly—although you will eventually be able to change the ownership on all of his or her files, you cannot immediately restart some production applications. In this case, you can temporarily disable logins to a specific account by using a command like this:

```
# passwd -l natashia
```

This command would lock *natashia*'s account until the *root* user once again used the `passwd` command on this account to set a new password.

A locked account can be identified in the password database by the characters *LK*:

```
# grep natashia /etc/shadow
natashia:*LK*:::::::
```

You can unlock the account by either removing the *LK* entry manually or by setting a password.

Once all of the user's files have been backed up, and any active processes have been killed by the superuser, the user account may be permanently deleted by using the `userdel` command. For example, to delete the user account *natashia* and remove that user's home directory and all the files underneath that directory, you would use this command:

```
# userdel -r natashia
```

Or, you could edit both the password and shadow password databases and remove the appropriate lines containing the entries for the user *natashia*. You would also need to manually remove the user's home directory and all of her files underneath that directory. Note that this procedure works only if the user database is the traditional UNIX local DB—it does not work with user DBs like LDAP and NIS/NIS+.

There are also several system accounts, including *adm, bin, listen, nobody, lp, sys,* and *uucp,* that should remain locked at all times to prevent interactive logins.

Adding Groups

To add a new group to the system, you may either manually edit the */etc/group* file or use the `groupadd` command, which has the following syntax:

```
/usr/sbin/groupadd -g gid   group_name
```

Thus, to add a group called managers to the system, with a GID of 500, you would use this command:

```
# groupadd -g 500 managers
```

You would then be able to verify the new group's existence by searching the groups database:

```
# grep managers /etc/group
managers::500:
```

The `groupadd` command will fail if the GID that you specify has already been allocated to an existing group or if the *group_name* is greater than eight characters.

Managing Groups

If you want to change your group from primary to secondary during an interactive session to ensure that all the files that you create are associated with the correct GID, you need to use the `newgrp` command. For example, the *root* user has the following primary group membership:

```
# id
uid=0(root) gid=0(root)
```

However, if the *root* user wishes to act as a member of another group, such as *sys*, you would have to use the following command:

```
# newgrp sys
```

The effective GID would then change to *sys*:

```
# id
uid=0(root) gid=3(sys)
```

NOTE   *If a password is set on the target group, a non-root user would have to enter that password to change the effective group.*

Any operations (such as creating files) that the root user performs after using `newgrp` will be associated with the GID of 3 (*sys*) rather than 0 (*root*). For example, if you created a new file with the primary group, the group associated with the new file would be GID 0:

```
# touch root.txt
 # ls -l root.txt
-rw-r--r--    1 root        root       0 Oct 12 11:17 root.txt
```

However, if the *root* user then changes groups to *sys* and creates a new file, the group associated with the file will be *sys* rather than *root*:

```
# newgrp sys
# touch sys.txt
# ls -l sys.txt
-rw-r--r--    1 root        sys        0 Oct 12 11:18 sys.txt
```

Starting the SMC

The SMC operates by collecting data from systems, providing an interface for viewing that data, and allowing administrative tasks to be executed on the basis of that data. Different servers can store localized toolboxes. Alternatively, if a high-resolution graphics card or monitor is not available, then SMC can be started with a command-line interface.

The command that starts the SMC is */usr/sadm/bin/smc*. This assumes that SMC is to be opened for operations. An alternative mode of operation is provided by the smc edit mode, where toolboxes can be modified or updated. The following options are available to the smc command when starting up:

- *–auth-data*   Allows authentication data to be read from a file.
- *–toolbox*   Stipulates the name of a toolbox to read in from a file. Alternatively, a URL can be specified that points to the location of a toolbox.
- *–domain*   Designates the domain name for the systems that are being managed. LDAP, DNS, NIS, and NIS+ domains are supported. The form of the URL for a DNS domain *cassowary.net* and the host *midnight* would be **dns:/midnight/cassowary.net**.
- *–hostname:port*   Nominates the hostname and port number of the server to manage. The default port number is 898.
- *–J*   Passes any command-line options to the Java Virtual Machine, such as the initial and maximum heap sizes.
- *–rolepassword*   Specifies a password for the role *rolename*.
- *–password*   Specifies a password for *username*.
- *–rolename*   Specifies a role to execute SMC.
- *–t*   Executes SMC in terminal mode.
- *–trust*   Allows all downloaded code to be trusted.
- *–tool*   Specifies a tool to be executed.
- *–username*   Specifies a username with which SMC is to be executed.
- *–yes*   Answers yes, by default, to all interactive questions.

The format of data in an *auth-data* file is as follows:

```
hostname=ivana
username=root
password=my1asswd
rolename=su
rolepassword=su1asswd
```

Of course, any *auth-data* file should be read-only by *root*, or by the user who is assigned the role of SMC management. However, there is always an inherent risk in storing passwords in plain text in a file on any file system, since it could be removed and mounted on another system and its contents read directly. Alternatively, gaining unauthorized access to the *auth-data* file may allow a cracker to obtain administrative access to a large number of servers whose authentication tokens are stored in the file. One file is normally created for every server whose credentials must be locally stored.

Examples

The following examples demonstrate how to work productively with SMC.

Working with the SMC

When you start the SMC, you are presented with a login screen (after a very long wait when used for the first time), as shown in Figure 12-1. This screen allows you to connect through to the server specified on the command line, or in the text box, and authenticate yourself as the administrator. Generally, the username will be *root*, but it could be any nonprivileged user who has been assigned administrative roles.

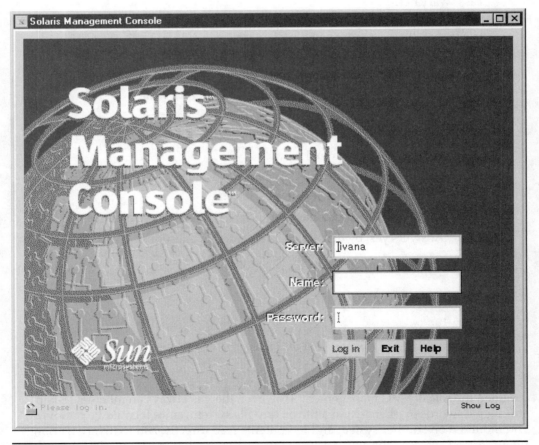

FIGURE 12-1   SMC login screen

The main screen for the SMC is shown in Figure 12-2. As you see, there are three menus (Console, View, and Help), two tabs (Applications View and SMC Server View), a navigation pane on the left side, a view pane on the right side, and a status and information pane in the lower-right corner. By default, Applications View is enabled. To switch to SMC Server View, simply click the SMC Server View tab.

In Applications View, shown in Figure 12-3, a number of broad headings are used to differentiate the applications used to manage the system. Each of these headings can be activated by clicking the appropriate text or folder icon in the navigation pane, after which a list of applications and application types appears in the view pane. As shown in the navigation pane, the classes of applications supported by SMC include Connectivity, Documentation, Infrastructure, Jobs, Security, Software, and User & Group.

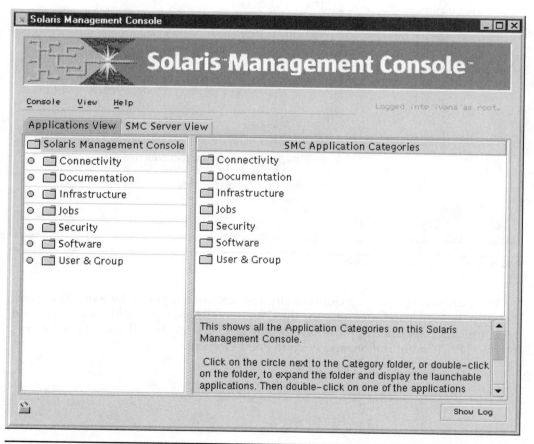

FIGURE 12-2   SMC main screen

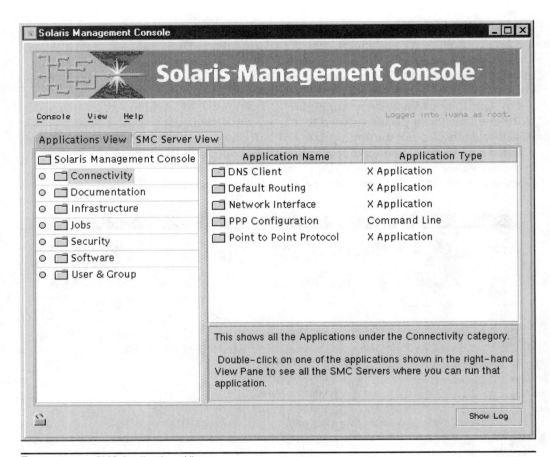

FIGURE 12-3   SMC Applications View

There are several different Connectivity applications supported by SMC. These are shown in the view pane after selecting the Connectivity heading or folder icon, as shown in Figure 12-3. Supported applications include DNS Client, Default Routing, Network Interface, PPP Configuration, and Point to Point Protocol.

In the Documentation class of applications, shown in Figure 12-4, only the Answerbook is supported.

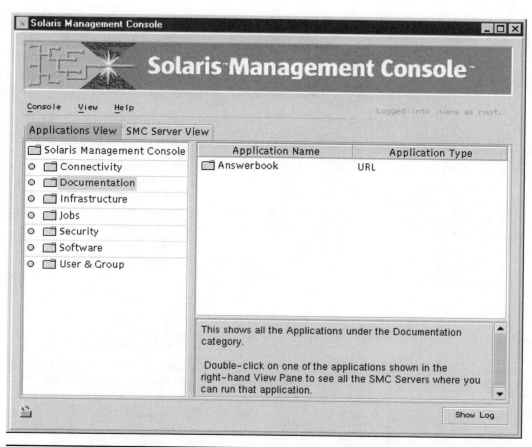

FIGURE 12-4   SMC Documentation applications

The Infrastructure class of applications, shown in Figure 12-5, includes AdminSuite, Admintool, Performance Meter, Shutdown/Restart Computer, Terminal, and Workstation Information.

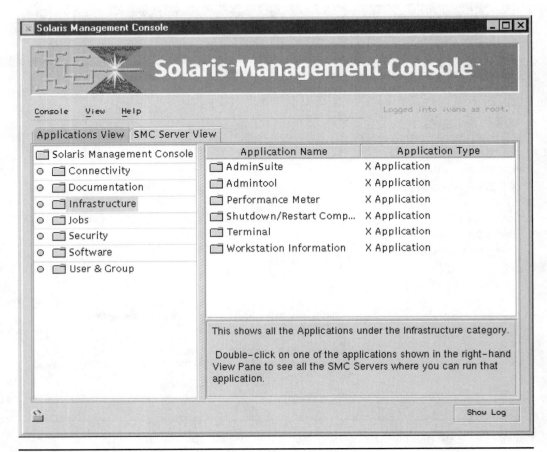

FIGURE 12-5 SMC Infrastructure applications

In the Jobs class of applications, shown in Figure 12-6, only the Process Manager is supported by default.

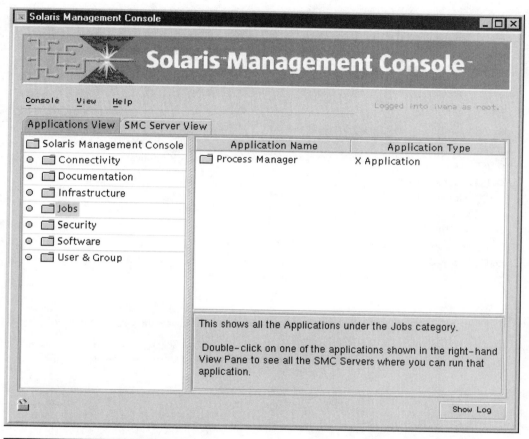

FIGURE 12-6   SMC Jobs applications

In the Security class of applications, shown in Figure 12-7, only the Kerberos v5 server (SEAM) is supported by default.

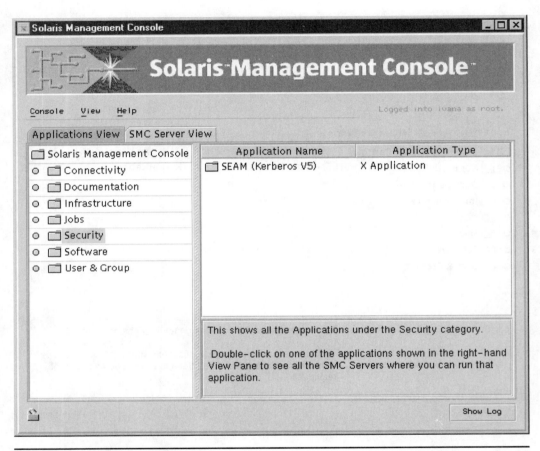

FIGURE 12-7   SMC Security applications

The Software class of applications, shown in Figure 12-8, supports DNS Server, Software Manager, and Solaris Product Registry.

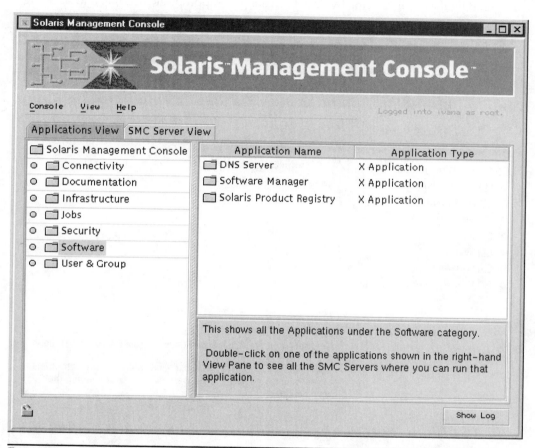

FIGURE 12-8   SMC Software applications

In the User & Group class of applications, shown in Figure 12-9, only the Change Root Password operation is supported by default.

Every application listed underneath each main application class heading can be configured by the administrator, by double-clicking the appropriate heading and selecting

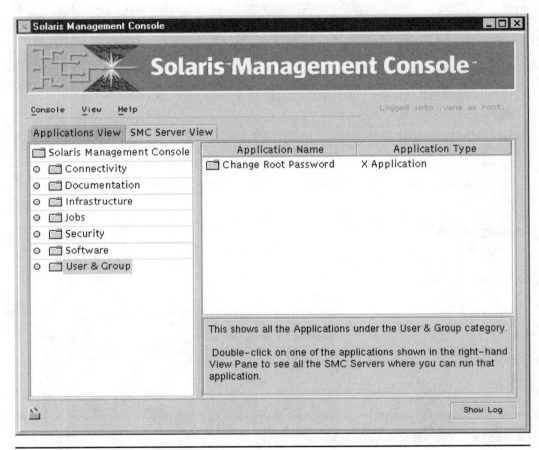

FIGURE 12-9   SMC User & Group applications

the software product to be configured. This operation is shown in Figure 12-10 for the DNS Server software package underneath the Software applications heading. The parameters that can be modified include the application name, the server name on which it is to be executed, and the user who will run the application.

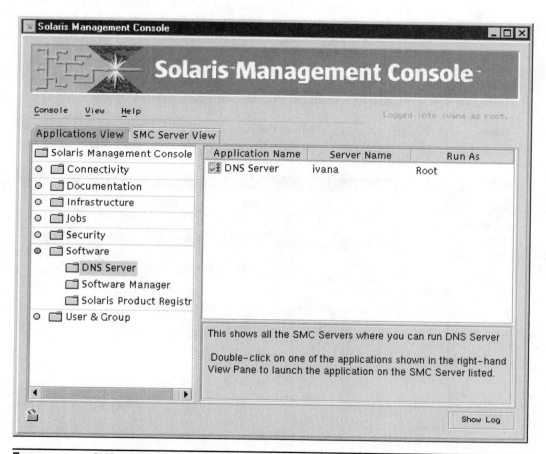

FIGURE 12-10   SMC application configuration

The list of applications in each category is limited to those installed by default in the Solaris installation. However, SMC becomes really useful only after a number of new applications are included in the toolbox. These can be configured on a per-system basis rather than having a "one size fits all" toolbox configuration. For example, a backup server might have Legato administration options added to SMC, while a database server might have the Oracle administration options integrated into SMC.

To add a new application to an existing category, select Console | Add Application, as shown in Figure 12-11. Alternatively, if you want to remove an existing application from an existing SMC category, select the application in the view pane and then select Console | Remove Application. Finally, if you just want to modify the configuration of an existing application in an existing application category, select Console | Modify Application.

When you choose to add an application, the Add Application dialog box appears, as shown in Figure 12-12. Here, you can choose the application type, application category,

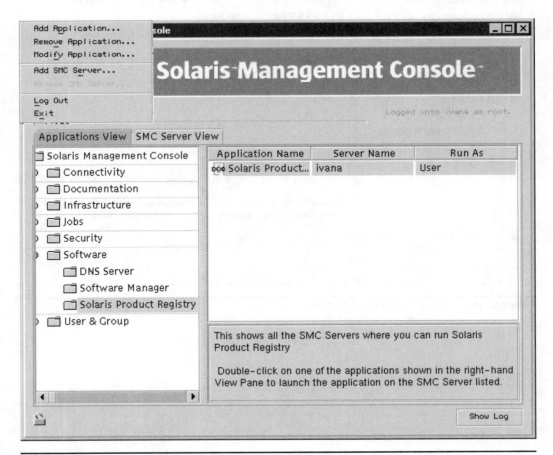

FIGURE 12-11   SMC Console menu

FIGURE 12-12
SMC Add
Application
dialog box

user to run the application as, and the application name. In addition, you can specify the executable path, any optional command-line arguments, and whether or not to use the default icon or a customized icon.

When removing an application, the Remove Application dialog box is displayed. Here, you must choose whether to remove the application's SMC entry or whether to cancel the application removal, as shown here:

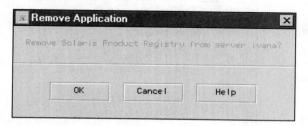

When you choose to modify an application, the Modify Application dialog box appears, as shown in Figure 12-13. Here, you can modify the application type, application category, user to run the application as, and the application name. In addition, you can modify the executable path, any optional command-line arguments, and whether or not to use the default icon or a customized icon.

FIGURE 12-13
SMC Modify
Application
dialog box

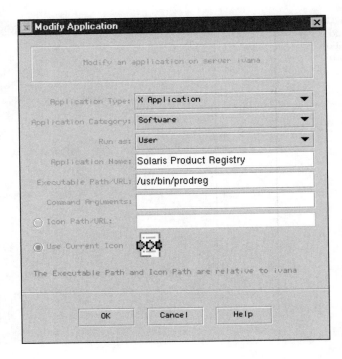

FIGURE 12-13
SMC Modify
Application
dialog box

One of the main benefits of the SMC application is that multiple servers can be added into the pool of servers managed from a single interface, as shown in Figure 12-14. This reduces administrative overhead, especially in large installations where literally hundreds of servers may need to be managed by a single administrator or team of administrators.

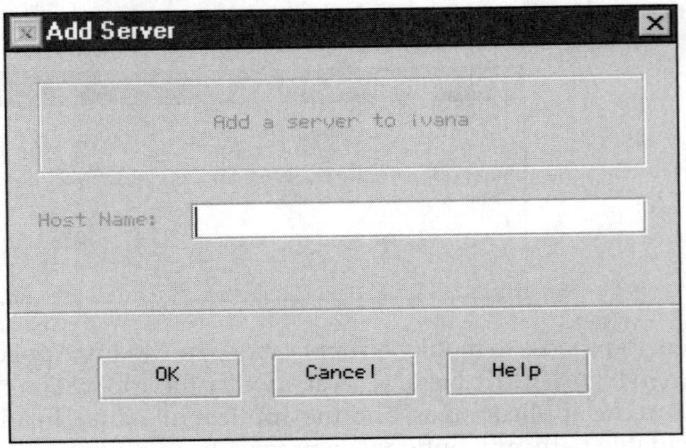

FIGURE 12-14
SMC Add Server
dialog box

Command Reference

The following commands are used to manage users on Solaris systems.

pwck

The pwck command is used to verify the accuracy of the password file. It reads */etc/passwd*, verifies that the expected number of fields exist for each entry in the file, and validates the contents of the username, UID, and GID fields. It also checks whether the home directory exists and whether the default shell noted is a valid shell.

grpck

The grpck command is similar to the pwck command; you can use it to verify the accuracy of the group file. It reads */etc/group*, verifies that the expected number of fields exist for each entry in the file, and validates the contents of the group name and GID fields. It also creates a list of usernames defined in the group and checks that these are contained in the */etc/passwd* file. If not, an error is reported, because an old user account may have been deleted from */etc/passwd* but may still be listed in a group.

pwconv

You can use the pwconv command to convert systems that do not have a shadow password file to use password shadowing. Most (if not all) modern systems would use password shadowing. However, if the */etc/shadow* file does not exist, the encrypted password is stripped from */etc/passwd*, and is replaced by *x*, indicating that the password for each user is shadowed. A shadow password file would then be created using the encrypted passwords extracted from the password file.

However, a more common use of pwconv is to update the shadow password file with entries that have been created manually in */etc/passwd*. Although this is not the recommended method of adding users to the system, some sites have scripts that create blocks of new user accounts by generating sequential usernames with generic group and password information. In such cases, it would be necessary to run pwconv after the script has been executed, to ensure that entries created in */etc/passwd* are correctly transferred to */etc/shadow*.

SMC Initialization

There are a number of different Java options that may be useful for the initialization of the SMC that can be passed using the *–J* option. These options include

- *–Xmixed*   Runs in mixed mode execution
- *–Xint*   Runs in interpreted mode

- *–Xbootclasspath*   Lists directories in which to search for classes for bootstrapping
- *–Xbootclasspath/a*   Appends directories in which to search for classes for bootstrapping
- *–Xbootclasspath/p*   Prepends directories in which to search for classes for bootstrapping
- *–Xnoclassgc*   Switches off garbage collection
- *–Xincgc*   Switches on progressive garbage collection
- *–Xbatch*   Switches off compilation in the background
- *–Xms*   Sets an initial size for the Java heap
- *–Xmx*   Sets a maximum size for the Java heap
- *–Xss*   Sets a size for the Java thread stack
- *–Xprof*   Displays CPU profiling output
- *–Xrunhprof*   Displays heap or monitor profiling output
- *–Xdebug*   Allows debugging remotely
- *–Xfuture*   Enforces strict checking
- *–Xrs*   Minimizes native calls

Summary

In this chapter, you have examined the basic procedures for managing users and groups on a Solaris system. Since all processes and threads are executed with a real or effective user and group ID, it's important for you to understand how to manage these entities effectively.

SMC is a powerful and versatile tool for managing multiple systems from a single interface where different systems can be customized to administer their own local applications as well as a set of common applications. This flexibility gives SMC a number of advantages over the `admintool`, or command-line administration. For more information on SMC, read the administrator's guide on **http://docs.sun.com**.

13
CHAPTER

Kerberos and Pluggable Authentication

Chapter 9 examined username and password authentication, in the context of system and network security, as a built-in feature of Solaris. However, in cross-platform environments, gaining access to more flexible and distributed authentication is necessary for scalability. In this chapter, the basic concepts of Sun's version of MIT Kerberos (known as the Sun Enterprise Authentication Mechanism, or SEAM), are introduced for distributed authentication, followed by a review of the Pluggable Authentication Module (PAM) that allows system administrators to specify the authentication that they want to use. PAM allows drop-in replacement for existing authentication systems without having to reconfigure services or applications that require authentication.

Key Concepts

The following concepts provide a foundation for implementing pluggable and distributed authentication services in Solaris. Note that related hardware authentication issues, such as the use of smart cards, are beyond the scope of this chapter. However, readers interested in the use of card-based credentials should read the *Solaris Smartcard Administration Guide* at **http://docs.sun.com**.

Kerberos

Distributed services and applications require distributed authentication. While single-purpose tools like the secure shell (SSH) can be used as tools for remote access between a single client and multiple servers, maintaining local databases of keys on every client machine is costly in terms of disk space and network traffic. There is an argument that such information should always be distributed across the network, but the level of redundancy that SSH requires for installations of 1,000+ clients is inefficient. For consistency's sake, providing a single sign-on mechanism ensures that credentials used by a number of common services are authenticated in a dependable way.

One alternative to using SSH servers as the primary means of authentication across a network is to use a centralized authentication system such as Kerberos, which grew out of the Athena Project at the Massachusetts Institute of Technology (MIT). Kerberos is a network authentication protocol that is designed to provide strong authentication for client/server applications by using secret-key cryptography, which is similar to that provided by SSH. However, the main difference between the two systems is that whereas authentication is performed by the target server when using SSH, a Kerberos authentication server can provide services to many different servers for a large number of clients by using a Key Distribution Center (KDC). Thus, the many-to-many relationships realized in the Kerberos authentication database makes the network authentication process more streamlined and efficient. Kerberos also supports data integrity checks through message digests and data transmission privacy through encryption.

Kerberos is also designed to provide authentication to hosts inside and outside a firewall, since many attacks may originate in internal networks that are normally considered trusted. In addition, Release 5 introduced the notion of *realms,* which are external but trusted networks, with authentication being extended beyond the firewall. Another advantage of the Kerberos system is that the protocol has been published and widely publicized, and a free implementation (including source code) is available from MIT (**http://web.mit.edu/network/kerberos-form.html**).

Kerberos is based around a key distribution, certificate granting, and a validation system called "tickets." If a client machine wants to make a connection to a target server, it requests a ticket from a centralized authentication server, which is physically the same machine as the target server, but is logically quite separate. An encrypted ticket is produced by the authentication server that authorizes the client to request a specific service from a specific host, generally for a specific time period. This is similar to a parking-ticket machine that grants the drivers of motor vehicles permission to park in a specific street for one or two hours only. Release 5 of Kerberos supports tickets that can be renewed on request. Tickets may also be transferred across different machines without reauthentication, and may be issued before they are valid timewise.

When authentication is requested from the authentication server, a session key is created by that server, which is based on your password that it retrieves from your username and a random value that represents the requested service. The session key is like a voucher that the client then sends to a ticket-granting server, which then returns a ticket that can be used to access the target server. Clearly, there is some overhead in making a request to an authentication server, a ticket-granting server, and a target server. However, the overhead is well worth the effort if important data is at risk of interception. The sequence of events leading to authentication is shown in Figure 13-1.

A significant limitation of Kerberos is that all applications that use its authentication services must be "Kerberized": that is, significant changes must be made to the application's source code in order for it to use Kerberos services. Solaris 10 provides Kerberized versions of the following applications:

- ftp
- rcp
- rdist
- rlogin
- rsh
- telnet

Every host, user, or service that interacts with the KDC is known as a *principal*. The principal includes both a user's realm and their current instance, or role. Thus, *pwatters/root@cassowary.net* identifies the user *pwatters* having the current instance *root* in the realm *cassowary.net*, while *pwatters/ftp@cassowary.net* would denote the same physical user with the current instance of an FTP user.

PAM

The goal of the Pluggable Authentication Module (PAM) is to enable a stack framework for providing authentication services without requiring applications themselves to be modified. Historically, gaining improvements in distributed authentication, for example, has been very difficult because clients and servers need to be modified at the source level. For example, to use Kerberos, clients need to be Kerberized, which is difficult if you

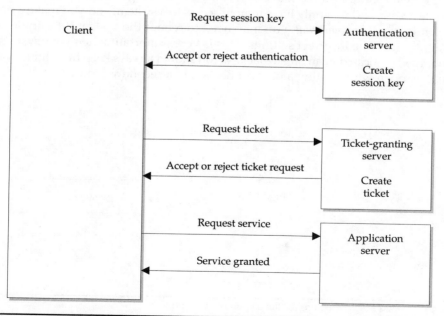

FIGURE 13-1 Distributed mechanisms for Kerberos 5 authentication

only have access to application binaries. PAM ensures that there is an appropriate level of abstraction between the interface for authentication and its underlying implementation. Thus, an authentication service can be modified, upgraded, or changed without disturbing the applications and services that utilize authentication services. PAM provides support for password, session, credential, and account management.

Let's look at an example of PAM usage. Applications that require user logins—such as telnet, ftp, login, etc.—require that users authenticate themselves with a username and password. But what if you want to apply a different authentication system for ftp logins compared to telnet logins? With the default Solaris authentication system, you can't, but PAM allows you to. PAM also supports the use of multiple passwords for sensitive applications, and possibly multiple authentication types. For example, you could be asked to supply a credential (something you own), such as a smart card, supply a password (something you know), and pass a biometric face scan (something you are). This three-way process would provide the highest level of authentication possible—but might land you in trouble if you forget your smart card!

PAM's stack is shown in Figure 13-2. You can see two applications (telnet and rsh) using the PAM library, which is configured by */etc/pam.conf*, making use of two alternative authentication systems—Kerberos (module *pam_krb5.so.1*) and LDAP (module *pam_ldap.so.1*). rsh could be configured to use LDAP, while telnet could be configured to use Kerberos (or both, if multiple authentication is required). If multiple authentication systems are used, then users may need to remember multiple passwords.

One very important problem to note is that if you change authentication services for remote access, and you only have remote access to a system, and you make a mistake when configuring */etc/pam.conf*, you may need to reboot the system into single-user mode and change the incorrect settings. This is very important when your systems are rack-mounted or located in an off-site facility. You should always keep the editing window for *pam.conf* open while testing a new connection in a second window.

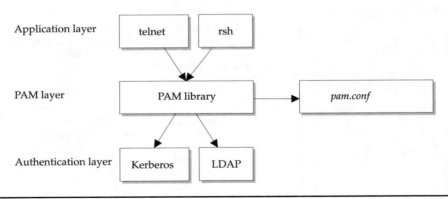

FIGURE 13-2   PAM stack structure for flexible authentication

Procedures

The following procedures demonstrate how to configure Kerberos and PAM services on Solaris systems.

Kerberos

Kerberos is managed by several different applications, including the following:

- The management daemon, `kadmind`
- The ticketing daemon, `krb5kdc`
- The management application, `kadmin`
- Utilities such as `ktutil` and `kdb5_util`
- A GUI for administration, `gkadmin`, shown in Figure 13-3

Kerberos configuration, shown next, is reasonably straightforward given appropriate network resources. All configuration files are stored in */etc/krb5*. The main configuration file is */etc/krb5/krb5.conf*, which contains entries that define the realms that the server

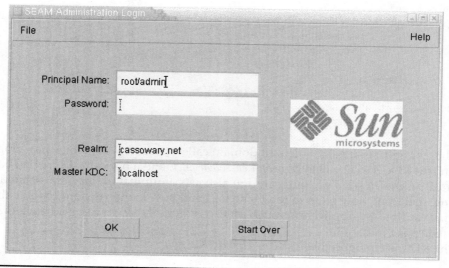

FIGURE 13-3   Kerberos management tool, gkadmin

is associated with, including the name of the primary and secondary KDC, and the admin server.

```
[libdefaults]
        default_realm = CASSOWARY.NET

[realms]
        CASSOWARY.NET = {
                kdc = KERBEROS1.CASSOWARY.NET
                KERBEROS2.CASSOWARY.NET
                admin_server = KERBEROS1.CASSOWARY.NET
        }

[logging]
        default = FILE:/var/krb5/kdc.log
        kdc = FILE:/var/krb5/kdc.log
        kdc_rotate = {
                period = 1d
                versions = 10
        }

[appdefaults]
        kinit = {
                renewable = true
                forwardable= true
        }
        gkadmin = {
                help_url = http://docs.sun.com:80/ab2/coll.384.1/SEAM/
@AB2PageView/1195
}
```

This configuration is for a default domain called *cassowary.net*, which has a logical admin and KDC server called *kerberos1.cassowary.net*, and a backup KDC server called *kerberos2.cassowary.net*. The configuration also sets a number of variables related to logging, including how often to rotate the logs and how many versions to retain before deletion. Individual applications such as kinit and gkadmin can also have their parameters set in the file.

The KDC is configured by the file */etc/krb5/kdc.conf*:

```
[kdcdefaults]
    kdc_ports = 88,750

[realms]
    CASSOWARY.NET = {
        profile = /etc/krb5/krb5.conf
        database_name = /var/krb5/principal
        admin_keytab = /etc/krb5/kadm5.keytab
```

```
        acl_file = /etc/krb5/kadm5.acl
        kadmind_port = 749
        max_life = 8h 0m 0s
        max_renewable_life = 7d 0h 0m 0s
        default_principal_flags = +preauth
  }
```

This configuration for CASSOWARY.NET defines the profile and database names, port numbers, etc. for the KDC administration. The access control list (ACL) file for administration authorizations within the domain is also contained in the *acl_file*.

To initialize the primary KDC, you use the `kdb5_util` command:

```
# /usr/sbin/kdb5_util create -r CASSOWARY.NET -s
Initializing database '/var/krb5/principal' for realm 'CASSOWARY.NET',
master key name 'K/M@CASSOWARY.NET'
You will be prompted for the database Master Password.
It is important that you NOT FORGET this password.
Enter KDC database master key:
Re-enter KDC database master key to verify:
```

Next, you add entries to the */etc/krb5/kadm5.acl* file for the principals who have permissions to administer the database. The following entry gives *pwatters/admin@ CASSOWARY.NET* unlimited authority to modify the database and associated policies:

```
pwatters/admin@CASSOWARY.NET     *
```

To add this principal to the database, you use the `kadmin.local` command, and type in **addprinc pwatters/admin** when prompted:

```
# kadmin.local
Authenticating as principal pwatters/admin@CASSOWARY.NET with password.
kadmin.local:    addprinc pwatters/admin
Enter password for principal "pwatters/admin@CASSOWARY.NET":
Re-enter password for principal "pwatters/admin@CASSOWARY.NET":
Principal "pwatters/admin@CASSOWARY.NET" created.
```

At the `kadmin.local` prompt, you next need to initialize the keytab files for basic administrative operations for the administrator:

```
kadmin.local: ktadd -k /etc/krb5/kadm5.keytab kadmin/
kerberos1.cassowary.net
Entry for principal kadmin/kerberos1.cassowary.net with kvno 3,
encryption type
DES-CBC-CRC added to keytab WRFILE:/etc/krb5/kadm5.keytab.
kadmin.local: ktadd -k /etc/krb5/kadm5.keytab changepw/kdc1.example.com
Entry for principal kadmin/kerberos1.cassowary.net with kvno 3,
```

```
encryption type
DES-CBC-CRC added to keytab WRFILE:/etc/krb5/kadm5.keytab.
kadmin.local: ktadd -k /etc/krb5/kadm5.keytab kadmin/changepw
Entry for principal kadmin/kerberos1.cassowary.net with kvno 3,
encryption type
DES-CBC-CRC added to keytab WRFILE:/etc/krb5/kadm5.keytab.
kadmin.local:quit
```

The KDC can now be started by using the following commands:

```
# /etc/init.d/kdc start
# /etc/init.d/kdc.master start
```

As with any security service, there are risks that should be noted before implementation. In particular, there have been bugs in syslog that can lead to a possible denial-of-service attack. This risk highlights the potential for attacks against a centralized service being the weakest point of the Kerberos system. Even if the authentication server and target server were operational, for example, a sustained flood of requests to a ticket-granting server can halt any network-based service that requires authentication.

PAM

The */etc/pam.conf* file contains a set of entries that associates services and applications requiring authentication with specific PAM modules. Each entry consists of a space or tab-limited tokens representing the following:

- The name of the application or service requiring authentication
- The type of PAM module required
- A flag that determines the failure modes for the entry
- The path to the PAM library
- Any other options

There are several module types that are supported by PAM, including the following:

- **Authentication modules (*auth*)**   Implement user-based authentication
- **Account modules (*account*)**   Implement more general account management activities, such as password aging
- **Password modules (*password*)**   Implement password modifications
- **Session modules (*session*)**   Support login sessions

Obviously, a service may require some or all of these functions—each module requires one entry for each service it is associated with in */etc/pam.conf*.

The following list shows some commonly used applications requiring authentication and their matching module types:

Application	Module Types
cron	*auth, account*
dtlogin	*auth, account, session*
dtsession	*auth*
ftp	*auth, account, session*
init	*session*
login	*auth, account, session*
passwd	*auth, password*
ppp	*auth, account, session*
rlogin	*auth, account, session*
rsh	*auth, account, session*
sac	*auth, account, session*
sshd	*auth, account, password, session*
telnet	*auth, account, session*

Five flags control operational and failure modes for PAM. These flags define how to handle a successful or failed authentication. For example, you may provide multiple means of authentication, but require only that one is satisfied for the user to be authenticated, or you might require that all must be satisfied before a user is authenticated. The following are the flags supported by PAM:

- **binding**   If authentication is successful, skip any other modules listed and report the user as authenticated, but return a failure if not authenticated.

- **required**   If authentication is not successful, check all others, but report the authentication as failed.

- **requisite**   If authentication is not successful, check no others, and report the authentication as failed.

- **optional**   If authentication is not successful, check all others, and report the authentication as successful if any other means succeeds.

- **sufficient**   If authentication is successful, skip any others listed and report the user as authenticated, but check all other means if failure is recorded.

The actual means of authentication supported by PAM include the following authentication modules:

Module	Description
pam_authtok_check.so.1	Manages passwords
pam_authtok_get.so.1	Implements password querying
pam_authtok_store.so.1	Supports authentication modifications
pam_dhkeys.so.1	Used for Diffie-Hellman authentication in secure RPC
pam_dial_auth.so.1	Supports login authentication
pam_krb5.so.1	Core Kerberos authentication modules
pam_ldp.so.1	Main LDAP authentication module
pam_passwd_auth.so.1	Supports `passwd` authentication
pam_rhosts_auth.so.1	Provides equivalent host and automatic logins using *~/.rhosts* and */etc/host.equiv* files
pam_roles.so.1	Role-based account management
pam_sample.so.1	Testing facility
pam_smartcard.so.1	Facilitates smart-card authentication
pam_unix_account.so.1	Provides UNIX-style password management
pam_unix_auth.so.1	Provides UNIX-style authentication support
pam_unix_cred.so.1	Provides UNIX-style credential support
pam_unix_session.so.1	Provides UNIX-style session administration

Examples

The following examples demonstrate how to configure PAM for both Kerberized and non-Kerberized services for distributed and flexible authentication services.

Non-Kerberized Services

The login service can be set up to invoke the *pam_authtok_get.so.1* module first and, if it succeeds, then invoke all the other modules. If invoking *pam_authtok_get.so.1* fails, then the other modules are not invoked—and because they must all succeed for the authentication to succeed, the authentication fails. The following example shows how this can be implemented in */etc/pam.conf*:

```
login     auth requisite     pam_authtok_get.so.1
login     auth required      pam_dhkeys.so.1
login     auth required      pam_unix_cred.so.1
login     auth required      pam_unix_auth.so.1
login     auth required      pam_dial_auth.so.1
```

The rlogin service is similar to the login configuration, but has a sufficient condition attached to the *pam_rhosts_auth.so.1* module that is invoked first. If this is successful, then no further modules are invoked; otherwise, the rlogin authentication sequence follows the standard login sequence previously described. The following example shows how this can be implemented in */etc/pam.conf*:

```
rlogin    auth sufficient    pam_rhosts_auth.so.1
rlogin    auth requisite     pam_authtok_get.so.1
rlogin    auth required      pam_dhkeys.so.1
rlogin    auth required      pam_unix_cred.so.1
rlogin    auth required      pam_unix_auth.so.1
```

The rsh service has fewer restrictions than rlogin—if the *pam_rhosts_auth.so.1* module fails to authenticate, then the *pam_unix_cred.so.1* module is invoked, as shown in the following */etc/pam.conf* example:

```
rsh    auth sufficient    pam_rhosts_auth.so.1
rsh    auth required      pam_unix_cred.so.1
```

Other services, such as PPP, follow their own paths—password prompting by *pam_authtok_get.so.1* is a prerequisite to the use of Diffie-Hellman key support for authentication, and so on, as shown in the following example:

```
ppp    auth requisite    pam_authtok_get.so.1
ppp    auth required     pam_dhkeys.so.1
ppp    auth required     pam_unix_cred.so.1
ppp    auth required     pam_unix_auth.so.1
ppp    auth required     pam_dial_auth.so.1
```

Kerberized Services

To configure broad support for Kerberized services in */etc/pam.conf*, the following configuration can be used:

```
login    auth optional        pam_krb5.so.1
other    auth optional        pam_krb5.so.1
cron     account optional     pam_krb5.so.1
other    account optional     pam_krb5.so.1
other    session optional     pam_krb5.so.1
other    password optional    pam_krb5.so.1
```

This links services like login and cron to the underlying Kerberos authentication module. For each Kerberized application, there is an *auth required* condition for *pam_authtok_get.so.1* and for *pam_unix_auth.so.1*, in addition to an *auth binding* condition for *pam_krb5.so.1*. The following examples show the configuration for `krlogin`, but it would be the same for `krsh` and `ktelnet` with the appropriate service name changes:

```
krlogin    auth required    pam_unix_cred.so.1
krlogin    auth binding     pam_krb5.so.1
krlogin    auth required    pam_unix_auth.so.1
```

Command Reference

The following commands are used to interact with Kerberos.

kadmin

The `kadmin` command is used to manage local Kerberos services, by administering keytabs, principals, and policies. There are two versions of `kadmin` available: `kadmin` `.local` is used only on the master KDC and does not require authentication. However, `kadmin`, when executed on any other server, requires Kerberos authentication across a secure link. Once logged in, the following prompt is displayed, ready for commands to be entered:

```
kadmin:
```

When `kadmin` starts up, it checks the value of the *USER* environment variable to determine the principal name. For example, if *USER=pwatters*, then the principal name would be *pwatters/admin*. Alternatively, the *–p* option can be passed to `kadmin` when starting up, followed by the principal name. In addition, if a realm other than the default is to be administered, the realm name must be supplied on the command line after the *–r* option is passed. The user will be prompted for a password, unless one has been passed on the command line with the *–w* option. Thus, to start `kadmin` for the realm *cassowary.net* with the principal *pwatters/admin* and the password *6fgj4gsd*, the following command would be used:

```
# kadmin -p pwatters/admin -r CASSOWARY.NET -w 6fgj4gsd
```

The following options are supported by `kadmin`:

Option	Description
list_requests	Displays all `kadmin` commands
add_principal	Adds a new principal
get_privs	Displays the ACLs for the current principal
–expire	Sets the principal's effective end date
–pwexpire	Sets the principal's password effective end date
–maxlife	Specifies an upper time limit for tickets

Option	Description
–maxrenewlife	Specifies an upper time limit for ticket renewal
–policy	Sets the policy name
–pw	Sets the principal's password
delete_principal	Completely removes a principal
modify_principal	Updates the principal's characteristics
get_principal	Displays the principal's characteristics
list_principals	Prints all known principal names
add_policy	Attaches a new policy
delete_policy	Completely removes a policy
get_policy	Displays the characteristics of a policy
list_policy	Displays policy names
ktadd	Attaches a principal to a keytab
ktadd	Removes a principal from a keytab

kdb5_util

The `kdb5_util` program is used to manage the Kerberos database files. It accepts the database name as an argument on the command line after the *–d* option has been passed. One of the following options must also be included to perform a specific action:

Option	Description
create	Creates a new database
destroy	Deletes an existing database
stash	Initializes a stash file to store the master key for the database
dump	Exports the database to ASCII format
load	Imports the database from ASCII format

Summary

In this chapter, you learned how to configure Kerberized applications for strong authentication. This is an important aspect of Solaris security; however, not all networked applications are Kerberized at this point in time.

PART III

Managing Devices

IV

PART

Device and Resource Management

One of the most important but most challenging roles of a system administrator is device management. Devices, in this context, can be defined as both physical and logical entities that together constitute a hardware system. Although some operating systems hide device configuration details from all users (even administrators!) in proprietary binary formats, Solaris device configuration is easy to use, with configuration information stored in special files known as *device files*. In addition to providing the technical background on how device files operate and how device drivers can be installed, this chapter provides practical advice on installing standard devices, such as new hard drives, as well as more modern media, like CD-Rs and Zip drives.

Solaris 10 now supports the dynamic reconfiguration of many systems' devices on some SPARC platforms, particularly in the medium-level server range and above. This allows administrators to remove faulty hardware components and replace them without having to power down a system or perform a reconfiguration boot, the latter of which is necessary for older systems. This is particularly significant for systems that have high redundancy of system components to guarantee uptime under all but the most critical of circumstances.

Key Concepts

The following key concepts are central to understanding devices.

Device Files

Device files are special files that represent devices in Solaris 10. Device files reside in the */dev* directory and its subdirectories (such as */dev/dsk*), while the */devices* directory is a tree that completely characterizes the hardware layout of the system in the file system namespace. Although initially it may seem confusing that separate directories exist for devices and for system hardware, the difference between the two systems will become apparent in the discussion that follows. Solaris 10 refers to both physical and logical devices in three separate ways: with physical device names, physical device files, and logical device names (which are described in the next section).

Physical device names are easily identified because they are long strings that provide all details relevant to the physical installation of the device. Every physical device has a physical name. For example, an SBUS could have the name */sbus@1f,0*, while a disk device might have the name */sbus@1f,0/SUNW,fas@2,8800000/sd@1,0*. Physical device names are usually displayed at boot time and when using selected applications that access hardware directly, such as `format`.

On the other hand, physical device files, which are located in the */devices* directory, comprise an instance name that is an abbreviation for a physical device name, which can be interpreted by the kernel. For example, the SBUS */sbus@1f,0* might be referred to as *sbus*, and a device disk */sbus@1f,0/SUNW,fas@2,8800000/sd@1,0* might be referred to as *sd1*. The mapping of instance names to physical devices is not hard-wired: the */etc/ path_to_inst* file always contains these details, keeping them consistent between boots, and is shown in Chapter 15.

/dev and /devices Directories

In addition to physical devices, Solaris 10 also needs to refer to logical devices. For example, physical disks may be divided into many different slices, so the physical disk device will need to be referred to using a logical name. Logical device files in the */dev* directory are symbolically linked to physical device names in the */devices* directory. Most user applications refer to logical device names. A typical listing of the */dev* directory has numerous entries that look like this:

```
arp        ptys0      ptyyb      rsd3a      sd3e       ttyu2
audio      ptys1      ptyyc      rsd3b      sd3f       ttyu3
audioctl   ptys2      ptyyd      rsd3c      sd3g       ttyu4
bd.off     ptys3      ptyye      rsd3d      sd3h       ttyu5
be         ptys4      ptyyf      rsd3e      skip_key   ttyu6
bpp0       ptys5      ptyz0      rsd3f      sound/     ttyu7
...
```

Many of these device filenames are self-explanatory:

- */dev/console* represents the console device—error and status messages are usually written to the console by daemons and applications using the `syslog` service. */dev/ console* typically corresponds to the monitor in text mode; however, the console is also represented logically in windowing systems, such as OpenWindows, where the command `server% cmdtool -C` brings up a console window.

- */dev/hme* is the network interface device file.

- */dev/dsk* contains device files for disk slices.

- */dev/tty*n and */dev/pty*n are the *n* terminal and *n* pseudo-terminal devices attached to the system.

- */dev/null* is the end point of discarded output; many applications pipe their output.

The `drvconfig` command creates the */devices* directory tree, which is a logical representation of the physical layout of devices attached to the system, and pseudo-drivers. `drvconfig` is executed automatically after a reconfiguration boot. It reads file permission information for new nodes in the tree from */etc/minor_perm*, which contains entries like

```
sd:* 0666 httpd staff
```

where *sd* is the node name for a disk device, *0666* is the default file permission, *httpd* is the owner, and *staff* is the group.

Storage Devices

Solaris 10 supports many different kinds of mass-storage devices, including SCSI hard drives (and IDE drives on the *x*86 platform), reading and writing standard and rewriteable CD-ROMs, Iomega Zip and Jaz drives, tape drives, DVD-ROMs, and floppy disks. Hard drives are the most common kinds of storage devices found on a Solaris 10 system, ranging from individual drives used to create system and user file systems, to highly redundant, server-based RAID systems. These RAID configurations can comprise a set of internal disks, managed through software (such as DiskSuite), or high-speed, external arrays, like the A1000, which include dedicated RAM for write-caching. Because disk writing is one of the slowest operations in any modern server system, this greatly increases overall operational speed.

Hard drives have faced stiff competition in recent years, with new media such as Iomega Zip and Jaz drives providing removable media for both random and sequential file access. This makes Zip and Jaz drives ideal media for archival backups, competing with the traditional magnetic tape drives. The latter have largely been replaced in modern systems by the digital audio tape (DAT) system, which has high reliability and data throughput rates (especially the DDS-3 standard).

This section looks at the issues surrounding the installation and configuration of storage devices for Solaris 10, providing practical advice for installing a wide range of hardware.

Hard Drives

When formatted for operation with Solaris 10, hard disks are logically divided into one or more slices (or partitions), on which a single file system resides. File systems contain sets of files, which are hierarchically organized around a number of directories. Solaris 10 contains a number of predefined directories that often form the top level of a file system hierarchy. Many of these directories lie one level below the *root directory*, often denoted by /, which exists on the primary system disk of any Solaris 10 system. In addition to a primary disk, many Solaris 10 systems have additional disks that provide storage space for user and daemon files. Each file system has a mount point that is usually created in the top level of the root file system. For example, the */export* file system is obviously mounted in the top level of /. The mount point is created by using the mkdir command:

```
# mkdir /export
```

In contrast, the */export/home* file system, which usually holds the home directories of users and user files, is mounted in the top level of the */export* file system. Thus, the mount point is created by using the following command:

```
# mkdir /export/home
```

A single logical file system can be created on a single slice, but cannot exist on more than one slice, unless there is an extra level of abstraction between the logical and physical file systems (for example, a virtual disk is created using DiskSuite, which spans many physical disks). A physical disk can also contain more than one slice. On SPARC architecture systems, eight slices can be used, numbered zero through seven. On Intel architecture systems, however, ten slices are available, numbered zero through nine.

The actual assignment of logical file systems to physical slices is a matter of discretion for the individual administrator, and although there are customary assignments recommended by Sun and other hardware vendors, a specific site policy, or an application's requirements, might necessitate the development of a local policy. For example, database servers often make quite specific requirements about the allocation of disk slices to improve performance. However, with modern, high-performance RAID systems, these recommendations are often redundant. Because many organization have many different kinds of systems deployed, it is useful to maintain compatibility between systems as much as possible. For more details, see the "Disk Space Planning" section of Chapter 3.

CD-ROMs

A popular format of read-only mass storage on many servers is the compact disc–read-only memory (CD-ROM). Although earlier releases of Solaris worked best with Sun-branded CD-ROM drives, as of Solaris 2.6, Solaris 10 fully supports all SCSI-2 CD-ROM drives. For systems running older versions of Solaris, it may still be possible to use a third-party drive, but the drive must support 512-byte sectors (the Sun standard). A second Sun default to be aware of is that CD-ROM drives must usually have the SCSI target ID of 6, although this limitation has again been overcome in later releases of the kernel. However, a number of third-party applications with "auto detect" functions may still expect to see the CD-ROM drive at SCSI ID 6.

A number of different CD-ROM drive formats are also supported with the mount command, which is used to attach CD-ROM drives to the file system. It is common to use the mount point */cdrom* for the primary CD-ROM device in Solaris 10 systems, although it is possible to use a different mount point for mounting the device by using a command-line argument to mount.

Zip and Jaz Drives

There are two ways to install Zip and Jaz drives: by treating the drive as a SCSI disk, in which case format data needs to be added to the system to recognize it, or by using Andy Polyakov's ziptool, which formats and manages protection modes supported by Zip 100 and Jaz 1GB/2GB drives. Both of these techniques support only SCSI and not parallel port drives.

Treating the Zip 100 SCSI drive or the Jaz 1GB drive as a normal SCSI device is the easiest approach, because there is built-in Solaris 10 support for these SCSI devices. However, only standard, non-write-protected disks can be used.

Tape Drives

Solaris 10 supports a wide variety of magnetic tapes using the remote magtape (rmt) protocol. Tapes are generally used as backup devices rather than as interactive storage devices. What they lack in availability they definitely make up for in storage capacity: many DAT drives have capacities of 24GB, making it easy to perform a complete backup of many server systems on a single tape. This removes the need for late-night monitoring by operations staff to insert new tapes when full, as many administrators will have experienced in the past.

Device files for tape drives are found in the *dev/rmt* directory. They are numbered sequentially from 0, so default drives generally are available as *dev/rmt/0*. Low-density drives can be specified by adding l to the device filename, with medium-density drives having *m* added. For example, a medium-density drive at location 0 would be written as *dev/rmt/0m*, and a low-density drive at location 1 would be written as *dev/rmt/1l*. By default, the tape will be rewound when being written to—to specify that a tape should not be rewound, simply add *n* to the device name. Thus, a medium-density drive at location 0 with no rewind would be written as *dev/rmt/0mn*.

To back up to a remote drive, use the command ufsdump, which is an incremental file system dumping program. For example, to create a full backup of the *dev/rdsk/c0t1d0s1* file system to the tape system *dev/rmt/0*, simply use the following command:

```
# ufsdump 0 /dev/rmt/0 /dev/rdsk/c0t1d0s1
```

This command specifies a level 0 (i.e., complete) dump of the file system, specifying the target drive and data source as *dev/rmt/0* and *dev/rdsk/c0t1d0s1*, respectively. To check the status of a tape drive at any time, you can use the mt command:

```
# mt -f /dev/rmt/0 status
```

Floppy Disks

Floppy disk drives (1.44MB capacity) are standard on both SPARC and Intel architecture systems. In addition, by using the Volume Manager, detecting and mounting floppy disks is straightforward. Insert the target disk into the drive, and use this command:

```
# volcheck
```

This checks all volumes that are managed by volume management and mounts any valid file system that is found. The mount point for the floppy drive is determined by the settings in */etc/vfstab*:

```
fd     -    /dev/fd    fd    -    no    -
```

Refer to the section "Adding Devices" for information on entering disk information into the virtual file system database and for more details on configuring the */etc/vfstab* file. A very useful feature of volcheck is to automatically check for new volumes; for example,

```
# volcheck -i 60 -t 3600 /dev/diskette0 &
```

works in the background to check every minute whether a floppy is in the drive. However, this polling takes place only for one hour unless renewed.

CD-ROMs and DVD-ROMs

CD-ROMs are supported directly by the operating system in SPARC architectures and do not require any special configuration, other than the usual process of initializing the system for a reconfiguration reboot, powering down the system, attaching the CD-ROM device to the SCSI bus, and powering on the system. It is not necessary to use format or newfs to read the files on the CD-ROM, nor is it usually necessary to manually mount the file system, because the Volume Manager (vold) is usually enabled on server systems.

A common problem for Solaris 10 *x86* users is that there are few tested and supported CD-ROM brands for installing the operating system (although most fully compliant ATA/ATAPI CD-ROMs should work). The older Sound Blaster IDE interface for CD-ROMs does not appear to be suitable, although support may be included in a later release (the Alternate Status register is apparently not implemented on the main integrated circuit for the controller board). It is always best to check the current Hardware Compatibility List (HCL) from the Sun site.

Many recent SPARC and Intel systems come installed with a DVD-ROM drive. Although the drive cannot be used yet to play movies, it can be effectively used as a mass-storage device, with a capacity equal to several individual CD-ROMs. Future releases of Solaris may include a DVD player and support for the newer DVD-RAM technology.

CD-Rs and CD-RWs

Solaris 10 supports both reading and writing to CD-ROMs. In addition to the CD-R (CD-recordable) format, Solaris 10 also supports CD-RW (CD-rewritable), previously known as CD-erasable. It is a new optical-disc specification created by the industry organization Optical Storage Technology Association (OSTA, **http://www.osta.org**). You can hook up many SCSI CD-R and CD-RW devices to a SPARC system to SCSI device ID 6, and they will function as a normal CD-ROM drives.

Although the technical capability to support any SCSI-based device is a given for the operating system, finding software to adequately support it usually is a potentially limiting factor for nonstandard hardware. Fortunately, many different open-source and commercial editions of CD-recording software are available for the Solaris 10 platform. The best application is cdrecord, by Jörg Schilling, which you can download from **ftp:// ftp.fokus.gmd.de/pub/unix/cdrecord/**. It is freeware, and it makes use of the real-time scheduler in Solaris 10. It also compiles on the Solaris 10 *x86* platform, and can create both music and data discs. Although it has a rather clunky command-line interface, it has more features than some of the commercial systems, including the ability to do the following:

- Simulate a recording for test purposes (*–dummy* option)
- Use a single CD for multiple recording sessions (*–multi* option)
- Manually fix the disk, if you want to view data from an open session on a normal CD–ROM (*–fix* option)
- Setting the recording speed factor (*–speed* option)

If you prefer a commercial system, GEAR PRO UNIX is also available (**http:// www.gearsoftware.com/products/prounix/index.cfm**), as well as Creative Digital Research's CDR Publisher (**http://www.cdr1.com/**), which is available through Sun's Catalyst program. For more general information about the CD recording process, see Andy McFadden's very comprehensive FAQ at **http://www.cdrfaq.org/**.

Procedures

The following procedures demonstrate how to manage system devices.

Adding Devices

In many cases, adding new devices to a Solaris 10 system is straightforward, because most devices connect to the SCSI bus, which is a standard interface. The steps involved usually include preparing the system for a reconfiguration boot, powering down the system, connecting the hardware device, noting the SCSI device number, powering on the system, and using the `zformat` command, if necessary, to create a file system. This section examines the procedure for adding disks to both SPARC and Intel architecture machines and highlights potential problems that may occur.

Hard Drives

Hard disk installation and configuration on Solaris 10 is often more complicated than on other UNIX systems. However, this complexity is required to support the sophisticated hardware operations typically undertaken by Solaris 10 systems. For example, Linux refers to hard disks using a simple BSD-style scheme: */dev/hdn* are the IDE hard disks on a system, and */dev/sdn* are the SCSI hard disks on a system, where *n* refers to the hard disk number. A system with two IDE hard disks and two SCSI hard disks will therefore have the following device files configured:

```
/dev/hda
/dev/hdb
/dev/sda
/dev/sdb
```

Partitions created on each drive are also sequentially numbered: if */dev/hda* is the boot disk, it may contain several partitions on the disk, reflecting the basic UNIX system directories:

```
/dev/hda1 (/ partition)
/dev/hda2 (/usr)
/dev/hda3 (/var)
/dev/hda4 (swap)
```

Instead of simply referring to the disk type, disk number, and partition number, the device filename for each partition (slice) on a Solaris 10 disk contains four identifiers: controller (*c*), target (*t*), disk (*d*), and slice (*s*). Thus, the device file,

```
/dev/dsk/c0t3d0s0
```

identifies slice 0 of disk 0, controller 0 at SCSI target ID 3. To complicate matters further, disk device files exist in both the */dev/dsk* and */dev/rdsk* directories, which correspond to block device and raw device entries, respectively. Raw and block devices refer to the same physical partition, but are used in different contexts: using raw devices allows only operations of small amounts of data, whereas a buffer can be used with a block device to increase the data read size. It is not always clear whether to use a block or raw device interface; however, low-level system commands (like the `fsck` command, which performs disk maintenance) typically use raw device interfaces, whereas commands that operate on the entire disk (such as `df`, which reports disk usage) most likely use block devices.

To install a new hard drive on a Solaris 10 system, just follow these steps:

1. Prepare the system for a reconfiguration boot by issuing the command

   ```
   server# touch /reconfigure
   ```

2. Synchronize disk data and power down the system using the commands

   ```
   server# sync; sync; sync; shutdown
   ```

3. Switch off power to the system and attach the new hard disk to the external SCSI chain, or install it internally into an appropriate disk bay.

4. Check that the SCSI device ID does not conflict with any existing SCSI devices. If a conflict exists, simply change the ID by using the switch.

5. Power on the system and use the boot command to load the kernel, if the OpenBoot monitor appears:

```
ok boot
```

The next step—assuming that you have decided which partitions you want to create on your drive, using the information supplied earlier—is to run the format program. In addition to creating slices, format also displays information about existing disks and slices and can be used to repair a faulty disk. When format is invoked without a command-line argument,

```
# format
```

it displays the current disks and asks the administrator to enter the number of the disk to format. Selecting a disk for formatting at this point is nondestructive, so even if you make a mistake, you can always exit the format program without damaging data. For example, on an Ultra 5 system with three 10G SCSI disks, format opens with this screen:

```
Searching for disks...done
AVAILABLE DISK SELECTIONS:
0. c0t1d0 <SUN10 cyl 2036 alt 2 hd 14 sec 72>
/iommu@f,e0000000/sbus@f,e0001000/espdma@f,400000/esp@f,800000/
sd@1,0
1. c0t2d0 <SUN10 cyl 2036 alt 2 hd 14 sec 72>
/iommu@f,e0000000/sbus@f,e0001000/espdma@f,400000/esp@f,800000/
sd@2,0
2. c0t3d0 <SUN10 cyl 2036 alt 2 hd 14 sec 72>
/iommu@f,e0000000/sbus@f,e0001000/espdma@f,400000/esp@f,800000/
sd@3,0
Specify disk (enter its number):
```

It is also possible to pass a command-line option to format, comprising the disk (or disks) to be formatted; for example:

```
# format /dev/rdsk/c0t2d0
```

After selecting the appropriate disk, the message

```
[disk formatted]
```

appears if the disk has previously been formatted. This is an important message, because it is a common mistake to misidentify a target disk from the available selection of both formatted and unformatted disks. The menu looks like this:

```
FORMAT MENU:
        disk       - select a disk
        type       - select (define) a disk type
        partition  - select (define) a partition table
```

```
current     - describe the current disk
format      - format and analyze the disk
fdisk       - run the fdisk program
repair      - repair a defective sector
show        - translate a disk address
label       - write label to the disk
analyze     - surface analysis
defect      - defect list management
backup      - search for backup labels
verify      - read and display labels
save        - save new disk/partition definitions
volname     - set 8-character volume name
!<cmd>      - execute <cmd>, then return
quit
```
format>

If the disk has not been formatted, the first step is to prepare the disk to contain slices and file systems by formatting the disk. To do so, issue the command format:

```
format> format
Ready to format. Formatting cannot be interrupted
and takes 15 minutes (estimated). Continue? yes
```

The purpose of formatting is to identify defective blocks and mark them as bad, and generally to verify that the disk is operational from a hardware perspective. Once this has been completed, new slices can be created and sized by using the *partition* option at the main menu:

```
format> partition
```

In this case, we want to create a new slice 5 on disk 0 at target 3, which will be used to store user files when mounted as */export/home*, and corresponding to block device */dev/dsk/c0t3d0s5*. After determining the maximum amount of space available, enter that size in gigabytes (in this case, 10GB) when requested to do so by the format program for slice 5 (enter 0 for the other slices). If the disk is not labeled, you will also be prompted to enter a label, which contains details of the disk's current slices, which is useful for recovering data. This is an important step, because the operating system will not be able to find any newly created slices if the volume is not labeled. To view the disk label, use the prtvtoc command. Here's the output from the primary drive in an *x86* system:

```
# prtvtoc /dev/dsk/c0d0s2
* /dev/dsk/c0d0s2 partition map
*
* Dimensions:
*       512 bytes/sector
*        63 sectors/track
*       255 tracks/cylinder
```

```
*     16065 sectors/cylinder
*      1020 cylinders
*      1018 accessible cylinders
*
* Flags:
*    1: unmountable
*   10: read-only
*
```

			First	Sector	Last	
* Partition	Tag	Flags	Sector	Count	Sector	Mount Directory
0	2	00	48195	160650	208844	/
1	7	00	208845	64260	273104	/var
2	5	00	0	16354170	16354169	
3	3	01	273105	321300	594404	
6	4	00	594405	1317330	1911734	/usr
7	8	00	1911735	14442435	16354169	/export/home
8	1	01	0	16065	16064	
9	9	01	16065	32130	48194	

The disk label contains a full partition table, which can be printed for each disk by using the print command:

```
format> print
```

For the 1.05GB disk, the partition table looks like this:

```
Part Tag Flag Cylinders Size Blocks
0 root wm 0 0 (0/0/0) 0
1 swap wu 0 0 (0/0/0) 0
2 backup wm 0 - 3732 (3732/0/0) 2089920
3 unassigned wm 0 0 (0/0/0) 0
4 unassigned wm 0 0 (0/0/0) 0
5 home wm 0 - 3732 1075MB (3732/0/0) 2089920
6 usr wm 0 0 (0/0/0) 0
7 unassigned wm 0 0 (0/0/0) 0
```

After saving the changes to the disk's partition table, exit the format program and create a new UFS file system on the target slice by using the newfs command:

```
# newfs /dev/rdsk/c0t3d0s5
```

After a new file system is constructed, it is ready to be mounted. First, a mount point is created:

```
# mkdir /export/home
```

followed by the appropriate mount command:

```
# mount /dev/dsk/c0t3d0s5 /export/home
```

At this point, the disk is available to the system for the current session. However, if you want the disk to be available after reboot, you need to create an entry in the virtual file systems table, which is created from the */etc/vfstab* file. An entry like this,

```
/dev/dsk/c0t3d0s5 /dev/rdsk/c0t3d0s5 /export/home ufs 2 yes -
```

contains details of the slice's block and raw devices, the mount point, the file system type, instructions for `fsck`, and, most importantly, a flag to force mount at boot.

For an *x86* system, the output of `format` looks slightly different, given the differences in the way that devices are denoted:

```
AVAILABLE DISK SELECTIONS:
       0. c0d0 <DEFAULT cyl 1018 alt 2 hd 255 sec 63>
          /pci@0,0/pci-ide@7,1/ata@0/cmdk@0,0
Specify disk (enter its number):
```

The partition table is similar to that for the SPARC architecture systems:

```
partition> print
Current partition table (original):
Total disk cylinders available: 1018 + 2 (reserved cylinders)

Part      Tag    Flag     Cylinders        Size            Blocks
  0      root    wm       3 -    12      78.44MB    (10/0/0)       160650
  1       var    wm      13 -    16      31.38MB    (4/0/0)         64260
  2    backup    wm       0 -  1017       7.80GB    (1018/0/0) 16354170
  3      swap    wu      17 -    36     156.88MB    (20/0/0)       321300
  4 unassigned   wm       0                   0     (0/0/0)             0
  5 unassigned   wm       0                   0     (0/0/0)             0
  6       usr    wm      37 -   118     643.23MB    (82/0/0)      1317330
  7      home    wm     119 -  1017       6.89GB    (899/0/0)    14442435
  8      boot    wu       0 -     0       7.84MB    (1/0/0)         16065
  9 alternates   wu       1 -     2      15.69MB    (2/0/0)         32130
```

Installing a Zip/Jaz Drive

The steps for installation are similar for both the Zip and Jaz drives:

1. Set the SCSI ID switch to any ID that is not reserved.

2. Attach the Zip or Jaz drive to your SCSI adapter or chain and ensure that it has power.

3. Create a device entry in */etc/format.dat* by editing the file and inserting the following for a Zip drive:

```
disk_type="Zip 100"\
                       :ctlr=SCSI\
                       :ncyl=2406:acyl=2:pcyl=2408:nhead=2\
                       :nsect=40:rpm=3600:bpt=20480
           partition="Zip 100"\
```

```
                          :disk="Zip 100":ctlr=SCSI\
                          :2=0,192480
                          :2=0,1159168
```

For a Jaz drive, enter the following information in */etc/format.dat*:

```
disk_type="Jaz 1GB"\
                          :ctlr=SCSI\
                          :ncyl=1018:acyl=2:pcyl=1020:nhead=64\
                          :nsect=32:rpm=3600:bpt=16384
          partition="Jaz 1GB"\
                          :disk="Jaz 1GB":ctlr=SCSI\
                          :2=0,2084864
```

4. Perform a reconfiguration boot by typing

```
ok boot -r
```

at the OpenBoot prompt, or by using these commands from a superuser shell:

```
server# touch /reconfigure
server# sync; sync; init 6
```

The drive should now be visible to the system. To actually use the drive to mount a volume, insert a Zip or Jaz disk into the drive prior to booting the system. After booting, run the format program:

```
# format
```

5. Assuming that the *sd* number for your drive is 3, select this *sd* as the disk to be formatted. Create the appropriate partition using the *partition* option, then create an appropriate label for the volume and quit the format program.

6. Next, create a new file system on the drive by using the newfs command; for example:

```
# newfs -v /dev/sd3c
```

7. After creating the file system, you can mount it by typing

```
# mount /dev/sd3c /mount_point
```

where */mount_point* is something self-documenting (such as */zip* or */jaz*). You need to create this before mounting by typing the following:

```
# mkdir /zip
```

or

```
# mkdir /jaz
```

An alternate and more flexible approach is to use the ziptool program, which is available at **http://fy.chalmers.se/~appro/ziptool.html**. For Solaris 2.6 and greater, ziptool supports all Zip and Jaz drive protection modes, permits unconditional low-level formatting of protected disks, and supports disk labeling and volume management. The program has to be executed with root privileges regardless of the access permissions

PART IV

set on the SCSI disk device driver's entries in */devices*. Consequently, if you want to let all users use `ziptool`, you must install it as *set-root-uid*:

```
# /usr/ucb/install -m 04755 -o root ziptool /usr/local/bin
```

NOTE *You should note that running setuid programs has security implications.*

After downloading and unpacking the sources, you can compile the program by using this command:

```
# gcc -o ziptool ziptool.c -lvolmgt
```

Of course, you need to ensure that the path to *libvolmgt.a* is in your *LD_LIBRARY_PATH* (usually */lib*):

```
ziptool device command
```

where *device* must be the full name of a raw SCSI disk file, such as */dev/rsdk/c0t5d0s2*, and *command* is one or more of the following:

`rw`	Unlocks the Zip disk temporarily
`RW`	Unlocks the Zip disk permanently
`ro`	Puts the Zip disk into read-only mode
`RO`	Puts the Zip disk into a read-only mode that is password protected
`WR(*)`	Protects the disk by restricting reading and writing unless a password is entered
`eject`	Ejects the current Zip disk
`noeject`	Stops the Zip disk from being ejected

You can find further information on installing Jaz and Zip drives on the Iomega support Web site.

Examples

The following examples demonstrate how to manage devices.

Checking for Devices

Obtaining a listing of devices attached to a Solaris 10 system is the best way to begin examining this important issue. In Solaris 10, you can easily obtain system configuration information, including device information, by using the print configuration command on any SPARC or Intel architecture system:

```
# prtconf
```

On an Ultra 5 workstation, the system configuration looks like this:

```
SUNW,Ultra-5_10
    packages (driver not attached)
        terminal-emulator (driver not attached)
        deblocker (driver not attached)
        obp-tftp (driver not attached)
        disk-label (driver not attached)
        SUNW,builtin-drivers (driver not attached)
        sun-keyboard (driver not attached)
        ufs-file-system (driver not attached)
    chosen (driver not attached)
    openprom (driver not attached)
        client-services (driver not attached)
    options, instance #0
    aliases (driver not attached)
    memory (driver not attached)
    virtual-memory (driver not attached)
    pci, instance #0
        pci, instance #0
            ebus, instance #0
                auxio (driver not attached)
                power (driver not attached)
                SUNW,pll (driver not attached)
                se, instance #0
                su, instance #0
                su, instance #1
                ecpp (driver not attached)
                fdthree (driver not attached)
                eeprom (driver not attached)
                flashprom (driver not attached)
                SUNW,CS4231, instance #0
            network, instance #0
            SUNW,m64B, instance #0
            ide, instance #0
                disk (driver not attached)
                cdrom (driver not attached)
                dad, instance #0
                atapicd, instance #2
        pci, instance #1
            pci, instance #0
                pci108e,1000 (driver not attached)
                SUNW,hme, instance #1
                SUNW,isptwo, instance #0
```

```
            sd (driver not attached)
            st (driver not attached)
SUNW,UltraSPARC-IIi (driver not attached)
pseudo, instance #0
```

Never panic about the message that a driver is "not attached" to a particular device. Because device drivers are loaded only on demand in Solaris 10, only those devices that are actively being used will have their drivers loaded. When a device is no longer being used, the device driver is unloaded from memory. This is a very efficient memory management strategy that optimizes the use of physical RAM by deallocating memory for devices when they are no longer required. In the case of Ultra 5, you can see in the preceding code that devices like the PCI bus and the IDE disk drives have attached device drivers, and they were being used while prtconf was running.

For an *x*86 system, the devices found are quite different:

```
System Configuration:  Sun Microsystems   i86pc
Memory size: 128 Megabytes
System Peripherals (Software Nodes):
i86pc
    +boot (driver not attached)
        memory (driver not attached)
    aliases (driver not attached)
    chosen (driver not attached)
    i86pc-memory (driver not attached)
    i86pc-mmu (driver not attached)
    openprom (driver not attached)
    options, instance #0
    packages (driver not attached)
    delayed-writes (driver not attached)
    itu-props (driver not attached)
    isa, instance #0
        motherboard (driver not attached)
        asy, instance #0
        lp (driver not attached)
        asy, instance #1
        fdc, instance #0
            fd, instance #0
            fd, instance #1 (driver not attached)
        kd (driver not attached)
        bios (driver not attached)
        bios (driver not attached)
        pnpCTL,0041 (driver not attached)
        pnpCTL,7002 (driver not attached)
        kd, instance #0
        chanmux, instance #0
    pci, instance #0
        pci8086,1237 (driver not attached)
```

```
       pci8086,7000 (driver not attached)
       pci-ide, instance #0
           ata, instance #0
                cmdk, instance #0
                sd, instance #1
       pci10ec,8029 (driver not attached)
       pci5333,8901 (driver not attached)
    used-resources (driver not attached)
    objmgr, instance #0
    pseudo, instance #0
```

At Boot Time

The OpenBoot monitor has the ability to diagnose hardware errors on system devices before booting the kernel. This can be particularly useful for identifying bus connectivity issues, such as unterminated SCSI chains, but also some basic functional issues, such as whether devices are responding. Issuing the command

```
ok reset
```

will also force a self-test of the system.

Just after booting, it is also useful to review the system boot messages, which you can retrieve by using the dmesg command or by examining the */var/log/messages* file. This displays a list of all devices that were successfully attached at boot time, and any error messages that were detected. The following is the dmesg output for a SPARC Ultra architecture system:

```
# dmesg
Jan 17 13:06
cpu0: SUNW,UltraSPARC-IIi (upaid 0 impl 0x12 ver 0x12 clock 270 MHz)
SunOS Release 5.10 Version Generic_103640-19
[UNIX(R) System V Release 4.0]
Copyright (c) 1983-2004, Sun Microsystems, Inc.
mem = 131072K (0x8000000)
avail mem = 127852544
Ethernet address = 8:0:20:90:b3:23
root nexus = Sun Ultra 5/10 UPA/PCI (UltraSPARC-IIi 270MHz)
pci0 at root: UPA 0x1f 0x0
PCI-device: pci@1,1, simba #0
PCI-device: pci@1, simba #1
dad0 at pci1095,6460 target 0 lun 0
dad0 is /pci@1f,0/pci@1,1/ide@3/dad@0,0
        <Seagate Medalist 34342A cyl 8892 alt 2 hd 15 sec 63>
root on /pci@1f,0/pci@1,1/ide@3/disk@0,0:a fstype ufs
su0 at ebus0: offset 14,3083f8
su0 is /pci@1f,0/pci@1,1/ebus@1/su@14,3083f8
su1 at ebus0: offset 14,3062f8
```

```
su1 is /pci@1f,0/pci@1,1/ebus@1/su@14,3062f8
keyboard is </pci@1f,0/pci@1,1/ebus@1/su@14,3083f8>
   major <37> minor <0>
mouse is </pci@1f,0/pci@1,1/ebus@1/su@14,3062f8>
   major <37> minor <1>
stdin is </pci@1f,0/pci@1,1/ebus@1/su@14,3083f8>
   major <37> minor <0>
SUNW,m64B0 is /pci@1f,0/pci@1,1/SUNW,m64B@2
m64#0: 1280x1024, 2M mappable, rev 4754.9a
stdout is </pci@1f,0/pci@1,1/SUNW,m64B@2> major <8> minor <0>
boot cpu (0) initialization complete - online
se0 at ebus0: offset 14,400000
se0 is /pci@1f,0/pci@1,1/ebus@1/se@14,400000
SUNW,hme0: CheerIO 2.0 (Rev Id = c1) Found
SUNW,hme0 is /pci@1f,0/pci@1,1/network@1,1
SUNW,hme1: Local Ethernet address = 8:0:20:93:b0:65
pci1011,240: SUNW,hme1
SUNW,hme1 is /pci@1f,0/pci@1/pci@1/SUNW,hme@0,1
dump on /dev/dsk/c0t0d0s1 size 131328K
SUNW,hme0: Using Internal Transceiver
SUNW,hme0: 10 Mbps half-duplex Link Up
pcmcia: no PCMCIA adapters found
```

dmesg first performs a memory test, sets the Ethernet address for the network interface, and then initializes the PCI bus. Setting the Ethernet address is critical on SPARC systems, because the Ethernet interfaces will have the same address stored in PROM. An IDE disk is then recognized and mapped into a physical device, and the appropriate partitions are activated. The standard input devices (keyboard and mouse) are then activated, and the boot sequence is largely complete. However, the output is slightly different for the x86 system:

```
Jan 17 08:32
SunOS Release 5.10 Version Generic [UNIX(R) System V Release 4.0]
Copyright (c) 1983-2004, Sun Microsystems, Inc.
mem = 130688K (0x7fa0000)
avail mem = 114434048
root nexus = i86pc
isa0 at root
pci0 at root: space 0 offset 0
        IDE device at targ 0, lun 0 lastlun 0x0
        model ST310230A, stat 50, err 0
                cfg 0xc5a, cyl 16383, hd 16, sec/trk 63
                mult1 0x8010, mult2 0x110, dwcap 0x0, cap 0x2f00
                piomode 0x200, dmamode 0x200, advpiomode 0x3
                minpio 240, minpioflow 120
                valid 0x7, dwdma 0x407, majver 0x1e
ata_set_feature: (0x66,0x0) failed
```

```
                 ATAPI device at targ 1, lun 0 lastlun 0x0
                 model CD-912E/ATK, stat 50, err 0
                         cfg 0x85a0, cyl 0, hd 0, sec/trk 0
                         mult1 0x0, mult2 0x0, dwcap 0x0, cap 0xb00
                         piomode 0x200, dmamode 0x200, advpiomode 0x1
                         minpio 209, minpioflow 180
                         valid 0x2, dwdma 0x203, majver 0x0
PCI-device: ata@0, ata0
ata0 is /pci@0,0/pci-ide@7,1/ata@0
Disk0:   <Vendor 'Gen-ATA ' Product 'ST310230A          '>
cmdk0 at ata0 target 0 lun 0
cmdk0 is /pci@0,0/pci-ide@7,1/ata@0/cmdk@0,0
root on /pci@0,0/pci-ide@7,1/ide@0/cmdk@0,0:a fstype ufs
ISA-device: asy0
asy0 is /isa/asy@1,3f8
ISA-device: asy1
asy1 is /isa/asy@1,2f8
Number of console virtual screens = 13
cpu 0 initialization complete - online
dump on /dev/dsk/c0d0s3 size 156 MB
```

Note that `dmesg` may be deprecated in future releases, with other applications writing to */var/adm/messages* through `syslogd`.

While the System Is Up

If you are working remotely on a server system, and you are unsure of the system architecture, the command

```
# arch -k
```

returns Sun4u on the Ultra 5 system, but *Sun4m* on a SPARC 10 system. For a complete view of a system's device configuration, you may also want to try the `sysdef` command, which displays more detailed information concerning pseudo-devices, kernel loadable modules, and parameters. Here's the `sysdef` output for an *x*86 server:

```
# sysdef
# sysdef
*
* Hostid
*
  0ae61183
*
* i86pc Configuration
*
*
* Devices
*
```

```
+boot (driver not attached)
        memory (driver not attached)
aliases (driver not attached)
chosen (driver not attached)
i86pc-memory (driver not attached)
i86pc-mmu (driver not attached)
openprom (driver not attached)
options, instance #0
packages (driver not attached)
delayed-writes (driver not attached)
itu-props (driver not attached)
...
*
* System Configuration
*
  swap files
swapfile               dev  swaplo blocks   free
/dev/dsk/c0d0s3        102,3      8 321288 321288
```

The key sections in the `sysdef` output are details of all devices, such as the PCI bus, and pseudo-devices for each loadable object path (including */kernel* and */usr/kernel*). Loadable objects are also identified, along with swap and virtual memory settings. Although the output may seem verbose, the information provided for each device can prove to be very useful in tracking down hardware errors or missing loadable objects.

Command Reference

The following command can be used to manage system devices.

format

The `format` command displays the following options:

disk	Nominates a disk to format
type	Specifies a disk type
partition	Specifies a partition table
current	Specifies the current disk
format	Formats the current disk
fdisk	Executes the `fdisk` program against the current disk
repair	Repairs a faulty sector on the current disk
show	Translates a disk address
label	Writes a disk label
analyze	Analyzes errors
defect	Lists problems

backup	Examines backup labels
verify	Verifies labels
save	Saves new partition data
volname	Sets a volume name
!<cmd>	Runs command in a shell
quit	Exits application

Summary

In this chapter, you have learned how to configure devices and manage system resources for the Intel and SPARC platforms. You have seen how mass storage devices such as hard drives can be easily configured and how you can review that configuration.

Summary

Installing Disks and File Systems

Disks are the most commonly used persistent storage devices attached to Solaris 10 systems. A wide variety of disks and disk types are available, including those using the Small Computer System Interface (SCSI, pronounced "scuzzy") and Integrated Device Electronics (IDE) interfaces, with a variety of sustained data transfer rates (exceeding 10,000 RPM in some cases). This chapter examines how to install disks and create file systems using standard Solaris 10 commands.

Key Concepts

Solaris file systems are generally of the type UFS (for UNIX File System), although other file system types can be defined in */etc/default/fs*. UFS file systems are found on hard disks that have both a raw and block device interface on Solaris, as found in the */dev/rdsk* and */dev/dsk* directories, respectively. Every partition created on a Solaris file system has its own entry in */dev/dsk* and */dev/rdsk*.

A UFS file system contains the following elements:

- A boot block, which contains booting data if the file system is bootable
- A super block, which contains the location of inodes, the size of the file system, the number of blocks, and the status
- Inodes, which store the details of files on the file system
- Data blocks, which store the files

Physical and Logical Device Names

One of the most challenging aspects of Solaris hardware to understand is the set of naming convention used by Solaris to refer to devices. Solaris uses a specific set of naming conventions to associate physical devices with instance names on the operating system. For administrators who are new to Solaris, these conventions can be incredibly confusing.

In addition, devices can also be referred to by their device name, which is associated with a device file created in the */dev* directory after configuration. For example, a hard disk may have the physical device name */pci@1f,0/pci@1,1/ide@3/dad@0,0*, which is associated with the device file */dev/dsk/c0t0d0*. In some versions of Microsoft Windows, disks are simply labeled by their drive letter (C:, D:, E:, and so on), while in Linux, device files are much simplified (for example, */dev/hda* for an IDE hard disk or */dev/sda* for a SCSI hard disk).

The benefit of the more complex Solaris logical device names and physical device references is that they make it easy to interpret the characteristics of each device by looking at its name. For the preceding disk name example (*/pci@1f,0/pci@1,1/ide@3/dad@0,0*), you can see that the IDE hard drive is located on a Peripheral Component Interconnect (PCI) bus at target 0. When you view the amount of free disk space on the system, for example, it is easy to identify slices on the same disk by looking at the device name:

```
# df -k
Filesystem              kbytes     used    avail capacity  Mounted on
/proc                        0        0        0      0%   /proc
/dev/dsk/c0t0d0s0      1982988   615991  1307508     33%   /
fd                           0        0        0      0%   /dev/fd
/dev/dsk/c0t0d0s3      1487119   357511  1070124     26%   /usr
swap                    182040      416   181624      1%   /tmp
```

Here, you can see that */dev/dsk/c0t0d0s0* and */dev/dsk/c0t0d0s3* are slice 0 and slice 3 of the disk */dev/dsk/c0t0d0*.

Creating a File System

To create a new UFS file system, you first must partition a disk into different slices. You can then use these slices to create new file systems by using the mkfs or newfs command. For example, the following two commands are equivalent for the purposes of creating a new file system on the partition *c0t0d0s1*:

```
# newfs /dev/rdsk/c0t0d0s1
# mkfs -F ufs /dev/rdsk/c0t0d0s1
```

Examples

The following sections provide some real-world examples for installing disks and file systems.

Monitoring Disk Usage

The most commonly used command for monitoring disk space usage is */usr/bin/df*, which by default displays the number of free blocks and files on all currently mounted volumes. Alternatively, many administrators create an alias for df in their shell initialization script (e.g., ~/.cshrc for C-shell), such as df -k, which displays the amount of free disk space in kilobytes. The basic output for df for a SPARC system looks like this:

```
server# df
Filesystem            kbytes     used     avail capacity  Mounted on
/dev/dsk/c0t0d0s0     245911    30754    190566    14%    /
/dev/dsk/c0t0d0s4    1015679   430787    523952    46%    /usr
/proc                      0        0         0     0%    /proc
fd                         0        0         0     0%    /dev/fd
/dev/dsk/c0t0d0s3     492871   226184    217400    51%    /var
/dev/md/dsk/d1       4119256  3599121    478943    89%    /opt
swap                  256000    43480    212520    17%    /tmp
/dev/dsk/c0t2d0s3    4119256  3684920    393144    91%    /disks/vol1
/dev/md/dsk/d0      17398449 12889927   4334538    75%     /disks/vol2
/dev/md/dsk/d3       6162349  5990984    109742    99%    /disks/vol3
/dev/dsk/c1t1d0s0    8574909  5868862   1848557    77%    /disks/vol4
/dev/dsk/c2t3d0s2    1820189  1551628    177552    90%    /disks/vol5
/dev/dsk/c1t2d0s0    4124422  3548988    575434    87%    /disks/vol6
/dev/dsk/c2t2d0s3    8737664  8281113    456551    95%    /disks/vol7
/dev/md/dsk/d2       8181953  6803556   1296578    84%    /disks/vol8
```

For an Intel system, the output is similar, although disk slices have a different naming convention:

```
server# df
Filesystem            kbytes     used     avail capacity  Mounted on
/proc                      0        0         0     0%    /proc
/dev/dsk/c0d0s0        73684    22104     44212    34%    /
/dev/dsk/c0d0s6       618904   401877    161326    72%    /usr
fd                         0        0         0     0%    /dev/fd
/dev/dsk/c0d0s1        29905     4388     22527    17%    /var
/dev/dsk/c0d0s7      7111598        9   7040474     1%    /export/home
swap                  222516      272    222244     1%    /tmp
```

df has a number of command-line options that can used to customize the collection and display of information. For example, this code prints usage data for all file systems:

```
server# df -a
Filesystem            kbytes     used     avail capacity  Mounted on
/dev/dsk/c0t0d0s0     245911    30754    190566    14%    /
/dev/dsk/c0t0d0s4    1015679   430787    523952    46%    /usr
/proc                      0        0         0     0%    /proc
fd                         0        0         0     0%    /dev/fd
/dev/dsk/c0t0d0s3     492871   226185    217399    51%    /var
/dev/md/dsk/d1       4119256  3599121    478943    89%    /opt
swap                  256000    43480    212520    17%    /tmp
/dev/dsk/c0t2d0s3    4119256  3684920    393144    91%    /disks/vol1
/dev/md/dsk/d0      17398449 12889927   4334538    75%     /disks/vol2
```

```
/dev/md/dsk/d3          6162349 5990984  109742    99%    /disks/vol3
/dev/dsk/c1t1d0s0       8574909 5868862 1848557    77%    /disks/vol4
/dev/dsk/c2t3d0s2       1820189 1551628  177552    90%    /disks/vol5
/dev/dsk/c1t2d0s0       4124422 3548988  575434    87%    /disks/vol6
auto_direct             4124560 3469376  613944    85%    /disks/www
auto_direct                   0       0       0     0%    /disks/ftp
server:vold(pid329)
                              0       0       0     0%    /vol
/dev/dsk/c2t2d0s3       8737664 8281113  456551    95%    /disks/vol7
/dev/md/dsk/d2          8181953 6803556 1296578    84%    /disks/vol8
```

It prints even those file systems that have their "ignore" option set in their entries in
/etc/mnttab:

```
server# cat /etc/mnttab
/dev/dsk/c0t0d0s0        /        ufs      rw,suid,dev=800000,
                                  largefiles    944543087
/dev/dsk/c0t0d0s4        /usr     ufs      rw,suid,dev=800004,
                                  largefiles    944543087
/proc   /proc   proc    rw,suid,dev=29c0000      944543087
fd      /dev/fd fd      rw,suid,dev=2a80000      944543087
/dev/dsk/c0t0d0s3        /var     ufs      rw,suid,dev=800003,
                                  largefiles    944543087
/dev/md/dsk/d1  /opt    ufs      suid,rw,largefiles,dev=1540001  944543105
swap    /tmp    tmpfs    ,dev=1 944543105
/dev/dsk/c0t2d0s3               /disks/vol1    ufs      suid,rw,
                                  largefiles,dev=800013    944543105
/dev/md/dsk/d0  /disks/vol2     ufs      nosuid,rw,
                                  largefiles, dev=1540000   944543105
/dev/md/dsk/d3  /disks/vol3     ufs      nosuid,rw,
                                  largefiles,dev=1540003         944543106
/dev/dsk/c1t1d0s0       /disks/vol4 ufs      nosuid,rw,
                                  largefiles,dev=800080 944543105
/dev/dsk/c2t3d0s2       /disks/vol5      ufs      nosuid,rw,
                                  largefiles,dev=80010a 944543106
/dev/dsk/c1t2d0s0       /disks/vol6 ufs      suid,rw,
                                  largefiles,dev=800088    944543106
auto_direct     /disks/www      autofs ignore,direct,
                                  nosuid,dev=2c00001         944543181
auto_direct     /disks/ftp autofs  ignore,direct,
                                  nosuid,dev=2c00002         944543181
server:vold(pid329)     /vol    nfs      ignore,
                                  dev=2bc0002       944543192
/dev/dsk/c2t2d0s3       /disks/vol7 ufs      nosuid,rw,
                                  largefiles,dev=800103 944548661
/dev/md/dsk/d2  /disks/vol8 ufs      nosuid,rw,
                                  largefiles, dev=1540002   944553321
```

To avoid delays in printing resource information on NFS-mounted volumes, it is also possible to check local file systems with this command:

```
# df -l
Filesystem          kbytes       used   avail capacity  Mounted on
/dev/dsk/c0t0d0s0    245911      30754  190566    14%    /
/dev/dsk/c0t0d0s4   1015679     430787  523952    46%    /usr
/proc                    0          0       0     0%     /proc
fd                       0          0       0     0%     /dev/fd
/dev/dsk/c0t0d0s3    492871     226184  217400    51%    /var
/dev/md/dsk/d1      4119256    3599121  478943    89%    /opt
swap                256000      43488  212512    17%     /tmp
/dev/dsk/c0t2d0s3   4119256    3684920  393144    91%    /disks/vol1
/dev/md/dsk/d0     17398449   12889901 4334564    75%    /disks/vol2
/dev/md/dsk/d3      6162349    5990984  109742    99%    /disks/vol3
/dev/dsk/c1t1d0s0   8574909    5868862 1848557    77%    /disks/vol4
/dev/dsk/c2t3d0s2   1820189    1551628  177552    90%    /disks/vol5
/dev/dsk/c1t2d0s0   4124422    3548988  575434    87%    /disks/vol6
/dev/dsk/c2t2d0s3   8737664    8281113  456551    95%    /disks/vol7
/dev/md/dsk/d2      8181953    6803556 1296578    84%    /disks/vol8
```

A block device can be specified on the command line, and its individual usage measured; for example, consider this code for a slice on controller 1:

```
# df /dev/dsk/c1d0d2
Filesystem          kbytes       used   avail capacity  Mounted on
/dev/dsk/c1t1d0s0   8574909    5868862 1848557    77%    /disks/vol4
```

Users can also check the status of the disks holding their individual user directories and files by using df. For example, this code will display the disk space usage for the disk on which the home directory exists for user *pwatters*:

```
# df /staff/pwatters
Filesystem          kbytes       used   avail capacity  Mounted on
/dev/md/dsk/d0     17398449   12889146 4335319    75%    /disks/vol2
```

The following code checks the size of the partition on which the temporary mailbox for the user *pwatters* was created by the elm mail-reading program. This is a good thing to check if you intend to send a lot of e-mail messages!

```
# df /tmp/mbox.pwatters
Filesystem          kbytes       used   avail capacity  Mounted on
swap                256000      45392  210608    18%     /tmp
```

PART IV

Another way of obtaining disk space usage information with more directory-by-directory detail is by using the */usr/bin/du* command. This command prints the sum of the sizes of every file in the current directory and performs the same task recursively for any subdirectories. The size is calculated by summing all of the file sizes in the directory, where the size for each file is rounded up to the nearest 512-byte block. For example, taking a du of the */etc* directory looks like this:

```
# cd /etc
# du
14       ./default
7        ./cron.d
6        ./dfs
8        ./dhcp
...
2429     .
```

Thus, */etc* and all of its subdirectories contain a total of 2,429 512-byte blocks of data. Of course, this kind of output is fairly verbose and is probably not much use in its current form.

Command Reference

The following commands are commonly used for managing and installing file systems.

The /etc/path_to_inst File

A list of mappings between physical devices to instance names is always kept in the */etc/path_to_inst* file. The following example reviews the device to instance name mapping for a SCSI-based SPARC system:

```
"/sbus@1f,0" 0 "sbus"
"/sbus@1f,0/sbusmem@2,0" 2 "sbusmem"
"/sbus@1f,0/SUNW,fas@2,8800000" 1 "fas"
"/sbus@1f,0/SUNW,fas@2,8800000/ses@f,0" 1 "ses"
"/sbus@1f,0/SUNW,fas@2,8800000/sd@1,0" 16 "sd"
"/sbus@1f,0/SUNW,fas@2,8800000/sd@0,0" 15 "sd"
"/options" 0 "options"
"/pseudo" 0 "pseudo"
```

You can see entries for the network interface */sbus@1f,0/SUNW,hme@2,8c00000*, as well as the floppy disk */sbus@1f,0/SUNW,fdtwo@f,1400000* and the SBUS *sbus@1f,0*.

For a PCI local bus–based system such as a Sun Blade 100, the output would look like this:

```
"/pci@1f,0" 0 "pcipsy"
"/pci@1f,0/isa@7" 0 "ebus"
```

```
"/pci@1f,0/isa@7/power@0,800" 0 "power"
"/pci@1f,0/isa@7/dma@0,0" 0 "isadma"
"/pci@1f,0/isa@7/dma@0,0/parallel@0,378" 0 "ecpp"
"/pci@1f,0/isa@7/dma@0,0/floppy@0,3f0" 0 "fd"
"/pci@1f,0/isa@7/serial@0,2e8" 1 "su"
"/pci@1f,0/isa@7/serial@0,3f8" 0 "su"
"/pci@1f,0/pmu@3" 0 "pmubus"
"/pci@1f,0/pmu@3/i2c@0" 0 "smbus"
"/pci@1f,0/pmu@3/i2c@0/temperature@30" 0 "max1617"
"/pci@1f,0/pmu@3/i2c@0/card-reader@40" 0 "scmi2c"
"/pci@1f,0/pmu@3/i2c@0/dimm@a0" 0 "seeprom"
"/pci@1f,0/pmu@3/fan-control@0" 0 "grfans"
"/pci@1f,0/pmu@3/ppm@0" 0 "grppm"
"/pci@1f,0/pmu@3/beep@0" 0 "grbeep"
"/pci@1f,0/ebus@c" 1 "ebus"
"/pci@1f,0/usb@c,3" 0 "ohci"
"/pci@1f,0/usb@c,3/mouse@2" 0 "hid"
"/pci@1f,0/usb@c,3/keyboard@4" 1 "hid"
"/pci@1f,0/firewire@c,2" 0 "hci1394"
"/pci@1f,0/ide@d" 0 "uata"
"/pci@1f,0/ide@d/dad@0,0" 0 "dad"
"/pci@1f,0/ide@d/sd@1,0" 0 "sd"
"/pci@1f,0/sound@8" 0 "audiots"
"/pci@1f,0/SUNW,m64B@13" 0 "m64"
"/pci@1f,0/network@c,1" 0 "eri"
"/pci@1f,0/pci@5" 0 "pci_pci"
"/options" 0 "options"
"/SUNW,UltraSPARC-IIe@0,0" 0 "us"
"/pseudo" 0 "pseudo"
```

You can see that all the sbus entries have been replaced by the pci entries and that the network interface is no longer a hme, but an eri (*"/pci@1f,0/network@c,1" 0 "eri"*). In addition, some completely new types of hardware, such as a smart-card reader (*"/pci@1f,0/pmu@3/i2c@0/card-reader@40" 0 "scmi2c"*), are also available.

dmesg

The dmesg command is often used to determine whether specific device drivers for network interfaces and mass-storage devices have been correctly loaded at boot time. While its functions have largely been taken over by the syslog daemon (syslogd), dmesg provides a useful record of error and status messages printed by the kernel.

When the system boots, several status messages of log level *kern.notice* will be recorded and can be subsequently retrieved by using dmesg:

```
Jan 15 14:23:16 austin genunix: [ID 540533 kern.notice] SunOS Release
        5.10 Version Generic_108528-06 64-bit
Jan 15 14:23:16 austin genunix: [ID 784649 kern.notice] Copyright
```

```
                1983-2001 Sun Microsystems, Inc.   All rights reserved.
Jan 15 14:23:16 austin genunix: [ID 678236 kern.info] Ethernet
        address = 0:3:ba:4:a4:e8
Jan 15 14:23:16 austin unix: [ID 389951 kern.info] mem =
        131072K (0x8000000)
Jan 15 14:23:16 austin unix: [ID 930857 kern.info] avail mem = 121085952
```

You can see that a 64-bit kernel has been loaded successfully, for SunOS 5.10 (Solaris 10). Sun's copyright banner is also recorded, along with the Ethernet address of the primary network interface card (*0:3:ba:4:a4:e8*), the amount of installed RAM, and the amount of currently available RAM after the kernel has been loaded.

Before the kernel begins loading device drivers, it performs an integrity check to determine whether any naming conflicts exist. If a conflict is found, it is logged for future reference and action:

```
May 15 14:23:16 austin genunix: [ID 723599 kern.warning]
        WARNING: Driver alias "cal" conflicts with an existing
        driver name or alias.
```

You can see that the device driver alias *cal* has been used more than once, giving rise to a naming conflict.

Next, details about the system architecture and its main bus type are displayed:

```
Jan 15 14:23:16 austin rootnex: [ID 466748 kern.info]
        root nexus = Sun Blade 100 (UltraSPARC-IIe)
Jan 15 14:23:16 austin rootnex: [ID 349649 kern.info]
        pcipsy0 at root: UPA 0x1f 0x0
Jan 15 14:23:16 austin genunix: [ID 936769 kern.info] pcipsy0 is /
pci@1f,0
Jan 15 14:23:16 austin pcipsy: [ID 370704 kern.info]
        PCI-device: pmu@3, pmubus0
Jan 15 14:23:16 austin pcipsy: [ID 370704 kern.info]
        PCI-device: ppm@0, grppm0
Jan 15 14:23:16 austin genunix: [ID 936769 kern.info]
        grppm0 is /pci@1f,0/pmu@3/ppm@0
```

You can see that the system is a Sun Blade 100 and that its PCI bus architecture has been correctly identified.

The next stage involves identifying the hard drives attached to the system, as follows:

```
Jan 15 14:23:27 austin pcipsy: [ID 370704 kern.info]
        PCI-device: ide@d, uata0
Jan 15 14:23:27 austin genunix: [ID 936769 kern.info]
        uata0 is /pci@1f,0/ide@d
```

```
Jan 15 14:23:28 austin uata: [ID 114370 kern.info] dad0 at pci10b9,52290
Jan 15 14:23:28 austin uata: [ID 347839 kern.info]  target 0 lun 0
Jan 15 14:23:28 austin genunix: [ID 936769 kern.info]
     dad0 is /pci@1f,0/ide@d/dad@0,0
Jan 15 14:23:28 austin dada: [ID 365881 kern.info]
     <ST315320A cyl 29649 alt 2 hd 16 sec 63>
Jan 15 14:23:29 austin swapgeneric: [ID 308332 kern.info]
     root on /pci@1f,0/ide@d/disk@0,0:a fstype ufs
```

The IDE hard drive installed on the system has been correctly detected (*/pci@1f,0/ide@d/dad@0,0*) and has the label *ST315320A cyl 29649 alt 2 hd 16 sec 63*. In addition, the file system type has been identified as native UFS.

The status of every device on the system is logged during device driver loading, so it's possible to use the dmesg command to determine whether drivers have been correctly loaded. In the following entry, the Fiber Distributed Data Interface (FDDI) cannot be activated because it is not correctly installed:

```
Jan 15 14:26:38 austin smt: [ID 272566 kern.notice]
     smt0: nf FDDI driver is not active.
     Initialization of this driver cannot be completed.
```

mkfile

The mkfile command creates a file of a specified size that is padded with zeros. File sizes can be specified in gigabytes (g), megabytes (m), bytes (b), or kilobytes (k). For example, to create a 1GB file in */tmp/newfile*, you would use the following command:

```
# newfile 1g /tmp/newfile
```

If disk blocks should not be allocated until a request from an application, then pass the –*n* option on the command line. This conserves disk space while ensuring that the file created does not exceed its maximum flagged size.

mkfs

The mkfs command creates a new file system on the raw disk device specified on the command line. The file system type is determined by the contents of the file */etc/default/fs*. In most Solaris systems, the contents of this file are "LOCAL=ufs", indicating that UFS file systems are the default. If a different file system type is to be created, then the –*F* option can be passed on the command line, followed by the file system type. For example, to create a file system of type *pcfs* which uses a standard FAT type on a floppy disk, you would use the following command:

```
# mkfs -F pcfs /dev/rdiskette
```

A number of aliases to the mkfs command are also available, which you can use to create file systems of different types directly. These commands include

- **mkfs_udfs** Creates a Universal Disk File System (UDFS) format file system
- **mkfs_pcfs** Creates a FAT format file system
- **mkfs_ufs** Creates a UFS format file system

In addition, passing the *–m* option displays the complete command string that was used to create the file system. This is useful for extracting and storing the command string in a script to re-create the file system on another disk.

newfs

The newfs command uses the mkfs command to create UFS file systems. The main difference between the two commands is the number of parameters that can be passed to newfs to tune the file system during creation. The following parameters can be used to specify file system parameters:

- *–a* n Specifies *n* blocks to be held in reserve to replace bad blocks
- *–b* n Sets the block size on the file system to be *n* bytes
- *–c* n Indicates that *n* cylinders should be allocated to each cylinder group
- *–C* n Specifies *n* as the maximum number of contiguous disk blocks per file
- *–d* n Sets the rotational delay to *n* milliseconds
- *–f* n Sets the smallest disk fragment for a single file to *n* bytes
- *–i* n Specifies that *n* bytes should be allocated to each inode
- *–m* n Specifies that *n* percent of the physical file system should be reserved as free
- *–n* n Sets the number of different group cylinder rotations to *n*
- *–r* n Sets the disk speed to *n* revolutions per minute
- *–s* n Sets the disk size to *n* sectors
- *–t* n Specifies that *n* tracks be allocated to each cylinder

For most applications, the defaults selected by newfs will provide adequate performance. However, some specialized applications do require smaller or larger disk minimum fragments or block size for their file systems, and these can easily be set during file system creation.

lofiadm

The lofiadm command is used to initialize a file on an existing partition that is labeled as a raw device, by using the loopback file device driver. You can then create a new file system on the device by using newfs or mkfs as if it were a separate partition. This can be useful if a new partition needs to be created, but the disk cannot be easily reformatted, particularly if it's only required temporarily.

To create a file system on a file, you should use the mkfile command to create a file to be a specific size. Next, you need to make the association between the file and the loopback file device driver. For example, if the file */tmp/datafile* was created with mkfile, the following command would create the association:

```
# lofiadm -a /tmp/datafile /dev/lofi/2
```

Finally, you can create a new file system by using the newfs command:

```
# newfs /dev/rlofi/2
newfs: construct a new file system /dev/rlofi/2: (y/n)? y
```

You can then mount the file system on a mount point (such as */testdata*) as required:

```
# mount /dev/lofi/2 /testdata
```

When the file system is no longer required, you can use the umount command to remove the file system from operation, while you can use the lofiadm command to remove the association between the file and the loopback file device driver:

```
# umount /testdata
# lofiadm -d /tmp/datafile
```

swap

The swap command is used to add virtual RAM to a system. Virtual RAM is typically used to provide memory for process execution when physical memory has been exhausted. Disk blocks are used to simulate physical memory locations, using an interface that is invisible to the user. Thus, users never need to be concerned about the type of RAM that their process is addressing. While virtual memory allows a system's effective capacity to be increased to many times its physical capacity, it is much slower than physical RAM. When a system experiences peak demands for memory, causing virtual memory to be used, the CPU must work harder to support virtual memory operations. Coupled with the relatively slow speed of disk writing, this has a significant impact on performance. When virtual memory is being utilized, and many new memory access calls are made along with normal file reading and writing, so-called "disk thrashing" (the excessive use of virtual memory) can occur, since the number of disk operations requested far exceeds the capacity of the disk to read and write. If this is a common occurrence, then you should install extra physical RAM into the system and/or tune the file system with tunefs.

Virtual memory should generally be added to the system at twice the physical RAM installed. Thus, for a 256MB system, you should initialize 512MB of virtual memory. To add virtual memory, you should use the mkfile command to create an empty file of the required size. Next, use the swap command to add the file into the pool of available disk space. For example, if two swap files are created on different file systems for redundancy (such as */u1/swap* and */u2/swap*), you can add them to the swap space pool by using the following commands:

```
# swap -a /u1/swap
# swap -a /u2/swap
```

To verify that the swap has been correctly added to the pool, use the following command:

```
# swap -l
```

If you have a dedicated slice set aside for swap, then you can simply pass the block device name on the command line:

```
# swap -a /dev/dsk/c1t1d2s1
```

To remove a file (or device) from the swap pool, you need to pass the –*d* option on the command line. Thus, to remove */u1/swap* and */dev/dsk/c1t1d2s1* from the swap pool, you would use the following commands:

```
# swap -d /u1/swap
# swap -d /dev/dsk/c1t1d2s1
```

The file */u1/swap* can now be safely deleted, and the slice */dev/dsk/c1t1d2s1* can be safely used for other purposes. Note that labeling a disk as a swap is very useful, as this allows you to use space near the center of the disk for swap.

sync

The sync command is generally executed prior to a shutdown or halt, to flush all disk buffers and to write the super block. This ensures that data integrity is preserved when the system is rebooted or where the run level is modified. It is simply executed without options, as shown here:

```
# sync
```

tunefs

The tunefs command allows you to tune a file system's performance to specific requirements. The key settings that can be modified are optimization for speed of execution or amount of disk space required. Generally, unless a system is critically low on disk space, it is best to optimize for speed. The following options are supported:

- *−a* n   Specifies that *n* blocks be written before a pause in rotation
- *−e* n   Specifies *n* as the maximum number of contiguous disk blocks per file
- *−d* n   Sets the rotational delay to *n* milliseconds
- *−m* n   Specifies that *n* percent of the physical file system should be reserved as free
- *−o* **key**   Optimizes the file system for a *key* that is either "time" or "space"

Summary

In this chapter, you have examined how to install, configure, and optimize file systems using UFS. In addition, when physical memory is lacking, virtual RAM can be configured to allow more applications to be executed at the expense of consuming disk space.

File System and Volume Management

O nce disks have been installed and formatted, a number of further operations must be performed to allow them to be used. For a start, the superuser must manually mount the disks and create an entry created in */etc/vfstab* for each new partition. Alternatively, disks may need to be unmounted for maintenance using the fsck program. However, if file system journaling is enabled in */etc/vfstab*, then the need for fsck is reduced. Finally, setting up volume management is critical to the enterprise, since the logical sizes of disks can be extended, and/or redundancy can be implemented.

All of these topics are examined in this chapter.

Key Concepts

The following concepts are required knowledge for managing disks, file systems, and volumes.

Mounting Local File Systems

Solaris (UNIX File System, or UFS) file systems are mapped in a one-to-one relationship to physical slices, which makes it easy for you to associate file systems with partitions, even if the physical and logical device references are complex. For example, the slice */dev/dsk/c0t3d0s5* may be mounted on the mount point */export/home*.

Mount points are simply empty directories that have been created using the mkdir command. One of the nice features of the UFS is that it has a one-to-many mapping to potential mount points: this means that a file system can be mounted, and its files and directories can be manipulated, unmounted, and then remounted on a different mount point. All of the data that was modified when the file system was mounted using a different mount point are retained. For example, if you mount */dev/dsk/c0t3d0s5* on */export/home*, create a directory called *pwatters* (that is, */export/home/pwatters*), unmount the file system, and then remount it on */usr/local*, the content of the folder *pwatters* will still be available, albeit with a new absolute path (*/usr/local/pwatters*).

Unmounting Local File Systems

In normal operations, a file system is mounted at boot time if its mount point and options are specified in the virtual file systems table (*/etc/vfstab*). The file system is unmounted before the system is shut down. However, at times, you may find it necessary to unmount a file system manually. For example, if you need to check the file system's integrity by using the `fsck` command, you must unmount the target file system. Alternatively, if you are going to modify the mount point of a file system, you need to unmount the file system from its current mount point and remount it on the new mount point. You cannot mount a file system on two different mount points.

Creating Entries in /etc/vfstab

Although you've used the `mount` command to manually mount file systems, it's preferable to simply create an entry in */etc/vfstab* to mount the file system automatically after boot. Alternatively, if you are going to make a number of entries in */etc/vfstab*, and the system is not going to be rebooted for some time, then you can use the following command to mount any entries in */etc/vfstab* that have not already been mounted:

```
# mountall
```

Take a look at an example entry in */etc/vfstab*:

```
#device               device               mount   FS    fsck   mount    mount
#to mount             to fsck              point   type  pass   at boot  options
/dev/dsk/c0t0d0s5 /dev/rdsk/c0t0d0s5 /usr    ufs   2      yes      -
```

This example shows an entry for the raw disk device */dev/rdsk/c0t0d0s5*, mounted on */usr*, standard UFS file system, mounted at boot time, with no options. In addition, the raw device on which `fsck` operates is */dev/rdsk/c0t0d0s5*, where an `fsck` file system check is required. The Options field contains a comma-delimited list of mounting options, which are equivalent to those used for the `mount` command (see the "Command Reference" section, later in the chapter, for details on the `mount` command). In addition to UFS file systems, file systems of other types can be mounted, including special types such as swap space or NFS-mounted volumes.

Fixing Problems by Using fsck

/usr/sbin/fsck is a file system checking and repair program that's commonly found on Solaris and other UNIX platforms. The program is usually executed by the superuser while the system is in a single-user mode state (for example, after you enter run-level S), but it can also be executed on individual volumes during multiuser run levels.

There is one "golden rule" of which you must be aware while using `fsck`: never apply `fsck` to a mounted file system. Doing so would leave the file system in an inconsistent state and cause a kernel panic—that's why running `fsck` on a mounted file system now causes the `fsck` command to abort with this message: */dev/dsk/...* Is a Mounted File System, Ignored. Any fixes to potential problems on a mounted file system could end up creating more damage than the original problem. This section examines the output of `fsck` and some examples of common problems. It also investigates how `fsck` repairs corrupt and inconsistent disk data.

Although Solaris 10 still retains `fsck`, the program is necessary only for Solaris 2.6 and previous releases—with later releases, logging is provided for UNIX file systems and should always be turned on. Thus, before any changes are made to a file system, details of the change are recorded in a log prior to their physical application. While this consumes some extra CPU and disk overhead (approximately 1 percent of disk space on each volume with logging enabled is required), it does ensure that the file system is never left in an inconsistent state. In addition, boot time is reduced, because `fsck` does not need to be executed.

Why do inconsistencies occur in the first place? In theory, they shouldn't, but they can occur under three common scenarios:

- If the Solaris server has been switched off like an old MS-DOS machine, without being powered down first

- If a system is halted without synchronizing disk data (it is advisable that you explicitly use `sync` before shutting down using `halt`)

- If hardware defects are encountered, including damage to disk blocks and heads, which can be caused by moving the system and/or by power surges

These problems are realized as corruption to the internal set of tables that every UNIX file system keeps to manage free disk blocks and inodes, which leads to blocks that are free being reported as already allocated and, conversely, to some blocks occupied by a program being recorded as free. This is obviously problematic for mission-critical data, which is a good reason to add RAID storage (or at least reliable backups). If you suspect physical damage, then you should perform surface analysis of the hard disk by using the `disckscan` command.

The first step to running `fsck` is to enable file system checking during bootup. To do this, you need to specify an integer value in the `fsck` field in the virtual file system configuration file */etc/vfstab*. Entering **1** in this field ensures sequential `fsck` checking, while entering **2** does not ensure sequential checking, as shown in the following example:

```
#device device mount FS fsck mount mount
#to mount to fsck point type pass at boot options
#
/dev/dsk/c1t2d1s3 /dev/rdsk/c1t2d1s3 /usr ufs 2 yes -/
-
```

After you enable `fsck` for a particular file system, you can execute it on that system. `fsck` checks the integrity of several features of the file system, the most significant of which is the superblock that stores summary information for the volume. Since the superblock is the most modified item on the file system being written and rewritten when data is changed on a disk, it is the most commonly corrupted feature. However, copies of the superblock are stored in many different locations to ensure that it can be reliably retrieved. The checks that `fsck` performs on the superblock include the following:

- A check of the file system size, which obviously must be greater than the size computed from the number of blocks identified in the superblock
- A check of the total number of inodes, which must be less than the maximum number of inodes
- A tally of reported free blocks and inodes

If any of these values is identified as corrupt by `fsck`, the superuser can select one of the many superblock backups that were created during initial file system creation as a replacement for the current superblock. We will examine superblock corruption and how to fix it in the section "fsck Operations," later in the chapter.

In addition to the superblock, `fsck` also checks the number and status of cylinder group blocks, inodes, indirect blocks, and data blocks. Since free blocks are located by maps stored in the cylinder group, `fsck` verifies that all the blocks marked as free are not actually being used by any files—if they are, files could be corrupted. If all blocks are correctly accounted for, `fsck` determines whether the number of free blocks plus the number of used blocks equals the total number of blocks in the file system. If `fsck` detects any incongruity, the maps of unallocated blocks are rebuilt, although there is obviously a risk of data loss whenever a disagreement over the actual state of the file system is encountered. `fsck` always uses the actual count of inodes and/or blocks if the superblock information is wrong, and it replaces the incorrect value if this is verified by the superuser.

When `fsck` examines inodes, it does so sequentially and aims to identify inconsistencies in format and type, link count, duplicate blocks, bad block numbers, and inode size. Inodes should always be in one of three states: allocated (used by a file), unallocated (not used by a file), or partially allocated. *Partially allocated* means that during an allocation or deallocation procedure, data has been left behind that should have been deleted or completed. Alternatively, partial allocation could result from a physical hardware failure. In both cases, `fsck` attempts to clear the inode.

The *link count* is the number of directory entries that are linked to a particular inode. `fsck` always checks that the number of directory entries listed is correct by examining the entire directory structure, beginning with the root directory, and tallying the number of links for every inode. Clearly, the stored link count and the actual link count should agree; however, the stored link count occasionally differs from the actual link count. This could result from a disk not being synchronized before a shutdown, for example, and while changes to the file system have been saved, the link count has not been correctly updated. If the stored count is not zero but the actual count is zero, disconnected files are placed in the *lost+found* directory found in the top level of the file system concerned. In other cases, the actual count replaces the stored count.

An *indirect block* is a pointer to a list of every block claimed by an inode. `fsck` checks every block number against a list of allocated blocks: if two inodes claim the same block number, that block number is added to a list of duplicate block numbers. The administrator may be asked to choose which inode is correct—obviously, picking the correct inode is a difficult and dangerous decision that usually indicates that it's time to verify files against backups.

`fsck` also checks the integrity of the actual block numbers, which can also become corrupt. Block numbers should always lie in the interval between the first data block and the last data block. If a bad block number is detected, the inode is cleared.

Directories are also checked for integrity by `fsck`. Directory entries are equivalent to other files on the file system, except they have a different mode entry in the inode. `fsck` checks the validity of directory data blocks, checking for the following problems: unallocated nodes associated with inode numbers; inode numbers that exceed the maximum number of inodes for a particular file system; incorrect inode numbers for the standard directory entries "." and ".."; and directories that have been accidentally disconnected from the file system.

`fsck` examines each disk volume in five distinct stages:

1. Checks blocks and sizes.
2. Verifies path names.
3. Examines connectivity.
4. Investigates reference counts.
5. Checks the cylinder groups.

What Is RAID?

Solaris servers are often set up to be *highly available*, which means that the databases, application servers, and distributed applications that they host must be accessible to clients at all times. Such applications and services are often deployed on Solaris because of the fail-over technologies provided by Sun's hardware offerings. For example, many high-end SPARC systems feature dual power supplies and allow for the installation of many hard disks in a single cabinet.

Production systems invariably experience two kinds of capacity problems. First, the largest file size that can be supported by the system is the size of an individual hard drive. This means, for example, that database servers that require multiple mount points must be located on a single file system for storing extremely large data files. Having 20 hard disks in this context is only as useful as having one. One solution is to wait until hard disks with higher capacities are manufactured; however, relying on future hardware updates is not feasible for systems that have immediate deployment requirements. What is required is some way of splitting physical data storage across several physical disk volumes, while providing a single logical interface for access.

The second problem that arises is that hard disks and other physical media inevitably fail after periods of heavy use. Even if quality hard drives have a mean time between failures (MTBF) of several years, this is an average figure: some drives last ten years, others last only one. Again, Sun Microsystems hardware provides some relief here: it is possible to "hot swap" hard drives, for example, without having to shut down the system and reboot. The faulty drive is simply removed and replaced by the new drive. Once backups have been loaded, the system will be available again. However, this is the best-case scenario, and the success of hot swapping ultimately depends on the RAID configuration.

Restoring disk contents from backups might take several hours, and customers often complain of downtime counted in minutes. While restoring from backups is an excellent strategy for countering catastrophic failure, it is simply not an option for a production system that is experiencing single disk failures. What is required is some level of content redundancy that retains more than one copy of a system's data across different disks.

To solve the capacity and redundancy problem, Solaris provides support for the redundant array of inexpensive disks (RAID) standard. RAID defines a number of different *levels* that provide various types of *striping* and *mirroring*. In this context, *striping* is the process of spreading data across different physical disks while presenting a single logical interface for the logical volume. Thus, a striped disk set containing four 18GB drives would have a total logical capacity of 72GB. This configuration is shown in Figure 16-1.

A different approach is offered by mirroring, with which a logical volume's contents are copied in real time to more than one physical device. Thus, four 18GB drives could be mirrored to provide two completely redundant 18GB volumes. This means that if one disk fails, its mirror is automatically used to continue to create, read, update, and delete operations on the file system, while the disk is physically replaced (again, with no reboot required). This kind of seamless operation requires minimal downtime. This configuration is shown in Figure 16-2.

FIGURE 16-1
Striped disk configuration

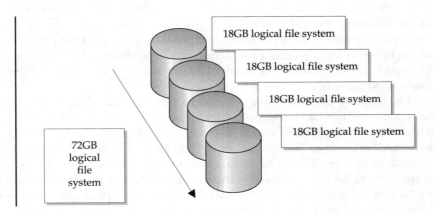

72GB logical file system

18GB logical file system

18GB logical file system

18GB logical file system

18GB logical file system

FIGURE 16-2
Mirrored disk
configuration

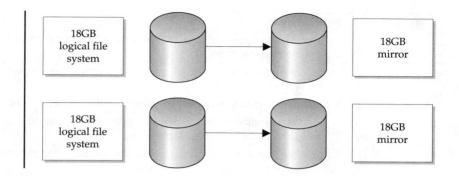

Alternatively, the four disks could be configured so that a 36GB striped volume could be created, combining the capacities of two disks, while the remaining two disks could be used to mirror this striped volume. Thus, the system is provided with a logical 36GB volume that also features complete redundancy. This configuration is shown in Figure 16-3.

Six major RAID levels are supported by DiskSuite, the tool used to set up mirrored and striped virtual file systems on Solaris. RAID Level 0 is the primary striping level and allows a virtual file system to be constructed of several physical disks. Their capacities are effectively combined to produce a single disk with a large capacity. In contrast, RAID Level 1 is the primary mirroring level: all data that is written to the virtual file system

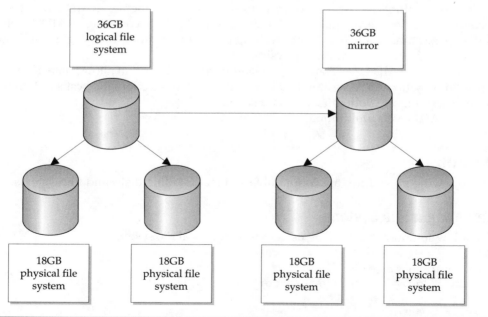

FIGURE 16-3   Striped and mirrored disk configuration

Level	Description
0	Primary striping level, allowing a single virtual file system to be constructed of multiple physical disks
1	Primary mirroring level, where all data written to a virtual file system is copied in real time to a separate mirroring disk
2	A secondary mirroring level, which uses Hamming codes for error correction
3	A secondary striping level, which writes parity information to a single drive, but writes all other data to multiple drives
4	A secondary striping level, which writes parity information to a single drive, but writes all other data to multiple drives
5	A striping and mirroring level, which allows data to be written to different disks, including parity information

TABLE 16-1   Commonly Used RAID Levels

is also copied in real time to a separate physical disk that has the same capacity as the original. This level has the slowest performance for writes, because all data must be written twice to two different disks; it also costs the most, because each drive to be mirrored uses a second drive that cannot be used for any other purpose. However, full redundancy can be achieved using RAID Level 1, and read performance is very good.

The remaining RAID levels are variations on these two themes. RAID Level 2 is a secondary mirroring level that uses Hamming codes for error correction. RAID Levels 3 and 4 are secondary striping levels, writing parity information to a single drive, but writing all other data to multiple physical disks.

In contrast, RAID Level 5 is a striping and mirroring level that allows data, including parity information, to be written to different disks. RAID 5 offers the best solution for systems that require both mirroring and striping.

The RAID levels are summarized in Table 16-1.

Procedures

The following procedures are commonly used for installing disks and file systems.

Mounting a File System

The following procedure can be used to mount a local file system:

```
# mkdir /export/home
# mount  /dev/dsk/c0t3d0s5 /export/home
# cd /export/home
# mkdir pwatters
# ls
pwatters
# cd /; umount /export/home
```

```
# mkdir /usr/local
# mount   /dev/dsk/c0t3d0s5 /usr/local
# cd /usr/local
# ls
pwatters
```

The mkdir command is used to create mount points, which are equivalent to directories. If you wish to make a mount point one level below an existing directory, you can use the mkdir command with no options. However, if you want to make a mount point several directory levels below an existing directory, you need to pass the option –p to the mkdir command. For example, the following command creates the mount point /staff, since the parent / directory already exists:

```
# mkdir /staff
```

However, to create the mount point /staff/nfs/pwatters, you would use the –p option if the directory /staff/nfs did not already exist:

```
# mkdir -p /staff/nfs/pwatters
```

Once a mount point has been created, you use the mount command to attach the file system to the mount point. For example, to mount the file system /dev/dsk/c0t3d0s5 on the mount point /export/home, you would use the following command:

```
# mount   /dev/dsk/c0t3d0s5 /export/home
```

The mount command assumes that a UFS file system will be mounted. If the target file system is non-UFS, you need to pass an option specifying the file system type on the command line by using the –F options. Supported file system types include the following:

- *nfs*   Network File System (NFS)
- *pcfs*   MS-DOS–formatted file system
- *s5fs*   System V–compliant file system

Details of all currently mounted files are kept in the /etc/mnttab file. This file should never be directly edited by the superuser. The /etc/mnttab file will contain entries similar to the following:

```
# cat /etc/mnttab
/dev/dsk/c0t0d0s0 / ufs rw,intr,largefiles,suid,dev=1100000 921334412
/proc /proc proc dev=2280000 922234443
fd /dev/fd fd rw,suid,dev=2240000 922234448
mnttab /etc/mnttab mntfs dev=2340000 922234442
swap /tmp tmpfs dev=1 922234451
/dev/dsk/c0t0d0s5 /usr ufs rw,intr,onerror=panic,suid,dev=1100005
922234441
```

Configuring /etc/vfstab

If you want a disk to be available after reboot, you must create an entry in the virtual file systems table (*/etc/vfstab*). An entry like this,

```
/dev/dsk/c0t3d0s5 /dev/rdsk/c0t3d0s5 /export/home ufs 2 yes -
```

contains details of the slice's block and raw devices, the mount point, the file system type, instructions for `fsck`, logging, and a flag to force mount at boot. These options are largely equivalent to those used with the `mount` command.

All file systems, including floppy disks, can be listed in the virtual file systems table. The mount point configuration for the floppy drive is typically similar to the following:

```
fd  -  /dev/fd  fd  -  no  -
```

Instead of mounting file systems individually by using the `mount` command, you can mount all file systems defined in */etc/vfstab* by using the `mountall` command:

```
# mountall
mount: /tmp already mounted
mount: /dev/dsk/c0t0d0s5 is already mounted
```

This attempts to mount all listed file systems, and reports file systems that have previously been mounted. Obviously, file systems that are currently mounted cannot be mounted twice.

Setting Up RAID

The first step in setting up any kind of RAID system is to install the DiskSuite packages and prepare the disks for mirroring or striping by formatting them. Primary disks and their mirrors must be set up with exactly the same partition structure to ensure that virtual file systems can be created that are compatible with both the primary and mirror.

Once you have installed the DiskSuite packages, you need to prepare disks that will be used with DiskSuite. This preparation includes creating state database replicas for virtual file systems used on the system. Ideally, these state database replicas will be distributed across each controller and/or disk so that maximum redundancy can be achieved. A small partition must be created on each disk that will contain the state database (typically around 5MB).

For example, to create a state database replica on the file system */dev/dsk/c1t0d0s7*, you would use the following command:

```
# metadb -c 3 -a -f /dev/dsk/c1t0d0s7 /dev/dsk/c0t0d0s7
```

This creates three replicas on each of the two disks specified (*/dev/dsk/c1t0d0s7* and */dev /dsk/c0t0d0s7*). Note that two controllers are used rather than one.

If no existing state database replicas can be found, the following message will be displayed:

```
metadb: There are no existing databases
```

Striping

To enable striping, you need to create configurations for the virtual file systems that you want to use. These can be permanently recorded in the DiskSuite configuration file (*md.tab*). For example, the striping configuration shown earlier in Figure 16-1 involving four 18GB disks could have its configuration recorded with the following entry, assuming the virtual file system (*s5*) has the path */dev/md/dsk/d5*:

```
d5 4 1 c1t1d0s5 1 c1t2d0s5 1 c2t1d0s5 1 c2t2d0s5
```

Here, the four physical disks involved are */dev/dsk/c1t1d0s5*, */dev/dsk/c1t2d0s5*, */dev/dsk /c2t1d0s5*, and */dev/dsk/c2t2d0s5*. To ensure that the virtual file system is mounted at boot time, it could be included in the */etc/vfstab* file, just like a normal file system. Indeed, only an entry for */dev/md/dsk/d5* should appear in */etc/vfstab* after striping is complete, and the entries for */dev/dsk/c1t1d0s5*, */dev/dsk/c1t2d0s5*, */dev/dsk/c2t1d0s5*, and */dev/dsk/c2t2d0s5* should be commented out.

To initialize the *d5* metadevice, use this command:

```
# metainit d5
```

If this commands succeeds, you simply treat the new metadevice as if it were a new file system and initialize a UFS on it:

```
# newfs /dev/md/rdsk/d5
```

Next, you create an appropriate mount point for the device (such as */staff*) and mount the metadevice:

```
# mkdir /staff
# mount /dev/md/dsk/d5 /staff
```

The striped volume *d5* is now ready for use.

Mirroring

To create a mirror between two file systems, you follow a procedure similar to creating an entry in the *md.tab* file. For example, if you want to create a mirror of */dev/dsk/c1t1d0s5* with */dev/dsk/c0t1d0s5* (note the different controller), you would need to create a virtual file system (*d50*) that mirrored the primary file system (*d52*) to its mirror (*d53*). You would need to make the following entries in *md.tab*:

```
d50 -m /dev/md/dsk/d52 /dev/md/dsk/d53
d52 1 1 /dev/dsk/c1t1d0s5
d53 1 1 /dev/dsk/c0t1d0s5
```

To initialize the *d5* metadevice, you would use this command:

```
# metainit d50
# metainit d52
# metainit d53
```

If this commands succeeds, you simply treat the new metadevice as if it were a new file system and initialize a UFS on it:

```
# newfs /dev/md/rdsk/d50
# newfs /dev/md/rdsk/d52
# newfs /dev/md/rdsk/d53
```

Next, you create an appropriate mount point for the device (such as */work*) and mount the metadevice:

```
# mkdir /work
# mount /dev/md/dsk/d50 /work
```

The mirrored volume *d50* is now ready for use. It is also possible to configure RAID 5 using a similar process.

Examples

The following examples provide some real-world cases for installing disks and file systems.

Using umount

Unmounting local file systems is easy using the umount command. You simply specify the file system to be unmounted on the command line. For example, to unmount the file system mounted on */export/home*, you would use the following command:

```
# umount /export/home
```

However, if there are open files on the file system, or users logging into their home directories on the target file system, it's obviously a bad idea to unmount the file system without giving users some kind of notice—in fact, it's just not possible. It's also important to determine whether other processes are using files on the file system. In fact, umount requires that no processes have files open on the target file system. You can use the fuser command to determine which users are accessing a particular file system. For example, to determine whether any processes have open files on the /export/home partition, you could use the following command:

```
# fuser -c /export/home
```

To give a listing of the UIDs associated with each process, the following command could be used:

```
# fuser -c -u /export/home
```

To warn users about the impending unmounting of the file system, you can use the wall command to send a message to all logged-in users. For example, the following message could be sent:

```
# wall
Attention all users
/export/home is going down for maintenance at 6:00 p.m.
Please kill all processes accessing this file system (or I will)
```

At 6 P.M., a fuser check should show that no processes are accessing the file system. However, if some users did not heed the warning, the fuser command can be used to kill all processes that are still active:

```
# fuser -c -k /export/home
```

This is obviously a drastic step, but it may be necessary in emergency or urgent repair situations.

To save time, if you wish to unmount all user file systems (excluding /, /proc, /usr, and /var), you could use the umountall command:

```
# umountall
```

This command unmounts only file systems that are listed in the virtual file system table, subject to the aforementioned exclusions.

fsck Operations

This section examines a full run of fsck, outlining the most common problems and how they are rectified. It also presents some examples of less-commonly encountered problems.

On a SPARC 20 system, fsck for the / file system looks like this:

```
** /dev/rdsk/c0d0s0
** Currently Mounted on /
** Phase 1 - Check Blocks and Sizes
** Phase 2 - Check Pathnames
** Phase 3 - Check Connectivity
** Phase 4 - Check Reference Counts
** Phase 5 - Check Cyl groups
FREE BLK COUNT(S) WRONG IN SUPERBLK
SALVAGE?
```

Clearly, the actual block count and the block count recorded in the superblock are at odds with each other. At this point, fsck requires superuser permission to install the actual block count in the superblock, which the administrator indicates by pressing Y.

The scan continues with the */usr* partition:

```
1731 files, 22100 used, 51584 free (24 frags, 6445 blocks,
  0.0% fragmentation)
** /dev/rdsk/c0d0s6
** Currently Mounted on /usr
** Phase 1 - Check Blocks and Sizes
** Phase 2 - Check Pathnames
** Phase 3 - Check Connectivity
** Phase 4 - Check Reference Counts
** Phase 5 - Check Cyl groups

FILE SYSTEM STATE IN SUPERBLOCK IS WRONG; FIX?
```

In this case, the file system state in the superblock records is incorrect, and again, the administrator is required to give consent for it to be repaired.

The scan then continues with the */var* and */export/home* partitions:

```
26266 files, 401877 used, 217027 free (283 frags, 27093 blocks,
  0.0% fragmentation)
** /dev/rdsk/c0d0s1
** Currently Mounted on /var
** Phase 1 - Check Blocks and Sizes
** Phase 2 - Check Pathnames
** Phase 3 - Check Connectivity
** Phase 4 - Check Reference Counts
** Phase 5 - Check Cyl groups
1581 files, 4360 used, 25545 free (41 frags, 3188 blocks,
  0.1% fragmentation)
** /dev/rdsk/c0d0s7
```

```
** Currently Mounted on /export/home
** Phase 1 - Check Blocks and Sizes
** Phase 2 - Check Pathnames
** Phase 3 - Check Connectivity
** Phase 4 - Check Reference Counts
** Phase 5 - Check Cyl groups
2 files, 9 used, 7111589 free (13 frags, 888947 blocks,
   0.0% fragmentation)
```

Obviously, the */var* and */export/home* partitions have passed examination by fsck and are intact. However, the fact that the / and */usr* file systems were in an inconsistent state suggests that the file systems were not cleanly unmounted, perhaps during the last reboot. Fortunately, the superblock itself was intact. However, this is not always the case.

In the following example, the superblock of */dev/dsk/c0t0d0s2* has a bad "magic number," indicating that it is damaged beyond repair:

```
# fsck /dev/dsk/c0t0d0s2
 BAD SUPER BLOCK: MAGIC NUMBER WRONG
 USE ALTERNATE SUPER-BLOCK TO SUPPLY NEEDED INFORMATION
eg. fsck [-F ufs] -o b=# [special ...]
where # is the alternate super block. SEE fsck_ufs(1M).
```

In this case, you need to specify one of the alternative superblocks that were created by the newfs command. When a file system is created, a message appears about the creation of superblock backups:

```
super-block backups (for fsck -b #) at:
32, 5264, 10496, 15728, 20960, 26192, 31424, 36656, 41888,
47120, 52352, 57584, 62816, 68048, 73280, 78512, 82976, 88208,
93440, 98672, 103904, 109136, 114368, 119600, 124832, 130064,
135296, 140528, 145760, 150992, 156224, 161456.
```

In the preceding example, you may need to specify one of these alternative superblocks so that the disk contents are once again readable. If you didn't record the superblock backups during the creation of the file system, you can easily retrieve them by using the newfs command (and using –N to prevent the creation of a new file system):

```
# newfs -Nv /dev/dsk/c0t0d0s2
```

Once you have determined an appropriate superblock replacement number (which should be a higher number, to prevent overwriting, such as 32 in this example), use fsck again to replace the older superblock with the new one:

```
# fsck -o b=32 /dev/dsk/c0t0d0s2
```

Disks that have physical hardware errors often report being unable to read inodes beyond a particular point. For example, this error message

```
Error reading block 31821 (Attempt to read from file system
resulted in short read) while doing inode scan. Ignore error
<y> ?
```

stops the user from continuing with the fsck scan and correcting the problem. This is probably a good time to replace a disk rather than attempt any corrective action. Never be tempted to ignore these errors and hope for the best—especially in commercial organizations; you will ultimately have to take responsibility for lost and damaged data. Users will be particularly unforgiving if you had advance warning of a problem.

Here is an example of what can happen if a link count problem exists:

```
# fsck /
** /dev/rdsk/c0t1d0s0
** Currently Mounted on /
** Phase 1 - Check Blocks and Sizes
** Phase 2 - Check Pathnames
** Phase 3 - Check Connectivity
** Phase 4 - Check Reference Counts
LINK COUNT DIR I=4  OWNER=root MODE=40700
SIZE=4096 MTIME=Nov  1 11:56 1999  COUNT 2 SHOULD BE 4
ADJUST? y
```

If the adjustment does not fix the error, use find to track down the problem file and delete it:

```
# find / -mount -inum 4 -ls
```

The problem file should be in the *lost+found* directory for the partition in question (in this case, */lost+found*).

Having duplicate inodes can also create a problem:

```
** Phase 1 - Check Blocks and Sizes
 314415 DUP I=5009
 345504 DUP I=12011
 345505 DUP I=12011
 854711 DUP I=91040
 856134 DUP I=93474
 856135 DUP I=93474
```

This problem is often encountered in systems using Solaris 2.5 and 2.6, although the problem is not usually seen in systems running Solaris 7, 8, or 9; an upgrade may correct the problem.

Command Reference

The following command is typically used to manage volumes and file systems.

mount

The mount command, executed without any options, provides a list of all mounted file systems:

```
# mount
/ on /dev/dsk/c0t0d0s0 read/write/setuid/intr/largefiles/onerror=
    panic on Tue Jul 10 09:10:01 2001
/usr on /dev/dsk/c0t0d0s6 read/write/setuid/intr/largefiles/
    onerror=panic on Tue Jul 10 09:10:02 2001
/proc on /proc read/write/setuid on Tue Jul 10 09:10:03 2001
/etc/mnttab on mnttab read/write/setuid on Tue Jul 10 09:10:04 2001
/tmp on swap read/write/setuid on Tue Jul 10 09:10:05 2001
/export/home on /dev/dsk/c0t0d0s7 read/write/setuid/intr/largefiles
    /onerror=panic on Tue Jul 10 09:10:06 2001
```

The mount command has several options, which are described next. These can also be used to specify mounting options in */etc/vfstab*.

bg	Specifies to continue to attempt mounting in the background if mounting initially fails. Useful for mounting NFS volumes where the server is temporarily unavailable. The default is *fg*, which attempts to mount in the foreground.
hard	Specifies that hard mounting will be attempted, where requests to mount are continually sent. The alternative is *soft*, which just returns an error message.
intr	Allows keyboard commands to be used during mounting. To switch this off, use *nointr*.
largefiles	Enables support for large file systems (those greater than 2GB). To remove support for large file systems, use the *nolargefiles* option.
logging	Allows a log of all UFS transactions to be maintained. In the event of a system crash, you can consult the log and verify all transactions. This virtually eliminates the need to run lengthy fsck passes on file systems at boot. The default option is *nologging*, because logs occupy around 1 percent of file system space.

PART IV

noatime	Prevents access timestamps from being touched on files. This significantly speeds up access times on large file systems with many small files.
remount	Permits a file system's properties to be modified while it is still mounted, reducing downtime.
retry	Specifies the number of attempts that should be made to remount a file system.
rw	Specifies that the file system is to be mounted as read-write. Some file systems, however, are read-only (such as CD-ROMs). In such cases, the *ro* option should be specified (writing to a read-only file system is not physically possible).
suid	Permits set user ID applications to be executed from the file system, while *nosuid* prevents set user ID applications from executing. This is an important feature that can be used to prevent misuse of SUID by ordinary systems users. It overrides the *suid* bit on files.

Summary

In this chapter, you have examined how to implement advanced file system repair and integrity checking, and how to configure RAID. Most enterprise systems use RAID to ensure high availability, especially in a shared disk environment.

Backup and Recovery

Software and hardware failures are an unfortunate fact of life in the IT industry, and panic can result when missing or corrupt data is revealed during a peak service period. However, a system crash or a disk failure should not be a cause for alarm: instead, it should be the signal to a well-armed and well-prepared administrator to determine the cause of the problem, rectify any hardware faults, and restore any lost data by using a recovery procedure. This general procedure can be followed regardless of whether user files or database tables have been lost or corrupted.

Fortunately, Solaris provides a wide variety of backup and restore software that can be used in conjunction with any number of media—for example, magnetic and digital audio tapes, writeable CD-ROMs, DVDs, and redundant hard drives. This chapter examines the development and implementation of snapshot, backup and recovery procedures with Solaris and reviews some of the popular backup and recovery freeware and commercial tools.

Key Concepts

The following concepts are required knowledge for implementing efficient backup and recovery services.

Understanding Backups

In many company networks, valuable data is stored on Solaris server systems in user files and database tables. The variety of information stored is endless: personnel files, supplier invoices, receipts, and all kinds of intellectual property. In addition, many organizations provide some kind of service that relies on server uptime and information availability to generate income or maintain prestige. For example, if a major business-to-consumer Web site like *Amazon.com* or business-to-business hub like *Office.com* experiences downtime, every minute that the system is unavailable costs money in lost sales, frustrated consumers, and reduced customer confidence. On the other hand, a government site such as the Government Accountability Office (**http://www.gao.gov/**) provides valuable advice to government, business, and consumers, and is expected to be available continuously. The reputation of online service providers can suffer greatly if servers go down. It is not enough, however, to ensure that a service is highly available; the data it provides also needs to be valid, which is why regular data backup needs to occur.

On a smaller scale, but just as significant, is a department server, which might provide file serving, authentication services, and print access for several hundred PC systems or Sun Rays. If the server hard disk crashes, the affected users who can't read their mail or retrieve their files are going to be inconvenienced if system data cannot be restored in a timely fashion.

This chapter examines the background and rationale for providing a reliable backup and restore service that will ensure a high level of service provision, even in the event of hardware failure.

Analyzing Backup Requirements

The first requirement of a backup service is the ability to restore a dysfunctional system to a functional state as quickly as possible. The relationship between time of restoration and user satisfaction is inverse, as shown in Figure 17-1: the longer a restore takes, the angrier users will become, while the rapid restoration of service will give users confidence. For this reason, many sites take incremental backups of their complete file systems each night but may take a weekly "full dump" snapshot that can be used to rapidly rebuild an entire system from a single tape or disk.

The second requirement for a backup service is data integrity: it is not sufficient just to restore some data and hope that it's close enough to the original. It is essential that all restored data actually be usable by applications as if no break in service had occurred. This is particularly important for database applications that may have several kinds of files associated with them. Table indices, data files, and rollback segments must all be

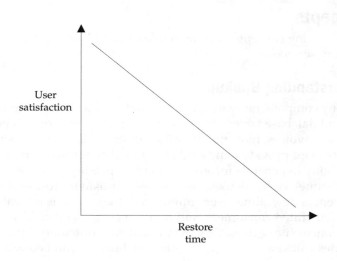

FIGURE 17-1
The relationship between time to restore and user satisfaction

User
satisfaction

Restore
time

synchronized if the database is to operate correctly, and user data must be consistent with the internal structure and table ownership rights. If files are simply backed up onto disk while the database is open, these files can be restored, but the database system may not be able to use them.

It is essential that you understand the restoration and data integrity requirements for all key applications on your system and identify any risks to service provision associated with data corruption. Thus, a comprehensive backup and restore plan should include provision for regular cold and warm dumps of databases to a file system that is regularly backed up.

A third requirement for a backup and restore service is flexibility: data should be recorded and compressed on media that can potentially be read on a different machine, using a different operating system. In addition, using alternative media for concurrent backups is also useful for ensuring availability in case of hardware failure of a backup device. For example, you may use a CD-ROM as your main backup device for nightly incremental backups, but you may also decide to use a DDS-3 DAT tape drive to create a full dump of the database on a weekly basis. If your server is affected by a power surge, the DAT drive is damaged, and a replacement will take one week to arrive, you can use the CD-ROM dump as a fallback, even though it may not be completely up-to-date.

Determining a Backup Strategy

Typical backup and restore strategies employ three related methods for recording data to any medium:

- Full dumps
- Incremental dumps
- Snapshots

A full dump involves taking a copy of an entire file system, or set of file systems, and copying it to a backup medium. Historically, large file systems take a long time to back up because of slow tape speeds and poor I/O performance, which can be improved by using the incremental method.

An incremental dump is an iterative method that involves taking a baseline dump on a regular basis (usually once every week) and then taking another dump of only those files that have changed since the previous full dump. Although this approach may require the maintenance of complex lists of files and file sizes, it reduces the overall time to back up a file system because, on most file systems, only a small proportion of the total number of files changes from week to week. This reduces the overall load on the backup server and improves tape performance by minimizing friction on drive heads. However, using incremental backups can increase the time to restore a system, as up to seven (one for each day of the week) backup tapes must be processed to restore data files fully. Seven tapes are required so that a single tape can be assigned to each day. Therefore, using incremental dumps enables you to strike a balance between convenience and the requirement for a speedy restore in the event of an emergency. Many sites use a combination of incremental and full daily dumps on multiple media to ensure that full restores can be performed rapidly and to ensure redundant recording of key data.

A snapshot is a very fast way to store recovery metadata for a UNIX File System (UFS) on a raw device or within an existing file system. Every time a change is made to data or metadata on the "snapped" file system, the original data is copied to the snapshot copy before the modification is processed. This means that if you overwrite or delete a file accidentally, you can easily retrieve it from the snapshot; so, a snapshot is more like a backup that occurs in real time. A snapshot is incremental, too, because it only occurs when data changes. Using snapshots for retrieval is much faster than going to backup tapes, because the data is stored on a mounted file system. However, as you can appreciate, if your disk contents change frequently, then a large amount of online storage is required to implement snapshotting.

After deciding on an incremental or full dump backup strategy, and appropriate use of snapshots, you need to plan how backups can be integrated into an existing network. There are four possible configurations that can be considered: The simplest approach is to attach a single backup device to each server so that the server acts as its own backup host:

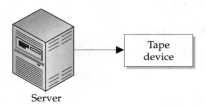

This approach is appealing because it allows data to be backed up and restored using the same device, without any requirement for network connectivity. However, this architecture has poor scaling capacity and does not provide for redundancy through the use of multiple backup devices. This can be rectified by including multiple backup devices for a single host:

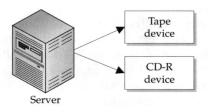

The cost of maintaining single or multiple backup devices for each server in an organization can be expensive. To reduce cost, many organizations centralize the management and storage of data for entire departments or sites on a single server. This approach is shown in Figure 17-2.

FIGURE 17-2
Centralized backup
server with multiple
storage devices

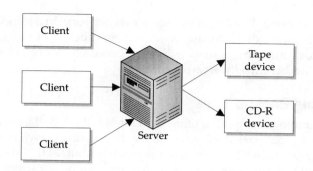

In this configuration, multiple client machines' hard drives are backed up to a central Solaris server, which can also be attached to multiple backup devices to provide various levels of redundancy for more- or less-significant data. For example, data from user PCs may not require the double or triple redundancy that financial records need. The freeware software product AMANDA, reviewed later in this chapter, is ideal for backing up multiple clients through a single server.

In recent years, storage area networks (SANs) have been employed to solve wide area storage problems. In a SAN, backup management and data storage is distributed across multiple backup hosts and devices. Thus, a client's data could potentially be stored on many different backup servers, and management of that data could be performed from a remote manager running on the client. This configuration is shown in Figure 17-3.

For example, a VERITAS client for Windows called Backup Exec can connect to many different Solaris servers through a Server Message Block (SMB), backing up data to multiple mediums. Other server-side packages, such as Legato NetWorker, offer distributed management of all backup services. Both products are reviewed later in this chapter. New to the game are Sun's Java-based Jiro and Jini technologies, which implement the proposed Federated Management Architecture (FMA) standard. FMA is a proposal

FIGURE 17-3
Distributed storage
and management
of backup services

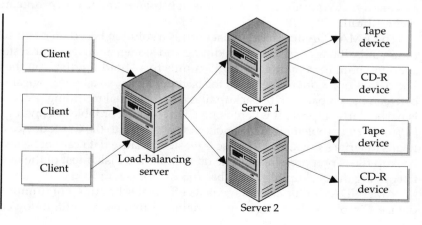

for implementing distributed storage across networks in a standard way, and it is receiving support from major hardware manufacturers such as Hitachi, Quantum, VERITAS, and Fujitsu for future integration with their products. More information on Jiro and FMA can be found at **http://www.jiro.com/**.

Selecting Backup Tools

If you want to use anything other than the standard UNIX backup tools, many freeware and commercial packages are available, depending on what facilities you require. For example, the AMANDA freeware program centralizes the storage and control for backup and restore of remote machines. However, it does not support distributed storage, in which the two commercial vendors, VERITAS Software and Legato Systems, specialize. VERITAS Software and Legato Systems are far and away the leading vendors in the automated enterprise-wide backup and restore application arena, since they provide failover and clustering capabilities along with backup and restore.

AMANDA

AMANDA, the Advanced Maryland Automatic Network Disk Archiver, is a backup system that follows the scheme of using a centralized backup server for multiple clients, shown previously in Figure 17-2. It can back up client drives from any operating system that supports SMB, including Solaris, Linux, and Windows NT clients. Although AMANDA was designed to operate with a single tape drive, it can be configured to use multiple tape drives and other backup devices.

One advantage of AMANDA over other backup systems is that it provides management of native Solaris backup and restore commands; this means that AMANDA backup files are `tar` files that can be manually extracted and viewed without using the AMANDA system if it is not available for some reason. This is particularly significant for full dumps that must be restored to a "green fields" server that does not yet have AMANDA installed. AMANDA can be downloaded from **http://www.amanda.org**, and answers to questions are available at **http://amanda.sourceforge.net/fom-serve/ cache/1.html**.

The AMANDA approach to backups is a solution based on `cron` scheduling of `tar` commands: It has an efficient scheduling and storage management system that involves spooling both incremental and full dumps to a "holding disk" on the backup server. The data is not written directly to the backup device, so a better logical separation exists between the preparation of backup files and the actual recording process. This separation is particularly important when using CD-R (CD-recordable) technology, because of the *buffer overrun* problem: If data is not made available to the CD-R device quickly enough, it fails to write a track, and the disc is wasted because data cannot be rewritten to it. If the backup file is prepared in advance on the holding disk, most of the overhead involved in copying the backup file to the backup device is removed.

AMANDA's other advantage is its efficient scheduling of dumps to the backup device. Simply performing an incremental dump each night, followed by a Sunday night full dump, is wasteful because only a few files may have changed on the server. While this approach is standard among many backup programs, AMANDA introduces the concept of a *dump cycle*, which minimizes the total number of dumps performed by estimating the time taken to dump any particular file. It attempts to balance total backup times across different days, based on past performance of a particular device.

While this feature is efficient, it may seem initially confusing to many administrators. Unfortunately, it is not possible to set up AMANDA in the traditional way, whereby a full dump is performed on weekends and incremental dumps are performed each weeknight, and this may be inappropriate for organizations that have a strict policy regarding backup scheduling. In addition, AMANDA has a further limitation in that it cannot back up a file system that is larger than the size of a single backup medium; for large disks (18GB and larger), AMANDA may be used only with the latest Digital Audio Tapes (DATs) and Digital Linear Tapes (DLTs), and not with quarter-inch cartridge (QIC) tapes or CD-R technology. While small drives and partitions can be backed up using these devices, it is obviously a limitation for organizations with large data-handling requirements.

Legato NetWorker

Legato's NetWorker storage management product is a commercial product that is often supplied with database server packages like Oracle. It is similar to AMANDA in that it prefers centralized over distributed control of all backup resources, in contrast to the VERITAS product, which is reviewed next. However, unlike AMANDA, multiple backup servers can exist as long as they are controlled by a central backup server. This approach was outlined in Figure 17-3. NetWorker is well known for its ability to back up data from and restore data to different clients, even those running different operating systems. This feature can be useful, for example, when you're upgrading client operating systems migrating from Linux to Solaris, because a complete reinstall of user packages and files is not necessary; they can be simply retrieved from a central NetWorker server.

To make it easy for Windows and other PC users to integrate neatly within an enterprise server environment, Legato also supplies a Windows NT client, which is shown in Figure 17-4.

For more information about Legato products, visit **http://www.legato.com/**.

VERITAS NetBackup

While AMANDA is focused on a single backup server that provides services to many clients, VERITAS provides a distributed backup management system, known as NetBackup, which can be used to process terabytes of data from many different clients across many different backup servers and multiple devices. This is similar to the approach outlined in Figure 17-3 and is aimed at maximizing the utilization of existing resources, such as tape drives and CD-R devices, no matter where they are located on a corporate intranet or even across the Internet. In addition, NetBackup provides the greatest amount

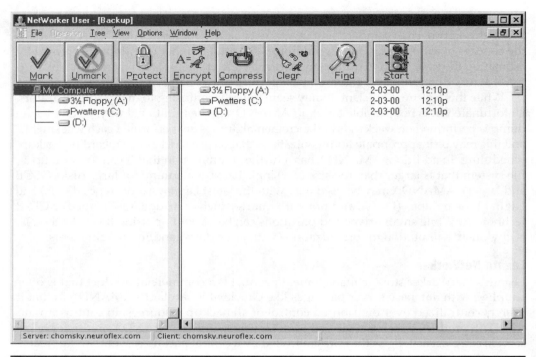

FIGURE 17-4 Legato NetWorker client

of choices for clients, who can seamlessly manage their own backups across multiple hosts and devices.

NetBackup also includes support for many server-side database systems, such as Oracle, dispensing with the need to perform separate warm dumps to backed-up files. NetBackup uses a set of storage rules on the server side to determine how files and data sources of various types are managed. These can be configured remotely by network administrators from any client that has access to the backup servers. VERITAS, like Legato, supplies several clients that make it easier for PC clients to operate within a larger storage management framework.

Backup Exec is the VERITAS Windows NT client that can be used to back up local files to a remote server running NetBackup. Figure 17-5 shows the easy-to-use interface for the Backup Exec client.

Similar to RAID, backup devices can be used concurrently to store data from different clients transparently through multiplexing; there is a logical separation between the client and what storage may be optimal with respect to the particular strengths and weaknesses of any one server. In addition, load can be balanced much more evenly across backup devices without concern for the capacity of any one particular drive. Thus, unlike AMANDA, it is easy to back up a single large partition using NetBackup.

Further information about NetBackup can be found at **http://www.veritas.com/**.

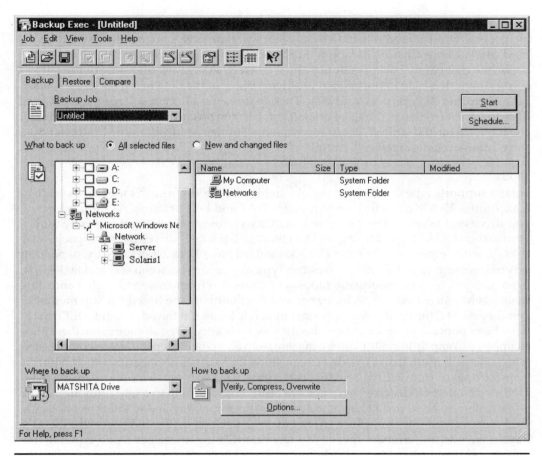

FIGURE 17-5   VERITAS Backup Exec client

Procedures

The following procedures should be followed to perform backup and restore operations.

Selecting a Backup Medium

When selecting a backup medium, you should always attempt to best meet the requirements of rapid restoration, data integrity, and flexibility. The following are the four main media currently in use:

- Tapes
- Disk drives
- CD writing and rewriting technologies (CD-R and CD-RW)
- DVD writing and rewriting technologies (DVD-R and DVD-RW)

Capacity and reliability criteria must also be considered: for example, while tapes are generally considered reliable for bulk storage, tape drives are much slower than a hard drive. However, a 20GB tape is much cheaper than an equivalent-capacity hard drive; the cost of any backup solution must be weighed against the value of the data being stored. It is also important to consider the size of the data being backed up, and how often data changes on a hard disk. These parameters affect how large the tapes need to be to store incremental dumps. For more information on choosing a bulk storage device, see the FAQ for the USENET forum comp.arch.storage at **http://alumni.caltech.edu/ ~rdv/comp-arch-storage/FAQ-1.html**.

Tapes

Solaris supports tape drives from the old archive QIC 150 1/4-inch tape drives (with a maximum 250MB capacity), up to modern DAT and DLT systems. A QIC is a low-end drive that takes a two-reel cassette; QICs were used widely in many early Sun workstations. DAT tapes for Digital Data Storage 2 (DDS-2) drives have a capacity of 4 to 8GB, while tapes for the newer DDS-3 standard have 12 to 24GB capacity, depending on compression ratios. DDS-2 drives can typically record between 400 and 800 KBps, again depending on compression ratios. The transition from analog to digital encoding methods has increased the performance and reliability of tape-based backup methods, and they are still the most commonly used methods today. On the other hand, DLT drives have been popular in the enterprise because of their very large storage capacities: for example, a Compaq 1624 DLT drive can store from 35 to 70GB, depending on compression, which is much more than DAT drives can store. DLT drives also feature much higher transfer rates of from 1.25 to 2.5 Mbps. Of course, DLT drives are more expensive than DAT drives, and DAT drives have always been more costly than a QIC, although a QIC is generally much too small to be useful for most systems today. Today's new technologies, such as Advanced Intelligent Tape (AIT), Linear Tape-Open (LTO), and SuperDLT (SDLT), have capacities and transfer speeds of a few hundred gigabytes per tape—equal to the performance and capacities of the hard disks used ten years ago.

Hard Drives

Because hard drives have the fastest seek times of all backup media, they are often used to store archives of user files that are copied from client drives using an SMB protocol service. In addition, hard drives form the basis of RAID systems. Thus, an array of RAID drives can work together as a single, logical storage device, collectively acting as a single storage system that can withstand the loss of one or more of its constituent devices. For example, if a single drive is damaged by a power surge, depending on the level of RAID protection, your system may be able to continue its functions with a minimum of administrator interference, with no impact on functionality, until the drive is replaced.

Many systems now support hot swapping of drives, so that the faulty drive can be removed and replaced, with the new drive coming seamlessly online. You may be wondering, in the days of RAID, why would anybody consider still using backups: the answer is that entire RAID arrays are just as vulnerable to power surges as a single drive, so in the event of a full hardware failure, all of your data could still be lost unless it is stored safely offsite on a tape or CD-ROM. To circumvent concurrent drive corruption at the end of a disk's life, many administrators use drives of equivalent capacities from different manufacturers, some new and some used, in a RAID array. This ensures that drives are least likely to fail concurrently.

RAID Levels 0 and 1 are most commonly used. RAID Level 0 involves parallelizing data transfer between disks, spreading data across multiple drives, thereby improving overall data transmission rates. This technique is known as *striping*. However, while RAID Level 0 can write multiple disks concurrently, it does not support redundancy, which is provided with RAID Level 1. This level makes an identical copy of a primary disk onto a secondary disk. This kind of *mirroring* provides complete redundancy: if the primary disk fails, the secondary disk is able to provide all data contained on the primary disk. Because striping and mirroring consume large amounts of disk space, they are costly to maintain per megabyte of actual data. Thus, higher RAID levels attempt to use heuristic techniques to provide similar functionality to the lower RAID levels, while reducing the overall cost. For example, RAID Level 4 stores parity information on a single drive, which reduces the overall amount of disk space required but is more risky than RAID Level 1.

Software RAID solutions typically support both striping and mirroring. This speeds up data writing and makes provisions for automating the transfer of control from the primary disk to the secondary disk in the event of a primary disk failure. In addition, many software solutions support different RAID levels on different partitions on a disk, which may also be useful in reducing the overall amount of disk space required to store data safely. For example, while users might require access to a fast partition using RAID Level 0, another partition may be dedicated to a financial database that requires mirroring (thus RAID Level 1). Sun's DiskSuite product is currently one of the most popular software RAID solutions.

Alternatively, custom hardware RAID solutions are also proving popular, because of the minimal administrative overhead involved with installing and configuring such systems. While not exactly "plug and play," external RAID arrays such as the StorEdge A1000 include many individual disks that can be used to support both mirroring and striping, with data transfer rates of up to 40 Mbps. In addition, banks of fast-caching memory (up to 80MB) speed up disk writes by temporarily storing them in RAM before writing them to one or more disks in the array. This makes the RAID solution not only safe but significantly faster than a normal disk drive.

CD-R, CD-RW, DVD-R, and DVD-RW

CD writing and rewriting devices are rapidly gaining momentum as desktop backup systems that are cheap, fast, and, in the case of CD-RW, reusable. CD-R and CD-RW devices are reviewed in Chapter 14. These devices serve two distinct purposes in backup systems: while CD-RW discs are useful for day-to-day backup operations because they can be reused, CD-R technology is more useful for archiving and auditing purposes. For example, many organizations outsource their development projects to third-party contractors; in such a case, it is useful for both the contractor and the client to have an archival copy of what has been developed, in case there is some later disagreement concerning developmental goals and milestones. On the other hand, contracts involved with government organizations may require regular snapshots to satisfy auditing requirements. Since CD-R is a write-once, read-only technology, it is best suited to this purpose. CD-R is wasteful as a normal backup medium, because CD-Rs can be used only once. CD-RWs can be rewritten hundreds of times, with more than 600MB of storage capacity.

DVD-R and DVD-RW are now replacing CD-R and CD-RW as the main distribution and backup media, respectively, for Solaris. These discs have approximately 4.7GB capacity in a single-layer drive, and more than 9GB in a dual-layer drive. While originally intended for storing video data, DVD-R and DVD-RW can now store any type of data.

Backup and Restore

Backup and restore software falls into three categories:

- Standard Solaris tools like `tar`, `dd`, `cpio`, `ufsdump`, and `ufsrestore`. These tools are quite adequate for backing up single machines with multiple backup devices.

- Centralized backup tools like AMANDA and Legato NetWorker, which are useful for backing up multiple machines through a single backup server.

- Distributed backup tools like VERITAS NetBackup, which are capable of remotely managing storage for multiple machines.

This section examines the standard Solaris backup and restore tools that are generally used for single machines with one or two backup devices. In addition, these tools are often useful for normal users to manage their own accounts on the server. For example, users can create tape archives using the `tar` command, whose output can be written to a single disk file. This is a standard way of distributing source trees in the Solaris and broader UNIX community. Users can also make copies of disks and tapes using the `dd` command. It is also possible to back up database files in combination with standard Solaris tools. For example, Oracle server is supplied with an `exp` utility, which can be used to archive the database while it is still running:

```
exp system/manager FULL=Y
```

Here, *system* is the username for an administrator with DBA privileges, and *manager* is the password. This will create a file called *expat.dmp*, which can then be scheduled to be backed up every night using a `cron` job, like so:

```
0 3 * * * exp system/manager FULL=Y
```

Some sites take full data dumps every night, which involves transferring an entire file to a backup medium. This produces a small amount of system overhead if the archive is only a few megabytes in size, but for a database with a tablespace of 50GB, this would place a great strain on a backup server, especially if it is being used for other purposes. Thus, it might be more appropriate to take an incremental dump that records only data that has changed. Incremental dumps will be discussed later in the "Using ufsdump and ufsrestore" section.

Using tar

The `tar` ("tape archive") command is used to create a tape archive or to extract the files contained on a tape archive. Although `tar` was originally conceived with a tape device in mind, any device can hold a `tar` file, including a normal disk file system. This is why many users have adopted `tar` as their standard archiving utility, even though it does not perform compression like the Zip tools for PCs. Tape archives are easy to transport between systems using FTP or secure copy in binary transfer mode, and they are the standard means of exchanging data between Solaris systems.

As an example, the following script creates a `tar` file of the */opt/totalnet* package. First, it checks the potential size of the tape archive by using the `du` command:

```
$ cd /opt/totalnet
$ du
4395     ./bin
367      ./lib/charset
744      ./lib/drv
434      ./lib/pcbin
777      ./lib/tds
5731     ./lib
5373     ./sbin
145      ./man/man1
135      ./man/man1m
281      ./man
53       ./docs/images
56       ./docs
15837    .
```

The estimated size of the archive is therefore 15,387 blocks. This could also have been achieved by using the command `du -s`, which just computes the size, without printing details of directory sizes. To create a tape archive in the */tmp* directory for the whole package, including subdirectories, you would execute the following command:

```
# tar cvf /tmp/totalnet.tar *
a bin/ 0K
a bin/atattr 54K
a bin/atconvert 58K
a bin/atkprobe 27K
```

```
a bin/csr.tn 6K
a bin/ddpinfo 10K
a bin/desk 17K
a bin/ipxprobe 35K
a bin/m2u 4K
a bin/maccp 3K
a bin/macfsck 3K
a bin/macmd 3K
a bin/macmv 3K
a bin/macrd 3K
a bin/macrm 3K
a bin/nbmessage 141K
a bin/nbq 33K
a bin/nbucheck 8K
a bin/ncget 65K
a bin/ncprint 66K
a bin/ncput 65K
a bin/nctime 32K
a bin/nwmessage 239K
a bin/nwq 26K
a bin/pfinfo 70K
a bin/ruattr 122K
a bin/rucopy 129K
a bin/rudel 121K
a bin/rudir 121K
a bin/ruhelp 9K
a bin/u2m 4K
a bin/rumd 120K
a bin/rumessage 192K
a bin/ruprint 124K
a bin/rurd 120K
a bin/ruren 121K
...
```

To extract the `tar` file's contents to disks, execute the following command:

```
# cd /tmp
 # tar xvf totalnet.tar
x bin, 0 bytes, 0 tape blocks
x bin/atattr, 54676 bytes, 107 tape blocks
x bin/atconvert, 58972 bytes, 116 tape blocks
x bin/atkprobe, 27524 bytes, 54 tape blocks
x bin/csr.tn, 5422 bytes, 11 tape blocks
x bin/ddpinfo, 9800 bytes, 20 tape blocks
x bin/desk, 16456 bytes, 33 tape blocks
x bin/ipxprobe, 35284 bytes, 69 tape blocks
x bin/m2u, 3125 bytes, 7 tape blocks
x bin/maccp, 2882 bytes, 6 tape blocks
```

```
x bin/macfsck, 2592 bytes, 6 tape blocks
x bin/macmd, 2255 bytes, 5 tape blocks
x bin/macmv, 2866 bytes, 6 tape blocks
x bin/macrd, 2633 bytes, 6 tape blocks
x bin/macrm, 2509 bytes, 5 tape blocks
x bin/nbmessage, 143796 bytes, 281 tape blocks
x bin/nbq, 33068 bytes, 65 tape blocks
x bin/nbucheck, 7572 bytes, 15 tape blocks
x bin/ncget, 66532 bytes, 130 tape blocks
x bin/ncprint, 67204 bytes, 132 tape blocks
x bin/ncput, 65868 bytes, 129 tape blocks
x bin/nctime, 32596 bytes, 64 tape blocks
x bin/nwmessage, 244076 bytes, 477 tape blocks
x bin/nwq, 26076 bytes, 51 tape blocks
x bin/pfinfo, 71192 bytes, 140 tape blocks
x bin/ruattr, 123988 bytes, 243 tape blocks
x bin/rucopy, 131636 bytes, 258 tape blocks
x bin/rudel, 122940 bytes, 241 tape blocks
x bin/rudir, 123220 bytes, 241 tape blocks
x bin/ruhelp, 8356 bytes, 17 tape blocks
x bin/u2m, 3140 bytes, 7 tape blocks
x bin/rumd, 122572 bytes, 240 tape blocks
x bin/rumessage, 195772 bytes, 383 tape blocks
x bin/ruprint, 126532 bytes, 248 tape blocks
x bin/rurd, 122572 bytes, 240 tape blocks
x bin/ruren, 123484 bytes, 242 tape blocks
...
```

Tape archives are not compressed by default in Solaris. However, they could be compressed with the normal Solaris `compress` utility:

```
$ compress file.tar
```

This will create a compressed file called *file.tar.Z*. Alternatively, the GNU `gzip` utility often achieves better compression ratios than a standard `compress`, so it should be downloaded and installed. When executed, the `gzip` command creates a file call *file.tar.gz*:

```
$ gzip file.tar
```

Although Solaris does come with `tar` installed, it is advisable to download, compile, and install GNU `tar`, because of the increased functionality that it includes with respect to compression. For example, to create a compressed tape archive *file.tar.gz*, use the z flag in addition to the normal `cvf` flags:

```
$ tar zcvf file.tar *
```

Using cpio

cpio is used for copying file archives and is much more flexible than tar, because a cpio archive can span multiple volumes. cpio can be used in three different modes:

- **Copy in mode (cpio –i)**   Extracts files from standard input, from a stream created by cat or similar
- **Copy out mode (cpio –o)**   Obtains a list of files from standard input and creates an archive from these files, including their path name
- **Copy pass mode (cpio –p)**   Equivalent to copy out mode, except that no archive is actually created

The basic idea behind using cpio for archiving is to generate a list of files to be archived, print it to standard output, and then pipe it through cpio in copy out mode. For example, to archive all the text files in your home directory and store them in an archive called *myarchive* in the */staff/pwatters* directory, you would use this command:

```
$ find . -name '*.txt' -print | cpio -oc > \
  /staff/pwatters/myarchive
```

Recording headers in ASCII is portable and is achieved by using the *–c* option. When the command completes, the number of blocks required to store the files is reported:

```
8048 blocks
```

The files themselves are stored in text format with an identifying header, which you can examine with cat or head:

```
$ head myarchive
0707010009298a00008180000011fc0000005400000001380bb9b600001e9b0
0000055000000000000000000000000000000000001f00000003Directory/file.
txtThe quick brown fox jumps over the lazy dog.
```

Since recording headers in ASCII is portable, files can actually be extracted from the archive by using the cat command:

```
$ cat myarchive | cpio -icd "*"
```

This extracts all files and directories as required (specified by using the *–d* option). It is just as easy to extract a single file. To extract *Directory/file.txt*, you use this command:

```
$ cat myarchive | cpio -ic "Directory/file.txt"
```

If you are copying files directly to tape, it is important that you use the same blocking factor when you retrieve or copy files from the tape to the hard disk that you used when you copied files from the hard disk to the tape. If you use the defaults, there should be no problems, although you can specify a particular blocking factor by using the –B directive.

Using dd

The dd program copies raw disk or tape slices block-by-block to other disk or tape slices; it is like cp for slices. It is often used for backing up disk slices to other disk slices and/or to a tape drive, and for copying tapes. To use dd, you must specify an input file, *if*, an output file, *of*, and a block size. For example, to copy the root partition (/) on */dev/rdsk/c1t0d0s0* to */dev/rdsk/c1t4d0s0*, you can use this command:

```
# dd if=/dev/rdsk/c1t0d0s0 of=/dev/rdsk/c1t4d0s0 bs=128k
```

To make the new partition bootable, you also need to use the installboot command after dd. Another use for dd is to back up tape data from one tape to another tape. This is particularly useful for re-creating archival backup tapes that may be aging. For example, to copy from tape drive 0 (*/devrmt/0*) to tape drive 2 (*/dev/rmt/2*), use this command:

```
# dd if=/dev/rmt/0h  of=/dev/rmt/1h
```

It is also possible to copy the contents of a floppy drive by redirecting the contents of the floppy disk and piping it through dd:

```
# dd < /floppy/floppy0 > /tmp/floppy.disk
```

Taking a Snapshot

The Solaris command for taking snapshots is fssnap. The following example shows a snapshot stored in the "backing-store" of */snap* for the / file system:

```
# fssnap -o backing-store=/snap /
/dev/fssnap/0
```

The path to the backing-store can be a local file system, or even one remotely mounted over NFS to a RAID file system, providing high availability and large amounts of storage for remote systems on a central server. The preceding operation can be repeated for each of the file systems you want to snap, as shown next for the */export* file system:

```
# fssnap -o backing-store=/snap /export
/dev/fssnap/1
```

To examine the status of the snapshot, you can use the enquiry mode of fssnap:

```
# fssnap -i /
Snapshot number              : 0
Block Device                 : /dev/fssnap/0
```

```
Raw Device                      : /dev/rfssnap/0
Mount point                     : /
Device state                    : idle
Backing store path              : /snap/snapshot0
Backing store size              : 4096 KB
Maximum backing store size      : Unlimited
Snapshot create time            : Wed Jun 30 12:05:02 2004
Copy-on-write granularity       : 64 KB
```

If you don't have access to a RAID system for storing snapshots, you can always archive them using a normal ufsdump backup, as shown next for the / file system snapshot:

```
# ufsdump 0cu /dev/rmt/0 'fssnap -F ufs -o raw,bs=/snap,unlink /dev/rdsk/c0t0d0s0'
```

Examples

The following examples show how to perform backup and restore operations.

Using ufsdump and ufsrestore

ufsdump and ufsrestore are standard backup and restore applications for UNIX file systems. ufsdump is often set to run from cron jobs late at night to minimize load on server systems. ufsrestore is normally run in single-user mode after a system crash. ufsdump can be run on a mounted file system; however, it may be wise to unmount it first, perform a file system check (using fsck), remount it, and then perform the backup.

The key concept in planning ufsdumps is the dump level of any particular backup. The dump level determines whether ufsdump performs a full or incremental dump. A full dump is represented by a dump level of 0, while the numbers 1 through 9 can be arbitrarily assigned to incremental dump levels. The only restriction on the assignment of dump level numbers for incremental backups is their numerical relationship to each other: a high number should be used for normal daily incremental dumps, followed once a week by a lower number that specifies that the process should be restarted. This approach uses the same set of tapes for all files, regardless of which day they were recorded on. For example, Monday through Saturday would have a dump level of 9, while Sunday would have a dump level of 1. After cycling through incremental backups during the weekdays and Saturday, the process starts again on Sunday.

Some organizations like to separate each day's archive in a single tape. This makes it easier to recover work from an incremental dump, where speed is important, and/or whether or not backups from a particular day need to be retrieved. For example, one user may want to retrieve a version of a file that was edited on a Wednesday and the following Thursday, but want only the version prior to the latest (Wednesday). The Wednesday tape can then be used in conjunction with ufsdump to retrieve the file. A weekly full dump is scheduled to occur on Sunday, when few people are using the system. Thus,

Sunday would have a dump level of 0, followed by Monday, Tuesday, Wednesday, Thursday, and Friday with dump levels of 5, 6, 7, 8, and 9, respectively. To signal the end of a backup cycle, Saturday then has a lower dump level than Monday, which could be 1, 2, 3, or 4.

Prior to beginning a ufsdump, it is often useful to estimate the size of a dump to determine how many storage tapes will be required. This estimate can be obtained by dividing the size of the partition by the capacity of the tape. For example, to determine how many tapes would be required to back up the */dev/rdsk/c0t0d0s4* file system, use this:

```
# ufsdump S /dev/rdsk/c0t0d0s4
50765536
```

The approximately 49MB on the drive will therefore easily fit onto a QIC, DAT, or DLT tape. To perform a full dump of an *x86* partition (*/dev/rdsk/e0d0s0*) at Level 0, you can use the following approach:

```
# ufsdump 0cu /dev/rmt/0 /dev/rdsk/c0d0s0
  DUMP: Writing 63 Kilobyte records
  DUMP: Date of this level 0 dump: Mon Feb 03 13:26:33 1997
  DUMP: Date of last level 0 dump: the epoch
  DUMP: Dumping /dev/rdsk/c0d0s0 (solaris:/) to /dev/rmt/0.
  DUMP: Mapping (Pass I) [regular files]
  DUMP: Mapping (Pass II) [directories]
  DUMP: Estimated 46998 blocks (22.95MB).
  DUMP: Dumping (Pass III) [directories]
  DUMP: Dumping (Pass IV) [regular files]
  DUMP: 46996 blocks (22.95MB) on 1 volume at 1167 KB/sec
  DUMP: DUMP IS DONE
  DUMP: Level 0 dump on Mon Feb 03 13:26:33 1997
```

The parameters passed to ufsdump include *0* (dump level), *c* (cartridge: blocking factor 126), and *u* (updates the dump record */etc/dumpdates*). The dump record is used by ufsdump and ufsrestore to track the last dump of each individual file system:

```
# cat /etc/dumpdates
/dev/rdsk/c0t0d0s0          0 Wed Feb  2 20:23:31 2000
/dev/md/rdsk/d0            0 Tue Feb  1 20:23:31 2000
/dev/md/rdsk/d2            0 Tue Feb  1 22:19:19 2000
/dev/md/rdsk/d3            0 Wed Feb  2 22:55:16 2000
/dev/rdsk/c0t0d0s3          0 Wed Feb  2 20:29:21 2000
/dev/md/rdsk/d1            0 Wed Feb  2 21:20:04 2000
/dev/rdsk/c0t0d0s4          0 Wed Feb  2 20:24:56 2000
/dev/rdsk/c2t3d0s2          0 Wed Feb  2 20:57:34 2000
/dev/rdsk/c0t2d0s3          0 Wed Feb  2 20:32:00 2000
/dev/rdsk/c1t1d0s0          0 Wed Feb  2 21:46:23 2000
```

PART IV

```
/dev/rdsk/c0t0d0s0                    3 Fri Feb  4 01:10:03 2000
/dev/rdsk/c0t0d0s3                    3 Fri Feb  4 01:10:12 2000
```

ufsdump is flexible because it can be used in conjunction with rsh (remote-shell) and remote access authorization files (*.rhosts* and */etc/hosts.equiv*) to log on remotely to another server and dump the files to one of the remote server's backup devices. However, the problem with this approach is that using *.rhosts* leaves the host system vulnerable to attack: if an intruder gains access to the client, he can remotely log onto a remote backup server without a username and password. The severity of the issue is compounded by the fact that a backup server that serves many clients has access to most of those clients' information in the form of tape archives. Thus, a concerted attack on a single client, leading to an unchallenged remote logon to a backup server, can greatly expose an organization's data. The problems associated with remote access and authorization are covered in depth in Chapter 16; however, a secure shell (SSH) tool can be used to overcome the need to use the remote commands. By combining ssh and ufsdump, you can create a full dump of a file system from a client, transfer it securely to the backup server, and then copy it to the backup server's remote devices:

```
# ufsdump 0f - / | ssh server "dd of=/dev/rmt/0 bs=24b conv=sync"
```

A handy trick often used by administrators is to use ufsdump to move directories across file systems. A ufsdump is taken of a particular file system, which is then piped through ufsrestore to a different destination directory. For example, to move existing staff files to a larger file system, use these commands:

```
# mkdir /newstaff
# cd /staff
# ufsdump 0f - /dev/rdsk/c0t0d0s2 | (cd /newstaff; ufsrestore xf -)
```

Users of ufsdump should be aware of the buffer overflow vulnerability that exists in some versions of ufsdump supplied with Solaris 2.6 and Solaris 7. This vulnerability permits rogue local users to obtain root access under some conditions. A patch is available from SunSolve (**http://sunsolve.sun.com/**), and a full explanation of the problem can be found at the SecurityFocus Web site, **http://www.securityfocus.com/bid/680**.

After backing up data using ufsdump, it easy to restore the same data using the ufsrestore program. To extract data from a tape volume on */dev/rmt/0*, use this command:

```
# ufsrestore xf /dev/rmt/0
You have not read any volumes yet.
Unless you know which volume your file(s) are on you should start
with the last volume and work towards the first.
Specify next volume #: 1
set owner/mode for '.'? [yn] y
```

ufsrestore then extracts all the files on that volume. However, you can also list the table of contents of the volume to standard output, if you are not sure of the contents of a particular tape:

```
# ufsrestore tf /dev/rmt/0
1          ./openwin/devdata/profiles
2          ./openwin/devdata
3          ./openwin
9          ./lp/alerts
1          ./lp/classes
15         ./lp/fd
1          ./lp/forms
1          ./lp/interfaces
1          ./lp/printers
1          ./lp/pwheels
36         ./lp
2          ./dmi/ciagent
3          ./dmi/conf
6          ./dmi
42         ./snmp/conf
```

Command Reference

The following command can be used to back up and restore Solaris file systems.

ufsrestore

ufsrestore supports an interactive mode, which has online help to assist you in finding the correct volume from which you can restore:

```
# ufsrestore i
ufsrestore > help
Available commands are:
        ls [arg] - list directory
        cd arg - change directory
        pwd - print current directory
        add [arg] - add 'arg' to list of files to be extracted
        delete [arg] - delete 'arg' from list of files to be
            extracted
        extract - extract requested files
        setmodes - set modes of requested directories
        quit - immediately exit program
        what - list dump header information
        verbose - toggle verbose flag (useful with ''ls'')
        help or '?' - print this list
If no 'arg' is supplied, the current directory is used
ufsrestore >
```

PART IV

Summary

In this chapter, you have examined the basic steps and technologies that can be used to back up a system offline. This approach to data integrity ensures that data can be retrieved in the case of catastrophic failure, but online (RAID) approaches may be more suited for mirroring data to protect against hardware failure.

Printer Management

Solaris supports a wide variety of printers, whose details are stored in the *terminfo* database (*/usr/share/lib/terminfo*). Most plaintext and PostScript printers are supported. However, some older SPARC-specific printing hardware, which relied on the proprietary NeWSPrint software, is no longer supported. To install a printer for Solaris correctly, you must verify that a driver exists in the *terminfo* database, as this defines printer interface data.

Key Concepts

This chapter examines printing using the `lp` command, checking printer status with `lpstat`, setting up printer classes, and using `lpadmin` to manage a printer. In addition, it explores supported Solaris printers and the *terminfo* database, configuring name services for printing, setting printer environment variables, and using tools to add and configure printers. Most commands used to manage print services are located in the */usr/lib/lp* and */usr/sbin* directories, while user print commands can be found in */usr/bin*.

You need to keep several important system configurations in mind when you're planning to set up printing services on a Solaris system. First, you must ensure that plenty of disk space is available in the */var* partition, so that print jobs may be spooled in */var/spool* (spool is an acronym for "system peripheral operation offline"). This is particularly important when your system is spooling PostScript print jobs, which may be several megabytes in size. When several PostScript jobs are submitted concurrently, the system will require 10 to 20MB of disk space. Second, you need to ensure that sufficient physical RAM is available; otherwise, spooling will be slowed down by the use of virtual RAM. If you must use virtual RAM for spooling, you need to ensure that enough virtual RAM is available (you can add more by using the `swap` command). In addition, if print jobs are spooling, invest in some fast Small Computer System Interface (SCSI) disks for the */var* partition: 10,000-RPM disks are now available as standard in all new UltraSPARC systems, and these give excellent print spooling performance.

A large set of configuration files for printing is located under the */etc/lp* directory. These files specify how print services are to be executed for all installed printers. The */etc/lp/classes* directory may contain files that define printer classes, while the */etc/lp/fd* directory may contain files that define print filters. A list of these filters is maintained in the file */etc/lp/filter.table*, while locally developed forms are stored in */etc/lp/forms*. Print cartridge data is located under the */etc/lp/pwheels* directory, while configuration data for supported printers is stored in the */etc/lp/printers* directory.

Procedures

The following procedures will enable you to install and configure a printer for Solaris.

Determining Whether a Printer Is Supported

The *terminfo* database is just a set of hierarchical directories that contains files that define communication settings for each printer type. Printers from different vendors are defined in files that sit in a subdirectory whose name is defined by the first letter of the vendor's name. Thus, the directory */usr/share/lib/terminfo* contains the following entries:

```
# ls /usr/share/lib/terminfo
1  3  5  7  9  a  b  d  f  g  h  j  l  m  o  p  r  s  u  w  y
2  4  6  8  A  B  c  e  G  H  i  k  M  n  P  q  S  t  v  x  z
```

For example, if you wanted to see which Epson printers are supported under Solaris 10, you would change to the root directory of the *terminfo* database and then to the subdirectory in which Epson drivers are found (*/usr/share/lib/terminfo/e*). This directory contains drivers for the following printers:

```
$ ls -l
total 80
-rw-r--r--   2 bin     bin        1424 Sep  1  1998 emots
-rw-r--r--   2 bin     bin        1505 Sep  1  1998 env230
-rw-r--r--   2 bin     bin        1505 Sep  1  1998 envision230
-rw-r--r--   1 bin     bin        1717 Sep  1  1998 ep2500+basic
-rw-r--r--   1 bin     bin        1221 Sep  1  1998 ep2500+color
-rw-r--r--   1 bin     bin        1093 Sep  1  1998 ep2500+high
-rw-r--r--   1 bin     bin        1040 Sep  1  1998 ep2500+low
-rw-r--r--   2 bin     bin         971 Sep  1  1998 ep40
-rw-r--r--   2 bin     bin         971 Sep  1  1998 ep4000
-rw-r--r--   2 bin     bin         971 Sep  1  1998 ep4080
-rw-r--r--   2 bin     bin         971 Sep  1  1998 ep48
-rw-r--r--   1 bin     bin        2179 Sep  1  1998 epson2500
-rw-r--r--   1 bin     bin        2200 Sep  1  1998 epson2500-80
-rw-r--r--   1 bin     bin        2237 Sep  1  1998 epson2500-hi
-rw-r--r--   1 bin     bin        2257 Sep  1  1998 epson2500-hi80
-rw-r--r--   2 bin     bin        1209 Sep  1  1998 ergo4000
-rw-r--r--   1 bin     bin        1095 Sep  1  1998 esprit
-rw-r--r--   1 bin     bin         929 Sep  1  1998 ethernet
```

```
-rw-r--r--   1 bin    bin         927 Sep  1  1998 ex3000
-rw-r--r--   2 bin    bin        1053 Sep  1  1998 exidy
-rw-r--r--   2 bin    bin        1053 Sep  1  1998 exidy2500
```

You can see that the Epson 2500, for example, has its settings contained within the file *ep2500+basic*. However, several other versions of the printer driver are available, including *ep2500+color* and *ep2500+high*.

Setting Up Printer Classes

A set of printers can be grouped together to form a *class*. When you set up a printer class, users can specify the class (rather than individual printers) as the destination for a print request. This can be useful, for example, when the printers are located in different buildings, or where the printing load needs to balanced across multiple printers. These class definitions are stored in the directory */etc/lp/classes*.

A file is created for each printer class, with the filename set to the name of the class. The file contains a list of all printers belonging to the class. To add a printer to the class, you can either manually edit the appropriate class file or use the lpadmin command. For example, either of the following commands would add the printer *hp2* to the class *bubblejets*:

```
# cat "hp2" >> /etc/lp/classes/bubblejets
# lpadmin -p hp2 -c bubblejets
```

Examples

The following examples demonstrate how to set up print services for Solaris.

Configuring Print Services

The place to start configuring print services is the configuration of the *printers* entry in the */etc/nsswitch.conf* file, where your local naming service is used to resolve printer names. For example, if you use only file-based naming resolution, the *printers* entry in */etc/nsswitch.conf* file would look like this:

```
printers: files
```

Alternatively, if you use Network Information Service (NIS), the entry would look like this:

```
printers: files nis
```

Finally, if you use NIS+, the entry would contain the following:

```
printers: nisplus files xfn
```

It is also possible that individual users will define printers in the file ~/.*printers*, in which case, the /*etc/nsswitch.conf* printer configuration entry determines the order in which the ~/.*printers* file should be consulted.

For individual users, the environment variables *LPDEST* and *PRINTER* can be set to indicate which printer should be used as the default. For example, the following command sets the default printer for the current user to be the local *hp1* printer:

```
$ PRINTER=hp1; export PRINTER
```

The *LPDEST* environment variable can be set in the same manner:

```
$ LPDEST=hp1; export LPDEST
```

Adding a Local Printer

Next, you need to examine entries within the /*etc/printers.conf* file, which determines, for file-based name resolution, which printers are available to users of the local system. These printers may be connected locally through the parallel port, or they could be mounted remotely by using the Network File System (NFS) or Samba. A typical /*etc/ printers.conf* file looks like this:

```
$ cat /etc/printers.conf
hp1:\
        :bsdaddr=pserver,hp1,Solaris:\
        :description=HP Primary:
hp2:\
        :bsdaddr=pserver,hp2,Solaris:\
        :description=HP Secondary:
_default:\
        :use=hp1:
```

There are two printers defined in the *printers.conf* file: *hp1* (default) and *hp2*. Each entry in the /*etc/printers.conf* file should have its own directory created under the /*etc/lp/ printers* directory. A number of files can exist in this directory for each printer, including the following:

- *alert.sh*   Shell script that responds to alerts
- *alert.var*   Contains alert variables
- *comment*   Name of printer
- *configuration*   Individual printer configuration file
- *users.deny*   List of users who are denied access to the printer
- *users.grant*   List of users who are granted access to the printer

A sample configuration file (*/etc/lp/printers/hp1*) for the printer *hp1* is shown here:

```
Banner: on: always
Content types: PS
Device: /dev/term/a
Interface: /usr/lib/lp/model/standard
Modules: default
Printer type: PS
```

This configuration states that banners are always printed, PostScript and ASCII files are supported, the device */dev/term/a* is used to send print output, and the standard interface (*/usr/lib/lp/model/standard*) will be used with default modules.

Accessing Remote Printers

To access a central print service from a client, you can use the `lpadmin` command to set up an association. To allow local access to a printer called *samuel* on the host *mason*, you would execute the following command from the client:

```
# lpadmin -p samuel -s mason
```

Optionally, you can associate a description with the printer *samuel*:

```
# lpadmin -p samuel -D "epson 2500 on mason"
```

Users on the local system should now be able to obtain status information for the printer *samuel*:

```
# lpstat -p samuel
printer samuel is idle. enabled since Jan 24 14:28 2004. available.
```

Using Forms and Filters

Many businesses deal with form letters as a matter of course. These are predesigned templates for creating bulk copies of letters and other types of forms. Users are responsible for creating their own forms, by defining characteristics such as character size, ink color, page length, and page width. Forms can be set up to support preprinted stationery, in which users insert text within predefined areas. The following form can be used to print a standard two-page financial summary, 48 lines length, and 80 characters in width. The character pitch size is 12, with characters being printed in black Courier.

```
Page length: 48
Page width: 60
Number of pages: 2
```

```
Line pitch: 6
Character pitch: 12
Character set choice: courier
Ribbon color: black
Comment:
Financial summary form
```

If the form is stored in the file */etc/lp/forms/financial.fmd*, then the lpforms command can be used to make the form available for use:

```
# lpforms -f financial -F /etc/lp/forms/financial.fmd
```

To use the form, any existing forms must first be unmounted and any jobs that have been sent to the printer must be rejected. This allows customized stationery to be loaded. Once the form has been loaded into the system, print requests can be accepted once again. The following example shows the command sequence for loading the form *financial.fmd* for the printer *ainsley*, after first unmounting the *bank.fmd* form:

```
# reject ainsley
# lpadmin -p ainsley -M -f bank
# lpadmin -p ainsley -M -f financial
# accept ainsley
```

Print filters extend the concept of a UNIX filter, since output from a print request is piped through a print filter as standard input, to produce a modified version of the original text. Typically, some kind of transposition or interpretation occurs between input and output. Commonly used filters include those that convert *ditroff, dmd, plot*, and *tek* files to PostScript. New filters can be added to the system by using the lpfilter command. For example, if you developed a new image processing system that prepared documents in a format called "fract," a new filter to convert these files to PostScript could be installed by using the following command:

```
# lpfilter -f fract -F /etc/lp/fd/fract.fd
```

You can use the following command to delete this filter when it is no longer required:

```
# lpfilter -f fract -x
```

Command Reference
The following commands can be used to manage Solaris printing.

Solaris Print Manager
The Solaris print manager provides a more sophisticated view of current printer settings by displaying a list of all printers that are known to the local system, as well as their

configuration settings. (There is an equivalent GNOME print manager.) You can set display options for the print manager that make it easy to customize views based on local site preferences. Figure 18-1, for example, shows the default view on a network that has three printers available: *yasimov, henryov,* and *prova.* The entry [Empty] appears next to the icon for each printer because no jobs are currently being processed by any of the printers. The details of print jobs can be minimized for each printer by clicking the minus (–) symbol next to the appropriate icon.

You can open the printer Properties window for each printer defined on the system. For the printer *yasimov,* the current properties are shown in Figure 18-2.

Several key characteristics are noted in the Properties window:

- The icon label, which is usually the name of the printer (*yasimov*)
- The icon set to be used for the printer
- A description of the printer
- The name of the printer queue
- The status of the printer queue
- The name of the printer device
- The status of the printer device

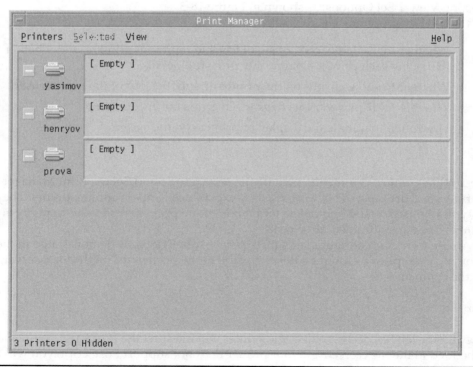

FIGURE 18-1   Viewing configured printers

FIGURE 18-2
Viewing printer
properties for
printer *yasimov*

It is possible to further modify the display of printer sets in print manager by selecting View | Set Options, as shown in Figure 18-3.

The following options are available:

- Whether to use large icons or small icons to represent printers, and whether to display each printer's name only or its full details
- Whether to show all jobs on the printer or only the jobs of the current user
- Whether to display various flags when errors are encountered
- How often to update the display of printers on the system

lp

The `lp` (line printer) commands predate the `admintool` and Solaris Print Manager interfaces and are most likely to be used by experienced Solaris administrators. They are typically used to add and delete local and remote printer entries and to perform a number of other administrative tasks.

After a printer is configured, it's then easy to submit jobs, as demonstrated in the following examples. To submit a PostScript job to the printer *hp1* on the local server, use the command

```
$ lp -d hp1 file.ps
```

After the job has been spooled, the printer will interpret the PostScript commands embedded in the file correctly. If your printer does not support PostScript, you will be printing the embedded PostScript codes and not the rendered document. The *–d* flag is

FIGURE 18-3
Setting print
manager options

used to specify the name of the printer (*hp1*). If a printer is not specified, the job will
be sent to the default printer.

A similar command can be used to spool a text file to the same printer:

```
$ lp file.txt
```

A large number of options can be passed to lp for various purposes. For example,
instead of issuing the lp command 50 times to print 50 copies of a report, you could
use the following command:

```
$ lp -n 50 report.txt
```

Alternatively, if you are printing a large job, you can use the –*m* option to specify
that you want to be notified by e-mail when the job has finished printing:

```
$ lp -m bigjob.ps
```

As an alternative to lp, you can use the POSIX style of printing to submit jobs. This
involves specifying both the print server and printer name, rather than just the printer
name. This ensures that no conflict exists between printers of the same name that are
attached to different hosts. For example, the server *admin* could have a printer called
hp1, as could the server *finance*: if you pass –*d hp1* on the command line with lp, which
printer would be selected for your job? To make sure the correct printer is used, you
need to specify both the server and printer on the command line.

For the host *admin*, here is the PostScript example again, this time using the POSIX-
compliant format:

```
$ lpr -P admin:hp1 file.ps
```

If you want to print to the *hp1* server attached to the server *finance*, you could use the following command instead:

```
$ lpr -P finance:hp1 file.ps
```

cancel

A print job can be easily cancelled by using the `cancel` command and passing the job's ID to the command. For example, to cancel the job *hp1-212*, you would use the following command:

```
# cancel hp1-212
```

lpadmin

`lpadmin` is a printing administration utility that is used to add and configure printers. Adding a printer or modifying its operating characteristics is usually performed with a number of `lpadmin` commands.

To set a printer name and port, use the following command:

```
# lpadmin -p hp2 -v /dev/null
```

This command sets the port to */dev/null* for the printer *hp2*.

To specify the printer software type to be used, use the following command:

```
# lpadmin -p hp2 -m netstandard
```

This command would force the *hp2* printer to use the netstandard printing software.

To set the protocol and timeout parameters, use the following command:

```
# lpadmin -p hp2 -o dest=montana:hp2 -o protocol=tcp -o timeout=5
```

This command specifies that *hp2* (being mounted from the server *montana*) would use the TCP protocol and would have a timeout of 5 seconds.

If the *hp2* printer is no longer attached to the system, its data could be removed with the following command:

```
# lpadmin -x hp2
```

If a printer is temporarily unavailable due to maintenance, you can use the `reject` command to prevent new jobs being sent to a local printer. In the following example, the *hp2* printer is temporarily removed from access:

```
# reject hp2
```

The `disable` command is used to stop all print jobs from proceeding. Thus, to disable all print jobs on the printer *hp2*, use the following command:

```
# disable hp2
```

To add a more meaningful description to a printer entry, you can include an optional description string. For example, to add the description "HP printer on montana" to the *hp2* printer, you would use the following command:

```
# lpadmin -p hp2 -D "HP printer on montana"
```

By default, a banner page is printed when using the `lp` print commands. To disable the banner page from printing, perhaps to conserve paper, you can set the *nobanner* option. For example, to set the *nobanner* option on *hp2*, you would use this command:

```
# lpadmin -p hp2 -o nobanner=never
```

Alternatively, to make banner printing optional on *hp2*, use the following command:

```
# lpadmin -p hp2 -o nobanner=optional
```

If you want to refer to a remote printer as if it were a locally attached printer, you can do so by using `lpadmin`. In the following example, the server *montana* has the printer *wyoming* attached, so you can add it using this command:

```
# lpadmin -p wyoming -s montana
```

lpstat

The `lpstat` command can be used to verify that a printer is available for printing. The following example verifies whether the printer *wyoming* is available for printing:

```
$ lpstat -D -p wyoming
printer wyoming is idle. enabled since Dec 07 17:23 2001. available.
```

The `lpstat` command returns a description of any error conditions that exist for the printer. For example, if there is a paper misfeed in the printer, the following error message will be displayed:

```
# lpstat -D -p wyoming
printer wyoming faulted. enabled since Dec 07 17:23 2001. available.
unable to print: paper misfeed jam
```

Summary

In this chapter, you have examined how to configure print services for a Solaris system. The Solaris Print Manager provides a convenient alternative to traditional command-line printer setup.

Pseudo File Systems and Virtual Memory

While file systems are designed to store files, they can also be used for a number of related purposes, such as storing the process tree or allowing virtual memory to be created from disk blocks; or they can be used in a process file system. This chapter examines these two novel applications of file systems.

Key Concepts

The following concepts are required knowledge for installing pseudo file systems and virtual memory.

Pseudo File Systems

A pseudo file system is a file system that is literally a file system but has a different purpose than just storing files. One of the core pseudo file systems used in Solaris is the process file system (PROCFS), which is mounted on /proc. Most modern operating systems have a process model. However, Solaris implements some of its own special features of processes, as described in this section. The PROCFS is one of the most innovative characteristics of processes in Solaris. The state of all normal threads and processes is stored on the PROCFS. Each entry in the top-level file system corresponds to a specific process ID (PID), under which a number of subdirectories contain all state details. Applications and system services can communicate with the PROCFS as if it were a normal file system. Thus, state persistence can be provided by using the same mechanism as normal file storage. Images of all currently active processes are stored in the /proc file system by their PID.

The internals of the PROCFS can seem a little complicated; fortunately, Solaris provides a number of tools to work with the /proc file system. Here's an example of how process state is persisted on the PROCFS. First, a process is identified, which in this example is the current Korn shell (ksh) for the user *pwatters* through a normal process list display:

```
# ps -eaf | grep pwatters
 pwatters 310    291  0   Mar 20 ?          0:04 /usr/openwin/bin/Xsun
 pwatters 11959 11934  0 09:21:42 pts/1    0:00 grep pwatters
 pwatters 11934 11932  1 09:20:50 pts/1    0:00 ksh
```

Now that you have a target PID (11934), you can change to the */proc/11934* directory and view the image of this process:

```
# cd /proc/11934
# ls -l
total 3497
-rw-------   1 pwatters     other      1769472 Mar 30 09:20 as
-r--------   1 pwatters     other          152 Mar 30 09:20 auxv
-r--------   1 pwatters     other           32 Mar 30 09:20 cred
--w-------   1 pwatters     other            0 Mar 30 09:20 ctl
lr-x------   1 pwatters     other            0 Mar 30 09:20 cwd ->
dr-x------   2 pwatters     other         1184 Mar 30 09:20 fd
-r--r--r--   1 pwatters     other          120 Mar 30 09:20 lpsinfo
-r--------   1 pwatters     other          912 Mar 30 09:20 lstatus
-r--r--r--   1 pwatters     other          536 Mar 30 09:20 lusage
dr-xr-xr-x   3 pwatters     other           48 Mar 30 09:20 lwp
-r--------   1 pwatters     other         2016 Mar 30 09:20 map
dr-x------   2 pwatters     other          544 Mar 30 09:20 object
-r--------   1 pwatters     other         2552 Mar 30 09:20 pagedata
-r--r--r--   1 pwatters     other          336 Mar 30 09:20 psinfo
-r--------   1 pwatters     other         2016 Mar 30 09:20 rmap
lr-x------   1 pwatters     other            0 Mar 30 09:20 root ->
-r--------   1 pwatters     other         1440 Mar 30 09:20 sigact
-r--------   1 pwatters     other         1232 Mar 30 09:20 status
-r--r--r--   1 pwatters     other          256 Mar 30 09:20 usage
-r--------   1 pwatters     other            0 Mar 30 09:20 watch
-r--------   1 pwatters     other         3192 Mar 30 09:20 xmap
```

Each of the directories with the name associated with the PID contains additional subdirectories that contain state information and related control functions. For example, the *status* file contains entries that refer to a structure that defines state elements, including the following:

- Process flags
- Process ID
- Parent process ID
- Process group ID
- Session ID

- Thread ID
- Process pending signal set
- Process heap virtual address
- Process stack size
- User and system CPU time
- Total child process user and system CPU time
- Fault traces

The process flag definitions contained in the structure define specific process state characteristics, including:

- **PR_ISSYS**   System process flag
- **PR_VFORKP**   Vforked child parent flag
- **PR_FORK**   Inherit-on-fork flag
- **PR_RLC**   Run-on-last-close flag
- **PR_KLC**   Kill-on-last-close flag
- **PR_ASYNC**   Asynchronous-stop flag
- **PR_MSACCT**   Microstate accounting on flag
- **PR_MSFORK**   Post-fork microstate accounting inheritance flag
- **PR_BPTADJ**   Breakpoint on flag
- **PR_PTRACE**   Ptrace-compatibility on flag

In addition, a watchpoint facility is provided, which is responsible for controlling memory access. A series of *proc* tools interprets the information contained in the */proc* subdirectories, which display the characteristics of each process.

Procedures

The following procedures allow you to work with pseudo file systems under Solaris.

proc Tools

The *proc* tools are designed to operate on data contained within the */proc* file system. Each utility takes a PID as its argument and performs operations associated with the PID. For example, the `pflags` command prints the flags and data model details for the PID in question. For the preceding Korn shell example, you can easily print out this status information:

```
# /usr/proc/bin/pflags 29081
29081:   /bin/ksh
```

```
            data model = _ILP32   flags = PR_ORPHAN
   /1:      flags = PR_PCINVAL|PR_ASLEEP [ waitid(0x7,0x0,0x804714c,0x7) ]
```

You can also print the credential information for this process, including the effective and real UID and group ID (GID) of the process owner, by using the `pcred` command:

```
# /usr/proc/bin/pcred 29081
29081:  e/r/suid=100  e/r/sgid=10
```

Here, both the effective and the real UID is 100 (user *pwatters*), and the effective and real GID is 10 (group *staff*).

To examine the address space map of the target process, you can use the `pmap` command:

```
# /usr/proc/bin/pmap 29081
29081:  /bin/ksh
08046000       8K read/write/exec       [ stack ]
08048000     160K read/exec             /usr/bin/ksh
08070000       8K read/write/exec       /usr/bin/ksh
08072000      28K read/write/exec       [ heap ]
DFAB4000      16K read/exec             /usr/lib/locale/en_AU/en_AU.so.2
DFAB8000       8K read/write/exec       /usr/lib/locale/en_AU/en_AU.so.2
DFABB000       4K read/write/exec       [ anon ]
DFABD000      12K read/exec             /usr/lib/libmp.so.2
DFAC0000       4K read/write/exec       /usr/lib/libmp.so.2
DFAC4000     552K read/exec             /usr/lib/libc.so.1
DFB4E000      24K read/write/exec       /usr/lib/libc.so.1
DFB54000       8K read/write/exec       [ anon ]
DFB57000     444K read/exec             /usr/lib/libnsl.so.1
DFBC6000      20K read/write/exec       /usr/lib/libnsl.so.1
DFBCB000      32K read/write/exec       [ anon ]
DFBD4000      32K read/exec             /usr/lib/libsocket.so.1
DFBDC000       8K read/write/exec       /usr/lib/libsocket.so.1
DFBDF000       4K read/exec             /usr/lib/libdl.so.1
DFBE1000       4K read/write/exec       [ anon ]
DFBE3000     100K read/exec             /usr/lib/ld.so.1
DFBFC000      12K read/write/exec       /usr/lib/ld.so.1
 total      1488K
```

It's always surprising to see how many libraries are loaded when an application is executed, especially something as complicated as a shell, leading to a total of 1,488KB memory used in the preceding example. You can use the `pldd` command to obtain a list of the dynamic libraries linked to each process:

```
# /usr/proc/bin/pldd 29081
29081:  /bin/ksh
```

```
/usr/lib/libsocket.so.1
/usr/lib/libnsl.so.1
/usr/lib/libc.so.1
/usr/lib/libdl.so.1
/usr/lib/libmp.so.2
/usr/lib/locale/en_AU/en_AU.so.2
```

Signals are the way in which processes communicate with each other, and can also be used from shells to communicate with spawned processes (usually to suspend or kill them). However, by using the psig command, it is possible to list the signals associated with each process:

```
# /usr/proc/bin/psig 29081
29081:   /bin/ksh
HUP      caught   RESTART
INT      caught   RESTART
QUIT     ignored
ILL      caught   RESTART
TRAP     caught   RESTART
ABRT     caught   RESTART
EMT      caught   RESTART
FPE      caught   RESTART
KILL     default
BUS      caught   RESTART
SEGV     default
SYS      caught   RESTART
PIPE     caught   RESTART
ALRM     caught   RESTART
TERM     ignored
USR1     caught   RESTART
USR2     caught   RESTART
CLD      default  NOCLDSTOP
PWR      default
WINCH    default
URG      default
POLL     default
STOP     default
TSTP     ignored
CONT     default
TTIN     ignored
TTOU     ignored
VTALRM   default
PROF     default
XCPU     caught   RESTART
XFSZ     ignored
WAITING  default
LWP      default
```

```
FREEZE    default
THAW      default
CANCEL    default
LOST      default
RTMIN     default
RTMIN+1 default
RTMIN+2 default
RTMIN+3 default
RTMAX-3 default
RTMAX-2 default
RTMAX-1 default
RTMAX     default
```

It is also possible to print a hexadecimal format stack trace for the lightweight processes (LWPs) in each process by using the pstack command. This can be useful in the same way that the truss command was used:

```
# /usr/proc/bin/pstack 29081
29081:   /bin/ksh
 dfaf5347 waitid    (7, 0, 804714c, 7)
 dfb0d9db _waitpid (ffffffff, 8047224, 4) + 63
 dfb40617 waitpid  (ffffffff, 8047224, 4) + 1f
 0805b792 job_wait (719d) + 1ae
 08064be8 sh_exec  (8077270, 14) + af0
 0805e3a1 ???????? ()
 0805decd main     (1, 8047624, 804762c) + 705
  0804fa78 ???????? ()
```

Perhaps the most commonly used *proc* tool is the pfiles command, which displays all of the open files for each process. This may be useful for determining operational dependencies between data files and applications, but is limited because the filenames are not listed:

```
# /usr/proc/bin/pfiles 29081
29081:   /bin/ksh
  Current rlimit: 64 file descriptors
    0: S_IFCHR mode:0620 dev:102,0 ino:319009 uid:6049 gid:7 rdev:24,8
       O_RDWR|O_LARGEFILE
    1: S_IFCHR mode:0620 dev:102,0 ino:319009 uid:6049 gid:7 rdev:24,8
       O_RDWR|O_LARGEFILE
    2: S_IFCHR mode:0620 dev:102,0 ino:319009 uid:6049 gid:7 rdev:24,8
       O_RDWR|O_LARGEFILE
   63: S_IFREG mode:0600 dev:174,2 ino:990890 uid:6049 gid:1 size:3210
       O_RDWR|O_APPEND|O_LARGEFILE FD_CLOEXEC
```

In addition, you can obtain the current working directory of the target process by using the pwdx command:

```
# /usr/proc/bin/pwdx 29081
29081:   /home/paul
```

If you need to examine the process tree for all parent and child processes containing the target PID, you can do so by using the ptree command. This is very useful for determining dependencies between processes that are not apparent by consulting the process list:

```
# /usr/proc/bin/ptree 29081
247   /usr/dt/bin/dtlogin -daemon
  28950 /usr/dt/bin/dtlogin -daemon
    28972 /bin/ksh /usr/dt/bin/Xsession
      29012 /usr/dt/bin/sdt_shell -c        unset DT;      DISPLAY=lion:0;
        29015 ksh -c        unset DT;      DISPLAY=lion:0;
/usr/dt/bin/dt
          29026 /usr/dt/bin/dtsession
            29032 dtwm
              29079 /usr/dt/bin/dtterm
                29081 /bin/ksh
                  29085 /usr/local/bin/bash
                    29230 /usr/proc/bin/ptree 29081
```

Here, ptree has been executed from the Bourne Again Shell (bash), which was started from the Korn shell (ksh), which was spawned from the dtterm terminal window, which was spawned from the dtwm window manager, and so on.

Although many of these *proc* tools may seem obscure, they are often very useful when you are trying to debug process-related application errors, especially in large applications like database management systems.

Virtual Memory

The swap command is used to add virtual RAM to a system. Virtual RAM is typically used to provide memory for process execution when physical memory has been exhausted. Disk blocks are used to simulate physical memory locations using an interface that is invisible to the user. Thus, users never need to be concerned about the type of RAM that their process is addressing.

While virtual memory allows a system's effective capacity to be increased to many times its physical capacity, it is much slower than physical RAM. When a system experiences peak demands for memory, causing virtual memory to be used, the CPU must work harder to support virtual memory operations. Coupled with the relatively slow speed of disk writing, this has a significant impact on performance. When virtual memory is being used, and many new memory access calls are made along with normal file reading and writing, so-called "disk thrashing" can occur, since the number of disk operations requested far exceeds the capacity of the disk to read and write. If disk thrashing is a common occurrence, then you should install extra physical RAM in the system or tune the file system with `tunefs`.

It is important to note that virtual memory should generally be added to the system at twice the physical RAM installed. Thus, for a 256MB system, 512MB of virtual memory should be initialized. To add virtual memory, you should use the `mkfile` command to create an empty file of the required size. For example, to create two swap files with 4,097,072KB each, you would use the following commands:

```
# mkfile 4097072k /u1/swap
# mkfile 4097072k /u2/swap
```

Next, you must use the `swap` command to add the file into the pool of available disk space. For example, if you create two swap files on different file systems for redundancy (such as */u1/swap* and */u2/swap*), you can use the following commands to add them to the swap space pool:

```
# swap -a /u1/swap
# swap -a /u2/swap
```

To verify that the swap file has been correctly added to the pool, use the following command:

```
# swap -l
swapfile              dev  swaplo blocks    free
/dev/dsk/c0t0d0s1    118,17      16 8194144 6240336
/dev/dsk/c3t4d0s1    118,1       16 8194144 6236384
```

In this example, you can see that the partitions *c0t0d0s1* and *c3t4d0s1* have 8,194,144 blocks each allocated for swap, and have 6,240,336 and 6,236,384 free blocks, respectively.

A summary of the swap space can also be printed by using the `swap –s` command:

```
# /usr/sbin/swap -s
total: 2360832k bytes allocated + 130312k reserved = 2491144k used,
7238792k available
```

In this example, you can see that 2,360,832KB has been allocated, while 130,312KB has been reserved.

If you have a dedicated slice set aside for swap, then you can simply pass the block device name on the command line:

```
# swap -a /dev/dsk/c1t1d2s1
```

To ensure that this partition is added as swap during boot, enter the following into the */etc/vfstab* file:

```
#device              device     mount    FS     fsck   mount    mount
#to mount            to fsck    point    type   pass   atboot   ops
/dev/dsk/c1t1d2s1    -          -        swap   -      no       -
```

To remove a file (or device) from the swap pool, you need to pass the *–d* option on the command line. Thus, to remove */u1/swap* and */dev/dsk/c1t1d2s1* from the swap pool, you would use the following commands:

```
# swap -d /u1/swap
# swap -d /dev/dsk/c1t1d2s1
```

You could then safely delete the file */u1/swap* and safely use the slice */dev/dsk/c1t1d2s1* for other purposes, as long as the */etc/vfstab* entries have been deleted.

An issue that commonly arises when swap partitions are enabled on production systems is whether or not swap space should be created on a mirrored partition (i.e., RAID level 1). Mirroring ensures that when data is written to a partition on one disk it is also copied in full to a sister partition on another drive. This ensures that if data on the first drive is destroyed, it can be recovered automatically from the mirrored volume.

Creating swap files on mirrored partitions ensures that virtual memory cannot be corrupted by a disk failure. Thus, if a disk containing virtual memory for a production system is corrupted while executing a critical application, such as a database server, then the correct data will automatically be read from the mirrored volume if corruption is detected. However, since RAID mirroring requires that all data written to the source volume also be written immediately afterward to the mirrored volume, this can significantly slow down effective write speeds for the entire system, since data must be written twice.

Summary

In this chapter, you have examined some novel uses of file systems—for storing process trees and simulating memory. Since file systems are generic persistence devices, they can be used in many different ways and not just for storing user and system files.

System Logging, Accounting, and Tuning

A well-managed system needs to be continuously monitored for security, accounting, and performance purposes. Solaris 10 provides several built-in mechanisms for accounting for resource usage, which you can then further use with an automated billing procedure. This is very useful for Internet service providers and shared-use systems that must account for the resources utilized by users or groups. In addition, you can easily detect inappropriate usage of resources by unauthorized individuals, and you can limit utilization by enforcing quotas.

Key Concepts

The following sections examine how to enable system logging, monitoring, and accounting.

System Logging

syslog is a centralized logging facility that provides different classes of events that are logged to a logfile. syslog also provides an alerting service for certain events. Because syslogd is configurable by root, it is very flexible in its operations. Multiple logfiles can exist for each daemon whose activity is being logged, or a single logfile can be created. The syslog service is controlled by the configuration file */etc/syslog.conf*, which is read at boot time, or whenever the syslog daemon receives a HUP signal. This file defines the facility levels or system source of logged messages and conditions. Priority levels are also assigned to system events recorded in the system log, while an action field defines what action is taken when a particular class of event is encountered. These events can range from normal system usage, such as FTP connections and remote shells, to system crashes.

The source facilities defined by Solaris are for the kernel (*kern*), authentication (*auth*), daemons (*daemon*), mail system (*mail*), print spooling (*lp*), user processes (*user*), and many others. Priority levels are classified as system emergencies (*emerg*), errors requiring immediate attention (*attn*), critical errors (*crit*), messages (*info*), debugging output (*debug*), and other errors (*err*). These priority levels are defined for individual systems and architectures in *<sys/syslog.h>*. It is easy to see how logging applications, such as TCP wrappers, can take advantage of the different error levels and source facilities provided by syslogd.

On the Solaris platform, the syslog daemon depends on the *m4* macro processor being present. *m4* is typically installed with the software developer packages and is usually located in */usr/ccs/bin/m4*. This version has been installed by default since Solaris 2.4. Note that the syslogd supplied by Sun has been error-prone in previous releases. With early Solaris 2.*x* versions, the syslog daemon left behind zombie processes when alerting logged-in users (e.g., notifying root of an *emerg*). If syslogd does not work, check that *m4* exists and is in the path for root, and/or run the syslogd program interactively by invoking it with a –*d* parameter. *m4* is discussed in detail in Chapter 27.

Quotas

Resource management is one of the key responsibilities of an administrator, particularly where the availability of a service is the organization's primary source of income (or recognition). For example, if an application server requires 10MB of free disk space for internal caching of objects retrieved from a database, performance on the client side will suffer if this space is not available (for example, because a user decided to dump his collection of MP3 music files onto the system hard drive). If external users cannot access a service because of internal resource allocation problems, they are unlikely to continue using your service. There is also a possibility that a rogue user (or competitor) may attempt to disrupt your service by attempting any number of well-known exploits to reduce your provision of service to clients. The "Implementing Quotas" section examines resource management strategies that are flexible enough to meet the needs of casual users yet restrictive enough to limit the potential for accidental or malicious resource misuse.

System Accounting

Solaris provides a centralized auditing service known as *system accounting.* This service is very useful for accounting for the various tasks that your system may be involved in— you can use it to monitor resource usage, troubleshoot system failures, isolate bottlenecks in the system, and assist in system security. In addition, system accounting acts as a real accounting service, and you can use it for billing in the commercial world. The "Collecting Accounting Data" section reviews the major components of system accounting, including several applications and scripts that are responsible for preparing daily reports on connections, process, and disk loads, and usage statements for users. Once you enable the appropriate script in */etc/init.d*, system accounting does not typically involve administrator intervention.

Performance

Measuring performance is a necessary task to determine whether current utilization levels require a system to be upgraded and whether user applications and system services are executing as quickly and efficiently as possible. Solaris provides a wide variety of tools to tune and monitor the operation of individual devices and core system elements, and other tools that can be applied to improve performance. These tools work with the kernel, disk, memory, network, compilers, applications, and system services. This chapter examines how to use some of the standard Solaris tools to monitor performance, identify performance issues and bottlenecks, and implement new settings.

NOTE   *An alternative to using the tools provided with Solaris is to use the SymbEL tools developed by Adrian Cockroft and Richard Pettit (**http://www.sun.com/sun-on-net/ performance/se3**), which are fully described in their book,* Sun Performance and Tuning, *published by Sun Microsystems Press (1998).*

Procedures

The following procedures are commonly used to manage logfiles, quotas, and accounting.

Examining Logfiles

Logfiles are fairly straightforward in their contents, and you can stipulate what events are recorded by placing instructions in the *syslog.conf* file. Records of mail messages can be useful for billing purposes and for detecting the bulk sending of unsolicited commercial e-mail (spam). The system log records the details supplied by `sendmail`: a message-id, when a message is sent or received, a destination, and a delivery result, which is typically "delivered" or "deferred." Connections are usually deferred when a connection to a site is down. `sendmail` usually tries to redeliver failed deliveries in four-hour intervals.

When using TCP wrappers, connections to supported Internet daemons are also logged. For example, an FTP connection to a server will result in the connection time and date being recorded, along with the hostname of the client. A similar result is achieved for Telnet connections.

A delivered mail message is recorded as

```
Feb 20 14:07:05 server sendmail[238]: AA00238: message-id=
 <bulk.11403.19990219175554@sun.com>
Feb 20 14:07:05 server sendmail[238]: AA00238: from=<sun-developers-1@sun.com>,
size=1551, class=0, received from gateway.site.com (172.16.1.1)
Feb 20 14:07:06 server sendmail[243]: AA00238: to=<pwatters@mail.site.com>,
 delay=00:00:01, stat=Sent, mailer=local
```

whereas a deferred mail message is recorded differently:

```
Feb 21 07:11:10 server sendmail[855]: AA00855: message
-id=<Pine.SOL.3.96.990220200723.5291A-100000@oracle.com>
Feb 21 07:11:10 server sendmail[855]: AA00855: from=<support@oracle.com>,
 size=1290, class=0, received from gateway.site.com (172.16.1.1)
Feb 21 07:12:25 server sendmail[857]: AA00855: to=pwatters@mail.site.com,
```

PART IV

```
delay=00:01:16, stat=Deferred: Connection timed out during user open with
mail.site.com, mailer=TCP
```

An FTP connection is recorded in a single line,

```
Feb 20 14:35:00 server in.ftpd[277]: connect from workstation.site.com
```

in the same way that a Telnet connection is recorded:

```
Feb 20 14:35:31 server in.telnetd[279]: connect from workstation.site.com
```

Implementing Quotas

Solaris provides a number of tools to enforce policies on disk and resource usage, based around the idea of *quotas*, or a prespecified allocation of disk space for each user and file system. Thus, a single user can have disk space allocated on different slices, and file systems can have quotas either enabled or disabled (they are disabled by default). Although many organizations disable disk quotas for fear of reducing productivity by placing unnecessary restrictions on the development staff, there are often some very good reasons for implementing quotas on specific slices. For example, if an open file area, like an anonymous FTP "incoming" directory, is located on the same partition as normal user data, a denial of service (DoS) attack could be initiated by a rogue user who decides to fill the incoming directory with large files, until all free space is consumed. A CGI application that writes data to a user's home directory (for example, a guestbook) can also fall victim to a DoS attack: a malicious script could be written to enter a million fake entries into the address book, thereby filling the partition to capacity. The result in both of these cases is loss of service and loss of system control. It is therefore important that networked systems have appropriate checks and balances in place to ensure that such situations are avoided.

Quotas are also critical to ensure fair resource sharing among developers. Otherwise, a developer who decides to back up her PC drive to her home directory on a server, completely filling the partition, could thereby prevent other users from writing data.

In addition to security concerns, enforcing quotas is also optimal from an administrative point of view: it forces users to rationalize their own storage requirements, so that material that is not being used can be moved offline or deleted. This saves administrators from having to make such decisions for users (who may be dismayed at the results if the administrator has to move things in a hurry!).

One simple policy is to enforce disk quotas on all public file systems that have network access. Increasing quotas for all users is easy, therefore the policy can be flexible. In addition, quotas can be hard or soft: *hard* quotas strictly enforce incursions into unallocated territory, whereas *soft* quotas provide a buffer for temporary violations of a quota, and the users are given warning before enforcement begins. Depending on the security level at which your organization operates (for example, C2 standards for military organizations), a quota policy may already be available for you to implement.

A total limit on the amount of disk space available to users can be specified using quotas for each user individually. Consider the user *pwatters* on *server* as an example.

You may allot this user, a Java developer, a quota of 10MB for development work on the */staff* file system. To set up this quota, you need to undertake the following steps:

1. Edit the */etc/vfstab* file as root, and add the `rq` flag to the *mount* options field for the */staff* file system. This enables quotas for the file system.
2. Change the directory to */staff*, and create a file called *quotas*.
3. Set permissions on */staff/quotas* to be read and write for root only.
4. Edit user quotas for user *pwatters* on file system */staff* by using the `edquota` command, and entering the number of inodes and 1KB blocks that will be available to user *pwatters*. For example, enter the following:

   ```
   # fs /staff blocks (soft = 10000, hard = 11000) inodes (soft = 0, hard = 0)
   ```

5. Check the settings that you have created by using the `quota` command.
6. Enable the quota for user *pwatters* by using the `quotaon` command.

You can implement these steps by entering the following:

```
# vi /etc/vfstab
# cd /staff
# touch quotas
# chmod u+rw quotas
# edquota pwatters
# quota -v pwatters
# quotaon /staff
```

When you verify the quotas using `quota -v`,

```
# quota -v pwatters
```

the output should look like the following:

```
Disk quotas for pwatters (uid 1001):
Filesystem      usage  quota  limit    timeleft  files  quota
/staff             0  10000  11000           0      0      0
```

Note that there may be a bug on the Intel version, since this command may hang indefinitely, but no problems have been reported on SPARC. You can see that a soft limit of 10MB and a hard limit of 11MB was entered for user *pwatters*. If halfway through the development project this user requests more space, you could adjust the quota by using the `edquota` command again. To check quotas for all users, use the `repquota` command:

```
# repquota /staff
```

```
Block limits
```

```
User            used    soft     hard
jsmith     --    2048    4096     8192
pwatters   --     131   10000    20000
qjones     --   65536   90000   100000
llee       --    4096    8192    10000
```

Again, there may be a bug on the Intel version, but no problems have been reported on SPARC. If a user attempts to exceed their quota during an interactive session, unless you've set up a warning to be issued under those circumstances, the first indication that the user will have often comes in the form of a "file system full" or "write failed" message. After checking the amount of free space on the partition where their home disk is located, many users are at a loss to explain why they can no longer edit files or send e-mail.

Collecting Accounting Data

Collecting data for accounting is simple: create a startup script (*/etc/rc2.d/S22acct*) to begin collecting data soon after the system enters multiuser mode and, optionally, create a kill script (*/etc/rc0.d/K22acct*) to turn off data collection cleanly before the system shuts down. When accounting is enabled, details of processes, storage, and user activity are recorded in specially created logfiles, which are then processed daily by the */usr/lib/acct/runacct* program. The output from runacct is also processed by */usr/lib/acct/prdaily*, which generates the reports described in the next section. There is also a separate monthly billing program called */usr/lib/acct/monacct*, which is executed monthly and generates accounts for individual users.

Collecting Performance Data

The following applications are commonly used to measure system performance:

iostat	Collects data about input/output operations for CPUs, disks, terminals, and tapes from the command line
vmstat	Collects data on virtual memory performance from the command line and prints a summary
mpstat	Breaks down CPU usage per operation type
sar	Runs through cron or the command line to collect statistics on disk, tape, CPU, buffering, input/output, system calls, interprocess communication, and many other variables

The following sections examine how each of these commands is used.

iostat

The kernel maintains low-level counters to measure various operations, which you can access by using iostat. When you first execute it, iostat reports statistics gathered since booting. Subsequently, the difference between the first report and the current state is reported for all statistics. Thus, when you run it at regular intervals (such as each minute), you can obtain high-resolution samples for establishing system performance within a specific epoch by using iostat. This can be very useful for gaining an accurate picture of how system resources are allocated.

To display disk usage statistics, the following command produces ten reports over epochs of 60 seconds:

```
# iostat -x 60 10
device r/s w/s kr/s kw/s wait actv svc_ t %w %b
sd0    0.2 0.4 12.2 9.0  1.0  2.0  38.6   0  1
...
device r/s w/s kr/s kw/s wait actv svc_t %w %b
sd0    0.3 0.3 12.5 8.0  2.0  1.0  33.2   0  1
...
```

The following describes what each column indicates for the disk device:

device	Shows the device name (*sd1* indicates a disk)
r/s	Displays the number of disk reads per second
w/s	Prints the number of disk writes per second
kr/s	Shows the total amount of data read per second (in kilobytes)
kw/s	Displays the total amount of data written per second (in kilobytes)
wait	Prints the mean number of waiting transactions
actv	Shows the mean number of transactions being processed
svc_t	Displays the mean period for service in milliseconds
%w	Prints the percentage of time spent waiting
%b	Shows the percentage of time that the disk is working

To display statistics for the CPU at one-second intervals 20 times, you could use the following command:

```
# iostat -c 1 20
```

The output would display four columns, showing user time, system time, I/O wait, and idle time, respectively, in percentage terms.

vmstat

One of the greatest performance issues in system tuning is virtual memory capacity and performance. Obviously, if your server is using large amounts of swap, running off a slow disk, the time required to perform various operations will increase. One application that reports on the current state of virtual memory is the vmstat command, which displays a large collection of statistics concerning virtual memory performance. As you can see from the following display, the virtual memory report on the server is not encouraging: 1,346,736,431 total address translation faults were recorded, as well as 38,736,546 major faults, 1,346,736,431 minor faults, and 332,163,181 copy-on-write faults. This suggests that more virtual memory is required to support operations or that, at least, the disk on which the swap partition is placed should be upgraded to 10,000 RPM.

```
# vmstat -s
        253 swap ins
    237 swap outs
    253 pages swapped in
 705684 pages swapped out
1346736431 total address trans. faults taken
 56389345 page ins
 23909231 page outs
152308597 pages paged in
 83982504 pages paged out
 26682276 total reclaims
 26199677 reclaims from free list
        0 micro (hat) faults
1346736431 minor (as) faults
 38736546 major faults
332163181 copy-on-write faults
316702360 zero fill page faults
 99616426 pages examined by the clock daemon
      782 revolutions of the clock hand
126834545 pages freed by the clock daemon
 14771875 forks
  3824010 vforks
 29303326 execs
160142153 cpu context switches
2072002374 device interrupts
3735561061 traps
2081699655 system calls
1167634213 total name lookups (cache hits 70%)
 46612294 toolong
964665958 user    cpu
399229996 system cpu
1343911025 idle    cpu
227505892 wait    cpu
```

mpstat

Another factor influencing performance is the system load—obviously, a system that runs a large number of processes and consistently has a load of greater than 1.0 cannot be relied upon to give adequate performance in times of need. You can use the mpstat command to examine a number of system parameters, including the system load, over a number of regular intervals. Many administrators take several hundred samples using `mpstat` and compute an average system load for specific times of the day when a peak load is expected (e.g., at 9 A.M.). This can greatly assist in capacity planning of CPUs to support expanding operations. Fortunately, SPARC hardware architectures support large numbers of CPUs, so it's not difficult to scale up to meet demand.

The output from `mpstat` contains several columns, which measure the following parameters:

- Context switches
- Cross-calls between CPUs
- Idle percentage of CPU time
- Interrupts
- Minor and major faults
- Sys percentage of CPU time
- Thread migrations
- User percentage of CPU time

For the server output shown next, the proportion of system time consumed is well below 100 percent—the peak value is 57 percent for only one of the CPUs in this dual-processor system. Sustained values of *sys* at or near the 100-percent level indicate that you should add more CPUs to the system:

```
# mpstat 5
CPU minf mjf xcal intr ithr  csw icsw migr smtx  srw syscl  usr sys  wt idl
  0   46   1  250   39  260  162   94   35  104    0    75   31  14   8  47
  1   45   1   84  100  139  140   92   35  102    0    14   35  13   7  45
CPU minf mjf xcal intr ithr  csw icsw migr smtx  srw syscl  usr sys  wt idl
  0  141   3  397  591  448  539  233   38  111    0 26914   64  35   1   0
  1  119   0 1136  426  136  390  165   40  132    0 21371   67  33   0   0
CPU minf mjf xcal intr ithr  csw icsw migr smtx  srw syscl  usr sys  wt idl
  0    0   0  317  303  183  367  163   28   63    0  1110   94   6   0   0
  1    0   0    4  371  100  340  148   27   86    0 56271   43  57   0   0
```

sar

The `sar` command is the most versatile method for collecting system performance data. From the command line, it produces a number of snapshots of current system activity over a specified number of time intervals. If you don't specify an interval, the current day's data extracted from `sar`'s regular execution by `cron` is used. For example, to display a summary of disk activity for the current day, you can use the following command:

```
# sar -d
SunOS 5.10 sun4u    01/25/04
09:54:33   device   %busy   avque   r+w/s   blk/s   avwait   avserv
              sd01      27     5.8       6       8     21.6     28.6
              sd03      17     2.4       4       7     14.2     21.2
              sd05      13     1.7       3       6      9.3     18.3
              sd06      35     6.9       8      10     25.7     31.8
```

In this example, you can see that several disk devices are shown with varying percentages of busy time, mean number of transaction requests in the queue, mean number of disk reads and writes per second, mean number of disk blocks written per second, mean time for waiting in the queue, and mean time for service in the queue.

When a new disk, new memory, or a new CPU is added to the system, you should take a baseline `sar` report to determine the effect on performance. For example, after adding 128MB RAM on the system, you should be able to quantify the effect on mean system performance by comparing `sar` output before and after the event during a typical day's workload.

Examples

The following examples show how to manage logfiles, quotas, and accounting.

Logging Disk Usage

For auditing purposes, many sites generate a `df` report at midnight or during a change of administrator shifts, to record a snapshot of the system. In addition, if disk space is becoming an issue and extra volumes need to be justified in a system's budget, it is useful to be able to estimate how rapidly disk space is being consumed by users. Using the `cron` utility, you can set up and schedule a script using `crontab` to check disk space at different time periods and to mail this information to the administrator (or even post it to a Web site, if system administration is centrally managed).

A simple script to monitor disk space usage and mail the results to the system administrator (*root@server*) looks like this:

```
#!/bin/csh -f
df | mailx -s "Disk Space Usage" root@localhost
```

As an example, if this script were named */usr/local/bin/monitor_usage.csh* and executable permissions were set for the *nobody* user, you could create the following `crontab` entry for the *nobody* user to run at midnight every night of the week:

```
0 0 * * * /usr/local/bin/monitor_usage.csh
```

or you could make the script more general, so that users could specify another user who would be mailed:

```
#!/bin/csh -f
df | mailx -s "Disk Space Usage" $1
```

The `crontab` entry would then look like this:

```
0 0 * * * /usr/local/bin/monitor_usage.csh remote_user@client
```

The results of the disk usage report would now be sent to the user *remote_user@client* instead of *root@localhost*.

Another way of obtaining disk space usage information with more directory-by-directory detail is to use the */usr/bin/du* command. This command prints the sum of the sizes of every file in the current directory and performs the same task recursively for any subdirectories. The size is calculated by adding together all of the file sizes in the directory, where the size for each file is rounded up to the next 512-byte block. For example, taking a du of the */etc* directory looks like this:

```
# du /etc

14       ./default
7        ./cron.d
6        ./dfs
8        ./dhcp
201      ./fs/hsfs
681      ./fs/nfs
1        ./fs/proc
209      ./fs/ufs
1093     ./fs

...
2429     .
```

Thus, */etc* and all of its subdirectories contains a total of 2,429KB of data. Of course, this kind of output is fairly verbose and probably not much use in its current form. If you were only interested in *recording* the directory sizes, in order to collect data for auditing and usage analysis, you could write a short Perl script to collect the data, as follows:

```
#!/usr/local/bin/perl
# directorysize.pl: reads in directory size for current directory
# and prints results to standard output
@du = `du`;
for (@du)
{
($sizes,$directories)=split /\s+/, $_;
print "$sizes\n";
}
```

If you saved this script as *directorysize.pl* in */usr/local/bin/directory* and set the executable permissions, it would produce a list of directory sizes as output, like the following:

```
# cd /etc
 # /usr/local/bin/directorysize.pl

28
14
12
16
402
1362
2
418
2186
...
```

Because you are interested in usage management, you might want to modify the script as follows to display the total amount of space occupied by a directory and its subdirectories, as well as the average amount of space occupied. The latter number is very important when evaluating caching or investigating load balancing issues.

```
#!/usr/local/bin/perl
# directorysize.pl: reads in directory size for current directory
# and prints the sum and average disk space used to standard output
$sum=0;
$count=0;
@ps = `du -o`;
for (@ps)
{
    ($sizes,$directories)=split /\s+/, $_;
    $sum=$sum+$sizes;
    $count=$count+1;
}
print "Total Space: $sum K\n";
print "Average Space: $count K\n";
```

Note that du -o was used as the command, so that the space occupied by subdirectories is not added to the total for the top-level directory. The output from the command for */etc* now looks like this:

```
# cd /etc
 # /usr/local/bin/directorysize.pl
Total Space: 4832 K
Average Space: 70 K
```

Again, you could set up a `cron` job to mail this information to an administrator at midnight every night. To do this, first create a new shell script to call the Perl script, which is made more flexible by passing as arguments the directory to be measured and the user to which to send the mail:

```
#!/bin/csh -f
cd $1
/usr/local/bin/directorysize.pl | mailx -s "Directory Space Usage" $2
```

If you save this script to */usr/local/bin/checkdirectoryusage.csh* and set the executable permission, you could then schedule a disk space check of a cache file system. You could include a second command that sends a report for the */disks/junior_developers* file system, which is remotely mounted from *client*, to the team leader on *server*:

```
0 0 * * * /usr/local/bin/checkdirectoryusage.csh /cache squid@server
1 0 * * * /usr/local/bin/checkdirectoryusage.csh /disks/junior_
developers
team_leader@server
```

Tools may already be available on Solaris to perform some of these tasks more directly. For example, `du -s` will return the sum of directory sizes automatically. However, the purpose of this section has been to demonstrate how to customize and develop your own scripts for file system management.

Generating Accounting Reports

Once you have enabled data collection, generating reports is a simple matter of setting up a `cron` job for a nonprivileged user (usually *adm*), typically at a time of low system load. In the following example, accounting runs are performed at 6 A.M.:

```
0 6 * * * /usr/lib/acct/runacct 2> /var/adm/acct/nite/fd2log
```

Accounting runs involve several discrete stages, which are executed in the following order:

SETUP	Prepares accounting files for running the report
WTMPFIX	Checks the soundness of the *wtmpx* file and repairs it, if necessary
CONNECT	Gathers data for user connect time
PROCESS	Gathers data for process usage
MERGE	Integrates the connection and process data
FEES	Gathers fee information and applies to connection and process data
DISK	Gathers data on disk usage and integrates with fee, connection, and process data
MERGETACCT	Integrates accounting data for the past 24 hours (*daytacct*) with the total accounting data (*/var/adm/acct/sum/tacct*)

CMS	Generates command summaries
CLEANUP	Removes transient data and cleans up before terminating

After each stage of `runacct` has been successfully completed, the *statefile* (*/var/adm/ acct/nite/statefile*) is overwritten with the name of that stage. Thus, if the accounting is disrupted for any reason, it can be easily resumed by rereading the *statefile*. On January 23, if the *statefile* contained *FEES*, but terminated during *DISK*, you could restart the accounting run for the day by using the following command:

```
# runacct 2301 DISK >> /var/adm/acct/nite/fd2log
```

Once the daily run has been completed, the *lastdate* file is updated with the current date in *ddmm* format, where *dd* is the day and *mm* is the month of the last run. In addition, you can review a number of files manually to obtain usage summaries. For example, the daily report is stored in a file called *rprtddmm*, which contains the CMS and *lastlogin* data, as well as a connection usage summary:

```
Jan 26 02:05 2002   DAILY REPORT FOR johnson Page 1
from Fri Jan 25 02:05:23 2002
to   Sat Jan 26 02:05:54 2002

TOTAL DURATION IS 46 MINUTES
LINE           MINUTES   PERCENT   # SESS   # ON   # OFF
/dev/pts/1     0         0         0        0      0
pts/1          46        0         8        8      8
TOTALS         46        --        8        8      8
```

Here, you can see that the total connection time for the previous day was 46 minutes.

Login Logging

The */var/adm/acct/sum/loginlog* file contains a list of the last login dates for all local users. Some system accounts appear as never having logged in, which is expected:

```
00-00-00   adm
00-00-00   bin
00-00-00   daemon
00-00-00   listen
00-00-00   lp
00-00-00   noaccess
00-00-00   nobody
00-00-00   nuucp
00-00-00   smtp
00-00-00   sys
02-01-20   root
02-01-26   pwatters
```

You should check the */var/adm/acct/sum/loginlog* file for access to system accounts, which should never be accessed, and for unexpected usage of user accounts. The file is created during the accounting run.

Command Summaries

A typical command summary (CMS) statement generated by the `runacct` program is shown in Table 20-1. It is located in the */var/adm/acct/sum* directory.

Once you know what each column in this report represents, it becomes obvious that in this example, reading, sending, and receiving mail are the main uses of this server, on a daily basis at least, while the `runacct` command, which actually performs the accounting, is one of the least-used programs. Here is an explanation of the columns in the preceding report:

- **COMMAND NAME**   Shows the command as executed. This can lead to some ambiguity, because different commands could have the same filename. In addition, any shell or Perl scripts executed would be displayed under the shell and Perl interpreter, respectively, rather than showing up as a process on their own.

- **NUMBER CMDS**   Displays the number of times that the command named under COMMAND NAME was executed during the accounting period.

- **TOTAL KCOREMIN**   Shows the cumulative sum of memory segments (in kilobytes) used by the process identified under COMMAND NAME per minute of execution time.

- **TOTAL CPU-MIN**   Prints the accumulated processing time for the program named under COMMAND NAME.

- **TOTAL REAL-MIN**   Shows the actual time in minutes that the program named in COMMAND NAME consumed during the accounting period.

- **MEAN SIZE-K**   Indicates the average of the cumulative sum of consumed memory segments (TOTAL KCOREMIN) over the set of invocations denoted by NUMBER CMDS.

- **MEAN CPU-MIN**   The average CPU time computed from the quotient of NUMBER CMDS divided by TOTAL CPU-MIN.

- **HOG FACTOR**   The amount of CPU time divided by actual elapsed time. This ratio indicates the degree to which a system is available compared to its use. The hog factor is often used as a metric to determine overall load levels for a system, and it is useful for planning upgrades and expansion.

- **CHARS TRNSFRD**   Displays the sum of the characters transferred by system calls.

- **BLOCKS READ**   Shows the number of physical block reads and writes that the program named under COMMAND NAME accounted for.

COMMAND NAME	NUMBER CMDS	TOTAL KCOREMIN	TOTAL CPU MIN	TOTAL REALMIN	MEAN SIZE-K	MEAN CPU-MIN	HOG FACTOR	CHARS TRNSFRD	BLOCKS READ
totals	1034	1843.03	0.46	546.88	4049.14	0.00	0.00	107141376	982
pine	5	1426.41	0.11	177.47	13477.87	0.02	0.00	72782400	237
sendmail	171	176.44	0.09	4.73	1873.71	0.00	0.02	14895311	306
sh	107	31.15	0.04	0.29	881.70	0.00	0.12	58380	0
uudemon	114	27.91	0.02	0.10	1154.92	0.00	0.24	67765	8
in.ftpd	1	23.20	0.02	0.69	1435.05	0.02	0.02	6422528	7
mail.loc	13	19.69	0.02	0.06	1193.21	0.00	0.27	11973498	57
tcsh	4	13.61	0.01	179.98	1361.33	0.00	0.00	153040	1
uuxqt	48	11.01	0.01	0.08	1159.30	0.00	0.13	35568	0
uusched	48	10.99	0.01	0.09	1014.52	0.00	0.13	36096	180
popper	9	7.84	0.01	1.55	1205.74	0.00	0.00	155107	32
sed	58	7.63	0.01	0.02	618.38	0.00	0.58	44907	2
date	34	7.26	0.01	0.01	821.74	0.00	0.72	26348	1
rm	36	5.68	0.01	0.02	681.44	0.00	0.45	0	8
acctcms	4	4.92	0.01	0.01	953.03	0.00	0.97	125984	1
in.telne	4	4.85	0.00	180.03	1076.74	0.00	0.00	55744	0
cp	42	4.47	0.01	0.02	525.65	0.00	0.36	14434	60
ckpacct	24	4.23	0.00	0.09	907.14	0.00	0.05	49200	0
awk	26	4.01	0.01	0.02	616.82	0.00	0.36	950	0
chmod	37	3.69	0.01	0.01	553.60	0.00	0.55	0	0
cat	22	3.58	0.00	0.01	825.54	0.00	0.55	1540	2
acctprc	1	2.98	0.00	0.00	744.00	0.00	0.96	46152	0

TABLE 20-1   A Typical Command Summary (CMS) Statement

Often, the values of these parameters are confusing. For example, let's compare the characteristics of `pine`, which is a mail client, and `sendmail`, which is a mail transport agent. `pine` was executed only five times, but accounted for 1426.41 KCOREMIN, while `sendmail` was executed 171 times with a KCOREMIN of 176.44. The explanation for this apparent anomaly is that users probably log in once in the morning and leave their *pine* mail client running all day. The users sent an average of 34.2 messages during this day, many of which contained attachments, thus accounting for the high CPU overhead.

monacct

When examined over a number of days, accounting figures provide a useful means of understanding how processes are making use of the system's resources. When examined in isolation, however, they can sometimes misrepresent the dominant processes that the machine is used for. This is a well-known aspect of statistical sampling: before you can make any valid generalizations about a phenomenon, your observations must be repeated and sampled randomly. Thus, it is useful to compare the day-to-day variation of a system's resource use with the monthly figures that are generated by */usr/lib/acct/monacct*. Compare these daily values with the previous month's values generated by `monacct` in Table 20-2.

As you can see in Table 20-2, the individual day's figures were misleading. In fact, spread over a whole month, the `netscape` program tended to use more resources than the *pine* mail client, being invoked 1,538 times, and using 163985.79 KCOREMIN, compared to 165 invocations and 43839.27 KCOREMIN for *pine*. Clearly, it is very useful to examine monthly averages for a more reliable, strategic overview of system activity, while daily summaries are useful for making tactical decisions about active processes.

Charging Fees Using Accounting

The previous section looked at the output for `monacct`, which is the monthly accounting program. To enable `monacct`, you need to create a `cron` job for the *adm* account, which is similar to the entry for the `runacct` command in the previous section:

```
0 5 1 * * /usr/lib/acct/monacct
```

In addition to computing per-process statistics, `monacct` also computes usage information on a per-user basis, which you can use to bill customers according to the number of CPU minutes they used. Examine the user reports in Table 20-3 for the same month that was reviewed in the previous section.

Of the nonsystem users, obviously *pwatters* is going to have a large bill this month, with 65 prime CPU minutes consumed. Billing could also proceed on the basis of KCORE-MINS utilized; *pwatters*, in this case, used 104572 KCORE-MINS. How an organization bills its users is probably already well established, but even if users are not billed for cash payment, examining how the system is used is very valuable for planning expansion and for identifying rogue processes that reduce the availability of a system for legitimate processes.

COMMAND NAME	NUMBER CMDS	TOTAL KCOREMIN	TOTAL CPU MIN	TOTAL REALMIN	MEAN SIZE-K	MEAN CPU-MIN	HOG FACTOR	CHARS TRNSFRD	BLOCKS READ
totals	513833	529119.94	262.83	632612.94	2013.17	0.00	0.00	8959614208	138299
nscp	1538	163985.79	6.77	59865.58	24233.18	0.00	0.00	4744854	720
installp	110508	58676.62	33.65	197.77	1743.57	0.00	0.17	27303024	139
sed	122726	45704.45	40.87	98.07	1118.16	0.00	0.42	20044188	171
pine	165	43839.27	3.88	1594.97	11304.12	0.02	0.00	1578316160	4675
project	13	37654.92	22.76	22.79	1654.41	1.75	1.00	6187332	106
ll-ar	4	24347.44	26.49	50.37	919.24	6.62	0.53	61351684	135
nawk	75544	21678.96	24.46	40.21	886.40	0.00	0.61	61351684	135
predict	289	16808.70	13.59	13.74	1236.66	0.05	0.99	38996306	293
sqpe	17	15078.86	4.15	10.30	3636.67	0.24	0.40	90547712	889
grep	71963	13042.15	18.69	26.47	697.69	0.00	0.71	377825714	3
pkgparam	24578	11360.71	9.11	9.68	1246.38	0.00	0.94	102325648	0
false_ne	7	10399.85	2.12	2.13	4899.81	0.30	1.00	212530	5
pkgremov	89	10073.67	8.95	22.70	1125.88	0.10	0.39	1129787392	18845
pkginsta	125	7163.67	4.75	38.21	1508.46	0.04	0.12	1912983552	4077
tee	8622	3237.38	2.03	2.30	1592.24	0.00	0.88	2134692	0
ls	8825	3133.31	2.59	3.31	1209.06	0.00	0.78	2038136	215

TABLE 20-2   Monthly Account Summary

UID	LOGIN NAME	CPU (MINS) PRIME	CPU (MINS) NPRIME	KCORE-MINS PRIME	KCORE-MINS NPRIME	CONNECT (MINS) PRIME	CONNECT (MINS) NPRIME	# DISK BLOCKS	# OF PROCS	# OF SESS	# DISK SAMPLES	FEE
TOTAL		233	30	363969	158762	1061	1005	11830502	513833	134	45	0
0	root	157	4	180984	3881	546	0	1858608	444602	3	3	0
1	daemon	0	0	0	0	0	0	6	0	0	3	0
2	bin	0	0	0	0	0	0	5759280	0	0	3	0
3	sys	0	0	114	89	0	0	18	51	0	3	0
4	adm	1	7	618	4856	0	0	15136	20005	0	3	0
5	uucp	1	4	1371	3557	0	0	5088	22036	68	3	0
10	pwatters	65	6	104572	15758	197	88	2026666	1842	0	3	0
12	llee	0	0	0	0	0	0	12	0	0	3	0
71	lp	0	0	0	26	0	0	13822	134	0	3	0
108	jsmith	0	0	0	0	0	0	318	0	0	3	0
436	dbrown	0	0	0	0	0	0	48	0	0	3	0
1001	bjones	0	0	16	9	0	2	78	21	2	3	0
1002	ledwards	0	0	130	21	0	0	34	102	0	3	0
1003	tgonzale	0	0	0	0	0	0	40896	0	0	3	0
1012	ljung	5	10	74282	130564	318	915	2110492	3521	61	3	0
60001	nobody	3	0	1883	0	0	0	0	21519	0	0	0

TABLE 20-3   Charging Fees Using Accounting

PART IV

Performance Tuning

Previous sections examined how to use tools such as `sar`, `vmstat`, and `iostat` to measure system performance before and after key events such as adding new RAM or CPUs or upgrading disks to faster speeds. In addition to these hardware changes, it is possible to increase the performance of an existing system by tuning the kernel. This could involve switching from a 32-bit to a 64-bit kernel, if supported by hardware, and setting appropriate parameters for shared memory, semaphores, and message queues in */etc/system*. However, note that the Solaris 10 kernel is self-tuning to some extent for normal operations. Once database servers with special requirements are installed, or many users must be supported on a single system, it may be necessary to tweak some parameters and reboot.

If a system is slow, the process list is the first place to look, as described in Chapter 8. One of the reasons that so much space is devoted to process management in this book is that it is often user processes, rather than system CPU time, that adversely impact system performance. The only time that kernel tuning will really assist is where shared memory and other parameters need to be adjusted for database applications, or where system time for processes far exceeds the user time. This can generally be established by using the `time` command. You can use some commonly modified parameters in the */etc/system* file, described shortly, to improve system performance. After you make changes to */etc/system*, you need to reboot the system, but you need to take caution: if a syntax error is detected in */etc/system*, the system may not be able to booted.

The first step in tuning the kernel is generally to set the maximum number of processes permitted per user to a sensible value. This is a hard limit that prevents individual users from circumventing limits imposed by quotas and nice values set by the superuser. To insert a maximum of 100 processes per user, make the following entry in */etc/system*:

```
set maxuprc=100
```

If you are running a database server, your manual will no doubt supply minimum requirements for shared memory for the server. *Shared memory* is memory that can be locked but can be shared between processes, thereby reducing overhead for memory allocation. You can set the following parameters to determine how shared memory is allocated:

shmmax	The peak shared memory amount
shmmin	The smallest shared memory amount
shmmni	The largest number of concurrent identifiers permitted
shmseg	The quantity of segments permitted for each process
semmap	The initial quantity of entries in the semaphore map

semmni	The largest number of semaphore sets permitted
semmns	The total number of semaphores permitted
semmsl	The largest number of semaphores in each semaphore set

The following example entry for */etc/system* allocates 128MB of shared memory and sets other parameters appropriately:

```
set shmsys:shminfo_shmmax=134217728
set shmsys:shminfo_shmmin=100
set shmsys:shminfo_shmmni=100
set shmsys:shminfo_shmseg=100
set semsys:seminfo_semmap=125
set semsys:seminfo_semmni=250
set semsys:seminfo_semmns=250
```

Command Reference

The following command is commonly used to manage logfiles, quotas, and accounting.

syslog

The file */etc/syslog.conf* contains information used by the system log daemon, `syslogd`, to forward a system message to appropriate logfiles and/or users. `syslogd` preprocesses this file through *m4* to obtain the correct information for certain logfiles, defining LOGHOST if the address of "loghost" is the same as one of the addresses of the host that is running `syslogd`.

The default `syslogd` configuration is not optimal for all installations. Many configuration decisions depend on whether the system administrator wants to be alerted immediately if an alert or emergency occurs or instead wants all auth notices to be logged, and a `cron` job run every night to filter the results for a review in the morning. For noncommercial installations, the latter is probably a reasonable approach. A `crontab` entry like this,

```
0 1 * * * cat /var/adm/messages | grep auth | mail root
```

will send the root user a mail message at 1 A.M. every morning with all authentication messages.

A basic *syslog.conf* should contain provision for sending emergency notices to all users, as well as alerts to the root user and other nonprivileged administrator accounts. Errors, kernel notices, and authentication notices probably need to be displayed on the system console. It is generally sufficient to log daemon notices, alerts, and all other authentication information to the system logfile, unless the administrator is watching for cracking attempts, as shown here:

```
*.alert                                          root,pwatters
*.emerg                                          *
*.err;kern.notice;auth.notice                    /dev/console
daemon.notice                       /var/adm/messages
auth.none;kern.err;daemon.err;mail.crit;*.alert  /var/adm/messages
auth.info                                        /var/adm/authlog
```

Summary

In this chapter, you have learned the basic procedures involved in system accounting and logging. Since these form the basis for billing and other reporting activities, they are a critical yet often ignored aspect of system administration.

PART

V

Networking

Basic Networking

Sun's view is that "The Network Is the Computer." However, while users often consider the "network" to be a single, heterogeneous medium, the process of transferring a packet of data from one host to another is not a trivial task. This is where conceptual protocol stacks such as the general Open Systems Interconnection (OSI) networking model are useful in encapsulating and dividing the labor associated with physical network transmission and its management by software. Solaris uses the four-layer TCP/IP suite of network protocols to carry out network operations, including the Transmission Control Protocol (TCP), User Datagram Protocol (UDP), and Internet Protocol (IP). These protocols and the layer in which they reside will be covered in depth in the following chapters. It's important to note that the IP stack was rewritten in Solaris 10 to enhance performance and security, so upgrading from Solaris 9 for this reason alone is worthwhile.

In this chapter, we examine how TCP/IP is implemented on Solaris, including the configuration of network interfaces, daemons, addresses, ports, and sockets. We also examine how to configure the Internet daemon (`inetd`) to support a number of separate network services that are centrally managed.

Key Concepts

A network is a combination of hardware and software that enables computers to communicate with each other. At the hardware level, building a network involves installing a network interface into each system ("host") to be networked, and implementing a specific network topology by using cables, such as Ethernet, or wireless. At the software level, representations of network devices must be created, and protocols for exchanging data between hosts must be established. Data is exchanged by dividing it into packets that have a specific structure, enabling large data elements to be exchanged between hosts by using a small amount of wrapping. This wrapping, based on various protocols, contains information about the order in which packets should be assembled when transmitted from one host to another, for example.

By supporting many different types of hardware devices and connection technologies, and by implementing standards-based networking software, Solaris provides a flexible platform for supporting high-level network services and applications. These will be explored in detail in the following chapters.

Network Topologies

The two most common forms of network topology are the star network and the ring network. The ring topology, shown in Figure 21-1, is a peer-to-peer topology, where neighboring hosts are connected and data is exchanged between distant hosts by passing data from the source host to the target host through all intermediate hosts. Ring networks are most suitable for networks in which long distances separate individual hosts. However, if only one of the links between hosts is broken, then data transmission between all hosts can be interrupted.

In contrast, a star network has a centralized topology, where all hosts connect to a central point and exchange data at that point, as shown in Figure 21-2. This topology has the advantage of minimizing the number of hops that data must travel from a source to a target host, compared to a ring network. In addition, if one link is broken, then only data originating from or sent to the host on that link will be disrupted. However, if the point at which hosts are connected breaks down, then all data transmission will cease.

In practice, most modern high-speed networks are based on star topologies. When connecting local area networks (LANs) together to form intranets, a star topology has the advantage of being able to interconnect networks by their central connection points. This means that data sent from a host on one network must travel to its central point, which then sends the data to the connection point on a remote network, which then passes the data to the remote target host. Thus, only three hops are required to exchange data between hosts on two networks when using a star topology. A sample data flow is shown in Figure 21-3.

Let's look at a specific example of how an internet can be laid out, before we examine how OSI and the Solaris implementation of TCP/IP make this possible. Imagine that a Web server runs on the host 203.54.68.21 while a Web client (such as Netscape Navigator) runs on the host 203.54.67.122. Since these two hosts are located on two different local

FIGURE 21-1
Ring network topology

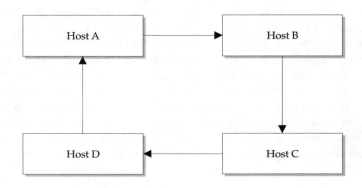

FIGURE 21-2
Star network
topology

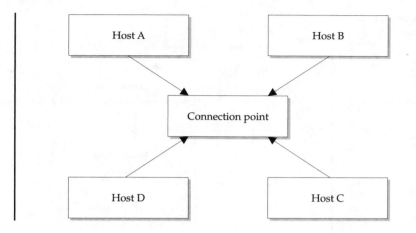

area (Class C) networks, they must be interconnected by a router. In the star topology, a connection point must allow a link to each host on the local network—in this example, a hub is used to connect each host, as well as to forward all data bound for nonlocal addresses to the router. Thus, when a high-level Hypertext Transfer Protocol (HTTP) request is sent from the client 203.54.67.122 to the server 203.54.68.21, a packet is sent to the hub, which detects that the destination is nonlocal and forwards the packet to the router. The router then forwards the packet to the router for the remote network, which detects that the destination is local and passes the packet to the hub, which in turn passes it to the server. Since HTTP is a request/response protocol, the backward path is traced when a response to the request is generated by the server. The configuration for this example is shown in Figure 21-4.

FIGURE 21-3
Interconnecting
networks

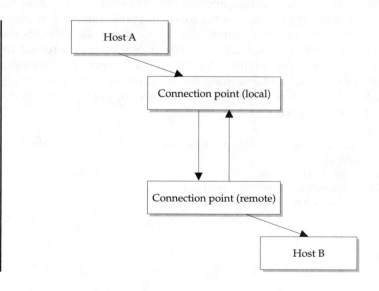

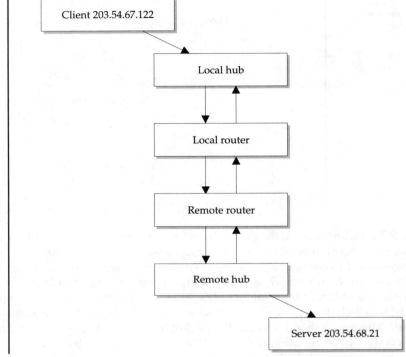

FIGURE 21-4
Supporting
high-level services

If this example seems complex, you'll be pleased to know that the implementation of many of these services is hidden from users, and most often from developers. This makes implementing networking applications very simple when using high-level protocols like HTTP. For example, consider the following Java code, which uses HTTP to make a connection to a remote server running an application called StockServer. After passing the name of a stock in the URL, the current price should be returned by the server. The code fragment shows the definition for the URL, a declaration for an input stream, reading a line from the stream and assigning the result to a variable (*stockPrice*), and closing the stream. If this code were contained in an applet, for example, the *stockPrice* for SUNW could then be displayed.

```
String stockURL="http://data.cassowary.net/servlet/StockServer?code=SUNW";
URL u = new URL(stockURL);
BufferedReader in = new BufferedReader(new
InputStreamReader(u.openStream()));
String stockPrice=in.readLine();
in.close();
```

A further level of abstraction is provided by Web Services and the Simple Object Access Protocol (SOAP), which uses HTTP as a transport protocol for transmitting requests to execute Remote Procedure Calls (RPCs) in a platform-independent way. This approach has some similarities to working directly at the HTTP level, since a URL can be used to execute the SOAP request, but the data is returned in a standard XML format. The following URL, for example, is used to retrieve the stock price for Sun Microsystems from XML Today:

http://www.xmltoday.com/examples/stockquote/getxmlquote.vep?s=*SUNW*

The data returned from this request can be parsed and its tags can be interpreted by a client program:

```
<stock_quotes>
    <stock_quote>
            <symbol>SUNW</symbol>
            <when>
                    <date>10/30/2002</date>
                    <time>3:06pm</time>
            </when>
            <price type="ask" value="2.50" />
            <price type="open" value="2.60" />
            <price type="dayhigh" value="2.60" />
            <price type="daylow" value="2.49" />
            <change>-0.10</change>
            <volume>5768644</volume>
    </stock_quote>
</stock_quotes>
```

As discussed in Chapter 33, Web Services will become more commonly used in future versions of Solaris, and related enterprise applications, so it's useful to understand how they work and how they relate to underlying networking protocols.

OSI Networking

Building networks is complex, given the wide array of hardware and software that can be used to implement them. The OSI networking model, shown in Figure 21-5, provides a framework for defining the scope of different layers of networking technology, which can be used to understand how different protocols and suites (such as TCP/IP) operate. Each layer of the model, starting from the bottom, supports the functionality required by the top levels. Moving from bottom to top, operations become more and more abstracted from their physical implementation. It is this abstraction that allows HTTP and other high-level protocols to operate without being concerned about low-level implementations. The OSI networking model allows for different instantiations of lower levels, without requiring higher-level code to be rewritten.

FIGURE 21-5
OSI networking
model

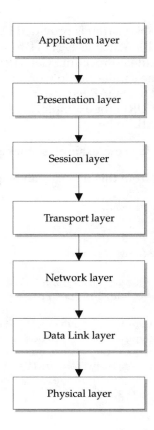

Starting from the bottom of the model, the following list describes the layers:

- **Physical (Layer 1)** Defines how data is exchanged at its very basic level (bits and bytes), as well as cabling requirements.

- **Data Link (Layer 2)** Defines the apparatus for transferring data, including error checking and synchronization.

- **Network (Layer 3)** Specifies operational issues, such as how networks can exchange data, as shown in Figures 21-3 and 21-4.

- **Transport (Layer 4)** Specifies how individual computers are to interpret data received from the network.

- **Session (Layer 5)** Determines how data from different sources can be separated, and how associations between hosts can be maintained.

- **Presentation (Layer 6)** Specifies how different types of data are formatted and how that data should be exposed.

- **Application (Layer 7)** Describes how high-level applications can communicate with each other in a standard way.

TCP/IP Networking

The TCP/IP suite of protocols forms the basis of all Internet communications, and was originally devised as part of the Defense Advanced Research Projects Agency (DARPA) for the ARPANET. While TCP/IP is the default networking protocol supported by Solaris, other operating systems also support TCP/IP, even if it is not their primary protocol. For example, Microsoft Windows networks support NetBEUI and IPX/SPX, while MacOS supports AppleTalk. The default networking protocol for Linux and Solaris is TCP/IP.

TCP/IP presents a simpler interface than OSI, since only the Application, Transport, Network, and Link layers need to be addressed. TCP/IP is layered, just like the OSI reference model. Thus, when a client application needs to communicate with a server, a process is initiated of passing data down each level on the client side, from the Application layer to the Physical layer, and up each level on the server side, from the Physical layer to the Application layer. Data is passed between layers in service data units. However, it's important to note that each client layer logically only ever communicates with the corresponding server layer, as demonstrated by the Java code presented earlier in the chapter: the Application layer is not concerned with logically communicating with the Physical layer, for example. Abstraction is the core benefit of TCP/IP in development and communication terms, since each level is logically isolated, while methods for supporting service data are also well defined.

We'll now review the key layers as they are implemented in the Solaris TCP/IP stack and Ethernet.

Ethernet

Robert Metcalfe at Xerox PARC developed Ethernet during the 1970s, although the major standards for Ethernet were not published until the 1980s. Ethernet is a type of physical network that supports virtually any type of computer system, unlike previous networks that supported only certain types of computers. The "ether" part of the name comes from the material that was thought, in the 19th century, to surround the earth and provide a medium for the transmission of radio waves. In the same way that radio became a ubiquitous mode for transmitting data, Ethernet has become the most commonly used medium for network transmission.

Ethernet is the most commonly used link technology supported by Solaris, and comes in five different speeds:

- **10Base2**   2 Mbps
- **10Base5**   5 Mbps
- **10Base-T**   10 Mbps
- **100Base-T**   100 Mbps
- **1000Base-T/FX**   1 Gbps

The 10, 100, and 1000 indicate the signaling frequency in MHz. There are different types of media that are supported for each baseband, such as 10Base. For example, the 10Base family supports the following media types:

- Thick coaxial cable
- Thin coaxial cable
- Twisted-pair cable
- Fiber-optic cable

Coaxial cable is a shielded, single-strand copper cable that is generally surrounded by an aluminum insulator. It is a highly insulated, reliable transmission medium. In contrast, twisted-pair cable can either be shielded or unshielded. Fiber-optic cable uses light as the transmission medium, and typically achieves the highest bandwidth. However, your choice of transmission media may depend on the distances that need to be covered for interconnection. The following restrictions are imposed on the most commonly used transmission media:

- **10Base2**   185 meters
- **10Base5**   500 meters
- **10Base-T**   150 meters

So, in a building where 500-meter cabling is required, only 10Base5 will be suitable, unless a *repeater* is used, which is a device like a hub that can be used to link different network branches together. Single-mode fiber may be used where long distances of 10 to 15 km are involved. Also, there are limitations on the number of hubs that can be used to extend the logical length of a segment—a packet cannot be transmitted through more than four hubs or three cable segments in total, to ensure successful transmission. There are some other restrictions that you should keep in mind when using specific media—for example, some types of cabling are more sensitive to electrical interference than others.

Solaris systems are typically supplied with a single Ethernet card, supporting 10/100 Mbps; however, server systems (such as the 420R) are supplied with quad Ethernet cards, supporting four interfaces operating at 10/100 Mbps. Although Ethernet (specified by the IEEE 802.3 standard)is the most common link type, other supported link types on Solaris include Fiber Distributed Data Interface (FDDI) and Asynchronous Transfer Mode (ATM). FDDI networks use a ring topology based on a transmitting and receiving ring, using high-quality fiber-optic cable, to support high-speed, redundant connections. However, FDDI is expensive compared to Ethernet, and gigabit FDDI is not available. ATM is designed for high quality of service applications, like video and audio streaming, that require a constant amount of bandwidth to operate. Data is transmitted in fixed-size cells of 53 bytes, and a connection is maintained between client and server only as required. Although ATM does not approach the speeds of Gigabit Ethernet, its quality of service provisions benefit certain types of data transmission.

In terms of the OSI networking model, Ethernet comprises both the Physical layer (Layer 1) and the Data Link layer (Layer 2), although a logical link control protocol is not logically defined.

Ethernet has become the technology of choice for LANs. Originally designed to transmit 3 Mbps, a base network interface using Ethernet can now transmit data at 10 Mbps. The latest Ethernet technology supports data transmission at 10 Gbps! Supported media for Ethernet includes thick and thin coaxial, fiber-optic, and twisted-pair cables.

The major reason for the success of Ethernet in industry was the adoption of the Ethernet standard (IEEE 802.3), allowing for interoperability between different vendors' products. Ethernet specifies the Carrier Sense Multiple Access with Collision Detection (CSMA/CD) access method, as well as physical layer specifications. The Ethernet specification allowed many different vendors to produce network interfaces and media that supported Ethernet. Ethernet is a very flexible system, since interfaces operating at different transmission rates can be connected to the same LAN.

There are three elements that comprise Ethernet:

- Physical media segments, which are used to interconnect systems
- The media access control (MAC) rules that implement access to Ethernet channels
- A frame that organizes data to be transmitted in a standard way

Systems connected to the Ethernet are technically known as *stations*. Every station on the network is independent—access is not centrally controlled, since the medium allows signaling to be received and interpreted by all stations. Transmission across Ethernet occurs in bitwise form. When transmitting data, a station must wait for the channel to be free of data before sending a packet formatted as a frame.

If a station has to wait for the channel to be free before sending its own packets, you can appreciate the potential for traffic congestion and a "broadcast storm" if one station has a lot of data to send. However, after transmitting one packet, each station then competes for the right to transmit each subsequent frame. The MAC access control system prevents traffic congestion from occurring. It is quite normal, for example, for collision rates of 50 percent to exist without any noticeable impact on performance.

A more insidious problem occurs with so-called late collisions. These are collisions that occur between two hosts that are not detected because the latency for transmission between the two hosts exceeds the maximum time allowed to detect a collision. If this occurs at greater than 1 percent of the time, serious problems may emerge in terms of data throughput and potential corruption.

CSMA/CD

The mechanism for preventing packet collision is the Carrier Sense Multiple Access with Collision Detection (CSMA/CD) method specified by the IEEE standard. Prior to data being transmitted, a station must enter Carrier Sense (CS) mode. If no data is detected on the channel, then all stations have an equal opportunity to transmit a frame, a condition known as Multiple Access (MA). If two or more stations begin transmitting frames and detect that they are transmitting at the same time, a state known as Collision Detection (CD), then the stations halt transmission, enter the CS mode, and wait for the next MA opportunity. Collisions can occur because there is a time difference between when two stations might detect MA, depending on their "distance" in the network. When a collision occurs, the frames must be re-sent by their respective parties. The process flow for CSMA/CD is shown in Figure 21-6.

When systematic problems emerge in a LAN, demonstrated by much lower than theoretical transmission rates, a design flaw in the network layout could be causing a large number of collisions. You might be wondering how, if a CD event occurs, two stations can prevent retransmitting at the same time in the future, thereby repeating their previous collision—the answer is that the delay between retransmission is randomized for each network interface. This prevents repetitive locking, and delivery of a packet will always be attempted 16 times before a failure occurs. When more stations are added to a single LAN, the number of collisions occurring will also increase. With high-speed networks, the delay caused by retransmission of a packet is usually in the order of microseconds rather than milliseconds. If the number of retransmissions escalates, then there is a planned, exponential reduction in network traffic, affecting all stations, until stable operation is restored.

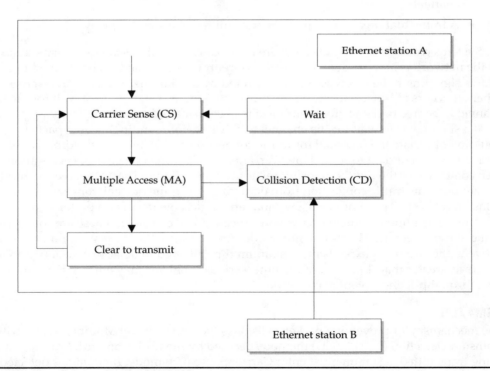

FIGURE 21-6   Process flow for CSMA/CD

One of the important things to note about Ethernet, with respect to quality of service issues, is that it is not a guaranteed delivery system, unlike some other networking systems. This is because Ethernet operates on the principle of best effort, given the available resources. Ethernet is susceptible to electrical artifacts, interference, and a number of other problems that may interfere with data transmission. However, for most practical purposes, Ethernet performs very well. If assured delivery is required, then higher-level application protocols, based on message queuing for example, would need to be implemented across Ethernet to have guaranteed delivery. Transport layer protocols such as TCP label each packet with a sequence number to ensure that all packets are received and reassembled in the correct order.

Ethernet has a logical topology, or tree-like structure, that is distinct from the set of physical interfaces that are interconnected using networking cable. One of the implications of this tree-like structure is that individual branches can be segmented in order to logically isolate structural groups. This structure also allows a large number of unrelated networks to be connected to each other, forming the basis of the Internet as we know it. Individual network branches can be linked together by using a repeater of some kind such as a hub. In contrast, a switch only takes traffic destined to one of its ports. The Ethernet channel can be extended beyond the local boundaries imposed by a single branch. A hub only connects interfaces on a single segment, while a switch can interconnect multiple LANs. A LAN router is needed when connecting multiple logical LANs.

Ethernet Frames

The main data structure utilized by Ethernet is the frame. The frame has a number of defined fields that specify elements like the MAC addresses for the destination and originating hosts in a packet transmission. The advantage in this ordering is that only the first 48 bits of a packet need to be read by a host to determine whether a packet received has reached its ultimate destination. If the destination MAC address does not match the local MAC address, then the contents of the packet do not need to be read. However, the snoop command can be used to extract the content of packets that are not destined for the local MAC address, assuming that you are using a hub and not a switch. This is why it's important to encrypt the contents of packets being transmitted across the Internet—they can be trivially "sniffed" by using programs like snoop. In addition to the destination and originating MAC addresses, the frame also contains a data field, of 46 to 1,500 bytes, and a cyclic redundancy check of 4 bytes. The data field contains all of the data encapsulated by higher-level protocols, such as IP.

Ethernet Addresses

One of the best features of Ethernet is that it enables a group of interfaces on a specific network to listen for broadcasts being transmitted to a specific group address, known as a multicast address. This allows a single host to originate a packet that is to be read by a number of different hosts, without having to retransmit the packet multiple times. In addition, each interface listens on its normal MAC address as well as on the multicast address.

A MAC address is a hexadecimal number that is set in the factory by every network interface manufacturer. It contains elements that allow an interface to be distinguished from those manufactured by other companies, and also allows individual interfaces from the same manufacturer to be distinguishable. It is possible, with SPARC systems, to set the MAC address manually in the PROM. However, this is generally not advisable, except in systems with multiple interfaces, where they might have the same MAC address by default. The format of the MAC address is usually a set of hexadecimal numbers delimited by colons. The MAC address 11:22:33:44:55:AA is one example. The initial three bytes identify a specific manufacturer—the list of manufacturers and their codes can be downloaded from **ftp://ftp.lcs.mit.edu/pub/map/ethernet-codes**.

In order to support IP and higher-level transport and application protocols, a mapping must be made between the MAC address and the IP address. This is achieved by the Address Resolution Protocol (ARP) and Reverse Address Resolution Protocol (RARP). The hardware address, otherwise known as the MAC address, is used to distinguish hosts at the link level. This is mapped to an IP address at the Network level, by using ARP and RARP.

IPv4

The basic element of IP version 4 (IPv4) is the IP address, which is a 32-bit number (4 bytes) that uniquely identifies network interfaces on the Internet. For single-homed hosts, which have only one network interface, the IP address identifies the host. However, for multihomed hosts, which have multiple network interfaces, the IP address does not uniquely identify the host. Even the domain name assigned to a multihost can be different, depending on which network the interface is connected to. For example, a router is a host that contains at least two interfaces, since it supports the passing of data between networks.

The IP address is usually specified in dotted decimal notation, where each of the bytes is displayed as an integer separated by a dot. An example IP address is 192.205.76.123, which is based on a Class C network. There are five classes of network defined by IP (A, B, C, D, E), although only three of these (A, B, and C) are actually used for the identification of hosts. Network classes can be identified by a discrete range of values; thus, if an address lies within a specific range, it can be identified as belonging to a network of a specific class. The following ranges are defined by IP:

- **Class A**   0.0.0.0–127.255.255.255
- **Class B**   128.0.0.0–191.255.255.255
- **Class C**   192.0.0.0–223.255.255.255
- **Class D**   224.0.0.0–239.255.255.255
- **Class E**   240.0.0.0–247.255.255.255

The different classes allow for ever decreasing numbers of hosts in each network, starting from class A, where networks can support millions of hosts, to class C networks, which can only support up to 254 hosts. Some address ranges have special purposes:

for example, the network 10.0.0.0 is reserved for private use, and is commonly used to define IP addresses for internal networks. This is a security feature, since 10.0.0.0 addresses are not resolvable from the Internet. In addition, the 127.0.0.0 addresses are used to refer to the localhost, with the most commonly used value being 127.0.0.1.

Subnets allow large networks to be divided into smaller, logical networks, by using a subnet mask. For class A networks, the mask is 255.0.0.0; for class B networks, the mask is 255.255.0.0; and for class C networks, the mask is 255.255.255.0.

Solaris 10 provides complete support for IPv6 and IPSec, discussed in Chapter 25. These innovations are designed to increase the capacity of the Internet, and secure packets transmitted by using transport protocols.

The IP layer sits between the Network ("Ethernet") and Transport layers in the stack. Thus, it provides the interface between the underlying physical transport and the logical transport used by applications. It manages the mapping between hardware (MAC) addresses and software addresses for network interfaces. To connect a LAN to the Internet, it is necessary to obtain an IP network number from the InterNIC. However, since most Solaris software uses TCP/IP for network operations, even when not connected to the Internet, it is necessary to become familiar with IP, including its configuration and its major operational issues.

IP carries out the following functions in the stack:

- **Addressing** Mapping hardware addresses to software addresses
- **Routing** Finding a path to transmit a packet from a source network interface to a destination network interface
- **Formatting** Inserting specific types of data into a packet to ensure that it reaches its destination
- **Fragmentation** Dividing packets into fragments in situations where a packet is too large to be transmitted using the underlying medium

IP relies on three other protocols for its operation: ARP ensures that datagrams are sent to the correct destination network interface from a source network interface by mapping IP addresses to hardware addresses. RARP is responsible for mapping hardware addresses to IP addresses. The Internet Control Message Protocol (ICMP) is involved with the identification and management of network errors, which result from packets being dropped, from physical disconnection of intermediate and destination routers, and from a redirection directive issued by an intermediate or destination router. Note that the ping command is typically used as the interface to check for errors on the network.

The key data structure used by IP is the datagram. Details about the datagram are recorded in the packet's header, including the addresses of the source and destination hosts, the size of the datagram, and the order in which datagrams are to be transmitted or received. The structure of the IP datagram is shown in Figure 21-7.

The Version is an integer that defines the current IP version (i.e., 4). The Header Length specifies the size, in bytes, of the packet header—generally, the header is 20 bytes in length, since IPv4 options are not often used. The Type of Service specifies, in 8 bits, what type of data is being handled. This allows packets to be designated as

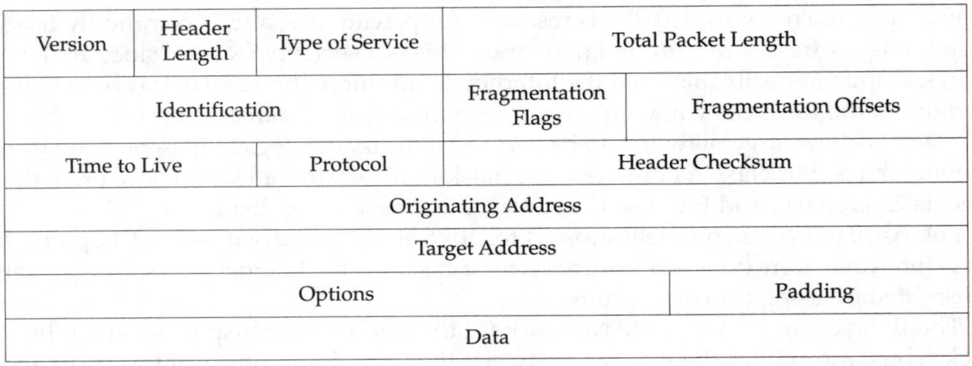

Version	Header Length	Type of Service	Total Packet Length	
Identification			Fragmentation Flags	Fragmentation Offsets
Time to Live		Protocol	Header Checksum	
Originating Address				
Target Address				
Options			Padding	
Data				

FIGURE 21-7   Structure of IP datagrams

requiring high-speed, high-reliability, or maximum bandwidth. Bits 0 through 2 are responsible for determining the message priority, with the following values being supported:

- **000**   Normal traffic
- **001**   Priority traffic
- **010**   Immediate traffic
- **011**   Flash traffic
- **100**   Flash override traffic
- **101**   Critical traffic
- **110**   Internet control traffic
- **111**   Network control traffic

Bits 3 through 5 specify whether low (0) or high (1) priority be given to speed, bandwidth, or reliability, respectively, while the last two bits are reserved.

The Total Packet Length is specified by a 16-bit number, which has a maximum of 65,535 bytes. However, this value is largely theoretical since framing through hardware layers (such as Ethernet and modems) sets this value to be much lower in practice. Large packets need to be fragmented—that's where the Identification, Fragmentation Flags, and Fragmentation Offsets come into play. The Identification field is a 16-bit identifying number for reassembly. The Fragmentation Flag is a 3-bit number that indicates whether a packet may or may not be fragmented, and whether the current fragment is the last fragment or other fragments are yet to be transmitted. The Fragmentation Offsets is a 13-bit number that indicates where a fragment lies in the sequence of fragments to be reconstructed.

The Time to Live specifies the number of hops permitted before the packet expires and is dropped. The Protocol number (defined in */etc/protocols*) specifies which protocol is to be used for data definition. The supported protocols are shown in Table 21-1.

Name	Number	Acronym	Description
ip	0	IP	Internet Protocol
icmp	1	ICMP	Internet Control Message Protocol
ggp	3	GGP	Gateway-Gateway Protocol
tcp	6	TCP	Transmission Control Protocol
egp	8	EGP	Exterior Gateway Protocol
pup	12	PUP	PARC Universal Packet Protocol
udp	17	UDP	User Datagram Protocol
hmp	20	HMP	Host Monitoring Protocol
xns-idp	22	XNS-IDP	Xerox Network System IDP
rdp	27	RDP	Reliable Datagram Protocol

TABLE 21-1   Supported Solaris Protocols

The Header Checksum determines whether the packet header has been corrupted, by using a cyclic redundancy check. The Originating Address and Target Address are the IP addresses of the source and destination hosts, respectively, for the packet.

A set of options up to 40 bytes can also be specified in the header, although these options are not always used. The following options are available:

- **End of Option list**   Marks the end of the list of options, since it can be a variable length list
- **No Operation**   Defines the boundary between options
- **Security**   Used to specify security levels for the traffic
- **Loose Source Routing**   The origin provides routing that may be followed
- **Strict Source Routing**   The origin provides routing that must be followed
- **Record Route**   Stores the route of a datagram
- **Stream Identifier**   Used to support streaming
- **Internet Timestamp**   Records the time in milliseconds since the start of UT

The following security levels are defined:

- **00000000 00000000**   Unclassified
- **11110001 00110101**   Confidential
- **01111000 10011010**   EFTO
- **10111100 01001101**   MMMM
- **01011110 00100110**   PROG
- **10101111 00010011**   Restricted

- **11010111 10001000**   Secret
- **01101011 11000101**   Top Secret

The correct interpretation of these levels can be determined from the *Defense Intelligence Agency Manual DIAM 65-19*. A more accessible reference is MIL-STD-2411-1, the *Registered Data Values for Raster Product Format* specification (**http://www.nima.mil/publications/specs/printed/2411/2411_1.pdf**).

The packet can be padded to ensure that the length of the header is 32 bits where necessary and that it separates the header from the packet data.

In order to check whether IP packets are being transmitted correctly between a source and destination network interface, and all intermediate routers, you can use the `traceroute` command. Note that `traceroute` does not display the contents of packet headers and data as does the `snoop` command.

Transport Layer

The interface between the Application layer and the Internet layer in the TCP/IP stack is the Transport layer. This layer implements protocols to transport packets in application-specific ways, depending on the individual requirements of the application. The two most commonly used transport protocols are TCP and UDP. TCP aims to provide reliable transmission, but is more heavyweight, while UDP is lightweight, but does not guarantee the delivery of packets. Thus, data-intensive applications that are error tolerant in terms of data transmission, such as video and data, tend to use UDP, as long as they are on reliable networks. On the Internet, applications that require the reliable transmission of data generally use TCP.

TCP and UDP are the two main transport protocols that support higher-level application protocols like the Simple Mail Transfer Protocol (SMTP) and HTTP. In turn, TCP and UDP sit on top of IP. The main feature of TCP is that it guarantees reliable delivery of packets, to the extent that dropped packets are retransmitted as required. However, reliable delivery in transport terms is different from reliable delivery assured by asynchronous messaging, as might be implemented by a message queue. It is up to the application to provide for the storaging and forwarding of packets if the network connection is broken.

However, it's important to note that while TCP aims for guaranteed delivery, UDP makes no such promises—indeed, the "User Datagram" Protocol may well be described as the "Unreliable Delivery" Protocol! The trade-off here is between guaranteed delivery and efficiency—UDP is more lightweight than TCP, and can significantly reduce bandwidth requirements. In some applications where bandwidth is limited and connectivity is transient, such as noisy wireless signals, UDP is much more appropriate for use at the Transport level.

As broadband, highly reliable Ethernet is rolled out, bandwidth-intensive applications such as audio/video, Voice over IP (VoIP), and video conferencing are all built on top of UDP, due to the reduced overhead. TCP is best suited to situations where a reliable network is always available, and where real-time interactions are necessary. For example, the `telnet` daemon uses TCP transport because interactive commands are issued in real time. In contrast, the `biff` daemon, which lets the user know that new mail has arrived, doesn't really require real-time access, since no interactive commands are issued. In this case, UDP is more appropriate than TCP.

In technical terms, TCP is a connection-oriented protocol, while UDP is a connectionless protocol. This means that where services use TCP to transmit data, a persistent connection must be maintained between the client and the server. There are some important differences in the way that data is packed using TCP and UDP. In TCP, sequence numbers are issued to ensure that packet delivery is consistent. UDP has much less restrictive requirements, which reduces the amount of bandwidth required to carry UDP traffic compared to equivalent services that utilize TCP.

Sockets provide a way to uniquely bind protocols to ports and addresses on the client and server. They consist of a five-tuple (host, address/host, port/client, address/client, port/protocol). While many sockets on a server can have the same host and address/port concurrently, they can be uniquely addressed because the client address is different for each client; thus the server always knows which client to interact with. But you can never create a socket with exactly the same tuple—otherwise, you'll generate a binding error.

All TCP and UDP services operate through a specific port. Sometimes, a service is offered over both TCP and UDP ports, such as the `ldap` daemon, which operates on port 389 TCP and port 389 UDP. However, many services operate only on TCP or UDP. One service may operate on a specific TCP port, while a separate service may operate on the same numbered port for UDP. There are conventions for operating services on specific ports, although these may be modified on a local system. For example, the default port number for operating the Apache Web server is port 80 TCP, but any other TCP port may be used, as long as it is not being used by another service. When a remote client connects to a locally operated service, a port listener receives the connection for the appropriate service, as defined by the port number. This prevents data destined for one service from being diverted to another (inappropriate) service. A server socket is formed by the service port and the local IP address for the server. A client socket is formed in the same way, by the client's IP address and the appropriate port. In this way, client-server interactions can be described by the two sockets. The kernel has a port table that it maintains to match up client and server ports and IP addresses, which can be viewed by using the `netstat` command:

```
# netstat

TCP: IPv4
    Local Address          Remote Address        Swind Send-Q Rwind Recv-Q  State
-------------------    -------------------    ----- ------ ----- ------  -------
ivana.telnet           austin.1040             8550      1 24820      0  ESTABLISHED
ivana.32807            ivana.32782            32768      0 32768      0  TIME_WAIT

Active UNIX domain sockets
Address    Type        Vnode        Conn   Local Addr      Remote Addr
30000b0dba8 stream-ord 300006cb810 00000000 /tmp/.X11-unix/X0
30000b0dd48 stream-ord 00000000 00000000
```

PART V

In this example, a socket comprised of the host *ivana* and the `telnet` port is servicing a `telnet` session for the client *austin* with the remote port 1040. All of the standard services are mapped in the services database (*/etc/services*). These ports are defined as part of the work of the Internet Engineering Task Force (IETF), and the Request For Comments (RFC) process for defining Internet standards (**http://www.rfc-editor.org/rfc.html**). Generally, standard services are defined for ports 1 to 1,024, which correspond to privileged ports on UNIX, since only the superuser may execute services that operate in this range. Any user may execute services that operate on ports 1,025 and above.

The following is an example entry in */etc/services*:

```
telnet           23/tcp
```

This entry defines the `telnet` service to run on port 23 TCP. A number of possible tokens can be contained within each service definition:

- Name of service
- Service port number
- Service transport type
- Aliases for service

Another convention in UNIX systems is to operate Internet services through a single super-daemon known as `inetd`. One advantage of running through `inetd` is that daemons can be configured using a single file (*/etc/inetd.conf*). However, with complex services like a Web server's, it's often preferable to configure daemons through their own configuration file.

Procedures

The following procedures show how to configure Solaris networking.

Hostnames and Interfaces

A Solaris network consists of a number of different hosts that are interconnected using a switch or a hub. Solaris networks connect through to each other by using routers, which can be dedicated hardware systems or Solaris systems that have more than one network interface. Each host on a Solaris network is identified by a unique hostname: these hostnames often reflect the function of the host in question. For example, a set of four Web servers may have the hostnames www1, www2, www3, and www4, respectively.

Every host and network that is connected to the Internet uses IP to support higher-level protocols such as TCP and UDP. Every interface of every host on the Internet has a unique IP address, which is based on the network IP address block assigned to the local network. Networks are addressable by using an appropriate netmask, which corresponds to a class A (255.0.0.0), class B (255.255.0.0), or class C (255.255.255.0) network, respectively.

Solaris supports multiple Ethernet interfaces, which can be installed on a single machine. These are usually designated by files like this:

```
/etc/hostname.hmen
```

or this:

```
/etc/hostname.len
```

where *n* is the interface number, and le and hme are interface types.

The network interface device name can be determined by using the `sysdef` or `prtconf` command. Interface files contain a single name, with the primary network interface being designated with an interface number of zero. Thus, the primary interface of a machine called *helium* would be defined by the file */etc/hostname.hme0*, which would contain the name *helium*. A secondary network interface, connected to a different subnet, might be defined in the file */etc/hostname.hme1*. In this case, the file might contain the name *helium1*. This setup is commonly used in organizations that have a provision for a failure of the primary network interface, or to enable load balancing of server requests across multiple subnets (for example, for an intranet Web server processing HTTP requests).

Subnets are visible to each other by means of a mask. Class A subnets use the mask 255.0.0.0. Class B networks use the mask 255.255.0.0. Class C networks use the mask 255.255.255.0. These masks are used when broadcasts are made to specific subnets. A class C subnet 134.132.23.0, for example, can have 255 hosts associated with it, starting with 134.132.23.1 and ending with 134.132.23.255. Class A and B subnets have their own distinctive enumeration schemes.

Internet Daemon

The `inetd` daemon is the "super" Internet daemon that is responsible for centrally managing many of the standard Internet services provided by Solaris through the application layer. For example, `telnet`, `ftp`, `finger`, `talk`, and `uucp` are all run from `inetd`. Even third-party Web servers can often be run through `inetd`. Both UDP and TCP transport layers are supported with `inetd`. The main benefit of managing all services centrally through `inetd` is reduced administrative overhead, since all services use a standard configuration format from a single file.

There are also several drawbacks to using `inetd` to run all of your services: there is now a single point of failure, meaning that if `inetd` crashes because of one service that fails, all of the other `inetd` services may be affected. In addition, connection pooling for services like the Apache Web server is not supported under `inetd`: high-performance applications, for which there are many concurrent client requests, should use a stand-alone daemon.

The Internet daemon (`inetd`) relies on two files for configuration. The */etc/inetd.conf* file is the primary configuration file, consisting of a list of all services currently supported,

PART V

and their run-time parameters, such as the file system path to the daemon that is executed. The */etc/services* file maintains a list of mappings between service names and port numbers, which is used to ensure that services are activated on the correct port.

Network Configuration Files

Independent of DNS is the local hosts file (*/etc/hosts*), which is used to list local hostnames and IP addresses. For a network with large numbers of hosts, using the */etc/hosts* file is problematic, since its values must be updated on every host on the network each time a change is made. This is why using DNS or NIS/NIS+ is a better solution for managing distributed host data. However, the */etc/hosts* file contains entries for some key services, such as logging, so it usually contains at least the following entries:

- The loopback address, 127.0.0.1, which is associated with the generic hostname localhost. This allows applications to be tested locally using the IP address 127.0.0.1 or the hostname localhost.

- The IP address, hostname, and FQDN of the localhost, since it requires this data before establishing a connection to a DNS server or NIS/NIS server when booting.

- An entry for a loghost, so that syslog data can be redirected to the appropriate host on the local network.

A sample */etc/hosts* file is shown here:

```
127.0.0.1        localhost
192.68.16.1      emu           emu.cassowary.net
192.68.16.2      hawk          hawk.cassowary.net        loghost
192.68.16.3      eagle         eagle.cassowary.net
```

In this configuration, the localhost entry is defined, followed by the name and IP address of the localhost (hostname *emu*, with an IP address 192.68.16.1). In this case, *emu* redirects all of its syslog logging data to the host hawk (192.68.16.2), while another host eagle (192.68.16.3) is also defined.

Configuring Network Interfaces

The ifconfig command is responsible for configuring each network interface at boot time. ifconfig can also be used to check the status of active network interfaces by passing the *–a* parameter:

```
# ifconfig -a
lo0: flags=849<UP,LOOPBACK,RUNNING,MULTICAST> mtu 8232
        inet 127.0.0.1 netmask ff000000
hme0: flags=863<UP,BROADCAST,NOTRAILERS,RUNNING,MULTICAST> mtu 1500
        inet 10.17.65.16 netmask ffffff00 broadcast 10.17.65.255
hme1: flags=863<UP,BROADCAST,NOTRAILERS,RUNNING,MULTICAST> mtu 1500
        inet 204.17.65.16 netmask ffffff00 broadcast 204.17.65.255
```

In this case, the primary interface hme0 is running on the internal network, while the secondary interface hme1 is visible to the external network. The netmask for a class C network is used on both interfaces, while both have a distinct broadcast address. This ensures that information broadcast on the internal network is not visible to the external network. There are several parameters shown with ifconfig –a, including whether or not the interface is UP or DOWN (that is, active or inactive). In the following example, the interface has not been enabled at boot time:

```
# ifconfig hme1
hme1: flags=863<DOWN,BROADCAST,NOTRAILERS,RUNNING,MULTICAST>
      mtu 1500 inet 204.17.64.16 netmask ffffff00          broadcast
204.17.64.255
```

The physical address can also be useful in detecting problems with a routing network interface to examine the ARP results for the LAN. This will determine whether or not the interface is visible to its clients:

```
# arp -a
Net to Media Table
Device   IP Address                 Mask       Flags   Phys Addr
------   -------------------        ---------------- ----  ----------------
hme0     server1.cassowary.net 255.255.255.255        00:c0:ff:19:48:d8
hme0     server2.cassowary.net 255.255.255.255   ·    c2:d4:78:00:15:56
hme0     server3.cassowary.net 255.255.255.255        87:b3:9a:c2:e9:ea
```

Modifying Interface Parameters

There are two methods for modifying network interface parameters. You can use the ifconfig command to modify operational parameters, and to bring an interface online (UP) or shut it down (DOWN). Secondly, you can use */usr/sbin/ndd* to set parameters for TCP/IP transmission, which will affect all network interfaces. In this section, we examine both of these methods, and how they may be used to manage interfaces and improve performance.

It is sometimes necessary to shut down and start up a network interface to upgrade drivers or install patches affecting network service. To shut down a network interface, for example, you can use the following command:

```
# ifconfig hme1 down
 # ifconfig hme1
hme1: flags=863<DOWN,BROADCAST,NOTRAILERS,RUNNING,MULTICAST>
     mtu 1500 inet 204.17.64.16 netmask ffffff00
     broadcast 204.17.64.255
```

PART V

It also possible to bring this interface back "up" by using `ifconfig`:

```
# ifconfig hme1 up
 # ifconfig hme1
hme1: flags=863<UP,BROADCAST,NOTRAILERS,RUNNING,MULTICAST>
        mtu 1500 inet 204.17.64.16 netmask ffffff00
        broadcast 204.17.64.255
```

To ensure that this configuration is preserved from boot to boot, it is possible to edit the networking startup file */etc/rc2.d/S69inet* and add this line to any others that configure the network interfaces.

It may be necessary to set several of these parameters in a production environment to ensure optimal performance, especially when application servers and Web servers are in use. For example, when a Web server makes a request to port 80 using TCP, a connection is opened and closed. However, the connection is kept open for a default time of two minutes to ensure that all packets are correctly received. For a system with a large number of clients, this can lead to a bottleneck of stale TCP connections, which can significantly impact the performance of the Web server. Fortunately, the parameter that controls this behavior (*tcp_close_wait_interval*) can be set using ndd to something more sensible (like 30 seconds):

```
# ndd -set /dev/tcp tcp_close_wait_interval 30000
```

To ensure that this configuration is preserved from boot to boot, it is possible to edit the networking startup file, */etc/rc2.d/S69inet*, and add this line to any others that configure the network interfaces.

You should be aware that altering ndd parameters will affect all TCP services, so while a Web server might perform optimally with *tcp_close_wait_interval* equal to 30 seconds, a database listener that handles large datasets may require a much wider time window. The best way to determine optimal values is to perform experiments with low, moderate, and peak levels of traffic for both the Web server and the database listener, to determine a value that will provide reasonable performance for both applications. It is also important to check SunSolve for the latest patches and updates for recently discovered kernel bugs.

Examples

The following examples show how to configure Solaris networking.

Configuring inetd

Services for `inetd` are defined in */etc/inetd.conf*. Every time you make a change to *inetd.conf*, you need to send a HUP signal to the `inetd` process. You can identify the process ID (PID) of `inetd` by using the `ps` command and then sending a kill SIGHUP signal to that PID from the shell. In addition, commenting an entry in the */etc/services* file will not necessarily prevent a service from running: strictly speaking, only services that make the `getprotobyname()` call to retrieve their port number require the */etc/services* file. So, for applications like `talk`, removing their entry in */etc/services* has no effect. To prevent the `talk` daemon from running, you would need to comment out its entry in */etc/inetd.conf* and send a SIGHUP to the `inetd` process.

A service definition in */etc/inetd.conf* has the following format:

```
service socket protocol flags user server_name arguments
```

where the service uses either datagrams or streams, and uses UDP or TCP on the transport layer, with the *server_name* being executed by the user. An example entry is the UDP `talk` service:

```
talk dgram udp wait root /usr/sbin/in.talkd in.talkd
```

The `talk` service uses datagrams over UDP and is executed by the root user, with the `talk` daemon being physically located in */usr/sbin/in.talkd*. Once the `talk` daemon is running through `inetd`, it is used for interactive screen-based communication between two users (with at least one user "talking" on the local system).

To prevent users from using (or abusing) the `talk` facility, you would need to comment out the definition for the `talk` daemon in the */etc/inetd.conf* file. Thus, the line shown earlier would be changed to this:

```
#talk dgram udp wait root /usr/sbin/in.talkd in.talkd
```

In order for `inetd` to register the change, it needs to be restarted by using the `kill` command. To identify the PID for `inetd`, the following command may be used:

```
# ps -eaf | grep inetd
   root    206    1   0    May 16 ?        30:19 /usr/sbin/inetd -s
```

To restart the process, the following command would be used:

```
kill -1 206
```

The daemon would then restart after reading in the modified *inetd.conf* file.

Configuring Services

TCP is a connection-oriented protocol that guarantees delivery of packets, where data has been segmented into smaller units. The benefit of transmitting small units in a guaranteed delivery scheme is that, if checksum errors are detected or some data is not received, the amount of data that needs to be transmitted is very small. In addition, if packet delivery times out, packets can then be retransmitted. By using sequence numbers,

TCP always manages to reassemble packets in their correct order. Port numbers for TCP (and UDP) services are defined in the /etc/services database. A sample database is shown here:

```
tcpmux          1/tcp
echo            7/tcp
echo            7/udp
discard         9/tcp           sink null
discard         9/udp           sink null
systat          11/tcp          users
daytime         13/tcp
...
```

Reading from left to right are the service name, port number, transport type, and service aliases. Other services defined in the preceding example include the `echo` service, which simply sends back the segment transmitted to it, the `daytime` service, which returns the current local time at the server, `ftp`, which supports the File Transfer Protocol (FTP) service, and `smtp`, which supports SMTP. If services are not to be supported on the localhost, then their entries should be commented in the service database. For example, to disable the service definition for the `finger` service, which allows remote users to check local user details, the `finger` entry would be modified as follows:

```
#finger         79/tcp
```

Port numbers 1 to 1024 are standard, as defined by RFC memos (**http://www.rfc-editor.org/rfc.html**). Nonstandard services can be run on ports above 1024. Some services have been standardized above this maximum by general convention, such as the X11 server.

Application Protocols

Services are implemented by daemons that listen for connections, and generate responses based on specific requests. Many of the TCP service definitions match up with an application supported by a daemon (server) process. There are two types of daemons supported by Solaris: standalone daemons and `inetd` daemons. Standalone daemons internally manage their own activities, while `inetd` allows daemons to be run through a single central server. This allows for centralization of administration and reduces the need for processes running on a system, since `inetd` can listen for connections, and invoke daemon processes as required. Definitions for services are contained in the /etc/inetd.conf file. A sample /etc/inetd.conf file is shown here:

```
ftp       stream  tcp   nowait  root    /usr/sbin/in.ftpd       in.ftpd -l
telnet    stream  tcp   nowait  root    /usr/sbin/in.telnetd    in.telnetd
name      dgram   udp   wait    root    /usr/sbin/in.tnamed     in.tnamed
shell     stream  tcp   nowait  root    /usr/sbin/in.rshd       in.rshd
```

```
login    stream  tcp     nowait  root    /usr/sbin/in.rlogind    in.rlogind
exec     stream  tcp     nowait  root    /usr/sbin/in.rexecd     in.rexecd
comsat   dgram   udp     wait    root    /usr/sbin/in.comsat     in.comsat
talk     dgram   udp     wait    root    /usr/sbin/in.talkd      in.talkd
uucp     stream  tcp     nowait  root    /usr/sbin/in.uucpd      in.uucpd
tftp     dgram   udp     wait    root    /usr/sbin/in.tftpd      in.tftpd -s
/tftpboot
finger   stream  tcp     nowait  nobody  /usr/sbin/in.fingerd    in.fingerd
systat   stream  tcp     nowait  root    /usr/bin/ps             ps -ef
netstat  stream  tcp     nowait  root    /usr/bin/netstat        netstat -f inet
...
```

Reading from left to right are the service name, socket type, transport protocol, flags, executing user, and daemon program to execute upon request. Socket types include streams or datagrams, transports include TCP and UDP, and flags include wait (wait after response) and nowait (exit after response).

A sample inetd application is the talk service. By examining its definition in */etc/inetd.conf*, you can see that it uses datagram sockets, runs on UDP, waits until timeout, is run by root, is implemented by the command */usr/sbin/in.talkd*, and has the name *in.talkd*. The talk service supports instant communications between users on the local system, or between any two systems on the Internet. To issue a talk request to a remote user, a local user would issue the talk command followed by the user's username and FQDN. For example, to talk to the user *shusaku* at the host *users.cassowary.net*, the following command would be used:

```
$ talk shusaku@users.cassowary.net
```

If the host *users.cassowary.net* is running inetd, and inetd supports *in.talkd*, then the following talk request would appear on the user *shusaku's* login shell:

```
Message from Talk_Daemon@db.cassowary.net at 10:50 ...
talk: connection requested by yasuanri@db.cassowary.net.
talk: respond with:  talk yasunari@db.cassowary.net
```

If the user *shusaku* wished to "talk" with *yasunari*, the following command would be used by *shusaku*:

```
$ talk yasunari@db.cassowary.net
```

If a service is to be disabled for security purposes, then its entry can simply be commented out, just like for the services database. For example, to disable the finger service, the finger entry would be commented as follows:

```
#finger  stream  tcp     nowait  nobody  /usr/sbin/in.fingerd    in.fingerd
```

Once changes have been made to *inetd.conf*, a SIGHUP signal should be sent to the inetd process, causing it to reread the *inetd.conf* file. To restart `inetd` with a PID of 186, the following command would be used:

```
# kill -1 186
```

Many of the services supported by `inetd` support remote access, and can possibly be deemed security risks.

/etc/inetd.conf

A sample *inetd.conf* file is shown next. It contains entries for the most commonly used Internet services.

```
ftp       stream  tcp   nowait  root   /usr/sbin/in.ftpd      in.ftpd -1
telnet    stream  tcp   nowait  root   /usr/sbin/in.telnetd   in.telnetd
name      dgram   udp   wait    root   /usr/sbin/in.tnamed    in.tnamed
shell     stream  tcp   nowait  root   /usr/sbin/in.rshd      in.rshd
login     stream  tcp   nowait  root   /usr/sbin/in.rlogind   in.rlogind
exec      stream  tcp   nowait  root   /usr/sbin/in.rexecd    in.rexecd
comsat    dgram   udp   wait    root   /usr/sbin/in.comsat    in.comsat
talk      dgram   udp   wait    root   /usr/sbin/in.talkd     in.talkd
uucp      stream  tcp   nowait  root   /usr/sbin/in.uucpd     in.uucpd
```

Some of these services are described here:

- **fingerd**   Checks to see who is logged into a system
- **rdisc**   Allows routes to be discovered on the network
- **rexecd**   Permits commands to be executed remotely
- **rlogind**   Allows a remote login to another server
- **rshd**   Spawns a shell on a remote system
- **rwhod**   Checks to see who is running processes
- **telnetd**   Connects to a remote host
- **tftpd**   Supports Trivial FTP for diskless clients
- **uucpd**   Implements the UNIX-to-UNIX Copy Program
- **pcmciad**   Manages PCMCIA operations
- **rstatd**   Allows system resources to be monitored remotely
- **rwalld**   Permits a message to be written to all logged-in users on a network
- **statd**   Allows system resources to be monitored locally
- **syslogd**   Configurable system log
- **talkd**   Allows remote users to chat in real time

/etc/services

Many `inetd` services must be mapped to a specific port number: a sample */etc/services* file, shown next, defines port numbers for most of the commonly used services:

```
tcpmux          1/tcp
echo            7/tcp
echo            7/udp
discard         9/tcp           sink null
discard         9/udp           sink null
systat          11/tcp          users
daytime         13/tcp
daytime         13/udp
netstat         15/tcp
```

Checking if a Host Is "Up"

The easiest way to check if a remote host is accessible is to use the `ping` command. The following example checks whether the host *emu* is accessible from the host *dingo*:

```
$ ping emu
```

If *emu* is accessible, the following output will be generated:

```
emu is alive
```

However, if *emu* is not accessible, an error message similar to the following will be seen:

```
Request timed out
```

If you need to determine at what point in the network the connection is failing, you can use the `traceroute` command to display the path taken by packets between the two hosts as they travel across the network. For example, to observe the route of the path taken by packets from AT&T to Sun's Web server, I would use the following command:

```
$ traceroute www.sun.com
Tracing route to wwwwseast.usec.sun.com [192.9.49.30]
over a maximum of 30 hops:
  1   184 ms    142 ms    138 ms   202.10.4.131
  2   147 ms    144 ms    138 ms   202.10.4.129
  3   150 ms    142 ms    144 ms   202.10.1.73
  4   150 ms    144 ms    141 ms   atm11-0-0-11.ia4.optus.net.au
       [202.139.32.17]
  5   148 ms    143 ms    139 ms   202.139.1.197
  6   490 ms    489 ms    474 ms   hssi9-0-0.sf1.optus.net.au
       [192.65.89.246]
```

```
 7   526 ms    480 ms    485 ms   g-sfd-br-02-f12-0.gn.cwix.net
     [207.124.109.57]
 8   494 ms    482 ms    485 ms   core7-hssi6-0-0.SanFrancisco.cw.net
     [204.70.10.9]
 9   483 ms    489 ms    484 ms   corerouter2.SanFrancisco.cw.net
     [204.70.9.132]
10   557 ms    552 ms    561 ms   xcore3.Boston.cw.net [204.70.150.81]
11   566 ms    572 ms    554 ms   sun-micro-system.Boston.cw.net
     [204.70.179.102]
12   577 ms    574 ms    558 ms   wwwwseast.usec.sun.com [192.9.49.30]
Trace complete.
```

If the connection was broken at any point, then * or ! would be displayed in place of the average connection times displayed. An asterisk would also appear if the router concerned was blocking connections for `traceroute` packets.

Command Reference

The following commands are useful for configuring Solaris networking.

arp

You can check the table of IP address–to–MAC address mappings by using the `arp` command:

```
$ arp -a
Net to Media Table
Device  IP Address            Mask             Flags  Phys Addr
------  --------------------  ---------------  -----  ---------------
hme0    www.cassowary.net     255.255.255.255         00:19:cd:e3:05:a3
hme0    mail.cassowary.net    255.255.255.255         08:11:92:a4:12:ee
hme0    ftp.cassowary.net     255.255.255.255  SP     08:12:4e:4d:55:a2
hme0    BASE-ADDRESS.MCAST.NET 240.0.0.0       SM     01:01:4e:00:00:00
```

Here, the network device is shown with the fully qualified hostname (or IP address), the netmask, any flags, and the MAC address. The flags indicate the status of each interface, including SP for the localhost, where an entry will be published on request, and SM for the localhost, supporting multicast. Alternatively, a specific host can be queried by passing its name on the command line:

```
$ arp mail
mail (204.67.34.12) at 08:11:92:a4:12:ee
```

ARP works by broadcasting to identify the appropriate channel on which to locate the target host. Conversely, RARP is used to map MAC addresses to IP addresses. RARP is typically used to supply IP addresses from boot servers to diskless clients. A database of Ethernet addresses is maintained in the */etc/ethers* table to support this activity.

snoop

Packet interception is performed by the `snoop` application, which reads raw packet data from a network interface operating in promiscuous mode. The following example shows ETHER (Link), IP (Network), TCP (Transport), and Telnet (Application) sections, respectively:

```
# snoop -v tcp port 23
Using device /dev/hme0 (promiscuous mode)
ETHER:  ----- Ether Header -----
ETHER:
ETHER:  Packet 1 arrived at 14:13:22.14
ETHER:  Packet size = 60 bytes
ETHER:  Destination = 1:58:4:16:8a:34,
ETHER:  Source     = 2:60:5:12:6b:35, Sun
ETHER:  Ethertype = 0800 (IP)
ETHER:
IP:   ----- IP Header -----
IP:
IP:   Version = 4
IP:   Header length = 20 bytes
IP:   Type of service = 0x00
IP:         xxx. .... = 0 (precedence)
IP:         ...0 .... = normal delay
IP:         .... 0... = normal throughput
IP:         .... .0.. = normal reliability
IP:   Total length = 40 bytes
IP:   Identification = 46864
IP:   Flags = 0x4
IP:         .1.. .... = do not fragment
IP:         ..0. .... = last fragment
IP:   Fragment offset = 0 bytes
IP:   Time to live = 255 seconds/hops
IP:   Protocol = 6 (TCP)
IP:   Header checksum = 11a9
IP:   Source address = 64.23.168.76, moppet.paulwatters.com
IP:   Destination address = 64.23.168.48, miki.paulwatters.com
IP:   No options
IP:
TCP:  ----- TCP Header -----
TCP:
TCP:  Source port = 62421
TCP:  Destination port = 23 (TELNET)
TCP:  Sequence number = 796159562
TCP:  Acknowledgement number = 105859685
TCP:  Data offset = 20 bytes
TCP:  Flags = 0x10
TCP:         ..0. .... = No urgent pointer
TCP:         ...1 .... = Acknowledgement
```

```
TCP:          .... 0... = No push
TCP:          .... .0.. = No reset
TCP:          .... ..0. = No Syn
TCP:          .... ...0 = No Fin
TCP:   Window = 8760
TCP:   Checksum = 0x8f8f
TCP:   Urgent pointer = 0
TCP:   No options
TCP:
TELNET:    ----- TELNET:    -----
TELNET:
TELNET:   "a"
TELNET:
```

The ETHER header defines many of the characteristics of the packet. In the `snoop` example, the packets arrival time, size (in bytes), and destination and source addresses (Ethernet format) are all noted. In addition, the network type is also supplied. This leads into the IP header, which shows the IP version (IPv4), the length of the header (in bytes), destination and source addresses (IP format), and a checksum to ensure data integrity. Also, the protocol for transport is defined as TCP. The TCP header shows the port on which the data is being sent and on which it should be received, in addition to the application type (Telnet). The sequence and acknowledgement numbers determine how packets are ordered at the receiving end, since TCP is connection-oriented and guarantees data delivery, unlike other transport protocols, such as UDP, which are connectionless and do not guarantee the delivery of data. Finally, the data being transported is displayed: "a". In addition to Telnet, other application protocols include SMTP, FTP, and NFS.

ndd

ndd is used to set parameters for network protocols, including TCP, IP, UDP, and ARP. It can be used to modify the parameters associated with IP forwarding and routing. For example, take a look at the set of configurable parameters for TCP transmission:

```
server# ndd /dev/tcp \?
?                              (read only)
tcp_close_wait_interval        (read and write)
tcp_conn_req_max_q             (read and write)
tcp_conn_req_max_q0            (read and write)
tcp_conn_req_min               (read and write)
tcp_conn_grace_period          (read and write)
tcp_cwnd_max                   (read and write)
tcp_debug                      (read and write)
tcp_smallest_nonpriv_port      (read and write)
tcp_ip_abort_cinterval         (read and write)
tcp_ip_abort_linterval         (read and write)
tcp_ip_abort_interval          (read and write)
tcp_ip_notify_cinterval        (read and write)
tcp_ip_notify_interval         (read and write)
```

```
tcp_ip_ttl                        (read and write)
tcp_keepalive_interval            (read and write)
tcp_maxpsz_multiplier             (read and write)
tcp_mss_def                       (read and write)
tcp_mss_max                       (read and write)
tcp_mss_min                       (read and write)
tcp_naglim_def                    (read and write)
tcp_rexmit_interval_initial       (read and write)
tcp_rexmit_interval_max           (read and write)
tcp_rexmit_interval_min           (read and write)
tcp_wroff_xtra                    (read and write)
tcp_deferred_ack_interval         (read and write)
tcp_snd_lowat_fraction            (read and write)
tcp_sth_rcv_hiwat                 (read and write)
tcp_sth_rcv_lowat                 (read and write)
tcp_dupack_fast_retransmit        (read and write)
tcp_ignore_path_mtu               (read and write)
tcp_rcv_push_wait                 (read and write)
tcp_smallest_anon_port            (read and write)
tcp_largest_anon_port             (read and write)
tcp_xmit_hiwat                    (read and write)
tcp_xmit_lowat                    (read and write)
tcp_recv_hiwat                    (read and write)
tcp_recv_hiwat_minmss             (read and write)
tcp_fin_wait_2_flush_interval     (read and write)
tcp_co_min                        (read and write)
tcp_max_buf                       (read and write)
tcp_zero_win_probesize            (read and write)
tcp_strong_iss                    (read and write)
tcp_rtt_updates                   (read and write)
tcp_wscale_always                 (read and write)
tcp_tstamp_always                 (read and write)
tcp_tstamp_if_wscale              (read and write)
tcp_rexmit_interval_extra         (read and write)
tcp_deferred_acks_max             (read and write)
tcp_slow_start_after_idle         (read and write)
tcp_slow_start_initial            (read and write)
tcp_co_timer_interval             (read and write)
tcp_extra_priv_ports              (read only)
tcp_extra_priv_ports_add          (write only)
tcp_extra_priv_ports_del          (write only)
tcp_status                        (read only)
tcp_bind_hash                     (read only)
tcp_listen_hash                   (read only)
tcp_conn_hash                     (read only)
tcp_queue_hash                    (read only)
tcp_host_param                    (read and write)
tcp_1948_phrase                   (write only)
```

PART V

Parameters can also be set for IP. For example, if the parameter *ip_forwarding* has a value of 2 (the default), it will perform routing only when two or more interfaces are active. However, if this parameter is set to zero, *ip_forwarding* will never be performed (that is, to ensure that multihoming is enabled rather than routing). This can be set by using the command

```
# ndd -set /dev/ip ip_forwarding 0
```

Summary

This chapter examined the basic principles and procedures of Solaris networking. While we have covered a lot of ground, it's worthwhile learning how to relate services and applications from different TCP/IP layers to ensure end-to-end network connectivity.

DHCP and NTP

This chapter examines the Dynamic Host Configuration Protocol (DHCP), which is an easy way to dynamically manage IP addresses in class A, class B, and class C networks, using time-based leases for client addresses. Since at any one time only a few IP addresses on a network may be in use, organizing their allocation dynamically makes more sense than statically assigning them to individual hosts. This is particularly important for popular class C networks, in which less than 300 addresses are available. In this chapter, you will learn the background of DHCP and similar protocols (RARP and BOOTP). In addition, this chapter walks you through how to install a Solaris DHCP server and how to configure DHCP clients. It also investigates the Network Time Protocol (NTP), which provides a framework for standardizing and synchronizing accurate time and date settings on individual systems and on networks of systems.

This chapter covers practical issues associated with installing DHCP servers and configuring DHCP clients on Windows, Linux, and Solaris systems. It is assumed that you are familiar with DNS and with TCP/IP stacks implemented on Solaris, Linux, or Windows systems. Starting with a description of the DHCP protocol and its historical roots in the BOOTP protocol, the chapter aims to provide a reference of the DHCP protocol and practical installation and configuration procedures for heterogeneous environments.

Key Concepts

The following key concepts are required knowledge for configuring DHCP and NTP.

Dynamic Host Configuration Protocol

The Internet is a worldwide, networked environment through which information can be exchanged by using a number of well-defined network protocols, such as the Transmission Control Protocol (TCP) and User Datagram Protocol (UDP). Each host on the Internet can be identified by a single machine-friendly number (e.g., 128.43.22.1), which is mapped to a human-friendly Fully Qualified Domain Name (e.g., *www.paulwatters.com*). This mapping is provided by a globally distributed database, known as the Domain Name

Service (DNS), which allows local networks to statically assign IP address ranges to all their local hosts.

When DNS was first introduced, the exponential growth of networks and hosts connected to the Internet was not anticipated. This means that IP address allocations initially reserved for class A, B, and C networks were rather generous in hindsight—many address ranges were not used to their full capacity. Nowadays, there is a critical shortage of available IP address space using the current IPv4 standard. Although the new IPv6 protocol (supported by Solaris 10) will provide many more potential addresses, organizations worldwide are seeking solutions to use their existing resources more efficiently. While IPv6 is currently being adopted by many organizations, widespread deployment is not anticipated in the near future.

As an alternative to static IP address allocation, a practical alternative IP address management strategy is to use DHCP. This protocol allows a server to dynamically allocate IP addresses from a central DHCP server to all configured DHCP clients on the local network. DHCP provides a mechanism by which computers using TCP/IP can obtain protocol configuration parameters automatically, by using a lease mechanism, without having to rely on static addresses, which could be incorrect or outdated. This means that only hosts that are "up" will take an IP address from the pool of existing addresses assigned to a particular network, by requesting and accepting an IP address lease from the DHCP server. However, if a machine has been assigned an IP address, then it is possible that the lease on that machine has still not expired. Thus the machine is not up but still has an IP address. For a class C network, the pool of available addresses is (at most) 254, excluding the broadcast address, which is insufficient for many growing organizations. In addition, if an organization changes ISP, the organization ordinarily needs to change the network configuration parameters for each client system, a manual and inefficient process that consumes the valuable time of network administrators.

DHCP is not the only protocol to lease out IP addresses in this way. Previously, Solaris clients used the Reverse Address Resolution Protocol (RARP) to obtain an IP address dynamically from a RARP server. This protocol is particularly important for diskless clients who cannot store their IP address locally. However, DHCP is better than RARP because it supports clients from Solaris, Linux, and Microsoft Windows and can serve more parameters than just an IP address. In addition, RARP servers can provide addresses to only a single network, whereas DHCP is capable of serving multiple networks from a single server, provided that routing is correctly set up. On the other hand, Microsoft Windows administrators should be familiar with the Bootstrap Protocol (BOOTP), which provided IP addresses dynamically in the same way that DHCP does. In fact, DHCP can be considered a superset of BOOTP, and DHCP servers are generally backward compatible with BOOTP. The relationship between DHCP and BOOTP is historical: the BOOTP protocol is the foundation on which DHCP was built. Many similarities remain: the packet formats for DHCP and BOOTP are the same, although BOOTP packets are fixed length and DHCP packets are variable length. The DHCP packet length is negotiated between the client and the server.

Another advantage of DHCP over proprietary protocols is that it is an open network standard, developed through the Internet Engineering Task Force (IETF). It is based on a client/server paradigm, in which the DHCP client (e.g., a PC running Microsoft Windows) contacts a DHCP server (e.g., a server running Solaris) for its network configuration parameters. The DHCP server is typically centrally located and is under the control of the network administrator. Since the server is secure, DHCP clients can obtain reliable information for dynamic configuration, with parameters that reflect up-to-date changes in the current network architecture. For example, if a client is moved to a new network, it must be assigned a new IP address for that new network. DHCP can be used to manage these assignments automatically. If you are interested in finding out more about how DHCP works, refer to RFC 2131. There is also a reference implementation of a DHCP server, client, and relay agent available from Internet Systems Consortium (ISC), a nonprofit corporation (**http://www.isc.org/**). The ISC implementation uses a modular API, which is designed to work with both POSIX-compliant and non-POSIX-compliant operating systems. It also includes source code, making it useful for understanding how DHCP works behind the scenes.

In addition to dynamically allocating IP addresses, DHCP serves other key network configuration parameters, such as the subnet mask, default router, and Domain Name System (DNS) server. Again, this goes beyond the capabilities of competing protocols like RARP. By deploying a DHCP server, network administrators can reduce repetitive client-based configuration of individual computers, often requiring the use of confusing OS-specific setup applications. Instead, clients can obtain all of their required network configuration parameters automatically, without manual intervention, from a centrally managed DHCP server.

Both commercial and freeware versions of DHCP clients and servers are available for all platforms. For example, Check Point's (**http://www.checkpoint.com/**) DHCP server can be integrated with its firewall product, Firewall-1, to maximize the security potential of centralized network configuration management. Advanced network management protocols are supported by DHCP, like the Simple Network Management Protocol (SNMP). In addition, configuration change-management issues, like IP mobility and managing addresses for multiple subnets, can all be handled from a single DHCP server.

Implementation of DHCP should always be evaluated in the context of other network management protocols, like SNMP, and other directory services, like the Lightweight Directory Access Protocol (LDAP). Both LDAP and SNMP are crucial to the management of hosts and users in large and distributed networks. Since DHCP is responsible for the allocation of network configuration parameters, it is essential that SNMP agents obtain the correct information about hosts that they manage. In addition, LDAP server administrators need to be aware that host IP addresses will change over time.

Network Time Protocol

Time may be relative to the observer, but keeping accurate and consistent time provides a critical frame of reference for applications running on a local server and across the network. For example, imagine a database application that records bank balances in a temporary database for an Internet banking system. The most recent bank balance for each account, when updated, would be always inserted into the Balance column of the

Accounts table, with two primary keys to identify the balances: account_name and timestamp. Whenever the latest balance is to be entered, a new row is inserted into the Accounts table with the account_name, balance, and timestamp. All other transactions, such as withdrawals, require that the most recent balance be determined from the timestamp (no updates of rows are permitted, for security reasons). If dates and times are not maintained consistently on the system, the potential exists for the true bank balance at the present time to be missed for selection based on the incorrect timestamp it may have been assigned.

This disparity would clearly render the application useless. Figure 22-1 demonstrates this scenario in action—two balances have been inserted into the Accounts table for account_name 95639656: $18,475.90 is the balance on January 1, 2002, at 18:54:21, and $17,475.90 is the balance on the same day at 18:54:22. This set of entries indicates that a withdrawal of $1,000 occurred one second after the first transaction. What if the system clock did not have accuracy to within one second? The incorrect balance of $18,475.90 might then be reported when future queries are run.

While most systems are capable of maintaining millisecond accuracy for time, a more complex situation arises when high availability and clustering become involved and different systems in the cluster have different times and dates. For example, imagine that a single database server receives updates from six Java 2 Enterprise Edition (J2EE) application servers on six different machines. These servers process requests from clients in a round-robin fashion, and all update the same table on the database server. This allows each application server to always retrieve the most up-to-date information for each client. However, if each server has a different date and time, they would be writing balances into the Accounts table with varying timestamps. Again, the fact that the timestamps varied would prevent the application from being used seriously.

Figure 22-2 again demonstrates this scenario—two balances have been inserted into the Accounts table for account_name 95639656: server1 inserted the balance $18,475.90 on January 1, 2002 at 18:54:21, and server2 inserted the balance $17,475.90 on January 1, 2002 at 18:54:22. This set of entries indicates that a withdrawal of $1,000 occurred one second after the first transaction. If the two clocks of server1 and server2

FIGURE 22-1
Inserting database records using timestamps requires accurate timekeeping.

account_name	Balance	timestamp
95639656	18475.90	01012002185421
95639656	17475.90	01012002185422

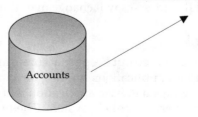

FIGURE 22-2
Inserting database
records from
multiple servers
using timestamps
requires even
more accurate
timekeeping.

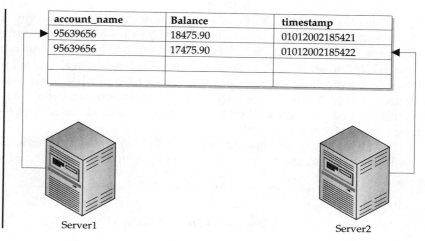

account_name	Balance	timestamp
95639656	18475.90	01012002185421
95639656	17475.90	01012002185422

were not synchronized with millisecond accuracy, we would never know which balance ($18,475.90 or $17,475.90) is actually correct. What if a leap second was observed on one server and not another? Clearly, there is a need for systems to be able to regularly synchronize their clocks to ensure consistency in enterprise applications.

One solution that solves the accuracy problem for single systems and for networks is the Network Time Protocol (NTP). The current production version of NTP is v3, specified in RFC 1305, which allows time to be synchronized between all systems on a network by using multicast, and also permits high-precision external hardware clock devices to be supported as authoritative time sources. These two approaches ensure that potential data-consistency problems caused by timestamps do not hamper online transaction processing and other real-time data-processing applications. By using a master-slave approach, one server on the network can be delegated the authority for timekeeping for all systems on that network. Using a master-slave approach ensures that multiple, potentially conflicting sources of authoritative time do not interfere with each other's operation. Note that Simple NTP (SNTP) version 4 is described in RFC 2030; however, it is still under development and is not a formal RFC yet.

NTPv3 provides a number of enhancements over previous versions—it supports a method for servers to communicate with a set of peer servers to average offsets and achieve a more accurate estimation of current time. This is a similar method used by national measurement laboratories and similar timekeeping organizations. In addition, network bandwidth can be preserved because the interval between client/server synchronizations has been substantially increased. This improvement in efficiency has been achieved because of the improvements to the local-clock algorithm's accuracy. In any case, NTP uses UDP to communicate synchronization data, minimizing any network overhead. In order for clients to access server data, the IP address or hostname of the server must be known—there is no mechanism for automatic discovery of a time server defined by NTP.

While NTP has a simple client/server interface, individual servers also have the ability to act as secondary servers for external, authoritative time sources. For example, a network might have a designated time server from which all clients retrieve the correct time, which the server in turn authoritatively receives from a national measurement laboratory. In addition, hardware clocks can be used as a backup in case of network failure between the local network and the measurement laboratory. When a connection is reestablished, the local server's time can simply be recalibrated with the authoritative time received from the laboratory.

This chapter examines how to configure NTP servers and clients to synchronize their timekeeping and examines strategies for maintaining accurate time on the server side.

Procedures

The following procedures are used to run DHCP and NTP.

DHCP Operations

The basic DHCP process is a straightforward, two-phase process involving a single DHCP client and at least one DHCP server. When the DHCP client (dhcpagent) is started on a client, it broadcasts a DHCPDISCOVER request for an IP address on the local network, which is received by all available servers running a DHCP server (in.dhcpd). Next, all DHCP servers that have spare IP addresses answer the client's request through a DHCPOFFER message, which contains an IP address, subnet mask, default router name, and DNS server IP address. If multiple DHCP servers have IP addresses available, it is possible that multiple servers will respond to the client request. The client simply accepts the first DHCPOFFER that it receives, upon which it broadcasts a DHCPREQUEST message, indicating that a lease has been obtained. Once the server whose IP is accepted has received this second request, it confirms the lease with a DHCPACK message. After a client has finished using the IP address, a DHCPRELEASE message is sent to the server.

In the situation where a server has proposed a lease in the first phase that it is unable to fulfill in the second phase, it must respond with a DHCPNACK message. This means that the client will then broadcast a DHCPDISCOVER message, and the process will start again. A DHCPNACK message is usually sent if a timeout has occurred between the original DHCPDISCOVER request and the subsequent reception at the server side of a DHCPREQUEST message. This is often due to network outages or congestion. The list of all possible DHCP messages is shown in Table 22-1.

The DHCPOFFER message specifies the lease period, after which the lease will be deemed to have expired and will be made available to other clients. However, clients also have the option of renewing an existing lease, so that their existing IP address can be retained. DHCP defines fixed intervals prior to actual lease expiry at which time a client should indicate whether or not it wishes to extend the lease. If these renewals are not made in time, a DHCPRELEASE message will be broadcast, and then the lease will be invalid.

TABLE 22-1
DHCP Codes and
Their Meanings

Code	Description
DHCPDISCOVER	Broadcast from client to all reachable servers
DHCPOFFER	Server responds to DHCPDISCOVER requests
DHCPREQUEST	Client accepts lease proposal from only one server
DHCPACK	Server acknowledges lease
DHCPNACK	Server refuses to accept DHCPREQUEST
DHCPRELEASE	Lease no longer required

DHCP has three ways to allocate leases to client. Automatic allocation grants an IP address permanently to a client. This is useful for granting IP addresses to servers that require a static IP address. A DNS server typically requires a static IP address, which can be registered in host records lodged with InterNIC. The majority of clients will have addresses assigned dynamically by the server, which allows the greatest reuse of addresses. Alternatively, an administrator may manually assign an address to a specific client.

The process of allocating a DHCP lease is shown in Figure 22-3.

Configuring an NTP Server

The Solaris NTP daemon is `xntpd`. It operates by listening for requests from NTP clients and sends responses appropriately. The server processes a request, modifies the appropriate fields with the correct time, etc., and then returns the modified request data as a response. The response allows the client to modify its clock settings appropriately. In addition, the server is able to provide data from a number of different authoritative sources.

FIGURE 22-3
How DHCP leases
IP addresses

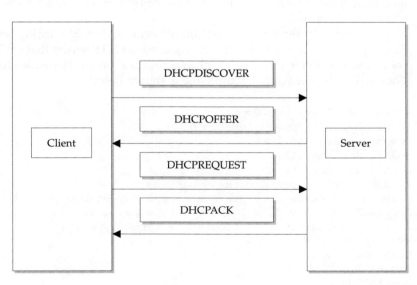

PART V

The accuracy of a client's time can be improved by selecting the most accurate server. Fortunately, there are measurements available to determine which clocks provide the most accurate data. Reliability and accuracy data is returned in the response data when a client makes a request to the server.

In a more complex network, where a time server must be highly available, it may be more appropriate to create a hierarchical system of NTP servers, where dynamic reconfiguration is possible. This is only necessary where hardware or software failures can affect a single production system's reliability. In this case, multiple servers can act as peers to each other. A primary time server in this setup obtains its time from a reference, such as an external clock device, and transmits it to other, secondary servers. Alternatively, there may be multiple primary time servers, and secondary servers must determine which server is most accurate. Clients then access secondary sources directly.

Of course, this creates a stratum of accuracy, with primary servers being the most accurate, secondary servers being the next most accurate, and clients being the least accurate. Millisecond accuracy should be possible with secondary servers. However, errors can be estimated even at the client level and corrections made to improve the overall accuracy of the time estimation.

The timestamp lies at the core of the NTP data model—it is the number of seconds that have elapsed since 01/01/1900 00:00 and is represented by a 64-bit unsigned floating-point number. The first 32 bits represent the integer portion of the number, while the last 32 bits represent the fractional portion of the number.

The number of seconds in one non-leap year is 31,536,000. Given that only 64 bits are available to store time data in the NTP timestamp format, the maximum value will be reached in the year 2036. Given the number of legacy applications even now that use timestamping, a significant amount of planning will be required over the next 30 years or so to develop a new, high-capacity timestamp format that is backward compatible with existing formats.

A sample NTP server configuration file is located in */etc/inet/ntp.server*. This file provides a pro forma template for configuring an NTP server that utilizes an external clock device, provides for local clock synchronization, and provides for broadcasting times across the network. A sample file is shown here:

```
server 127.127.XType.0 prefer
fudge 127.127.XType.0 stratum 0
broadcast 224.0.1.1 ttl 4
enable auth monitor
driftfile /var/ntp/ntp.drift
statsdir /var/ntp/ntpstats/
filegen peerstats file peerstats type day enable
filegen loopstats file loopstats type day enable
filegen clockstats file clockstats type day enable
keys /etc/inet/ntp.keys
trustedkey 0
requestkey 0
controlkey 0
```

TABLE 22-2
XTypes Available
Through xntpd

XType	Device	RefID	Description
1	local	LCL	Undisciplined Local Clock
2	trak	GPS	TRAK 8820 GPS Receiver
3	pst	WWV	PSTI/Traconex WWV/WWVH Receiver
4	wwvb	WWVB	Spectracom WWVB Receiver
5	true	TRUE	TrueTime GPS/GOES Receivers
6	irig	IRIG	IRIG Audio Decoder
7	chu	CHU	Scratchbuilt CHU Receiver
8	parse	—	Generic Reference Clock Driver
9	mx4200	GPS	Magnavox MX4200 GPS Receiver
10	as2201	GPS	Austron 2201A GPS Receiver
11	arbiter	GPS	Arbiter 1088A/B GPS Receiver
12	tpro	IRIG	KSI/Odetics TPRO/S IRIG Interface
13	leitch	ATOM	Leitch CSD 5300 Master Clock Controller
15	*	*	TrueTime GPS/TM-TMD Receiver
17	datum	DATM	Datum Precision Time System
18	acts	ACTS	NIST Automated Computer Time Service
19	heath	WWV	Heath WWV/WWVH Receiver
20	nmea	GPS	Generic NMEA GPS Receiver
22	atom	PPS	PPS Clock Discipline
23	Ptb	TPTB	PTB Automated Computer Time Service
24	Usno	USNO	USNO Modem Time Service
25	*	*	TrueTime generic receivers
26	Hpgps	GPS	Hewlett Packard 58503A GPS Receiver
27	Arc	MSFa	Arcron MSF Receiver

The `server` entry indicates the primary server that this system prefers. The `broadcast` entry directs the server to broadcast messages to clients. The `driftfile` entry relates to a local clock's accuracy and its frequency offset.

In both cases where *XType* appears in the first two lines, a legal value for a clock device must be inserted. The clock device could be one of the devices shown in Table 22-2.

Once the settings for the NTP server have been modified, they should be saved in the file */etc/inet/ntp.conf*. When started in debug mode, the NTP server produces the following output:

```
/usr/lib/inet/xntpd -d
tick = 10000, tickadj = 5, hz = 100
kernel vars: tickadj = 5, tick = 10000
adj_precision = 1, tvu_maxslew = 495, tsf_maxslew = 0.002070b9
create_sockets(123)
```

```
bind() fd 19, family 2, port 123, addr 00000000, flags=1
bind() fd 20, family 2, port 123, addr 7f000001, flags=0
bind() fd 21, family 2, port 123, addr 0a401203, flags=1
init_io: maxactivefd 21
getconfig: Couldn't open </etc/inet/ntp.conf>
report_event: system event 'event_restart' (0x01) status 'sync_alarm,
sync_unspec, 1 event, event_unspec' (0xc010)
```

In this output, an error message is generated because the file */etc/inet/ntp.conf* could not be found—it's a common mistake not to copy across the template */etc/inet/ntp.server* file to */etc/inet/ntp.conf*! To observe the set of internal variables used by xntpd during its operation, the ntpq command can be used.

NTP Security

One of the main problems in tying all production time-management operations to a single primary server is the potential for crackers to either spoof a legitimate primary server and pretend to be the primary server or undertake a denial of service attack. Fortunately, NTP provides authentication procedures to ensure that only authorized servers and clients can access their peers and/or the primary server. In addition, the use of multiple authoritative sources, including a backup external hardware clock, can remove some of the problems associated with denial of service attacks—after all, if an external network port is being blocked by an attacker or group of attackers, then the local standby can always be used.

NTP security is ultimately based on trust relationships that are developed as part of an overall network design. In addition, a number of innovations in the NTP authentication system make it very difficult for a cracker to spoof a primary server. For example, the originate timestamp (the time at which the message was transmitted from a client) is equivalent to a one-time pad, although if the cracker has knowledge of previous timestamps, it may be possible, with sufficient CPU power, to successfully spoof a server. However, given the error-estimation procedures and methods for clients to select the most accurate server, it's unlikely that an attack would succeed.

Examples

The following examples show how to set up DHCP and NTP clients and servers.

Configuring a Solaris DHCP Server

The Solaris client (dhcpagent) and server (in.dhcpd) solution features backward compatibility with other methods already in use, particularly RARP and static configurations. In addition, the address of any workstation's network interfaces can be changed after the system has been booted. The dhcpagent client for Solaris features caching and automated lease renewal and is fully integrated with IP configuration (ifconfig). The in.dhcpd server for Solaris can provide both primary and secondary

DHCP services and is fully integrated with NIS+. The Solaris DHCP server has the ability to handle hundreds of concurrent requests and to boot diskless clients. Multiple DHCP support is provided through the Network File System (NFS). Although this chapter does not cover these advanced features, it's worthwhile to consider them when you are making a decision to use RARP or DHCP (or some other competing dynamic IP allocation method).

The main program used to configure DHCP under Solaris is */usr/sbin/dhcpconfig*, which is a shell script that performs the entire configuration for you. Alternatively, you can use the dhtadm or pntadm applications to manage the DHCP configuration table (*/var/dhcp/dhcptab*). The dhcpconfig program is menu-based, making it easy to use. The first menu displayed when you start the program looks like this:

```
***                     DHCP Configuration                    ***
    Would you like to:
    1)          Configure DHCP Service
    2)          Configure BOOTP Relay Agent
    3)          Unconfigure DHCP or Relay Service
    4)          Exit
    Choice:
```

The first menu option configures the DHCP service for initial use. If your system has never used DHCP, then you must start with this option. You will be asked to confirm DHCP startup options, such as the timeout periods made on lease offers (i.e., between sending DHCPOFFER and receiving a DHCPREQUEST), and whether or not to support legacy BOOTP clients. You will also be asked about the bootstrapping configuration, including the following settings:

- Timezone
- DNS server
- NIS server
- NIS+ server
- Default router
- Subnet mask
- Broadcast address

These settings can all be offered to the client as part of the DHCPOFFER message.

The second menu option configures the DHCP server to act simply as a relay agent. After you enter a list of BOOTP or DHCP servers to which requests can be forwarded, the relay agent should be operational.

Finally, you may choose to unconfigure either the full DHCP service or the relay service, which will revert all configuration files.

If you selected option 1, you will first be asked if you want to stop any current DHCP services:

```
Would you like to stop the DHCP service? (recommended) ([Y]/N)
```

Obviously, if you are supporting live clients, then you should not shut down the service. This is why DHCP configuration needs to take place outside normal business hours, so that normal service is not disrupted. If you have ensured that no clients are depending on the in.dhcpd service, you can answer yes to this question, and proceed.

Next, you are asked to identify the datastore for the DHCP database:

```
### DHCP Service Configuration ###
### Configure DHCP Database Type and Location ###
Enter datastore (files or nisplus) [nisplus]:
```

The default value is NIS+ (*nisplus*), covered in Chapter 29. However, if you are not using NIS+ to manage network information, then you may choose the *files* option. If you choose the *files* option, you need to identify the path to the DHCP datastore directory:

```
Enter absolute path to datastore directory [/var/dhcp]:
```

The default path is the */var/dhcp* directory. However, if your */var* partition is small or running low on space and you have a large network to manage, you may wish to locate the datastore directory somewhere else.

You will then be asked if you wish to enter any nondefault DHCP options:

```
Would you like to specify nondefault daemon options (Y/[N]):
```

Most users will choose the standard options. However, if you wish to enable additional facilities like BOOTP support, then you will need to answer yes to this question. You will then be asked whether you want to have transaction logging enabled:

```
Do you want to enable transaction logging? (Y/[N]):Y
```

Transaction logs are very useful for debugging, but grow rapidly in size over time, especially on a busy network. The size of the file will depend on the syslog level that you wish to enable as well:

```
Which syslog local facility [0-7] do you wish to log to? [0]:
```

Next, you will be asked to enter expiry times for leases that have been offered to the client:

```
How long (in seconds) should the DHCP server keep outstanding OFFERs? [10]:
```

The default is ten seconds, which is satisfactory for a fast network. However, if you are operating on a slow network, or expect to be servicing slow clients (like 486 PCs and below), then you may wish to increase the timeout. In addition, you can also specify that the *dhcptab* file be reread during a specified interval, which is useful only if you have made manual changes using dhtadm:

```
How often (in minutes) should the DHCP server rescan the dhcptab? [Never]:
```

If you wish to support BOOTP clients, you should indicate this at the next prompt:

```
Do you want to enable BOOTP compatibility mode? (Y/[N]):
```

After configuring these nondefault options, you will be asked to configure the standard DHCP options. The first option is the default lease time, which is specified in days:

```
Enter default DHCP lease policy (in days) [3]:
```

This value is largely subjective, although it can be estimated from the address congestion of your network. If you are only using an average 50 percent of the addresses on your network, then you can probably set this value to seven days without concern. If you are at the 75 percent level, then you may wish to use the default value of three days. If you are approaching saturation, then you should select daily lease renewal. If the number of hosts exceeds the number of available IP addresses, you may need to enter a fractional value, to ensure the most equitable distribution of addresses.

Most sites will wish to allow clients to renegotiate their existing leases:

```
Do you want to allow clients to renegotiate their leases? ([Y]/N):
```

However, just like a normal landlord, you may sometimes be compelled to reject requests for lease renewal, especially if your network is saturated.

You must now enable DHCP support for at least one network for DHCP to operate:

```
Enable DHCP/BOOTP support of networks you select? ([Y]/N):
```

For an example local network of 192.65.34.0, you will be asked the following questions:

```
Configure BOOTP/DHCP on local LAN network: 192.65.34.0? ([Y]/N):
```

You should (of course!) answer yes, if this is the network that you wish to configure DHCP for.

PART V

Next, you need to determine whether you wish DHCP to insert hostnames into the *hosts* file for you, based on the DHCP data:

```
Do you want hostnames generated and inserted in the files hosts table? (Y/[N]):
```

Most sites will use DNS or similar for name resolution, rather than the *hosts* file, so this option is not recommended. One situation in which you may wish to generate hostnames is if you are using a terminal server or Web server pool, where the hostnames are arbitrary and frequently change in number. In this case, you simply need to enter a sensible base name for the hostnames to be generated from:

```
What rootname do you want to use for generated names? [yourserver-]:
```

For a Web server bank, you could use a descriptive name like *www-*.

Next, you will be asked to define the IP address range that you want the DHCP server to manage, beginning with the starting address:

```
Enter starting IP address [192.65.34.0]:
```

Next, you must specify the number of clients. In the example class C network, this will be 254:

```
Enter the number of clients you want to add (x < 65535):
```

Once you have defined the network that you wish to support, you're ready to start using DHCP. An alternative method for invoking dhcpconfig is to do so from the command line, passing key parameters as arguments. For example, to set up a DHCP server for the domain *paulwatters.com*, with the DNS server 204.56.54.22, with a lease time of 14,400 seconds (4 hours), you would use the following command:

```
# dhcpconfig -D -r SUNWbinfiles -p /var/dhcp -l 14400 \
  -d paulwatters.com -a 204.56.54.22 -h dns -y paulwatters.com
```

To unconfigure a DHCP server, execute the following command:

```
# dhcpconfig -U -f -x -h
```

This command removes host entries from the name service, the *dhcptab* file, and the network tables.

An alternative to the dhcpconfig command is the dhcpmgr GUI, which performs the following operations:

- Configures DHCP
- Configures BOOTP
- Administers DHCP
- Administers BOOTP
- Administers DHCP addresses and macros
- Administers DHCP options
- Migrates DHCP data stores
- Moves data from one DHCP server to another

Figure 22-4 shows the GUI for dhcpmgr.

Manual DHCP Server Configuration

Although most administrators use dhcpconfig or dhcpmgr to manage DHCP services, it is also possible to manually edit the DHCP configuration database, *dhcptab*, by using the dhtadm command. You can install macros and set server options by using dhtadm.

FIGURE 22-4
DHCP
Configuration
Wizard

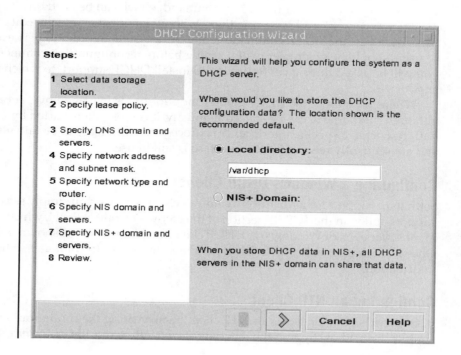

In the first instance, dhtadm can be used to create a new *dhcptab* file:

```
# dhtadm -C
```

The following options can be passed to dhtadm to perform various tasks:

- *–A* Define a macro or symbol.
- *–B* Perform batch processing.
- *–C* Create the service configuration database.
- *–D* Remove a macro or symbol.
- *–M* Update a macro or symbol.

Configuring a Solaris DHCP Client

Once the DHCP server has been configured, it is then very easy to configure a Solaris client. When installing the client, you will be asked whether you wish to install DHCP support. At this point, you should answer yes. Accordingly, you will not be asked to enter a static IP address as per a normal installation, as this will be supplied by the DHCP server with the DHCPOFFER message.

If you wish to enable support for DHCP on a client that has already been installed, you need to use the sys-unconfig command, which can be used on all systems to reconfigure network and system settings, without having to manually edit configuration files. The sys-unconfig command reboots the system in order to perform this task, so users should be given plenty of warning before reconfiguration commences. Again, you will be asked during configuration to install DHCP support, to which you should answer yes.

When configured, the DHCP client (dhcpagent) is managed by ifconfig— although dhcpagent can be started manually, it is most often started by ifconfig with respect to a specific interface. This process allows a lease to be initially obtained, and subsequently renewed if the interface is still in use.

Configuring a Windows DHCP Client

Setting up support for a Microsoft Windows client is easy—you simply select the DHCP support option in the TCP/IP section of the Network Control Panel, which can be found in most versions of Windows. A DHCP client for Windows 95 is shown in Figure 22-5. Once DHCP support is enabled, it is no longer necessary to enter any static IP address information.

Configuring an NTP Client

If a system is going to act as an NTP client, then creating the configuration file is much simpler. Instead of copying the template */etc/inet/ntp.server* file to */etc/inet/ntp.conf*, the

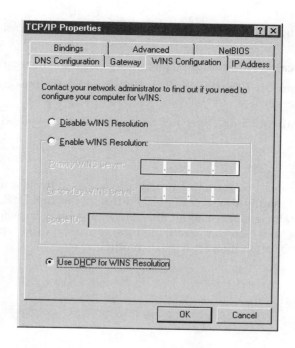

FIGURE 22-5
DHCP client for
Microsoft Windows

template */etc/inet/ntp.client* file is copied to */etc/inet/ntp.conf.* By default, this file contains
a list that listens for multicast broadcasts on the local subnet:

```
multicastclient 224.0.1.1
```

NTP clients send and receive NTP message data in a specific format. The main fields
transmitted include the following:

- **Leap Indicator**   Flag that indicates a leap year at the end of the day.
- **Version Number**   NTPv3.
- **Mode**   Determines whether the message is symmetric active, symmetric
  passive, client, server, broadcast, or an NTP control message.
- **Stratum**   Level of accuracy for the message, with 1 being a primary server
  and 2–255 indicating secondary servers of decreasing accuracy.
- **Poll Interval**   Maximum time separating messages.
- **Precision**   Local clock precision.
- **Root Delay**   Delay anticipated between the primary and other sources.
- **Root Dispersion**   Error estimate from the primary source.
- **Reference Clock Identifier**   Allows the primary source clock to be identified.
- **Reference Timestamp**   The last time the local clock was updated.

- **Originate Timestamp** The time at which the message was transmitted from a client.
- **Receive Timestamp** The time at which the message was received.
- **Transmit Timestamp** The time at which the message was transmitted from a server.
- **Authenticator** Specifies the authentication method used.

Summary

In this chapter, you have examined core issues in hosts as distributed systems by allowing dynamic assignment of IP addresses through DHCP. You have also learned how to obtain agreement about time. Since time is the basis for synchronized operations, it is critical that a common reliable time source be used when building networked systems that must interact with each other.

CHAPTER

Routing and Firewalls

In this chapter, we examine how to connect multiple machines in subnets, and how to connect subnets to form local area networks (LANs) through routers. Inter-router connection allows the formation of wide area networks (WANs) and, ultimately, the Internet. Communication between different machines, through the transmission of data packets, can only take place through the process of routing. Routing involves finding a route between two hosts, whether they exist on the same network or are separated by thousands of miles and hundreds of intermediate hosts. Fortunately, the basic principles are the same in both cases. However, for security reasons, many sites on the Internet have installed packet filters, which deny certain packet transmissions on a host or port basis. In this chapter, we examine static and dynamic methods for configuring routes between hosts, and examine the mechanisms of IP filtering and firewalls.

Key Concepts

The key concepts for network routing are discussed in this section.

Network Interfaces

Solaris supports many different kinds of network interfaces, for local- and wide-area transmission. Ethernet and FDDI are commonly used to create networks of two or more systems at a single site through a LAN, while supporting high-speed, wide-area connections through T1 and X.25 lines. A switch is a device that can interconnect many devices so that they can be channeled directly to a router for wide-area connection. For example, a building may have a switch for each of its physical floors, and each of these switches may connect to a single switch for the whole building that is connected to a data circuit, through a router (*router.company.com*). A general rule of thumb for connecting routable networks is not to have more than three levels of connection between a server and a router, because otherwise the number of errors increases dramatically. Figure 23-1 shows a possible class C network configuration for this building.

This configuration is fine if a single company (*company.com*) owns and occupies this building, and both floors use the same data circuit. However, imagine that *company.com*

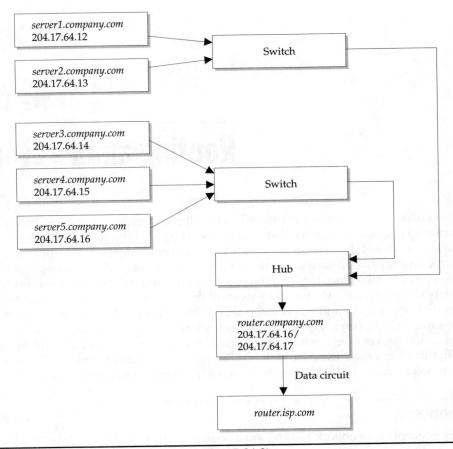

FIGURE 23-1 Class C network configuration (204.17.64.0)

expands and leases the second floor to a subsidiary company called *subsidiary.com*. The subsidiary company wants to use the existing data circuit arrangements and is happy to share the cost of the Internet connection. However, the subsidiary company wants to logically isolate its network from that of *company.com*, and needs to protect its data: it intends to install on its own router a packet filter that explicitly denies or allows packets to cross into its own network.

This logical separation can be easily achieved by separating the existing network into two subnets, allowing the subsidiary company to install its own router, and then connecting the two networks through that router. Traffic to the data circuit can still flow through the existing connection, even though they are now separated from the router. How the subsidiary's traffic "finds" the data circuit is the kind of problem that routing can solve. More generally, routing allows one host to find a path to any other host on the Internet. Figure 23-2 shows the revised configuration for this building, incorporating

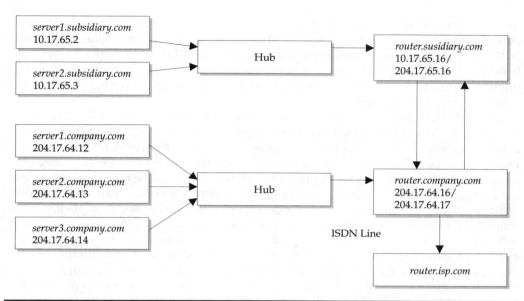

FIGURE 23-2 Connecting two class C networks (204.17.64.0 and 204.17.65.0)

the changes required by the subsidiary company, forming two class C networks whose routers are connected to each other.

It should be clear from these examples that from a network perspective, a Solaris 10 system must be either a router or a host. A router may be a Solaris server that performs other functions (e.g., DNS server, NIS server, and so on), or it may be a dedicated, hardware-based system supplied by another manufacturer (e.g., Cisco, Ascend). In this chapter, we examine ways of setting up and configuring a Solaris host to be a router, although your organization may prefer to use a dedicated system for routing.

The basic function of a router, as displayed in Figures 23-1 and 23-2, is to pass information from one network to another. In the examples, information is passed from one class C network to another, but also to the router of the data circuit. The router on the other end then connects with many other routers, eventually giving global coverage. The information passed between networks is contained in discrete packets. Because the router passes this information along, it can potentially make a copy of the data and save it to a local disk. This is the basis of many security-related problems on the Internet, since usernames and passwords are also transmitted as packets and can be intercepted by any intermediate router between client and server.

To be a router, a system must have multiple physical network interfaces. This is distinct from a system that has one or more virtual interfaces defined for a single physical interface card. Thus, the router for *company.com* has the interfaces hme0 and le0. The first interface accepts traffic from the internal network and passes it to the second interface, while the second interface accepts traffic from the other routers and passes it to the internal network, or to other routers as appropriate. Having two network interfaces allows data to be passed through the machine and exchanged across different networks. In the preceding example, the *company.com* router was able to exchange information between the *subsidiary.com* router and the external router. Thus, many routers can be interconnected to form networks in which packets can be passed from a source to a destination host transparently.

Since the *subsidiary.com* router serves as a packet-filtering firewall, it is likely that the network has a nonroutable internal structure that is not directly accessible to the external network but is visible from the router (the 10.17.65.0 network). Thus, a rogue user from *company.com* will be able to "see" the external interface for the *subsidiary.com* router but will not be able to see the internal interface, or any of the hosts beyond, unless she manages to break into the router through the external interface. This adds a second layer of protection against intrusion. A packet filter can then be used to explicitly deny connections to machines in the internal network, except for very specific system or network services. For example, a departmental mail server may reside on *server1.subsidiary.com*, and external machines will ultimately need access to the sendmail ports on this server. This can be achieved by port forwarding, the ability of the router to map a port on its external interface to a port on a machine on the internal network. For example, a Web server on *server1.subsidiary.com:80* could be accessed from the external network by connecting to *router.subsidiary.com:8080* if the mapping was enabled. These techniques can achieve the necessary logical isolation between external users and actual network configuration, which can be useful for security planning. Packet filtering, port forwarding, and nonroutable networks are discussed later in the chapter.

A machine with more than one network interface may not be configured to act as a router, in which case it is referred to as a multihomed host. Multihoming can be useful for performing such functions as load balancing, and directly serving different class C networks without passing information between them.

IP Routing

Now that you have reviewed how to install, configure, and tune network interfaces, this section describes how to set up routing, by explaining how packets are transferred from hosts to routers and exchanged between routers. This section also examines how to troubleshoot routing problems with traceroute, and introduces the different routing protocols that are currently being used on the Internet.

There are two kinds of routing, static and dynamic. Static routing is common in simple networks with only a few hosts and networks interconnected. Static routing is much simpler to implement than dynamic routing, which is suitable for large networks, where the routes between networks cannot be readily specified. For example, if your organizational network has only 2 routers connecting three networks, then the number of routes that need to be installed statically is 4 (i.e., the square of the number of routers). In contrast, for a building with 5 routers, the number of routes that need to specified statically is 25. However, by using the default route facility, the number of routes to be specified drops significantly, as shown in the following example:

{data circuit}------R1---------R2------------R3-------{stub}
R1 routes = default route to data circuit route to R2 and R3 (3 routes)
R2 routes = default route to R1 & route to R3 (2 routes)
R3 routes = default route to R2 (1 routes)
Total routes = 3 + 2 + 1 = 6

If a router configuration changes, then all the static configuration files on all the routers need to be changed (i.e., there is no mechanism for the "discovery" of routes). Alternatively, if a router fails because of a hardware fault, then packets may not be able to be correctly routed. Dynamic routing solves all of these problems, but requires more processing overhead on each router. There are two related dynamic routing daemons— in.rdisc, the router discovery daemon, and in.routed, the route daemon—whose configuration will be discussed at length in this section.

Overview of Packet Delivery

Before we examine the differences between static and dynamic routing in detail, let's take a step back and consider how information is passed between two systems, whether the exchange is host to host, host to router, or router to router. All information is exchanged in the form of discrete packets. A packet is the smallest unit of information transmitted between hosts using TCP/IP and contains both a header and a message component, as shown in Figure 23-3. In order to deliver packets from one host to another host successfully, each packet contains information in the header, which is similar to an envelope. Among many other fields, the header contains the address of the destination machine and the address of the source machine. The message section of the packet contains the actual data to be transferred.

Packets are often transferred on the transport layer using the Transmission Control Protocol (TCP), which guarantees the delivery of packets, although some applications use the User Datagram Protocol (UDP), where the continuity of a connection cannot be

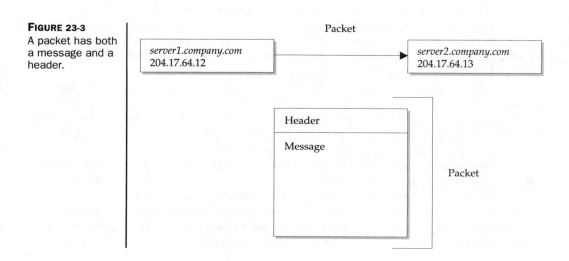

FIGURE 23-3
A packet has both a message and a header.

Packet

server1.company.com
204.17.64.12

server2.company.com
204.17.64.13

Header

Message

Packet

guaranteed. In normal TCP transmission mode, only 64KB of data can be transferred in a single session, unless large window support is enabled, in which case up to 1GB of data may be transmitted. The header may also have information inserted by the source machine, which is referred to as *data encapsulation*. The action of passing a packet is referred to as a *hop*, so routing involves enabling packets to hop from a source host to any arbitrary host on the Internet.

In order for packets to be delivered correctly between two hosts, all intermediate routers must be able to determine where the packets have come from and where they must be delivered to. This can be achieved by referring to a host by using its IP address (e.g., 204.16.42.58) or its Fully Qualified Domain Name (e.g., *server.company.com*). Although it is also possible to refer to a machine by its Ethernet (hardware) address, a logical rather than a physical representation of a machine's network interface card is always used.

Sending a packet across a network makes full use of all network layers. For example, if a telnet session is to be established between two machines, the application protocol specifies how the message and header are to be constructed, information which is then passed to the transport layer protocol. For a telnet session, the transport layer protocol is TCP, which proceeds with encapsulation of the packet's data, which is split into segments. The data is divided depending on the size of the TCP window allowed by the system. Each segment has a header and a checksum. The checksum is used by the destination host to determine whether a received packet is likely to be free of corruption.

When a segment is due to be transmitted from the source host, a three-way handshake occurs between the source and destination: a SYN segment is sent to the destination host to request a connection, and an acknowledgement (ACK) is returned to the source when the destination host is ready to receive. When the ACK is received by the source host, its receipt is acknowledged back to the destination, and transmission proceeds with data being passed to the IP layer, where segments are realized as IP datagrams. IP also adds a header to the segment, and passes it to the physical networking layer for transport.

A common method of enacting a denial-of-service (DoS) attack on a remote host involves sending many SYN requests to a remote host, without completing the three-way handshake. Solaris now limits the maximum number of connections with incomplete handshakes to reduce the impact of the problem. When a packet finally arrives at the destination host, it travels through the TCP/IP protocol stack in the reverse order from which it took on the sender: just like a deck of cards that has been dealt onto a playing table and retrieved from the top of the pack.

The story becomes more complicated when packets need to be passed through several hosts to reach their ultimate destination. Although the method of passing data from source to destination is the same, the next hop along the route needs to be determined somehow. The path that a packet takes across the network depends on the IP address of the destination host, as specified in the packet header.

If the destination host is on the local network, the packet can be delivered immediately without intervention of a separate router. For example, a source host 204.12.60.24 on the class C network 204.12.60.0 can directly pass a packet to a destination 204.12.60.32.

However, once a packet needs to be delivered beyond the local network, the process becomes more complicated. The packet is passed to the router on the local network (which may be defined in */etc/defaultrouter*), and a router table is consulted. The router table contains a list of the hosts on the local network and other routers to which the router has a connection. For example, the router for the 204.12.60.0 network might be 204.12.60.64. Thus, a packet from 204.12.60.24 would be passed to 204.12.60.64, assuming a class C subnet, if the destination host is not on the 204.12.60.0 network. The router 204.12.60.64 may have a second interface, 204.12.61.64, that connects the 204.12.60.0 and 204.12.59.0 networks. If the destination host is 204.12.59.28, the packet could now be delivered directly to the host because the router bridges the two networks. However, if the packet is not deliverable to a host on the 204.12.59.0 network, then it must be passed to another router defined in the current router's tables.

IP Filtering and Firewalls

After going to all the trouble of making routing easy to use and semi-automated with the dynamic routing protocols, some situations require that the smooth transfer of packets from one host to another via a router be prevented, usually because of security concerns about data that is contained on hosts on a particular network. For example, Microsoft Windows networks broadcast all kinds of information about workgroups and domains that is visible to any computer that can connect through the network's router. However, if the network's router prevents a computer from another network from listening to this information, it can still be broadcast internally without being visible to the outside world. Fortunately, this kind of "packet filtering" is selective: only specific ports are blocked at the router level, and they can also be blocked in only direction. For example, a database listener operating on a router could accept connections from machines that are internal to the network, but external access would be blocked. For large organizations that have direct connections to the Internet, setting up a corporate firewall at the router level has become a priority to protect sensitive data while providing employees with the access to the Internet that they require. This section examines the basics of packet filtering. The "Configuring the IPFilter Firewall" section, later in the chapter, reviews the installation and configuration of the popular `ipfilter` package for Solaris 10.

IP filtering involves the selective restriction and permission of access to TCP and UDP ports on a system. IP filtering is commonly used for two purposes: to secure a network from attacks and intrusion from rogue users on outside hosts, and to prevent the broadcast and transmission of unauthorized data from an internal network to the rest of the Internet. In the former case, an attacker may attempt to gain entry to your system by using an application like `telnet`, or may try to insert or retrieve data from a database by connecting to a database listener and issuing SQL commands from a client application. Both of these scenarios are common enough to motivate many sites to restrict all incoming traffic to their networks, except on a very small number of specific ports. Commonly allowed ports include

- Secure shell (`ssh`) on port 22
- Secure copy (`scp`) on port 24
- Mail server (`sendmail`) on port 25
- DNS server on port 53

- Web server (apache) on port 80

This may seem like a very minimal list to many administrators, but the fact is that almost every UNIX daemon has been discovered to suffer from "buffer overflow" problems in recent years, as discussed in Chapter 9, leaving systems open to exploitation. A rule of thumb is to only allow services that users definitely need to be productive and that have been approved by management. Some users might argue that allowing the finger service is useful, but it also gives away a lot of information about home directories and valid usernames that can be exploited by rogue users. In addition, some users may set up Web and FTP servers without permission. Because Solaris only restricts ports below 1024 for the superuser and system accounts, all ports above 1024 are available for users to engage in unauthorized activities for which your company may be held responsible. For example, a user might run a Web server on port 8080 that distributes pirate software: if a software manufacturer discovers this operation, it will most likely sue your company rather than the individual involved. Blocking access to all ports, unless they are specifically required or sanctioned, limits these kinds of problems.

What is less intuitive than restricting incoming traffic is the notion of also restricting outgoing traffic. Firewalls are able to manage both incoming and outgoing traffic because a firewall may also act as a router, and routers always have at least two network interfaces. One good reason to consider blocking outgoing network on some ports is that users may engage in leisure activities, such as playing networked adventure games, when they should be working. Since you don't really want to be the police officer "patrolling" the system for violators, it is best just to restrict any access in the first place to avoid any problems down the track. It's also possible to use a firewall to accept or deny connections based on IP address: obviously, a machine making a connection from the external network, but pretending to have an address from inside the network, should be identified and its attempts rejected (this is known as *IP spoofing*). Figure 23-4 summarizes the functions of a router that acts as a packet-filtering firewall. Permitted ports are labeled OK, while denied ports are labeled NO. All connections for sendmail (25) are accepted, as are ssh connections. However, external connections to a database listener are rejected (port 1521), and a machine on the external network that is spoofing an internal network IP address has all its connections rejected.

The Kernel Routing Table

The routing table maintains an index of routes to networks and routers that are available to the local host. Routes can be determined dynamically, by using RDISC for example, or can be added manually, by using route or ifconfig. These commands are normally used at boot time to initialize network services. There are three kinds of routes:

- **Host routes**   Map a path from the local host to another host on the local network.
- **Network routes**   Allow packets to be transferred from the local hosts to other hosts on the local network.

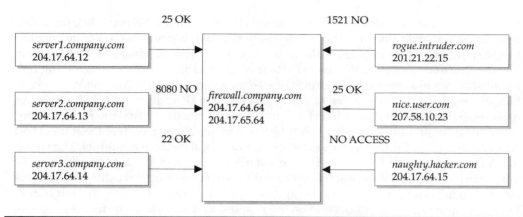

FIGURE 23-4   Basic firewall configuration blocking incoming and outgoing ports

- **Default routes**   Pass the task of finding a route to a router. Both RIP and RDISC daemons can use default routes.

Dynamic routing often causes changes in the routing table after booting, when a minimal routing table is configured by `ifconfig` when initializing each network interface, as the daemons manage changes in the network configuration and router availability.

Procedures

The basic procedures for router configuration are provided in this section.

Configuring a Router

In order to configure routing, it is necessary to enable the appropriate network interfaces. In this chapter, we will assume that an Ethernet network is being used, thus, each system that acts as a router must have at least two Ethernet interfaces installed. In addition, Solaris also supports multiple Ethernet interfaces to be installed on a single machine. These are usually designated by files like */etc/hostname.hmen* for dual-homed systems, */etc/hostname.qen* for quad-homed hosts, or */etc/hostname.len* for older machines, where *n* is the interface number. Interface files contain an FQDN, with the primary network interface being designated with an interface number of 0. Thus, the primary interface of a machine called *server* would be defined by the file */etc/hostname.hme0,* which might contain the FQDN *external.server.com.* A secondary network interface, connected to a different subnet, might be defined in the file */etc/hostname.hme1.* In this case, the file might contain the address *internal.server.com.*

A system with a second network interface can act either as a router or as a multihomed host. Hostnames and IP addresses are locally administered through a naming service, which is usually the Domain Name Service (DNS) for companies connected to the Internet, and the Network Information Service (NIS/NIS+) for companies with large internal networks that require administrative functions beyond what DNS provides, including centralized authentication. It is also worth mentioning at this point that it is quite possible to assign different IP addresses to the same network interface, which can be useful for hosting "virtual" domains that require their own IP address, rather than relying on application-level support for multihoming (e.g., when using the Apache Web server). Simply create a new */etc/hostname.hme*X:Y file for each IP address required, where X represents the physical device interface, and Y represents the virtual interface number.

In the examples presented in the introduction to this chapter, each of the routers had two interfaces, one for the internal network and one for the external Internet. The subnet mask used by each of these interfaces must also be defined in */etc/netmasks*. This is particularly important if the interfaces lie on different subnets or serve different network classes. In addition, it might also be appropriate to assign an FQDN to each of the interfaces, although this will depend on the purpose to which each interface is assigned. For the system *router.subsidiary.com*, there will be two hostname files created in the */etc* directory.

When installing a system as a router, it is necessary to determine which network interface to use as the external interface for passing information between networks. This interface must be defined in the file */etc/defaultrouter*, by including that interface's IP address. These addresses can be matched to hostnames if appropriate. For example, the interfaces for *router.subsidiary.com* will be defined in */etc/hosts* as

```
127.0.0.1    localhost    loghost
10.17.65.16    internal
204.17.65.16    router    router.subsidiary.com
```

If the server is to be multihomed instead of being a router, ensure that */etc/defaultrouter* does not exist, and create an */etc/notrouter* file:

```
server# rm /etc/defaultrouter
server# touch /etc/notrouter
```

Note that the */etc/defaultrouter* file lists a default route and does not make the system a router, even if it is multihomed. To force a system to be a router, you must ensure that the */etc/gateways* file has been created empty:

```
server# touch /etc/gateways
```

Normally, only static routes for single-homed hosts are defined in the */etc/gateways* file.

Viewing Router Configuration

The ifconfig command is responsible for configuring each network interface at boot time. ifconfig can also be used to check the status of active network interfaces by passing the *–a* parameter:

```
router# ifconfig -a
lo0: flags=849<UP,LOOPBACK,RUNNING,MULTICAST> mtu 8232
        inet 127.0.0.1 netmask ff000000
hme0: flags=863<UP,BROADCAST,NOTRAILERS,RUNNING,MULTICAST> mtu 1500
        inet 10.17.65.16 netmask ffffff00 broadcast 10.17.65.255
hme1: flags=863<UP,BROADCAST,NOTRAILERS,RUNNING,MULTICAST> mtu 1500
        inet 204.17.65.16 netmask ffffff00 broadcast 204.17.65.255
```

In this case, the primary interface hme0 is running on the internal network, while the secondary interface hme1 is visible to the external network. The netmask for a class C network is used on both interfaces, while both have a distinct broadcast address. This ensures that information broadcast on the internal network is not visible to the external network. There are several parameters shown with ifconfig -a, including whether or not the interface is UP or DOWN (i.e., active or inactive). In the following example, the interface has not been enabled at boot time:

```
server# ifconfig hme1
hme1: flags=863<DOWN,BROADCAST,NOTRAILERS,RUNNING,MULTICAST> mtu 1500
        inet 204.17.64.16 netmask ffffff00 broadcast 204.17.64.255
```

Static Routes

On hosts, routing information can be extracted in two ways: by building a full routing table, exactly as occurs on a router, or by creating a minimal kernel table, containing a single default route for each available router (i.e., static routing). The most common static route is from a host to a local router, as specified in the */etc/defaultrouter* file. For example, for the host 204.12.60.24, the entry in */etc/defaultrouter* might be

```
204.12.60.64
```

This places a single route in the local routing table. Responsibility for determining the next hop for the message is then passed to the router.

Static routes can also be added for servers using in.routed, by defining them in the */etc/gateways* file. When using static routing, routing tables in the kernel are defined when the system boots, and do not normally change, unless modified by using the route or ifconfig command. When a local network has a single gateway to the rest of the Internet, static routing is the most appropriate choice.

Routing Protocols

The Routing Information Protocol (RIP) and the Router Discovery Protocol (RDISC) are two of the standard routing protocols for TCP/IP networks, and Solaris supports both. RIP is implemented by in.routed, the routing daemon, and is usually configured to start during multiuser mode startup. The routing daemon always populates the routing table with a route to every reachable network, but whether or not it advertises its routing availability to other systems is optional.

Hosts use the RDISC daemon (in.rdisc) to collect information about routing availability from routers and should run on both routers and hosts. in.rdisc typically creates a default route for each router that responds to requests: this "discovery" is central to the ability of RDISC-enabled hosts to dynamically adjust to network changes. Routers that only run in.routed cannot be discovered by RDISC-enabled hosts. For hosts running both in.rdisc and in.routed, the latter will operate until an RDISC-enabled router is discovered on the network, in which case RDISC will take over routing.

Viewing the Routing Table (netstat –r)

The command netstat –r shows the current routing table. Routes are always specified as a connection between the local server and a remote machine, via some kind of gateway. The output from the netstat –r command contains several different flags: flag U indicates that the route between the destination and gateway is up; flag G shows that the route passes through a gateway; flag H indicates that the route connects to a host; and flag D signifies that the route was dynamically created using a redirect. There are two other columns shown in the routing table: Ref indicates the number of concurrent routes occupying the same link layer, while Use indicates the number of packets transmitted along the route (on a specific Interface).

The following example shows an example server (*server.company.com*) that has four routes: the first is for the loopback address (lo0), which is Up and is connected through a host. The second route is for the local class C network (204.16.64.0), through the gateway *gateway.company.com*, which is also Up. The third route is the special multicast route, which is also Up. The fourth route is the default route, pointing to the local network router, which is also Up.

```
$ netstat -r

Routing Table:
  Destination          Gateway             Flags  Ref   Use    Interface
-------------------- -------------------- ----- ----- ------ ---------
127.0.0.1            localhost            UH       0   877  lo0
204.17.64.0          gateway.company.com  U        3    85  hme0
BASE-ADDRESS.MCAST.NET host.company.com   U        3     0  hme0
default              router.company.com   UG       0   303
```

Manipulating the Routing Table (route)

The route command is used to manually manipulate the routing tables. If dynamic routing is working correctly, manual manipulation should not normally be necessary. However, if static routing is being used, or the RDISC daemon does not discover any routes, it may be necessary to add routes manually. In addition, it may also be necessary to delete routes explicitly for security purposes. You should be aware, though, that except for interface changes, the routing daemon may not respond to any modifications to the routing table that may have been enacted manually. It is best to shut down the routing daemon first before making changes, and then restart it after all changes have been initiated.

Adding Host Routes

To add a direct route to another host, you use the `route` command with the following syntax:

```
route add -host destination_ip local_ip -interface interface
```

Thus, if you wanted to add a route between the local host (e.g., 204.12.17.1) and a host on a neighboring class C network (204.12.16.100), for the primary interface hme0, you would use the following command:

```
add -host 204.12.16.100 204.12.17.1 -interface hme0
```

Adding Network Routes

To add a direct route to another network, you use the `route` command with the following syntax:

```
route add -net destination_network_ip local_ip" -netmask mask
```

If you wanted to add a route between the local host (e.g., 204.12.17.1) and the same network as for the host in the preceding section (204.12.16.0), for the class C netmask (255.255.255.0), you would use this command:

```
route add -net 204.12.16.0 204.12.17.1 -netmask 255.255.255.0
```

Adding a Default Route

To add a default route, you can use the `route` command with the following syntax:

```
route add default hostname -interface interface
```

For example, to add a default route to a local router (204.54.56.1) for a secondary interface hme1, you can use the following command:

```
route add default 204.54.56.1 -interface hme1
```

PART V

Dynamic Routing

In this section, we will look more closely at the RIP and RDISC dynamic routing protocols. A prerequisite for dynamic routing to operate is that the */etc/defaultrouter* file must be empty.

routed

`in.routed` is the network routing daemon and is responsible for dynamically managing entries in the kernel routing tables. It is usually started from a line during multiuser boot (`/etc/rc2.d/S69inet`) using the following command:

```
/usr/sbin/in.routed -q
```

The routing daemon uses UDP port 520 to route packets and to establish which interfaces are currently Up and which are Down. `in.routed` listens for requests for packets and for known routes from remote hosts. This supplies hosts on a network with the information they need to determine how many hops to a host. When it is initialized, the routing daemon checks both gateways specified in */etc/gateways*. It is also possible to run the routing daemon in a special memory-saving mode that retains only the default routes in the routing table. While this may leave a system at the mercy of a faulty router, it does save memory and reduces the resources that `in.routed` requires to maintain lists of active routes that are periodically updated. This can be enabled by initializing `in.routed` with the –*S* parameter.

RDISC

The RDISC daemon uses the ICMP router discovery protocol and is usually executed on both hosts and routers at boot time, at which time routers broadcast their availability and hosts start listening for available routers. Routers broadcast their availability using the 224.0.0.1 multicast address. Routers that share a network with a host are selected first as the default route, if one is found. Another approach is for the host to send out a broadcast on the 224.0.0.2 multicast address, to solicit any available routers. In either case, if a router is available, it will accept packet forwarding requests from the host concerned.

Configuring the IPFilter Firewall

IPFilter is a popular freeware packet-filtering package for Solaris. It is a kernel-loadable module that is attached at boot time. This makes IPFilter very secure, because it cannot be tampered with by user applications. However, as you will read in this section, this approach also has problems, because loading unstable modules into the kernel can cause a Solaris system to crash. Solaris 10 now ships with the packages SUNWipfr and SUNWipfu, with updates available from **http://coombs.anu.edu.au/~avalon/**.

The first step in creating an IPFilter configuration file is to consult with users and managers to determine a list of acceptable services. Many companies already have an acceptable-use policy that governs which ports should be available and what permissions should be given for user-initiated services. After you determine a list of ingoing and outgoing port requirements, it is best to write a rule that denies all packets, and then to write rules following that which explicitly allow the services you have identified. It is also important to enable allowed services in both directions: for example, it is usually necessary for users to both receive and send e-mail, so an inbound and outbound rule needs to be included for `sendmail` (port 25).

IPFilter rules are processed in the order in which they are specified in the configuration file. Every rule is processed, which means that more general rules (like blocking all connections) should precede specific rules (like allowing bidirectional `sendmail` connections) in the configuration file. If you have a very complicated configuration, it is also possible to specify that processing terminate at any point in the file, if a condition is met, by using the "quick" keyword. Other important keywords include "block", "to", and "from" to construct rules for limiting packet transmission. The "block" command blocks packets from a particular source to a particular destination. The "from" command specifies the source of these packets, while the "to" command specifies the destination of these packets. The following example prevents any packets from the class B network 178.222.0.0:

```
block in quick from 178.222.0.0/16 to any
```

The `pass` command allows packets to pass the firewall. For example, the rule

```
pass in all
```

allows all packets to pass. Since routers by definition have more than two interfaces, it is also possible to specify a network interface to which a specific rule applies. For example, the following rule

```
block in quick on hme2 all
```

prevents all transmissions on the `hme2` interface.

An interface specification can be mixed with a normal rule, so that one interface accepts traffic from one class C network (178.222.1.0), but another interface may accept traffic only from a different class C network (178.221.2.0):

```
block in quick on hme2 from 178.222.1.0/24 to any
block in quick on hme1 from 178.222.2.0/24 to any
```

All of the examples so far have focused on inbound traffic using the "in" command. As mentioned earlier, it is also possible to restrict outbound traffic in the same way, by using the "out" command. The following example prevents traffic from the internal, nonroutable network (10.222.1.0) to pass through:

```
block out quick on hme0 from 10.222.1.0/24 to any
```

PART V

The rule shown in this example would be applied only to organizations that didn't want their employees using the Internet. Perhaps it could be combined with a `cron` job, which would reconfigure the firewall to allow access during lunch time and after work. It is also possible to limit particular protocols, so that TCP applications (like SSH) would be allowed, but UDP applications (like some streamed audio applications) would be banned, by specifying `proto udp` in the rule:

```
block in quick on hme0 proto udp from 10.222.1.0/24 to any
```

The most complicated rule comes in the form of a port-by-port specification of what is allowed and disallowed on a protocol-by-protocol basis. For example, the following rule blocks all Web server requests from the internal network from reaching their destination:

```
block in quick on hme0 proto tcp from any to 10.222.1.0/24 port = 80
```

This would allow Telnet and FTP connections to proceed freely, as TCP is only restricted on port 80.

Although firewall technology is very comprehensive and is very useful in placing specific restrictions on network transmission, there are some drawbacks with configuring firewalls in general, and IPFilter in particular. Since firewall configuration involves writing rules, and the syntax of the commonly used rule languages is often difficult to understand, packet filters can be difficult to configure correctly. Once you've created a configuration, there is also no test bed provided that determines that your configuration is satisfactory. There may be contention between one or more rules that is incorrectly resolved. There is a very active discussion group on IPFilter, with searchable archives, available at **http://false.net/ipfilter/**. The firewall mailing list is also good for more general discussion of firewall-related issues, and the contents are available at **http://www.greatcircle.com/firewalls/**. If you are more interested in commercial firewall products, check out the comparisons with freeware at **http://www.fortified.com /fwcklist.html/**.

Configuring the SunScreen Firewall

The best system for users who are new to Solaris is Sun's own SunScreen firewall (**http://www.sun.com/software/securenet/lite/download.html**). It comes in both a free and commercial edition, with the former being more than adequate for protecting small networks. It is available for both Solaris Intel and Solaris SPARC. The current release version is 3.1, which supports Gigabit Ethernet, SNMP management, and direct editing of security policy tables. However, it does not currently support IPv6. The firewall may be administered locally or remotely, by using a secure session.

There are several important limitations that are placed on the Lite version of SunScreen:

- It is designed to work with a system that is already acting as a router (if it wasn't, why would you want SunScreen anyway?).

- It does not operate in the special "stealth" mode employed by the commercial edition.

- It does not support any of the High Availability features of the commercial version.

- It does not support more than two network interfaces. However, as most routers have only two interfaces, this should not be an issue for small networks.

- It does not provide support for proxying.

SunScreen can be operated in either GUI mode, through a standard Web browser such as Netscape Navigator, or by directly editing the system's configuration files. It is easy to install using the Web Start Wizard, which is provided with the installation package.

To install the software, you need to run the */opt/SUNWicg/SunScreen/bin/ss_install* script, which is extracted from the SunScreen distribution. There are several options that you need to configure for SunScreen to operate as desired:

- Routing or stealth mode operation

- Local or remote administration

- Restrictive, secure, or permissive security level

- Support for DNS resolution

After choosing the appropriate option for your system, the following message will be displayed:

```
--Adding interfaces & interface addresses
--Initialize 'vars' databases
--Initialize 'authuser' & 'proxyuser' databases
--Initialize 'logmacro' database
--Applying edits
--Activating configuration
loading skip keystore.
Successfully initialized certificate database in /etc/skip/certdb
starting skip key manager daemon.
Configuration activated successfully on cassowary.
Reboot the machine now for changes to take effect.
```

After rebooting the system, the firewall software will be loaded into the kernel, after which you will need to add rules to the firewall, by using your browser to set the appropriate administration options. Figure 23-5 shows the browser starting on port 3852 on the localhost.

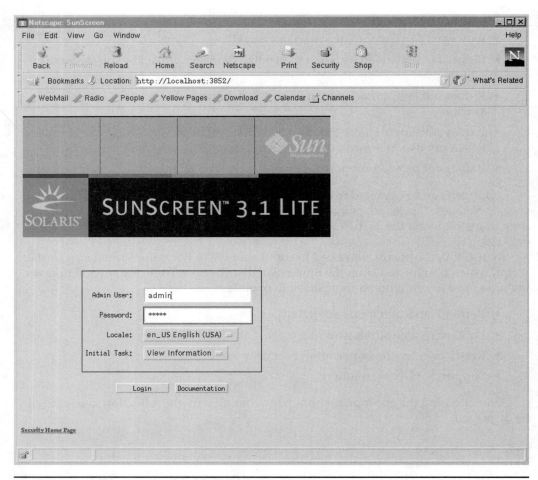

FIGURE 23-5 Starting the SunScreen administrative interface

When first installed, the SunScreen username and password will be "admin" and "admin", respectively. These should be entered into the Admin User and Password fields. After you click the Login button, the SunScreen Information page is displayed, as shown in Figure 23-6. At this point, you may view firewall logs, view connection statistics, and so on. However, most users will want to create a set of security policies immediately upon starting the firewall service.

Security policies are based on rules that either ALLOW or DENY a packet to be transmitted from a source to a destination address. Alternatively, an address class may be specified by using wildcards. The main actions associated with ALLOW rules are

- LOG_NONE

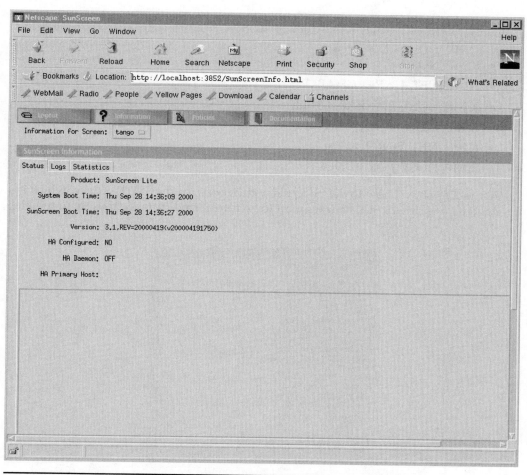

FIGURE 23-6   SunScreen Information interface

- LOG_SUMMARY
- LOG_DETAIL
- SNMP_NONE
- SNMP

The main actions associated with DENY rules are

- LOG_NONE
- LOG_SUMMARY
- LOG_DETAIL

- SNMP_NONE
- SNMP
- ICMP_NONE
- ICMP_NET_UNREACHABLE
- ICMP_HOST_UNREACHABLE
- ICMP_PORT_UNREACHABLE
- ICMP_NET_FORBIDDEN
- ICMP_HOST_FORBIDDEN

Figure 23-7 shows how to define a rule with actions for the SMTP service, which is operated by sendmail. This allows mail to be transferred from local users to remote

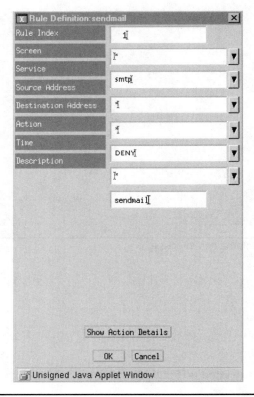

FIGURE 23-7   Rule definition

hosts. However, it you wanted to block all mail being sent to and from your network, you could create a DENY action within the rule for the SMTP service. The rule could be applied selectively to specific local subnets or remote destinations. Another useful feature is the ability to apply rules only for specific time periods. For example, if you worked in a bank, you could prevent all e-mail from being sent externally after 5 P.M. and before 9 A.M.

Once you have entered a new rule, you can view it on the Policy Rules page, along with any other rules, as shown in Figure 23-8. The Policy Rules page enables you to add new rules and edit, move, or delete existing rules. For each packet-filtering rule, the service, source address, destination address, action timeframe, and name are shown.

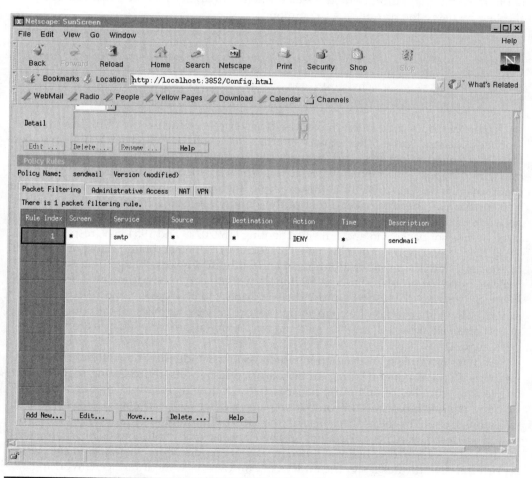

FIGURE 23-8   Policy Rules interface

SunScreen performs more than just packet filtering—it can be used to set up a virtual private network (VPN), and can perform advanced network address translation (NAT) functions. Further discussion of these concepts is beyond the scope of this book.

Examples

The following examples show how to work with a router.

Viewing Router Status

For both routing and multihomed hosts, the status of all network interfaces can be checked by using the netstat -i command:

```
router# netstat -i
Name  Mtu   Net/Dest      Address         Ipkts    Ierrs  Opkts    Oerrs Collis Queue
lo0   8232  loopback      localhost       199875   0      199875   0     0      0
hme0  1500  204.17.65.0   subsidiary.com  16970779 623190 19543549 0     0      0
hme1  1500  10.17.65.0    internal.gov    68674644 54543  65673376 0     0      0
```

In this example, mtu is the maximum transfer rate, which is much higher for the loopback address than for the network interface (as would be expected), and the number of Ipkts (inbound packets) and Opkts (outbound packets) is equivalent for lo0 (as one would hope). The loopback interface significantly increases the efficiency of a host that transmits packets to itself: in this example, there is an almost sixfold increase in the mtu for the lo0 interface over either of the standard network interfaces. The primary network interface hme0 is connected to the 204.17.65.0 network, and has transmitted a large number of packets in and out since booting (16970779 and 19543549, respectively). There have been a number of inbound errors (623190), but no outbound errors or collisions. Examining how the number of inbound and outbound errors change over time may indicate potential problems in network topology that need to be addressed. For example, if you are testing a Web server and it doesn't appear to be working, the Ipkts count can reveal whether or not the connections are actually being made: if the counter does not increase as expected, an intermediate hardware failure may be indicated (e.g., a dead switch).

Another example of a situation in which you might identify intermittent hardware failure is if you discover a large number of inbound packets, representing requests, but only a small number of outbound packets. In the following example, there are 1000847 inbound packets but only 30159 outbound packets since boot. Since it is unlikely in most situations that a 33:1 imbalance exists in the ratio of inbound to outbound packets, you would check the hme0 network interface. There are also many collisions being experienced by the hme0 interface: collisions between packets render them useless, and the figure reported here indicates a significant loss of bandwidth. If the interface is working as expected, it can also be worthwhile to investigate other causes arising from software (e.g., incorrect configuration of a packet filter).

```
server# netstat -i
Name  Mtu   Net/Dest     Address       Ipkts  Ierrs Opkts  Oerrs Collis Queue
lo0   8232  loopback     localhost     7513   0     7513   0     0      0
hme0  1500  204.17.64.0  1000847 5     30159  0     3979   0
```

netstat -s also allows these per-interface statistics to be viewed on a per-protocol basis, which can be very useful in determining potential problems with routing, especially if the router is packet filtering. The following example shows output from the netstat -s command, which displays the per-protocol statistics for the UDP, TCP, and ICMP protocols:

```
router# netstat -s
UDP
        udpInDatagrams      =502856      udpInErrors      =      0
        udpOutDatagrams     =459357
```

The following output from netstat -s begins with the UDP statistics, including the number of datagrams received and the number transmitted. The In/Out ratio is fairly even at 1.09, and the networking appears to be working well: there were no detected UDP errors (i.e., udpInErrors=0).

```
TCP     tcpRtoAlgorithm     =      4     tcpRtoMin          =      200
        tcpRtoMax           =240000      tcpMaxConn         =       -1
        tcpActiveOpens      =  33786     tcpPassiveOpens    =  12296
        tcpAttemptFails     =    324     tcpEstabResets     =    909
        tcpCurrEstab        =    384     tcpOutSegs         =19158723
        tcpOutDataSegs      =13666668    tcpOutDataBytes    =981537148
        tcpRetransSegs      =  33038     tcpRetransBytes    =41629885
        tcpOutAck           =5490764     tcpOutAckDelayed   =462511
        tcpOutUrg           =     51     tcpOutWinUpdate    =    456
        tcpOutWinProbe      =    290     tcpOutControl      = 92218
        tcpOutRsts          =   1455     tcpOutFastRetrans  = 18954
        tcpInSegs           =15617893
        tcpInAckSegs        =9161810     tcpInAckBytes      =981315052
        tcpInDupAck         =4559921     tcpInAckUnsent     =      0
        tcpInInorderSegs    =5741788     tcpInInorderBytes  =1120389303
        tcpInUnorderSegs    =  25045     tcpInUnorderBytes  =16972517
        tcpInDupSegs        =4390218     tcpInDupBytes      =4889714
        tcpInPartDupSegs    =    375     tcpInPartDupBytes  =130424
        tcpInPastWinSegs    =     17     tcpInPastWinBytes  =1808990872
        tcpInWinProbe       =    162     tcpInWinUpdate     =    270
        tcpInClosed         =    313     tcpRttNoUpdate     = 28077
        tcpRttUpdate        =9096791     tcpTimRetrans      = 18098
        tcpTimRetransDrop   =     26     tcpTimKeepalive    =    509
        tcpTimKeepaliveProbe=     76     tcpTimKeepaliveDrop =     1
        tcpListenDrop       =      0     tcpListenDropQ0    =      0
        tcpHalfOpenDrop     =      0
```

The TCP statistics are more mixed: there were 324 `tcpAttemptFails`, but given that there were 33,786 `tcpActiveOpens` at the time `netstat` was run, this is quite reasonable. The ratio of `tcpInInorderSegs` to `tcpInUnorderSegs` (i.e., received in order vs. not received in order) was 229:1, which is not uncommon.

```
IP      ipForwarding        =        2   ipDefaultTTL        =      255
        ipInReceives        =16081438    ipInHdrErrors       =        8
        ipInAddrErrors      =        0   ipInCksumErrs       =        1
        ipForwDatagrams     =        0   ipForwProhibits     =        2
        ipInUnknownProtos   =      274   ipInDiscards        =        0
        ipInDelivers        =16146712    ipOutRequests       =19560145
        ipOutDiscards       =        0   ipOutNoRoutes       =        0
        ipReasmTimeout      =       60   ipReasmReqds        =        0
        ipReasmOKs          =        0   ipReasmFails        =        0
        ipReasmDuplicates   =        0   ipReasmPartDups     =        0
        ipFragOKs           =     7780   ipFragFails         =        0
        ipFragCreates       =    40837   ipRoutingDiscards   =        0
        tcpInErrs           =      291   udpNoPorts          =144065
        udpInCksumErrs      =        2   udpInOverflows      =        0
        rawipInOverflows    =        0
```

There are some IP errors but they were quite minor: there were eight `ipInHdrErrors` but only one `ipInCksumErrs`, and two `udpInCksumErrs`.

```
ICMP    icmpInMsgs          = 17469      icmpInErrors        =        0
        icmpInCksumErrs     =     0      icmpInUnknowns      =        0
        icmpInDestUnreachs  =  2343      icmpInTimeExcds     =       26
        icmpInParmProbs     =     0      icmpInSrcQuenchs    =        0
        icmpInRedirects     =    19      icmpInBadRedirects  =       19
        icmpInEchos         =  9580      icmpInEchoReps      =     5226
        icmpInTimestamps    =     0      icmpInTimestampReps =        0
        icmpInAddrMasks     =     0      icmpInAddrMaskReps  =        0
        icmpInFragNeeded    =     0      icmpOutMsgs         =    11693
        icmpOutDrops        =140883      icmpOutErrors       =        0
        icmpOutDestUnreachs =  2113      icmpOutTimeExcds    =        0
        icmpOutParmProbs    =     0      icmpOutSrcQuenchs   =        0
        icmpOutRedirects    =     0      icmpOutEchos        =        0
        icmpOutEchoReps     =  9580      icmpOutTimestamps   =        0
        icmpOutTimestampReps=     0      icmpOutAddrMasks    =        0
        icmpOutAddrMaskReps =     0      icmpOutFragNeeded   =        0
        icmpInOverflows     =     0
```

On the ICMP front, `icmpOutErrors` and `icmpInErrors` are both 0, although there were 2,113 `icmpOutDestUnreachs`, indicating that at some point a network connection was not able to made when requested. This can be checked with the `traceroute` utility. Running a `cron` job to extract these figures to a file and then writing a PERL script to compare the values of concern is also often useful, because it is possible that errors could be masked by integers being "wrapped around" and starting at zero, after they reach values that are greater than the maximum available for a machine's architecture. However, this should not be a problem for the 64-bit Solaris kernel.

Summary

In this chapter, you have learned about static and dynamic routing systems and how to configure two basic firewall systems. These systems are complex, and before implementing either one you should review each product's documentation.

Remote Access

The service access facility (SAF) is a port management system that manages requests and responses for access to system ports. In this case, a port is defined as the physical connection between a peripheral device and the system. For example, most systems have one or more serial ports that allow for sequential data transmission effectively down a single line. In contrast, a parallel port allows for several lines of data to be transmitted bidirectionally. The SAF system is designed to allow requests to be made to the system from peripheral devices through ports, and to ensure that these requests are appropriately serviced by the relevant port monitor.

Modems, which allow Solaris 10 systems to connect to the Internet over a phone line, require SAF to operate through system serial ports. Thus, it's important to understand how to configure ports, port monitors, and listeners in preparation for making an Internet connection using a modem. Note that most Solaris systems are never accessed through a modem; however, if a system's only network card has died, and the console is physically inaccessible, a modem can be a lifesaver.

The Point-to-Point Protocol (PPP) daemon (pppd) is commonly used to set up modem access to an Internet service provider (ISP). PPP supports TCP/IP, and provides the Challenge Handshake Authentication Protocol (CHAP), which provides a higher level of security than is usually found on modem links. The PPP daemon relies on the chat program to perform dial-up and handle connections. In this chapter, we examine how to set up PPP for Internet connections.

Key Concepts

The following key concepts are required to understand how Solaris supports modems and Internet access.

Internet Access

Remote access is the hallmark of modern multiple-user operating systems such as Solaris and its antecedents, such as VAX/VMS. Unlike the single-user Windows NT system, users can concurrently log into and interactively execute commands on Solaris server systems from any client that supports Transmission Control Protocol/Internet Protocol (TCP/IP), such as Solaris, Windows NT, and Macintosh. Solaris can support hundreds to thousands of interactive user shells at any one time, constrained only by memory and CPU availability.

In this section, we examine several historically popular methods of remote access, such as `telnet`. We also outline the much-publicized security holes and bugs that have led to the innovation of secure remote access systems, such as secure shell (SSH). These "safer" systems facilitate the encryption of the contents of user sessions and/or authentication sequences and provide an important level of protection for sensitive data. Although remote access is useful, the administrative overhead in securing a Solaris system can be significant, reflecting the increased functionality that remote access services provide.

telnet

`telnet` is the standard remote access tool for logging into a Solaris machine from a client using the original DARPA Telnet protocol. A client can be executed on most operating systems that support TCP/IP. `telnet` is a terminal-like program that gives users interactive access to a login shell of their choice (for example, the C shell, or csh). Most `telnet` clients support VT100 or VT220 terminal emulations. The login shell can be used to execute scripts, develop applications, and read e-mail and news—in short, everything a Solaris environment should provide to its users, with the exception of X11 graphics and OpenWindows, or more recently the common desktop environment (CDE). A common arrangement in many organizations is for a Solaris server to be located in a secure area of a building, with `telnet`-only access allowed.

The sequence of events that occur during a `telnet` session begins with a request for a connection from the client to the server. The server responds (or times out) with a connection being explicitly accepted or rejected. A rejection may occur because the port that normally accepts `telnet` client connections on the server has been blocked by a packet filter or firewall. If the connection is accepted, the client is asked to enter a username followed by a password. If the username and password combination is valid, a shell is spawned and the user is logged in. The standard port for `telnet` connections is 23. Thus, a command like this,

```
$ telnet server
```

is expanded to give the effective command

```
$ telnet server 23
```

This means that `telnet` can be used as a tool to access a service on virtually any port. `telnet` is controlled by the super Internet daemon (`inetd`), which invokes the in.telnetd server. An entry is made in */etc/services* that defines the port number for the `telnet` service, which looks like this:

```
telnet     23/tcp
```

The configuration file */etc/inetd.conf* also contains important details of the services provided by `inetd`. The `telnet` daemon's location and properties are identified here:

```
telnet stream tcp nowait root /pkgs/tcpwrapper/bin/tcpd in.telnetd
```

In this case, you can see that in.telnetd is protected by the use of TCP *wrappers*, which facilitate the logging of `telnet` accesses through the Solaris `syslog` facility. In addition, `inetd` has some significant historical security holes and performance issues that, although mostly fixed in recent years, have caused administrators to shy away from servers invoked by `inetd`. The Apache Web server (**http://www.apache.org**), for example, runs as a stand-alone daemon process and does not use `inetd`.

Port Monitors

Central to the idea of providing services through serial ports is the port monitor, which continuously monitors the serial ports for requests to log in. The port monitor doesn't process the communication parameters directly, but accepts requests and passes them to the operating system. Solaris 10 uses the `ttymon` port monitor, which allows multiple concurrent `getty` requests from serial devices.

To configure the port for a terminal, start up `admintool` and enter the user mode, which can be either Basic, More, or Expert. In most cases, Basic setup will be sufficient. `admintool` allows the configuration of most parameters for the port, including the baud rate for communications, default terminal type, flow control, and carrier detection; but note that it is being deprecated. The values entered here should match those on the matching VT-100 terminal. Once you have saved the settings, it is possible to check the validity of the settings by using the `pmadm` command:

```
# pmadm -l -s ttyb
```

The Service Access Facility

The process that initiates the SAF is known as the service access controller (*/usr/lib/saf/sac*). It is started when the system enters run level 2, 3, or 4, as shown in this */etc/inittab* entry:

```
sc:234:respawn:/usr/lib/saf/sac -t 300
```

Here, the `respawn` entry indicates that if a process is not running when it should be, it should be respawned. For example, if a system changes from run level 2 to run level 3, sac should be running. If it is not present, it will be restarted.

When sac is started, it reads the script */etc/saf/_sysconfig*, which contains any local configurations tailored for the system. Next, the standard configuration file */etc/saf/_sactab* is read and sac spawns a separate child process for each of the port monitors it supports (`ttymon` and `listen`). A sample *_sactab* file is shown here:

```
# VERSION=1
zsmon:ttymon::0:/usr/lib/saf/ttymon #
```

PART V

Port monitors also read a configuration file (*/etc/saf/zsmon/_pmtab*) that is used to configure the `ttymon` and `listen` port monitors. The following is a sample *_pmtab* file:

```
# VERSION=1
ttya:u:root:reserved:reserved:reserved:/dev/term/a:I::
/usr/bin/login::9600:ldterm,ttcompat:ttya login\: ::tvi925:y:#
ttyb:u:root:reserved:reserved:reserved:/dev/term/b:I::
/usr/bin/login::9600:ldterm,ttcompat:ttyb login\: ::tvi925:y:#
```

The point of this hierarchical configuration file structure is that values read from */etc/saf/_sysconfig* and */etc/saf/_sactab* by sac are inherited by the spawned port monitor processes, which then have the ability to configure their own operations.

The SAF has two types of port monitors: the terminal port monitor (`ttymon`) and the network port monitor (`listen`). For example, the `ttymon` port monitor for the console is started in run levels 2, 3, and 4, through an */etc/inittab* entry like the following:

```
co:234:respawn:/usr/lib/saf/ttymon -g -h -p
    "`uname -n` console login: " -T vt100 -d
    /dev/console -l console -m ldterm,ttcompat
```

The `ttymon` process is active when a monitor is connected to a server, such as a dumb terminal, rather than a graphics monitor.

Point-to-Point Protocol

PPP is the most commonly used protocol for connecting modems over a phone line (or, uncommonly, over a normal serial line) to support TCP/IP. It replaces the earlier Serial Line Interface Protocol (SLIP), which did not provide any level of security or authentication for serial line services. The Solaris 10 implementation of PPP is based on the ANU version (**ftp://cs.anu.edu.au/pub/software/ppp**). PPP provides reliable access to the Internet because it includes error correction and the ability to autodetect some network parameters.

All of the parameters for the PPP daemon are stored in */etc/ppp/options*. Alternatively, for options that are specific to each serial port, a new configuration file can be created (such as */etc/ppp/options.cua.a* for the serial port */dev/cua/a*). This is useful where two modems are connected to the two standard serial interfaces on a SPARC system that are connected to two separate modems, which in turn dial completely different ISPs—the lesson for high availability is to "be prepared" for the worst-case scenario. Supporting network operations through a 56 Kbps modem is going to be challenging, but not impossible, in an emergency.

Procedures

The following procedures are commonly used to set up remote access.

Command	Description
close	Quit `telnet` session
logout	Close connection
display	Print connection characteristics
mode	Change mode
open	Open connection
quit	Quit `telnet` session
send	Send special characters
set	Set connection characteristics
unset	Unset connection characteristics
status	Display connection status
toggle	Change connection characteristics
slc	Toggle special character mode
z	Suspend connection
!	Spawn shell
environ	Update environment variables
?	Display help
ENTER key	Return to session

TABLE 24-1 Telnet Client Commands

Using telnet

The Solaris `telnet` client has an extensive help facility available, which can be viewed by pressing the escape sequence (usually ^-]), and typing the command **help**. The main `telnet` commands are shown in Table 24-1.

As an example of how these commands work, the `display` command will print all of the current settings being used by your terminal:

```
telnet> display
will flush output when sending interrupt characters.
won't send interrupt characters in urgent mode.
won't skip reading of ~/.telnetrc file.
won't map carriage return on output.
will recognize certain control characters.
won't turn on socket level debugging.
won't print hexadecimal representation of network traffic.
won't print user readable output for "netdata".
won't show option processing.
won't print hexadecimal representation of terminal traffic.
```

```
echo            [^E]
escape          [^]]
rlogin          [off]
tracefile       "(standard output)"
flushoutput     [^O]
interrupt       [^C]
quit            [^\]
eof             [^D]
erase           [^?]
kill            [^U]
lnext           [^V]
susp            [^Z]
reprint         [^R]
worderase       [^W]
start           [^Q]
stop            [^S]
forw1           [off]
forw2           [off]
ayt             [^T]
```

Alternatively, the status command reveals the characteristics of the current telnet connection:

```
telnet> status
Connected to currawong.cassowary.net.
Operating in single character mode
Catching signals locally
Remote character echo
Escape character is '^]'.
```

To resume the telnet session, simply press the ENTER key at the telnet> prompt.

Remote Logins

inetd controls the standard remote access clients, including the so-called r-commands, including the remote login (rlogin) and remote shell (rsh) applications. The rlogin application is similar to telnet in that it establishes a remote connection through TCP/IP to a server, spawning an interactive login shell. For example, the command

```
$ rlogin server
```

by default produces the response

```
password:
```

after which the user enters a password, which the server then authenticates and either denies or grants access. If the target user account has a different name than your current user account, you can try this:

```
$ rlogin server -l user
```

However, there are two main differences between `telnet` and `rlogin` that are significant. The first is that `rlogin` attempts to use the username on your current system as the account name to connect to the remote service, whereas `telnet` always prompts for a separate username. This makes remotely logging into machines on a single logical network with `rlogin` much faster than with `telnet`. Second, on a trusted, secure network, it is possible to set up a remote authentication mechanism by which the remote host allows a direct, no-username/no-password login from authorized clients. This automated authentication can be performed on a system-wide level by defining an "equivalent" host for authentication purposes on the server in */etc/hosts .equiv*, or on a user-by-user basis with the file *.rhosts*. If the file */etc/hosts.equiv* contains the client machine name and your username, you will be permitted to automatically execute a remote login. For example, if the */etc/hosts.equiv* file on the server contains the line

```
client
```

any user from the machine *client* may log into a corresponding account on the server without entering a username and password. Similarly, if your username and client machine name appear in the *.rhosts* file in the home directory of the user with the same name on the server, you will also be permitted to remotely log in without an identification/authentication challenge. This means that a user on the remote system may log in with all the privileges of the user on the local system, without being asked to enter a username or password—clearly a dangerous security risk.

Remote-shell (rsh) connects to a specified hostname and executes a command. `rsh` is equivalent to `rlogin` when no command arguments are specified. `rsh` copies its standard input to the `remote` command, the standard output of the `remote` command to its standard output, and the standard error of the `remote` command to its standard error. Interrupt, quit, and terminate signals are propagated to the `remote` command. In contrast to commands issued interactively through `rlogin`, `rsh` normally terminates when the `remote` command does.

As an example, the following executes the command df –k on the server, returning information about disk slices and creating the local file *server.df.txt* that contains the output of the command:

```
$ rsh server df -k > server.df.txt
```

Clearly, `rsh` has the potential to be useful in scripts and automated command processing.

PART V

Testing Service Connectivity

Because a port number can be specified on the command line, `telnet` clients can be used to connect to arbitrary ports on Solaris servers. This makes a `telnet` client a useful tool for testing whether services that should have been disconnected are actually active. For example, you can interactively issue commands to an FTP server on port 21:

```
$ telnet server 21
Trying 172.16.1.1...
Connected to server.
Escape character is '^]'.
220 server FTP server (UNIX(r) System V Release 4.0) ready.
```

and on a `sendmail` server on port 25:

```
$ telnet server 25
Trying 172.16.1.1...
Connected to server.
Escape character is '^]'.
220 server ESMTP Sendmail 8.9.1a/8.9.1; Mon, 22 Nov 1999
    14:31:36 +1100 (EST)
```

Interactive testing of this kind has many uses. For example, if you `telnet` to port 80 on a server, you are usually connected to a Web server, where you can issue interactive commands using the Hypertext Transfer Protocol (HTTP). For example, to GET the default index page on a server, you could type **get index.html**:

```
Trying 172.16.1.1...
Connected to server.
Escape character is '^]'.
GET index.html
<!DOCTYPE HTML PUBLIC "-//IETF//DTD HTML 2.0//EN">
<HTML><HEAD>
<TITLE>Server</TITLE></HEAD>
<h1>Welcome to server!</h1>
```

This technique is useful when testing proxy server configurations for new kinds of HTTP clients (for example, a HotJava browser) or the technique can be executed during a script to check whether the Web server is active and serving expected content.

Using Remote Access Tools

With the increased use of the Internet for business-to-business and consumer-to-business transactions, securing remote access has become a major issue in the provision of Solaris services. Fortunately, solutions based around the encryption of sessions and authentication of clients has improved the reliability of remote access facilities in a security-conscious operating environment.

Secure Shell (SSH)

Open Secure Shell, OpenSSH, or just plain SSH is a secure client and server solution that facilitates the symmetric and asymmetric encryption of identification and authentication sequences for remote access. It is designed to replace the `telnet` and `rlogin` applications on the client side with clients available for Solaris, Windows, and many other operating systems. On the server side, it improves upon the nonsecure services supported by `inetd`, such as the r-commands.

SSH uses a generic transport layer encryption mechanism over TCP/IP, which uses the popular Blowfish or U.S. government–endorsed triple-DES (Data Encryption Standard) algorithms for the encryption engine. This is used to transmit encrypted packets whose contents can still be sniffed like all traffic on the network by using public-key cryptography, implementing the Diffie-Hellman algorithm for key exchange. Thus, the contents of encrypted packets appear to be random without the appropriate "key" to decrypt them.

The use of encryption technology makes it extremely unlikely that the contents of the interactive session will ever be known to anyone except the client and the server. In addition to the encryption of session data, identification and authentication sequences are also encrypted using RSA encryption technology. This means that username and password combinations also cannot be sniffed by a third party. SSH also provides automatic forwarding for graphics applications, based around the X11 windowing system, which is a substantial improvement over the text-only `telnet` client.

It is sensible in a commercial context to enforce a policy of SSH-only remote access for interactive logins. This can easily be enforced by enabling the SSH daemon on the server side and removing entries for the `telnet` and `rlogin` services in */etc/services* and */etc/inetd.conf*. Now that OpenSSH is supplied with Solaris, there is no excuse for not deploying SSH across all hosts in your local network.

Setting Up Port Listeners

The `listen` port monitor is managed by the `listen` and `nlsadmin` commands. In contrast to `ttymon`, the `listen` port monitor manages network ports and connections by listening for requests to access services and daemons. The `listen` monitor uses the Transport Layer Interface (TLI) and STREAMS to implement OSI-compliant network service layers. STREAMS provides a framework for writing network-enabled applications, giving access to the kernel, system calls, and a set of standard network libraries. STREAMS applications have many advantages over non-STREAMS applications, including the ability to collect performance data and analyze it in a standard way.

Specific network ports are assigned to the `listen` monitor, and child processes are spawned to handle each client request. One of the key features of `listen` is that it can provide services that are not managed by `inetd`—since all daemons can be accessed through a `listen` service. This is an important feature for the different users accessing services on a Solaris system. For example, a network connection could serve Web traffic, while a dial-in connection could cater to `telnet` or SSH access.

The `nlsadmin` command is used to set up transport providers for STREAMS-compatible network services. In order to configure a TLI listener database, you can use the `nlsadmin` command to configure the listener. First, you create the TCP/IP database:

```
# nlsadmin -i tcp
```

Next, you set the local hexadecimal address:

```
# nlsadmin -l \x11331223a11a58310000000000000000 tcp
```

All services that need to be run will then need to be entered into the TLI listener database.

Adding a Serial Port

Like any modern server system, Solaris 10 supports the connection of simple external devices through both a serial (RS-232-C or RS-423) and a parallel port. The two most common uses for serial devices on a SPARC system are connecting a VT-100 terminal or equivalent, to operate as the system console if no graphics device is installed, and as a modem, enabling dial-up Internet access using PPP. The former is a common practice in many server rooms, where the expense of a monitor and video card can be eliminated by using a VT-100 terminal as the console, because many SPARC machines require a display device to boot at all. On *x*86 systems, there are many more devices available that often have drivers available only for other operating systems. Sun and other third-party hardware vendors are slowly making releases available for these devices through the Solaris Developer Connection. If you need to obtain an updated copy of the Solaris Device Configuration Assistant, and any updated device drivers for supported external devices, these are currently available for download at **http://soldc.sun.com/support/drivers/boot.html**.

Adding a Modem

Solaris 10 works best with external Hayes-compatible modems, which are also supported by other operating systems such as Microsoft Windows. However, modems that require specific operating system support (such as so-called "WinModems"), will not work with Solaris 10. In addition, internal modem cards are generally not supported by Solaris 10. While older modems tend to use external (but sometimes internal!) DIP switches, modern modems can be configured using software to set most of their key operational parameters.

Modem access can be configured to allow inbound-only, outbound-only, and bidirectional access, which allows traffic in both directions, using a similar scheme. The following example considers the scenario of dial-out-only access. The modem should be connected to one of the system's serial ports (A or B) and switched on. The A and B serial ports map to the devices */dev/cua/a* and */dev/cua/b*, respectively.

To test the modem, use the `tip` command:

```
# tip hardwire
```

where `hardwire` should be defined in /etc/remote, similar to

```
hardwire:\
        :dv=/dev/cua/a:br#19200:el=^C^S^Q^U^D:ie=%$:oe=^D:
```

where 19,200 bps is the connection speed between the modem and the serial port. In addition, /etc/remote should have a connection string associated with each modem that's connected to the system. For example, the string

```
cua1:dv=/dev/cua/a:p8:br#19200
```

specifies that 19,200 bps is the connection speed between the modem and the serial port, with 8-bit transmission and with no parity enabled. To use this entry specifically, you would use the command

```
# tip cua1
```

If the message

```
connected
```

appears on your terminal, the system is able to communicate successfully with the modem. For Hayes-compatible modems, command strings can be entered directly like this:

```
ATE1V1
```

If you see "ok", the modem is communicating as expected and can be configured to run PPP.

Setting Up PPP

The first step in configuring PPP is to insert appropriate configuration information in /etc/ppp/options. The following options are the most commonly used:

- **<tty_name>**   Name of the terminal device to use for communication.
- **<speed>**   Speed at which to transmit data.
- *auth*   Specifies that authentication is required (`noauth` specifies that no authentication is required).

- *callback* Requests a callback from the remote server. Useful for saving on long-distance charges!

- *connect* or *init* Specifies the chat script to configure line communications.

- *mru* Sets a maximum receive unit (MRU) value that specifies a limit on the packet size transmitted by the server.

- *mtu* Sets a maximum transmission unit (MTU) value that specifies a limit on the packet size transmitted by the client.

Other options may be required, especially for authentication, but using these options is generally sufficient to make a connection. For further information, you should consult Celeste Stokely's PPP guide: **http://www.stokely.com/unix.serial.port.resources/ppp.slip.html**.

Examples

The following examples demonstrate how to set up modems and Internet access.

Using ttymon

The `ttymon` port monitor is managed by the `ttyadm` command. `ttymon` is designed to monitor requests from ports to allow remote access to the system. `ttymon` operates continually, spawning child processes when appropriate in order to service requests, which are sequentially numbered (for example, `ttymon1`, `ttymon2`, and so forth). The most common request for terminals is probably for an interactive login; thus, */usr/bin/login* is requested. The `sacadm` command can be used to list all current `ttymon` processes:

```
# sacadm -l
PMTAG     PMTYPE   FLGS   RCNT   STATUS    COMMAND
ttymon1   ttymon   -      2      ENABLED   /usr/lib/saf/ttymon #ttymon1
ttymon2   ttymon   -      2      ENABLED   /usr/lib/saf/ttymon #ttymon2
ttymon3   ttymon   -      2      ENABLED   /usr/lib/saf/ttymon #ttymon3
```

To view the services currently being provided through a particular monitor, you can use the `pmadm` command for each monitor process:

```
# pmadm -l -p ttymon2
PMTAG     PMTYPE   SVCTAG      FLGS     ID      <PMSPECIFIC>
ttymon2   ttymon   11          u        root    /dev/term/11
   -   -   /usr/bin/login - 9600 - login:   -tvi925
ttymon2   ttymon   12          u        root    /dev/term/12
   -   -   /usr/bin/login - 9600 - login:   -tvi925
ttymon2   ttymon   13          u        root    /dev/term/13
   -   -   /usr/bin/login - 9600 - login:   -tvi925
ttymon2   ttymon   14          u        root    /dev/term/14
   -   -   /usr/bin/login - 9600 - login:   -tvi925
```

Here, you can see that ports */dev/term/11* through */dev/term/14* are being serviced using the login service.

Connecting to an ISP

Once you have set up the */etc/ppp/options* file, you can make a connection from the command line. For example, to connect using a 56 Kbps modem using the chat script *emergency1.chat*, the following command will establish a connection without authentication:

```
# pppd connect 'chat -f emergency1.chat' /dev/cua/a 57600 noauth
```

Command Reference

The following commands can be used to support modem services and Internet access.

pmadm

The port monitors are managed by the pmadm command. Port services can be managed by using the following commands:

pmadm -a	Adds a port monitor service
pmadm -d	Disarms a port monitor service
pmadm -e	Enables a port monitor service
pmadm -r	Removes a port monitor service

sacadm

The sacadm command is used to manage port monitors. The following functions are available:

sacadm -a	Attaches a new port monitor
sacadm -e	Arms a port monitor
sacadm -d	Disarms a port monitor
sacadm -s	Initializes a port monitor
sacadm -k	Kills a port monitor
sacadm -l	Lists port monitor details
sacadm -r	Deletes a port monitor

tip

tip is a command that acts like a terminal. It can be used, for example, to access remote systems directly through a serial port, where one system acts as the console for the other.

`tip` uses the */etc/remote* file to enable it to make connections through the serial port. For example, if you have a profile set up in */etc/remote*, it's possible to fire up a terminal session immediately by using the command

```
# tip profile
```

where *profile* is the name of the profile that you've set up with all the settings that the port requires to operate. `tip` also uses initialization settings in the *.tiprc* file to specify its operational parameters.

The following table shows the most commonly used `tip` commands:

Command	Description
~.	Exits the session
~c	Changes directory
~!	Spawns a shell
~>	Sends a local file
~<	Receives a remote file
~p	Sends a local file
~t	Receives a remote file
~C	Allows a local application to connect to a remote system
~#	Issues a `break` command
~s	Defines a variable
~^z	Suspends `tip`

Summary

In this chapter, you have learned how to configure and perform remote logins to other networked systems, using both secure and nonsecure (traditional) methods. Although you will almost certainly use an Ethernet card to connect your systems to the Internet, a modem may well be required for backup purposes, so it's useful to understand how these can be configured.

Internet Layer (IPv6)

The TCP/IP protocol suite relies on the Internet Protocol to provide the lower-level services required to support the Transport and Application layers in the stack. However, the current version of IP (IPv4) is now approximately 20 years old, and much has changed in the network world since it was introduced—the Internet has become globally distributed, commercial transactions are conducted on the Internet, and the sheer number of connected hosts has given rise to routing, configuration, and address allocation problems. If these problems are not fixed, then the Internet in its present form may cease to function at some future time, as it reaches capacity. The Internet Engineering Task Force (IETF) predicts that this may occur in 2008.

IPv6 Motivation

The maximum number of IP addresses that can be created using IPv4 is 4.3 billion. While this number must have seemed very large when IPv4 was developed, it now represents a fraction of the potential human users of the Internet. While the Dynamic Host Configuration Protocol (DHCP) has alleviated the address availability problem, by leasing out addresses dynamically instead of assigning them statically, the "always connected, always available" broadband world will monopolize these leases. In addition, with the introduction of "smart spaces" filled with embedded devices with their own IP address, one human may potentially be associated with dozens if not hundreds of different devices. So, one key requirement for an improved IP is the ability to massively increase the pool of available IP addresses.

A related requirement has arisen by the effective breaking of end-to-end communication by the introduction of network address translation (NAT). Like DHCP, NAT was introduced to alleviate the IP address availability problem, by assigning a router a public, routable IP address, while assigning all hosts behind the router a private, nonroutable IP address. This reduced the number of public IP addresses required by organizations to connect their hosts to the Internet. NAT also shielded private computers from attacks originating from the Internet, because their IP addresses were nonroutable. However, NAT also made it impossible to perform peer-to-peer authentication, because the router running NAT software essentially acts as a proxy for the client system. Thus, using NAT can break security initiatives like the IP Security Protocol (IPSec) that require source and destination IP addresses for integrity checking, because there is no end-to-end connectivity. However, some implementations, such as Cisco's VPN solution and Nortel's VPN solution, work fine with IPSec and NAT. Another requirement for an improved IP is to remove the reliance on NAT for building secure networks.

A more practical problem also exists at the hardware level for IPv4 routers—since routing tables are growing exponentially, as new networks are added to the Internet, the physical memory capacity of many routers to hold and process this information is limited. If the routing structure is not simplified, then many routers may simply fail to route any packets correctly. However, as memory becomes cheaper, then routers may be able to handle future capacities.

IPv6 attempts to address the core issues of the small IP address space, end-to-end communication, and the unwelcome mass of routing data. IPv6 is based on a 128-bit address space, rather than a 32-bit address space, providing a large pool of addresses for future computer systems and embedded devices to utilize. The 128 bits are divided into 8 × 16-byte integers expressed using hexadecimal (e.g., 1072:3B:BED3:1:0:2:220:B6EB). In addition, end-to-end communications can be preserved by the use of flow labels that can be used to identify the true end parties to a specific real-time communication. Routing has been dramatically overhauled to ensure that addresses and routes can be more efficiently stored and utilized.

IPv6 has been supported by Sun since Solaris 8, in the form of a dual stack, whereby IPv4 and IPv6 traffic can be supported on a single network. This ensures that new applications requiring the use of IPv6 can coexist alongside legacy IPv4 applications. The following sections examine each of the key areas of IPv6 and discuss their implementation in Solaris.

Addressing

IPv6 increases the IP address size for each network interface from 32 bits to 128 bits, giving a total address space of 2^{32} and 2^{128}, respectively. To give you an idea of the difference between these two spaces, $2^{32} = 4,294,967,296$ (about 1 billion less than the world's population), while $2^{128} = 3.402 \times e^{38}$, which is billions of times greater! This expansion not only will support the massive expansion of the Internet through the connection of billions of embedded devices, it will also ensure that many stop-gap measures such as DHCP and NAT can be disbanded, if they serve no other purpose in a specific environment. Although some competing proposals argued for only a 64-bit IPv6 address space, this would not have enabled some of the useful features of IPv6, including the ability to do away with subnet masks. This allows autoconfiguration of network interfaces without the user having to know what class of subnet (A, B, or C) their local area network belongs to.

Using 128-bit addressing makes autoconfiguration much easier in IPv6 compared to IPv4: the lower 64 bits are composed of the hardware (MAC) address for the network interface, while the upper 64 bits comprise a router message. Since every subnet now has an equivalent-sized subnet prefix, it is no longer used to distinguish different subnet classes.

IPv6 has three different interface types that addresses can be identifiers for:

- **Unicast**   An identifier for a single, specific interface
- **Multicast**   A broadcast-like identifier for all interfaces belonging to a set
- **Anycast**   An identifier for only one interface that belongs to a set, usually the member that is closest to the source

While unicast and multicast addressing are readily identifiable from IPv4, the inclusion of anycast addressing provides the foundation for significant advances in the area of high availability, redundancy, and network storage, since any member of a set of interfaces designed by their addresses can be selected based on some distance metric, or availability at run time. For example, a storage area network (SAN) may support distributed backup services for a multinational organization. When a client has a backup scheduled, it is directed to the nearest server node based on geographical distance. If that node is unavailable, the next available server node in the set of server nodes is selected, and so on. While this sort of decision logic can be programmed in at the Application layer, its inclusion in the Internet layer makes it ubiquitous across all applications and services operating on a network.

Like IPv4, IPv6 has a number of special addresses that have specific purposes and that administrators should be aware of:

- **Loopback address**   0:0:0:0:0:0:0:1
- **IPv4 address**   96 bits zero-padded to the 32-bit original address
- **Local site address**   1111 1110 11
- **Local link address**   1111 1110 10
- **Multicast address**   1111 1111
- **Unspecific address**   0:0:0:0:0:0:0:0

IPv6 addresses are being allocated by using a simple formula:

Field Name	Provider-Based	Registry	Provider	Subscriber	Subnet	Interface
Number of Bits	3 (e.g., 010)	a	b	c	d	128-b-a-c-d-3

In this scheme, the registry is one of the following organizations that cater to a specific region:

- **10000**   Multiregional (IANA)
- **01000**   RIPE NCC (Europe)
- **11000**   InterNIC (North America)
- **10100**   APNIC (Asia/Pacific)

The provider is some network service provider within a specific region, and the subscriber is the end-user organization. Within the organization, subnets can still exist, within which individual network interfaces will belong. At present, provider-based prefixes are being used to utilize a subset of all available address sets for the current range of networks connected to the Internet.

Because IPv6 addresses are much longer than IPv4 addresses, they are difficult for humans to learn and use. The IPv6 address space is so large that large portions of the address are presently zero padded. Thus, a notation has been introduced to simplify the representation of repeated sections of zeros. To eliminate any ambiguity in the resolution of zero-padded sections, only one set of zeros may be represented by the dual-colon token :: in each address. For example, the address 1080:0:0:0:0:711:100D:306B could also be represented as 1080::711:100D:306B, or the address 1080:0:0:0:0:0:100D:306B could be represented as 1080::100D:306B. However, it would not be possible to represent the address 1080:0:208:0:711:0:0:306B as 1080::208::711::306B, since the position of each non-zero bit is ambiguous.

For further information, read the "IP Version 6 Addressing Architecture" RFC at **ftp://ftp.isi.edu/in-notes/rfc2373.txt**.

IPv6 Routing

Internet routing is based on the idea that optimal paths can be dynamically calculated because routers carry information about all network paths in memory. With the massive number of possible paths and new networks being introduced daily, it's impractical to dynamically calculate optimal paths, so most routers fall back on a set of default routes to handle most of their traffic. While a system to optimize routing is theoretically possible, the very flat organization of networks and domains means that it's not practically possible with IPv4. The exception here is the set of backbone Internet servers who must carry the load and determine all network paths that cannot be computed by individual nodes, placing an onerous burden on some service providers.

IPv6 aims to change this situation by implementing a hierarchical model for addressing, providing an explicit set of domains in the address to ensure that destinations can be resolved at a more local level. Thus, a router does not need to have knowledge of a large set of possible network destinations—the appropriate destination router can be determined from the address. The provider field in the address takes on the role of providing a first glance indication of a packet's ultimate destination. At the same time, changes in the structure of the Internet cannot be reliably predicted, so any routing system must be flexible enough to support structural changes down the line.

A number of different routing algorithms are supported by IPv6, including the following that are compatible with IPv4:

- Open Shortest Path First (OSPF)
- Routing Information Protocol (RIP)
- Inter-Domain Routing Protocol (IDRP)
- Intermediate System to Intermediate System Protocol (ISIS)

Routing extensions are also available through a header in the IPv6 Extended Header segment. These extensions include the ability to specify intermediate hosts or specific packet paths, which can then be reversed to ensure that a reply packet is delivered back to the sender using the same path. This approach has great benefits to users of mobile telecommunications technologies such as mobile phones, since the highly dynamic path back to its source does not need to be recomputed by intermediate routers.

Headers

IPv6 introduces a number of changes to the format of headers contained in a standard IPv4 packet. The following fields are common to IPv4 and IPv6:

- Version
- Length
- Service Type
- Packet Length
- Identification
- Fragment Offset
- TTL
- Transport
- Header Checksum
- Source Address
- Destination Address
- Options
- Padding

However, there are several brand new headers that contain important information in standard format:

- **Version Number**   A "6" identifies IPv6
- **Priority**   Sets a priority value depending on whether a packet is non–congestion (priority) controlled or congestion-controlled
- **Flow Label**   Sets a QualityOfService parameter for the packet
- **Payload Length**   Size of the packet's data
- **Next Header**   Determines whether an Extension Header follows
- **Hop Limit**   Sets a limit on the number of nodes that can handle the packet (graceful degradation)

A number of extensions to the standard headers are available in the Extended Header if flagged in the Next Header field of the standard header. The following extensions are currently being developed:

- Authentication and security
- Confidentiality
- Destination data
- Extended routing
- Hop-by-hop processing
- Reassembly

Quality of Service

Quality of service (QoS) is very much a missing component of IPv4. When IPv4 was developed, there was no such thing as "mission critical e-commerce data" being exchanged between organizations on the Internet. However, with the rise of B2B e-commerce and the development of digital virtual enterprises, ensuring QoS is critical to the operation of certain classes of applications and services (such as Web Services).

IPv6 provides QoS through a priority and flow label system of packet prioritization defined within the packet header. There are several different priority values that have been suggested for congestion-controlled traffic, which has a lower priority than non-congestion-controlled traffic:

- 0   Unclassified
- 1   Bulk traffic
- 2   Noninteractive bulk data transfer
- 3   Undefined
- 4   Interactive bulk data transfer
- 5   Undefined
- 6   Interactive non-bulk data transfer
- 7   Control traffic

Security

All IPv6 stacks must implement IPSec. IPSec provides security at the Internet layer rather than at the Transport layer (like the Secure Sockets Layer currently provides for secure e-commerce). IPSec provides facilities for encryption, authentication, implementation of security policies, and data compression. The two main components of IPv6 security are packet encryption through the Encapsulated Security Payload (ESP) and source authentication through the Authentication Header (AH).

The ESP provides confidentiality, authentication, and integrity checks, while the AH only supports authentication and integrity, and works at the packet level—it uses strong cryptography to ensure that a packet can be authentically exchanged between two interfaces by sharing a secret key. This allows the two parties to be assured that the packet has not been tampered with in transit, and that the packet originated from the source interface as described in the packet's header.

The ESP provides a different level of security than the AH, by ensuring that the data contained within a packet has not been intercepted and decrypted by a third party, as long as the secret key protecting the data has not been given to a third party.

Key management is clearly a central issue in the provision of a secure platform for IPv6. That's why the Internet key exchange (IKE) system is important to the success of IPSec. IKE makes it possible for two systems to share secret keys in a secure environment. However, if a cracker discovers a secret key, then all of the traffic previously protected by the key will be open for reading by that hacker. This is why secret keys cannot be used indefinitely, and should be regularly modified. One of the benefits of using Solaris IPSec is that it incorporates IKE—Solaris 8 IPSec did not support IKE, since it was not part of the IPSec standard at the time, leading to cross-platform incompatibilities.

Summary

This chapter examined the future of the Internet Protocol as embodied by IPv6, which is the next-generation IP. The areas in which IPv6 introduces the greatest changes are security, addressing, routing, and quality of service. Much of the detail in IPv6 differs from IPv4, and these changes were covered in detail in this chapter.

VI

PART

Services, Directories, and Applications

26

Network File System and Caching File System

This chapter examines Sun's Network File System (NFS), which is a distributed file system architecture based on the Remote Procedure Call (RPC) protocol. RPC is a standard method of allocating and managing shared resources between Solaris systems. Although NFS is similar to Samba in concept, supporting transparent file system sharing between systems, NFS features high data throughput because of dedicated support in the Solaris kernel, and support for both NFS 2 and 3 clients.

NFS was one of the first distributed network applications to ever be successfully deployed on local area networks. It allows users to mount volumes of other systems connected to the network, with the same ability as any other locally mounted file system to change permissions, delete and create files, and apply security measures. One of the great advantages of NFS is its efficient use of network bandwidth, by using RPC calls. In Solaris 10, the NFS concept has been extended to the Internet, with the new WebNFS providing file system access through a URL similar to that used for web pages. This chapter examines the theory behind distributed file systems and examines how they can best be established in practice.

Prior to Solaris 2.5, NFS 2 was deployed, which used the unreliable User Datagram Protocol (UDP) for data transfer, hence NFS 2's poor reputation for data integrity. However, the more modern NFS 3 protocol, based around TCP, has been implemented in all new Solaris releases since Solaris 2.5.1. NFS 3 allowed an NFS server to cache NFS client requests in RAM, thus speeding up disk writing operations and the overall speed of NFS transactions. In addition, Solaris 2.6 and above provides support for WebNFS. The WebNFS protocol allows file systems to be shared across the Internet, as an alternative to traditional Internet file-sharing techniques, like FTP.

Solaris 10 is supplied the new NFS 4. NFS 4 has many improved features compared to NFS 3, which will be examined in this chapter.

In this chapter, you learn how to set up and install an NFS server and an NFS client, and how to export file systems. In addition, this chapter examines how to set up the `automounter`, so that a user's home directory across all machines on an intranet is automatically shared and available, irrespective of the user's login host.

Key Concepts

The following concepts are required knowledge for installing and managing NFS.

NFS Architectures

A Solaris 10 system can share any of its locally mounted file systems with other systems, making them available for remote mounting. NFS considers the system that shares the file system to be a server, and the system that remotely mounts the file system as a client. When an NFS client mounts a remote file system, it is connected to a mount point on the local file system, which means it appears to local users as just another file system. For example, a system called *carolina* may make its mail directory */var/mail* available for remote mounting by NFS clients. This would allow users on machines like *georgia*, *virginia*, and *fairfax* to read their mail, actually stored on *carolina*, locally from their own machines without having to explicitly log in to *carolina*. This means that a single mail server that acts as an NFS server can serve all NFS clients on a LAN with mail. Figure 26-1 shows this configuration.

However, one important aspect of NFS is that it enables you to export file systems and mount them on a remote mount point that is different from the original shared directory. For example, the NFS server *carolina* may also export its Sun Answerbook files (from the directory */opt/answerbook*) to the clients *virginia, georgia,* and *fairfax.* However, *virginia* mounts these files in the */usr/local/www/htdocs* directory, as it publishes them via the Web, whereas *georgia* mounts them in */opt/doc/answerbook.* The client *fairfax* mounts them in */opt/answerbook* using the same mount point name as *carolina.* The point is that the remote mount point can be completely different from the actual directory exported by an NFS server. This configuration is shown in Figure 26-2.

Remote Procedure Calls

NFS uses RPC technology, which makes it easy for systems to make requests for remote execution of procedures on server systems. RPC is currently supported across a number of different operating systems, including Solaris, Linux, and Microsoft Windows. The purpose of RPC is to abstract the connection details and methods required to access

FIGURE 26-1
NFS server *carolina* exports its mail directory to NFS clients *georgia, fairfax,* and *virginia,* using the same mount point as the exported file system.

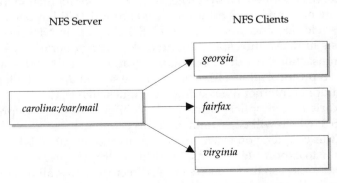

FIGURE 26-2
NFS server *carolina* exports its mail directory to NFS clients *georgia, fairfax,* and *virginia,* using their own mount points.

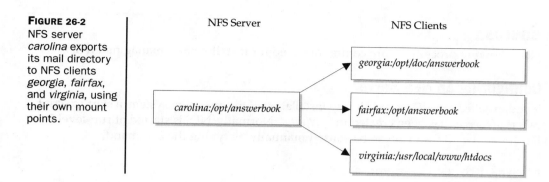

procedures across networks—that is, the client and server programs do not need to implement separate networking code, as a simple API is provided for finding services through a service called the `portmapper` (or `rpcbind`). The portmapper should be running on both the client and server for NFS to operate correctly. The portmapper is registered with both UDP and TCP 111, since requests may be generated for or received using NFS 2 or NFS 3, respectively.

automounter

The `automounter` is a program that automatically mounts NFS file systems when they are accessed and then unmounts them when they are no longer needed. It allows you to use special files, known as *automounter maps,* that contain information about the servers, the pathname to the NFS file system on the server, the local pathname, and the mount options. By using the `automounter`, you don't have to manually update the entries in */etc/vfstab* on every client every time you make a change to the NFS servers.

Normally, only root can mount file systems, so when users need to mount an NFS file system, they need to find the system administrator. The main problem is that once users are finished with a file system, they rarely tell the system administrator—even if they were to do so, manually mounting and unmounting resources at the request of users would create an administrative burden that is not scalable. In addition, if the NFS server containing that file system ever crashed, you may be left with one or more hanging processes. This can easily increase your workload if you are responsible for maintaining an NFS server. The `automounter` can solve both of these problems, because it automatically mounts an NFS file system when a user references a file in that file system, and it will automatically unmount the NFS file system if it is not referenced for more than five minutes.

The `automounter` is an RPC daemon that services requests from clients to mount and unmount remote volumes using NFS. During installation, a set of server-side maps are created that list the file systems to be automatically mounted. Typically, these file systems include shared user home directories (under */home*) and network-wide mail directories (*/var/mail*).

Procedures

The following procedures are commonly used for installing and managing NFS.

Configuring an NFS Server

If you installed the NFS server during installation of the operating system, a startup script called *nfs.server* has been created in */etc/init.d*. Normally, NFS is started at run-level 3. However, the NFS server can be started manually by typing the command

```
# /etc/init.d/nfs.server start
```

This command will start at least two daemons: the NFS server nfsd daemon (*/usr/lib/nfs/nfsd*) and the mount daemon (*/usr/lib/nfs/mountd*). The nfsd daemon is responsible for answering access requests from clients for shared volumes on the server, while the mountd daemon is responsible for providing information about mounted file systems.

To check whether or not the NFS server has started correctly, it is possible to examine the process list for nfsd and mountd by using the following commands:

```
# ps -eaf | grep nfsd
   root 19961     1  0   Aug 31 ?        0:09 /usr/lib/nfs/nfsd -a 16
# ps -eaf | grep mountd
   root   370     1  0   May 16 ?        2:49 /usr/lib/nfs/mountd
```

In this case, both nfsd and mountd are operating correctly. To stop the NFS server, you use the following command:

```
# /etc/init.d/nfs.server stop
```

There are some optional services started by the NFS server startup script, including daemons that support diskless booting (the Reverse Address Resolution Protocol daemon, */usr/sbin/in.rarpd*, and the boot parameter server, */usr/sbin/rpc.bootparamd*). In addition, a separate daemon for *x*86 boot support (*/usr/sbin/rpld*), using the Network Booting RPL (Remote Program Load) protocol, may also be started. You need to configure these services only if you wish to provide diskless booting for local clients; otherwise, they can be safely commented from the */etc/init.d/nfs.server* script.

Sharing File Systems

To actually share file systems and directories, you can use the share command. For example, if you want to share the */var/mail* directory from *carolina* to *georgia*, you could use the command

```
# share -F nfs -o rw=georgia /var/mail
```

In this example, -F nfs stands for "a file system of type NFS."

Of course, you really want to share the volume to *virginia* and *fairfax* as well, so you would probably use the command

```
# share -F nfs -o rw=georgia,virginia,fairfax /var/mail
```

The */var/mail* volume is shared to these clients because users on these systems need to read and write their e-mail. However, if you need to share a CD-ROM volume, you obviously need to share it read-only:

```
# share -F nfs -o ro /cdrom
```

Normally, the volumes to be shared are identified in the */etc/dfs/dfstab* file. Note that if this file contains no entries, then the NFS server will not start, with the message:

```
NFS service was not started because /etc/dfs/dfstab has no entries.
```

One of the really innovative features of NFS is that a system that shares volumes to other systems can actually remotely mount shared volumes from its own clients. For example, *carolina* might share the volume */cdrom* to *georgia*, *fairfax*, and *virginia*.

In contrast, *virginia* might share the */staff* directory, which contains home directories, to *carolina*, *georgia*, and *fairfax*, using the command

```
# share -F nfs -o rw=georgia,carolina,fairfax /staff
```

File systems can be unshared using the unshare command. For example, if you are going to change a CD-ROM on *carolina* that is shared to clients using NFS, it might be wise to unmount it first:

```
# unshare -F nfs /cdrom
```

To unshare all volumes that are currently being shared from an NFS server, you can use the following command:

```
# unshareall
```

The command dfmounts shows the local resources shared through the networked file system that are currently mounted by specific clients:

```
# dfmounts
RESOURCE   SERVER PATHNAME                CLIENTS
   -           carolina /cdrom            virginia,georgia
   -           carolina /var/mail         fairfax,virginia,georgia
   -           carolina /opt/answerbook   fairfax
```

However, dfmounts does not provide information about the permissions with which directories and file systems are shared, nor does it show those shared resources that have no clients currently using them. To display this information, you need to use the share command with no arguments. On *virginia*, this looks like

```
# share
/staff rw=georgia,fairfax,carolina  "staff"
```

while on *carolina*, the volumes are different:

```
# share
-                      /cdrom  ro=georgia,fairfax,carolina "cdrom"
-                      /var/mail  rw=georgia,fairfax,carolina "mail"
```

Conversely, as a client, you want to determine which volumes are available for you to mount from NFS servers. This can be achieved by using the dfshares command. For example, to view the mounts available from the server *virginia*, executed on *carolina*, the following output would be displayed:

```
# dfshares -F nfs virginia
RESOURCE                   SERVER          ACCESS        TRANSPORT
virginia:/staff            virginia        -             -
```

Installing an NFS Client

In order to access file systems that are being shared from an NFS server, a separate NFS client must be operating on the client system. There are two main daemon processes that must be running in order to use the mount command to access shared volumes: the NFS lock daemon (*/usr/lib/nfs/lockd*), and the NFS stat daemon (*/usr/lib/nfs/statd*). The lockd daemon manages file sharing and locking at the user level, while the statd daemon is used for file recovery after connection outage.

If NFS was installed during the initial system setup, then a file called *nfs.client* should have been created in */etc/init.d*. Normally, NFS clients are started at run-level 2. However, to manually run the NFS client, you need to execute the following command:

```
# /etc/init.d/nfs.client start
```

Just like the NFS server, you can verify that the NFS daemons have started correctly by using the following commands:

```
# ps -eaf | grep statd
  daemon    211    1  0   May 16 ?           0:04 /usr/lib/nfs/statd
# ps -eaf | grep lockd
    root    213    1  0   May 16 ?           0:03 /usr/lib/nfs/lockd
```

If these two daemons are not active, then the NFS client will not run.

The next step is for the client to consult the */etc/vfstab* file, which lists both the UFS and NFS file systems that need to be mounted and attempts to mount the latter if they are available by using the `mountall` command.

To stop the NFS client once it is operating, you may use the following command:

```
# /etc/init.d/nfs.client stop
```

The NFS server is usually started automatically during run-level 3.

Configuring a CacheFS File System

In general terms, a cache is a place where important material can be placed so that it can be quickly retrieved. The location of the cache may be quite different from the normal storage location for the specified material. For example, field commanders in the army may store ammunition in local caches, so that their forces can obtain their required materiel quickly in case of war. This ammunition would normally be stored securely well away from the battlefield, but must be "highly available" when required. The state of the battlefield may make it difficult to access outside sources of ammunition during live fire, so a sizable cache of arms is always wise.

This analogy can be easily extended to client/server scenarios in which an unreliable or slow data link may give rise to performance issues. A cache, in this case, can be created to locally store commonly used files, rather than retrieving them each time they are requested from a server. The cache approach has the advantage of speeding up client access to data. However, it has the disadvantage of data asynchronization, in which a file is modified on the server after it has been stored in the cache. Thus, if a local file retrieved from the cache is modified before being sent back to the server, any modifications performed on the server's copy of the file would be overwritten. Conversely, cached data may be out of date by the time it is retrieved by the local client, meaning that important decisions could be made based on inaccurate information.

Many Internet client/server systems, involved in the exchange of data across an HTTP link, use a cache to store data. This data is never modified and sent back to the server, so overwriting server-side data is never an issue. Small ISPs with limited bandwidth often use caches to store files that are commonly retrieved from a server. For example, if the ISP has 1,000 customers who routinely download the front page of the *Sydney Morning Herald* each morning, it makes sense to download the file once from the *Sydney Morning Herald* Web site and store it locally for the other 999 users to retrieve. Since the front page may only change from day to day, the page will always be current, as long as the cache purges the front page file at the end of each day. The daily amount of data to be downloaded from the *Sydney Morning Herald* Web site has been reduced by 99.9 percent, which can significantly boost the ISP's performance in downloading other noncached files from the Internet, as well as reduce the overall cost of data throughput.

Solaris provides a cache file system (CacheFS) that is designed to improve NFS client/ server performance across slow or unreliable networks. The principles underlying CacheFS are exactly the same as the principles underlying the preceding two cache examples: locally stored files that are frequently requested can be retrieved by users on the client system without having to download them again from the server. This approach minimizes the number of connections required between an NFS client and server to retrieve the same amount of data, in a manner that is invisible to users on the client system. In fact, if anything, users will notice that their files are retrieved more quickly than before the cache was introduced.

CacheFS seamlessly integrates with existing NFS installations, with only simple modifications to mount command parameters and /etc/vfstab entries required to use the facility. The first task in configuring a cache is to create a mount point and a cache on a client system. If a number of NFS servers are to be used with the cache, it makes sense to create individual caches underneath the same top-level mount point. Many sites use the mount point /cache to store individual caches. This example assumes that a file system from the NFS server *yorktown* will be cached on the local client system *midway*, so the commands to create a cache on *midway* are

```
midway# mkdir /cache
midway# cfsadmin -c /cache/yorktown
```

Here, the `cfsadmin` command is used to create the cache once the mount point /cache has been created.

Now, take a look at how you would force the cache to be used for all accesses from *midway* to *yorktown* for the remote file system /staff, which is also mounted locally on /staff:

```
# mount -F cachefs -o backfstype=nfs,cachedir=/cache/yorktown yorktown:/
staff /staff
```

Once the *yorktown:/staff* file system has been mounted in this way, users on *midway* will not notice any difference in operation, except that file access to /staff will be much quicker.

It is possible to check the status of the cache by using the `cachefsstat` command. To verify that /cache/yorktown is operating correctly, you would use the following command:

```
# cachefsstat /cache/yorktown
```

Alternatively, you can use the `cfsadmin` command:

```
# cfsadmin -l /cache/yorktown
cfsadmin: list cache FS information
maxblocks 80%
minblocks 0%
threshblocks 75%
maxfiles 80%
minfiles 0%
threshfiles 75%
maxfilesize 12MB
yorktown:_staff:_staff
```

Note the last line, which is the current cache ID. You need to use the cache ID if you ever need to delete the cache. If you do need to delete a cache, you can use the cfsadmin command with the –d option:

```
# umount /staff
# cfsadmin -d yorktown:_staff:_staff /cache/yorktown
```

This example unmounts the /staff volume on merlin locally, before attempting to remove the cache by providing its ID along with its mount point.

Enabling the automounter

The automount command installs autofs mount points and associates an automounter map with each mount point. This requires that the automount daemon be running (automountd). When the automount daemon is initialized on the server, no exported directories are mounted by the clients: these are mounted only when a remote user attempts to access a file on the directory from a client. The connection eventually times out, in which case the exported directory is unmounted by the client. The automounter maps usually work with a network information service, like NIS+, to manage shared volumes, meaning that a single home directory for individual users can be provided on request from a single server, no matter which client machine they log into. Connection and reconnection is handled by the automount daemon. If automount starts up and has nothing to mount or unmount, this is reported, and is quite normal:

```
# automount
automount: no mounts
automount: no unmounts
```

Automounter Maps

The behavior of the automounter is determined by a set of files called automounter maps. There are two main types of maps—indirect and direct:

- **Indirect map**   Useful when you are mounting several file systems that will share a common pathname prefix. As you will see shortly, an indirect map can be used to manage the directory tree in /home.

- **Direct map**   Used to mount file systems where each mount point does not share a common prefix with other mount points in the map.

This section looks at examples of each of these types of maps. An additional map, called the master map, is used by the automounter to determine the names of the files corresponding to the direct and indirect maps.

Indirect Maps

The most common type of automounter maps are indirect maps, which correspond to "regularly" named file systems like /home, or /usr directory trees. Regularly named file systems share the same directory prefix. For example, the directories /home/jdoe and /home/sdoe are regularly named directories in the /home directory tree.

Normally, indirect maps are stored in the /etc directory, and are named with the convention auto_directory, where directory is the name of the directory prefix (without slashes) that the indirect map is responsible for. As an example, the indirect map responsible for the /home directory is usually named auto_home. An indirect map is made up of a series of entries in the following format:

```
directory      options      host:filesystem
```

Here, directory is the relative pathname of a directory that will be appended to the name of the directory that corresponds to this indirect map, as specified in the master map file. (The master map is covered later in this section.) For options, you can use any of the mount options covered earlier in this chapter. To specify options, you need to prefix the first option with a dash (–). If you do not need any extra options, you can omit the options entirely. The final entry in the map contains the location of the NFS file system.

Here is an example of the indirect map that is responsible for the directories in /home:

```
# /etc/auto_home - home directory map for automounter
jdoe        orem:/store/home/jdoe
sdoe        orem:/store/home/sdoe
kdoe -bg srv-ss10:/home/kdoe
```

Here, the entries for jdoe, sdoe, and kdoe correspond to the directories /home/jdoe, /home/sdoe, and /home/kdoe, respectively. The first two entries indicate that the automounter should mount the directories /home/jdoe and /home/sdoe from the NFS server orem, while the last one specifies that the directory /home/kdoe should be mounted from the NFS server srv-ss10. The last entry also demonstrates the use of options.

Now that you have taken a look at an indirect map, you are ready to walk through what happens when you access a file on an NFS file system that is handled by the automounter. For example, consider the following command that accesses the file /home/jdoe/docs/book/ch17.doc:

```
$ more /home/jdoe/docs/book/ch17.doc
```

Because the directory /home/jdoe is automounted, the following steps are used by the automounter to allow you to access the file:

1. The automounter looks at the pathname and determines that the directory /home is controlled by the indirect map auto_home.

2. The automounter looks at the rest of the pathname for a corresponding entry in the auto_home map. In this case it finds the matching entry, jdoe.

3. Once a matching entry has been found, the automounter checks to see if the directory /home/jdoe is already mounted. If the directory is already mounted, you can directly access the file; otherwise, the automounter mounts this directory and then allows you to access the file.

Direct Maps

When you use an indirect map, the `automounter` takes complete control of the directory corresponding to the indirect map. This means that no user, not even root, can create entries in a directory corresponding to an indirect map. For this reason, directories specified in an indirect map cannot be automounted on top of an existing directory. In this case you need a special type of map known as a direct map. A direct map allows you to mix `automounter` mount points and normal directories in the same directory tree. The directories specified in a direct map have "nonregular" mount points, which simply means that they do not share a common prefix. A common use for direct maps is to allow for directories in the /usr directory tree to be automounted.

The direct map is normally stored in the file /etc/auto_direct. The format of this file is similar to the format of the indirect maps:

```
directory      options    host:filesystem
```

Here, *directory* is the absolute pathname of a directory. For *options*, you can use any of the mount options covered earlier in this chapter. To specify options, you need to prefix the first option with a dash (–). If you do not need any extra options, you can omit the options entirely. The final entry in the map contains the location of the NFS file system. Here is an example of the direct map that is responsible for some of the directories in /usr:

```
# /etc/auto_direct - Direct Automount map
/usr/pubsw/man  orem:/internal/opt/man
/usr/doc        orem:/internal/httpd/htdocs
```

When any files in the directories /usr/pubsw/man or /usr/doc are accessed, the `automounter` automatically handles the mounting of these directories.

Master Maps

When the `automounter` first starts, it reads the file /etc/auto_master to determine where to find the direct and indirect map files. The *auto_master* file is known as the master map. It consists of lines whose format is as follows:

```
directory      map
```

Here, *directory* is the name of the directory that corresponds to the indirect map. For a direct map, this entry is /–. The *map* is the name of the map file in the /etc directory corresponding to the *directory* given in the first column.

The following example shows a master map file for the direct and indirect maps given earlier in this section:

```
# Master map for automounter
/home           auto_home
/-                auto_direct
```

Other entries can also be made in the master map. For example, to share a common directory for mail between a number of clients and a mail server, you would enter the following definition:

```
/-                  /etc/auto_mail
```

This creates a share called *auto_mail* that makes mail on a single server accessible to all client machines upon request. The `automounter` permits two kinds of shares that can be defined by direct and indirect maps: a direct map is a set of arbitrary mount points that are listed together, while an indirect map mounts everything under a specific directory. For example, *auto_home* mounts user directories and all subdirectories underneath them. If an automounted share is available on the server, then you should see its details being displayed in the */etc/mnttab* file:

```
burbank:/var/mail    /var/mail nfs      nosuid,dev=2bc0012      951071258
```

Continuing with the example of *auto_mail*, as defined in the master map, a file named */etc/auto_mail* would have to contain the following entry:

```
# cat /etc/auto_mail
  /var/mail     burbank:/var/mail
```

This ensures that the *burbank* server knows where to find the */var/mail* directory physically, and that `automount` can mount the shared volume at will.

Sometimes, the network load caused by mounting and unmounting home directories can lead to an increase in I/O load, and reduce the effective bandwidth of a network. For this reason, only volumes that need to be shared should be shared. Alternatively, the *timeout* parameter for `automount` can be modified to extend its latency for mounting and unmounting directories.

automount and NIS+

A common problem with *auto_home* is that systems in an NIS+ environment may create user accounts on a file system mounted as */home*. This means that if *auto_home* is active, as defined by */etc/auto_master*, then after rebooting, the shared home directories are mounted on */home*, and when the local */home* attempts to mount the same point, it fails. This is one of the most frequently asked questions about Solaris 10, as the convention was different for earlier Solaris systems, which used local */home* directories. The recommended practice is now to create home directories under */export/home*, on the local file system if required, or to use *auto_home* in an NIS+ environment. However, if you wish to disable this feature altogether and stick with a local */home*, then simply remove "+auto_master" from the master map (*/etc/auto_master*).

Starting and Stopping the automounter

Starting and stopping the automounter is normally handled by your system at boot and shutdown time, but you will have to start and stop the automounter manually if you make changes to any of its map files.

The automount daemon is typically started from /etc/init.d/autofs during the multiuser startup, with a command like

```
# /etc/init.d/autofs start
```

You can confirm that it started correctly by using the following command:

```
# /bin/ps -ef | grep automountd
```

The output should look like the following:

```
root 21642    1  0 11:27:29 ?         0:00 /usr/lib/autofs/automountd
```

If you receive no output, then the automounter has not started correctly. In that case you should run the startup script again.

Stopping the autofs client is similar to starting it:

```
# /etc/init.d/autofs stop
```

The stop script usually stops the automounter, but you can confirm this by using the command

```
# /bin/ps -ef | grep automountd
```

This is the same command that is used to check whether the automounter is running, except that once you stop it, this command should not produce any output. If you do see some output and it contains a grep command, you can ignore those lines. Any other output indicates that the automounter has not stopped, in which case you should execute the NFS client stop command again.

If you receive a message similar to the following:

```
/home: busy
```

then you need to determine if anyone is logged onto the system and is using files from /home. If you cannot determine this, you can use the following command to get a list of all the mounted directories in the directory that caused the error message (in this case /home):

```
$ df -k -F nfs
/home/jdoe
```

Just replace /home with the name of the directory that produced the error message. In this case only one directory, /home/jdoe, was automounted. Once you have a list of these directories, try unmounting each one with the umount command. When you receive an error message, you will know which directory contains the files that are in use. You can ask the user to finish with those files, and then proceed to stop the automounter.

Examples

The following examples provide some real-world cases for installing and managing NFS.

Checking portmapper Status

If you're having trouble starting the NFS daemon, it's often a Remote Procedure Call (RPC) problem. In order to determine whether an RPC portmapper is running, you may use the rpcinfo command:

```
# rpcinfo -p
   program vers proto   port  service
    100000   4   tcp    111   rpcbind
    100000   3   tcp    111   rpcbind
    100000   2   tcp    111   rpcbind
    100000   4   udp    111   rpcbind
    100000   3   udp    111   rpcbind
    100000   2   udp    111   rpcbind
    100007   3   udp  32774   ypbind
    100007   2   udp  32774   ypbind
    100007   1   udp  32774   ypbind
    100007   3   tcp  32771   ypbind
    100007   2   tcp  32771   ypbind
    100007   1   tcp  32771   ypbind
    100011   1   udp  32785   rquotad
    100024   1   udp  32789   status
    100024   1   tcp  32775   status
    100021   1   udp   4045   nlockmgr
    100021   2   udp   4045   nlockmgr
    100021   3   udp   4045   nlockmgr
    100021   4   udp   4045   nlockmgr
    100068   2   udp  32809
    100068   3   udp  32809
    100068   4   udp  32809
    100068   5   udp  32809
    100083   1   tcp  32795
    100021   1   tcp   4045   nlockmgr
    100021   2   tcp   4045   nlockmgr
    100021   3   tcp   4045   nlockmgr
    100021   4   tcp   4045   nlockmgr
    100005   1   udp  32859   mountd
```

```
100005    2   udp   32859   mountd
100005    3   udp   32859   mountd
100005    1   tcp   32813   mountd
100005    2   tcp   32813   mountd
100005    3   tcp   32813   mountd
100026    1   udp   32866   bootparam
100026    1   tcp   32815   bootparam
```

In this example, both `mountd` and `nfsd` are running, along with several other services, so the NFS daemon should have no problems executing. However, the RPL service is not active, since it is not displayed in the `rpcinfo` list, so *x86* clients would not be able to use the local server as a boot server.

Mounting Remote File Systems

On the client side, if you want to mount a volume that has been shared from an NFS server, you use the `mount` command. For example, if you want to mount the exported CD-ROM from *carolina* on the NFS client *virginia*, you would use the command

```
# mount -F nfs -o ro carolina:/cdrom /cdrom
```

Like the */etc/dfs/dfstab* file, which records a list of volumes to be exported, the */etc/vfstab* file can contain entries for NFS volumes to be mounted from remote servers. For example, on the machine *fairfax*, if you wanted the */var/mail* volume on *carolina* to be mounted locally as */var/mail*, you would enter the following line in */etc/vfstab*:

```
carolina:/var/mail   -        /var/mail      nfs     -      yes    rw
```

This line can be interpreted as a request to mount */var/mail* from *carolina* read/write on the local mount point */var/mail* as an NFS volume that should be mounted at boot time. If you make changes to the */etc/vfstab* file on *virginia*, and you want to mount the */var/mail* partition, you can use the command

```
# mount /var/mail
```

which will attempt to mount the remote */var/mail* directory from the server *carolina*.
Alternatively, you can use the command

```
# mountall
```

which will mount all partitions that are listed in */etc/vfstab* but have not yet been mounted. This should identify and mount all available partitions.

File systems can be unmounted by using the `umount` command. For example, if the */cdrom* file system on *carolina* is mounted on *virginia* as */cdrom*, then the command

```
# umount /cdrom
```

will unmount the mounted NFS volume. Alternatively, the `unmountall` command can be used, which unmounts all currently mounted NFS volumes. For example, the command

```
# umountall -F nfs
```

unmounts all volumes that are currently mounted through NFS.

When a remote volume is mounted on a local client, it should be visible to the system just like a normal disk, as shown by `df`:

```
# df -k
carolina:/cdrom           412456 341700   70756     83%     /cdrom
carolina:/var/mail        4194304 343234  3851070   8%      /var/mail
carolina:/opt/answerbook       2097152 1345634    750618 64%     /opt/
answerbook
```

Enhancing Security

So far, NFS has been examined without consideration of the security implications of sharing a file system to clients. In a local intranet environment, with protection from a firewall, some administrators implement open NFS sharing, where client lists are not supplied to share commands to limit access to server volumes. The problem with this approach is spoofing: an external system may be able to "pretend" to be part of your local network, thereby gaining access to globally shared NFS volumes. Given that NFS authentication is usually based on mappings of usernames on the client to the server, if a spoofed system contains equivalent user accounts to those found on the server, then unauthorized clients will be able to read and write data at will. This is why it's critical to only share volumes to specific client systems, using the appropriate read-write or read-only designation.

The other key parameter for the `share` command is *sec*, which specifies the type of authentication required to access server volumes. By default, the *sys* level is used, whereby usernames and groups are mapped between client and the server. Thus, the user *lynda* on the client will have the same access permissions as *lynda* on the server. However, other alternatives are available, depending on the relative risks involved in data loss. If sensitive data is being shared by an NFS server, it may be wise to implement a more sophisticated authentication method, including one based on DES public key cryptography (the *dh* level, standing for Diffie-Hellman) or the Kerberos 4 authentication method (the *krb4* level). If a volume is exported with the *dh* or *krb4* authentication levels, then all clients must use the method specified to access data on the volume specified. To support the *dh* or *krb4* authentication levels, secure RPC must be running. User keys can be updated by using the `chkey` command. For more information on security, see Chapter 9.

Performance

NFS performance is determined by a number of factors, including

- Server CPU speed, and number of server CPUs
- Server physical RAM and virtual RAM
- Server disk speed
- Server system load
- Server CacheFS capacity
- Server network interfaces
- Number of clients
- Speed of local network
- Domain Name Lookup Cache (DNLC) speed

Many sites develop NFS services incrementally—as the number of users grows, so does the number of CPUs, the amount of memory, the number of network interfaces, and the number of faster disks allocated to improving NFS performance. In addition, a number of software methods, including the CacheFS and DNLC settings, can be modified to improve data throughput.

One of the best methods for determining how NFS is performing, from both a client and server perspective, is to use the nfsstat command to gather performance statistics over a period of weeks or months. In particular, counting the number of calls and bad calls can show the proportion of successful to unsuccessful requests, respectively, to the server. To run nfsstat on the server, use the following command:

```
# nfsstat -s
...
Server nfs:
calls badcalls
575637455 3433
...
```

Here, you can see that the proportion of bad calls to the total number of calls is 3433 ÷ 575637455, which is much less than 1 percent. After gathering statistics for each interval, the counters can be reset to zero by using the following command:

```
# nfsstat -z
```

nfsstat now provides output showing separate statistics for NFS versions 2, 3, and 4.

Command Reference

The following commands are commonly used to install and manage NFS.

share

Table 26-1 shows the most common options for the `share` command.

mount

The main options available for mounting NFS file systems are shown in Table 26-2.

Parameter	Description
anon=username	Sets the username of unknown users to *username*
log	Starts NFS logging
nosuid	Prevents applications from executing as *setuid*
nosub	Prevents client access to subdirectories of exported server volumes
ro	Prevents writing to an exported file system
root	Allows remote access by remote root users as the local root user
rw	Permits reading and writing to an exported file system
sec	Specifies the authentication level (*sys, dh,* or *krb4*)

TABLE 26-1   NFS Server Options

Option	Description
ro	Mounts a file system with read-only permissions.
rw	Mounts a file system with read/write permissions.
hard	No timeouts permitted—the client will repeatedly attempt to make a connection.
soft	Timeouts permitted—the client will attempt a connection, and give an error message if the connection fails.
bg	Attempts to mount a remote file system in the background if the connection fails.

TABLE 26-2   NFS Client Options

Summary

In this chapter, you have examined how to share file systems with other servers by using NFS. New initiatives like WebNFS will ensure that NFS will not disappear, even though CIFS is now being used widely.

## 27

CHAPTER

Sendmail

E lectronic mail was one of the first applications to be widely adopted across the Internet, and despite changes in technology and a shift toward information delivery via the Web, e-mail has managed to hold its ground. E-mail has undergone many changes in recent years: instead of plain-text messages being sent from command-line clients (or mail user agents, MUAs), there are many different mail protocols that enable remote clients to retrieve their e-mail from a centralized server (e.g., POP, IMAP), and multimedia content is now supported through Multipurpose Internet Mail Extensions (MIME).

Although desktop clients are technically capable of running mail servers, most organizations still prefer to run a single main mail server, running a mail-transport agent (MTA), such as the traditional `sendmail` daemon, or a newer replacement (e.g., `qmail`). The reason for this preference is that server systems, such as Solaris, have high uptime and better security features than the average desktop client, and because the security of mail services can be managed centrally. For example, if a security vulnerability is revealed in `sendmail`, then a patch can be freely downloaded from SunSolve and applied to the server, with minimal disruption to users. If everyone ran their own mail server, new security problems could take weeks if not months per incident to rectify, in a large organization.

This chapter examines the background to how e-mail is addressed and delivered, and the configuration of the popular `sendmail` MTA. It then shifts focus to the client side, examining local and remote MUAs that use the Post Office Protocol (POP) and Internet Message Access Protocol (IMAP) to retrieve their mail from a dedicated mail server.

Key Concepts

The following concepts are required knowledge for configuring and managing e-mail services.

Understanding E-Mail Protocols

Transferring e-mail between servers on the Internet is largely conducted using the Simple Mail Transfer Protocol (SMTP). The advantage of using SMTP is that mail transfer can be initiated by a local third-party MUA, such as elm or pine, or it can be performed manually by a user using telnet.

If your users are not logged in through a shell on the local mail server, you need to provide a means by which they can send and retrieve mail through the server by using a remote mail client. Two protocols support this: POP, which is the oldest client/server mail-transfer protocol and supports only offline mail reading, and IMAP, which supports both offline and online mail reading. The choice between the two often comes down to which MUAs your users are comfortable with, and which protocol their favorite client supports. However, other considerations, such as authentication, authorization, and security, may sway an administrator to stipulate that IMAP be used over POP, even for offline mail reading. Note that POP is generally easier to install and configure than IMAP.

Simple Mail Transfer Protocol

SMTP allows servers to exchange mail with each other, on a message-by-message basis. Standardized since the publication of RFC 821, SMTP has become the dominant Internet mail-transfer protocol, at the expense of earlier transfer methods, such as the ancient UNIX-to-UNIX Copy (UUCP) program and the X.400 protocol, the latter of which is still popular with intranet-and LAN-based e-mail. SMTP allows sendmail and other MTAs, such as qmail, to accept connections on port 25 and "speak" to each other in a language that is interpretable by humans. In fact, as you will see later, it is actually possible for an administrator to manually test sendmail by telnetting to port 25 and issuing SMTP commands directly. This is very useful for troubleshooting and testing existing configurations. Unfortunately, SMTP has been used frequently by malicious users to forge e-mail headers to make their e-mail messages appear to come from other users.

SMTP supports a sender/receiver model of host-to-host e-mail transactions. For example, a host, such as the server *mail.companyA.com*, may wish to transfer a message to *mail.companyB.com*. This transaction takes place as follows (see Figure 27-1):

1. *mail.companyA.com* makes a connection to port 25.

2. *mail.companyB.com* acknowledges.

3. *mail.companyA.com* identifies the sender of the message.

4. *mail.companyB.com* acknowledges.

5. *mail.companyA.com* states the recipient of the message.

6. *mail.companyB.com* acknowledges. If the local user exists or is listed in the */etc/aliases* database, the acknowledgement is in the affirmative. However, if no local user can be matched to the intended recipient, the acknowledgement is in the negative.

7. If a user is found, the message is transmitted from *mail.companyA.com* to *mail.companyB.com*.

8. *mail.companyB.com* acknowledges receipt (with a receipt number).

9. *mail.companyA.com* requests a disconnection.

10. *mail.companyB.com* complies.

11. Mail is held on the MTA until the RECV command to retrieve the message is sent by the MUA.

This kind of transaction is conducted millions of times every day on mail servers around the world, and is very fast. In the example, each of the acknowledgements from *mail.companyB.com* is associated with a three-digit numeric code: for example, a successful command from *mail.companyA.com* is always acknowledged with a code of 250 from *mail.companyB.com*. Alternatively, if a user is not local, the code 551 is returned.

There are a number of standard SMTP commands, which are summarized here:

- **HELO**   Identifies the mail-sending host to the mail-receiving host
- **MAIL**   Identifies the remote user who is sending the mail to the mail-receiving host
- **RCPT**   Indicates the local user to whom the mail is to be delivered
- **DATA**   Precedes the body of the mail message
- **VRFY**   Checks that a particular local user is known to the mail system
- **EXPN**   Expands local mailing lists
- **QUIT**   Terminates a session

FIGURE 27-1
Mail exchange
transaction between
mail.companyA.com
and
mail.companyB.com

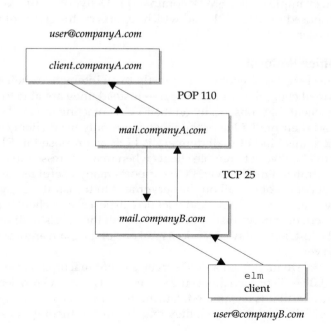

In addition to the standard SMTP commands presented here, RFC 1869 proposed extensions to SMTP called ESMTP. ESMTP allows developers to extend the services currently provided by SMTP. MTAs that support ESMTP commands will attempt to greet each other with the EHLO command. If ESMTP is supported, a list of implemented commands on the remote server is returned. For example,

```
server% telnet server.companyB.com 25
Trying 192.68.232.45...
Connected to server.companyB.com.
Escape character is '^]'.
220 server.companyB.com ESMTP Sendmail 8.9.1a/8.9.1; Fri, 18 Feb 2000 13:05:14
+1100 (EST)
EHLO server.companyA.com
250-server.companyB.com Hello pwatters@server.companyA.com [192.68.231.64],
pleased to meet you
250-EXPN
250-VERB
250-8BITMIME
250-SIZE
250-DSN
250-ONEX
250-ETRN
250-XUSR
250 HELP
```

One example of an ESMTP command is Delivery Status Notification (DSN), which was proposed in RFC 1891, and which reports on the status of remote mail deliveries to local users.

Post Office Protocol

Many users today do not log in directly to an interactive shell on a mail server and run a local mail client like `mailx` or `elm`—instead, they are able to use a GUI-based mail-reading client that runs locally on their PC, contacting the mail server directly to retrieve and send their mail. One of the most commonly used client/server protocols that facilitates this kind of mail delivery is POP, as proposed in RFC 1725. POP supports offline mail delivery to remote clients when mail addressed to a user account is delivered via a centralized mail server. POP supports many useful features, including the ability to retain copies of e-mail on the server and to transmit a copy to the client. This can be very useful for auditing and backup purposes, as a client machine may have to be reinstalled, or it may crash, in which case, all the user's mail (including unread mail) might be lost. Reliability of service is still one of the main arguments for using a centralized mail server.

To retrieve mail from a POP server, a client machine makes a TCP connection to port 110. The client then greets the server, receives an acknowledgement, and the session continues until it is terminated. During this time, a user may be authenticated. If a user is successfully authenticated, they may begin conducting transactions in the form of retrieving messages, until the QUIT command is received by the server, in which case the session is terminated. Errors are indicated by status codes like –ERR for negative responses and +OK for positive responses. POP is deliberately SMTP-like in its command set and operation, making it easier for administrators to apply their skills to configuring both kinds of systems.

One of the drawbacks of POP is its lack of security: although users are authenticated using their username and password on the mail server, this exchange is not encrypted, and so anyone "snooping" the network might be able to retrieve this username and password. This would allow a rogue user to log into the mail server as the mail user— perhaps without the mail user realizing this for a long time, because they themselves never log in directly to the mail server. Since telnet and ftp use exactly the same method of authentication, it's certainly no worse than many standard network applications.

To obtain a free POP server for Solaris, download the freeware Qpopper server from QUALCOMM at **http://www.eudora.com/qpopper/index.html**. Alternatively, Netra systems are supplied with the SUNWipop package, which provides a POP service for that platform. QUALCOMM also has a free POP MUA called Eudora, which is very popular in educational institutions and is available for both Macintosh and Windows platforms. Figure 27-2 shows the main user screen for Eudora: users can retrieve their mail from a remote server and display it ordered by date, sender, and subject. In addition, files from the local Macintosh or Windows file system can be sent as attachments by using the MIME extensions. Software like Eudora makes it easy for Macintosh and Windows users to have the convenience of local file access and GUI-based interfaces while retaining the security and reliability of the Solaris server platform. However, note that browsers such as Netscape and other command-line MUAs (such as elm or pine) may be more appropriate than Eudora for some environments.

Internet Message Access Protocol

IMAP, proposed in RFC 2060, is intended to replace POP. While IMAP can perform offline processing, it is primarily intended for remote clients to retain some of the features of online processing enjoyed by MUAs like mailx and elm. A remote MUA using IMAP has the ability to perform more sophisticated transactions than those performed by a POP-based client: while POP caters to requests like retrieving all new messages on the server and passing them to the client, IMAP supports requests of just headers, just message bodies, or both. In addition, a search can be made for messages that match a particular criterion: for example, a request could be made to find all messages received by a particular user, or all messages received on a particular day. Although a POP-based MUA can perform these operations on its local copy of mail messages, IMAP can perform these operations remotely on the server. In addition, server-side messages can be marked with different flags to indicate, for example, whether they have been replied to. Again, this is the kind of functionality often supplied by server-side MUAs like mailx or elm, but IMAP allows these operations to be performed by remote, easy-to-use GUIs. IMAP users can also store their files locally, as with a POP-based service—but, significantly, IMAP has a synchronization feature whereby the local mailbox contents can be regularly matched with the mailbox on the server, to ensure that no data corruption occurs due to errors on the client machine.

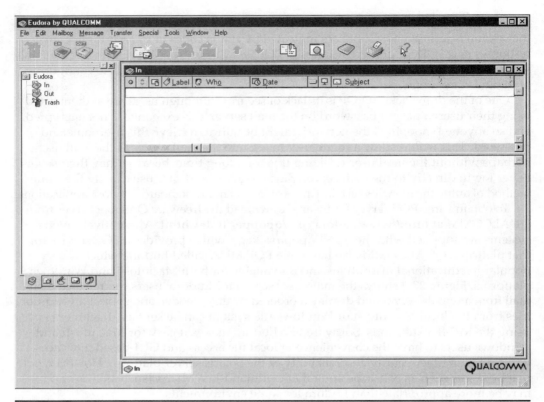

FIGURE 27-2   The POP-based Eudora client for Microsoft Windows, which receives mail from a centralized and secure Solaris mail server

In summary, POP and IMAP offer significantly different functions, and the use of either protocol depends on the MUAs that are supported and the needs of the users. Many mail clients only support POP, and your organization may stay with the POP platform for this reason alone, even though IMAP offers many more features.

Mail Headers

When a mail message is delivered into a user's mailbox, it contains a history of its delivery process in the headers that precede the message body. These headers include

- **From**   Records the mail-sending user and the date and time at which the mail was received.

- **Received**   Provides details of how the mail was received by the MTA on the mail server, including the remote computer's name, MTA name, and identification.

- **Date**   Indicates the time and date at which the message was received.

- **Message-Id** A unique number generated by the sending host that identifies the message.

- **To** Indicates the user to whom the message was addressed—usually a user on the local machine.

- **Content-Type** Indicates the MIME type in which the message was encoded. This is usually text, but could contain multimedia types as well.

- **Content-Length** The number of lines making up the body of the message.

- **Subject** Subject of the mail message as entered by the sender.

sendmail

Now that you have reviewed how mail is transferred between the client and the server, the focus now shifts to server-to-server mail communications. Mail exchange between servers is performed by using MTAs, such as `sendmail`, which implement the SMTP protocol. `sendmail` is the most popular MTA for Solaris and many other UNIX systems, even though newer systems, such as `qmail`, make it easier to configure an MTA. This section cannot cover all material relating to `sendmail`, because it is one of the most complex Solaris programs to master. However, this section provides sufficient detail so that most administrators working in a standard environment will be able to configure and test their mail-transfer environment.

`sendmail` is the default MTA supported by Solaris, although it is certainly possible to install an alternative third-party MTA like `qmail` (see **http://www.qmail.org/** for details). Solaris 10 supports `sendmail` version 8.

In most Solaris installations, the `sendmail` MTA relies on a single configuration file (*sendmail.cf*) that contains sets of rules to determine how e-mail is to be sent from the local host to any arbitrary remote host, and which mailer is to be used (e.g., for local versus remote delivery). The rules are used to choose the mechanism by which each message is delivered, while mail addresses are often rewritten to ensure correct delivery. For example, a mail message sent from a server command line may not include the Fully Qualified Domain Name in the Reply To field, in which case a remote user would not be able to reply to a message sent to them. The `sendmail` MTA ensures that the "virtual envelopes" that contain e-mail messages are addressed correctly, by inserting headers where appropriate to identify senders and recipients.

Although `sendmail` is highly customizable, it is also difficult to configure and test, because a single error in the rules can produce unexpected results. `sendmail` reads and processes every rule in *sendmail.cf*, so in order to speed up the process, the rules are written in a "computer friendly" format. Unfortunately, like assembly language, computer-friendly rules are rarely human-friendly! The next section reviews the configuration of `sendmail` and highlights some of the security issues that continue to surround its deployment. Fortunately, the public version of `sendmail` allows you to use simple configuration rules to create a *sendmail.cf* file, which is easier than working directly on the *sendmail.cf* file.

m4 Configuration

The m4 macro language can be used to create a *sendmail.cf* file, by using a set of predefined macros that has been developed for use with `sendmail`. In order to create a *sendmail.cf* file using m4 macros, a text file containing a list of macros to run, and the appropriate parameter values for your site, needs to be created (typically called *sendmail.mc*). Once you have installed this file into the *cf/cf* subdirectory underneath the main `sendmail` directory, then you can use the following command from that directory to build a new *sendmail.cf* file:

```
# cp /etc/sendmail.cf /etc/sendmail.orig
# m4 ../m4/cf.m4 sendmail.mc > /etc/sendmail.cf
```

The first command backs up the current production *sendmail.cf* file, while the next command builds a new production *sendmail.cf* file. After you start `sendmail`, by using the command defined in the previous section, `sendmail` will be running with the new configuration.

Before you examine a sample *sendmail.mc* file, take a closer look at the macros and parameters that can be used to configure `sendmail`.

Macros

The following macros are defined for use with *sendmail.mc*:

- **DOMAIN**   Used to define common elements for mail servers with the same domain name
- **EXPOSED_USER**   Prevents domain masquerading for specific users
- **FEATURE**   Enables a specific `sendmail` feature
- **MAILER**   Specifies the mail-delivery program to use on the server (`local`, `smtp`, or `procmail`)
- **MASQUERADE_AS**   Inserts an effective domain on all outgoing e-mail rather than the real domain
- **OSTYPE**   Defines the host operating system type

Features

Once the basic domain and operating system parameters have been generated, the next step is to enable specific `sendmail` features by using the FEATURE macro. One instance of FEATURE is required for every feature that is to be enabled. Commonly used features include

- **accept_unqualified_senders**   Accepts messages for delivery from users with e-mail addresses that do not have an FQDN.
- **accept_unresolvable_domains**   Accepts messages for delivery from users with e-mail addresses whose FQDN is not resolvable.
- **access_db**   Enables a database of senders and domains to be maintained from whom mail is automatically bounced or rejected.

- **always_add_domain**   Inserts FQDN onto all e-mails sent through `sendmail`, even those that are being delivered to local users.

- **blacklist_recipients**   Defines a list of recipients who are not allowed to receive e-mail.

- **domaintable**   Substitutes a new domain name for a previous domain name.

- **mailertable**   Allows a different mail server to be associated with each virtual domain supported.

- **nullclient**   Allows local `sendmail` instances to forward all messages to a single outbound `sendmail` server for delivery.

- **promiscuous_relay**   Allows relay of mail from any site through the local server. This should never be used, because of the risk that spam merchants will find your server and use it to relay spam to obscure its true origin.

- **redirect**   Redirects messages destined for users who no longer exist on the system. Requires a corresponding entry in /etc/aliases with the name of the former user and his/her new e-mail address.

- **relay_based_on_mx**   Uses the MX record defined in DNS to determine if the local `sendmail` server is the correct server to relay messages from other servers.

- **relay_entire_domain**   Permits all hosts within the local domain to route e-mail through the local `sendmail` server.

- **smrsh**   A functionally limited shell that can be used to restrict system access by the `sendmail` daemon.

- **use_ct_file**   Prevents users from changing the username part of their e-mail addresses on outbound e-mails.

- **use_cw_file**   Contains a list of all DNS aliases for the mail server.

- **virtusertable**   Supports routing of e-mail for user accounts with the same username that actually belongs to different virtual domains. Thus, *joe@domainone.com* is not confused with *joe@domaintwo.com*, even though both domains use the same `sendmail` instance.

Parameters

Specific parameters can be set for `sendmail`'s operation with the m4 `define` command. Although most of the values set by default within `sendmail` will be satisfactory for normal use, you may occasionally need to change a value. `sendmail` defines a very large number of parameters, but only some of the most commonly modified parameters are examined here:

- *confDOMAIN_NAME*   If your DNS server is unreliable, then you might want to set the default domain name here.

- *confLOG_LEVEL*   Specifies the logging level for `sendmail` from 0 (minimal) to 13 (everything).

- *confMAILER_NAME* The alias used for returning messages and other automatically generated mail sent by the system. This is generally set to MAILER-DAEMON, which is typically aliased to root. So, it's possible to just set the value to root.
- *confMAX_MESSAGE_SIZE* The maximum size, in bytes, of any message that is accepted for delivery. Although large attachments are common these days, an upper limit of a few megabytes should be set, to prevent a denial of service attack.
- *confSMTP_LOGIN_MSG* Replaces the standard `sendmail` version banner with a local (usually nondescript) message. Can be useful in preventing would-be crackers from attempting an exploit that is specific to your version of `sendmail`.

Sample sendmail.mc File

The following is a sample *sendmail.mc* file that contains some of the parameters, features, and macros discussed in the previous sections:

```
OSTYPE('solaris2')
define('confDOMAIN_NAME', 'cassowary.net')
define('confLOG_LEVEL', '13')
define('confMAILER_NAME', 'root')
define('confMAX_MESSAGE_SIZE', '1048576')
define('confSMTP_LOGIN_MSG', 'No Name Mail Server')
FEATURE('smrsh','/usr/sbin/smrsh')
FEATURE(redirect)
FEATURE(always_add_domain)
FEATURE(blacklist_recipients)
FEATURE('access_db')
```

There are more extensive examples for many different configuration files supplied with the `sendmail` source. In particular, Eric Allman's excellent *readme* file should be read by anyone who is seriously contemplating extensive `sendmail` configuration.

Procedures

The following procedures are commonly used for configuring and managing e-mail services.

Configuring sendmail (sendmail.cf)

The *sendmail.cf* file consists of single-line commands, which can range from rules and macros to options and headers. Some of these commands must appear only once if they specify a directive that affects the interpretation of rules (there can, however, be many rules in a *sendmail.cf* file). The main kinds of commands in a *sendmail.cf* file are

- **C** Specifies a class that can contain more than one item. For instance, `C{MAILCLIENTS} mars venus pluto` specifies an array that contains a list of mail clients (*mars, venus,* and *pluto*).

- **D** Specifies a macro. For example, `DR mail.companyA.com` specifies a macro named R whose contents is *mail.companyA.com*.

- **E** Specifies an environment variable. As a security measure, `sendmail` does not use environment information passed to it, preferring to use values specified in the *sendmail.cf* file. To set the location of a Java Virtual Machine (JVM), which may be used to support some mail-related applications, use the variable specification `EJVM=/usr/local/java/bin/java`.

- **H** Specifies a header, such as the Received: header. These definitions now can be very complex because of the inclusion of multipart MIME messages.

- **M** Specifies the mail-delivery agent. For instance, `Mlocal, P=/bin/mail` specifies that */bin/mail* is the mail-delivery agent, which is usually the case under Solaris.

- **O** Specifies an option. For example, setting `O SendMimeErrors=True` enables the sending of MIME-encapsulated error messages.

- **P** Sets message precedence. For example, first-class mail is set with a precedence of zero (`Pfirst-class=0`), while junk mail is set with a precedence of −100 (`Pjunk=-100`).

- **R** Specifies a rule. For example, the rule `R$- $@ $1 @ ${Mydomain} Rewrite address` appends the FQDN defined by the macro ${Mydomain} to a username.

- **S** Indicates the start of a rule set, which can be specified either as a number (e.g., S2 for ruleset 2) or with a label (e.g., SDomainRules for the DomainRules rule set).

Six kinds of system-defined rule sets are contained in the *sendmail.cf* file:

- **S0** Handles basic address parsing. For example, if a user address is not specified, the error message User Address Required is returned.

- **S1** Processes the e-mail sender's address.

- **S2** Processes the e-mail recipient's address.

- **S3** Performs name canonicalization and initiates the rewriting rules. For example, invalid addresses are checked (e.g., those with colons), and any angle brackets (<>) are stripped from the address.

- **S4** Performs the final output post-rewriting, including conversion of expanded addresses like *pwatters%mail@companyA.com* to *pwatters@mail.companyA.com*.

- **S5** The final rewriting rule set that occurs after all aliases, defined in */etc/aliases*, have been expanded.

User-defined rule sets can occupy S6 and above. For example, ruleset 33 is defined in Solaris to support Sun's RemoteMode. A typical `sendmail` rule takes the form

```
Rlhs rhs     description
```

where R indicates that the line is a rule, *lhs* is the left-hand side of the rule, *rhs* is the right-hand side of the rule, and description is a comment that is useful for humans to interpret what action the rule performs. The left-hand side is a specification for matching a particular mail header, while the right-hand side specifies the action to be taken if a match is found for the rule.

Just as `lex`, `yacc`, and JavaCC can be used to specify actions based on matched tokens, so does the `sendmail` parser. When the *sendmail.cf* file is parsed by `sendmail`, it recognizes several specifiers on the left-hand side:

- **$–** Matches a single token.
- **$*** Matches any number of tokens, including zero tokens.
- **$+** Matches any number of tokens greater than zero.
- **$=*character*** Matches any token equal to *character*.

If any rule stated using these specifiers finds a match, then one or more actions may be performed by one or more right-hand side specifiers:

- **$@** Rewrite-and-return.
- **$>*integer*** Rewrite using the rule set specified by *integer*.
- **$#** Deliver through the specified mailer.
- **$*character*** and **$*integer*** Actions can be performed on variables defined on the left-hand side.

As an example, consider a rule that adds an FQDN onto a mail *servermail*, where a message is destined for external delivery. In this case, $h (*host*) is set to *mail* and $d (*domain*) is set to *companyA.com*. Thus, a rule to match a username with no FQDN specified would be

```
R$+    $@$1<@$h.$d>    Add a FQDN to username
```

Thus, any valid Solaris username like *pwatters* will have *mail*, a dot ("."), and *companyA.com* appended to it for external delivery, giving:

```
paul<@mail.companyA.com>
```

A more complex rule for a more complex organization that has multiple internal networks might have a second level in the FQDN above the company name (for example, the mail server for the sales department of companyA.com would have the FQDN *mail.sales.companyA.com*). In this case, you define $o (organization level), set $o to *sales*, and change the rule to

```
R$+      $@$1<@$h.$o.$d>      Add a FQDN to username, including organization level
```

Hence, any valid Solaris username like *neil* will have *mail*, a dot (.), *sales*, another dot, and *companyA.com* appended to it for external delivery:

```
neil<@mail.sales.companyA.com>
```

Thus, the combination of rules, macros, and options can successfully create and resolve most e-mail addresses. If all of the rule writing and option setting seems daunting to a first-time `sendmail` administrator, it is possible to use GUI-based configuration tools to ease the burden. One of the easiest ways to run and configure `sendmail` is to use `webmin`, which is freely available at **http://www.webmin.com/webmin/**. `webmin` is a web-based interface for system administration for Solaris, including `sendmail`. Using any browser that supports tables and forms, you can use the `sendmail` configuration module, which allows administrators to manage `sendmail` aliases, masquerading, address rewriting, and other features. `webmin` can also use SSL to secure connections between your Web browser and the `webmin` server, which is especially useful for remote administration. Figure 27-3 shows the `webmin` interface and the options it supports for configuring `sendmail`.

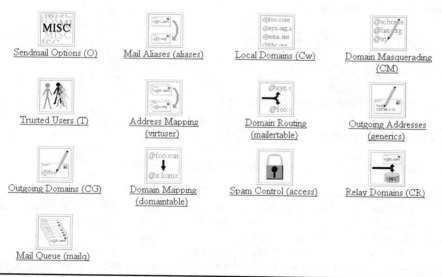

FIGURE 27-3 webmin GUI for configuring sendmail

Running sendmail

`sendmail` is started as a daemon process from scripts that are usually activated during multiuser startup (*/etc/rc2*). To stop `sendmail` manually, use the following command:

```
/etc/init.d/sendmail stop
```

To start `sendmail`, use this command:

```
/etc/init.d/sendmail start
```

Troubleshooting

Since `sendmail` can be a difficult program to configure, `sendmail` also includes some provision for troubleshooting. For example, the command

```
server# sendmail -bt
```

causes `sendmail` to execute in address-testing mode, which is very useful for testing rule sets interactively before including them in a production system. Keep in mind that ruleset 3 is no longer invoked automatically in address-testing mode: thus, to test the address

```
Paul.Watters.1996@pem.cam.ac.uk
```

you should use the test string

```
"3,0 Paul.Watters.1996@pem.cam.ac.uk"
```

instead of just using

```
"0 Paul.Watters.1996@pem.cam.ac.uk"!
```

As a complete example:

```
ADDRESS TEST MODE (ruleset 3 NOT automatically invoked)
Enter <ruleset> <address>
> 0 Paul.Watters.1996@pem.cam.ac.uk
rewrite: ruleset   0   input: Paul . Watters . 1996 @ pem . cam . ac . uk
rewrite: ruleset 199   input: Paul . Watters . 1996 @ pem . cam . ac . uk
rewrite: ruleset 199 returns: Paul . Watters . 1996 @ pem . cam . ac . uk
rewrite: ruleset  98   input: Paul . Watters . 1996 @ pem . cam . ac . uk
rewrite: ruleset  98 returns: Paul . Watters . 1996 @ pem . cam . ac . uk
rewrite: ruleset 198   input: Paul . Watters . 1996 @ pem . cam . ac . uk
rewrite: ruleset 198 returns: $# local $: Paul . Watters . 1996 @ pem . cam .
ac . uk
```

```
rewrite: ruleset    0 returns: $# local $: Paul . Watters . 1996 @ pem . cam .
ac . uk
> 0,3 Paul.Watters.1996@pem.cam.ac.uk
rewrite: ruleset    0   input: Paul . Watters . 1996 @ pem . cam . ac . uk
rewrite: ruleset 199   input: Paul . Watters . 1996 @ pem . cam . ac . uk
rewrite: ruleset 199 returns: Paul . Watters . 1996 @ pem . cam . ac . uk
rewrite: ruleset  98   input: Paul . Watters . 1996 @ pem . cam . ac . uk
rewrite: ruleset  98 returns: Paul . Watters . 1996 @ pem . cam . ac . uk
rewrite: ruleset 198   input: Paul . Watters . 1996 @ pem . cam . ac . uk
rewrite: ruleset 198 returns: $# local $: Paul . Watters . 1996 @ pem . cam .
ac . uk
rewrite: ruleset    0 returns: $# local $: Paul . Watters . 1996 @ pem . cam .
ac . uk
rewrite: ruleset    3   input: $# local $: Paul . Watters . 1996 @ pem . cam .
ac . uk
rewrite: ruleset    3 returns: $# local $: Paul . Watters . 1996 @ pem . cam .
ac . uk
```

In addition to `sendmail`-based troubleshooting, the `mailx` MUA has a *–v* (verbose) switch, which tracks the process of mail delivery directly after mail has been sent. For example, if a message is sent from *user@companyA.com* to *user@companyB.com*, from the machine *client.companyA.com*, the process of delivery is displayed to the sender:

```
client% mailx -v user@companyB.com
Subject: Hello
Hi user@companyB.com. This is a test.
^D
EOT
client% user@companyB.com... Connecting to mailhost (mail)...
220 mail.serverB.com ESMTP Sendmail 8.12.10; Sat, 19 Feb 2004 12:13:22 +1100 (EST)
>>> HELO mail.companyA.com
250 mail.serverB.com Hello mail.companyA.com (moppet.companyA.com), pleased
to meet you
>>> MAIL From:<user@companyA.com>
250 <user@companyA.com>... Sender ok
>>> RCPT To:<user@companyB.com>
250 <user@companyA.com>... Recipient ok
>>> DATA
354 Enter mail, end with "." on a line by itself
>>> Hi user@companyB.com. This is a test.
>>>.
250 Ok
>>> QUIT
221 mail.companyB.com closing connection
user@companyB.com... Sent (Ok)
```

In the preceding example, the local mail server (*mail.companyA.com*) contacts the remote mail server (*mail.companyB.com*) and delivers the mail correctly to the user. Used in this way, `mailx` can provide immediately useful hints for users and administrators to identify delivery problems with particular user addresses or remote network problems.

Since e-mail is a key Internet service, and since `sendmail` is the most widely deployed MTA, `sendmail` is often associated with security warnings and issues. This has led some developers to develop alternative MTA systems like `qmail`, while many organizations worldwide devote the appropriate resources to tracking down and solving bugs in `sendmail`. If you are a `sendmail` administrator, it pays to watch the headlines at sites like the Sendmail Consortium (**http://www.sendmail.org/**).

For example, `sendmail` has been shown to suffer from the "buffer overflow" problem that allows remote users to execute arbitrary commands on a server running `sendmail`. This is a common problem for UNIX applications written in the C language, but only if proper bounds checking on array sizes is not correctly implemented. In the case of `sendmail`, very long MIME headers could be used to launch an attack—a patch is available that allows `sendmail` to detect and deny messages that might be associated with such an attack.

Examples

The following examples provide some real-world cases for configuring and managing e-mail services.

An Example SMTP Transaction

This section walks you through an actual SMTP session so that you can see how straightforward the procedure is. For example, it is possible to initiate message transfer from a client machine to a user on *mail.companyB.com*, by using the following commands:

```
client% telnet mail.serverB.com 25
Trying 192.68.232.41...
Connected to mail.serverB.com.
Escape character is '^]'.
220 mail.serverB.com ESMTP Sendmail 8.9.1a/8.9.1; Fri, 18 Feb 2000 10:25:59 +1100
(EST)
```

If you now type **help**, you will receive a list of SMTP commands that can be used to transfer mail interactively:

```
214-This is Sendmail version 8.9.1a
214-Topics:
214-    HELO    EHLO    MAIL    RCPT    DATA
214-    RSET    NOOP    QUIT    HELP    VRFY
214-    EXPN    VERB    ETRN    DSN
214-For more info use "HELP <topic>".
214-To report bugs in the implementation send email to
214-    sendmail-bugs@sendmail.org.
214-For local information send email to Postmaster at your site.
214 End of HELP info
```

Note that HELP is turned off by default, so you may not always see this response.

To actually send a message, you can use a combination of the HELO, MAIL, RCPT, and QUIT commands. HELO introduces the hostname that you are connecting from:

```
HELO client.companyB.com
250 server.companyB.com Hello client.companyB.com [192.68.232.45], pleased to
meet you
```

Next, you need to specify a sender by using the MAIL command:

```
MAIL FROM: <pwatters@companyB.com>
250 <pwatters@companyB.com>... Sender ok
```

You should then specify a recipient for the mail by using the RCPT command:

```
RCPT TO: <postmaster@server.companyB.com>
250 <postmaster@server.companyB.com>... Recipient ok
```

After you transmit the sender and recipient information, it's time to actually send the body of the message by using the DATA command:

```
DATA
354 Enter mail, end with "." on a line by itself
Hello,
My mail client is not working so I had to send this message manually - can you
help?
Thanks.
.
250 KAA11543 Message accepted for delivery
```

After the message has been accepted for delivery, you can then terminate the session by using the QUIT command:

```
QUIT
221 server.company.com closing connection
Connection closed by foreign host.
```

The message has now been successfully transmitted.

Mail Headers

Mail headers are useful in understanding how mail is transferred. For example, if a message is sent from a mail client on the local server to another user on the local server, the headers are easy to interpret:

```
From pwatters@companyA.com Fri Feb 18 13:31 EST 2000
Received: (from pwatters@localhost)
        by mail.companyA.com (8.9.1a/8.9.1) id NAA17837
        for pwatters; Fri, 18 Feb 2000 13:31:34 +1100 (EST)
Date: Fri, 18 Feb 2000 13:31:34 +1100 (EST)
```

```
From: WATTERS Paul Andrew <pwatters@companyA.com>
Message-Id: <200002180231.NAA17837@mail.companyA.com>
To: pwatters@companyA.com
Subject: Testing Local Delivery
Content-Type: text
Content-Length: 5
This is a test of local delivery.
```

These headers can be interpreted thus: the local user *pwatters@localhost* sent the remote user *pwatters@companyA.com* a five-line message, encoded as text, on the subject of Testing Local Delivery. The message was serviced by the `sendmail` MTA version 8.12.10, and had an ID of 200002180231.NAA17837@mail.CompanyA.com. If mail is forwarded from another host, then the headers become more complicated, but follow the same general principles.

Using Multipurpose Internet Mail Extensions

As you saw in the previous example concerning mail headers, there was a header that specified the content type (Content-Type), which was text in the example but could have conceivably been any kind of digital medium, thanks to MIME, as proposed in RFC 2045. MIME is very useful for sending multimedia files through e-mail; it eliminates the worry about the specifics of encoding. Since many multimedia files are binary, and e-mail message bodies are transmitted as text, MIME encodes the files as text and sends them as normal messages. In addition, MIME supports the notion of multipart messages— that is, a single e-mail message may contain more than one encoded file. This is very useful for sending a number of documents to another user: it is not necessary to overburden `sendmail` by sending a new message for each document (recall that `sendmail` processes e-mail messages one at a time). MIME also provides support for languages that are encoded in ASCII but that need to be displayed in another script (e.g., Japanese kanji).

MIME defines how a Content-Type header can be used to specify a particular character set or other nontextual data type for an e-mail message. For example, the e-mail header

```
Content-Type: text/plain; charset=us-ascii
```

indicates that the message consists of plain text in the US-ASCII character set. MIME also specifies how to encode data when necessary. MIME also stipulates that the receiving user is responsible for interpreting the encoded information so that it correctly displays the encoded message in a form that is understood by the user. Here is an example MIME-encoded message:

```
This is a multi-part message in MIME format.
------=_NextPart_000_01A6_01BF7314.FF804600
Content-Type: text/plain;
        charset="iso-8859-1"
Content-Transfer-Encoding: 7bit
```

```
Joe,
Just confirmed the latest sales figures.
See the attached report.
Jane
------=_NextPart_000_01A6_01BF7314.FF804600
Content-Type: application/msword;
        name="report.doc"
Content-Disposition: attachment;
        filename="report.doc"
Content-Transfer-Encoding: base64
0M8R4KGxGuEAAAAAAAAAAAAAAAAAAAAAPgADAP7/CQAGAAAAAAAAAAAAACAAAAmQAAAAAAAAAA
EAAAmwAAAEAAAD+////AAAAJcAAACYAAA////////////////////////////////////////////
////////////////////////////////////////////////////////////////////////////
////////////////////////////////////////////////////////////////////////////
////////////////////////////////////////////////////////////////////////////
////////////////////////////////////////////////////////////////////////////
////////////////////////////////////////////////////////////////////////////
////////////////////////////////////////////////////////////////////////////.
```

After the headers are printed, indicating the number and type of attachments, the actual encoded data is printed (which is what all the forward slashes represent, in case you were wondering!). When you run `metamail` on this file, since it contains MIME-encoded data, the user is prompted to save any detected attachments:

```
This message contains data in an unrecognized format, application/msword,
which can either be viewed as text or written to a file.
What do you want to do with the application/msword data?
1 -- See it as text
2 -- Write it to a file
3 -- Just skip it
```

At this point, the user enters 2, and they are then prompted to save the file:

```
Please enter the name of a file to which the data should be written
(Default: report.doc) >
```

The data is then saved to the file specified. MIME is thus very useful for encoding data from several binary files into a portable format that can be transmitted as an e-mail message.

Using Mail Clients

Mail clients can be local or remote. Local clients have online access to many Solaris commands, including `.forward` and `vacation`, while remote clients are GUI-based and are often easier to use. Remote clients can use either the IMAP or POP protocol to communicate with the server-based MTA, as reviewed earlier in the chapter. This section introduces a popular local client, `elm`, and an equally popular remote client, Netscape mail, and examines how each client is configured.

Local Clients (elm)

Although Solaris is supplied with the `mailx` program, a local user agent developed by the University of California at Berkeley, many sites choose to install the `elm` MUA, which was originally developed by Hewlett-Packard. `elm` is now freeware and supports many advanced features such as MIME and DSN. `elm` is highly configurable and can operate in beginner's, intermediate, and advanced user modes. `elm` can be started with the following command:

```
client% elm
```

The user interface for `elm` is shown in Figure 27-4. Using `elm`, users can issue most commands by typing a single letter from the main menu:

- | Pipes the displayed message through a user-defined command
- !   Executes a shell process
- ?   Obtains help for `elm` commands
- *<n>*   Sets the current message number to *n*
- */pattern*   Searches for pattern *pattern* in message
- **a**   Creates alias for sender of the current message in the address book
- **b**   Bounces the current message to a user to make it appear as if it hasn't been delivered
- **c**   Changes to a folder other than the inbox
- **d**   Deletes the current message from the inbox
- **f**   Forwards the current message to another user
- **m**   Creates a new mail message
- **o**   Sets options for skill level and general `elm` options (saved in *elmrc*)
- **p**   Prints current message
- **q**   Exits `elm` and saves changes to inbox
- **s**   Saves current message to a specific folder
- **u**   Undeletes a message marked for deletion
- **x**   Exits without saving changes to inbox

By default, `elm` uses the `vi` editor to edit messages, but if this is too daunting for you, you can set the editor to `emacs` or `pico` by editing the defaults in the *elmrc* configuration file. By convention, it is normal to include a signature at the bottom of every message, containing contact details. This is usually kept in *~/.signature*. A typical signature file might contain the following:

```
--
Paul A. Watters
```

Principal Consultant, Cassowary Computing Pty Ltd
Sydney NSW Australia
Paul.Watters.1996@pem.cam.ac.uk

This allows readers of your messages to quickly identify you and your role in the organization that you may represent. Since you may already be known to local users, `elm` actually has the ability to automatically attach a different signature to messages addressed to either local or remote users. This is but one of the many features that has ensured `elm`'s continued success in the age of GUI-based remote clients.

Remote Clients (Netscape Mail)

GUI-based mail clients, operating on a remote PC, have become commonplace in offices in which mail is centralized on a Solaris server but a desktop system is used to read mail. Popular choices for reading e-mail remotely include the Netscape mail client and the Eudora mail client, both of which are freely available from **http://www.netscape.com/** and **http://www.eudora.com/**, respectively. Both Eudora and Netscape use POP to retrieve their mail from a remote POP server. This section reviews the configuration of the POP-based Netscape mail client, as this is more complicated than a local client like `elm` that reads mail directly from the spooler.

The first step after installing the Netscape Mail software is to set the user preferences. In the Preferences dialog box, shown in Figure 27-5, the user needs to set up in the Mail & Newsgroups section basic information about their contact details: full name, e-mail address, Reply-To address (if it is different from their e-mail address), organization, and the location of their signature file on the local file system. This enables e-mails that are sent from the client to be identified easily.

```
      Mailbox is '/usr/spool/mail/pacific' with 2 messages [ELM 2.4 PL11]

  N  1    Jan 10  neil@studiob.com     (22)
     2    Jan 9   Oracle Corporation (30)    Oracle Registration Information

















        |=pipe, !=shell, ?=help, <n>=set current to n, /=search pattern
 a)lias, C)opy, c)hange folder, d)elete, e)dit, f)orward, g)roup reply, m)ail,
   n)ext, o)ptions, p)rint, q)uit, r)eply, s)ave, t)ag, u)ndelete, or e(x)it

Command: ▌
```

FIGURE 27-4   The elm mail user agent

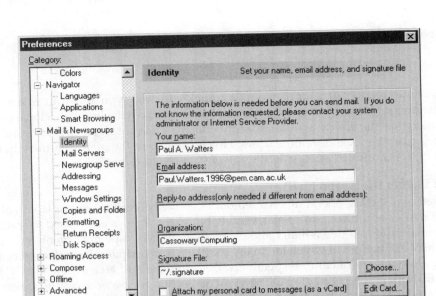

FIGURE 27-5 Configuring user preferences in Netscape Mail

The next step is to configure the POP settings. The POP server name is recorded on the General Preferences tab, shown in Figure 27-6, along with the server type (in this case, POP-3). The remote username is also recorded, along with an instruction to remember

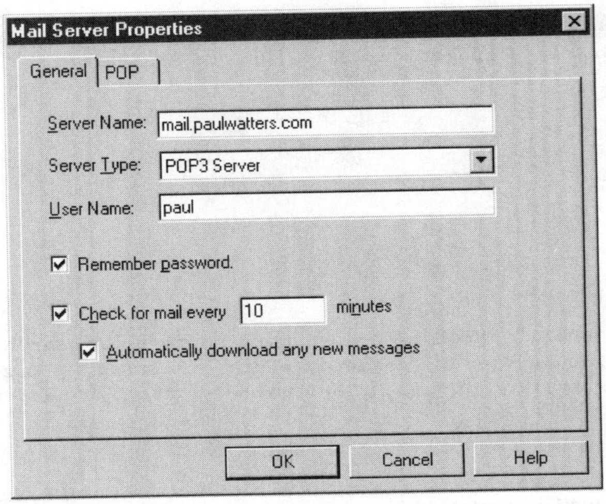

FIGURE 27-6 Configuring POP settings in the Netscape mail client

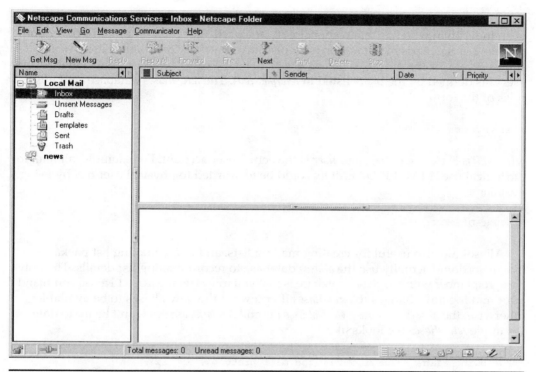

FIGURE 27-7 Sending mail in the Netscape mail client

the remote password and to automatically check for and retrieve mail every ten minutes. The POP tab contains an option to leave the mail on the server or to store it on the local file system.

The Netscape mail client main GUI is shown in Figure 27-7. The left pane displays the different supported mailboxes: inbox, unsent mail, draft e-mails, templates, sent mail, and a trash folder. In addition, messages can be ordered by subject, sender, date, or priority level.

Command Reference

The following command is commonly used to configure e-mail on Solaris.

alias

E-mail addresses typically correspond to a local Solaris user: for example, for the user account *pwatters* on host *mail.companyA.com*, the e-mail address would naturally be *pwatters@mail.companyA.com*. However, in many situations, mail needs to be addressed to a user who may not have a user account as such. In addition, there are often aliases required by application programs and daemons as administrative contacts, which should not go a specific individual, but rather should be forwarded to the user account of an individual who has that responsibility at a particular point in time. To cover both of these cases, Solaris maintains an administrative database of e-mail aliases, which allows a user for the purposes of `sendmail` to be logically different from actual Solaris users (as defined by the users listed in *etc/passwd*). The *etc/aliases* database contains rules of the form

```
alias: user
```

where *alias* is the user alias, and *user* is the actual user account. For example, all mail for the logical user MAILER-DAEMON could be forwarded to physical user *root* by using the alias

```
MAILER-DAEMON: root
```

Aliases are also useful for creating mailing lists, and many mailing list packages like majordomo actually use the *aliases* database to record mailing list details. The only tip to remember with the *aliases* database is that you must run the `newaliases` command after making any changes to *etc/aliases* if you want the new aliases to be available; otherwise, the *aliases* database (*etc/aliases.dir* and *etc/aliases/pag*) won't be up to date. A sample *etc/aliases* file looks like

```
# Following alias is required by the mail protocol, RFC 822
# Set it to the address of a HUMAN who deals with this system's mail problems.
Postmaster: root
# Alias for mailer daemon; returned messages from our MAILER-DAEMON
# should be routed to our local Postmaster.
MAILER-DAEMON: postmaster
# Aliases to handle mail to programs or files, eg news or vacation
nobody: /dev/null
# To be specified in as sender in USENET postings (anti-UCE trap)
spam: /dev/null
# Alias for staff distribution list, members specified here:
staff:  pwatters,neil@indiana,maya@sydney,greg@sydney,lori@sydney
# Alias for a person, so they can receive mail by several names:
paul:   pwatters
root:   maya@sydney
help:   greg@sydney
helpdesk:  help
support:  neil@indiana
abuse:  spam
```

Summary

In this chapter, you have learned how to configure `sendmail` and some of the popular client systems reading e-mail. While `sendmail` is very complicated to learn, it is the industry standard, and using macros is much easier than modifying *sendmail.cf* manually.

Domain Name Service

Although Solaris 10 has its own naming service, known as the Network Information Service (NIS), support is also provided for DNS, which maps IP addresses to hostnames. Every computer that is connected to the Internet must have an IP address, which identifies it uniquely within the network. For example, 192.18.97.241 is the IP address of the Web server at Sun. IP addresses are hard for humans to remember, and they don't adequately describe the network on which a host resides. Thus, by examining the Fully Qualified Domain Name (FQDN) of 192.18.97.241—*www.sun.com*— it's immediately obvious that the host, *www*, lies within the *sun.com* domain. The mapping between human-friendly domain names and machine-friendly IP addresses is performed by a distributed naming service known as the Domain Name Service (DNS). This chapter examines how DNS servers manage records of network addresses, and how this information can be accessed by Solaris applications. In addition, this chapter examines how to build and configure the latest version of the Berkeley Internet Daemon (BIND) from source, if security issues leave your existing BIND service vulnerable to attack.

Key Concepts

The following key concepts are central to understanding the role of DNS as a naming service.

Overview of DNS

The Domain Name Service is a distributed database that maps human-friendly fully qualified hostnames, like *paulwatters.com*, to a numeric IP address, like 209.67.50.203. In the early days of the Internet, a single file was distributed to various hosts (called the *HOSTS.TXT* file), which contained an address-to-hostname mapping for known hosts. Administrators would periodically upload a list of any new hosts added to their networks, after which they would download the latest version of the file. However, as the Internet grew, maintaining this text database became impossible.

A new system for mapping addresses to names was proposed in RFCs 882 and 883, based around information about local networks being sourced from designated servers for each network. It should be noted that Solaris retains a variant of the *HOSTS.TXT* file in the form of the */etc/hosts* file, which is typically used to map IP addresses to domain names for the localhost, as well as key network servers such as the local domain name server. This is very useful in situations where the DNS server is not responding while the system is being booted. The */etc/hosts* file is consulted by some applications, such as the syslog daemon (syslogd), to determine which host (the "loghost") should be used for system logging. A typical */etc/hosts* file looks like this:

```
127.0.0.1          localhost
204.168.14.23      bryce       bryce.paulwatters.com      loghost
204.168.14.24      wasatch     wasatch.paulwatters.com
```

Of course, only key servers and the localhost should be defined in the */etc/hosts* file—otherwise, any change in IP address for that server will not be reflected in the value resolved from */etc/hosts*.

DNS works on a simple client/server principle: if you know the name of a DNS server for a particular network, you will be able to retrieve the IP address of any host within that network. For example, if you know that the name server for the domain *paulwatters.com* is *dns20.register.com*, you can contact *dns20.register.com* to retrieve the address for any host within the *paulwatters.com* domain (including *www.paulwatters.com*, or 209.67.50.203). Of course, this leads you to a classic "chicken and egg" problem—how do you know, in the first instance, that the DNS server *dns20.register.com* is authoritative for *paulwatters.com*? The answer is that, in the same way that the addresses of all hosts under *paulwatters.com* are managed by its DNS server, the address of the DNS server is managed by the next server along the chain—in this case, the DNS server for the *.com* domain.

There are many such top-level domains now in existence, including the traditional *.edu* (educational organizations), *.com* (commercial organizations), and *.net* (network) top-level domains. Most countries now have their own top-level domains, including *.au* (Australia), *.ck* (Cook Islands), and *.ph* (Philippines). Underneath each top-level domain are several second-level domains: for example, Australia has *.com.au* (Australian commercial organizations), *.edu.au* (Australian educational organizations), and *.asn.au* (Australian nonprofit associations). The organizations that manage each top-level and second-level domain can also be quite different: while Network Solutions (**http://www .nsi.com/**) is responsible for the wholesale allocation of domain names for the *.com* top-level domain, the *.com.au* second-level domain is managed by Melbourne IT (**http://www .melbourneit.com.au/**).

As an example, take a look at how the hostname *www.finance.saltlake.com* is resolved: the client resolver needs to determine which DNS server is authoritative for *.com* domains, followed by the DNS server that is authoritative for *saltlake.com* domains, potentially followed by the DNS server that is authoritative for the *finance.saltlake.com* domain, if all mappings for *saltlake.com* are not stored on a single server. The *.com* resolution is taken care of by the list of root servers provided by the whois database (**ftp://ftp.rs.internic.net/domain/named.root**):

```
>>> Last update of whois database: Mon, 9 Oct 2000 09:43:11 EDT <<<
The Registry database contains ONLY .COM, .NET, .ORG, .EDU domains and
Registrars.
ftp://ftp.rs.internic.net/domain/named.root
;       This file holds the information on root name servers needed to
;       initialize cache of Internet domain name servers
;       (e.g. reference this file in the "cache  .  <file>"
;       configuration file of BIND domain name servers).
;
;       This file is made available by InterNIC registration services
;       under anonymous FTP as
;           file            /domain/named.root
;           on server       FTP.RS.INTERNIC.NET
;       -OR- under Gopher at    RS.INTERNIC.NET
;           under menu      InterNIC Registration Services (NSI)
;               submenu     InterNIC Registration Archives
;           file            named.root
;
;       last update:    Aug 22, 1997
;       related version of root zone:   1997082200
.                           3600000 IN  NS  A.ROOT-SERVERS.NET.
A.ROOT-SERVERS.NET.         3600000     A   198.41.0.4
.                           3600000     NS  B.ROOT-SERVERS.NET.
B.ROOT-SERVERS.NET.         3600000     A   128.9.0.107
.                           3600000     NS  C.ROOT-SERVERS.NET.
C.ROOT-SERVERS.NET.         3600000     A   192.33.4.12
.                           3600000     NS  D.ROOT-SERVERS.NET.
D.ROOT-SERVERS.NET.         3600000     A   128.8.10.90
.                           3600000     NS  E.ROOT-SERVERS.NET.
E.ROOT-SERVERS.NET.         3600000     A   192.203.230.10
.                           3600000     NS  F.ROOT-SERVERS.NET.
F.ROOT-SERVERS.NET.         3600000     A   192.5.5.241
.                           3600000     NS  G.ROOT-SERVERS.NET.
G.ROOT-SERVERS.NET.         3600000     A   192.112.36.4
.                           3600000     NS  H.ROOT-SERVERS.NET.
H.ROOT-SERVERS.NET.         3600000     A   128.63.2.53
.                           3600000     NS  I.ROOT-SERVERS.NET.
I.ROOT-SERVERS.NET.         3600000     A   192.36.148.17
.                           3600000     NS  J.ROOT-SERVERS.NET.
J.ROOT-SERVERS.NET.         3600000     A   198.41.0.10
.                           3600000     NS  K.ROOT-SERVERS.NET.
K.ROOT-SERVERS.NET.         3600000     A   193.0.14.129
.                           3600000     NS  L.ROOT-SERVERS.NET.
L.ROOT-SERVERS.NET.         3600000     A   198.32.64.12
.                           3600000     NS  M.ROOT-SERVERS.NET.
M.ROOT-SERVERS.NET.         3600000     A   202.12.27.33
```

The preceding *named.root* file can be used by servers to resolve IP addresses for root DNS servers, if they do not run a local DNS server. After obtaining an IP address for a root server for the *.com* domain, a query is then made to the DNS server that is authoritative for *saltlake.com* for the address *www.finance.saltlake.com*. Either of two possible scenarios may occur at this point: the DNS server that is authoritative for the entire *saltlake.com* domain can resolve the address, or the query is passed to a DNS server for the *finance* *.saltlake.com* domain, if the root server has delegated authority to another server. In the latter situation, the *saltlake.com* DNS server does not know the IP address for any hosts within the *finance.saltlake.com* domain, except for the address of the DNS server. DNS is therefore a very flexible system for managing the mapping of domain names to IP addresses.

The software that carries out the client request for, and server resolution of, IP addresses is BIND. Although most vendors, including Sun, ship their own customized version of BIND, it is possible to download, compile, configure, and install your own version of BIND (available for download from Internet Systems Consortium at **http://www.isc.org/**).

Examples

The following examples demonstrate how to install and configure DNS client tools and the DNS server.

DNS Client Tools

Configuring a DNS client in Solaris is very easy, and can be accomplished in a few easy steps. First, you must have installed the BIND package during system installation to use the DNS client tools. Second, you must configure the name service switch (*/etc/ nsswitch.conf*) to consult DNS for domain name resolution, in addition to checking the */etc/hosts* file and/or NIS/NIS+ maps or tables for hostnames. The following line must appear in */etc/nsswitch.conf* for DNS to work correctly:

```
/etc/nsswitch.conf hosts:  dns [NOTFOUND=return] files
```

If you have NIS+ running, the line would look like this:

```
/etc/nsswitch.conf hosts:  dns nisplus nis [NOTFOUND=return] files
```

Next, enter the name of the local domain into the file */etc/defaultdomain*. For example, the */etc/defaultdomain* file for the host *www.paulwatters.com* should have the following entry:

```
paulwatters.com
```

Finally, add to the */etc/resolv.conf* file the name of the local domain, the IP addresses of the local primary DNS server, and the IP address of a secondary (offsite) DNS server. This means that even if your local DNS server goes down, you can rely on the secondary DNS server to provide up-to-date information about external hosts, relying on data within the */etc/hosts* file to resolve local addresses. The following example demonstrates how the */etc/resolv.conf* file might look for the host *www.finance.saltlake.com*:

```
domain finance.saltlake.com
domain saltlake.com
nameserver 204.168.12.1
nameserver 204.168.12.16
nameserver 64.58.24.1
```

The domain belongs to two domains: the subdomain *finance.saltlake.com*, as well as the domain *saltlake.com*. Thus, two primary DNS servers are listed within the local domain (204.168.12.1 and 204.168.12.16). In addition, an external secondary is also listed, corresponding to *ns.utahisp.com*, or 64.58.24.1.

Once the client resolver is configured in this way, you can use a number of tools to test whether DNS is working, and also to further examine how IP addresses are resolved.

nslookup

The most important tool for performing DNS resolutions is `nslookup`, which can be used in a simple command-line mode to look up FQDNs from IP addresses, and vice versa. However, `nslookup` also features an interactive mode that is very useful for retrieving name server characteristics for a particular domain, and to determine which DNS servers are authoritative for a specific host or network.

The following is a simple example—if you wanted to determine the IP address of the host *www.paulwatters.com*, using a client on the host *provo.cassowary.net*, you would use the following command:

```
$ nslookup www.paulwatters.com
```

The following response would be returned:

```
Server:   provo.cassowary.net
Address:  206.68.216.16

Name:     paulwatters.com
Address:  209.67.50.203
Aliases:  www.paulwatters.com
```

This means that the primary DNS server for the local (*cassowary.net*) domain is *provo.cassowary.net* (206.68.216.16). This server then makes a connection through to the DNS server, which is authoritative for the domain paulwatters.com (*dns19.hostsave.com*). This server then returns the canonical (actual) name for the host (*paulwatters.com*), the alias name (*www.paulwatters.com*), and the desired IP address. If you reversed the process and instead supplied the IP address 209.67.50.203 on the command line, you would be able to perform a reverse lookup on that address, which would resolve to the domain name *paulwatters.com*.

If you want to verify that your DNS server is returning the correct IP address, or if you want to verify an address directly yourself, then running `nslookup` in interactive mode allows you to set the name of the DNS server to use for all lookups. For example, if you wanted to resolve the domain name for the Web server of the University of Sydney, you could use the following command:

```
$ nslookup www.usyd.edu.au
```

The following response would then be returned:

```
Server:    provo.cassowary.net
Address:   206.68.216.16

Name: solo.ucc.usyd.edu.au
Address:   129.78.64.2
Aliases:   www.usyd.edu.au
```

However, you could verify that this IP address is indeed correct by setting your DNS server to be the DNS server that is authoritative for the *ucc.usyd.edu.au* domain:

```
$ nslookup
Default Server:  provo.cassowary.net
Address:  206.68.216.16
```

Next, enter the name of the DNS server that is authoritative for the target domain:

```
> server metro.ucc.su.oz.au
Default Server:  metro.ucc.su.oz.au
Address:  129.78.64.2
```

Next, enter the name of the host to resolve:

```
> www.usyd.edu.au
Server:  metro.ucc.su.oz.au
Address:  129.78.64.2
```

And the IP address is returned correctly:

```
Name:       solo.ucc.usyd.edu.au
Address:    129.78.64.24
Aliases:    www.usyd.edu.au
```

If you want to determine some of the key characteristics of the DNS entry for *www.usyd.edu.au*, such as the DNS server that is authoritative for the host, and the mail address of the administrator who is responsible for the host, it is possible to retrieve the Start of Authority (SOA) record through `nslookup`:

```
$ nslookup
Default Server:  provo.cassowary.net
Address:  206.68.216.16

> server metro.ucc.su.oz.au
Default Server:  metro.ucc.su.oz.au
Address:  129.78.64.2
> set q=soa
> www.usyd.edu.au
Server:  metro.ucc.su.oz.au
Address:  129.78.64.2

www.usyd.edu.au canonical name = solo.ucc.usyd.edu.au
ucc.usyd.edu.au
        origin = metro.ucc.usyd.edu.au
        mail addr = root.metro.ucc.usyd.edu.au
        serial = 316
        refresh = 3600 (1 hour)
        retry   = 1800 (30 mins)
        expire  = 36000 (10 hours)
        minimum ttl = 43200 (12 hours)
```

This SOA record indicates the following:

- The canonical name of *www.usyd.edu.au* is *solo.ucc.usyd.edu.au*.

- The origin of the DNS record is *metro.ucc.usyd.edu.au* (and this server is authoritative for the host *solo.ucc.usyd.edu.au*).

- The serial number for the current record is 316. Next time a change is made to the record, the serial number should be incremented.

- The refresh rate is 1 hour.

- The retry rate in 30 minutes.

- The expiry rate is 10 hours.

- The TTL is 12 hours.

The meaning of each field is examined later in the chapter, in the "Configuring a DNS Server" section, which discusses how to create DNS records for the server. The use of `nslookup` to determine which servers are authoritative for a particular query is

576 Part VI: Services, Directories, and Applications

not limited to individual hosts—in fact, the authoritative servers for entire networks can be determined by using `nslookup`. For example, if you wanted to determine which servers were authoritative for the Cook Islands top-level domain (*.ck*), you would use the following command:

```
$ nslookup
> set type=ns
> ck.
Server:   provo.cassowary.net
Address:  206.68.216.16

Non-authoritative answer:
ck        nameserver = DOWNSTAGE.MCS.VUW.AC.NZ
ck        nameserver = NS1.WAIKATO.AC.NZ
ck        nameserver = PARAU.OYSTER.NET.ck
ck        nameserver = POIPARAU.OYSTER.NET.ck
ck        nameserver = CIRCA.MCS.VUW.AC.NZ

Authoritative answers can be found from:
DOWNSTAGE.MCS.VUW.AC.NZ internet address = 130.195.6.10
NS1.WAIKATO.AC.NZ       internet address = 140.200.128.13
PARAU.OYSTER.NET.ck     internet address = 202.65.32.128
POIPARAU.OYSTER.NET.ck  internet address = 202.65.32.127
CIRCA.MCS.VUW.AC.NZ     internet address = 130.195.5.12
```

Some servers that are authoritative for the top-level domain of the Cook Islands are located in New Zealand. This geographic separation may seem strange, and may not be the norm, but it makes sense if you've ever lived through a tropical storm in Rarotonga—if the power to the *OYSTER.NET.ck* network is disrupted, hostnames can still be resolved through the backup servers at *WAIKATO.AC.NZ*.

It's sometimes possible to obtain a list of all the networks and hosts within a particular top-level domain by using the `ls` command—but be warned, the output can be verbose, and security settings may prohibit you from doing this:

```
$ nslookup
> set type=ns
> ls ck.
[DOWNSTAGE.MCS.VUW.AC.NZ]
 ck.                            server = parau.oyster.net.ck
 parau.oyster.net               202.65.32.128
 ck.                            server = poiparau.oyster.net.ck
 poiparau.oyster.net            202.65.32.127
 ck.                            server = downstage.mcs.vuw.ac.nz
 ck.                            server = circa.mcs.vuw.ac.nz
 sda.org                        server = parau.oyster.net.ck
 parau.oyster.net               202.65.32.128
 sda.org                        server = poiparau.oyster.net.ck
```

whois

The next tool that is often useful for resolving hostnames is the `whois` command. This command uses InterNIC servers to perform all of the resolutions for you, and includes useful information, like the registrar of the domain name (useful when making complaints about spam or harassment on the Internet!). Here's the `whois` entry for *paulwatters.com*:

```
$ whois paulwatters

Whois Server Version 1.3

Domain names in the .com, .net, and .org domains can now be
registered with many different competing registrars. Go to
http://www.internic.net for detailed information.

    Domain Name: PAULWATTERS.COM
    Registrar: REGISTER.COM, INC.
    Whois Server: whois.register.com
    Referral URL: www.register.com
    Name Server: DNS19.REGISTER.COM
    Name Server: DNS20.REGISTER.COM
    Updated Date: 30-may-2000
```

dig

Finally, `dig` (domain information groper) is an application that ships with Solaris 10 that returns IP addresses from domain name queries. It returns details of many hosts on a network, as shown in the following example:

```
$ dig mq.edu.au
 ; <<>> DiG 9.1.3 <<>> mq.edu.au ANY
 ;; global options:  printcmd
 ;; Got answer:
 ;; ->>HEADER<<- opcode: QUERY, status: NOERROR, id: 30758
 ;; flags: qr rd ra; QUERY: 1, ANSWER: 6, AUTHORITY: 2, ADDITIONAL: 2

 ;; QUESTION SECTION:
 ;mq.edu.au.                     IN       ANY

 ;; ANSWER SECTION:
 mq.edu.au.              82400   IN       A       137.111.1.11
 mq.edu.au.              82400   IN       MX      10 sunb.ocs.mq.edu.au.
 mq.edu.au.              82400   IN       MX      10 baldrick.ocs.mq.edu.au.
 mq.edu.au.              82400   IN       SOA     sunb.ocs.mq.edu.au.
 hostmaster.mq.edu.au. 2004110800 7200 1800 3600000 82400
 mq.edu.au.              82400   IN       NS      baldrick.ocs.mq.edu.au.
 mq.edu.au.              82400   IN       NS      sunb.ocs.mq.edu.au.

 ;; AUTHORITY SECTION:
 mq.edu.au.              82400   IN       NS      sunb.ocs.mq.edu.au.
```

```
mq.edu.au.                82400    IN      NS       baldrick.ocs.mq.edu.au.

;; ADDITIONAL SECTION:
sunb.ocs.mq.edu.au.    82383    IN      A        137.111.1.11
baldrick.ocs.mq.edu.au.          82383    IN      A        137.111.1.12

;; Query time: 319 msec
;; SERVER: 127.0.0.1#53(127.0.0.1)
;; WHEN: Wed Nov 10 03:48:28 2004
;; MSG SIZE  rcvd: 228
```

Procedures

The following procedures show how to configure a DNS server.

Configuring a DNS Server

Now that you've examined DNS from a client viewpoint and explored concepts like SOAs, IP-to-address mapping, and address-to-IP mapping, it should be obvious what kind of services a DNS server needs to provide to clients. In addition, DNS servers need to be able to support both primary and secondary services as described earlier.

BIND is the most commonly used DNS server for Solaris. It is supplied in a package that is generally installed during initial system configuration. Its main configuration file is */etc/named.conf*, for BIND 8 supplied with Solaris 8. BIND 4 and earlier used a configuration file called */etc/named.boot*; however, these versions are no longer supported by the ISC, and administrators running BIND 4 should upgrade to BIND 9.

The */etc/named.conf* file is responsible for controlling the behavior of the DNS servers and provides the following keywords, which are used to define operational statements:

acl	Defines an access control list that determines which clients can use the server.
include	Reads an external file that contains statements in the same format as */etc/named.conf*. This is very useful when your configuration file becomes very large, as different sections can be divided into logically related files.
logging	Determines which activities of the server are logged in the logfile specified by the statement.
options	Defines local server operational characteristics.
server	Defines operational characteristics of other servers.
zone	Creates local DNS zones.

Each of the following sections examines a sample statement involving one of these keywords.

acl

If you want to define an access control list for all hosts on the local network (10.24.58.*), you would insert this statement:

```
acl local_network {
10.24.58/24
};
```

Here, 24 indicates the netmask 255.255.255.0 in prefix notation. If your router is the host 10.24.58.32 and you want to prevent any access to the DNS server from that address, you would amend the preceding statement to the following:

```
acl local_network {
!10.24.58.32; 10.24.58/24
};
```

Note that the negation of a specific address from a subnet that is also permitted must precede the definition of that subnet in the statement.

include

Since the definitions for configuring DNS zones (discussed a bit later in the "zone" section) can be very long for large networks, administrators often place them in a separate file so that they can be managed separately from ACL definitions and system options. Thus, to include all of the zone definitions from the file */var/named/zones.conf*, you would insert the following statement into the */etc/named.conf* file:

```
include "/var/named/zones.conf"
```

options

The *options* section sets key parameters that affect the run-time behavior of the BIND server. Typically, these are the directories in which the zone databases are stored, and the file in which the process ID of the named process is stored. The following example gives the standard options for BIND 8:

```
options {
directory "/var/named";
pid-file "/var/named/pid";
}
```

server

The *server* statement defines characteristics of remote name servers. There are two main options that can be set with a *server* statement: whether or not a remote server is known to transmit incorrect information, and whether or not the remote server can answer multiple queries during a single request. A sample *server* statement would look like this:

```
server 10.24.58.32
{
    bogus yes;
    transfer-format many-answers;
}
```

zone

A zone must be created for each network or subdomain that your DNS server manages. Zones can be created either as primary or secondary, depending on which server is authoritative for a particular domain. Entries for IP-to-name and name-to-IP mappings must also be included to correctly resolve both IP address and domain names. For the domain *cassowary.net*, the following zone entries would need to be created:

```
zone "cassowary.net"
{
    type master;
    file "cassowary.net.db";
}
zone "58.24.10.in-addr.arpa"
{
    type master;
    file "cassowary.net.rev";
}
```

In this case, the two zone files */var/named/cassowary.net.db* and */var/named/cassowary.net.rev* need to be populated with host information. A sample */var/named/cassowary.net.db* file would contain SOA entries like this:

```
@    IN    SOA    cassowary.net.    root.cassowary.net.    (
        2000011103    ;serial number
        10800         ;refresh every three hours
        1800          ;retry every 30 mins
        1209600       ;Two week expiry
        604800)       ;Minimum one week expiry
        IN    NS    ns.cassowary.net.
        IN    MX    10    firewall.cassowary.net.
```

```
firewall      IN    A       10.24.58.1      ;firewall
emu           IN    A       10.24.58.2      ;webserver
quoll         IN    A       10.24.58.3      ;webserver
tazdevil      IN    A       10.24.58.4      ;kerberos
security      IN    CNAME       tazdevil
```

A sample */var/named/cassowary.net.rev* file would contain SOA entries like this:

```
@    IN    SOA    58.24.10.in-addr.arpa.      root.cassowary.net.   (
          2000011103    ;serial number
          10800         ;refresh every three hours
          1800          ;retry every 30 mins
          1209600       ;Two week expiry
          604800)       ;Minimum one week expiry
          IN    NS     ns.cassowary.net.
1         IN    PTR    firewall.cassowary.net.
2         IN    PTR    emu.cassowary.net.
3         IN    PTR    quoll.cassowary.net.
4         IN    PTR    tazdevil.cassowary.net.
```

Each host within the domain must have an IP-to-domain mapping as well as a domain-to-IP mapping. Once a change is made to the zone file, you should increment the serial number as appropriate. Note that in addition to address (A) and pointer (PTR) records for IP address and domain names, respectively, it is also possible to identify hosts as mail exchangers (MX) and by canonical names (CNAME). The former is required to define which host is responsible for handling mail within a domain, while the latter is used to create aliases for specific machines (thus, the *tazdevil* Kerberos server is also known as *security.cassowary.net*).

DNS provides a number of security features, such as options for disabling zone transfers and implementing transaction signatures. Disabling zone transfers ensures that a hacker cannot retrieve a detailed zone list and thereby identify targets to attack. Requesting many zone transfers concurrently is also a popular denial of service attack. Using transaction signatures, on the other hand, ensures that both parties in a DNS exchange (client and server) can be mutually authenticated by using digital signatures. This prevents spoofing of DNS entries from a non-authentic DNS server to clients.

Summary

In this chapter, you have learned how to configure a DNS server and how to retrieve DNS information manually using various client tools. Since DNS is the naming service for the entire Internet, you need to master the skills presented in this chapter before configuring workstations or DNS services.

Network Information Service (NIS/NIS+)

C hapter 28 examined the Domain Name Service (DNS), which allows hosts around the Internet to be easily and consistently identified by user-friendly "names" rather than computer-friendly IP addresses. However, while DNS is a very common network information service, it is not the only kind of service available. Solaris 10 supports NIS+, which is an improved version of the Network Information Service (which was popular with Solaris 1). However, NIS/NIS+ will eventually be deprecated in favor of the Lightweight Directory Access Protocol (LDAP), which is an industry standard, and may be deprecated in future Solaris releases in favor of LDAP.

NIS+ is composed of a centralized repository of information about hosts, networks, services, and protocols on a local area network. This information is physically stored in a set of maps that are intended to replace the network configuration files usually stored in a server's /etc directory. The set of all maps on a NIS+ network is known as a namespace, supporting large networks of up to 10,000 hosts where responsibilities can be delegated to local servers. NIS+ improves upon the standard NIS by allowing enhancements to authentication processes, combined with sophisticated resource authorization. This allows NIS+ namespaces to exist over public networks like the Internet without risk of data loss or interception, with the caveat that NIS+ relies on the relatively weak DES encryption algorithm.

This chapter examines the process of setting up a NIS+ server and highlights the differences between NIS+ and NIS, and between NIS+ and other naming services like DNS. In fact, many sites choose to run DNS alongside NIS+, which is also possible. In addition, this chapter reviews the role and configuration of primary and slave servers, and walks through the installation of NIS+ using the script method.

Key Concepts

The following concepts are required knowledge for installing and running NIS/NIS+.

Managing Resources

NIS+ is a Solaris network information service whose primary focus is the management of users, hosts, networks, services, and protocols. NIS+ does not replace DNS, which is still required for host addressing and identification. However, NIS+ namespaces can be constructed to parallel the host designations assigned through DNS, to simplify operations and to make the integration of both services more seamless. NIS+ gives networks more than just DNS: namespaces are used as centralized repositories of shared network information that can be used to more effectively manage large networks. However, many organizations choose not to use NIS+ because it has some overlap with DNS, and because of the extra administrative burden involved in installing and configuring NIS+ primary and slave servers. However, if you use the NIS+ scripts to install and configure namespaces, instead of using NIS+ commands directly, NIS+ can be much easier to configure.

NIS revolves around the idea of maps: a map is generally a database with two columns, of which one is a primary key that is used to retrieve an associated value. This associative nature makes the storage and retrieval of group, mail, passwords, and Ethernet information fast for small networks, but can rapidly become difficult to manage (not to mention slow) for large networks. NIS+, in contrast, uses tables, of which 16 are defined by the system. Tables store information such as server addresses, time zones, and networks services. This section reviews the most commonly used types of NIS maps and NIS+ tables.

First, however, consider this conceptual overview of how NIS+ could be used to better manage an organization's network data. Suppose that you're setting up a Solaris network for an imaginary college called Panther College, which has a DNS domain of *panther.edu*. Panther has two teaching divisions: an undergraduate school (*undergrad .panther.edu*) and a graduate school (*graduate.panther.edu*). The *panther.edu* domain has a class C network (192.12.1.0), as do each of the undergraduate (192.12.2.0) and graduate schools (192.12.3.0). Each of these networks can have up to 255 hosts, which more than adequately covers the staff members in both teaching divisions. To support DNS, there may be a campus-wide DNS server *ns.panther.edu* at 192.12.1.16, while the *undergrad.panther .edu* network has its own DNS servers at *ns.undergrad.panther.edu* (192.12.1.16), and *ns.graduate.panther.edu* (192.12.2.16). This is a fairly standard setup for a medium-sized network like a college campus, and is demonstrated in Figure 29-1.

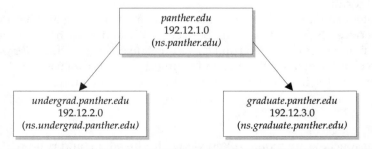

FIGURE 29-1   DNS configuration for a fictional college with two divisions—graduate and undergraduate—both of which have their own name server

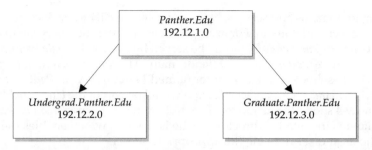

FIGURE 29-2   NIS+ domains for Panther College

The NIS+ domains for Panther College can exactly mirror the DNS configuration, as shown in Figure 29-2. However, some differences in naming are immediately apparent: whereas DNS names are all lowercase and do not end in a period, NIS+ names use initial capitalization for each part of the name and end in a period.

In addition, the second-level domain identified in DNS as *panther.edu* would be the "root domain" in an NIS+ network, and the third-level domains *undergrad.panther.edu* and *graduate.panther.edu* would be described as "nonroot domains." Each of these domains would be associated with a server, in which case the existing DNS servers would double up as NIS+ servers. In fact, in normal NIS+ usage, each of the three domains at Panther College would require two servers: a master server and at least one replica, or slave, server. This ensures that if the master server is disrupted or experiences hardware failure, the replica server holds copies of network service information and service continues. The expanded NIS+ domains for Panther College, with a master and slave server each (called *Master* and *Replica*), are shown in Figure 29-3.

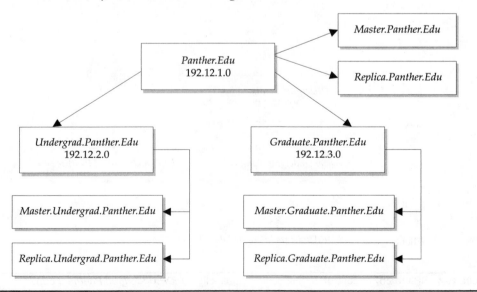

FIGURE 29-3   NIS+ domains with a master and a slave server each

In addition to domains and servers, NIS+ also caters to clients. Each client is associated with a specific server and domain. For example, a client in the chemistry lab in the graduate school (*Curie.Graduate.Panther.Edu.*) would be served by *Master.Graduate.Panther.Edu.*, and would be part of the *Graduate.Panther.Edu.* domain. Alternatively, a history professor in the undergraduate school with a computer named *FDR.Undergrad.Panther.Edu.* would be served by *Master.Undergrad.Panther.Edu.*, and would be part of the *Undergrad.Panther.Edu.* domain. Figure 29-4 shows the hierarchy of control for the *FDR.Undergrad.Panther.Edu.* client. When each client is installed, a directory cache is created, which enables the client to locate other hosts and services via the appropriate server.

So far, only one of the many kinds of namespace components has been mentioned: the domain. However, there are many other components that exist in the namespace, including group objects, directory objects, and table objects. The following sections examine these important features of the namespace, as well as the specific configuration of NIS maps and NIS+ tables.

It is worth mentioning at this point that one of the main reasons that organizations choose to implement NIS+ is the improved security that accompanies the system. For example, NIS+ tables are not directly editable, unlike their normal Solaris counterparts in the */etc* directory. Requests to change or even access information in the namespace can only take place once a user has been authenticated. In addition to authentication, each user must be authorized to access a particular resource. This doubly protects sensitive and organizational data in a networked environment. The main authentication exchange takes place when either a user presents their credentials or a host presents its credentials, in the form of an unencrypted LOCAL form or a more secure DES-encrypted

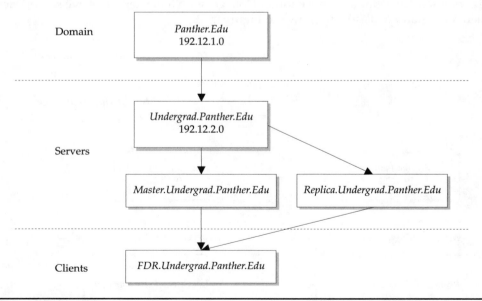

FIGURE 29-4   Hierarchy of control for a specific domain client (*FDR.Undergrad.Panther.Edu.*)

exchange. The former is used for testing, while the latter is always used for deployment. After authentication, authorization for the requested resource is checked. Access rights can always be examined by using the `niscat` command, which is discussed later in this chapter.

NIS Maps

As previously mentioned, NIS uses a series of maps to encode data about the network structure. Many of these maps are in a form that can be accessed through an address key (having a *byaddr* suffix) or through a name (with a *byname* suffix). Whenever a client needs to find information about a particular host, service, group, network, or netgroup, it can retrieve it by consulting the appropriate map as defined in the namespace. The main system maps are listed in this table:

bootparams	Contains a list of diskless clients for a domain
ethers.byaddr	Contains a list of the Ethernet addresses of all hosts in the domain, and their hostnames
ethers.byname	Contains a list of the hostnames of all hosts in the domain, and their Ethernet addresses
group.bygid	Contains a list of groups, indexed by group ID (GID)
group.byname	Contains a list of groups, indexed by group name
hosts.byaddr	Contains a list of the addresses of all hosts in the domain, and their hostnames
hosts.byname	Contains a list of the hostnames of all hosts in the domain, and their addresses
mail.aliases	Contains a list of mail aliases within the namespace, indexed by name
mail.byaddr	Contains a list of mail aliases within the namespace, indexed by address
netgroup	Contains netgroup information, indexed by group name
netgroup.byhost	Contains netgroup information, indexed by hostname
netgroup.byuser	Contains netgroup information, indexed by username
netid.byname	Contains the netname of hosts and users
netmasks.byaddr	Defines the netmasks defined in the domain namespace
networks.byaddr	Defines the networks in the domain namespace, sorted by address
networks.byname	Defines the networks in the domain namespace, sorted by name
passwd.byname	Defines the password database, sorted by username
passwd.byuid	Defines the password database, sorted by user ID
protocols.byname	Defines the network protocols used in the domain, sorted by name
protocols.bynumber	Defines the network protocols used in the domain, sorted by number
publickey.byname	Contains public keys for RPC
rpc.bynumber	Contains RPC details, indexed by number
services.byname	Defines all available Internet services, sorted by name
ypservers	Contains a list of all NIS servers available

As you can see, there are many similarities in name and function between the NIS maps and the */etc* system files they are intended to replace. However, both the */etc* files and NIS maps perform poorly under heavy loads, when the number of hosts defined in a specific namespace exceeds several hundred. In this case, it is much more appropriate to bypass NIS and */etc*, and move directly to a NIS+ installation where a single table (such as *Ethers*) replaces the dual lookup system used by NIS (such as *ethers.byname* and *ethers.byaddr*).

NIS+ Tables

Namespace information in NIS+ is stored in tables, which are based around a centralized administration model (even though particular functions can be delegated to specific servers). NIS+ is similar to DNS because it arranges hosts and resources hierarchically into domains, has inbuilt redundancy with master and slave servers, and can store much more information about a network than just its hosts. However, since each host in a domain has many different characteristics and user details that must be recorded and stored centrally, updating these details can be time consuming, and issues like contention in the recording of user and host data often arise. However, NIS+ namespaces can be updated incrementally, as changes occur, so that the entire database does not need to be updated immediately. Changes are entered into a master domain server and are then propagated through time to the rest of the domain. This process is governed by a time-to-live setting similar to that used for DNS. These are the key NIS tables:

- *Auto_Home*   Comprises an automounter map that facilitates the mounting of a home directory for any user in the local domain. It is commonly used to share a common home directory for a user who has accounts on multiple machines. It is also the cause of some consternation among administrators who attempt to create their users' home directories under */home* but don't use the automounter! The *Auto_Home* table has two columns: a common username that is consistent across all machines in a domain, and a physical location for the user's shared home directory. For example, the home directory of user *pwatters* might be located physically on the server *winston*, in the directory */u1/export/pwatters*. In this case, the entry in *Auto_Home* would be

```
pwatters  winston:/u1/export/pwatters
```

- *Auto_Master*   Maps the physical mount points of all the NFS automounter maps in a particular domain to a name. For example, it can be used to map user home directories to */home* or */staff* using *Auto_Home*, with either of the following mount points, respectively:

```
/home  auto_home
/staff  auto_home
```

- *Bootparams*   Contains the necessary information to boot and configure any diskless clients in the domain. It contains entries for server-based dump and swap, as well as a root directory, for each client. For example, if there is a diskless client called *pembroke* and it is configured by the server *downing*, the *Bootparams* table would contain the following entry:

```
pembroke   root=downing:/export/root/pembroke \
               swap=downing:/export/swap/pembroke \
               dump=downing:/export/dump/pembroke
```

Thus, each diskless client will have its own *Bootparams* table entry and resources available on the server.

- *Ethers*   Contains entries that associate a hostname with a specific hardware address. For example, if the host *freycinet* has an Ethernet address of 00:ff:a1:b3:c4:6c, the *Ethers* table entry would look like this:

```
00:ff:a1:b3:c4:6c   freycinet
```

For this to be useful, a corresponding entry for *freycinet* must exist in */etc/hosts*.

- *Group*   Consists of a group name, group password, group ID number, and member list, and stores information about the three kinds of groups accessible by NIS+ clients: Solaris groups (such as *staff*), NIS+ groups, and netgroups.

- *Hosts*   Lists all the hosts in a particular domain, matching their IP address with a hostname and an optional nickname. For example, if the host *maria* has an alias called *bruny* and has the IP address 192.34.54.3, then the entry in the *Hosts* table would look like this:

```
192.34.54.3   maria   bruny
```

- *Mail Aliases*   Replicates the functionality of the old */etc/aliases* file for the local mail transport agent (MTA), which is typically `sendmail`. An *Aliases* table can store an alias for a specific user, or it can be used to construct a mailing list. For example, if the user *bounty* wants to receive mail as *endeavour*, the *Mail Aliases* table entry would look like this:

```
endeavour:bounty
```

However, if an advertising company has a local mailing list for *newclients*, these messages could be distributed nationally to local offices by using an alias like this:

```
newclients:layton,miami,oakton,sanfran
```

- *Netgroups*   Defines a group of hosts and users that is authorized to perform specific operations on one or more other hosts within a group. The table format contains entries that identify the name of the group, as well as its members. For small organizations, everyone belongs to a single group, perhaps called *everyone*:

```
everyone   paulwatters.com
```

- *Netmasks*   Specifies the netmasks for all local class A, class B, and class C networks. For example, if the network 192.12.34.0 has a netmask of 255.255.255.0, the entry would look like this:

```
192.12.34.0   255.255.255.0
```

- *Networks*   Contains details of the local networks and their IP addresses. For example, if a class B network 192.12.0.0 is known on the Internet as *brunswick*, but has an alias of *essendon*, it would be entered into the *Networks* table as

```
brunswick  192.12.0.0  essendon
```

- *Passwd*   Stores all the standard user information expected on Solaris hosts, including username, encrypted password, user ID, group ID, and user's real name, home directory, and login shell. A typical entry may look like this:

```
pwatters:8dfjh4h.rj:101:10:Paul A. Watters:/home/pwatters:/bin/
tcsh:10905:-1:-1:-1:-1::0
```

In addition to the standard details, there is extra information that specifies how often a password must be changed, or how many days until it must next be changed. This significantly increases the functionality of NIS+ over standard Solaris password authorization.

- *Protocols*   Defines the protocols available to the network. A necessary entry for Internet use would be the Internet Protocol (IP),

```
ip  0  IP
```

which identifies *ip* as protocol number 0, which also has the alias *IP*.

- *RPC*   Defines the RPC programs available to the network. An entry consists of a name, a program number, and an alias. For example, rpcbind is also known as portmap, sunrpc, and the portmapper. The entry for rpcbind looks like this:

```
rpcbind  100000  portmap  sunrpc  portmapper
```

- *Services*   Contains a list of the IP services that are available through both TCP and UDP. For example, the HTTP service provided by many Web servers, such as Apache, is usually available through TCP port 80. This would be defined in the *Services* table as

```
http  80/tcp
```

- *Timezone*   Defines the local time zone, which affects all system settings and applications, such as sendmail. For example, the entry

```
hartog Australia/NSW
```

allows the host *hartog* to be identified as belonging to the New South Wales time zone in Australia. In addition, time zones can be specified on a host-by-host basis. This allows systems that exist in different time zones to belong to the same domain. For example, a SPARCstation in Sydney can belong to the same domain as an UltraSPARC in San Francisco. The *Timezone* table consists of entries that relate a time zone to a specific host.

Procedures

The following procedures are commonly used to install and run NIS/NIS+. This section walks through a configuration session with NIS+, focusing on using a script-based installation, which makes using NIS+ much easier. The main tasks involved in setting up NIS+ are to configure the domains, master servers, slave servers, and users. These tasks can be performed only after a network has been designed along the lines discussed in previous sections.

Whether or not you are setting up a root or a nonroot domain, the basic process is the same: after initializing a master server and creating the appropriate administrative groups, you populate the NIS+ tables and then install the clients and servers. In the case of a root domain, these servers can then act as master servers for lower-level domains. This section reviews the process of setting up a master server, populating the NIS+ tables, configuring clients and servers, and setting up other domains.

Setting Up a Root Domain

The first step in creating a NIS+ namespace is to create the root master server for the new domain. Continuing with the example for the *Panther.Edu.* domain, you create the root master server for *Panther.Edu.* by using the `nisserver` command. The server will be known in DNS as *ns.panther.edu*. This command is used for most server configuration operations. In this case, you use the command

```
ns.panther.edu# nisserver -r -d Panther.Edu.
```

This creates a root domain master server without backward compatibility with NIS. To enable NIS support, you need to use the command

```
ns.panther.edu# nisserver -Y -r -d Panther.Edu.
```

Populating Tables

After you create the master root server for the *Panther.Edu.* domain on *ns.panther.edu*, the next step is to populate the NIS+ tables. To achieve this, you need to use the `nispopulate` command:

```
ns.panther.edu# nispopulate -F -p /nis+files -d Panther.Edu.
```

This populates all the tables for the *Panther.Edu.* domain and stores the information on the master server. Again, if you need to support NIS, you need to include the *–Y* option:

```
ns.panther.edu# nispopulate -Y -F -p /nis+files -d Panther.Edu.
```

To administer the NIS+ namespace, you need to add administrators to the admin group. You can achieve this by using the `nisgrpadmin` command. In the *Panther.Edu.* example, imagine that you have two administrators, *michael* and *adonis*. To add these administrators, use this command:

```
ns.panther.edu# nisgrpadm -a admin.Panther.Edu. michael.Panther.Edu.
adonis.Panther.Edu.
```

If you are satisfied with the configuration, then it is best to checkpoint the configuration by transferring the domain configuration information to disk copies of the tables. This can be achieved by using the `nisping` command:

```
ns.panther.edu# nisping -C Panther.Edu.
```

Now that you have successfully created the root domain, you can create clients that will act as master and slave servers for the two subdomains in the *Panther.Edu.* root domain: *Graduate.Panther.Edu.* and *Undergrad.Panther.Edu.*

Setting Up Clients

To create master servers for the nonroot domain *Undergrad.Panther.Edu.*, you first need to set up the client within a domain by using the `nisclient` command. For the host *client1.panther.edu,* which will become the master server for the nonroot domain, the command is

```
client1.panther.edu# nisclient -i -d Panther.Edu. -h Ns.Panther.Edu
```

To actually set up the client's user within the domain, you can also use the `nisclient` command, when executed from a nonprivileged user's shell:

```
client1.panther.edu% nisclient -u
```

If this was for the user *maya*, then *maya* would now be able to access the namespace. Next, you need to turn the client host you have initialized into a nonroot domain master server.

Setting Up Servers

After the root server is created, most organizations will want to create new master servers for each of the subdomains that form the domain. For example, in the *Panther.Edu.* domain, there are two subdomains: *Undergrad.Panther.Edu.* and *Graduate.Panther.Edu.* In this case, two clients must be created from the root master server and then converted to be servers. Initially, these are root server replicas, but their designation then changes to a nonroot master server for each of the subdomains. Replica servers for the subdomain master servers can also be enabled.

The following example designates two client machines, whose DNS names are *client1.panther.edu* and *client2.panther.edu* (recall that the master server for the root domain is *ns.panther.edu*). These two clients will actually become the master and slave servers for the subdomain *Undergrad.Panther.Edu.* To begin the server creation process, a similar approach is followed as for the creation of the master server for the root domain:

1. Start the rpc daemon on the client machine, which will become the master server for the nonroot domain:

   ```
   client1.panther.edu# rpc.nisd
   ```

2. Convert the *client1* server to a root replica server in the first instance, which ensures that the subdomain inherits the appropriate settings from the top-level domain:

   ```
   ns.panther.edu# nisserver -R -d Panther.Edu. -h client1.panther.edu
   ```

3. After replicating the settings from the root master server, the new nonroot master server is ready to begin serving the new subdomain. In this case, the root master server (*ns.panther.edu*) must delegate this authority explicitly to the master of *Undergrad.Panther.Edu.*, which is *client1.panther.edu*:

   ```
   ns.panther.edu# nisserver -M -d Undergrad.Panther.Edu. \
     -h client1.panther.edu
   ```

4. Following the same routine previously outlined for the root master server, populate the tables of the new subdomain server *client1.panther.edu*:

   ```
   client1.panther.edu# nispopulate -F -p /nis+files \
     -d Undergrad.Panther.Edu.
   ```

5. Having created a new master server for the new subdomain, create a replica server to ensure service reliability in the event of failure:

   ```
   client1.panther.edu# nisclient -R -d Undergrad.Panther.Edu. \
     -h client2.panther.edu
   ```

You would need to adapt the process of installing a server for the *Undergrad.Panther.Edu.* subdomain to create the other subdomain (*Graduate.Panther.Edu.*), but the general process of setting up a client, converting it to a replica server, and populating the tables would be very similar to this domain. Now that you have investigated how to create subdomains, the next section covers the day-to-day usage of NIS+, and the most commonly used commands that access tables, groups, and objects in the namespace.

Examples

The following examples provide some real-world cases for installing and running NIS/NIS+, using the name service switch. You might be wondering—in a mixed network information service environment comprising NIS maps, NIS+ tables, and DNS servers— how name services are selected to resolve particular requests. The answer provided in Solaris 2.*x* is the name service switch, whose configuration is specified in the file */etc/ nsswitch.conf*. The name service switch is very useful because it enables you to configure which name service handles specific kinds of requests. It is also possible to specify more than one kind of service for every kind of request: thus, if a request fails on the default service, it can be applied to a different service. For example, to resolve hostnames, many sites have at least some local hostnames statically hardwired into the */etc/hosts* database. In addition, many sites connected to the Internet use DNS to resolve hostnames.

Where does this leave the relative sophistication of NIS+ namespaces, or the legacy of NIS maps? The answer is that files, DNS, NIS, and NIS+ can be configured to be selected as the first, second, third, and fourth choices as the default name service for resolving hosts in */etc/nsswitch.conf*. For example, the line

```
hosts: files dns nisplus nis
```

indicates that the */etc/hosts* file should be consulted first, and if a match cannot be found for a hostname, try DNS second. If DNS fails to resolve, then NIS+ should be tried. As a last resort, NIS map resolution can be attempted. This is a useful setup for a network that makes great use of the Internet and relies less on NIS+ and NIS. Of course, many NIS+ advocates would suggest using the line

```
hosts: nisplus nis files dns
```

since this ensures that NIS+ is always selected over the */etc/hosts* database or DNS.

In addition to host resolution, *nsswitch.conf* also allows the configuration of 14 other options, which roughly correspond to the contents of the NIS+ tables and/or the NIS maps. A NIS+ oriented *nsswitch.conf* file would look like this:

```
passwd:       files nisplus
group:        files nisplus
hosts:        nisplus dns [NOTFOUND=return] files
services:     nisplus [NOTFOUND=return] files
networks:     nisplus [NOTFOUND=return] files
protocols:    nisplus [NOTFOUND=return] files
rpc:          nisplus [NOTFOUND=return] files
ethers:       nisplus [NOTFOUND=return] files
netmasks:     nisplus [NOTFOUND=return] files
bootparams:   nisplus [NOTFOUND=return] files
publickey:    nisplus
netgroup:     nisplus
automount: nisplus files
aliases: nisplus files
sendmailvars: nisplus files
```

In most of the resolution scenarios shown in this listing, NIS+ is consulted before the files, except for the password and group information. In addition, DNS is listed as a host resolution method after NIS+. However, it would also be possible to implement a bare-bones system that relies only on files for most resource information and DNS for name resolution:

```
passwd:        files
group:         files
hosts:         dns [NOTFOUND=return] files
networks:      files
protocols:     files
rpc:           files
ethers:        files
netmasks:      files
bootparams:    files
publickey:     files
netgroup:      files
automount:     files
aliases:       files
services:      files
sendmailvars:    files
```

The [NOT FOUND=return] entry ensures that if the first source fails (*dns* in this case), the second source is consulted (in this case, files). Before any other services may be installed, NIS+ requires that the master server for the root domain be created. The master server will primarily be responsible for the management of the NIS+ namespace. For example, for the *Panther.Edu.* domain, the DNS server (*ns.panther.edu*) will also be used for NIS+. This means that the nisserver script can be executed on the DNS server system (*ns.panther.edu*) in order to initialize the master server for the root domain:

```
ns.panther.edu# nisserver -r -d Panther.Edu.
This script sets up this machine "ns" as an NIS+
root master server for domain Panther.Edu..

Domain name              : Panther.Edu.
NIS+ group               : admin.Panther.Edu.
NIS (YP) compatibility   : OFF
Security level           : 2=DES

Is this information correct? (type 'y' to accept, 'n' to change) y
This script will set up your machine as a root master server for
domain Panther.Edu. without NIS compatibility at security level 2.

Use "nisclient -r" to restore your current network service environment.

Do you want to continue? (type 'y' to continue, 'n' to exit this script)
```

```
setting up domain information "Panther.Edu." ...

setting up switch information ...

running nisinit ...
This machine is in the "Panther.Edu." NIS+ domain.
Setting up root server .

starting root server at security level 0 to create credentials...

running nissetup to create standard directories and tables ...

running nissetup to create standard directories and tables ...
org_dir.Panther.Edu. created
groups_dir.Panther.Edu. created
passwd.org_dir.Panther.Edu. created
group.org_dir.Panther.Edu. created
auto_master.org_dir.Panther.Edu. created
auto_home.org_dir.Panther.Edu. created
bootparams.org_dir.Panther.Edu. created
cred.org_dir.Panther.Edu. created
ethers.org_dir.Panther.Edu. created
hosts.org_dir.Panther.Edu. created
ipnodes.org_dir.Panther.Edu. created
mail_aliases.org_dir.Panther.Edu. created
sendmailvars.org_dir.Panther.Edu. created
netmasks.org_dir.Panther.Edu. created
netgroup.org_dir.Panther.Edu. created
networks.org_dir.Panther.Edu. created
protocols.org_dir.Panther.Edu. created
rpc.org_dir.Panther.Edu. created
services.org_dir.Panther.Edu. created
timezone.org_dir.Panther.Edu. created
client_info.org_dir.Panther.Edu. created
auth_attr.org_dir.Panther.Edu. created
exec_attr.org_dir.Panther.Edu. created
prof_attr.org_dir.Panther.Edu. created
user_attr.org_dir.Panther.Edu. created
audit_user.org_dir.Panther.Edu. created

adding credential for ns.Panther.Edu...
Enter login password:
creating NIS+ administration group: admin.Panther.Edu. ...
adding principal ns.Panther.Edu. to admin.Panther.Edu. ...

restarting NIS+ root master server at security level 2 ...
starting NIS+ password daemon ...
starting NIS+ cache manager ...
```

This system is now configured as a root server for domain Panther.Edu.

You can now populate the standard NIS+ tables by using the
nispopulate script or /usr/lib/nis/nisaddent command.

That's all that is required for NIS+ support. However, to enable support for NIS clients within the domain, you would need to use the following command instead:

ns.panther.edu# nisserver -Y -r -d Panther.Edu.

Command Reference

Now that you have reviewed the configuration of NIS+, and the main tables that are used to define a NIS+ domain, you are ready to examine how to use NIS+ effectively to manage hosts and resources within a domain. As you have seen, many different objects can be managed and identified within a NIS+ domain, and there are several commands that are used to access them:

- **nisdefaults**   Displays the NIS+ settings for the local client system
- **nischmod**   Used to set access rights on NIS+ objects
- **nisls**   Used to perform object lookups and queries
- **niscat**   Displays the contents of table entries and can be used to examine NIS+ objects in detail

nisdefaults

The current settings for a local client system and the active user can be displayed by using the nisdefaults command. The nisdefaults command is commonly used when attempting to troubleshoot an error, such as a user's credentials not being correctly authenticated from the *Passwd* table. As an example, take a look at the nisdefaults command for the host *comorin* when executed by the user *walter*:

```
comorin$ nisdefaults
Principal Name : walter.develop.panther.edu.
Domain Name    : develop.panther.edu.
Host Name      : comorin.develop.panther.edu.
Group Name     : develop
Access Rights  : ----rmcdr---r---
Time to live   : 11:00:00
Search Path    : develop.panther.edu. panther.edu.
```

The output of the nisdefaults command can be interpreted in the following way:

- The principal user is *walter*, who belongs to the NIS+ domain *develop.panther.edu*.
- The primary domain name is *develop.panther.edu*.

- The hostname of the local system is *comorin.develop.panther.edu*.
- The user *walter*'s primary group is *develop*.
- The time-to-live setting is *11* hours.
- The client's access rights within the domain are stated.
- The search path starts with the current nonroot domain (*develop.panther.edu*), followed by the root domain (*panther.edu*).

The access rights stated for the user in this example are outlined in more detail in the next section.

nischmod

Every user has a set of access rights for accessing objects within the network. The notation for setting and accessing object permissions is very similar to that used for Solaris file systems. The following permissions may be set on any object, or may be defined as the default settings for a particular client:

c	Sets create permission
d	Sets delete permission
m	Sets modify permission
r	Sets read permission

The `nischmod` command is used to set permissions on objects within the domain. The following operands are used to specify access rights for specific classes of users:

a	All (all authenticated and unauthenticated users)
g	Group
n	Nobody (all unauthenticated users)
o	Object owner
w	World (all authenticated users)

There are two operators that can be used to set and remove permissions:

+	Sets a permission
–	Removes a permission

Some examples of how permission strings are constructed will clarify how these operators and operands are combined for use with the `nischmod` command. The following command removes all modify (*m*) and create (*c*) access rights on the *Passwd* table for all unauthenticated (*n*) users:

```
moorea# nischmod n-cm passwd.org_dir
```

Even unauthenticated users require read (*r*) access to the *Passwd* table for authentication, which can be granted with the following command:

```
moorea# nischmod n+r passwd.org_dir
```

To grant modify (*m*) and create (*c*) access rights to the current user (in this case, root) and their primary group on the same table, you would use the command

```
moorea# nischmod og+cm passwd.org_dir
```

Although NIS+ permission strings are easy to remember, they are hard to combine into single commands in which some permissions are granted while others are removed, unlike the octal codes used to specify absolute permissions on Solaris file systems. However, it is possible to combine permission strings by using a comma to separate individual strings. The following complex-string example shows how to set permissions within a single string but equally shows how challenging it is to interpret:

```
moorea# nischmod o=rmcd,g=rmc,w=rm,n=r hosts.org_dir
```

This command grants the following permissions to four different categories of users:

owner	Read, modify, create, and delete
group	Read, modify, and create
world	Read and modify
nobody	Read only

nisls

The `nisls` command is used as a lookup and query command that can provide views on NIS+ directories and tables. For example, to view all the NIS+ directories that have been populated within the local namespace, you can use the `nisls` command:

```
moorea# nisls
develop.panther.edu.:
org_dir
groups_dir
```

There are two directory object types listed here: *org_dir*, which lists all the tables that have been set up within the namespace, and *groups_dir*, which stores details of all NIS+ groups. You can view a list of tables by using the `nisls` command once again on the *org_dir* directory:

```
moorea# nisls org_dir
org_dir.sales.panther.edu.:
```

```
auto_home
auto_master
bootparams
client_info
cred
ethers
group
hosts
mail_aliases
netgroup
netmasks
networks
passwd
protocols
rpc
sendmailvars
services
timezone
```

A large number of tables have been populated for this domain. The *groups* directory contains the *admin* group created earlier, which lists all the administrators, as well as several other groups that are based on distinct organizational units within the current domain:

```
moorea# nisls groups_dir
groups_dir.sales.panther.edu.:
admin
adverts
legal
media
```

niscat

The `niscat` command is used to retrieve the contents of objects within the domain—primarily the data contained within NIS+ tables. For example, all hosts listed within the domain can be listed by using the following command:

```
moorea$ niscat -h hosts.org_dir
moorea.panther.edu moorea 10.58.64.16
borabora.panther.edu borabora 10.58.64.17
tahiti.panther.edu tahiti 10.58.64.18
orana.panther.edu orana 10.58.64.19
```

Alternatively, you can use the `niscat` command to examine the contents of the *Passwd* table:

```
moorea$ niscat passwd.org_dir
moppet:*LK*:1001:1:moppet:/staff/moppet:/bin/tcsh:10910:-1:-1:-1:-1::0
```

```
miki:*LK*:1002:1:miki:/staff/miki:/bin/bash:10920:-1:-1:-1:-1::0
maya:*LK*:1003:1:maya:/staff/maya:/bin/sh:10930:-1:-1:-1:-1::0
paul:*LK*:1004:1:paul:/staff/paul:/bin/csh:10940:-1:-1:-1:-1::0
```

Next, you can examine which groups these users belong to by using the `niscat` command once again:

```
moorea$ niscat group.org_dir
root::0:root
staff::1:moppet,miki,maya,paul
bin::2:root,bin,daemon
sys:*:3:root,bin,sys,adm
adm::4:root,adm,daemon
uucp::5:root,uucp
mail::6:root
```

All of the hosts that form part of the local domain can be examined based on their Ethernet address, which is extracted from the *Ethers* table, as shown in the following example:

```
moorea$ niscat ethers.org_dir
1:4a:16:2f:13:b2 moorea.panther.edu.
1:02:1e:f4:61:2e borabora.panther.edu.
f4:61:2e:1:4a:16 tahiti.panther.edu.
2f:13:b2:1:02:1e orana.panther.edu.
```

To get an idea of the services that are offered to these hosts, you can examine the *Services* table:

```
moorea$ niscat services.org_dir
tcpmux tcpmux tcp 1
echo echo tcp 7
echo echo udp 7
discard discard tcp 9
discard sink tcp 9
discard null tcp 9
discard discard udp 9
discard sink udp 9
discard null udp 9
systat systat tcp 11
systat users tcp 11
daytime daytime tcp 13
daytime daytime udp 13
```

Every other table that is defined within the domain may be viewed by using the `niscat` command in this way.

Summary

In this chapter, you have examined how to configure the NIS and NIS+ naming services. While these are presently widely deployed in the enterprise, they will likely be replaced by LDAP or some other standard naming service in the future.

Lightweight Directory Access Protocol (LDAP)

L DAP is a "white pages" type of service, similar to the older X.500 standard for managing organization-wide directory information, for which it originally acted as a front end. X.500 was based on the "heavyweight" Directory Access Protocol (DAP), whereas LDAP, as a "lightweight" protocol, sits directly on top of TCP/IP. Operations on LDAP servers such as iPlanet Directory Server (iDS) are of two kinds: data management operations, which insert, update, or delete records, and queries, which retrieve authentication and identification tokens from the organization's database. In theory, the LDAP protocol allows for a lot of different types of data about individuals and groups to be stored, including sounds, images, and text.

In Solaris 8, only an LDAP client was supplied with the operating environment release, making it less attractive to use than NIS/NIS+, since a separate LDAP server had to be purchased and installed. However, Solaris 10 has integrated iDS into the core architecture, meaning that LDAP servers and clients can be installed and configured directly after and during installation, respectively. iDS is a key component of the iPlanet software suite, which provides centralized authentication and authorization services for other iPlanet applications, and for third-party applications. For example, access to the Internet mediated through the iPlanet Proxy Server can be gained only by being an attribute of a group defined within the local iDS database, demonstrating the key role that iDS plays in supporting enterprise applications. Similarly, access to scheduling and event notification facilities through the iPlanet Calendar Server can be provided only to users who are authenticated through the iDS database. Many Solaris applications can use LDAP for authentication and authorization.

iDS does not use a proprietary protocol to store user and group data or to communicate with clients: instead, iDS uses the LDAP standard to authenticate users. This is an open standard, meaning that a Solaris-based LDAP server can authenticate some Microsoft Windows clients. In addition, it means that iDS can act as a drop-in replacement for any other LDAP-compliant server, enabling you to standardize directory services across a single platform. Alternatively, multiple server types from different vendors can be combined to form an integrated solution. For example, you might choose to use iDS in mission-critical applications, because of its clustering and high-availability features, which might be overkill in other situations. It is also possible to use the LDAP client software supplied with Solaris to connect to an LDAP server running on a different platform.

Two key benefits to switching from NIS/NIS+ to LDAP are the ease of replication and the assurance of high availability. While NIS/NIS+ architecture is based on the idea of a primary server, backed up by some slaves, LDAP servers can be replicated across subnets and domains, to servers known as *replicas*, increasing the number of servers available for authoritative lookups and reducing the burden on any one server. In addition, updates occur rapidly between LDAP servers compared to an NIS/NIS+ architecture, which relies on uploads of all data between primary and slave servers.

Although LDAP has many features, the most important of which iDS implements, LDAP also has a number of limitations. It does not have an interface defined to store data in a relational database, nor does it store data internally in a relational way. Although queries can be performed on the directory, these are not performed by using a query language (like SQL). LDAP is better designed for a reference data environment, where the types of lookups are well defined and data updates are infrequent.

However, LDAP's power lies in its capability to store and manage names and data in a flexible way. While there are predefined schema elements, such as users and organizations, other elements can be added where necessary. In addition, developers can write client programs that can easily access the directory and retrieve authoritative data. Since most networked applications perform some kind of authentication, a single, centralized source of authentication data can be accessed, reducing administrative overhead.

This chapter examines how to configure LDAP servers and a wide range of client services.

Key Concepts

Since LDAP is a directory service, its basic data element is known as an *entry*. Like a phone book entry, there are a number of attributes that are associated with the entry, when regarded as an object. For example, a phone directory object has a surname, first name, address, and phone number, which together comprise a single entry when instantiated. The overall organization of entries in an LDAP directory is defined by a schema, which consists of a rule set that determines what attributes can be associated with different object types. Although it is possible to define your own schemas and data models, all LDAP servers support a standard schema that promotes interoperability and is the basis for the LDAP standard, as proposed in RFC 2307. Alternatively, your application can extend the standard schema with some additional object attributes, although these may not be accessible by other servers.

LDAP is used in Solaris 10 as a naming service that is compatible with existing NIS and NIS+ services. This allows integration at the present time, but also suggests future deprecation of the NIS and NIS+ services in Solaris. iDS contains a set of objects and their attributes that is able to store all of the data contained within NIS/NIS+ maps and tables. Additional schema data must also be stored within the LDAP directory to support client operations.

The directory structure for LDAP is arranged hierarchically, from a single top node within the Directory Information Tree (DIT), to as many levels of abstraction as are required to support an organization's directory requirements. The tree structure might, for example, be based on purely geographical information, with the top node representing a country, or it might be based on organizational lines, with the top node corresponding to a company name. All entries within the tree can be identified by their Distinguished Name (DN), and each attribute of the entry can be described as a Relative Distinguished Name (RDN). Figure 30-1 shows an example DIT, with all of the common elements found therein.

At the first level, the country, c, is defined as *US*, so the DN would simply be *c=US*. At the second level, the organization, o, is defined as *cassowary.net*, so the DN is defined as *dc=cassowary, dc=net, c=US*, where dc represents the Domain Component (DC). On the third level, the Organizational Unit, ou, is defined as *Engineering*, so the DN is defined as *ou=Engineering, dc=cassowary, dc=net, c=US*. On the fourth level, an individual user is identified by a Common Name (CN) of *Paul Watters*, and a corresponding UID of *paul*. Thus, the DN is *uid=paul, ou=Engineering, dc=cassowary, dc=net, c=US*. As you can see, it is possible to clearly distinguish individuals belonging to organizations and departments in specific countries from each other, by simply using a DN, if the DIT is defined at a fine-grained level, and assuming that no two users in the same department have exactly the same name.

iDS stores all data in LDIF (LDAP Data Interchange Format) files. This standard is used by all LDAP directory servers and many messaging systems to store user and group data. Thus, it is possible to export an LDIF file with an organization's data from a previous version of iDS and import it here. Alternatively, third-party products may be able to export LDIF files that can also be read into iDS, to initialize the directory

FIGURE 30-1

Example Directory Information Tree (DIT)

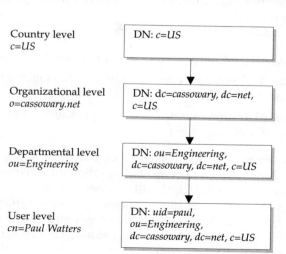

Country level
c=US

DN: *c=US*

Organizational level
o=cassowary.net

DN: *dc=cassowary, dc=net, c=US*

Departmental level
ou=Engineering

DN: *ou=Engineering, dc=cassowary, dc=net, c=US*

User level
cn=Paul Watters

DN: *uid=paul, ou=Engineering, dc=cassowary, dc=net, c=US*

PART VI

structure. The following is an example entry in an LDIF file for the directory entry previously defined:

```
dn: cn=Paul Watters, o=cassowary.net, c=US
cn: Paul Watters
sn: Watters
mail: paul@cassowary.net
objectClass: people
```

As you can see, the LDIF file structure simply reflects the attributes that are defined within the directory, written sequentially to the file immediately following the DN.

Procedures

The following procedures are required to configure directory services.

Configuring iDS

Configuring iDS is a two-stage process: the first stage involves installing and configuring the server to run iDS, and the second stage involves setting up iDS to support LDAP clients (as described in the next section). To begin the process of configuring the server to run iDS, you must execute the `directoryserver` program:

```
# /usr/sbin/directoryserver setup
```

You can install either iDS or the standalone iPlanet Console. After selecting iDS, you are presented with three different installation options: Express, which presents few opportunities for customization but is very fast; Typical, which offers some configuration before installation; and Custom, which offers maximum flexibility but is the slowest installation method.

Three packages comprise the iDS installation:

- **Server Core Components**   Comprises all the common objects used by iDS
- **iPlanet Directory Suite**   Contains the management console and the iDS software
- **Administration Server**   Contains packages for system administration and directory management

After selecting the appropriate packages to install, you need to indicate whether the current installation will store configuration information, or whether this will be stored in another server. If data will be stored in another server, then you must enter the hostname, port number, directory manager/administrator username, and password so that the correct target iDS installation for configuration can be identified.

Following the selection of the configuration iDS target, you need to indicate whether the current installation will store user and group information, or whether this will be stored in another server. Again, if data will be stored in another server, then you must enter the hostname, port number, DN, password, and suffix so that the correct target iDS installation for user and group data can be identified.

Next, you need to set up the new iDS server with a unique server identifier, a port number that is not used by any other application, and the appropriate suffix for the local installation. The default port number for LDAP is 389, while LDAP over SSL typically runs on port 636.

Next, you must select and enter the administrator ID and password for the local iDS installation. This ID and password are also used to manage the local LDAP server via the management console. Since the administrator ID and password can be used to gain access to the iDS server, and modify user and group data without restriction, it's important that you choose these credentials carefully, to avoid easy guessing by rogue users.

The Administration Domain must be entered next. Since iDS can manage multiple domains simultaneously from a single server, you must keep their data functionally and physically separate. Typically, the Administration Domain matches the Internet domain name. However, each server needs to have a separate Administration Domain if it is located underneath a top-level domain. For example, if there are two separate iDS servers running in the *cassowary.net* domain, one for Engineering and one for Sales, then the Administration Domains could be named *engineering.cassowary.net* and *sales .cassowary.net*, respectively.

Next, you must select and enter the directory manager's password for the local iDS installation. Since the Directory Manager ID and password can be used to gain access to the iDS server, and modify user and group data with few restrictions, you must choose these credentials carefully, to avoid dictionary-based cracking.

The iDS Administration Server is used to manage all aspects of the LDAP service. The Administration Server runs as a Web server, meaning that you can use any HTML browser to view and configure all current settings for the iDS Administration Server. You must choose a port to access the iDS Administration Server. The URL for the Administration Server is then given by appending the port number with a colon to the hostname. For example, the URL **http://ldap.cassowary.net:38575/** suggests an LDAP server running on port 38575 of the host *ldap.cassowary.net*.

Supporting LDAP Clients

In order to configure iDS to provide services to clients, you use the `idsconfig` command. You can either manually enter the service configuration on the command line or supply it from an external file by passing the *–i* option. Alternatively, a configuration file from one system (generated by passing the *–o* option) can also be read in from an external file. If multiple iDS instances are installed, then configuration information from the first installation can be used by subsequent installations. You can start `idsconfig` with the following command:

```
# /usr/lib/ldap/idsconfig
```

The following output shows a sample `idsconfig` session for *sales.cassowary.net*. In the first section, you are required to review the basic configuration of the directory service, including the port number, directory manager DN, and its password:

```
Enter the port number for iDS (h=help): [389]
Enter the directory manager DN: [cn=Directory Manager]
Enter passwd for cn=Directory Manager :
Enter the domainname to be served (h=help): [sales.cassowary.net]
```

Next, you need to review the directory and server details, including the base DN, profile name, and list of servers:

```
Enter LDAP BaseDN (h=help): [dc=sales,dc=cassowary,dc=net]
Enter the profile name (h=help): [default]
Are you sure you want to overwrite profile cn=default? y
Default server list (h=help): [192.64.18.1]
Preferred server list (h=help):
Choose desired search scope (one, sub, h=help): [one]
```

You must make security choices next, including the credential level and authentication method:

```
The following are the supported credential levels:
1 anonymous
2 proxy
3 proxy anonymous
Choose Credential level [h=help]: [1] 1
The following are the supported Authentication Methods:
1 none
2 simple
3 sasl/DIGEST-MD5
4 tls:simple
5 tls:sals/DIGEST-MD5
Choose Authentication Method (h=help): [1] 2
Current authenticationMethod: simple
Do you want to add another Authentication Method? N
```

Note that setting credential levels and authentication methods is a major decision, and these settings are difficult to roll back after installation. After reviewing the server configuration, you now need to configure client access. This includes setting timeouts for profile and directory access, password formats, and time and size limits:

```
Do you want the clients to follow referrals (y/n/h)? [n] n
Do you want to modify the server timelimit value (y/n/h)? [n] n
Do you want to modify the server sizelimit value (y/n/h)? [n] n
Do you want to store passwd's in "crypt" format (y/n/h)? [n] y
Do you want to setup a Service Authentication Method (y/n/h)? [n] n
Search time limit in seconds (h=help): [60]
```

```
Profile Time To Live in seconds (h=help): [3600]
Bind time limit in seconds (h=help): [10] 2
Do you wish to setup Service Search Descriptors (y/n/h)? [n] n
```

Finally, you are presented with a configuration summary, before any actions are performed by `idsconfig`:

```
Summary of Configuration
1 Domain to serve : sales.cassowary.net
2 BaseDN to setup : dc=sales,dc=cassowary,dc=net
3 Profile name to create : default
4 Default Server List : 192.64.18.1
5 Preferred Server List :
6 Default Search Scope : one
7 Credential Level : anonymous
8 Authentication Method : simple
9 Enable Follow Referrals : FALSE
10 iDS Time Limit :
11 iDS Size Limit :
12 Enable crypt passwd storage : 1
13 Service Auth Method pam_ldap :
14 Service Auth Method keyserv :
15 Service Auth Method passwd-cmd:
16 Search Time Limit : 30
17 Profile Time to Live : 43200
18 Bind Limit : 2
19 Service Search Descriptors Menu
```

Creating LDAP Entries

The `ldapaddent` command is used to create entries in the LDAP container for all of the standard system databases stored in files underneath the */etc* directory. All of the following Solaris databases (with the corresponding ou) can be transferred into LDAP by this method:

- *aliases (ou=Aliases)*
- *bootparams (ou=Ethers)*
- *ethers* (requires *bootparams* database to be installed first) *(ou=Ethers)*
- *group (ou=Group)*
- *hosts (ou=Hosts)*
- *netgroup (ou=Netgroup)*
- *netmasks* (requires *networks* database to be installed first) *(ou=Networks)*
- *networks (ou=Networks)*
- *passwd (ou=People)*
- *shadow* (requires *passwd* database to be installed first) *(ou=People)*

- *protocols (ou=Protocols)*
- *publickey (ou=Hosts)*
- *rpc (ou=Rpc)*
- *services (ou=Services)*

A simple script can be created to automate the process of adding each of these databases to LDAP, when the bindDN password is supplied on the command line:

```
#!/bin/sh
ldapaddent -D "cn=directory manager" -w $1 -f /etc/aliases aliases
ldapaddent -D "cn=directory manager" -w $1 -f /etc/bootparams bootparams
ldapaddent -D "cn=directory manager" -w $1 -f /etc/ethers ethers
ldapaddent -D "cn=directory manager" -w $1 -f /etc/group group
ldapaddent -D "cn=directory manager" -w $1 -f /etc/hosts hosts
ldapaddent -D "cn=directory manager" -w $1 -f /etc/netgroup netgroup
ldapaddent -D "cn=directory manager" -w $1 -f /etc/networks networks
ldapaddent -D "cn=directory manager" -w $1 -f /etc/netmasks netmasks
ldapaddent -D "cn=directory manager" -w $1 -f /etc/passwd passwd
ldapaddent -D "cn=directory manager" -w $1 -f /etc/shadow shadow
ldapaddent -D "cn=directory manager" -w $1 -f /etc/protocols protocols
ldapaddent -D "cn=directory manager" -w $1 -f /etc/publickey publickey
ldapaddent -D "cn=directory manager" -w $1 -f /etc/rpc rpc
ldapaddent -D "cn=directory manager" -w $1 -f /etc/services services
```

This script can be used on all client systems that will use LDAP.

Starting a Client

The `ldapclient` program can be used for several purposes, including to start LDAP client services on client systems and to review the LDAP cache. In order to initialize a client, you must enter on the command line the address of the LDAP server, where its profile is stored. The LDAP cache manager (`ldap_cachemgr`) is responsible for ensuring that the correct configuration data is returned to a client upon initialization, especially if changes have been made to the profile. One of the following subcommands must be supplied on the command line to specify the behavior of `ldapclient`:

- **genprofile**   Creates an LDIF format configuration file that can be exported to another system, or imported at some future time
- **init**   Initializes an LDAP client from an LDAP server using a profile
- **list**   Prints a list of entries stored in the client cache to standard output
- **manual**   Initializes an LDAP client from an LDAP server using parameters specified on the command line
- **mod**   Permits the modification of parameter values after initialization has been completed
- **uninit**   Uninitializes an LDAP client from an LDAP server

The following parameters can be modified by using the `ldapclient mod` command, or passed directly for manual initialization using the `ldapclient manual` command:

- *attributeMap*   Used to modify the default schema for a specific service.

- *authenticationMethod*   Stipulates the authentication method to be used (none, simple, sasl/CRAM-MD5, sasl/DIGEST-MD5, tls:simple, tls:sasl/CRAM-MD5, or tls:sasl/DIGEST-MD5). None means no security at all, while simple means that a password is sent in the clear and thus is vulnerable to interception. The other methods use a message digest algorithm to enhance security.

- *bindTimeLimit*   Specifies the maximum number of seconds allowed for a bind operation to be performed.

- *certificatePath*   Specifies the full path to the certificate database.

- *credentialLevel*   Specifies the type of credential required for authentication (either anonymous or proxy).

- *defaultSearchBase*   Specifies the baseDN for searching.

- *defaultSearchScope*   Determines the scope for searching on the client side.

- *domainName*   Specifies the Fully Qualified Domain Name.

- *followReferrals*   Determines whether the referral setting is used for DIT partitioning.

- *objectclassMap*   Designates a different schema.

- *preferredServerList*   Lists a set of alternative LDAP servers to be contacted prior to the default.

- *profileName*   Determines the name of the client profile.

- *profileTTL*   Specifies the refresh epoch for the client cache to obtain new information from the server.

- *proxyDN*   Specifies the DN for the proxy server.

- *proxyPassword*   States the password for the proxy server.

- *searchTimeLimit*   Restricts the amount of time for each LDAP search.

- *serviceAuthenticationMethod*   Determines the authentication method for the `passwd-cmd`, `keyserv`, and `pam_ldap` services.

- *serviceCredentialLevel*   Specifies the type of credential required for service authentication (either anonymous or proxy). Proxy access for clients can occur only if a proxy account has previously been created in the directory and the *proxyDN* and *proxyPassword* attributes have been defined. Anonymous is not recommended, since it provides no security at all.

- *serviceSearchDescriptor*   Allows a different baseDN to be specified on a per-service basis.

Some examples follow of how LDAP clients can be initialized by using `ldapclient`. In the first example, the LDAP server 192.64.18.1 will be used to initialize the local client by using the `init` subcommand:

```
# ldapclient init 192.64.18.1
```

No additional parameters are necessary. However, a manual installation is much more complex, as all nondefault parameters must be specified. Sometimes, only a single parameter will differ from the default: for example, if simple authentication was required, instead of no authentication (the default), the following command would be used:

```
# ldapclient manual -a authenticationMethod=simple \
          -a defaultServerList=192.64.18.1
```

Alternatively, if you need to specify a higher-level search base, you could use the following command:

```
# ldapclient manual -a authenticationMethod=simple \
          -a defaultSearchBase=dc=cassowary,dc=net       \
          -a defaultServerList=192.64.18.1
```

To generate an LDIF format configuration file, you would use the `genprofile` subcommand and redirect the output to a file (*/tmp/default.ldif*):

```
# ldapclient genprofile -a profileName=default \
-a defaultSearchBase=dc=cassowary,dc=net       \
-a defaultServerList=192.64.18.1      \
> /tmp/default.ldif
```

Using the LDAP-NIS+ Interface

The `nisldapmaptest` command is used to operate on data stored within LDAP by using an NIS+ interface. This is particularly important when testing to see that NIS+ and LDAP services are correctly integrated. It can also be useful for experienced NIS+ administrators who want to add, delete, or modify LDAP records by using a familiar NIS+ interface. There are several options that can be passed to the `nisldapmaptest` command, including

- *–d* Enables deletion of data
- *–r* Updates data or adds new data
- *–s* Searches for existing data
- *–t* Contains the name of the target NIS+ object

Some examples of using `nisldapmaptest` follow. First, to determine whether a user entry (*pwatters*) exists in the password table, use the following:

```
# nisldapmaptest -t passwd.org_dir name=pwatters
```

Any of the following tables can be queried in this way:

- *auto_home*
- *auto_master*
- *bootparams*
- *client_info*
- *cred*
- *ethers*
- *group*
- *hosts*
- *mail_aliases*
- *netgroup*
- *netmasks*
- *networks*
- *passwd*
- *protocols*
- *rpc*
- *sendmailvars*
- *services*
- *timezone*

For example, to obtain a list of hosts stored in the *hosts* table, you would use the following command:

```
# nisldapmaptest -t hosts.org_dir
```

If an invalid host was found in the table, you could delete it by using the following command:

```
# nisldapmaptest -d -t hosts.org_dir name=oldhost
```

Example

This example demonstrates how to manage iDS by using the console. Once the iDS server has been installed, you should be able to start the console by using the following command:

```
# directoryserver startconsole
```

The appropriate admin port number and hostname will be displayed on the login window, as shown in the following illustration. In this case, 14462 is the admin port for the LDAP server that was specified during install. You must enter the administration user ID and corresponding password to open the main administration server window.

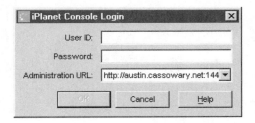

The main iDS console is then displayed, as shown in Figure 30-2. The two main functions of the console are organized into two tabs: Servers and Applications, and Users and Groups.

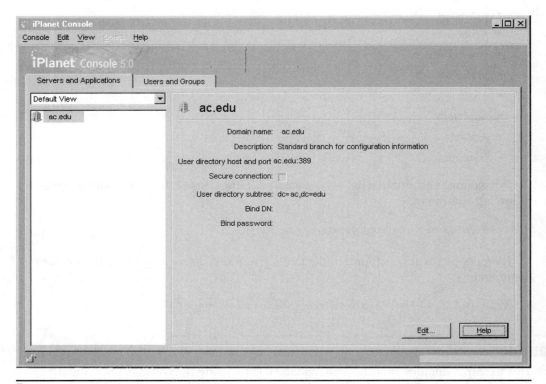

FIGURE 30-2   Main console window

The Servers and Applications tab has two separate panes. The first pane is a hierarchical object list of all servers and their respective databases that have been configured for the network. The local server group is displayed, along with entries for the local administration server and the actual directory server. By clicking the icon associated with the localhost, the hostname, description, physical location, platform, and operating system are displayed. Clicking the server group icon displays the group name, description, and installation path.

The second pane shows the domain name, description, port number, and user directory structure for the iDS server. In addition, the DN and password are displayed, as well as an option to encrypt connections to the server. You can edit these details by clicking the Edit button.

By clicking the Directory Server icon in the Servers and Applications tab, a list of configured items for the local server is displayed, as shown in Figure 30-3. For example, the server name, description, installation date, product name, vendor name, version number, build number, revision level, security level, server status, and port are all displayed. Again, you can edit all of these entries by clicking the Edit button.

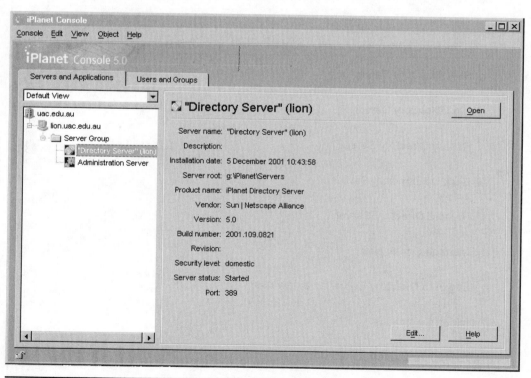

FIGURE 30-3   Main directory server window

By double-clicking the Directory Server icon, a new window is displayed, as shown in Figure 30-4, which is used to configure the directory server's operation. There are four tabs available, each with a number of different operations, but only Tasks and Configuration are relevant. The Tasks tab defines nine different operations:

- **Start Directory Server**   Initializes the local iDS server and launches it.
- **Stop Directory Server**   Shuts down all local services and stops the iDS processes.
- **Restart Directory Server**   Shuts down all local services, stops the iDS processes, initializes the local iDS server, and relaunches it.
- **Back Up Directory Server**   Backs up the local iDS database.
- **Restore Directory Server**   Restores the local iDS database from a backup.

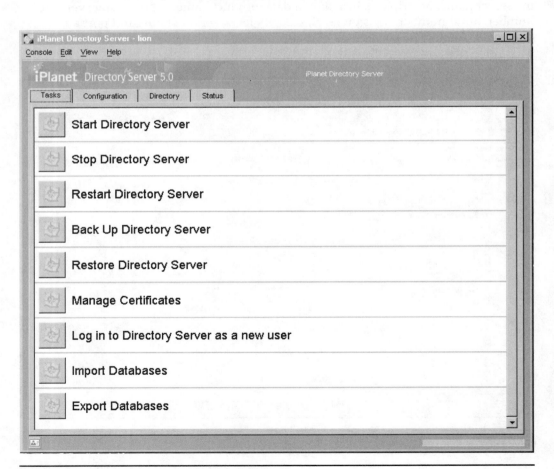

FIGURE 30-4   Directory server configuration window

- **Manage Certificates** Manages certificates for security.
- **Log In to Directory Server as a New User** Logs in to iDS as a different user.
- **Import Databases** Imports a new iDS database from a different system.
- **Export Databases** Exports an existing local iDS database to a different system.

The Configuration tab contains a hierarchical list of objects associated with the iDS database, including tables, replication features, the database schema, logs, and optional plug-ins. In addition, a set of tabs allows you to configure various options. The Settings subtab allows you to set the unencrypted port, encrypted port, and referrals, as shown in Figure 30-5. In addition, you can set up the server as read-only and track entry modification times and various schema checks.

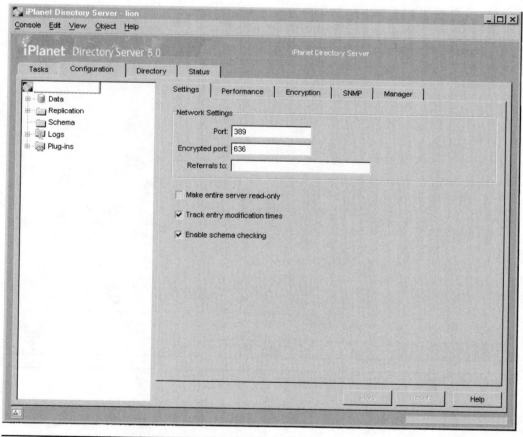

FIGURE 30-5   Settings configuration window

The Performance subtab sets limits on the size of the directory, a time limit for access, and an idle timeout, as shown in Figure 30-6. These settings need to be modified for local use, but are set at 2000 entries, one hour, and zero, respectively.

The Encryption subtab has two main tasks: setting options for server security and setting options for client authentication, as shown in Figure 30-7. On the server side, access can be granted using SSL, thereby protecting authentication tokens from interception by a third party. In this case, you need to set RSA options, including the name of the

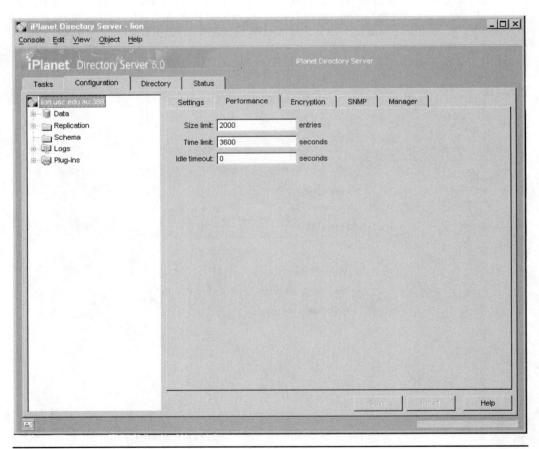

FIGURE 30-6   Performance configuration window

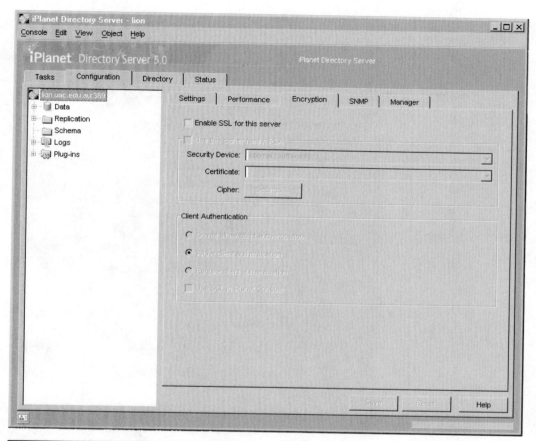

FIGURE 30-7   Encryption configuration window

security device (by default, internal/software-based), the certificate location, and the cipher. On the client side, authentication can be disallowed, allowed, or required, depending on the application's requirements. In addition, using SSL can be made mandatory within the iPlanet console.

The SNMP subtab, as shown in Figure 30-8, provides an interface to the Simple Network Management Protocol, allowing you to monitor service status remotely by using a third-party SNMP monitoring product. When alarm events are triggered

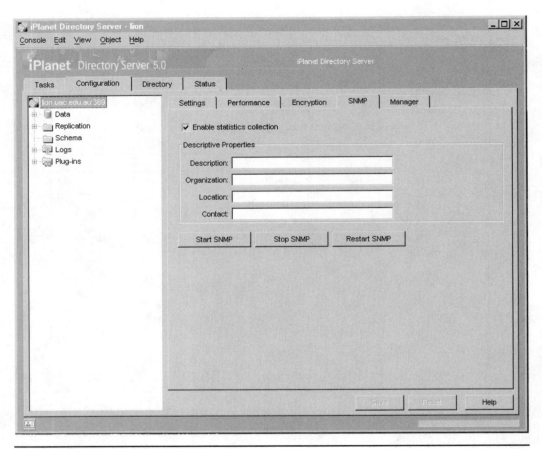

FIGURE 30-8   SNMP configuration window

because of run-time errors, you and other administration staff can be notified by pager, phone, or e-mail, enabling you to quickly take appropriate action to rectify the problem. The SNMP tab also enables you to enter descriptive properties, including the organization, location, and support contact, and start, stop, or restart the service by clicking the corresponding three buttons.

The Manager subtab, as shown in Figure 30-9, sets several options for the Directory Manager role. This includes the DN of the Directory Manager, the algorithm used to encrypt the Directory Manager's password (by default, the Salted Secure Hashing

Algorithm, SSHA), and the Directory Manager's password. You can also choose and confirm a new password by entering it into the New Password field Confirm Password field.

You can configure the administration server by double-clicking the Administration Server icon in the Servers and Applications tab, which produces the window shown here:

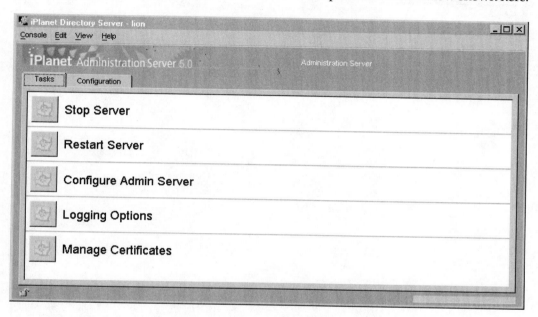

This window is used to configure the administration server's operation. Two tabs are available, each with a number of different operations. The Tasks tab defines five different operations:

- **Start Server**   Initializes the local iDS server and launches it.
- **Restart Server**   Shuts down all local services, stops the iDS processes, initializes the local iDS server, and relaunches it.
- **Configure Admin Server**   Configures the local administration server.
- **Logging Options**   Sets up local logging options.
- **Manage Certificates**   Manages certificates for security.

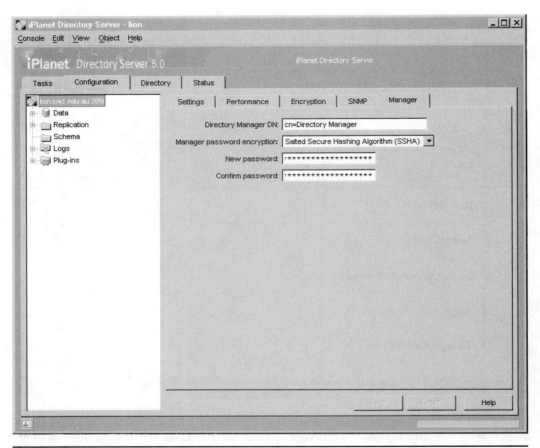

FIGURE 30-9   Manager configuration window

The console provides an interface for querying the directory and for adding new entries at the user, group, and OU levels. The search facility allows you to enter a search string that consists of a full or partial username, group name, or OU. For example, to find the user Paul Watters in the directory, you could search on "Paul" or "Watters". Figure 30-10 shows the searching interface and the result of a search on "watters" (no

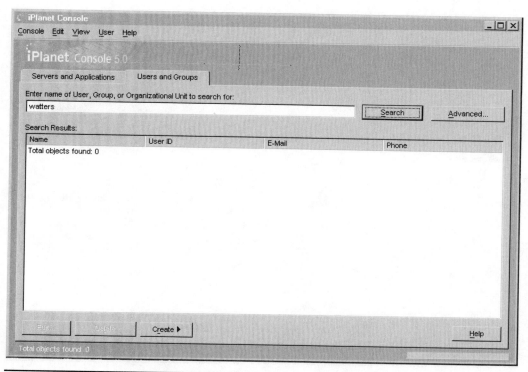

FIGURE 30-10   Searching the directory

matches were found in the directory). If a match had been found, the name, user ID, e-mail address, and phone number would have been displayed. In addition, you can modify each entry found as the result of a search by clicking the Edit button.

If an entry is not found, it can be searched for by clicking the Create button, as shown in Figure 30-11. A drop-down list of all possible entry types is shown, including users, groups, and OUs.

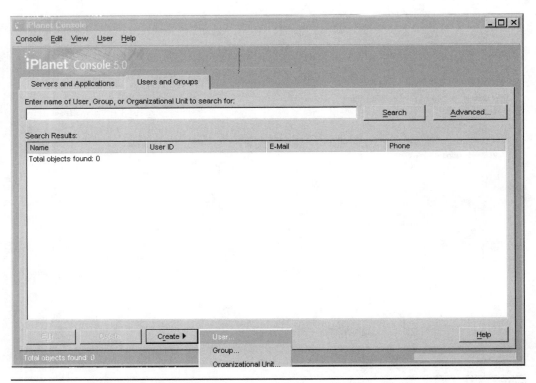

FIGURE 30-11   Adding a directory entry

After choosing to create a new user, group, or OU, you need to indicate the directory subtree under which the entry will appear, as shown in the following illustration. There are four options: Base DN (i.e., the top level of the directory), Groups, People (users), or Special Users.

You can create a new user by using the Create User screen, as shown in Figure 30-12. You may enter the user's first name, last name, common name, user ID, password, e-mail address, phone number, and fax number into their respective fields. In addition, a target language can be entered for the user, and Windows NT or POSIX-specific user data can be stored. Since this iDS installation is based on Solaris, POSIX should be selected.

Once you have entered the user's details, return to the user search screen, enter in the name of the user whose details have been stored, and you should be able to retrieve their complete record, as shown in Figure 30-13. Once retrieved, you can modify the user's details or delete their record.

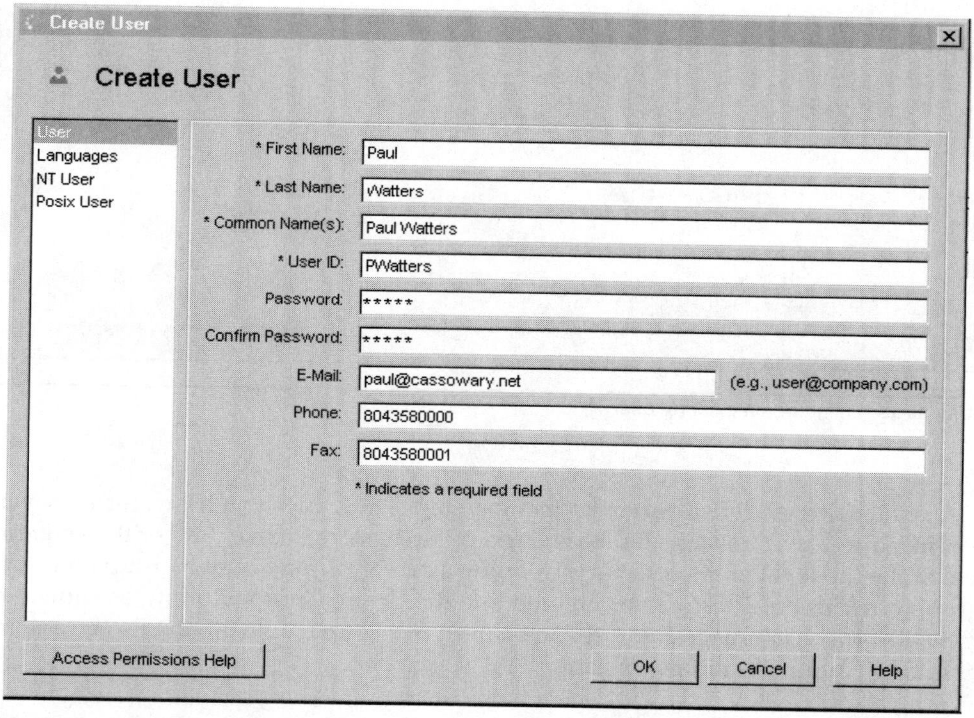

FIGURE 30-12   Creating a new user

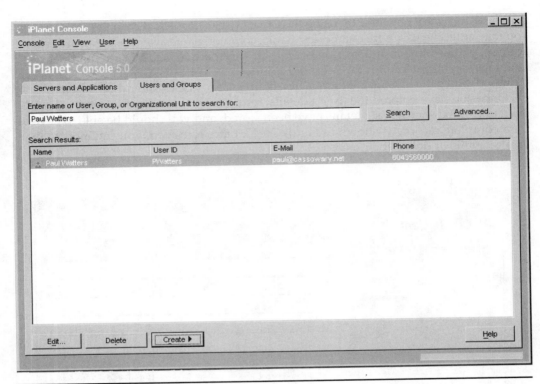

FIGURE 30-13 Finding an existing user

A key user characteristic is group membership. Thus, after you have created several users in a directory, it makes sense to create a group to store them in, rather than entering them at the top level of the directory. Defining a new group requires a group name and a group description. These can be entered into the Create Group window, as shown in Figure 30-14. The languages required to be used by group members can also be entered by clicking Languages in the left pane.

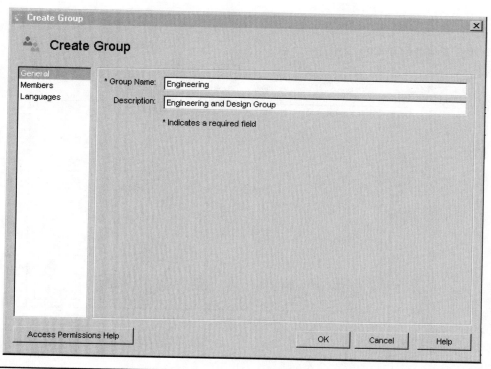

FIGURE 30-14   Creating a group

Once a group has been defined, you can add members individually by clicking Members in the left pane and clicking the Add button, as shown in Figure 30-15. Alternatively, group members, once created using this screen, can be easily removed by clicking the Remove button.

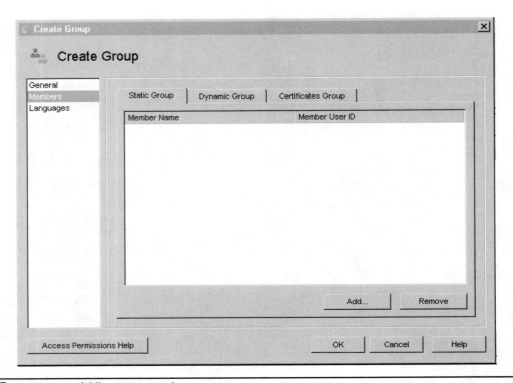

FIGURE 30-15   Adding group members

After members have been added to groups, it's then possible to search on a user and group basis, rather than just on a user basis, as shown in Figure 30-16. The search string can either be a group name or a username. Once group members have been selected on the basis of the search term, their details are displayed sorted by name, with user ID, e-mail address, and phone number also appearing.

At the top level, you can define a new OU. The OU's entry can contain its name, a description, phone number, fax number, alias, and full address, as shown in Figure 30-17. In addition, you can define the language support required for the OU by clicking Languages in the left pane.

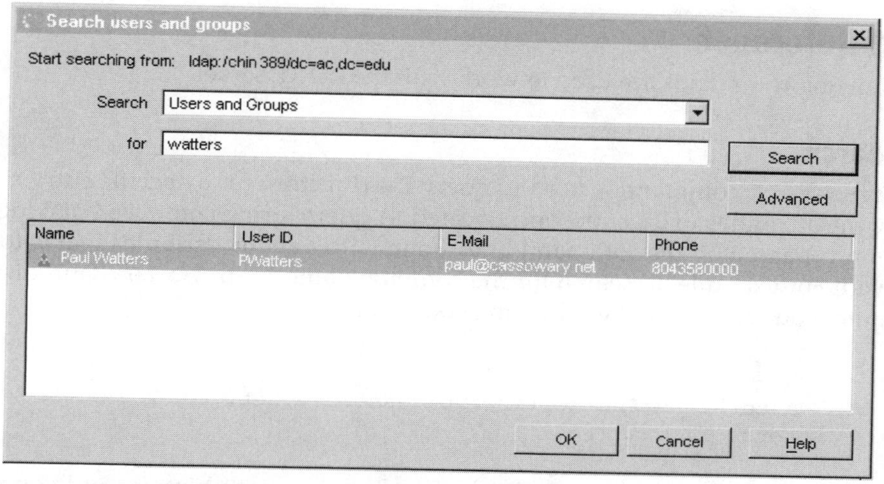

FIGURE 30-16   Searching users and groups

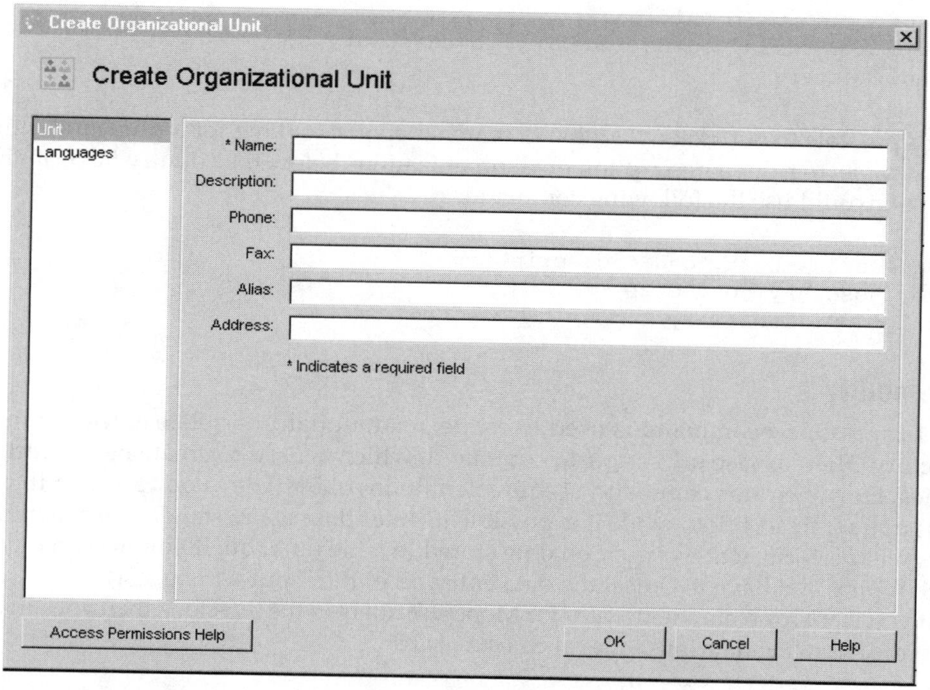

FIGURE 30-17   Creating an OU

Command Reference

The following commands are used to work with the LDAP server.

ldapsearch

The `ldapsearch` command is used to query the directory for a specific entry and to display the attributes of an entry once located. A query string composed of a logical condition is passed on the command line, along with a set of attributes that is to be displayed. For example, to search for the common name "Paul Watters" and display the results, you would use the following command:

```
$ ldapsearch -u "cn=Paul Watters" cn
cn=Paul A Watters, ou=Engineering, o=cassowary.net, c=US
cn=Paul Watters
```

Alternatively, if you know the UID of the user you are searching for and you want to look up the common name, you could use the following command:

```
$ ldapsearch -u -t "uid=paul" cn
cn=Paul A Watters, ou=Engineering, o=cassowary.net, c=US
cn=Paul Watters
```

It's possible to perform a wider area search than just looking for a single individual. For example, to print a description of all organizations below the country "US" in the DIT, you would use the following command:

```
$ ldapsearch -L -b "c=US" description
dn: o=cassowary.net, c=US
description: Cassowary Computing Pty Ltd
```

ldapmodify

The `ldapmodify` command is used to create, read, update, or delete entries in the directory. There is also an `ldapadd` command, which is used to create new directory entries. However, this command is equivalent to invoking `ldapmodify` with the *–a* (add) option. In addition, while it is possible to enter data using standard input, most users will perform actions based on data stored in a file (after all, if you make a mistake when typing and have to cancel the data entry, all of the input will be lost).

If you want to create a new entry for Moppet Watters in the directory, then you should insert the following data into a file called *newdata.txt*:

```
dn: cn=Moppet Watters, o=cassowary.net, c=US
objectClass: person
cn: Mopster Watters
sn: Watters
```

```
title: Mascot
mail: moppet@cassowary.net
uid: moppet
```

To insert this data into the directory, you would use the following command:

```
# ldapmodify -a -f newdata.txt
```

To delete this entry from the directory, you would first insert the following data into *delentry.txt*:

```
dn: cn=Moppet Watters, o=cassowary.net, c=US
changetype=delete
```

Then, you could delete the entry from the directory by using the following command:

```
# ldapmodify -f delentry.txt
```

Summary

In this chapter, you have learned how to configure the Solaris LDAP server. LDAP will almost certainly replace NIS/NIS+ in the future, so it's worthwhile planning to transition existing directory services to the new platform.

CHAPTER

Samba

One of the most commonly used file- and print-sharing protocols is the Server Message Block (SMB) protocol, developed by Microsoft, and used extensively in Windows systems. SMB allows file systems and printers to be shared with a number of remote clients, with full access rights. For example, in a Windows NT domain, printing access rights to networked printers may be granted, but read-only access rights may be provided to a shared CD-ROM on the server. It is also possible to mount remotely exported file systems as virtual local drives, making it easy to integrate centralized data storage with local data management systems (such as databases). Fortunately, Solaris supports SMB networking through the Samba suite of programs, which even includes a NetBIOS name service.

This chapter examines how you can use Samba to share Solaris 10 file systems and printers with any client that supports SMB networking, including Windows, Linux, and MacOS clients. This means that you can use Solaris 10 as a reliable, centralized file server, replacing unreliable servers running other operating systems. Although Samba had to be installed as a third-party package in previous versions of Solaris, Solaris 10 includes Samba 3. In this chapter, you will learn how to export file systems, share printers, and share file systems between Samba servers.

Key Concepts

The key concepts of installing, configuring, and tuning Samba are discussed in this section.

Samba Server

Samba is a package that makes it easy to bring the Windows and Solaris networking environments closer together. Although both Windows and Solaris support standard TCP/IP networking, both Microsoft and Sun have tended to develop their own versions of file system and printer sharing. Windows Explorer, shown in Figure 31-1, is used to create combined views of all local and remote file systems within a domain. The example given shows two local drives (C and D), a local CD-ROM drive, as well as the computer

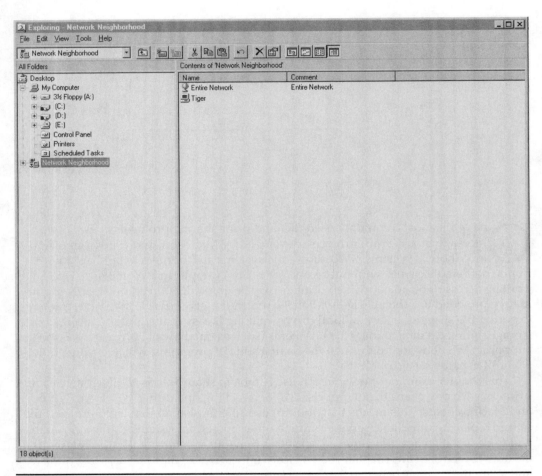

FIGURE 31-1   Viewing the Network Neighborhood in Microsoft Windows Explorer

Tiger, as shown in the Network Neighborhood. If the entry for *Tiger* were expanded, several shared disks could potentially be mounted, if access rights were granted to the local user for the remote volumes, through Security Access Manager (SAM). In addition, printers attached to *Tiger* could be accessed, and print jobs could be managed using the Printers control panel.

Figure 31-2 shows how easy it is to share file systems using Windows 2000: you simply right-click the drive you want to share in the Explorer window, select the Sharing tab, and define the authentication procedures and access rights for the shared volume. Consumer versions of Windows, such as XP, have a slightly different perspective, but the underlying operations are similar.

FIGURE 31-2
Sharing a drive
in Microsoft
Windows 2000

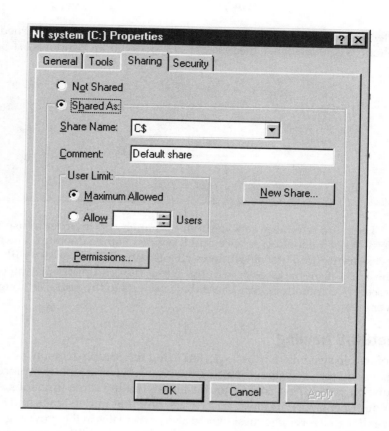

In contrast, Sun developed the Network File System (NFS) protocol, which also allows file systems and printers to be shared with other clients. There are even Windows-based NFS clients that allow Windows clients to access Solaris NFS shares. However, the choice between using NFS and Samba in a heterogeneous network may be one of cost (PC-NFS costs money, Samba is free), but is more likely a question of numbers: Would you rather install NFS client software on hundreds of Windows systems that already have SMB support or install a single SMB-compliant server (like Samba)? Using Samba as a centralized Windows server reduces the need to buy extra server licenses for file and print servers, because these functions could be provided by a Solaris Intel or Solaris SPARC system running Samba. Samba also runs on Linux systems.

The following illustration shows a concrete example of how Samba can be useful on the (Microsoft Windows) client side: a remote file system (*elp**servlets*) being exported using Samba running on Solaris allows a Microsoft Windows user to map a local drive letter (K) to that file system. As far as the Windows client is concerned, the Solaris Samba volume is equivalent to a file system being shared from Windows NT Server or equivalent.

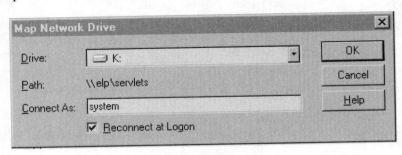

There are two main services that you must run in order to use Samba: the nmbd NetBIOS name lookup service and the smbd Samba daemon. The NetBIOS service is necessary to "find" local Windows clients and all SMB servers within the local domain. The smbd daemon takes care of the actual file- and print-sharing operations. A new process is created for every client that connects to the smbd, although only one nmbd is ever created.

NetBIOS Naming

Before file systems may be exported using the Samba daemon, you need to locate the client and server systems by using the NetBIOS name lookup protocol. The nmbd service runs on port 137 on Solaris, and it carries out the same functions as NetBIOS naming under Microsoft Windows. nmbd is a server that understands and can reply to NetBIOS over IP name service requests. nmbd also participates in the browsing protocols that make up the Windows Network Neighborhood view. In addition, you can use nmbd as a WINS (Windows Internet Name Server) server for resolution of hostnames. You can best gain an insight into how this operates by looking at some of the Windows NT commands that you can use to browse SMB shares and compare these commands with the equivalent Linux commands that perform the same tasks.

In order to view a list of client systems that are currently accessing a Windows NT Server system, you would use this command:

```
C:\WINNT\SYSTEM32>nbtstat -s
```

The following output would then be displayed:

```
                  NetBIOS Connection Table

Local Name   State      In/Out   Remote Host        Input    Output
---------------------------------------------------------------------
SYDNEY <00>  Connected  Out      HUNTER    <20>     101KB    15KB
SYDNEY <00>  Connected  Out      MELBOURNE  <20>     1MB     100MB
SYDNEY <00>  Connected  Out      WGONG     <20>     203KB    205KB
```

This output states that the server called SYDNEY is serving the remote systems HUNTER, MELBOURNE, and WGONG. You can examine how much data has been uploaded and downloaded to and from the server by looking at the *Input/Output* column. In the case of HUNTER, the input is greater than the output, whereas for MELBOURNE, the output greatly exceeds the input, which would be expected of a file-serving system. In contrast, WGONG has approximately similar levels of input and output.

In order to "view" all of the hosts available for connections within a specific Windows NT domain, you can use the `net view` command:

```
C:\WINNT\SYSTEM32>net view
```

This produces output similar to the following:

```
Server Name              Remark

-------------------------------------------------------
\\HUNTER      Regional Server
\\SYDNEY      Capital Server
\\WGONG       Regional Server
\\BRISBANE    Capital Server
\\BATHURST    Web Server
\\ORANGE      Web Server
\\DINGO       Kerberos Server
\\DINGBAT     Anonymous FTP Server
The command completed successfully.
```

Here, you can see that a number of systems are available within the local EASTAUS domain. There are several file servers for capital cities and regional cities, as well as two Web servers, a Kerberos server, and an anonymous FTP server. These kinds of systems would typically be found in a modern network, and all would potentially require remote file access to other systems. For example, the two Web servers might require access to some files on the anonymous FTP server; this access could be provided by Samba.

Solaris systems don't have the `net view` command. However, Samba does provide a number of tools, such as `nmblookup`, that you can use to list all of the systems within a specific domain. For example, to display all of the systems within the EASTAUS domain, you would use the following command:

```
$ nmblookup EASTAUS
Added interface ip=62.12.48.43 bcast=62.12.48.255 nmask=255.255.255.0
Sending queries to 62.12.48.255
Got a positive name query response from 62.12.48.39 (62.12.48.39)
Got a positive name query response from 62.12.48.41 (62.12.48.41)
Got a positive name query response from 62.12.48.42 (62.12.48.42)
Got a positive name query response from 62.12.48.43 (62.12.48.43)
Got a positive name query response from 62.12.48.50 (62.12.48.50)
Got a positive name query response from 62.12.48.57 (62.12.48.57)
Got a positive name query response from 62.12.48.58 (62.12.48.58)
```

Remember that any of these hosts could be Samba servers running on Linux or Solaris, as well as Microsoft Windows servers and clients using native SMB networking. You can start the nmbd daemon with the following command:

```
# /usr/local/samba/bin/nmbd -D
```

The *-D* option specifies that the NetBIOS name service daemon should run as a standalone daemon rather than as a service through the Internet super daemon inetd.

Samba Clients

There are a number of ways to make a client connection to a Samba server. If you are using an NT Workstation system or similar, the Solaris Samba server should simply appear as a normal NT Server, with individual file systems listed as shares (as determined by the *smb.conf* file). In addition, Solaris file systems may be mapped as local NT drives. This makes Solaris Samba an ideal solution for servicing multiple NT Workstation systems as a reliable file server.

Linux users can use the smbmount command to mount shared Solaris file systems, to maintain a single protocol for file sharing rather than, say, use NFS and Samba. To mount the *answerbook* share on the Solaris Samba server SYDNEY, for example, you would issue the following command from a Linux system:

```
# smbmount //SYDNEY/answerbook /usr/local/answerbook
```

This would mount the remote *answerbook* share onto the local file system on the mount point */usr/local/answerbook*. Of course, the mount point would need to be created prior to mounting by using this command:

```
# mkdir -p /usr/local/answerbook
```

To unmount the share once it is no longer required, you would use the following command:

```
# smbumount /usr/local/answerbook
```

Solaris users who wish to access remote Samba shares (from Solaris, NT, or Linux servers) typically use the smbclient program, which runs from the command line and has a simple command set that is similar to that used by FTP. smbclient provides a very useful and compact way to upload, download, and delete files on a remote server. To make an initial connection, you would use a command of the form

```
# smbclient -L system
```

where *system* is the name of the remote Samba server. To determine which shares were available on the server SYDNEY, you would use this command:

```
# smbclient -L SYDNEY
Added interface ip=62.12.48.43 bcast=62.12.48.43 nmask=255.255.255.0
Domain=[EASTAUS] OS=[Unix] Server=[Samba 3.0.6]

        Sharename       Type        Comment
        ---------       ----        -------
        answerbook      Disk        Sun Answerbooks
        homes           Disk        User Home Directories
        IPC$            IPC         IPC Service (Samba 3.0.6)

        Server                  Comment
        ---------               -------
        SYDNEY                  Samba 3.0.6

        Workgroup               Master
        ---------               -------
        EASTAUS                 WGONG
```

To make a connection to the share *//SYDNEY/answerbook*, use this command:

```
# smbclient //SYDNEY/answerbook
```

smbclient provides its own shell, so you would then be able to use one of the commands listed in Table 31-1 to list directory contents, change working directories, and upload and download files.

Accessing a remote printer using Samba is slightly different: you must supply the *–P* option to the smbclient command to identify that target share as a printer. For example, to mount the printer called *hp* on the Samba server SYDNEY, you would use the command

```
$ smbclient -P //SYDNEY/hp
```

TABLE 31-1
Basic smbclient
Commands

Command	Action
cd <*dir*>	Changes working directory
dir <*dir*>	Displays directory contents
get <*file*>	Retrieves a single file from the server
ls <*dir*>	Displays directory contents
mget <*files*>	Retrieves multiple files from the server
mput <*files*>	Stores multiple files on the server
put <*file*>	Stores a single file on the server

You may then print a local file (such as *address_book.txt*) by using a command such as the following:

```
smb:\> print address_book.txt
```

You can then use the standard printing tools to examine print queues to determine whether the print job was successfully completed.

Procedures

The following procedures are required to configure the Samba daemon.

Configuring the Samba Daemon

You can start the smbd daemon with this command:

```
# /usr/local/samba/bin/smbd -D
```

Again, the *–D* option specifies that the NetBIOS name service daemon should run as a standalone daemon rather than as a service through the Internet super daemon inetd. Note that you should create a startup file for smbd and nmbd at the appropriate run level, if you want Samba to start at boot time.

The Samba daemon has a special configuration file, called *smb.conf*. It is usually stored in the */usr/local/samba/lib* directory. The *smb.conf* file can either be very short or very long, depending on the extent to which your local system requires customization and how many file systems need to be exported. A sample *smb.conf* file is shown here:

```
[global]
workgroup = EASTAUS
netbios name = SYDNEY
server string = Solaris Samba Server V3.0.6
interfaces = 62.12.48.43
security = SHARE
log file = /usr/local/samba/log/log.%m
max log size = 500
socket options = TCP_NODELAY SO_RCVBUF=4096 SO_SNDBUF=4096
dns proxy = Yes
guest account = guest
hosts allow = localhost, 62.12.48.43/255.255.255.0

[printers]
comment = SYDNEY HP Printer
path = /var/spool/hp
print ok = Yes
browseable = Yes
```

```
[homes]
comment = User Home Directories
read only = No
browseable = Yes

[answerbook]
comment = Sun Answerbook Docs
path = /usr/answerbook/
guest ok = Yes
```

The *global* section defines several key parameters that affect the operation of smbd, including the name of the workgroup (EASTAUS), the name of the local server (SYDNEY), the server string that identifies the system (Solaris Samba Server V3.0.6), the primary network interface IP address (62.12.48.43), the security level (standard share level), the path to the Samba log file (*/usr/local/samba/log*), TCP transmission parameters (such as send and receive buffer sizes in bytes), and the name of the guest account (*guest*). Next, the local *hp* printer is specified as a share in the *printers* section. In addition, two different file systems are shared: the *homes* file system shares the local home directory for each user on the system, while the *answerbook* file system shares the local copy of Sun's Answerbooks. Although NFS provides the automounter service, which makes it easy for users to retrieve files from a single home directory on a server, the *homes* facility on Samba can be just as versatile. Although most of the settings in *smb.conf* are easy to interpret, you can find the complete Samba manual online at the Samba site (**http://www.samba.org/**).

One of the nice features of Samba is the configuration script–checking program testparm. The testparm program will alert you to any configuration errors prior to starting a Samba service. In addition, testparm prints out *all* of the Samba parameters associated with the system in general, and for each share, not just those that were explicitly declared in the *smb.conf* file:

```
$ testparm
Load smb config files from /usr/local/samba/lib/smb.conf
Processing section "[printers]"
Processing section "[homes]"
Processing section "[answerbook]"
Loaded services file OK.
WARNING: You have some share names that are longer than 8 chars
These may give errors while browsing or may not be accessible
to some older clients
Press enter to see a dump of your service definitions
# Global parameters
[global]
        workgroup = EASTAUS
        netbios name =
        netbios aliases =
        server string = Samba 3.0.6
        interfaces =
        bind interfaces only = No
```

```
          security = USER
          encrypt passwords = Yes
          update encrypted = No
          allow trusted domains = Yes
          hosts equiv =
          min passwd length = 5
          map to guest = Never
          null passwords = No
          password server =
[printers]
comment = SYDNEY HP Printer
path = /var/spool/hp
print ok = Yes
browseable = Yes

 [homes]
comment = User Home Directories
read only = No
browseable = Yes

 [answerbook]
comment = Sun Answerbook Docs
path = /usr/answerbook/
guest ok = Yes
```

Samba Daemon Status

After the Samba server has been started on port 139, it is easy to keep track of the server status by using the smbstatus command:

```
$ smbstatus
```

This will return a list of all current clients accessing data through the local Samba system:

```
Samba version 3.0.6
Service      uid      gid      pid     machine
------------------------------------------------
answerbook   root     root     344     MELBOURNE   Wed Nov 1 10:45:00 2000
homes        root     root     345     MELBOURNE   Wed Nov 1 10:45:30 2000
homes        julian   staff    1023    HUNTER Thu Nov 2 00:15:34 2000
answerbook   steve    staff    2333    WGONG Wed Nov 1 10:45:30 2000
```

In addition to the share name being accessed, the UID, GID, and PID of the smbd process associated with the client are shown along with the client system name and the date the connection was established. For example, the root user from the system MELBOURNE opened the *answerbook* and the root home directory on Wednesday, November 1, 2000, at 10:45 A.M.

The `smbstatus` command also displays details of actual files being opened by the users who have established a connection to the local Samba server. This can be very useful when trying to determine why a file on the local server file system can't be modified— a remote user may have placed a lock on it, which will not be released until the user has closed the file:

```
Locked files:
Pid     DenyMode      R/W      Oplock  Name
------------------------------------------------
345     DENY_NONE     RDWR     NONE    /root/data.txt     Wed Nov 1 10:51:34 2000
345     DENY_NONE     RDONLY   NONE    /root/db.txt       Wed Nov 1 10:56:21 2000
1023    DENY_NONE     RDWR     NONE    /home/julian/address_book.txt
   Thu Nov 2 00:20:34 2000
```

The details of all currently locked files are displayed, along with the PID of the Samba daemon spawned for each client process, the read/write status and full path to the locked file, and the time and date that the file was first opened.

Finally, `smbstatus` displays some useful statistics regarding shared memory usage, which can be useful when trying to size the amount of RAM required by a departmental server or similar system that services a large number of Samba clients:

```
Share mode memory usage (bytes):
  2096928(99%) free + 112(0%) used + 112(0%) overhead = 2097152(100%) total
```

In this situation, almost all of the allocated memory is free, meaning that many more Samba clients may be serviced.

Troubleshooting

Samba problems can be difficult to isolate, because you have to deal with both Microsoft Windows and Solaris issues and their integration. For example, Windows and Solaris use completely different authentication systems, particularly with respect to encrypted passwords. Thus, you need to choose whether to enable Windows-style authentication in *smb.conf* for password encryption or modify the Windows Registry to transmit passwords in the clear. If you suspect a password-related problem, you can disable the use of passwords for authentication by entering the string "NOPASSWORDXXXXXXXXXXXXXXXXXXX". By temporarily removing the password on the Solaris side, you can determine whether an authentication issue is password-related. However, allowing logins to Solaris without passwords is a very bad idea on production systems or those connected to the Internet, so it would be wise to create a special account with */bin/false* as the shell, which you must remove after testing.

In the first instance, the Samba daemons can be restarted. This can assist you if the daemon has "hung," because of a name conflict, timeout, or some other reason. In addition, the daemons must be restarted every time a change is made to the *smb.conf* file.

Examples

The following examples show how Samba works in action.

Samba GUIs

If manually configuring Samba by using the *smb.conf* file is a bit daunting, you can use one of several third-party GUIs to automate the process of creating an *smb.conf* through a browser. One of the most popular tools is the Samba Web Administration Tool (SWAT), which runs as a service through the Internet super daemon (inetd) on port 901. It can be administered locally, through a browser running on Solaris, or remotely, through a browser running on Microsoft Windows. The current Samba source distribution will build SWAT by default; however, you need to make a number of configuration changes to enable the SWAT service:

1. Map the SWAT service name to the required TCP port (901), by adding the following line to the */etc/services* files:

   ```
   swat    901/tcp
   ```

2. Add the following line to the */etc/inetd.conf* file:

   ```
   swat    stream  tcp  nowait  root   /usr/local/samba-3.0.5/bin/swat
   swat
   ```

3. For the changes to take effect, restart the inetd service:

   ```
   # ps -eaf | grep inetd
       root    200    1  0    Nov 1 ?        01:25 /usr/sbin/inetd -s
   ```

4. The PID of inetd is *200*, so use the following command to restart the service with the modified *inetd.conf* file:

   ```
   kill -1 200
   ```

5. After opening a browser, you can then access the SWAT interface by using the URL **http://SYDNEY:901/**, as shown in Figure 31-3.

NT Authentication

In order to allow users to be authenticated from an NT domain and access Samba shares, insert the following lines into *smb.conf*:

```
encrypt passwords = yes
security = server
password server = "pdc"
```

In this example, the server name *pdc* corresponds to the NetBIOS name of the PDC.

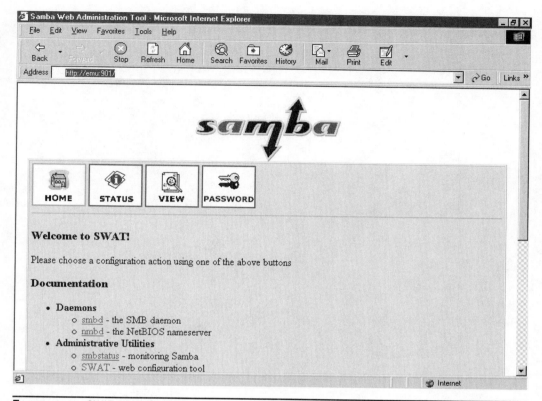

FIGURE 31-3   SWAT GUI for Samba

Summary

In this chapter, you have examined the basic elements of Samba configuration for Solaris. While Solaris provides NFS as its native distributed file system protocol, SMB makes Solaris more compatible with the Microsoft Windows environment.

Application Development and Debugging

A lthough most system administrators are not application developers, in many situations they can make administration tasks much simpler by using a Perl script or small C program that includes system calls. A key challenge of system management involves the automation of as many mundane, repetitive tasks as possible. Although shell or Perl scripting can be useful in this context, as described in Chapter 6, sometimes complete programs are required. This chapter examines how to develop, compile, and execute C applications.

Programming Languages

There are many ways to develop software for Solaris, all of which depend on the internal representation of data and executable code. At the most basic level, all data and instructions are encoded as binary data—quite literally, sets of 1's and 0's that represent data words. For example, a processor with an 8-bit word length means that integers between 0 and 255 can be directly addressed by the CPU, without any kind of intermediate translation. Most Intel CPUs today have a word length of 32 bits, while UltraSPARC processors have a 64-bit word length, making it easier (and faster) to directly process large numbers. This ability is very important in scientific applications, like processing data from human genomes, or in database applications, where transactions of financial data associated with many billions of dollars are performed constantly.

In the early days of computing, a new, "higher level" programming interface was developed, called assembly language. By using assembly language to write programs, instead of directly writing binary code, developers were able to use an interface that was one level of abstraction away from the hardware. They could use English-like statements and identifiers to move and address blocks of memory, for example. This increased productivity and decreased production time. However, anyone who has ever written an assembly language program knows that it is still far from easy. In addition, a different assembly language existed for every processor in existence, meaning that skills developed for a Z80 processor were completely different from those for a 2650 CPU. This made it difficult for programmers to transfer their skills to other systems.

A third level of abstraction was realized by early application development languages like C, in which the original UNIX kernel and, later, the Solaris kernels were written. Although C can contain inline assembly language, it was designed to be independent of the CPU on which its compiled instructions are executing. A compiler translates the English-like instructions written into binary code for a specific CPU, but the actual C source code is highly portable: as long as the program was written to conform to the ANSI standard for C, and as long as a compiler exists for the target platform, the source of a C application can be copied to that platform, compiled, and executed. C++ is a language based around C that has object-oriented data structures, which, at the time of its introduction, improved design processes and made implementation of complex software easier.

However, this ideal was far from the reality: differences in C and C++ compilers across vendors made it very difficult to maintain compatibility, particularly with the rise of graphical user interfaces (GUIs). GUIs had to deal with creating binary code not only for different CPU types, but also for the broad spectrum of display devices on the market, which had little in common with each other. Particularly in the 1980s and early 1990s, it became fashionable to ditch cross-platform products like C to focus specifically on application development for a particular platform. For example, Microsoft developers used Visual Basic to create applications that would run only on the Microsoft Windows or MS-DOS platforms, and UNIX developers wrote applications for the X11 environment that were not necessarily designed to be cross-platform. Although these applications worked well for their target environments, it also meant that markets for software were constrained by the development platform. Many excellent desktop products never made it to UNIX, and several well-known data processing systems were unable to run on Windows.

This situation seemed to reflect the frustration felt when development was performed using assembly language: different codebases were required for the same product on different platforms, and a separate development team was required for each platform. It was often very difficult to synchronize these efforts in any realistic way—so, an application with the same version number in Microsoft Windows might have completely different functionality than an equivalent product for the MacOS. One solution to this problem was to begin looking at what went wrong with C and other third-generation languages that promised cross-platform run-time abilities. A solution was required that ensured that source distributions could be copied to a target platform and executed with little or no modification. One possibility was the Perl programming environment. Here, developers created Perl source, which could then be copied to any machine with a Perl interpreter, and it would be parsed and compiled just prior to execution. However, Perl (at that stage) was not object-oriented, and it did not have support for graphical environments.

On the other hand, the Java programming language (which grew out of the Oak project) promised a full cross-platform graphical environment, which was based around the idea of a "virtual machine." If programmers focused on writing applications based around an API (Application Programming Interface) for the virtual machine, the application would execute on any platform for which there was a Java Virtual Machine (JVM) that met the specifications developed by Sun Microsystems, the creator of Java. Java also featured single-process multithreading, which is very important in applications like Web servers, because traditional Web servers create a new process for each client connection, while a Java Web server runs in a single process and creates internal threads for each client to execute in. This is much more memory- and CPU-efficient than creating and destroying processes for each client in high-transaction-volume environments.

Unlike Perl, Java applications were compiled on the development platform into an intermediate bytecode format, which could then be executed on any target platform. This reduced the run-time compilation overhead associated with Perl. Unfortunately, some vendors decided to innovate and create their own extensions to the JVM, which has created some uncertainty about the future of the Java language. In addition, Sun Microsystems has refused to hand the control of Java over to an independent body, so that an ANSI standard could be created, for example. Even with these caveats, however, Java is being rapidly adopted worldwide as the platform in which to deploy networked applications.

C Programming

Most Solaris developers use the GNU C (gcc) or C++ (g++) compiler for their development work, because, unlike some vendor-supplied compilers in the UNIX world, gcc is 100-percent ANSI-compliant with the C language specification. It is available for Solaris, Linux, and Microsoft Windows, meaning that applications can be relatively easily ported between different platforms, with some modifications. In addition, g++ brings object-oriented data structures and methods to the world of Solaris. The GNU C compiler development project now falls under the broader banner of the GNU Compiler Collection, which aims to integrate the existing GNU development environments (including Fortran, Pascal, and so on) into a single development suite. C is the language in which the Solaris kernel and many other applications are written, including many of the applications in the GNU suite, such as flex and bison. You can find more information about the GNU Compiler Collection project at **http://www.gnu.org/software/gcc/**.

As mentioned earlier, C is a language that requires a compiler to convert a source file, containing legal C language statements, into binary code that is suitable for execution. Because C applications require no run-time interpretation at all (like Java or Perl), C is often the language of choice where fast performance is required. However, it is also true that writing C programs reduces the level of abstraction between the developer and the system, thereby making it easier to make mistakes with programming constructs such as pointers to locations of data elements in memory, for example. A common problem that was examined in Chapter 9 involves "buffer overflow," which results from a C program overwriting the bounds of a fixed-size array. C will not prevent you from making these kinds of mistakes, because the compiler assumes that you know what you are doing. Java is much better suited to catching run-time exceptions such as these. Indeed, you can define customized exception handling in Java, which can be modified to suit the application at hand. For example, if your application is mission critical, it may not be appropriate to terminate a service just because unexpected input is encountered. The application might instead shift into a failsafe mode and e-mail the system administrator for attention.

A C application can consist of up to five different components:

- **Source files**   Usually have .c extensions and contain the C language instructions necessary to execute the application.
- **Any local "include" files**   Define application-wide constants and declarations that are related to user library functions.
- **System-wide header files**   Define all of the declarations related to system library functions.
- **Local libraries**   Contain precompiled functions and components that can be called from a user application.
- **System libraries**   Precompiled functions and components that are required to operate the Solaris kernel and that form the basis for system functions.

When compiling a C program, you may need to define particular paths and directories where system or user-supplied libraries can be located by the linker, which is responsible for combining local object files to form an executable. An application can either be statically linked, in which case all components are combined to form a single executable, or dynamically linked, in which case libraries are loaded from their own separate files at run time. For example, the shell environment variable *LD_LIBRARY_PATH* is usually set to */lib*, which is the directory that contains the majority of system libraries under Solaris. Many C developers use a local library directory to store user-developed application libraries, so it's often useful to replace the default *LD_LIBRARY_PATH* with a replacement like this:

```
$ USER_LIBRARY_PATH=/staff/pwatters/lib; export USER_LIBRARY_PATH
$ SYS_LIBRARY_PATH=/lib; export SYS_LIBRARY_PATH
$ LD_LIBRARY_PATH=$USER_LIBRARY_PATH:$ SYS_LIBRARY_PATH;
  export LD_LIBRARY_PATH
```

Using gcc

Creating and compiling a simple C program is straightforward: simply call the compiler with the command gcc, supply the source filename and, optionally, an executable filename (the default is *a.out*), and press RETURN. For example, let's create a file called *helloworld.c* with the following contents:

```
#include <stdio.h>
main()
{
    printf("Hello World!\n");
}
```

This is about the simplest program possible in C. The standard input/output (I/O) header file *stdio.h* is "included" in the compilation process to ensure that the correct libraries that support functions like *printf* are dynamically linked. To compile this program, simply type

```
$ gcc helloworld.c -o helloworld
```

This produces an executable called `helloworld`. If all goes well, no error messages will be printed. To execute the program, you simply need to type this command:

```
$ ./helloworld
Hello World!
```

Let's take a slightly more complicated example that implements the C arithmetic operators to print out the result of a set of simple operations:

```
#include <stdio.h>
main()
{
     int val1=10;
     int val2=20;
printf("%i + %i = %i\n", val1, val2, (val1+val2));
printf("%i - %i = %i\n", val1, val2, (val1-val2));
printf("%i * %i = %i\n", val1, val2, (val1*val2));
printf("%i / %i = %i\n", val1, val2, (val1/val2));
}
```

If you save this program in a file called *operators.c*, you can compile it with the command

```
$ gcc operators.c -o operators
```

You can now execute the program with the following command:

```
$ ./operators
10 + 20 = 30
10 - 20 = -10
10 * 20 = 200
10 / 20 = 0
```

Oops! 10 divided by 20 is not 0: let's revisit the program. Although Perl allows all variables to be simply defined by the $ operator, C requires that explicit types be declared for all variables and for the results of all operations performed on variables (even simple arithmetic operations!). Thus, it would be more appropriate (and correct) to continue to define integer variables as integers, but floating-point variables, or operations that return floating-point values, should be explicitly cast as floating-point types. So, the preceding application could be rewritten as follows:

```
#include <stdio.h>
main()
{
    int val1=10;
    int val2=20;
printf("%i + %i = %i\n", val1, val2, (val1+val2));
printf("%i - %i = %i\n", val1, val2, (val1-val2));
printf("%i * %i = %i\n", val1, val2, (val1*val2));
printf("%i / %i = %2.2f\n", val1, val2, (float)(val1/val2));
}
```

You can now execute the modified program and obtain the correct results:

```
$ ./operators
10 + 20 = 30
10 - 20 = -10
10 * 20 = 200
10 / 20 = 0.5
```

When you create programs that have a lot of iterative operations, or that are intended for a production environment, you can enable an optimization mode in gcc by using the –O or –O2 option. Because code is generated by default to contain debugging information, you can remove it by specifying the optimization option. In addition, you can specify many other tweaks and tricks individually or in combination. You can utilize spare CPU registers for arithmetic operations, for example. However, keep in mind for large programs that turning on optimization can slow down compilation time considerably, thus, you should only enable optimization just prior to production.

System Calls, Libraries, and Include Files

The example presented in the previous section used only one function (*printf*) contained within a single system library, whose functions are all prefaced in the file *stdio.h*. It is a typical C convention to include constants and interface definitions for precompiled libraries in header files. As you've probably guessed, there are many more system libraries than the single one you have examined so far. In addition, it is possible (and often desirable) to create and distribute your own libraries, which can also make use of header files.

Although you can write your own functions and libraries, you can speed up application development time considerably by reusing many of the components that are supplied with Solaris. In particular, you must use system calls in order to access system and kernel functions. These can be important when building server-side software, although they are less important for GUI-based applications. However, note that system calls, when directly accessing data within the kernel, can cause buffer overflows if you don't correctly preprocess arguments. For example, if a string passed to a system call has a maximum length of 1,024 bytes, but a 1,025-byte string is passed, a kernel panic is possible if the executing user has privileges (real or effective).

Solaris provides manual pages for all system calls and functions in the third group of man pages. These provide invaluable information about function and library interfaces, including the number of required parameters, return types, and other dependencies. This section walks you through the development of a simple application (a horserace winner predictor) that makes use of two system calls (*rand()* and *srand()*). The aim of the program is to randomly select a winning horse from a variable-sized field of horses— although this may seem like a trivial example, it is a simple application whose development touches on the basic elements of constructing a C program.

The first step in developing the application is to investigate the system calls and functions that will be used to generate the random numbers. You can start by reading the Solaris documentation, where you'll find that the *rand()* function is an ANSI-compliant, suitable method to use. Through the man pages, you can check the required parameters to pass to *rand()*, the name of the include file that defines the interface, and any information that is relevant to calling the function. For example, you can display the man page for *rand()* by typing this command:

```
$ man 3 rand
```

The man page for *rand()* identifies the system header file as *<stdlib.h>*, so all programs that use the *rand()* function must "include" the relevant include file, by specifying this header file in the C source:

```
#include <stdlib.h>
```

The man page for *rand()* specifies that the return type of the *rand()* function is an integer (*int*), and it doesn't require any parameters to be passed in order to return a randomly generated number (*void*). The man page also states that the *rand()* function returns a pseudo-random integer, lying on the interval between 0 and *RAND_MAX*. By convention, nonchanging numerical values such as *RAND_MAX* are defined as constants and cannot be modified by a program.

A second important requirement for generating random numbers is also displayed on the man page: a seeding function must be called by any program before calling the *rand()* function. This is because random-number generation by digital computers is only pseudo-random—it generates a series of potentially predictable numbers, using a linear congruential algorithm. Although it is possible to guess a random sequence if you know the seed value, the trick is to use a seed number that changes constantly—retrieving the second or millisecond value from a time-of-day system call is a popular choice. The man page for *rand()* states that the *srand* function takes an unsigned integer argument, representing the seed, and does not return a value. However, if a seed is not supplied, the default value of 1 is used.

Let's have a look at how to put all of these requirements together to form a program that uses random numbers. This example is a program that guesses a winning horse number from a field of horses in a race:

```
#include <stdio.h>
#include <stdlib.h>
main(int argc, char *argv[])
{
   int numberOfHorses, horsePicked, seed;
   printf("Horses 1.0\n");
   printf("This program picks a winning horse \n");
   if (argc != 3)
   {
     printf("usage: horses number_of_horses seed\n");
     exit(1);
   }
   numberOfHorses=atoi(argv[1]);
   seed=atoi(argv[2]);
   if (numberOfHorses>24)
   {
     printf("Sorry - the maximum number of horses is 24\n");
     exit(1);
   }
   else
   {
     printf("Number of horses: %i\n", numberOfHorses);
   }
   srand(seed);
   horsePicked=1+(int)((float)numberOfHorses*rand()/(RAND_MAX+1.0));
   printf("Horse number %i shall win the race\n",horsePicked);
}
```

The program begins by including the header files for the standard I/O and standard C libraries. Next, we declare the *main()* function, which is the exclusive entry point into the program. We pass two parameters to the *main()* function: an integer called *argc* and a pointer to an array of characters called *argv*. These two functions are used to enumerate and pass in command-line parameters, respectively. Because we want to pass in two variables (the *number_of_horses* in a race and the random-number seed, *seed*), *argc* should equal 3 (the extra parameter is the name of the program, in this case *horses*).

Next, we declare internal variables representing the number of horses (*numberOfHorses*), the horse selected (*horsePicked*), and the random-number seed (*seed*). After a banner is printed, the number of command-line arguments is checked. If it is not equal to 3, the application terminates. Checking the bounds of arguments prevents any nasty problems arising later on (including overwriting the boundary of an array—a situation that is examined later with respect to the GNU debugger, gdb). Next, we check that the number of horses is not greater than a typical field—say, 24 horses. If the parameter passed on the command line is greater than 24, the program exits with a value of 1—the exit value of a program can be checked by a shell script, for example, to determine whether an application has failed.

If all the parameters have been passed to the application as expected, the main body of the program can be executed. The random-number generator is seeded with the variable called *seed*, and the winning horse number is then randomly selected by using the formula supplied—the *numberOfHorses* multiplied by the number returned by the *rand()* function, scaled appropriately by the *RAND_MAX* constant. Finally, the number of the winning horse is printed on standard output.

This line-by-line explanation may seem long-winded, and it certainly won't teach you to be a C programmer. However, it does introduce the essential elements of a C program and highlights the evaluation of logical expressions at all points in an application, in order to carry out some specified task. Although the number and type of system calls on a Solaris system is very large (several hundred, in fact), they can all be accessed using the general approach used in developing this small application.

To compile the program using gcc, use the following command:

```
$ gcc horses.c -o horses -lm
```

This command string compiles the source file *horses.c*, to produce the executable file *horses*, and forces the math library to be linked, so that any mathematical functions can be accessed at run time. If an application uses system calls, and the appropriate libraries are not linked in, the application will fail when executed. Let's see what happens when we execute the *horses* program, with a field of 12 horses and a seed value of 769:

```
$ ./horses 12 769
Horses 1.0
This program picks a winning horse from a dynamic field size
Number of horses: 12
Horse number 7 shall win the race
```

This program suggests that horse number 7 shall win the horse race. However, if we supply a new random-number seed, we may receive a completely different prediction:

```
bash-2.03# ./horses 12 768
Horses 1.0
This program picks a winning horse from a dynamic field size
Number of horses: 12
Horse number 3 shall win the race
```

We really shouldn't be basing our bets using the results computed by the program. In any case, we definitely don't want to take a bet on a field with many horses running, otherwise the odds of guessing the correct horse are way too high:

```
bash-2.03# ./horses 1000
Horses 1.0
This program picks a winning horse from a dynamic field size
Sorry - the maximum number of horses allowed in a race is 24
```

The random-number generator used in this demonstration is not really suitable for production use; you should consult the "bible" of numerical computing, which is *Numerical Recipes*. The source code, and many book chapters, are now freely available online at **http://nr.harvard.edu/nr/nronline.html**.

High-Level Input/Output

Solaris applications make extensive use of standard input and standard output streams, so that they can be executed on the command line. For example, the cat program displays the contents of files, which can then be piped through a filter (like more or grep) on the command line. Many Solaris scripts combine a number of small utilities to create complex applications. Understanding input and output streams is critical to developing utilities that can interoperate with existing Solaris applications.

The specific functions for operating on standard input and standard output are defined in the *<stdio.h>* header file. The most commonly used input and output routines are these:

- **fgetc**   Reads a single character from a file
- **fgets**   Reads a string from a file
- **getchar**   Reads in a single character from standard input

Other supported I/O functions, such as getc, are less commonly used, because they may be equivalent to another function, or may simply not be applicable to a wide range of situations.

Let's look at a simple example of a program that uses the fgetc routine to read all characters from a file, character by character, using the fgetc command:

```c
#include <stdio.h>
main(int argc, char *argv[])
{
    FILE *fp;
    int character;

    if ((fp=fopen(argv[1],"r"))==NULL)
    {
        fprintf(stderr, "Cannot open file %s for input\n",
                argv[1]);
```

```
            exit(1);
    }
    do
    {

            character=fgetc(fp);
            if (character!=EOF)
            {
                    printf("%c",character);
            }
    } while (character!=EOF);
    fclose(fp);
}
```

This program acts very much like the *cat* utility, because it requires the name of a file to be passed on the command line. The program begins by reading in the *<stdio.h>* header file, which determines the scope for resolving all I/O routines contained in the program (in this case, `fgetc`). After the *main()* function is declared with the number of arguments to be passed from the command line (*argc*), and the arguments themselves (**argv[]*), a file-opening function is called (`fopen`). In contrast to the low-level file handling discussed later, `fopen` can open an input stream for reading, writing, and appending, by using the FILE type. In this example, a file handle (*fp*) is declared, and it is opened for reading by the `fopen` command, using the *r* (read-only) attribute. If the file cannot be opened for reading, an appropriate error message is printed to standard error. Finally, a *do...while* loop is constructed, so that every character in the named file is printed to standard output, until the condition has been violated that the read character is not the end-of-file (EOF) character. After the file is closed using the *fclose()* function, the program ends, having successfully printed the entire contents of the named file to the screen.

A related example comes from the *fgets* function, which reads in strings of a predetermined buffer size from a named file. In the following example, we read all data from the named file by using *fgets* rather than *fgetc* because *fgets* reduces the overall number of input operations by a factor proportional to the size of the buffer. Thus, a buffer size of eight characters requires eight times fewer read operations for *fgets* than the equivalent *fgetc* operation:

```
#include <stdio.h>
main(int argc, char *argv[])
{
        FILE *fp;
        char *buf;
        int size=8;
        if ((fp=fopen(argv[1],"r"))==NULL)
        {
                fprintf(stderr, "Cannot open file %s for input\n",
                        argv[1]);
                exit(1);
        }
        do
```

```
                {
                        buf=fgets(buf, size, fp);
                        if (buf!=NULL)
                        {
                                printf("%s",buf);
                        }
                } while (buf!=NULL);
                fclose(fp);
        }
```

In this example, a pointer to a file handle (*fp*) is declared, as well as a pointer to a string of characters (*buf*). In addition, a buffer size of eight is allocated. After a file-open operation is performed by `fopen` and the appropriate error handling is implemented through *stderr*, a *do...while* loop is implemented, which contains the decision logic of the program. This reads a buffer of size eight from the file *fp* and stores the contents in the character array *buf*. The *printf* function is then used to display the contents of the buffer as a string. The loop continues until a NULL is returned from the *fgets* read. After the file is closed using the *fclose()* function, the program ends, having successfully printed the entire contents of the named file to the screen.

One of the most common problems associated with standard I/O libraries is boundary violations. These typically occur when the size of an input stream exceeds what has been declared in the application. If no appropriate boundary checking is performed on the size of the input before it is processed, unexpected behavior can occur, usually in the form of a segmentation violation. Let's examine how this can occur:

```
#include <stdio.h>
#define MAX_SIZE 16

main()
{
    int character=0, i=0, j=0;
    char buf1[MAX_SIZE];
    do
    {
        character=getchar();
        if (character!=EOF)
        {
            buf1[i]=character;
            i++;
        }
    } while (character!=EOF);
    do
    {
        printf("%c", buf1[j]);
        j++;
    } while (j<i);
}
```

This program reads in a set of characters from standard input, stores them in a character array of static size (defined by *MAX_SIZE*), and then prints out the characters individually to standard output. If the application was executed, and the characters 1234567 were typed in, they would be dutifully printed to standard output. However, if the characters 12345678901234567890 were typed in, the message "Segmentation fault (core dumped)" would appear (along with a very large core file!). If this application was running as root, or any other privileged user, the unpredictable behavior of the program may have serious security implications, as well as potentially violating the integrity of kernel and user memory.

To remove the problem, we simply need to add an appropriate boundary-checking condition to the input routine. In this case, we simply check that the number of characters being read does not exceed the number specified by *MAX_SIZE*. We don't need to do the same check when printing the characters to standard output, because we know that there will never be an inappropriate number of characters stored in the character buffer in the first place:

```c
#include <stdio.h>
#define MAX_SIZE 16

main()
{
    int character=0, i=0, j=0;
    char buf1[MAX_SIZE];
    do
    {
        character=getchar();
        if (character!=EOF)
        {
            buf1[i]=character;
            i++;
        }
    } while ((character!=EOF)&&(i<MAX_SIZE));
    do
    {
        printf("%c", buf1[j]);
        j++;
    } while (j<i);
}
```

If the application was executed now, and the characters 1234567 were typed in, they would be dutifully printed to standard output. If the characters 12345678901234567890 were typed in, however, only 1234567890123456 would be displayed, and no core file would be dumped. A *core file* is an image of memory dumped when a process terminates abnormally. Because some applications can consume many megabytes of RAM, core files can become very large and waste valuable disk space. If you don't intend to use core files for debugging, you can safely remove them.

Regardless of whether standard input or another stream is used (such as a file), it is critical to check that boundaries have not been overwritten, especially where arrays and pointers are concerned.

We've so far looked at some simple cases involving text files. However, more complex applications that use *structs* to create database-like records usually require faster read/write access provided by binary data streams. Using a binary stream makes it impossible to use `cat` or `grep` to examine the contents of a file, but it does allow a valuable abstraction from files on a character-by-character basis. Complex data structures can be easily serialized and written to a binary file.

In the following example program, we define a struct called *dbRecord*, which contains some of the user data typically stored in the password file (*/etc/passwd*). Many applications use this data for authentication purposes. Imagine that we were going to write a new, improved version of */etc/passwd* that uses a binary data format rather than the existing cumbersome (and slow) text format. We'd need an administrative interface to allow new records to be easily added, because they could no longer be added by manually editing the */etc/passwd* file. Let's have a look at how this could be achieved:

```c
#include <stdio.h>

void printMenu();
char getInput();
void enterData(FILE *fp);

struct dbRecord
{
     int uid;
     int gid;
     char username[8];
     char homeDirectory[64];
     char shell[64];
     char comment[64];
};

main(int argc, char *argv[])
{
     FILE *dbFile;
     char menuChoice;
     if ((dbFile=fopen(argv[1],"a+"))==NULL)
     {
          fprintf(stderr, "Cannot open database file %s\n",
               argv[1]);
          exit(1);
     }
     do
     {
          printMenu();
          menuChoice=getInput();
```

```
        switch (menuChoice)
        {
            case 'e':
                enterData(dbFile);
                break;
            case 'q':
                printf("Session terminated\n");
    fclose(dbFile);
exit(1);
                break;
        }
    } while (menuChoice!='q');
}

void printMenu()
{
    printf("Database Main Menu\n");
    printf("------------------\n");
    printf("(e)nter new dbRecord\n");
    printf("(q)uit\n");
}

char getInput()
{
    char answer;
    printf("\nYour Choice: ");
    answer=getchar();
    return answer;
}

void enterData(FILE *fp)
{
    struct dbRecord user;
    printf("Data Entry\n");
    printf("----------\n\n");
    printf("Enter UID: ");
    scanf("%i",&user.uid);
    printf("Enter GID: ");
    scanf("%i",&user.gid);
    printf("Enter username: ");
    scanf("%s",user.username);
    printf("Enter full name: ");
    scanf("%s",user.comment);
    printf("Enter shell: ");
    scanf("%s",user.shell);
    printf("Enter home directory: ");
    scanf("%s",user.homeDirectory);
    fwrite((char *)&user, sizeof(struct dbRecord), 1, fp);
}
```

Let's walk through the code and see how we've implemented the data structures and decision procedures required to implement the password database administration interface. We start by declaring three functions: *printMenu()*, *getInput()I*, and *enterData(FILE *fp)*. These will be used to print the application menu to standard output, process user menu selections, and solicit user data, respectively. Next, we define a struct called *dbRecord*, which resembles the user record type employed by the */etc/passwd* file. This struct contains the following variables:

int uid	Stores the user's ID
int gid	Stores the user's primary group ID
char username[8]	Defines the login for the user
char homeDirectory[64]	Stores the full path to the user's home directory
char shell[64]	Contains the full path to the user's default shell
char comment[64]	Stores the user's full name and optionally a description of some kind

Next, we introduce the main body of the program, beginning with the declaration of a file handle *dbFile*. This is a file in which user data will be stored using a binary format, and its name is retrieved from *argv[1]* (i.e., passed on the command line). After the file is opened for appending and reading, as signified by the permission string *a+*, a *do...while* loop is constructed. The loop iterates until *menuChoice*, as entered by the user after the menu is printed, is *q*. In practice, this condition is never reached, because the *q* is caught by the *switch* statement, and the case *q* immediately exits from the program. If the case *e* is encountered, the function *enterData(FILE *fp)* is called. This function proceeds by asking the user to enter all data elements that are defined for *dbRecord*. Each entry is read in by using the *scanf* function. Once the data has been collected, a record is written to the specified file by using the *fwrite()* function.

Let's see how a data operation performs in practice:

```
$ ./database database.txt
Database Main Menu
------------------
(e)nter new record
(q)uit

Your Choice:
```

After selecting *e*, the Data Entry menu is displayed, and a new record can be inserted:

```
Data Entry----------
Enter UID: 1001
Enter GID: 100
Enter username: pwatters
Enter full name: Paul
Enter shell: /bin/sh
Enter home directory: /home/paul
```

After the record has been inserted, the main menu is displayed once again. Further records can be inserted, or you can simply quit the application:

```
Database Main Menu
------------------
  (e)nter new record
  (q)uit

Your Choice:q
Session terminated
```

Here, we started the database application by passing the filename *database.txt*, which is to contain the user data entered through the application. After the welcome banner is printed, we enter *e* to go to the data entry screen. Here, we enter data for the user *pwatters*, including UID *1001*, GID *100*, full name *Paul*, shell */bin/sh*, and home directory */home/paul*. After all of the data has been accepted and the entry has been written to the database file, we are returned to the main menu.

Low-Level Input/Output

The *open()* system call is used to open a file using a low-level call. The file remains open until it is closed with a *close()* system call. When the *open()* system call is called, a file descriptor is returned, which is a unique integer that distinguishes the current open file from other opened files. A pool of available file descriptor integers is maintained, and the next integer in the queue is selected. Recall that there are three file descriptors that are defined by the low-level interface: standard input (*0*), standard output (*1*), and standard error (*2*).

The named file is always opened at its beginning, so subsequent operations are operating sequentially on the data contained in the file. The *open()* function opens the file named in the string pathname, with the permissions specified by primary flags. These flags include the following:

- **O_RDONLY**   Opens the file read-only.
- **O_WRONLY**   Opens the file write-only.
- **O_RDWR**   Opens the file read/write.

In addition, the following secondary flags may be bitwise-OR'ed with the secondary flags to extend the functionality of the *open()* call:

- **O_CREAT**   Creates the file on the file system if it does not already exist.
- **O_EXCL**   The reverse of O_CREAT: if a file already exists, the call will fail.
- **O_NOCTTY**   Prevents the process from being overtaken by a terminal (tty) device that is specified by pathname.
- **O_TRUNC**   Allows a file to be truncated.
- **O_APPEND**   Allows data to be appended to the end of a file.

- **O_NONBLOCK**   Prevents waiting.
- **O_SYNC**   Enforces synchronous I/O.
- **O_NOFOLLOW**   Prevents the opening of a file if it is a symbolic link.
- **O_DIRECTORY**   Fails if the named file is not a directory.
- **O_LARGEFILE**   Allows large files whose sizes cannot be addressed (in 32-bit systems) to be opened.

The *open()* function always returns an integer, which is the file descriptor (if positive), or an error (if negative). The errors associated with *open()*, which are set by *errno*, include EEXIST, EISDIR, EACCESS, ENAMETOOLONG, ENOENT, ENOTDIR, ENODEV, EROFS, ETXTBSY, EFAULT, ELOOP, ENOSPC, ENOMEM, EMFILE, and ENFILE.

Two operations are supported by low-level I/O: reading (with the *read()* function) and writing (with the *write()* function). The main difference between high- and low-level reading and writing functions is that the latter require you to specify your own buffer size, and the type of data being read and written is not assumed.

The *read()* call has the form

```
ssize_t read(int fd, void *buf, size_t count)
```

where *fd* is a file descriptor, *buf* is a pointer to a (variable-sized) buffer, and *count* is the number of bytes to be read from the file. If the call is successful, the number of bytes read successfully is returned. If the call fails, one of the following codes is returned by *errno*: EINTR, EAGAIN, EIO, EISDIR, EBADF, EINVAL, or EFAULT. These are defined and described at the end of this chapter.

The *write()* call has the form

```
ssize_t write(int fd, void *buf, size_t count)
```

where *fd* is a file descriptor, *buf* is a pointer to a (variable-sized) buffer, and *count* is the number of bytes to be written to the file. If the call is successful, the number of bytes written successfully is returned. If the call fails, one of the following codes is returned by *errno*: EINTR, EAGAIN, EIO, EISDIR, EBADF, EINVAL, EPIPE, or EFAULT. These are defined and described at the end of this chapter.

A file opened with *open()* can be closed with *close(int fd)*, where *fd* is the file descriptor.

Let's examine how these low-level calls can be used in practice. We revisit the user database application and modify the file operations to use low-level rather than high-level routines.

```
#include <stdio.h>
#include <sys/types.h>
#include <sys/stat.h>
#include <unistd.h>
#include <fcntl.h>
```

```
void printMenu();
char getInput();
void enterData(int fd);

struct dbRecord
{
     int uid;
     int gid;
     char username[8];
     char homeDirectory[64];
     char shell[64];
     char comment[64];
};

main(int argc, char *argv[])
{
     int fd;
     char menuChoice;
     if ((fd=open(argv[1],O_RDWR|O_CREAT|O_APPEND))<0)
     {
          fprintf(stderr, "Cannot open database file %s\n",
                  argv[1]);
          exit(1);
     }
     do
     {
          printMenu();
          menuChoice=getInput();
          switch (menuChoice)
          {
               case 'e':
                    enterData(fd);
                    break;
               case 'q':
                    printf("Session terminated\n");
                    exit(1);
                    break;
          }
     } while (menuChoice!='q');
     close(fd);
}

void printMenu()
{
     printf("Database Main Menu\n");
     printf("------------------\n");
     printf("(e)nter new dbRecord\n");
```

```
        printf("(q)uit\n");
}

char getInput()
{
        char answer;
        printf("\nYour Choice: ");
        answer=getchar();
        return answer;
}

void enterData(int fd)
{
        struct dbRecord user;
        printf("Data Entry\n");
        printf("----------\n\n");
        printf("Enter UID: ");
        scanf("%i",&user.uid);
        printf("Enter GID: ");
        scanf("%i",&user.gid);
        printf("Enter username: ");
        scanf("%s",user.username);
        printf("Enter full name: ");
        scanf("%s",user.comment);
        printf("Enter shell: ");
        scanf("%s",user.shell);
        printf("Enter home directory: ");
        scanf("%s",user.homeDirectory);
        write(fd, (char *)&user, sizeof(struct dbRecord));
}
```

The first thing to notice is that we've added in several different header files, including *sys/types.h*, *sys/stat.h*, *unistd.h*, and *fcntl.h*. These are all necessary to support low-level I/O. Next, we've changed the declaration of the *enterData()* function from a pointer to type FILE, to a single integer. This is the integer that contains the file descriptor. This means we must also change the *fopen()* request to an *open()* call. This specifies the name of the file to be opened, along with three OR'ed flags: O_RDWR, O_CREAT, and O_APPEND. This ensures that the database file will be opened read/write, will be created if it doesn't already exist, and will be opened for appending. In addition, note that the error-checking condition has now changed: instead of checking to see whether the return value of *fopen()* is NULL, we now simply check to see whether the returned integer value from *open()* is positive (success) or negative (failure).

Finally, the *write()* call is similar to the original: a file descriptor is passed, using the instantiation of *dbRecord* (user), where each record is written individually (i.e., the size of the buffer being written is defined by the record size).

Performance Optimization and Debugging

If you write your own programs, or if you compile those written by others, speed of execution and size of executables are often major considerations. For example, if you are writing a program that attempts to solve differential equations or perform highly complex numerical operations, you will obviously want to optimize for speed of execution. If you're a Java applet developer, your codebase must be downloaded to remote Web browser clients before it can be executed, so you'd definitely be more interested in optimizing for executable size rather than speed. Any kind of optimization performed on source code during compilation will almost certainly increase compilation time, so this needs to be factored into plans for code optimization during early phases of development.

The Solaris development environment and the GNU compilers provide several ways in which you can monitor and enhance performance. The best way to evaluate application performance is to time the application. You can use the `time` command to measure the actual time taken to execute the application; it breaks this down into user and system components. Let's run the `time` command on the compiler command string used earlier to build the *horses* program from source:

```
$ time gcc horses.c -o horses -lm
real    0m0.547s
user    0m0.450s
sys     0m0.100s
```

The total time taken to compile the command was 0.547 seconds ("real time"), made up of approximately 0.45 second of user time, and 0.1 second of system time. In this context, user time is the number of seconds that the CPU spent processing instructions in user mode, while system time is the number of seconds the kernel was running on the CPU. It is also possible to measure the execution time of the application itself:

```
$ time ./horses
real    0m0.031s
user    0m0.020s
sys     0m0.000s
```

Here, you can see that the execution time of the application is many times faster than the compilation process: the real time used was 0.031 second, of which the user component was 0.02 second, and the system component was negligible. However, let's examine how long it actually took to compile the program:

```
$ time gcc -O2 horses.c -o horses -lm
real    0m0.895s
user    0m0.740s
sys     0m0.150s
```

The compilation time of 0.895 second was around 50 percent longer than an unoptimized compile. However, the execution time of the optimized program was less than half that required by the unoptimized program:

```
$ time ./horses
real    0m0.014s
user    0m0.010s
sys     0m0.010s
```

Using optimization can also have an effect on the size of a binary—a faster application is usually larger in executable size, as loops are unrolled and external functions are moved inline. In addition, producing debugging and profiling data for later examination using the GNU debugger (gdb) also increases the application binary size. For example, if we compile the *horses* program using the standard options, we can examine the size of the executable by using the ls command:

```
$ gcc horses.c -o horses -lm
$ ls -l horses
-rwxr-xr-x   1 root     root         11533 Jul 18 19:37 horses
```

However, when we specify debugging information to be included in the binary, we can use the *–pg* option with gcc—this also produces a much larger binary, as we can see using ls:

```
$ gcc -pg horses.c -o horses -lm
$ ls -l horses
-rwxr-xr-x   1 root     root         21215 Jul 18 19:37 horses
```

In this case, the object file contains the executable code as well as the types associated with all functions and variables in the program. In addition, the mapping between line numbers in the source and memory addresses in the object code is retained, making the executable almost twice as large as a binary with no debugging information.

When we write C programs, we're often faced with the difficult task of debugging an application that produces unexpected behavior. Integrated development environments (IDEs) are generally quite good at picking up syntax errors, but they cannot always diagnose what will occur at run time, because of differences in environment, system load, virtual memory and system library availability, and so on. That's where gdb really comes into its own.

Let's examine a simple program that declares an array of integers, assigns a value to the first and last elements of the array, and then prints it out:

```
#include <stdio.h>

main()
```

```
{
        int i[10];
        i[0]=1;
    printf("%i \n",i[0]);
        i[9]=1;
        printf("%i \n",i[9]);
}
```

If we compile and run the program, we would expect to see the output

```
$ ./array_test
1
1
```

However, a common problem with C programming is overwriting the boundaries of an array. You would think that, having declared the array to have ten elements, only ten elements would be addressable—accessing elements outside this range should cause a compile error. However, in our ten-element array declared in the preceding code example, most compilers will allow us to address the eleventh, twelfth, or thirteenth element, even though they don't "exist." In fact, if we modify our program to write to the twelfth element of the array, we will get a run-time error:

```
#include <stdio.h>
main()
{
        int i[10];
        i[0]=1;
        printf("%i \n",i[0]);
        i[11]=1;
        printf("%i \n",i[11]);
}
```

Let's see what happens when we run the program:

```
$ ./array_test
1
Segmentation fault
```

Although we can write off such errors easily by going back to the source and checking for programming errors, this can be a long and tedious process in large applications. In addition, it may not always be clear why a segmentation fault (or any other memory access violation error) is occurring at all. In these cases, it can be useful to get a snapshot of memory contents associated with a specific program, by using the GNU debugger (gdb). This can help determine the circumstances under which a program crashed and pinpoint any offending commands or variable values that were invalid at the time of execution. In addition, the specific values of variables in your programs can be "watched" while stepping through line-by-line execution of the program. This also gives developers an indication of where an error occurs in the source. It's even possible to pass new values of variables to the application while it is running, to "fix" any problems in real time. You can find the gdb manual online at **http://www.cis.ohio-state.edu/htbin/info/info/gdb.info**.

The main commands used in a gdb session are shown in Table 32-1.

We can use the gdb to trace the error in our application:

```
$ gdb array_test
GNU gdb 4.17.0.11 with Solaris/x86 hardware watchpoint and FPU support
Copyright 1998 Free Software Foundation, Inc.
GDB is free software, covered by the
GNU General Public License, and you are
welcome to change it and/or distribute copies
of it under certain conditions.
Type "show copying" to see the conditions.
There is absolutely no warranty for GDB.  Type "show warranty" for details.
This GDB was configured as "i386-Solaris"...
(gdb)
```

Command	Action
break	Sets a breakpoint at a specific point in a program prior to stepping. Breakpoints can be set on functions and source line numbers.
clear	Clears breakpoints specified for functions and line numbers in source files.
continue	Continues execution of a program after a breakpoint has been met, until the next breakpoint.
delete	Deletes breakpoints by breakpoint number.
display	Displays the value of an expression every time program execution is halted.
finish	Continues execution of a program after a breakpoint, until the program has completed.
info	Prints details of breakpoints and watchpoints set during a gdb session.
lisxt	Displays specific lines of source code.
next	Continues execution of a program to the next source line, if step mode has been set.
print	Displays the value of an expression.
run	Begins execution of a program under gdb.
step	Steps through code line-by-line, so that the effect of individual statements and expressions in the source can be evaluated.
watch	Halts execution if the value of a variable is modified.

TABLE 32-1   Basic GNU Debugger (gdb) Commands

First, we read in the content's executable file:

```
(gdb) file array_test
Reading symbols from array_test...done.
```

Next, we attempt to re-create the error, by executing the program within gdb:

```
(gdb) run
Starting program: /tmp/array_test
1

Program received signal SIGSEGV, Segmentation fault.
0x1 in ?? ()
```

This is the same point at which the application failed when executed within the shell. Because we have received a segmentation violation, we need to determine the circumstances under which it arose. When the *main()* function is called, details about the function call are generated, including the location of the call in the source file, its arguments (if any), and details of any local variables. This set of information is known as the *stack frame*, and all stack frames are stored in memory in a *call stack*. We can use the bt command to display the trace of the current call stack, with one line displayed for each stack frame. In our application, we had only a single function (the *main()* function), so only a single line is displayed:

```
(gdb) bt
#0  0x1 in ?? ()
```

At any point of execution, you can generate a list all of the variables used in an application by using the list command:

```
(gdb) list 'array_test.c'
There are 365 possibilities.  Do you really
wish to see them all? (y or n)
Letext                              __DTOR_LIST__
_CS_LFS64_CFLAGS                    __EH_FRAME_BEGIN__
_CS_LFS64_LDFLAGS                   __FRAME_END__
_CS_LFS64_LIBS                      __bb
_CS_LFS64_LINTFLAGS                 __blkcnt64_t
_CS_LFS_CFLAGS                      __blkcnt_t
_CS_LFS_LDFLAGS                     __bss_start
_CS_LFS_LIBS                        __caddr_t
_CS_LFS_LINTFLAGS                   __clock_t
_CS_PATH                            __compar_fn_t
                                    __daddr_t
```

```
_CS_XBS5_ILP32_OFF32_CFLAGS            __data_start
_CS_XBS5_ILP32_OFF32_LDFLAGS           __deregister_frame_info
_CS_XBS5_ILP32_OFF32_LIBS              __dev_t
_CS_XBS5_ILP32_OFF32_LINTFLAGS         __do_global_ctors_aux
_CS_XBS5_ILP32_OFFBIG_CFLAGS           __do_global_dtors_aux
_CS_XBS5_ILP32_OFFBIG_LDFLAGS          __fd_mask
_CS_XBS5_ILP32_OFFBIG_LIBS             __fd_set
_CS_XBS5_ILP32_OFFBIG_LINTFLAGS        __fsblkcnt64_t
_CS_XBS5_LP64_OFF64_CFLAGS             __fsblkcnt_t
_CS_XBS5_LP64_OFF64_LDFLAGS            __fsfilcnt64_t
```

You can also retrieve and set the values of these variables. More usefully, you can extract the values of the CPU registers by using the `info all-registers` command:

```
(gdb) info all-registers
      eax:        0x3             3
      ecx:        0x0             0
      edx:        0x2             2
      ebx: 0x400f6618    1074751000
      esp: 0xbffff874   -1073743756
      ebp: 0xbffff8a8   -1073743704
      esi: 0x4000aa20    1073785376
      edi: 0xbffff8d4   -1073743660
      eip:        0x1             1
   eflags:     0x10282  IOPL: 0; flags: SF IF RF
 orig_eax: 0xffffffff            -1
       cs:        0x23            35
       ss:        0x2b            43
       ds:        0x2b            43
       es:        0x2b            43
       fs:        0x0             0
       gs:        0x0             0
      st0: 0x3fff8000000000000000 Empty Normal 1
      st1: 0x00000000000000000000 Empty Zero   0
      st2: 0x3fff8000000000000000 Empty Normal 1
      st3: 0x00000000000000000000 Empty Zero   0
      st4: 0x00000000000000000000 Empty Zero   0
```

Setting a breakpoint for a function is easy when using the `break` command. In the case of our test program, we have only a single function (*main()*), so this will be reached almost as soon as the program is executed. Better symbolic information, including the code and line numbers concerned, can be obtained by compiling the application with the –*g* option. We can set a breakpoint on *main()* by using the following command:

```
(gdb) break main
Breakpoint 1 at 0x8048536
```

Next, we need to run the program again, and it will be halted once the declared breakpoint has been reached:

```
(gdb) run
Starting program: /tmp/array_test

Breakpoint 1, 0x8048536 in main ()
(gdb)
```

At this point, we can examine the values of all declared variables, and set watches appropriately. One issue when stepping through applications using gdb is referring to source files that are not in your path:

```
(gdb) s
Single stepping until exit from function main,
which has no line number information.
printf (format=0x80485d0 "%i \n") at printf.c:30
printf.c:30: No such file or directory.
```

Fortunately, you can obtain the source for many Solaris libraries, so it is often feasible to debug to the level of the standard I/O libraries and similar.

Summary

In this chapter, you have examined how to compile and build C applications on Solaris. Since the Solaris kernel originally was built using C, it makes sense for system administrators to understand how system calls and libraries work, even if they do not develop software themselves.

PART VI

Web Applications and Services

A large area of growth for Solaris implementations has been supporting Web operations based on Java 2 Enterprise Edition (J2EE) architectures. This chapter reviews several key J2EE technologies bundled with Solaris, with a focus on the Sun Java System Application Server and the widely used open-source Apache HTTP Server (**http://httpd.apache.org/**).

Apache Web Server

Apache is a multiprocess Web server that is supplied with the Solaris 10 distribution. It is used by the majority of Web servers in the world to serve HTTP (insecure) and HTTPS (secure) content. Apache also performs a number of different tasks, including

- Provides a Common Gateway Interface (CGI) to provide client access to server-side processes and applications. CGI applications can be written in C, C++, Perl, Bourne shell, or the language of your choice.

- Supports the hosting of multiple sites on a single server, where each site is associated with a unique Fully Qualified Domain Name (FQDN). Thus, a single Solaris system, in an ISP environment, can host multiple Web sites, such as *http://www.learnteach.com*, *http://www.paulwatters.com*, and so forth, using a single instance of Apache.

- Secures the transmission of credit card details and other sensitive data by supporting Secure Sockets Layer (SSL). This allows for key-based encryption of the HTTP protocol (called HTTPS), with key sizes of up to 128 bits.

- Provides a fully featured proxy/cache server, which provides an extra level of protection for clients behind a firewall, and also keeps a copy of the most commonly retrieved documents from the Web.

- Provides customized access, agent, and error logs that can be used for marketing and reporting purposes.

The main Apache configuration file is *httpd.conf*, which contains three sections:

- **Global environment configuration**   Sets key server information, such as the root directory for the Apache installation, and several process-management settings, such as the number of concurrent requests permitted per server process.

- **Main server configuration**   Sets run-time parameters for the server, including the port on which the server listens, the server name, the root directory for the HTML documents and images that comprise the site, and the server authorization configuration, if required.

- **Virtual hosts configuration**   Configures the Apache HTTP Server to run servers for multiple domains. Many of the configuration options that are set for the main server can also be customized for each of the virtual servers.

The following sections examine the configuration options in each of these sections in detail, after which you are shown how to start Apache.

Global Environment Configuration

The following options are commonly set in the global environment configuration section:

```
ServerType standalone
ServerRoot "/opt/apache1.3.9"
PidFile /opt/apache1.3.9/logs/httpd.pid
ScoreBoardFile /opt/apache1.3.9/logs/apache_status
Timeout 300
KeepAlive On
MaxKeepAliveRequests 100
KeepAliveTimeout 15
MaxRequestsPerChild 0
LoadModule auth_module        modules/mod_auth.so
```

The server configuration shown here does not run as a service of the Internet super daemon (`inetd`), rather, Apache runs as a standalone daemon. This gives Apache more flexibility in its configuration, as well as better performance than running through `inetd`. Since Apache is able to service more than one client through a single process (using the KeepAlive facility), no production system should ever use the `inetd` mode.

The ServerRoot for the Apache installation is set to */opt/apache1.3.9* in this installation. All of the key files required by Apache are located below this directory root, such as the lock file, the scoreboard file, and the file that records the PID of the current Apache process.

Each of the clients that connect to the server has an expiry date, in the form of a timeout. In this configuration, the timeout is set to 300 seconds (5 minutes). This is the period of inactivity after which a client is deemed to have timed out. Requests are kept alive, with up to 100 requests. There is no limit to the number of requests per child process.

Main Server Configuration

The following options are commonly set in the main server configuration section:

```
Port 80
ServerAdmin paul@paulwatters.com
ServerName www.paulwatters.com
DocumentRoot "/opt/apache1.3.9/htdocs"
<Directory/>
    Options FollowSymLinks
    AllowOverride None
</Directory>
<Directory "/opt/apache1.3.9/htdocs">
    Options Indexes FollowSymLinks MultiViews
    AllowOverride None
    Order allow,deny
    Allow from all
</Directory>
UserDir "/opt/apache1.3.9/users/"
DirectoryIndex index.html
AccessFileName .htaccess
<Files .htaccess>
    Order allow,deny
    Deny from all
</Files>
```

The parameters in this section determine the main run-time characteristics of the Apache HTTP Server. The first parameter is the port on which the Apache HTTP Server will run. If the server is being executed by an unprivileged user, then this port must be set to port 1024 or higher. However, if a privileged user like *root* is executing the process, then any unreserved port may be used (you can check the services database, */etc/services*, for ports allocated to specific services). By default, port 80 is used.

Next, some details about the server are entered, including the hostname of the system, which is to be displayed in all URLs, and a contact e-mail address for the server. This address is usually displayed on all error and CGI misconfiguration pages. The root directory for all HTML and other content for the Web site much also be supplied. This allows for both absolute and relative URLs to be constructed and interpreted by the server. In this case, the *htdocs* subdirectory underneath the main Apache directory is used. Thus, the file *index.html* in this directory will be the default page displayed when no specific page is specified in the URL. There are several options that can be specified for the *htdocs* directory, including whether or not to ignore symbolic links to directories that do not reside underneath the *htdocs* subdirectory. This is useful when you have available on CD-ROMs and other file systems files that do not need to be copied onto a hard drive, simply to be served through the Web.

Apache has a simple user authentication system available, which is similar to the Solaris password database (*/etc/passwd*) in that it uses encrypted passwords, but it does not use the Solaris password database. This means that a separate list of users and passwords must be maintained. Thus, when a password-protected page is requested by a user, the user must enter a username and matching password into a dialog box. By using the appropriate modules, a connection to LDAP or some other directory can be made. Any directory that appears underneath the main *htdocs* directory can be password protected using this mechanism.

Next, the various MIME types that can be processed by the server are defined, in a separate file called *mime.types*. The following are some examples of the MIME types defined for the server:

```
application/mac-binhex40        hqx
application/msword              doc
application/x-csh               csh
```

You can see the file types defined here for many popular applications, including compression utilities (Macintosh BinHex, *application/mac-binhex40*, with the extension .hqx), word processing documents (Microsoft Word, *application/msword*, with the extension .doc), and C shell scripts (*application/x-csh*, with the extension .csh).

The next section deals with logfile formats, as shown here:

```
HostnameLookups Off
ErrorLog /opt/apache1.3.9/logs/error.log
LogLevel warn
LogFormat "%h %l %u %t \"%r\" %>s %b \"%{Referer}i\" \"%{User-Agent}i\"" combined
LogFormat "%h %l %u %t \"%r\" %>s %b" common
LogFormat "%{Referer}i -> %U" referer
LogFormat "%{User-agent}i" agent
CustomLog /opt/apache1.3.9/logs/access.log common
CustomLog /opt/apache1.3.9/logs/access.log combined
```

The first directive switches off hostname lookups on clients before logging their activity. Since performing a reverse DNS lookup on every client making a connection is a CPU- and bandwidth-intensive task, many sites prefer to switch it off. However, if you need to gather marketing statistics on where your clients are connecting from (e.g., by geographical region or by second-level domain type), then you may need to switch hostname lookups on. In addition, an error log is specified as a separate entity to the access log. A typical set of access log entries looks like this:

```
192.64.32.12 - - [06/Jan/2002:20:55:36 +1000]
  "GET /cgi-bin/printenv HTTP/1.1" 200 1024
192.64.32.12 - - [06/Jan/2002:20:56:07 +1000]
  "GET /cgi-bin/Search.cgi?term=solaris&type=simple HTTP/1.1" 200 85527
192.64.32.12 - - [06/Jan/2002:20:58:44 +1000]
```

```
"GET /index.html HTTP/1.1" 200 94151
192.64.32.12 - - [06/Jan/2002:20:59:58 +1000]
  "GET /pdf/secret.pdf HTTP/1.1" 403 29
```

The first example shows that the client 192.64.32.12 accessed the CGI application `printenv` on January 6, 2002, at 8:55 P.M. The result code for the transaction is 200, which indicates a successful transfer. The `printenv` script comes standard with Apache, and displays the current environment variables being passed from the client. The output is very useful for debugging, and looks like this:

```
DOCUMENT_ROOT="/usr/local/apache-1.3.9.12/htdocs"
GATEWAY_INTERFACE="CGI/1.1"
HTTP_ACCEPT="image/gif, image/x-xbitmap, image/jpeg, image/pjpeg,
application/vnd.ms-excel, application/msword,
application/vnd.ms-powerpoint, */*" HTTP_ACCEPT_ENCODING="gzip, deflate"
HTTP_ACCEPT_LANGUAGE="en-au"
HTTP_CONNECTION="Keep-Alive"
HTTP_HOST="www"
HTTP_USER_AGENT="Mozilla/4.75 (X11; I; SunOS 5.10 i86pc; Nav)"
 PATH="/usr/sbin:/usr/bin:/bin:/usr/ucb:/usr/local/bin:
/usr/openwin/bin:/usr/dt/bin:/usr/ccs/bin"
QUERY_STRING=""
REMOTE_ADDR="209.67.50.55"
REMOTE_PORT="3399"
REQUEST_METHOD="GET"
REQUEST_URI="/cgi-bin/printenv"
SCRIPT_FILENAME="/usr/local/apache/cgi-bin/printenv"
SCRIPT_NAME="/cgi-bin/printenv"
SERVER_ADDR="209.67.50.203"
SERVER_ADMIN="paul@paulwatters.com"
SERVER_NAME="www.paulwatters.com"
SERVER_PORT="80"
SERVER_PROTOCOL="HTTP/1.1"
SERVER_SIGNATURE="Apache/1.3.9.12 Server at www.paulwatters.com Port 80\n"
SERVER_SOFTWARE="Apache/1.3.9.12 (Unix)" TZ="Australia/NSW"
```

The second example from the log shows that a client running from the same system successfully executed the CGI program `search.cgi`, passing two GET parameters: a search term of *solaris* and a search type of *simple*. The size of the generated response page was 85,527 bytes. The third example shows a plain HTML page being successfully retrieved, with a response code of 200 and a file size of 94,151 bytes.

The fourth example demonstrates one of the many HTTP error codes being returned, instead of the 200 success code. In this case, a request to retrieve the file */pdf/secret.pdf* is denied with a 403 code being returned to the browser. This code would be returned if the file permissions set on the */pdf/secret.pdf* file did not grant read access to the user executing Apache (e.g., *nobody*).

Virtual Hosts Configuration

The following options are commonly set in the virtual hosts configuration section:

```
<VirtualHost www.cassowary.net>
    ServerAdmin webmaster@paulwatters.com
    DocumentRoot /opt/apache1.3.9/htdocs/www.cassowary.net
    ServerName www.cassowary.net
    ErrorLog /opt/apache1.3.9/logs/www.cassowary.net-error_log
    CustomLog /opt/apache1.3.9/logs/www.cassowary.net-access_log common
</VirtualHost>
```

This example defines a single virtual host (called *www.cassowary.net*), in addition to the default host for the Apache HTTP Server. Virtual host support allows you to keep separate logs for errors and access, as well as a completely separate document root to the default server. This makes it very easy to maintain multiple virtual servers on a single physical machine.

Starting Apache

Apache is bundled with a control script (*apachectl*) that can be used to start, stop, and report on the status of the server. To obtain help on the *apachectl* script, use the following command:

```
$ /opt/apache1.3.9/apachectl help
usage: /opt/apache1.3.9/apachectl
(start|stop|restart|fullstatus|status|graceful|configtest|help)

start      - start httpd
stop       - stop httpd
restart    - restart httpd if running by sending a SIGHUP or start if
             not running
fullstatus - dump a full status screen; requires lynx and mod_status enabled
status     - dump a short status screen; requires lynx and mod_status enabled
graceful   - do a graceful restart by sending a SIGUSR1 or start if not running
configtest - do a configuration syntax test
help       - this screen
```

To start Apache, you simply need to issue the following command from the same directory:

```
$ /opt/apache1.3.9/apachectl start
```

To stop the service, you may use the following command from the same directory:

```
$ /opt/apache1.3.9/apachectl stop
```

If you change the Apache configuration file and need to restart the service so that the server is updated, simply use the following command from the same directory:

```
$ /opt/apache1.3.9/apachectl restart
```

Once Apache is running on port 80, clients will be able to begin requesting HTML pages and other content.

Sun Java System Application Server

The Sun Java System Application Server is a J2EE-compliant platform for deploying enterprise Java applications, in conjunction with existing CGI and Netscape Server API (NSAPI) applications. By integrating all server-side application support under a single service regime, it is possible to minimize administration overhead, achieve better scaling through tight integration, and provide combined monitoring and event notification support. Historically, server-side applications providing back-end and middleware services have used front-end presentation layers, in the form of HTML pages, JSP pages, applets, and applications to give users combined access to numerous data sources. By implementing business logic using the J2EE model, you can avoid the pitfalls associated with multiprocess applications, such as those written for use with Web servers that support CGI, by using Java's multithreading capabilities.

Enterprise JavaBeans (EJBs) are one of the key technologies supported by J2EE. These distributed components are of three varieties:

- **Stateless session beans**   Store data and perform operations that are not stateful
- **Stateful session beans**   Store data and perform operations that are stateful
- **Entity beans**   Allow object operations to be easily mapped onto relational database tables

By using stateful session beans to support user sessions, entity beans to persist data, and stateless session beans to provide a low-overhead interface to entity beans, you can build entire applications on the EJB infrastructure. While the myriad layers and parameters associated with an EJB deployment can be mind-boggling, fortunately the Sun Java System Application Server provides advanced deployment tools to ease and automate many aspects of this process. By implementing a distributed object platform, server-side applications can be expanded to span across multiple servers and clusters, improving scalability and reducing bottlenecks. The relationships between the various layers of EJB technology are shown in Figure 33-1.

Although most Java application servers support the J2EE specification, given the wide variety in licensing costs, it's important to understand what features set the Sun Java System Application Server apart from the competition.

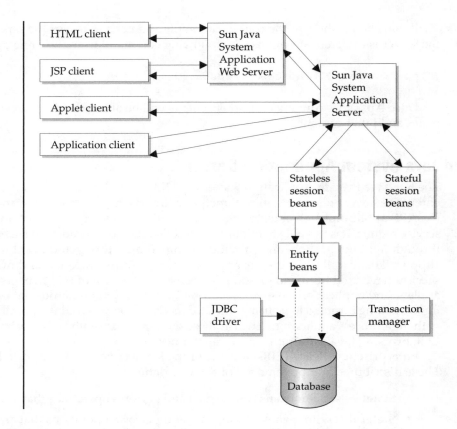

FIGURE 33-1
EJB layers

Performance is the number one goal of the Sun Java System Application Server: in addition to featuring multithreading within Java applications that it's hosting, the Sun Java System Application Server uses multithreading internally. In addition, some tasks can be executed in parallel by using multiple threads. Alternatively, multiprocessing is supported by virtue of data and process sharing across multiple systems: as an application grows, various tasks can be assigned to specific servers. For example, one server might handle authentication, while another might process all JDBC requests to a database server. One reason for implementing applications in this way is that not all servers required to run an application may be located in the same subnet: indeed, it is likely that an authentication server would sit outside a firewall, while a database server would be the most difficult system to access externally.

Since Java, CGI, NSAPI, and other server-side technologies can be handled by the same application server, rather than by several independent servers, it follows that performance improvements can be obtained by integration, since only one server needs to be running.

The Sun Java System Application Server provides high availability by supporting failover of stateful session beans. This means that if a system that is storing data for an interactive user session crashes for some reason, another server can recover the beans and continue. This is particularly useful when running applications that persist data in stateful session beans for long periods—since entity beans and stateless session beans do not store user state in the same way as stateful session beans, this reduces a key risk in supporting EJB technology. A similar facility is provided for Common Object Request Broker Architecture (CORBA) clients that connect through to EJBs.

Object caching is performed by the Sun Java System Application Server at several levels, to ensure efficient resource usage. This includes caching of JDBC connections to all databases, caching of JSP and HTML output, and various other tasks. While this approach has the inherent risks of object mismatching and incorrect retrieval, the caching features of the Sun Java System Application Server are generally robust, and can be switched on or off if desired. In addition, the Sun Java System Application Server features some preemptive strategies for streamlining data processing operations, including being able to view result sets before they have been completely retrieved from a database table.

The Sun Java System Application Server is a highly scalable system: it works on single-CPU systems running Windows, as well as on high-end E10000 systems running Solaris, with 64 CPUs. In addition to making optimal use of a single system's resources, the Sun Java System Application Server is able to scale across multiple systems, making the potential pool of CPU resources virtually unlimited. Since the Sun Java System Application Server uses its own Distributed Data Synchronization (DSync) system to share data among its configured servers, any overhead involved in swapping tasks across different systems is minimized. No additional installation or reconfiguration is required—new servers are added using the Sun Java System Application Server Administration Tool as required. Once you have added new servers to the pool of available systems, load balancing across all systems is performed automatically, without your intervention, by using round-robin and other algorithms for computing load sharing. This does not require external load balancing, as the load-balancing function is integrated within the application server.

Security is a key concern for application services, and the Sun Java System Application Server provides the best set of security offered in the J2EE market, since it is integrated with the Sun Java System Directory Server. By using LDAP for authentication and authorization, and single sign-on across all supported applications, you can reduce security risks significantly.

The Sun Java System Application Server supports JDBC and database access by using the standard Java SQL API, as well as a Unified Integration Framework API, that further abstracts vendor-specific operations from individual JDBC drivers. The Sun Java System Application Server supports DB2, Informix, Oracle, Sybase, and SQL Server, by supplying highly optimized, multithreaded drivers that work with a single transaction manager, which coordinates many low-level activities required to process transactions. In addition, the Sun Java System Application Server now features an integrated version of the PointBase database, which has support for relational and object storage. PointBase has its own JDBC driver, and can be used during development and testing without a third-party database being present.

Another key advantage of the Sun Java System Application Server over its competitors is the Sun Java System Application Server Administration Tool, which provides real-time management capabilities over all aspects of server operations. By using the Administration Tool, it's possible to manage services, monitor system activity, administer databases, review transaction progress, check system logs, handle events using SNMP, configure load balancing and clustering, and configure individual applications. Its intuitive, Swing-based interface makes the Administration Tool easy to use, which is particularly important for system administrators who are not J2EE developers, but who are responsible for managing an organization's J2EE environment. In addition, the Administration Tool can be used to manage security, authorization, and access, and perform application performance tuning and partitioning across multiple servers.

Architecture

Each Sun Java System Application Server instance has a number of services associated with it, typically including an Executive Server (KXS), a Java Server (KJS), a C++ Server (KCS), and a CORBA Executive Server (CXS). These are responsible for managing system services, Java applications, C++ applications, and CORBA services, respectively. The performance of KXS depends on a number of parameters, including the following:

- CPU activity
- Disk I/O activity
- Mean response time
- Number of requests ready
- Number of requests waiting
- Number of requests waiting to be serviced
- Number of results cached
- Number of threads available for processing requests
- Number of unserviced thread requests
- Number of user sessions currently supported
- Peak number of requests
- Total data throughput
- Total number of requests
- Virtual memory swapping in/out

Similarly, the performance of KJS, KCS, and CXS in providing application services is dependent on several factors, including

- Current requests waiting to be processed
- Mean response time

- Number of active database connections
- Number of available database connections
- Number of database commits
- Number of database rollbacks
- Number of requests ready
- Number of requests received
- Number of requests waiting
- Number of threads available for processing requests
- Number of unserviced thread requests
- Total data throughput
- Total number of database queries
- Total number of threads created

Server Configuration

To administer the server, you need to start up the Sun Java System Application Server Administration Tool. The interface consists of three main areas. The first area is a row of buttons that determines the type of actions to be performed. These actions include setting general options, monitoring services, managing databases, reviewing transactions, configuring logging, monitoring events, setting up load balancing, applying security measures, and configuring individual applications for deployment (in conjunction with the deployment tool).

Below the row of buttons are two panes: the left pane gives a tree view of the object hierarchy associated with each action, while the right pane contains a number of tabs that perform specific actions. In the General section, the object hierarchy in the left pane displays a list of all configured instances of the Sun Java System Application Server, since there can be several instances managed by the Administration Tool at one time. Each server instance has a number of servers associated with it, including KXS, KJS, KCS, and CXS. In the right pane, there are several tabs displayed, including Server, Request Manager, SNMP, LDAP, EJB, and Cluster.

The Server tab, shown in Figure 33-2, contains fields that display the name of the server instance, the hostname, the server's IP address, the port on which the server listens, and the current server version. In addition, you may enter the maximum number of server engine restarts and a specific cache size for JSP pages. You must explicitly enable internalization support for the server instance and enter the maximum server and engine shutdown times. In addition, the set of buttons at the bottom of the screen enables you to start, disable, or stop the server instance. If you make any configuration changes on the screen, you must either explicitly apply them by clicking the Apply Changes button or explicitly undo them by clicking the Undo Changes button. If you want to use the default values, click the Default Values button.

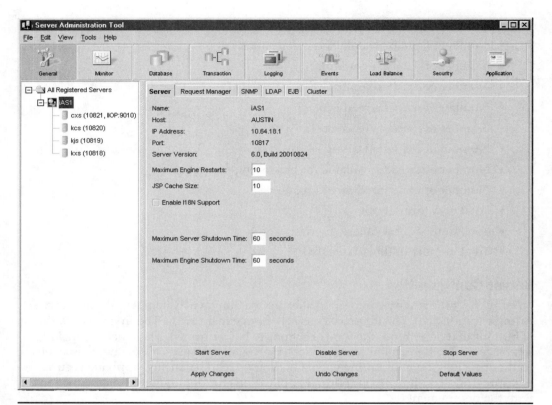

FIGURE 33-2   Server tab

The Request Manager tab, shown in Figure 33-3, allows you to enable or disable request flow control and enter values to set default request queue high- and low-water marks if appropriate. In addition, you must enter the minimum and maximum number of threads for the server. For low-volume servers, you can use the default values of 8 (minimum) and 64 (maximum) threads. However, high-volume sites will require some tuning of these parameters. For example, setting the minimum number of threads too low will reduce response time for new clients, since new threads must be spawned rather than drawn from the pool. In addition, if the maximum number of threads is set too low, then clients will be locked out! In general, you should perform load testing to determine an optimal threading configuration for the peak conditions experienced by your applications. A set of buttons at the bottom of the screen allows you to start, disable, or stop the server instance. If you make any configuration changes on the screen, you must either explicitly apply them by clicking the Apply Changes button or explicitly undo them by clicking the Undo Changes button. If you want to use the default values, click the Default Values button.

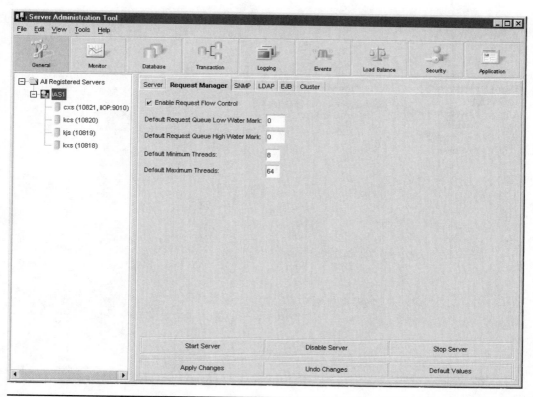

FIGURE 33-3   Request Manager tab

The Sun Java System Application Server supports the Simple Network Management Protocol (SNMP), which enables you to have specific services monitored and, if an error is detected, to be notified through e-mail, phone, fax, pager, or cell phone—that is, if you provide the appropriate SNMP monitoring software (note that the Sun Java System Application Server does *not* provide SNMP server functionality). The SNMP tab, shown in Figure 33-4, allows you to enable SNMP administration and monitoring, along with SNMP debugging features. In addition, you can set the connection attempt interval to a reasonably high figure, allowing reconnections to occur after a connection fault has been detected. In addition, a set of buttons at the bottom of the screen enables you to start, disable, or stop the server instance. If you make any configuration changes on the screen, you must either explicitly apply them by clicking the Apply Changes button or explicitly undo them by clicking the Undo Changes button. If you want to use the default values, click the Default Values button.

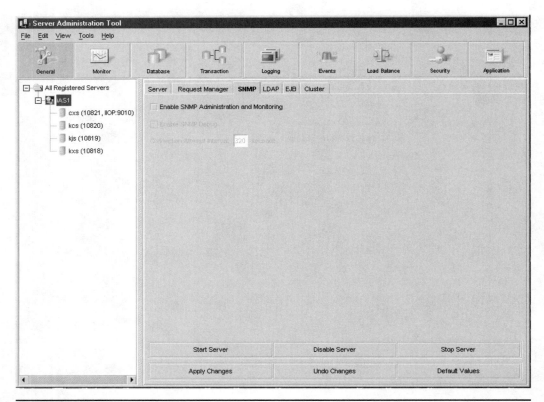

FIGURE 33-4   SNMP configuration

A key feature of the Sun Java System Application Server is its integration with the LDAP directory service. This allows users to be authenticated against a centralized service, and enables you to base access to resources on access control lists (ACLs) based on LDAP groups stored in the LDAP server. Since the Sun Java System Directory Server is bundled with the Sun Java System Application Server, it makes sense to use the integrated package for user management. The LDAP tab, shown in Figure 33-5, contains a list of all valid directory services that have been configured on the tab. The hostname, port number, user DN, and user path are all displayed, along with an optional group path. In addition, a set of buttons at the bottom of the screen allows you to add, modify, or remove LDAP services from the list. If you make any configuration changes on the screen, you must either explicitly apply them by clicking the Apply Changes button or explicitly undo them by clicking the Undo Changes button. If you want to use the default values, click the Default Values button.

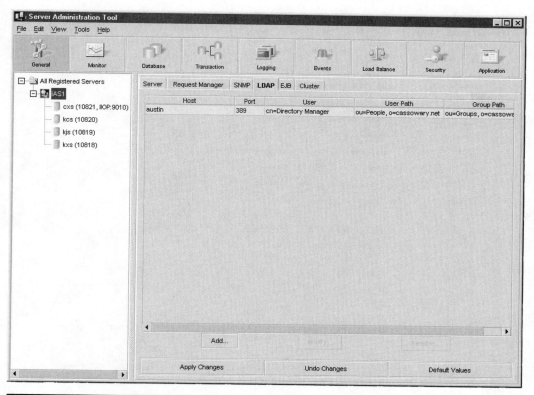

FIGURE 33-5   LDAP configuration

EJBs are the core programmable component technology used by the Sun Java System Application Server, as per the J2EE specification. A number of low-level parameters for EJB performance can be set from the EJB tab, as shown in Figure 33-6. These parameters include the default session timeout, the default object passivation timeout, the metadata cache size, the implementation cache size, the timer interval, and the failover save interval. Tuning these parameters will ensure that your application performs in line with its requirements. For example, if failover of persistent stateful session bean data is a high priority for an application, then you should set the failover safe interval to only a few seconds. This places a heavy toll on the server but improves data reliability. In contrast, if data loss is not critical to an application, then set the failover safe interval to a matter of minutes. This reduces the load on the server considerably but exposes your users to data-loss scenarios. In addition, a set of buttons at the bottom of the screen allows you to start, disable, or stop the server instance. If you make any configuration changes on the screen, you must either explicitly apply them by clicking the Apply Changes button or explicitly undo them by clicking the Undo Changes button. If you want to use the default values, click the Default Values button.

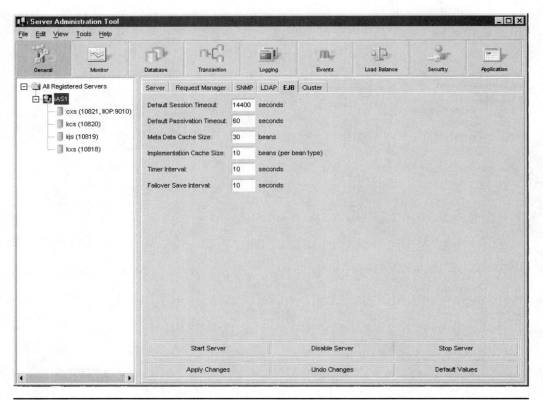

FIGURE 33-6   EJB configuration

The Cluster tab, shown in Figure 33-7, allows you to set a number of distributed computing parameters and provide a priority list of servers to be used in production. You can also set the maximum number of sync backups and an abnormal cluster restart flag. In addition, you can set the priority of different servers that are already in the pool. Thus, if your pool is composed of four Sun 220R systems and four Sun 420R systems, then the higher-end 420R systems should be given priority over the lower-end 220R systems. A set of buttons at the bottom of the screen allows you to start, disable, or stop the server instance. If you make any configuration changes on the screen, you must either explicitly apply them by clicking the Apply Changes button or explicitly undo them by clicking the Undo Changes button. If you want to use the default values, click the Default Values button.

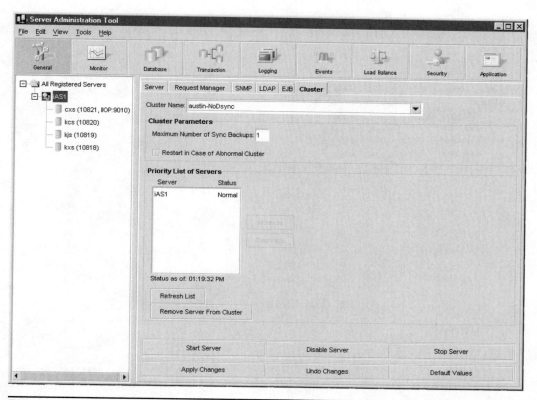

FIGURE 33-7   Cluster configuration

In the General section, you can use the Engine Information tab for CXS, KCS, KJS, and KXS, shown in Figure 33-8, to display the engine name, hostname on which the engine runs, the IP address of the server, the port number on which the engine listens, the IIOP port number, and the engine status. IIOP is the Inter-ORB protocol, which underlies all CORBA operations. In addition, a set of buttons at the bottom of the screen allows you to start, disable, or stop the process. If you make any configuration changes on the screen, you must either explicitly apply them by clicking the Apply Changes button or explicitly undo them by clicking the Undo Changes button. If you want to use the default values, click the Default Values button.

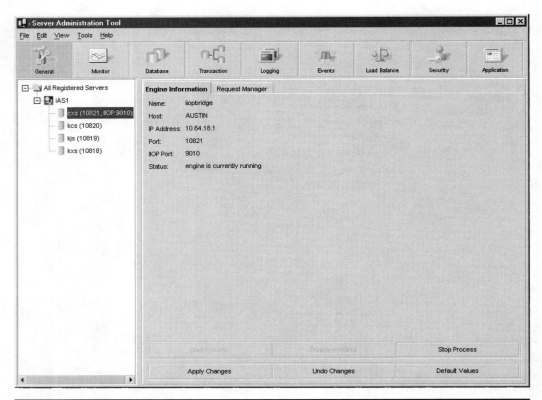

FIGURE 33-8 Application server engine configuration

You can use the Request Manager tab for CXS, KCS, KJS, and KXS, shown in Figure 33-9, to enable or disable request flow control and enter values to set default request queue high-and low-water marks, if appropriate. In addition, you must enter the minimum and maximum number of threads for the server. A set of buttons at the bottom of the screen allows you to start, disable, or stop the process. If you make any configuration changes on the screen, you must either explicitly apply them by clicking the Apply Changes button or explicitly undo them by clicking the Undo Changes button. If you want to use the default values, click the Default Values button.

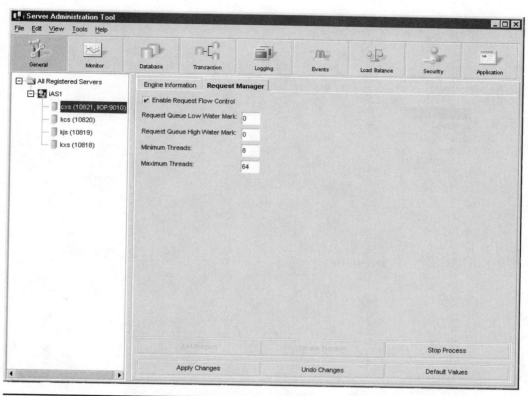

FIGURE 33-9   Request Manager configuration

Monitoring

In the Monitoring section, the object hierarchy in the left pane displays a list of all configured instances of the Sun Java System Application Server and their associated KXS, KJS, KCS, and CXS servers. In the right pane is a display of all processes to monitor for each server type. Attributes that can be monitored include average execution time, requests per interval, queries per interval, transactions committed per interval, transactions rolled back per interval, total number of threads, total number of requests, current number of requests, number of requests waiting, number of requests ready, number of current request threads, current number of request threads waiting, number of active data connections, and number of cached data connections. A set of buttons at the bottom of the screen allows you to add new plots, modify existing plots, and set various options, including the logfile name. Figure 33-10 shows the Monitoring screen for the CXS server.

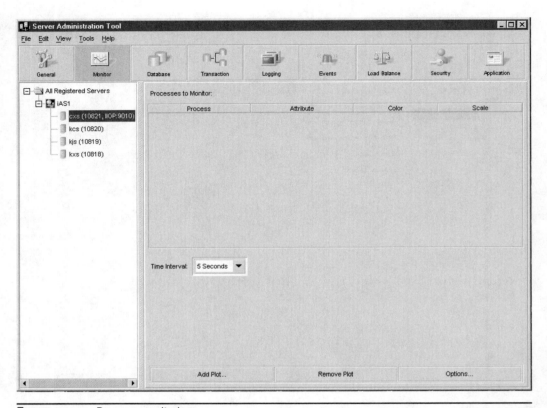

FIGURE 33-10   Process monitoring

Once you have selected a set of processes to monitor, you can set the operational monitoring parameters. These include the sampling interval (default is five seconds), the color of the attribute when plotted, and the scale of the plot. A sample is shown in Figure 33-11, where several *iiopbridge* attributes are plotted alongside each other.

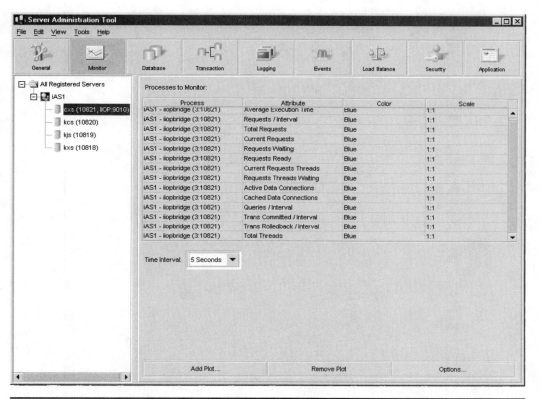

FIGURE 33-11   Attribute monitoring

After you select the attributes to be plotted, simply click the icon in the left pane that matches the server whose activity is to be monitored. This opens a new external window that contains the attribute plots, appropriately scaled and colored, as shown in Figure 33-12. By default, every tick mark represents 25 seconds of elapsed time.

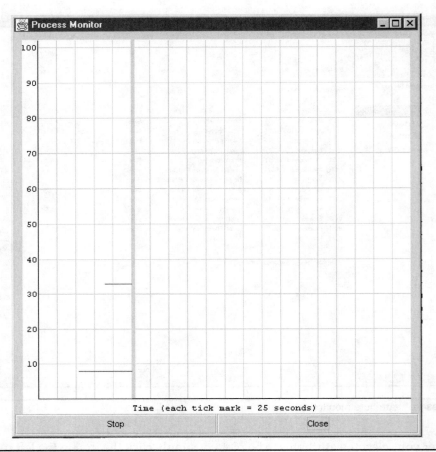

FIGURE 33-12 Graphing process activity

Databases

In the Database section, the object hierarchy in the left pane displays a list of all configured instances of the Sun Java System Application Server, as shown in Figure 33-13. In addition, under the Server Instance icon lies a list of all external JDBC data sources configured, external JDBC drivers installed, Sun Java System Application Server Type 2 data sources configured, and Sun Java System Application Server Type 2 JDBC drivers installed and activated.

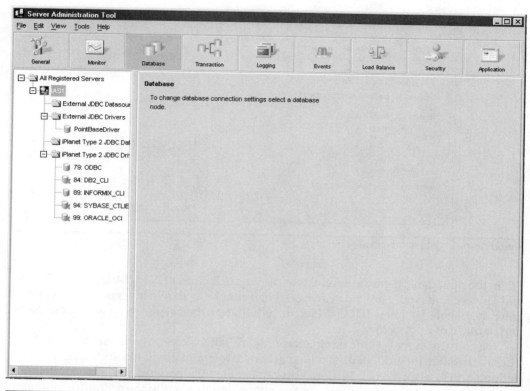

FIGURE 33-13   JDBC configuration

In order to make use of JDBC technology, especially when using entity beans, you must specify a JDBC driver that not only contains all the classes required to operate on a specific vendor's database but also supports a common API, which enables applications to be easily ported to a different vendor platform. In conjunction with entering a database URL, username, and password, it's easy to configure a data source to which an application can connect. New data sources can be easily registered, as shown in Figure 33-14.

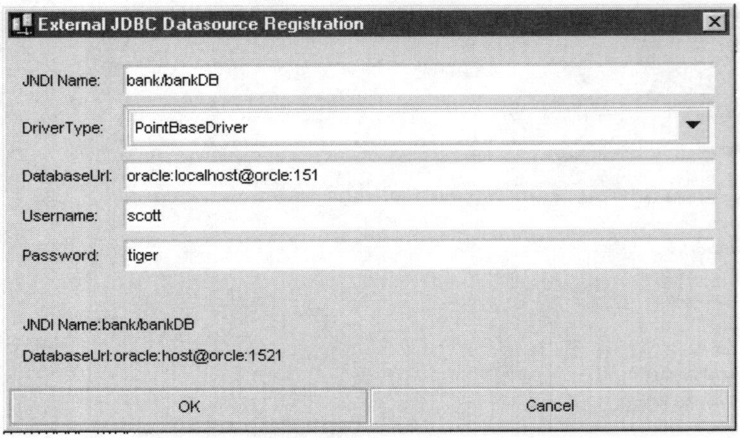

FIGURE 33-14 Data source configuration

In the right pane, there are several tabs displayed, including Add/Modify Data Sources and Drivers, and Apply or Undo Changes. For example, as shown in Figure 33-15, you can enter the details for a new JDBC driver, including the driver type, class name, class path, and native driver directory.

You can also enter specific parameters for each JDBC driver, as shown in Figure 33-16. These attributes include loading a data access driver and client library, along with a defined access priority. In addition, you can enable SQL parsing and have all debug messages logged to a file. You can set the connection timeout to the server (default is 60 seconds) and specify the maximum and minimum number of threads. In terms of the cache, you can set the maximum number of connections, minimum number of free slots, and connection timeout and interval. If you make any configuration changes on the screen, you must either explicitly apply them by clicking the Apply Changes button or explicitly undo them by clicking the Undo Changes button. If you want to use the default values, click the Default Values button.

Transactions

In the Transaction section, the object hierarchy in the left pane displays a list of all configured instances of the Sun Java System Application Server, under which lies a KJS instance where appropriate. By selecting either the Instance icon or the KJS icon, you can set parameters for each version. In the right pane, there are several tabs displayed, including Configuration, Resource Manager, and Transaction Manager. The Configuration tab, shown in Figure 33-17, allows you set server transaction properties appropriately, including options such as whether global transactions are enabled or whether the root and mirrored root directories are used. If you make any configuration changes on the screen, you must either explicitly apply them by clicking the Apply Changes button or explicitly undo them by clicking the Undo Changes button. If you want to use the default values, click the Default Values button.

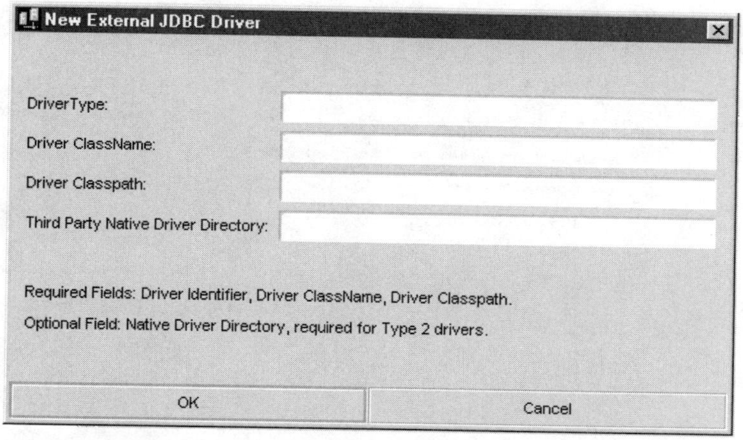

FIGURE 33-15   JDBC driver selection

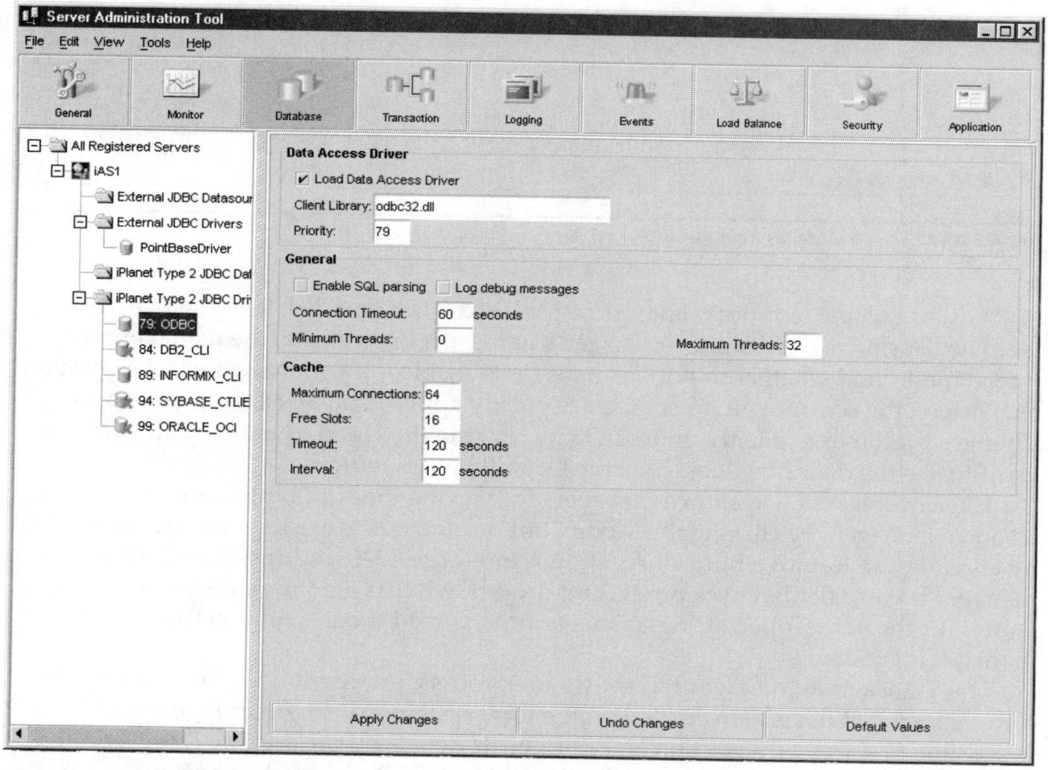

FIGURE 33-16   Selecting an existing JDBC configuration

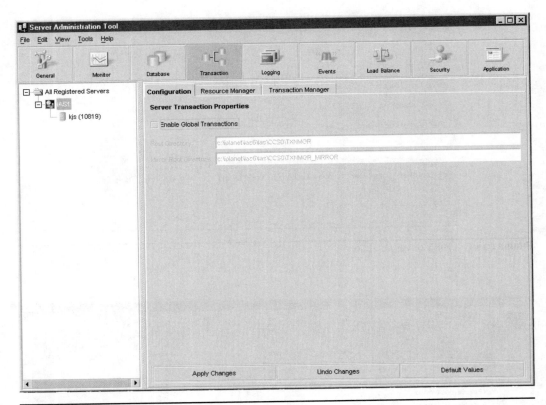

FIGURE 33-17 Transaction configuration

A list of existing resource managers is displayed when you click the Resource Manager tab. The list shows the resource manager's name, the open string, the manager type, thread mode, and whether or not the manager is enabled. If you make any configuration changes on the screen, you must either explicitly apply them by clicking the Apply Changes button or explicitly undo them by clicking the Undo Changes button. If you want to use the default values, click the Default Values button.

You can create new resource managers by clicking the Add button, modify existing resource managers by clicking the Modify button, and delete existing resource managers by clicking the Remove button. As shown in Figure 33-18, adding a new resource manager is easy: fields, check boxes, and drop-down lists are provided for you to enter values for the name, open string, manager type, thread mode, and whether or not the manager is enabled.

The Transaction Manager tab shows the process, transaction ID, and state of all transactions that have been created on the local system. As shown in Figure 33-19, it is possible to select a transaction and retrieve its details by clicking the Details button, or to update the list of transactions displayed by clicking the Update button.

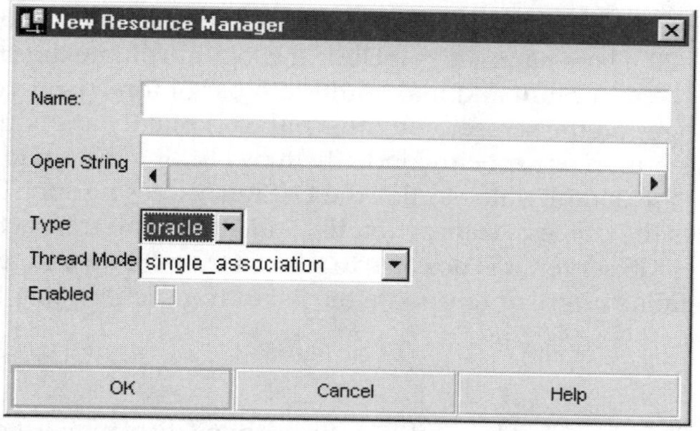

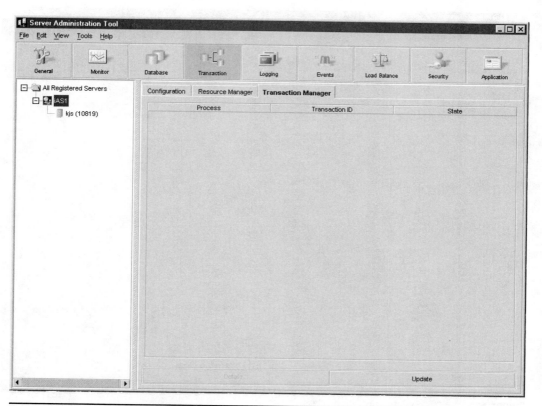

FIGURE 33-18   Adding a resource manager

FIGURE 33-19   Reviewing transactions

By clicking the KJS icon, you can set configuration parameters for the KJS server, as shown in Figure 33-20. These parameters include the logical volume directory, the amount of free space, and the minimum and maximum number of threads. If you make any configuration changes on the screen, you must either explicitly apply them by clicking the Apply Changes button or explicitly undo them by clicking the Undo Changes button. If you want to use the default values, click the Default Values button. The Transaction Manager tab shows the process, transaction ID, and state of all transactions that have been created on the KJS server. It is possible to select a transaction and retrieve its details by clicking the Details button, or to update the list of transactions displayed by clicking the Update button.

Logging

In the Logging section, the object hierarchy in the left pane displays a list of all configured instances of the Sun Java System Application Server. In the right pane, there are several tabs displayed, including Server Event, HTTP, and DSync, as shown in Figure 33-21.

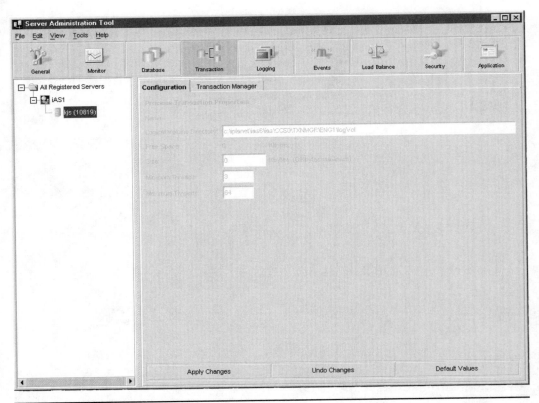

FIGURE 33-20 KJS configuration

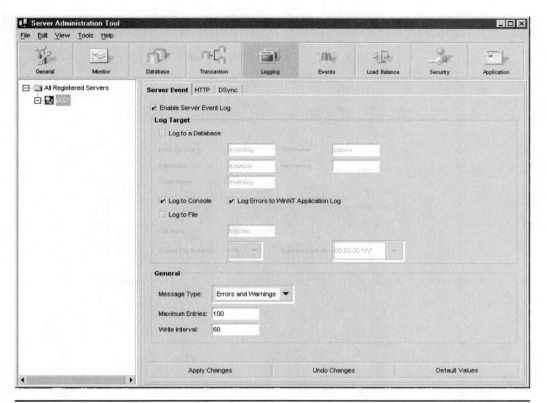

FIGURE 33-21   Server event configuration

The Server Event tab allows server events to be logged to one of three targets: a database table, the console, or a file. If you select a database, then you must enter the data source, database name, table name, username, and password for the database. If you select file logging, then you must enter the filename, and you may schedule log file rotation to occur on a regular basis. If you make any configuration changes on the screen, you must either explicitly apply them by clicking the Apply Changes button or explicitly undo them by clicking the Undo Changes button. If you want to use the default values, click the Default Values button.

The HTTP tab allows HTTP logging to occur, with the only target available being a database table. To configure database HTTP logging, you must enter the data source, database, table name, username, and password, as shown in Figure 33-22. In addition, you must enter the maximum number of entries in the log, as well as the write interval. If you make any configuration changes on the screen, you must either explicitly apply them by clicking the Apply Changes button or explicitly undo them by clicking the Undo Changes button. If you want to use the default values, click the Default Values button.

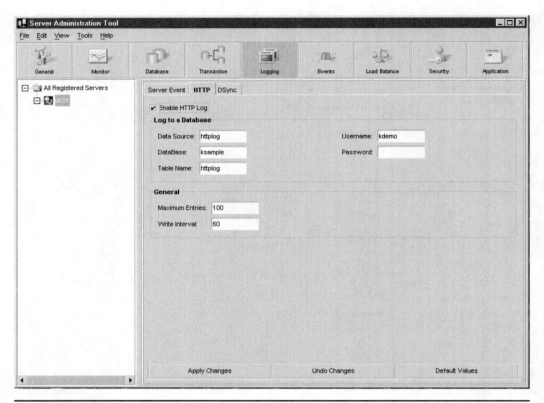

FIGURE 33-22   HTTP configuration

The DSync tab allows you to set a number of logging options for the DSync feature, as shown in Figure 33-23. You can enable logging on any or all of the following levels: module, failover, token, timeout, and messenger. If you want to save clusters, click the Dump Cluster Info button, or if you want to save node information, click the Dump Node Info button. If you make any configuration changes on the screen, you must either explicitly apply them by clicking the Apply Changes button or explicitly undo them by clicking the Undo Changes button. If you want to use the default values, click the Default Values button.

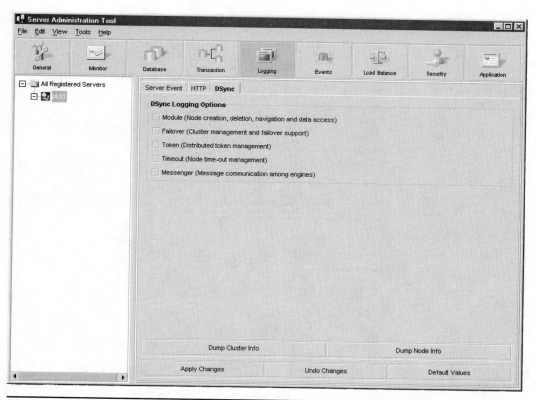

FIGURE 33-23   DSync configuration

Events

In the Events section, the object hierarchy in the left pane displays a list of all configured instances of the Sun Java System Application Server. In the right pane, there is a single screen displayed, which defines actions to be performed on the basis of specified events. The events that are notifiable are shown in Figure 33-24, and include the KXS, KJS, and KCS servers being down, the number of process restarts exceeding the set maximum, and the detection of an abnormal cluster. Variables that can be specified include a list of e-mail addresses to whom alerts should be sent, and a mail server through which all messages are transferred. Optionally, a script file can be included. If you make any configuration changes on the screen, you must either explicitly apply them by clicking the Apply Changes button or explicitly undo them by clicking the Undo Changes button. If you want to use the default values, click the Default Values button.

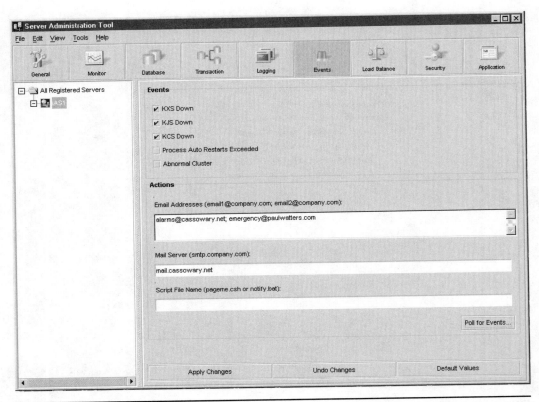

FIGURE 33-24   Event configuration

Load Balancing

In the Load Balance section, the object hierarchy in the left pane displays a list of all configured instances of the Sun Java System Application Server. In the right pane, there is a single screen displayed, which shows the various load-balancing methods implemented by the Sun Java System Application Server, as shown in Figure 33-25, even though only one server is configured. These include Sun Java System Application Server–driven methods, such as user-defined criteria, and Web container methods, comprising round robin, per component response time, and per server response time methods. If you make any configuration changes on the screen, you must either explicitly apply them by clicking the Apply Changes button or explicitly undo them by clicking the Undo Changes button. If you want to use the default values, click the Default Values button.

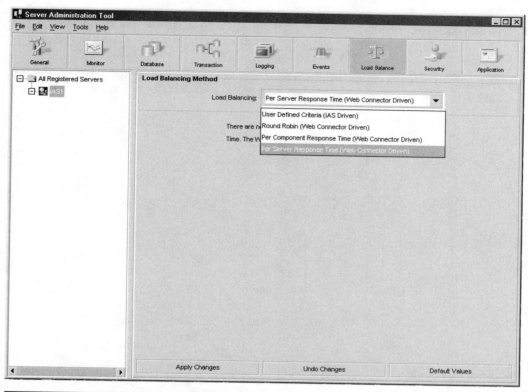

FIGURE 33-25 Load-balancing configuration

Security

In the Security section, the object hierarchy in the left pane displays a list of all configured instances of the Sun Java System Application Server. In the right pane, there is a single screen displayed, which displays all configured ACLs, as shown in Figure 33-26. You can create new ACLs by clicking the New button, modify existing ACLs by clicking the Modify button, and delete existing ACLs by clicking the Remove button.

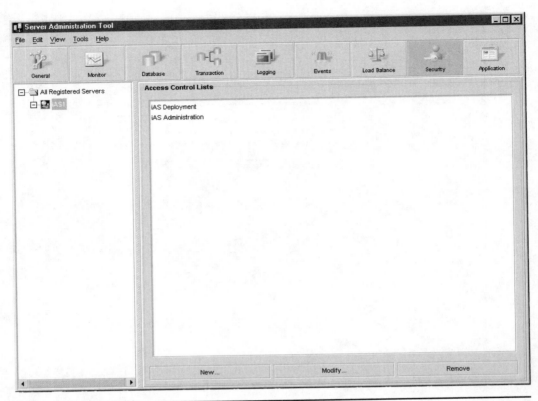

FIGURE 33-26 Security configuration

When you click the Modify button, a list of users and groups is displayed, as shown in Figure 33-27. It is then possible to add a new user or group, set a new permission, or remove an existing user or group from the list displayed.

Applications

In the Application section, the object hierarchy in the left pane displays a list of all configured instances of the Sun Java System Application Server, and all installed applications. Each installed application has its own icon, under which lie several nodes that represent different installed modules (such as *system*, *Default*, or a user-defined

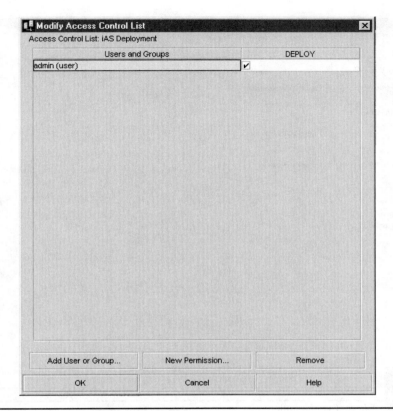

FIGURE 33-27   Access control list modification

module, such as *fortune*). In the right pane, there is a single screen displayed, which allows the file root directories for each type of file to be set. As shown in Figure 33-28, supported file types include Java components, queries, HTML pages, HTML templates, and application JAR files. If you make any configuration changes on the screen, you must either explicitly apply them by clicking the Apply Changes button or explicitly undo them by clicking the Undo Changes button. If you want to use the default values, click the Default Values button. You can easily deploy applications by clicking the Launch iASDT button.

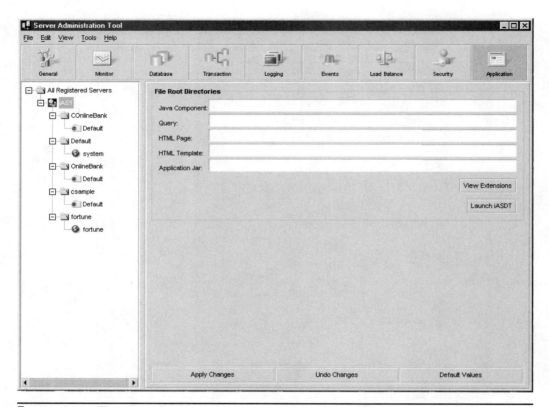

FIGURE 33-28   File root configuration

If you click an application group icon, a list of application group components is listed. As shown in Figure 33-29, this could include C++ type components or Java components. In addition, you can set access control to the application group by clicking the Set Application Group Access Control button. By clicking the appropriate check box, located next to each component, you can enable the component. If you make any configuration changes on the screen, you must either explicitly apply them by clicking the Apply Changes button or explicitly undo them by clicking the Undo Changes button. If you want to use the default values, click the Default Values button.

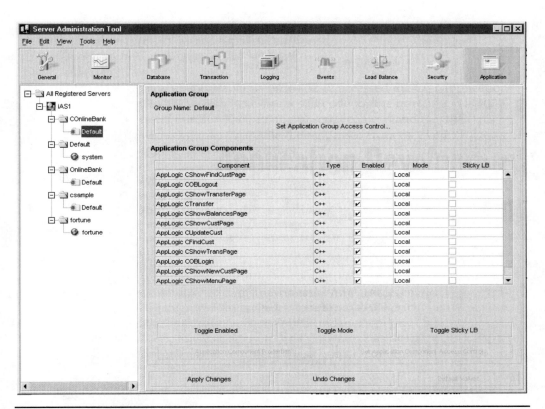

FIGURE 33-29   Application group configuration

Summary

This chapter examined how to configure simple Web applications through the open-source Apache HTTP Server and how to configure basic J2EE services within the Sun Java System Application Server that is shipped with the Solaris 10 distribution. These two services represent two extremes in the Web application market—the Apache HTTP Server is lightweight, providing access to Web pages, CGI scripts, and Java servlets (with the appropriate connector), while the Sun Java System Application Server can support the most complex Web applications, making use of distributed transactions, directory services, asynchronous message queues, and the emerging XML Web Services.

Summary

Index

INTERNATIONAL CONTACT INFORMATION

AUSTRALIA
McGraw-Hill Book Company
Australia Pty. Ltd.
TEL +61-2-9900-1800
FAX +61-2-9878-8881
http://www.mcgraw-hill.com.au
books-it_sydney@mcgraw-hill.com

CANADA
McGraw-Hill Ryerson Ltd.
TEL +905-430-5000
FAX +905-430-5020
http://www.mcgraw-hill.ca

**GREECE, MIDDLE EAST, & AFRICA
(Excluding South Africa)**
McGraw-Hill Hellas
TEL +30-210-6560-990
TEL +30-210-6560-993
TEL +30-210-6560-994
FAX +30-210-6545-525

MEXICO (Also serving Latin America)
McGraw-Hill Interamericana Editores
S.A. de C.V.
TEL +525-1500-5108
FAX +525-117-1589
http://www.mcgraw-hill.com.mx
carlos_ruiz@mcgraw-hill.com

SINGAPORE (Serving Asia)
McGraw-Hill Book Company
TEL +65-6863-1580
FAX +65-6862-3354
http://www.mcgraw-hill.com.sg
mghasia@mcgraw-hill.com

SOUTH AFRICA
McGraw-Hill South Africa
TEL +27-11-622-7512
FAX +27-11-622-9045
robyn_swanepoel@mcgraw-hill.com

SPAIN
McGraw-Hill/
Interamericana de España, S.A.U.
TEL +34-91-180-3000
FAX +34-91-372-8513
http://www.mcgraw-hill.es
professional@mcgraw-hill.es

**UNITED KINGDOM, NORTHERN,
EASTERN, & CENTRAL EUROPE**
McGraw-Hill Education Europe
TEL +44-1-628-502500
FAX +44-1-628-770224
http://www.mcgraw-hill.co.uk
emea_queries@mcgraw-hill.com

ALL OTHER INQUIRIES Contact:
McGraw-Hill/Osborne
TEL +1-510-420-7700
FAX +1-510-420-7703
http://www.osborne.com
omg_international@mcgraw-hill.com

Sound Off!

Visit us at **www.osborne.com/bookregistration** and let us know what you thought of this book. While you're online you'll have the opportunity to register for newsletters and special offers from McGraw-Hill/Osborne.

We want to hear from you!

Sneak Peek

Visit us today at **www.betabooks.com** and see what's coming from McGraw-Hill/Osborne tomorrow!

Based on the successful software paradigm, Bet@Books™ allows computing professionals to view partial and sometimes complete text versions of selected titles online. Bet@Books™ viewing is free, invites comments and feedback, and allows you to "test drive" books in progress on the subjects that interest you the most.